THE BIG BOOK OF
AUSTRALIA'S
WAR
STORIES

A collection of stories of Australia's iconic battles,
heroes and campaigns from the Boer War to Vietnam

JIM HAYNES

ALLEN&UNWIN
SYDNEY·MELBOURNE·AUCKLAND·LONDON

This book is for two of my most supportive friends—Chrissy Eustace and Max Ellis OAM

Allen & Unwin
83 Alexander Street
Crows Nest NSW 2065
Australia
Phone: (61 2) 8425 0100
Email: info@allenandunwin.com
Web: www.allenandunwin.com

 A catalogue record for this book is available from the National Library of Australia

ISBN 978 1 76087 561 9

Maps by Mapgraphics
Set in 11.5/14.5 pt Minion Pro by Midland Typesetters, Australia
Printed and bound in Australia by Griffin Press, part of Ovato.

10 9 8 7 6 5 4 3 2 1

The paper in this book is FSC® certified. FSC® promotes environmentally responsible, socially beneficial and economically viable management of the world's forests.

CONTENTS

PART III Fighting the Führer

PART IV Fighting the Emperor

PART V Fighting the Communists

INTRODUCTION

Here, put into their historical and social context and, I hope, told simply in layman's terms, are more than 100 stories and poems about Australia's battles, heroes, tragedies and campaigns, from the time of Federation to the Vietnam War. Many concern events that are still household names in Australia today, although often their historical significance is a mystery to most Aussies. Others concern events, characters and heroes that and who are barely remembered now, but are, for better or worse, an important part of our history. These are stories that played a part in creating the rich tapestry of our collective memory and our military and social history. Things that help us make sense of what happened in the past and who we are—they are stories that deserve to be told.

In some ways, writing, collecting and collating these stories over the past year has been a harrowing experience. I have been forced, almost daily, to confront the tragic reality and heartbreaking poignancy of the results of war, along with some of the baser and most deplorable aspects of human nature. I have had to attempt to research and explain the results of humankind's ability to demonstrate inhumanity towards fellow human creatures, with apparent impunity and lack of feeling or regret.

On the other hand, and far more importantly, this collection of stories also demonstrates the extraordinary courage, resilience, stoic humour, personal heroism and sacrifice that inevitably appear in times of war. These are the very aspects of humanity that created the legend of the Aussie digger, soldiers, sailors and airmen, and women like Sister Bullwinkel and Nancy Wake, who did things their own way and earned the undying respect of both their allies and their enemies.

Perhaps this collection of stories will help us to understand why, fifteen years before Gallipoli, Sir Arthur Conan Doyle, writing of stoic Australian courage, would say, 'When the ballad makers of Australia seek for a subject, let them turn to Elands River'—or why a British officer called the cheerful, insubordinate Australian troops at Gallipoli 'the bravest thing God ever made'. It may also explain why Field Marshal Montgomery's Chief of Staff remarked, before the Normandy invasion, 'I only wish we had the Australian 9th Division with us this morning.'

Of all the fields of human endeavour, there is none that produces more truly strange and unbelievable stories than war—and Australia's military history is no exception. There are many, stirring, tragic, amusing and incredible stories from our involvement in conflict here. My problem with this collection was most often what to leave out—rather than what stories to include.

I tried not to write a book of military history—a list of battles—but rather to explore, in chronological order, some of the great stories of our involvement in wars. I wanted to look at the events that most Aussies 'know happened', but don't really know much about. At the same time I have tried to put our military past into a context that explores the reasons why we acted as we did and what our decision-makers were thinking at the time.

I tried to examine, for instance, the way in which our national character was influenced by the fact that our nation was born during our involvement in the Boer War. I have tried to show why the bravery of Australians at the Battle of Villers-Bretonneux was such an astonishingly important event in World War I and why the Battle of the Coral Sea was one of the strangest ever fought, and why we celebrate it to this day.

———

Events that shocked and puzzled Australians when they occurred, like the 'Battle of Brisbane' and the Cowra breakout, are fascinating to look at in retrospect and analyse in an effort to see what it was about them that seemed, at the time, so obviously understandable on the one hand, or so strangely inexplicable, on the other.

I certainly found it obsessively interesting and often enlightening to research these events, attempt to explain why they occurred, demystify them and see why they were so puzzling or so seemingly justifiable to our forebears' generation. But, most of all, I just wanted to tell the stories. Some may shock you, some, I am sure, will sadden you, and others will hopefully make you proud to be Australian and even bring a smile to your face as you recognise something intrinsically human and 'Australian' about them.

If nothing else, these stories certainly help us to understand the sacrifices made by many thousands of Australians that allowed us to become the nation we are today. As you read them, you can decide whether those sacrifices were worthwhile—and whether we, as a nation, are worthy beneficiaries of those sacrifices.

PART I

FIGHTING
THE BOERS

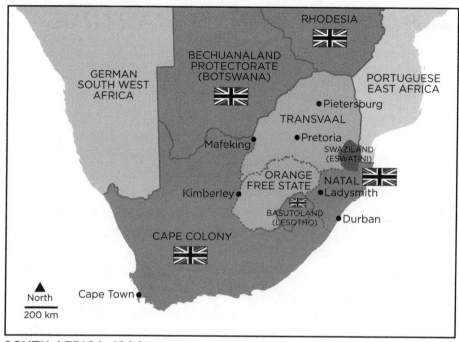

SOUTH AFRICA, 1900

A NATION BORN IN WARTIME

The Second South African (Anglo-Boer) War was the first time we fought as 'Australians', as our nation federated and was born during the course of the conflict.

The first contingents sent to fight in South Africa were raised by the Australian colonies in response to the outbreak of war in 1899. Mostly these contingents were men in the militia of the various colonial forces. The next lot to go were what were called the 'Bushmen' contingents, recruited from more diverse sources and paid for by public subscription or by gifts from wealthy individuals.

The next groups to be recruited were the 'Imperial Bushmen' contingents, which were raised in a similar way, but paid for by the British government in London. Then there were 'draft contingents', which were raised by the state governments after Federation on behalf of the new Commonwealth government, which as yet didn't have the infrastructure to do so. These were, technically, the first 'Australian' military units to fight for their country—well, the British Empire, anyway.

As far as the population of the Australian continent was concerned, there was no distinction between being an Australian and being British. Australia may have been a nation in 1901, but her people were all subjects of the Queen (for 22 days at least, until Victoria died and we became subjects of the King). The Australian Constitution does not mention the word 'citizen', referring only to the Australian people as 'subjects' of the monarch. Australian travellers all held British passports until it became possible to be an 'Australian' when overseas. The first Australian passports were issued in 1949.

About 16,000 Australians fought in what was almost always called 'The Boer War' by Australians. They were under British command and contingents were often broken up and attached to British forces. Towards the end of the war, Australian Commonwealth mounted contingents fought in the counter-offensive of 1900, when the Boer capitals fell, and then on through the guerrilla phases of the war which lasted until 1902.

During the war, a total of 282 Australian troops died in action or from wounds sustained in battle, while 286 died from disease and another 38 in accidents or of unknown causes. Six Australians received Victoria Crosses during the fighting in South Africa.

In many ways Australia's participation in the Second South African (Anglo-Boer) War serves as a reminder of just how 'British' Australians were at the time we became a nation. It is interesting to consider just how much influence this had in shaping Australian attitudes to being an independent, indivisible nation.

On the other hand, the way the Australians fought in South Africa was an indication of just how different those men were from their British counterparts. One obvious reason for this difference is the fact that the British troops were all regular army, while the Australians were all volunteers and a large majority of them were bushmen.

The stereotype of the Australian soldier as a fearless, laconic, reckless and extremely efficient fighting man with a wry sense of black humour, which would become a source of great pride to Australians in both world wars, had its foundations in the Second South African War. There is no better example of this than the Battle at Molopo River, 8 kilometres (5 miles) north-west of Mafeking, in the far north of Cape Colony, on 16 May 1900.

Colonel Plumer's relief column, approaching the besieged British garrison, encountered a force of 2000 Boers and a five-hour long battle took place. The 100 men of the 3rd Queensland Mounted Infantry, led by Captain Charles Kellie, had been assigned the task of protecting the supply wagons, well to the rear of the action.

Military historian, Chris Coulthard-Clark, described what happened next:

> Late in the day, however, when the infantry was sent to clear the enemy from trenches near a farmhouse with the bayonet, they refused to be so constrained and, in defiance of the orders, joined in the assault.

As the British troops rose in extended order to make their final dash to the enemy lines 400 metres off, they heard fiendish yells like the sounds of a band of Red Indians from behind and found the Queenslanders running alongside them as they completed the remaining distance. Although a daring exhibition of brave spirit, the Australian bushmen's wild rush had also been an act of folly. Whereas the British troops had been carefully advancing in bounds, making maximum use of cover, the Queenslanders had thrown caution to the winds and would have suffered accordingly if they had been attacking a more disciplined foe.

As it was, British losses were minor (seven killed and 24 wounded) and the battle was won. The siege of Mafeking was lifted the following day and there was jubilation throughout the British Empire.

Unlike many other nations, ours was not born out of conflict or disagreement with the 'motherland'. Quite the opposite is true, in fact, our nation formed at a time when support for Britain among Australians was at its absolute peak and men were clamouring to fight *for* the 'Old Country', certainly not against it!

In retrospect, it may seem odd to some that while the Australian British colonies were in the process of becoming a nation and thus asserting some level of independence, the 'motherland' had never been more popular and Australians have, arguably, never been prouder of being British than they were in 1901.

On the other hand, the court martial of four Australian officers and the execution by firing squad of lieutenants Peter Handcock and Harry Morant are incidents that have fuelled the fires of republicanism in Australia for more than a century and still serve today as a rallying point for anti-British sentiment in Australia.

QUEENSLAND MOUNTED INFANTRY

A.B. 'Banjo' Paterson

There's a very well-built fellow, with a swinging sort of stride,
About as handy sort as I have seen.
A rough-and-tumble fellow that is born to fight and ride,
And he's over here a-fighting for the Queen.

He's the Queensland Mounted Infantry—compounded horse and
    foot.
He'll climb a cliff or gallop down a flat.
He's cavalry to travel but he's infantry to shoot,
And you'll know him by the feathers in his hat.

THE SECOND SOUTH AFRICAN (ANGLO-BOER) WAR

The first European settlement on the southern tip of Africa was set up by the Dutch East India Company in 1652, in order to serve as a staging post in the spice trade between Europe and the Dutch East Indies (now Indonesia), where the Dutch had established control by defeating the Portuguese in a series of wars over several decades of the 17th century.

The population of the Cape Colony, 200 years after its beginning, consisted of a mixture of the descendants of Dutch settlers, along with some Protestant Germans and French Huguenots and many people of mixed race, descendants of the European settlers, Malay and Central African slaves imported into the colony over several centuries, and the many indentured servants from the local Khoi and San peoples. These people were often referred to as 'Cape Coloureds', although many of the rural-dwelling farmers of the colony, known as 'Boers', were also of mixed-race ancestry.

During the French Revolutionary and Napoleonic wars, factions developed in the colony supporting either side and this led the British to intervene and seize the colony in 1803, give it back in 1805, and finally take control in 1806. In 1815 the Dutch accepted a payment of £6 million for the colony and it became an undisputed British possession.

The British administration immediately banned the Dutch language and established British customs and this, in turn, led to many of the Boer colonists 'trekking' away to the north-east to be out of reach of the British administration. This movement increased after 5000 middle-class Britons migrated in the 1820s to help establish the colony as a British trading centre and the 'trek' became a flood after 'Emancipation Day' in 1838 when the British declared all slaves to be free. Boer farmers relied on slaves and many had purchased slaves on credit or used them as security for loans.

The treks resulted in the displacement of some African tribes from their homelands and led to the establishment of independent 'Afrikaner' colonies, which became the Boer Republics. The British recognised the Republic of South Africa (the Transvaal) in 1852 and granted sovereignty of part of the expanded Cape Colony to the Boers to become part of the Orange Free State after a savage war with the Besotho people in 1854.

By the late 19th century 'South Africa' was made up of four major territories. The British Cape Colony extended along the western, southern and eastern coasts and up to the north, and the smaller British Colony of Natal lay on the east coast. In between these British colonies were the land-locked Boer republics of the Orange Free State and, further north, the Transvaal (South African Republic).

The discovery of diamonds at Kimberley in 1869 led to a dispute over the sovereignty of the area, which was settled in favour of the Griqua mixed-race colonists who had arrived there in the late 1820s. Fearing the Boers, just across the border in the Orange Free State, the Griqua accepted British protection and the protectorate was then made part of the Cape Colony in 1871.

A British attempt to unite the colonies led to the annexation of the Transvaal in 1877 and a rebellion against British control three years later then led to the First South African War in 1880, which resulted in a British defeat and the republic regaining its independence in 1881.

The discovery of gold near Johannesburg in 1886 resulted in large numbers of British and other migrants heading north into the Transvaal and this gave the British a reason to interfere in the affairs of the republic on the excuse that migrants were being denied civil rights.

In 1895 an incident known as the 'Jameson Raid' occurred. It was an abortive attempt by 600 mercenaries employed by Cecil Rhodes, the Prime Minister of the Cape Colony, part-owner of a Kimberley mine and creator of the British colony of Rhodesia, to start an uprising on the gold-fields in the Transvaal and it caused international outrage and led the Transvaal government, led by Paul Kruger, to form an alliance with the Orange Free State and seek help from Germany to arm the republic and prepare for war. A telegram of congratulations to Kruger from the Kaiser after the Jameson Raid had deeply offended the British and, later in the war, a German volunteer unit fought for the Boers, as did several units from the Netherlands.

In 1899, when Britain demanded that Kruger give the 60,000 foreign whites at the Witwatersrand Goldfields voting rights, he refused and demanded the withdrawal of British troops from the borders of the South African Republic. When the British ignored the demand, Kruger declared war.

At first the Boer 'army', which was made up of 25,000 Transvaal commandos, 15,000 Orange Free State commandos and 5000 Cape Colony Boers (later supplemented by 5000 European mercenaries), outnumbered the British troops—but enlistment in Britain was rapid and this soon changed. Eventually some 340,000 British and British Empire troops were involved in the conflict. The Boer troops were members of civilian militias, organised into military units called *commandos*. They elected their officers and a leader, titled *Veldkornet*, who called the men to arms when required. In the early phases of the war, the artillery and state-of-the-art weaponry was provided by the governments of the Transvaal and the Orange Free State and mostly supplied by German companies Mauser and Krupp.

1st Phase—The Boer commando forces of the Transvaal, 25,000 trained men equipped with 55,000 Mauser rifles, 50 million rounds of ammunition and the latest heavy artillery and Maxim guns, invaded the British colony of Natal to the east of the Orange Free State and laid siege to the town of Ladysmith. To the west, Boer commandos from the Transvaal and the Orange Free State invaded Cape Colony and cut off the British garrisons at Kimberley and Mafeking. The British, fighting mainly as infantry, won battles at Talana and Elandslaagte in Natal, but suffered a series of defeats at Stormberg and Magersfontein in Cape Colony and Colenso in Natal during the second week of December 1899. At Spion Kop, in the British Natal Colony, 8000 Boer commandos defeated 20,000 British infantry attempting to lift the siege at Ladysmith, in January 1900.

2nd Phase—Lord Roberts, with Lord Kitchener as his Chief of Staff, replaced British General Sir Redvers Buller and British troops turned the tide of the war. The three major sieges were lifted at Ladysmith in Natal (28 February 1900), and in Cape Colony at Kimberley (15 February 1900) and Mafeking (18 May 1900). The retreating Boer armies were pursued and, in March 1900, the British took Bloemfontein, the capital of the Orange Free State. In May, the Orange Free State was annexed as the

British Orange River Colony and British troops entered Johannesburg in the Transvaal. Pretoria fell in June and the Transvaal was annexed on 1 September 1900. Officially, as far as Britain was concerned, the war was won.

3rd Phase—Some of the Boers signed allegiance to Britain and became known as 'hands uppers'. When the war was rekindled, some of these men switched sides, fought with the British, and were known as 'joiners'. Others again took up arms against the British and joined those who had refused to surrender and were known as 'bitter enders'. Boer leaders Christiaan de Wet, in the Orange Free State, and Louis Botha, Jan Smuts and Koos de la Rey in the Transvaal, set up small and mobile commando units to attack supply depots, disrupt communications and make raids on outposts of the British 'army of occupation'. Tactics were for the men to gather, make a raid and then disappear back into the farming communities. Units of the 250,000-strong British army would respond in force but, as soon as the troops left the area, the British again lost control of the district. This was especially the case in the frontier areas of the Transvaal. Each commando unit was made up of men from the district who had local support and knew the area.

The British response, under Lord Kitchener, who had taken over from Lord Roberts, was to form 'irregular' mobile regiments and establish outposts in forts and blockhouses protected by barbed wire. The British then embarked on a scorched-earth campaign to deny support to the local commandos—30,000 farms were burned, 8000 blockhouses were built and occupied by 50,000 troops, and 25,000 captured Boers were sent overseas to POW camps in Bermuda, Ceylon (now Sri Lanka), India and St Helena to prevent them escaping and rejoining the war. Then 200,000 displaced members of Boer and African families were moved forcibly into more than 60 concentration camps, where a quarter of them died. These harsh tactics finally prevailed and the last of the Boers surrendered in May 1902.

The peace terms offered by the British were generous: £3 million were given for reconstruction and the Boer republics were promised and granted limited self-government within the British Empire in 1906 and 1907. Finally all the colonies and republics combined to become the Union of South Africa and remained part of the British Empire and later, the British Commonwealth of Nations, until voting to withdraw in 1960.

THE FAT MAN AND THE WAR

'Magnet'

They sing of the pride of battle,
They sing of the dogs of war,
And the men that are slain like cattle
On African soil afar.

They sing of the gallant legions
Bearing the battle's brunt
Out in the torrid regions
Fighting the foe in front.

They sing of Mauser and Maxim,
And their doings across the foam,
But I hear none sing of The Fat Man
Who sits at his ease at home.

Contriving another measure
For scooping a lump of tin,
New coffers to hoard the treasure
That his brothers' blood sweeps in;

Chock-full of zeal for speeding
The sword of his Queen's behest,
But other men's legs to bear it
Is the notion that suits him best.

Nothing he knows of fighting;
He never was built that way;
But the game of war is exciting,
When the stake's worth more than the play.

And a fat little time is coming
When the turmoil has settled down,
And the dogs of war are silent
And the veldt is bare and brown.

When the sun has licked the blood up
And the brown earth hid the bones,
His miners will go out seeking
For gold and precious stones.

Like a ghoul from the reeking shambles
He grubs out his filthy pelf,
Reaping a cursed harvest
Where he daren't have sown himself.

Now, this is one man's opinion,
And I think it is fair and right,
If he wants the land of the Dutchman,
Let him go like a man and fight.

If African mines have treasure,
And the Fat Man wants a bone,
Let him go by himself and find it,
Let him trek to the front alone!

'FIGHTING CHARLIE'

Charles Frederick Cox was born in 1863 in Pennant Hills. His father was a butcher and orchardist who was several times Mayor of Parramatta and established citrus growing in the area. On leaving school in 1881 Charlie became a clerk with the New South Wales railways. He joined the volunteer regiment, the New South Wales Lancers, in 1891 and was commissioned second lieutenant in 1894, the same year that he married Minnie Gibbons in All Saints Anglican Church in Parramatta.

Charlie cut quite a dashing figure on a horse and his advancement in the lancers was rapid. He was made a lieutenant in 1896, was given command of the lancer detachment that went to London for Queen Victoria's Diamond Jubilee celebrations in April 1897, and was promoted to captain upon his return in November.

He resumed work with the railways but spent much of his time developing and promoting a scheme to take a contingent of New South Wales Lancers to Britain to train with British regiments as cavalry. Two years later the plan came to fruition and Charlie commanded a squadron of 106 lancers who went to England, at their own and their regiment's expense, to train with regular cavalry south of London at the British military training camp at Aldershot, which had been established in 1854, during the Crimean War.

The group left Sydney in March, arrived in London in April and paraded proudly through the streets accompanied by the band of the Royal Artillery. At Aldershot, it took Charlie's young troopers a little while to adapt to the British regimental style of training and drill. During the first parade, one trooper fell off his horse when it stumbled on the parade ground, and there were complaints from some of the young colonials that the British style of riding made their legs ache.

When war was declared in October, there was a wave of jingoism and Charlie made a big decision. He went to the War Office and volunteered his men to serve in South Africa.

At first his plan was met with resistance, possibly because the British army had other matters to deal with at the time, such as planning a campaign in South Africa. Charlie, however, persevered and called for help from Lord Carrington, who had been Governor of New South Wales from 1885 to 1890. Carrington made a few calls and cabled Sir William Lyne, Premier of New South Wales, requesting official sanction for the men to offer their services. Approval was granted and soon the British press was praising the brave colonials who had volunteered to fight for the motherland.

The troopers of the New South Wales Lancers became minor celebrities and were overwhelmed with invitations and praise as a wave of patriotic euphoria swept through Britain. One evening, while they were guests of the Alhambra Theatre in London, the spotlight was put on them and the audience cheered wildly. One of the troopers stood and sang the popular song 'Soldiers of the Queen' and the audience then joined him in stirring renditions of 'Rule Britannia', 'God Save the Queen' and 'Auld Lang Syne'.

There was, however, another side to the story. Several of the men, travelling on a train between London and Aldershot, happened to strike up a conversation with the Anglican Archdeacon of London, who was a little disturbed to hear that some of the 'volunteer soldiers' felt that they had not exactly been asked how they felt about being 'volunteered' to go to war. He was apparently concerned enough to mention this conversation to someone at the War Office.

Just four days before the regiment was due to embark for Cape Town, they were asked to parade at Aldershot and found that a small tent had been set up, which contained a table manned by several staff officers. The 100 colonials were lined up and entered the tent one at a time. There they were offered the choice of two slips of paper, one blue and one white, and asked to sign one. One stated that they had volunteered to fight in South Africa; the other stated that they did not wish to do so.

The following day Captain Charlie Cox was informed that one-third of the 100 troopers did not wish to go to war at all, which caused a good deal of embarrassment all round. The Commander in Chief of the British Army, Lord Wolseley, was reported to be furious, as were many members of the New South Wales parliament. Lord Carrington was left feeling a little silly, but probably no one was as red in the face as Charlie Cox.

The matter was kept secret until the troopers had all participated in the planned ceremonial parade through the streets of London to their departure point at Tilbury Docks, accompanied by the band of the Grenadier Guards.

On the voyage to Cape Town, Charlie did his best to convince the more recalcitrant members of his regiment to change their minds. On arrival 75 men stepped ashore to fight for Queen and Country, while 31 continued on to Sydney, where a board of inquiry classified the men who had returned and found that things were not quite as bad as they seemed.

Eight of the troopers were under 21 years of age and did not have parental permission to sign up. Nine of the men were found to be medically unfit for active service, two had been found guilty of misconduct and would not have been accepted anyway, and five were judged to have 'good reasons for not volunteering'. The remaining seven were listed as refusing to volunteer due to 'motives of a purely private nature'.

Most of the contingent that disembarked at Cape Town on 2 November 1899 joined General John French's force at Colesberg, in the Border District of the Cape Colony.

However, 29 of the lancers, led by Lieutenant John Osborne, were sent as part of an advance force to take part in the Battles of Belmont and Graspan and went into action as part of Field Marshal Methuen's force on 23 November 1899. Two days later the same 29 men were part of the follow-up action to Belmont, the hard-fought Battle of Graspan Siding.

Methuen bungled both battles and there were heavy losses and fierce hand-to-hand fighting at Graspan, but the New South Wales Lancers bravely held a small gully against a determined Boer advance and earned the nickname 'the Fighting 29'.

Captain Charlie Cox was attached to the Inniskilling Dragoons, and served under Major (later Field Marshal) Allenby before returning to Australia briefly at the end of his year's service. Promoted to major, he was given command of the 3rd New South Wales Mounted Rifles and was back in South Africa in April 1901. In June he was made an honorary lieutenant colonel and served under Colonel Rimington in the guerrilla phase of the war.

'Fighting Charlie' Cox certainly lived up to the nickname he earned in the Second South African War. He saw action at the Battles of Arundel, Riet River, De Klipdrift, Modder River, the Relief of Kimberley, Dronfield, Paardeberg, Poplar Grove, Driefontein, Bloemfontein, Brandfort, Ventersburg Road, Klipriviersberg, Doornkop, Diamond Hill, Olifantsfontein, Langkloof, Swartkop, Barberton and Colesberg, as well as many others classified in the official history of the Boer War as 'minor engagements'!

He was awarded the rare honour of being made a Companion of the Order of the Bath while only holding the rank of major, was Mentioned in Despatches and received the Queen's Medal with six clasps and the King's Medal with two clasps.

When the war ended in 1902, Cox became an inspector in the traffic and audit branch of the New South Wales Railways and was commander of the 1st Australian Light Horse from 1906. At the start of World War I he resigned from the railways and commanded the 6th Australian Light Horse Regiment, which fought as infantry at Gallipoli, where he was wounded in May. As honorary brigadier general, he succeeded Brigadier Chauvel and led the 1st Light Horse Brigade until the end of the war.

When an order came to withdraw just as Charlie was about to attack a Turkish position at the Battle of Magdhaba, on 23 December 1916, he famously told the dispatch rider, 'Take that damned thing away and let me see it for the first time in half an hour.' He then led his 3rd Regiment into battle and broke the Turkish resistance at Magdhaba.

He was famous also for having two dozen chooks with him throughout the campaign in Palestine. They pecked around his tent and were transported everywhere with his gear, so that he had eggs for breakfast every day. He was made a Companion of the Order of St Michael and St George (CMG) in 1918 and served as a conservative Nationalist Party senator in the Australian parliament from 1919 to 1938.

Although he was never in the Cabinet or particularly active in debates, he always received the most primary votes at election time, was a champion of retired servicemen and a very popular public figure. When the 6th Division had their farewell march through Sydney in 1940, Charlie took the salute and remarked that 'they looked splendid' but said 'he missed the horses'. He died, aged 81, in 1944.

MAXIMS OF WAR

A.B. 'Banjo' Paterson

Firstly, when fighting the Dutchman,
Make it your cardinal rule—
Think he's a rogue if it please you:
Never believe he's a fool.

Never be needlessly reckless—
He who does this is a dunce—
Stopping a bullet is easy—
But you don't stop 'em well more than once.

Make better use of your cover—
Don't ride around in full view,
God made the kopjes for Dutchmen—
Likewise he made 'em for you.

Parties of twenty for scouting—
Easy to see and to smother:
Neither can fight nor keep hidden—
Neither one thing nor the other.

If reconnoitring a kopje,
you feel the least shadow of a doubt,
Send up one man to inspect it—
send up a Rimington Scout!

Don't send a troop as a target
For Dutchmen to hustle about.

Never hold more than you've need of—
kopjes all round you are strown.
If they can't help you, they'll hurt you—
leave 'em severely alone.

If you should find a position,
When it would suit you to fight,
Keep it! Don't shift! If you leave it,
The Boers will come down in the night.
Then you'll go back and they'll shoot you—
And serve you most damnably right!

Why should you load up the 'Bully'
Bringing your transport to grief?
Look at the veldt all around you,
stocked with the primest of beef!

Finally never get jumpy—
E'en though the fighting is hot!
Think of how often you're shot at—
Think of how seldom you're shot!

GRASPAN

Chris Coulthard-Clark

This was an action, also referred to as the Battle of Enslin, fought on 25 November 1899 by a British force of 8500 men under Lieutenant General Lord Methuen while attempting to break the Boer siege of Kimberley. After an earlier engagement at Belmont, 18 kilometres to the south along the single-track railway line which formed the axis of the British advance, Methuen found the Boers occupying a line of kopjes (small hills) about 60 metres high to the east of the railway station at Graspan.

Information from British reconnaissance parties indicated that only about 400 enemy were present, supported by two guns. To prevent the enemy escaping as had happened at Belmont, Methuen decided to engage the Boer position first with artillery fire while working the 900 mounted troops available to him around both flanks. Once these were in position, a frontal assault was to be mounted by the small Naval Brigade operating with his force. Unfortunately for this plan of attack, unknown to Methuen—whose scouts were unable to observe into the enemy position from closer than about 2 kilometres—the original Boer defenders were reinforced late on the afternoon of 24 November by 2000 Orange Free State burghers under Commandant Jacobus Prinsloo.

When the British field batteries opened up soon after 6 am the next morning, the answering fire from the Boers came from five guns instead of two—not including a Hotchkiss quick-fire weapon and a Maxim machine gun. Realising that his original scheme was unworkable, Methuen promptly opted for an all-out attack on conventional lines. This effort would pit the Naval Brigade with some infantry detachments against the Boers' eastern (left) flank, while the rest of the British force sought to immobilise the enemy elsewhere and prevent reinforcement of the sector under attack.

This plan worked, but not before the 245-strong assault force had lost fifteen killed and 79 wounded. By the time the crest of the hill was reached, the enemy had all gone except for a small group, which resisted until only one man remained alive. The British could observe the Boers retiring in good order across the plain back into Orange Free State territory, but a shortage of mounted troops meant that a vigorous pursuit was not possible. The British weakness in this regard was graphically demonstrated at one point during the Boer retreat, when a large body of burghers suddenly turned and attempted to ride down the lesser number of British horsemen from the 9th Lancers trying to follow them.

The threat was averted by the response of some mounted infantry who, along with a detachment of 29 members of the New South Wales Lancers under Lieutenant S.F. Osborne, occupied a fold in the ground and poured a heavy fire into the advancing Boers. The incident reportedly won for Osborne and his men the nickname of 'the Fighting 29'.

The engagement had demonstrated once again that the Boers were more than a match for Methuen despite his numerical superiority. While he responded by complaining about the deficiency in the number of mounted troops available to him, and confirmed his disappointment in the part played by his cavalry by removing the commander of the 9th Lancers, nothing could disguise his own tactical incompetence which saw his force suffer total casualties at Graspan of seventeen dead and 168 wounded.

Among the dead of the Naval Brigade was nineteen-year-old Midshipman C. Huddart of Ballarat, Victoria.

I KILLED A MAN AT GRASPAN

Monty Grover

I killed a man at Graspan,
I killed him in fair fight;
And the Empire's poets and the Empire's priests
Swear blind I acted right.
The Empire's poets and the Empire's priests
Make out my deed was fine,
But they can't stop the eyes of the man I killed
From starin' into mine.

I killed a man at Graspan,
Maybe I killed a score;
But this one wasn't a chance-shot, home
From a thousand yards or more.
I fired at him when he'd got no show,
We were only a pace apart,
With the cordite scorchin' his old worn coat
As the bullet drilled his heart.

I killed a man at Graspan;
I killed him fightin' fair.
We came on each other face to face,
An' we went at it then and there.
Mine was the trigger that shifted first,
His was the life that sped,
An' a man I'd never a quarrel with
Was spread on the boulders, dead.

I killed a man at Graspan;
I watched him squirmin' till
He raised his eyes and they met with mine;
An' there they're starin' still.
The cut of my brother, Tom, he looked,
Hardly more'n a kid;
An', Christ, he was stiffenin' at my feet,
Because of the thing I did.

I killed a man at Graspan;
Seems an hour ago about,
For there he lies with his starin' eyes,
An' his blood still tricklin' out.
I know it was either him or me,
I know that I killed him fair,
But, all the same, wherever I look,
The man I killed is there.

I killed a man at Graspan;
I told the camp that night,
An' of all the lies that ever I told,
That was the poorest skite.
I swore I was proud of my hand-to-hand
An' the Boer I chanced to pot,
An' all the time I'd ha' gave my eyes
To never have fired that shot.

I killed a man at Graspan;
My first and, God! my last.
Harder to dodge than my bullet is
The look his dead eyes cast.
If the Empire asks for me, later on,
It'll ask for me in vain,
Before I reach for my bandolier
And fire on a man again.

OFF TO THE WAR

A.B. 'Banjo' Paterson

Banjo Paterson was not only a war correspondent at the Second South African War, he travelled across from Sydney with the first contingent of New South Wales Mounted Infantry and their horses on the troopship and livestock transport SS *Kent* in November 1899. Here is his account of the trip.

Our day commences at six o'clock; when the trumpeters are hustled out of their bunks and blinking sleepily, they tramp up to the deck and blow the reveille. Our trumpeters were by no means champions at first and every day they are taken to the extreme end of the ship for instruction, where they bray away to their hearts' content, and they are rapidly improving.

At the sound of the reveille the troops come gaping and stretching up from their quarters. The hose is played across the deck and all hands are supposed to go under it daily, but with a lot of influenza on board, the rule is not strictly enforced. At 6:30 the men are dressed and ready for work and the bugle goes for 'stables'. All hands set briskly to work taking down the rails between the horses, sweeping out the stalls, clearing up the deck, and throwing the litter overboard.

The forage is got up from below and apportioned out, and carried to the tubs where it is mixed. As the men go past with their bundles of forage on their backs the horses lean out of the stalls and grab at the bags with their teeth. As feed time gets near and the feed is mixed into huge tubs, the horses keep up a constant volley of applause, pawing at the floor with their front feet and taking their feed boxes in their teeth and rattling them.

The feed boxes are hung at the rail in front of them, and if a horse picks up the box in his teeth and lets it drop again it makes a great rattle, and they learn this trick very soon. Also they have a marvellous faculty for estimating time. They know the time for feed as well as the men. At any other time a man can walk up and down the row of stalls without attracting any attention; but at feed time every head is thrust out, all sorts of clutches are made at clothing, and a regular pandemonium is started by the animals trampling the floor, rattling their boxes, and biting each other.

After breakfast comes the first parade, and it really is wonderful to see the eagerness with which the backward men are trying to learn their work. All sorts of parades are going on at once all over the ship and are as keenly done as if under the eye of a general. Major Lee and Colonel Williams have a steady morning's work inspecting and checking stores, inspecting kits, dealing with defaulters and generally managing the economy of the expedition.

Major Fiaschi has charge of the sick, and, as we have an epidemic of influenza on board, there are always four or five men with lung or throat troubles that require watching. At any spare moment that the medical men have they read up on surgery, practise flag signalling, or, when a horse dies, they practise sutures and operations on his interior under the tuition of Major Fiaschi.

After parades and ship inspection there are more stables, and horses are fed. Fifteen men are detailed each day as pickets. They are divided into three watches of five men each. The first five have four hours' watch, then they are relieved by the second five for four hours and they are relieved by the third five. Then the first lot come on again and so on until 24 hours is completed. These men have to keep constant supervision over the horses; but all hands turn out to clean stables and feed horses.

After lunch we seize a half hour in which the lecture to officers is delivered, either on military law, outpost duty, cavalry tactics or surgical treatment. Then comes another parade, which may take the form of cleaning and drying troops' quarters and ventilating bedding or volley firing over the stern, or revolver practice at bottles in the water. This takes us to tea and after tea the concertinas are got out and the men sit in the hatchway and sing.

After 30 days of weary steaming we at last sighted the South African coast. We saw a line of low scrub-covered hills, without any sign of habitation. At the edge of the sea were sand hills, snowy white, with streaks of white sand and running back among the low timber—a barren uninviting coast. There was no sign of life anywhere, no houses, nor any traces of a settlement. The great African continent lay sleeping in the sun and peacefully as if war had never been heard of.

We were soon nearing the anchorage off Port Elizabeth and coasting down the South African shore, a coast exceedingly like the shore at Bondi, except that there are no houses. Our feeling of monotony changed to one of great expectancy, and by midnight we were at anchor. Next morning at grey dawn we steamed into Port Elizabeth.

THERE'S ANOTHER BLESSED HORSE FELL DOWN

A.B. 'Banjo' Paterson

(Banjo prefaced this poem with, 'Written in bad weather aboard the troopship
S.S.Kent taking horses to the Boer War').

When you're lying in your hammock, sleeping soft and sleeping
    sound,
Without a care or trouble on your mind,
And there's nothing to disturb you but the engines going round,
And you're dreaming of the girl you left behind;
In the middle of your joys you'll be wakened by a noise,
And a clatter on the deck above your crown,
And you'll hear the corporal shout as he turns the picket out,
'There's another blessed horse fell down.'

You can see 'em in the morning, when you're cleaning out the
    stall,
A-leaning on the railings nearly dead,
And you reckon by the evening they'll be pretty sure to fall,
And you curse them as you tumble into bed.
Oh, you'll hear it pretty soon, 'Pass the word for Denny Moon,
There's a horse here throwing handsprings like a clown;'
And it's 'Shove the others back or he'll cripple half the pack,
There's another blessed horse fell down.'

And when the war is over and the fighting all is done,
And you're all at home with medals on your chest,
And you've learnt to sleep so soundly that the firing of a gun
At your bedside wouldn't rob you of your rest;
As you lie in slumber deep, if your wife walks in her sleep,
And tumbles down the stairs and breaks her crown,
Oh, it won't awaken you, for you'll say, 'It's nothing new,
It's another blessed horse fell down.'

STINKHOUTBOOM FARM

Chris Coulthard-Clark

Located some 70 kilometres north of Kroonstad in the Orange Free State and just 10 kilometres south of the Vaal River, Stinkhoutboom Farm was the scene of an action during the Second South African War fought on 24 July 1900. British forces had pursued the Boer commando force led by General Christiaan de Wet north to this point, seeking to prevent his passage into the adjoining Transvaal republic and forcing him to take refuge in the Reitzburg Hills beyond the town of Vredefort.

On 24 July elements of Brigadier General C.P. Ridley's mounted infantry brigade (which included both the New South Wales Mounted Rifles and Army Medical Corps) learned that de Wet had passed through the town the previous night, commandeering men, food and horses. Ridley's men sped on in pursuit. At a farm called Stinkhoutboom some of the New South Wales Mounted Rifles, working with men from other units in the brigade, came upon part of de Wet's rear-guard with six grain wagons. In the farmhouse they also captured several exhausted Boers who were asleep in bed still fully clothed.

De Wet responded to the sound of firing by sending back scouts to make a counter-attack, supported by two guns, which opened fire from concealed positions on high ground to the right. The hour-long action which followed saw the small open plain near the farm filled with several hundred men from both sides, who engaged each other at a distance often no more than 200 metres.

Initially the mounted infantry were unable to hold their ground, and were forced to make an orderly retreat with the captured wagons. The end came when two guns from Ridley's brigade arrived on the scene and began shelling the Boers, forcing them to withdraw with seventeen casualties, including two men killed. The British suffered 39 casualties, reportedly including three South Australians killed and several wounded.

The engagement was principally notable for the act of a medical officer with the New South Wales Army Medical Corps, Lieutenant Neville Howse, who—at the height of the fighting—rescued a young trumpeter who lay wounded without shelter in the field of fire. This act of gallantry earned Howse the Victoria Cross, the first awarded to a member of any Australian unit.

OUR FIRST VC

On 24 July 1900, during action at Stinkhoutboom Farm, near Vredefort, in the Orange Free State, Lieutenant Neville Howse, a 36-year-old officer in the NSW Army Medical Corps, saw a trumpeter fall wounded in a fierce encounter with the enemy. He rode through very heavy cross-fire to rescue the man. When his horse was shot from under him, Howse continued on foot, reached the wounded man, dressed his wound and carried him back to safety.

For valour under fire, Lieutenant Howse, a non-combatant officer who did not carry weapons, became the first member of the Australian military to be awarded the Victoria Cross (VC). Although his act of bravery occurred before Federation, his Victoria Cross, Australia's first, was officially gazetted on 4 June 1901 . . . five months after we became a nation.

Neville Howse was born in Somerset, trained as a doctor and came to Australia in 1889 because of his poor health. He set up a medical practice in Orange, New South Wales, and was twice mayor of that city. He served in WWI at the capture of New Guinea, at Gallipoli and on the Western Front. He took charge of evacuating wounded men from the beach at Gallipoli and described the arrangements for dealing with wounded Anzacs as 'inadequate to the point of criminal negligence'. He became director of the AIF's medical services, with the rank of surgeon general and later rose to the rank of major general.

Howse was elected to federal parliament in 1922, was knighted twice, and became the Australian Minister for Defence in the Scullin government. He died of cancer in 1930, aged 66.

THE CARCASS-COVERED
KOPJE—ELANDS RIVER

When it comes to major conflicts involving Australian troops overseas, the first remarkable story that springs to my mind is that of the Battle of Elands River.

During August 1900, a Boer commando force of around 3000 men surrounded and laid siege to a storage post, which was defended by 200 Rhodesian militiamen and 300 Australian militia fighting as the Australian Imperial Bushmen. These were all citizen militiamen, made up of 141 Queenslanders, 105 men from New South Wales, 42 Victorians, nine Western Australians and two Tasmanians, none of whom had ever been shot at before.

It's strange how history changes from generation to generation, as new events become 'famous' and others fade away in the mists of time. Before the landing at Gallipoli on 25 April 1915, the iconic event in military history, well known to all Australians, was the Battle of Elands River. In fact, the famous writer Sir Arthur Conan Doyle, who was a war correspondent during the Boer War, once said:

> When the ballad makers of Australia seek for a subject, let them turn
> to Elands River.

Elands River was a staging post and supply depot on a rocky ridge in the Western Transvaal that was set up as the British army moved eastwards into Boer territory in June 1900, after the lifting of the siege of Mafeking in May.

By August, when the Siege of the Elands River Post began, there were 1500 horses, oxen and mules, together with 100 wagons and enough supplies stored there to maintain a force of 3000 for a month.

The British force, led by Colonel Baden-Powell, had set up head-quarters at Zeerust, about 48 kilometres (30 miles) west of Elands River, which was to be used as a staging point between Zeerust and the next British objective, the township of Rustenburg 128 kilometres (80 miles) to the east.

On 1 June Colonel Airey took a detachment of New South Wales Citizens' Bushmen to scout the road to Rustenburg and left two officers and 40 troops to establish the outpost at Elands River camp. It was a suitable spot, a shallow depression surrounded by ridges on three sides a kilometre from the river and it became a storage depot to supply troops moving east into the Transvaal.

Airey's men were part of the third contingent sent to the war by New South Wales. The 30 officers, 500 troops and 570 horses sailed from Sydney on 28 February 1900, on board two transports, arrived in Cape Town on 2 April and rode north-east to join the war. The small force at Elands River was joined on 7 June by 70 British South African Police and another detachment of New South Wales Citizens' Bushmen arrived the next day.

Meanwhile, news was spreading among the towns and farms in the area that Pretoria had fallen to the British on 6 June and the Boers began to surrender their weapons and return to their farms. A British garrison was set up at Elands River and as many as 1500 men camped there on the way to Rustenburg, which was occupied on 14 June. By the end of June, six garri-sons had been established between Mafeking and Rustenburg, and British patrols disarmed the Boers who had not surrendered their weapons.

It was noticed by some officers, including Captain Thomas of the New South Wales Citizens' Bushmen, that very few rifles had been handed in and, by mid July, it became obvious that the Boers were forming guer-rilla units and continuing to fight. It is estimated that about 90 per cent of those who had surrendered in the Western Transvaal had joined a commando army of around 7000 men led by Colonel de la Rey and gone back to war against the British.

On 3 July Baden-Powell, worried that his small force could not hold all the garrisons along the 192 kilometres (120 miles) of enemy territory, ordered the garrison commander at Rustenburg, Colonel Hore, to retire to Zeerust but, two days later, Field Marshal Lord Roberts ordered that Rustenburg be re-occupied. Colonel Hore's retreating troops met two more squadrons of New South Wales Citizens' Bushmen, led by Colonel Holdsworth, on the road past Elands River camp and the combined forces rode back to Elands River.

Colonel Hore, suffering badly from malaria, could go no further and the horses of A Squadron of the Citizens' Bushmen were unfit to travel, so it was decided that colonels Airey and Holdsworth would continue on to Rustenburg, leaving the bedridden Colonel Hore in command at Elands River.

On 10 July a force of Rhodesian Volunteers led by Captain Butters was sent to reinforce the Elands River garrison and help protect the supplies needed by the troops at Rustenburg. But the Boers cut the telegraph wires between Rustenburg and Zeerust, and all contact with Elands River was lost.

On 20 July Major Walter Tunbridge arrived at the Elands River garrison with 120 Queensland Mounted Infantry, but the tide of the war was turning. The following day the force led by Airey and Holdsworth was soundly routed by the Boers at Koster River, east of Elands River. Seventeen men, fleeing the Boers after the battle, made their way to Elands River.

The Boers were now fighting a full-scale guerrilla war. They desperately wanted the supplies at Elands River, which were valued at more than £100,000. On 4 August 1900, a commando force of around 3000 men, led by Boer General Jacobus Herculaas 'Koos' de la Rey, surrounded and laid siege to the post which was now defended by 200 Rhodesian militiamen and 300 Australians from the various colonies.

The Boers had twelve modern artillery pieces, which pounded the post in its exposed position. They also had snipers positioned on three sides of the camp. The defenders had one Maxim gun and one old 7-pound muzzle-loader. Unfortunately for them, the supplies at Elands River post did not include ammunition.

With Colonel Hore suffering from malaria, the command of the defence at Elands River was mostly in the hands of Major Walter Tunbridge, who led the Queensland Mounted Infantry contingent.

More than 2500 shells landed on the post during the first two days of the siege. Most of the 1500 horses, mules and oxen were killed in the horrific bombardment.

Queenslander Lieutenant James Annat led a patrol of 25 men that crawled 200 metres through the grass and attacked one gun position, forcing the Boers to retire. Annat asked permission to lead a patrol out at night to try to capture the gun but he was killed in the bombardment on 6 August.

The one artillery piece the defenders had was old and faulty. Major Tunbridge had to dismantle it for repairs and reassemble it four times during the siege and spent a day and a night with a file repairing and reshaping the garrison's small store of shells, which had been damaged in transit. The 7-pounder, which sat in a 9-pounder gun carriage, was of little use to the defenders anyway, as all the Boers' superior artillery were well out of its range. But the defenders did manage one direct hit on a farmhouse being used by snipers.

During the bombardment the 500 trapped men desperately dug trenches and erected earthen ramparts. Eyewitness accounts of the siege tell of the unprotected animals being killed 20 and 30 at one time by artillery shells and hundreds of maimed beasts being put down after every artillery barrage.

Baden-Powell knew Elands River would be a prime target for the Boers and sent Major General Sir Frederick Carrington with a force of 1000 men, made up of Carrington's Rhodesian Field Force troops and Australian Imperial Bushmen, to the aid of the garrison on 1 August.

The defenders on the ridge at Elands River post saw their comrades approaching along the Reit Valley and observed the Boers moving guns and rifle regiments into higher positions to trap them.

Carrington had left a third of his column guarding the wagons at the entrance to the valley and advanced slowly. De la Rey sent a commando unit to move around the column and attack with rifle fire from the hills on both sides.

Lieutenant Granville Ryrie, who was one of the Australians in the relief column that day, said later that bullets 'seemed to whistle about in all directions'.

Carrington realised his force was outnumbered and, having made it to within almost a mile of the besieged post, backed out of the valley and withdrew as Boer artillery successfully targeted his headquarters and artillery positions. He then retreated all the way to Zeerust with a Boer commando unit in hot pursuit and was eventually driven all the way back to Mafeking.

Carrington sent a dispatch to Roberts stating that he was sure the garrison had surrendered and that, faced by vastly superior forces, he had retreated to save his men. He attempted to burn his stores as he retreated, but the Boers were close behind and managed to put out the fires and salvage significant quantities of supplies.

The 500 men defending the post, however, were now trapped without cover under the blazing sun, with the stench of 1500 dead animals in the air. They had no access to water except by night patrol and they had seen their 'rescuers' retreat.

Baden-Powell was, however, approaching from the west with 2000 mounted troops to reinforce Carrington's units on 6 August. The sound of heavy artillery to the east mistakenly convinced him that Carrington had arrived and would lift the siege. At that point, a message from Field Marshal Lord Roberts ordered Baden-Powell to hasten towards Pretoria where his troops were required to help in the action against another Boer commando force led by Colonel de Wet near Magaliesberg to the west of Pretoria.

When Roberts received Carrington's dispatch, he congratulated him on not sacrificing his men in a futile attempt to lift the siege and decided to leave Hore's garrison to its fate, assuming it had already been overrun. He later commented that he 'was told that all sounds of firing at Elands River post had ceased'.

On 8 August, de la Rey sent a messenger under a flag of truce and offered to escort the force to the nearest British post, provided that none of the supplies within the camp were destroyed, 'in recognition of your courage in defence of your camp'. He even offered to let the officers retain their weapons.

Australian officers sent a written reply, which read:

If de la Rey wants our camp, why does he not come and take it? We will be pleased to meet him and his men, and promise them a great reception at the end of a toasting fork. Australians will never surrender. Australia forever!

The birth of our nation was still five months away. The 'Australians' fighting at Elands River were actually part-time militiamen from different colonies who had volunteered to go to the war.

When de la Rey sent a second offer of honourable surrender and safe passage, Colonel Hore replied: 'Even if I wished to surrender to you—and

I don't—I am commanding Australians who would cut my throat if I accepted your terms.'

After 11 August the siege became a stalemate. De la Rey left with his senior commanders to meet General Smuts and plan the future of Boer resistance in the Western Transvaal. A force of Boer commandos was left to keep the garrison surrounded and pinned down by sniper fire, but water parties were now able to get in and out at night and each man now had one quart of water a day.

On the evening of 10 August, Tunbridge sent a dispatch rider who made it through enemy lines and reached Carrington's position, and on 14 August, a week after Roberts had left 'the garrison to its fate', Carrington informed him that it was still holding on.

Meanwhile, a messenger carrying a dispatch from de la Rey to de Wet was captured by one of Lord Kitchener's scouts. The dispatch stated that Elands River had not yet surrendered and Kitchener, who had been chasing de Wet with a force comprising the 2nd and 3rd Cavalry Brigades, mounted infantry and two infantry battalions with another brigade as rear-guard, detoured to Elands River on 15 August. The siege was lifted early on 16 August when Kitchener's column, which was 16 kilometres (10 miles) long, arrived at Elands River.

Carrington's previously excellent military reputation was shattered by his retreat from Elands River. According to reports that surfaced later, the Australians in the relief party had wanted to make another attempt to reach the beleaguered post, but their request was denied. In 1901 some Australians managed to send Carrington a white feather. He asked to be relieved of his command and returned to Britain soon after.

Tunbridge was awarded the Queen's South Africa Medal with five clasps and promoted to lieutenant colonel. He became aide-de-camp to the governor-general on his return to Australia and later served as overall commander of Australian mechanical transport in WWI. He was made a Companion of the Order of the Bath and the Order of St Michael and St George and Commander of the Order of the British Empire. He resumed his career as an architect in Melbourne and died in 1943. He is buried at Box Hill cemetery.

General Jan Smuts, who would later serve two terms as prime minister of South Africa, made the following comments about the defence of the Elands River post:

There can only be one opinion about the fine determination and pluck of these stalwart Colonials, to many this terrific bombardment must have been their first experience of serious warfare. Deserted by their friends and then, owing to unreasonable obstinacy, abandoned by their disappointed enemies, they simply sat tight until Kitchener's column, which was in pursuit of General de Wet, finally disinterred them from the carcass-covered Kopje, into which they had burrowed so effectually that it seemed unlikely they would ever come out of it.

One of the Boer commandos in the force attacking the garrison later wrote:

For the first time in the war we were fighting men who used our own tactics against us. They were Australian volunteers and although small in number we could not take their position. They were the only troops who could scout into our lines at night and kill our sentries. Our men admitted that the Australians were more formidable and far more dangerous than any British troops.

Sir Arthur Conan Doyle, as already noted, wrote in praise of the Australians:

They were sworn to die before the white flag would wave above them. And so fortune yielded, as fortune will when brave men set their teeth ... when the ballad makers of Australia seek for a subject, let them turn to Elands River, for there was no finer fighting in the war.

Fifteen years after the Anglo-Boer War, the Anzacs landed at Gallipoli and the story of the colonial Australian troops at Elands River faded from the memory of most Australians.

ELANDS RIVER

George Essex Evans

It was on the fourth of August, as five hundred of us lay
In the camp at Elands River, came a shell from de la Rey.
We were dreaming of home faces, of the old familiar places,
And the gum trees and the sunny plains five thousand miles away.
But the challenge woke and found us
With four thousand rifles round us;
And Death stood laughing at us at the breaking of the day.

Hell belched upon our borders, and the battle had begun.
Our Maxim jammed: We faced them with one muzzle-loading gun.
East, south, and west, and nor'ward
Their shells came screaming forward
As we threw the sconces round us in the first light of the sun.
The thin air shook with thunder
As they raked us fore and under,
And the cordon closed around us, as they held us—eight to one.

We got the Maxim going, and the field-gun into place
(She stilled the growling of the Krupp upon our southern face);
Round the crimson ring of battle
Swiftly ran the deadly rattle
As our rifles searched their fore-lines with a desperate menace;
Who would wish himself away
Fighting in our ranks that day
For the glory of Australia and the honour of the race?

38

But our horse-lines soon were shambles, and our cattle lying dead
(When twelve guns rake two acres there is little room to tread)
All day long we heard the drumming
Of the Mauser bullets humming,
And at night their guns, day-sighted, rained fierce havoc
    overhead.
Twelve long days and nights together,
Through the cold and bitter weather,
We lay grim behind the sconces, and returned them lead for lead.

They called on us to surrender, and they let their cannon lag;
They offered us our freedom for the striking of the flag—
Army stores were there in mounds,
Worth a hundred thousand pounds,
And we lay battered round them behind trench and sconce and
    crag.
But we sent the answer in,
They could take what they could win—
We hadn't come five thousand miles to fly the coward's rag.

We saw the guns of Carrington come on and fall away;
We saw the ranks of Kitchener across the kopje grey—
For the sun was shining then
Upon twenty thousand men—
And we laughed, because we knew, in spite of hell-fire and delay,
On Australia's page forever
We had written Elands River—
We had written it for ever and a day.

UNDER RULE 303

THE SHORT AND SHAMEFUL HISTORY OF THE BUSHVELDT CARBINEERS

Of all the Australian stories associated with the Second South African War, none has received as much attention or caused as much anger, anguish, debate or public interest as the complex and tangled tale of the court martial of four Australian officers of the Bushveldt Carbineers—and the subsequent execution by firing squad of lieutenants Peter Handcock and Harry Morant. It is a story of murder and mayhem, plots and politics, treachery and cover-ups, and the characters involved seem to rise from the pages of history and become 'larger than life', colourful, colonial caricatures—mass murderers, wild colonial boys, cloak and dagger mystery men or comic colonial moustachioed 'Hooray Henrys' (who always remind me immediately of fictional comic stereotype 'Colonel Ponsonby', or Major Dennis Bloodnok from *The Goon Show*).

Many Australians believe that Handcock and Morant were truly Scapegoats of the Empire, which happens to be the title of a book written about the case in 1907 by the third man sentenced to death, Lieutenant George Witton. The execution of these two officers, which was carried out with unseemly haste within eighteen hours of the court's decision being handed down and without any attempt to inform Australian authorities of the decision, has been regarded by many as yet another example of British perfidy and criminal disregard for Australian soldiers, who were treated as mere 'expendable colonials'.

The question of the measure of British unfairness, or even treachery, hinges upon the fact that the accused stated time and again in their own defence that they were certain they had been ordered to behave and fight in a particular way but were being tried and judged by a completely different set of military rules.

The *moral* debate over the case centres around the dilemma as to whether it is just and reasonable to select and punish a few individual soldiers for what were obviously criminal acts, while ignoring the fact that hundreds of other troops were doing exactly the same and not being required to answer for their actions. Put simply, had the accused men made criminal decisions of their own volition? Or were they following 'orders' that were not in the British military handbook and, if so, how far up the chain of command did those orders originate?

Everyone who researches this case inevitably ends up with a theory, and I am no exception. I am of the opinion that British army intelligence constructed their case with the specific aim of ridding the army and the empire of one man, who was not even a member of the Bushveldt Car-bineers but was, in effect, the commanding officer of the Bushveldt Carbineer troopers at Fort Edward. That man was Captain Alfred 'Bulala' Taylor who, having resigned his commission when arrested, was tried by a British military court under martial law—rather than a court martial. I believe that the four Australian officers found guilty were the 'small fry' in the case being built against Taylor and, when the case against him failed to produce the desired result, they became 'collateral damage' and ended up being the victims, token examples of efforts to show that the British were fighting a fair and civilised war in the Transvaal—which they undoubtedly and patently were not.

Why did British intelligence want to 'get' Bulala Taylor?

Well, strange as it may seem, there was an unwritten gentlemen's agreement between the Boers and the British that the war should be fought as a 'white man's war'. Both sides were terrified of the results of mobilising and arming African tribes and involving them in the conflict. In spite of 300 years of European occupation, the white population was still vastly outnumbered in South Africa and there were many long-standing historical grudges to be settled, and the memories of conflicts such as the Zulu, Matabele (Ndebele) and Besotho Wars, and many others, were still fresh in the minds of white South Africans.

Both sides recognised that whoever won by using such methods would then have to deal with the consequences of the threat to white dominance that it would entail, not to mention any tribal wars that would result. When the war began, British officials instructed all white magistrates in the Natal colony to appeal to Zulu chiefs to remain neutral, and, in the Transvaal, President Kruger sent emissaries asking local tribes to stay out of it. However, some tribes were eager to enter the war with the specific aim of reclaiming land confiscated by the Boers, and certain 'rogue elements' within British Intelligence were actively aiding and abetting that possibility: none more so than Captain Alfred Taylor.

The Bushveldt Carbineers Regiment was a unit raised in February 1901 by Major Robert Lenehan, along with other 'irregular' units, in response to the guerrilla tactics being used by the Boers in the Transvaal. The recruiting base was Durban and 660 men served during the unit's eighteen-month history—43 per cent were Australian, 31 per cent English, and the rest were native South Africans, Americans, New Zealanders, Canadians and even a German. Although the unit's authorised strength was 500, its actual fighting strength was never more than about 350.

In many ways the history of the Bushveldt Carbineers serves as a microcosm from the last phase of the Second South African War and exposes to scrutiny Kitchener's policy of 'clearing out the Boers', and answering the guerrilla-style war being waged by Boer farmers with tactics like 'scorched earth', concentration camps, murder and deportation.

Most of the men who joined the regiment were colonial troopers who had been released from their units after the British victory over the Boers in the second phase of the war. Most were attracted by the prospect of further action, and by the high rate of pay of five shillings a day. It was a tough unit with a tough leader, Major Robert William Lenehan.

'Bob' Lenehan was born in 1865 in Petersham, Sydney, educated at St Ignatius College, Riverview, studied law, married Harriett Hodge in 1889, and was practising as a solicitor in 1890—the same year that he was commissioned as a second lieutenant in the 1st Infantry Regiment. Promoted to captain in 1896 in the New South Wales Field Artillery, he dropped a rank to serve as a captain with the 1st New South Wales Mounted Infantry and embarked for South Africa in January 1900.

For the next year Lenehan was constantly engaged in the action. From February to May 1900 he served in the Orange Free State and then in the Transvaal until June. He was present at the siege of the Elands River staging post in August and, from September 1900 to February 1901, was again part of operations in the Orange Free State. This service saw him awarded the Queen's South Africa Medal with six clasps.

Lenehan was given command of the Bushveldt Carbineers with the rank of major. There were several other Australian officers with the unit, including Veterinary Lieutenant Peter Handcock, who was born near Bathurst, New South Wales, in 1868, apprenticed to a blacksmith when he was twelve years old and worked as a blacksmith on the railways. He arrived in South Africa with the New South Wales Mounted Rifles and was promoted to farrier sergeant. When his regiment returned home, he obtained a commission as veterinary and transport officer in the Bushveldt Carbineers.

Lieutenant Harry Morant, who had known Lenehan in Sydney, joined the unit in May and Lieutenant George Witton joined in June.

These four men, all Australians, would later be the only ones, of the eight officers charged and six court-martialled, to be found guilty of war crimes in the Spelonken district during 1901.

Harry Harbord 'Breaker' Morant claimed that he was born in Devon and was the illegitimate son of Admiral Morant sent to Australia in disgrace as a 'remittance man' to be kept out of the way of the family after some sexual scandal.

However, both *The Northern Miner* and *The Bulletin* newspapers identified him as Edwin Henry Murrant, who had arrived in Townsville in Queensland on the SS *Waroonga* in 1883.

Murrant was the son of Edwin and Catherine Murrant, Master and Matron of the Union Workhouse at Bridgwater in Somerset, and it seems that Edwin died in August 1864, four months before the birth of his son, and his wife, Catherine, continued her employment as matron until her retirement in 1882. When Catherine died in 1899, Harry Morant was in Adelaide, where he had joined the Second Contingent South Australian Mounted Rifles, as Harry Harbord Morant, and was about to leave for South Africa to fight the Boers.

Records show that an Edwin Henry Murrant, son of Edwin Murrant, and his wife, Catherine, née O'Reilly, married Daisy May O'Dwyer on 13 March 1884, in Charters Towers. Daisy May O'Dwyer would later become known as the famous anthropologist and champion of the Aborigines, Daisy Bates.

The two separated within months after Morant was arrested on a charge of stealing pigs and a saddle. He was acquitted and went to work further west at Winton, then later he began overlanding cattle south, through the Channel Country. Daisy moved south, was employed as a governess at Berry, New South Wales, and, in February 1885 in Nowra, married cattleman Jack Bates. When he went off droving, she travelled to Sydney where, on 10 June 1885, she married again, to Ernest Baglehole.

Morant developed a legendary and romantic reputation as a hard-drinking horse-breaker, bush poet and ladies' man. A fearless and expert horseman, he was one of the few horsemen who managed to ride the notorious buckjumper, Dargin's Grey, and once jumped his horse Cavalier over a 6-foot (1.8 metre) fence to win a bet. He contributed bush ballads to *The Bulletin* and used the pen-name 'The Breaker'.

His skill as a horseman, and qualities of education and manners, led to him becoming a dispatch rider for General French, and he also worked as an aide and guide for Bennet Burleigh, a famous British war correspondent and also, at some point, met Captain Percy Hunt. Morant served with the South Australian Second Contingent for nine months, during which time he was promoted to the rank of sergeant. At the end of his one-year enlistment, his work was highly commended and he was offered a commission.

Morant, however, was not committed to the war and decided to take the opportunity to return 'home' to England, and spent six months there. During that time he linked up with Hunt and the two men became best friends and were engaged to two sisters. Hunt was still 'signed on' and returned to South Africa in March 1901. Morant followed and the two were commissioned into the Bushveldt Carbineers.

The regiment was part of General Plumer's column of 1300 men, which left Pretoria in March 1901 and advanced to capture Pietersburg, 288 kilometres (180 miles) to the north. The Bushveldt Carbineers' first job was to ensure the British supply trains were safe from the Boers' attempts to blow up all trains on the Pietersburg–Pretoria line. This they did by placing Boer prisoners in the second carriage of a train and telling them that if they did not reveal the location of the explosive mines on the line, they would be blown up with the train. The Carbineers ran the train until the first wagon was blown up and the Boers then revealed the positions of all the mines.

Pietersburg was taken on 14 April and the regiment established headquarters in the wild northern frontier Spelonken district of the Transvaal where A Squadron, under Captain James Robertson, was stationed at Fort Edward, north of Pietersburg, with an outpost at Sweetwaters Farm and Hotel, 2 kilometres (1.2 miles) away. This had been the site of a Boer commando camp but, when the Bushveldt Carbineers moved into the district, the Boers had withdrawn from the area, so as not to cause any problems for the farm and hotel owners, Charlie and Olivia Bristow.

B Squadron, under Lieutenant Harry Morant, was established further south on the other side of Pietersburg, in an area rather easier for the British to control.

Although the regiment was answerable to Area Commandant Colonel F.H. Hall at Pietersburg, the squadron at Fort Edward was greatly influenced by Captain Alfred Taylor, a British intelligence officer at Spelonken, 145 kilometres (90 miles) to the north, who was in the area inciting the local tribes to attack the Boer farms. Taylor was directed by Kitchener to 'liaise with' the Bushveldt Carbineers.

Born into a middle-class Protestant family in Dublin in 1861, Taylor went to sea as a young man and arrived in Africa in 1886. He then served as a mercenary for Cecil Rhodes' British South Africa Company and was instrumental in the success of the company's invasion and conquest of Matabeleland and the creation of Rhodesia as a British colony.

Taylor has been variously described by historians as a 'sadistic, ruthless mass murderer', 'war profiteer', 'cattle thief' and 'war criminal'. He was notorious for his atrocities against the Ndebele people, who gave him the name *Bulala* (The Killer). In May 1901 he led a party of six soldiers from the British Army Intelligence Department to the Transvaal to get information on Boer commando activity. British troops led by Taylor sacked the town of Louis Trichardt and arrested 90 men suspected of being Boer commandos. Taylor then ordered the town to be burned by native South African 'Irregulars' and had the remaining townspeople force-marched to the concentration camp at Pietersburg.

In his role as Acting District Native Commissioner, Taylor waged a war of extermination against the Tsonga people who had a close association with the local Boers. He also encouraged the local Venda and Sotho tribesmen to kill Boer farmers and help themselves to the land and whatever else they wanted, as 'the Boers would not be returning after the war'. Tribesmen from these groups were allowed to follow British soldiers into action and loot farms and massacre local Afrikaners after the troops departed. On at least two occasions the Bushveldt Carbineers 'raised the natives', as this action was called, to help them attack farms.

Captain James Robertson, leader of A Squadron, acknowledged that Taylor, who was not a member of the Bushveldt Carbineers, was 'in charge' in the Spelonkon district and it seems that, under his influence, discipline was a constant problem and the regiment's rules of engagement were vague and arbitrary at best and criminal at worst.

In May 1901, when Captain Frederick de Bertodano, an experienced intelligence officer attached to Lord Kitchener's staff, sought out Major Lenehan at Pietersburg, he was shocked to find Taylor filling in for Lenehan who was away from his headquarters. Back in Pretoria, de Bertodano informed Colonel Henderson, Director of Military Intelligence, that Taylor's reputation 'stank to Heaven', warned him that 'trouble was bound to ensue' and advised that he 'keep an eye on *Bulala* Taylor'.

Frederick Ramon Lopez de Bertodano, 8th Marquis of Moral, was born in 1871 in Lismore, New South Wales. He was the grandson of a Spanish nobleman, Ramon Roman de Bertodano y Lopez, who, in 1837, married Henrietta, daughter of James Pattison, the Governor of the Bank of England. Frederick's father was a well-known colonial racehorse breeder in northern New South Wales and Frederick inherited the rather useless title.

Educated at Armidale Grammar School and Sydney University, he passed his law exams, left for England and trained as a lawyer. He travelled to Rhodesia and took part in the fighting against the Matabele (Ndebele) in 1896 and was a solicitor in Bulawayo. Back in England he joined the Manchester Regiment as second lieutenant in 1899, was promoted to captain in January 1900 and seconded to South Africa.

As de Bertodano predicted, trouble began on 2 July 1901 when Taylor received word that a group of six Boers accompanied by two covered wagons and a large herd of cattle were coming into the fort either to surrender or seek a truce for medical treatment. He told Robertson the fort was possibly going to be attacked and ordered Sergeant Major Morrison to intercept the group, ignore any white flags, take no prisoners and 'make it look like a fight'. Morrison apparently turned to Captain Robertson and asked if he should obey Taylor's orders and Robertson replied, 'Certainly, he is commanding officer here.' Morrison then sent Sergeant Oldham, Corporal Primrose and five other troopers from Sweetwaters Hotel to meet the group.

The party consisted of two ox-wagons driven by two boys aged twelve and eighteen carrying 65-year-old farmer Jan Geyser and three other men who had been members of the local Boer commando unit. All were suffering from malaria and seeking treatment. They had a large herd of valuable cattle with them and a wooden cash box containing a large sum in paper money and gold bars, possibly being taken to safety away from the farm raids and burnings then sweeping the district.

What happened next was later reported by witnesses at the Court of Inquiry. The patrol fired on the wagons and a white flag was raised. Believing that women and children might be present, Sergeant Oldham called 'cease fire', disarmed the Boers and then followed Taylor's orders by having each member of his patrol execute one of the group. Jan Geyser was found lying sick in one of the wagons and Trooper Eden 'climbed into the wagon and shot him where he lay on his bed'.

Corporal Primrose returned to Sweetwaters to report and most of A Squadron then rode to the scene where, according to later witness testimony, five unarmed Boers were lying on the road 'shot in the head save one who was shot in the neck'. Another was 'lying dead in the wagon under his blankets never having got out of bed ... shot in the head'. Trooper Cochrane testified that the oxen and cattle were 'stolen by Captain Taylor, secretly driven to Rhodesia, and sold at Bulawayo'. Lieutenant Handcock took possession of the cash box and the bodies were buried in a mass grave at the site.

After the war, Jan Geyser's daughter wrote a letter describing the number of cattle involved and the contents of the wagons. Nothing was ever returned to the Geyser family. Captain Robertson reported to Major Lenehan that six 'train-wreckers and murderers' had been shot.

Later that day, back at Fort Edward, Trooper van Buuren, an Afrikaner member of the Bushveldt Carbineers, was seen talking to some women from the families of the victims, who were being held for transport to the concentration camp at Pietersburg. Local men who signed up with the British were known as 'joiners' and Taylor often made use of them in his 'intelligence' work. He was, however, worried about van Buuren and ordered Handcock to 'attend to the matter'.

Two days later Handcock took a patrol of four men, including van Buuren, scouting for Boer commandos. At the Court of Inquiry later that year, Trooper Churton testified that he saw Handcock ride up behind van Buuren and shoot him three times in the back. Handcock then said to Churton, 'Keep a sharp lookout. We just lost a man back there.' Handcock wrote a report that Captain Robertson amended as he 'deemed it unsuitable'. Robertson reported to Lenehan at Pietersburg that van Buuren was 'shot in contact with some Boers'.

Major Lenehan and Colonel Hall were aware of the 'poor discipline, unconfirmed murders, drunkenness, and general lawlessness' at Fort Edward. When it was reported that a local woman had accused a British officer of rape, an investigation revealed that the alleged rapist was Captain James Robertson; he was given a choice of being court-martialled or resigning his commission, and chose the latter option.

Lenehan then withdrew the whole detachment from Fort Edward with the exception of Handcock, who, as the station's veterinary officer, was responsible for the horses. Lenehan appointed Captain Percy Hunt, formerly of the 10th Hussars and a good friend of Harry Morant, to 'straighten out' the station. Morant and 60 men were also sent to Fort Edward with Hunt.

Lieutenant Witton's assessment of the situation, as it existed before he and Morant arrived at Fort Edward, was that Robertson:

> . . . was altogether unfit to command such a body of men, and allowed his detachment to drift into a state of insubordination verging on mutiny. The men did almost as they liked, and horses and other captured stock were being divided amongst themselves, while stills on neighbouring farms were freely made use of.

Any consideration of what later became generally known as the 'Breaker Morant Affair' should take into account the fact that all of the events described above occurred before Morant was ever stationed at Fort Edward.

Over the next month eighteen Boers were captured and 500 cattle and fifteen wagons were confiscated. Taylor was still playing an active role in directing activities at Fort Edward and problems continued under Hunt's command, although he made an effort to improve discipline. He had the confiscated cattle disposed of correctly through military channels, he had Morant and Handcock locate and destroy stills the men were using to make spirits, and he had a group of troopers arrested for stealing rum and threatening to shoot Lieutenant Picton for reporting the theft to Hunt. When the men involved absconded, Lenehan had them caught and charged, but they made accusations of misconduct against the officers at Fort Edward and Colonel Hall ordered them to be discharged from service without a full inquiry.

Hunt at this time also admonished Morant for 'bringing in prisoners' on several occasions and instructed him verbally that Kitchener's orders were to 'take no prisoners' and that any Boer prisoners found wearing items of British uniform could be executed by firing squad without being brought in for trial.

A new detachment of twenty men under Lieutenant Witton arrived at Spelonken on 4 August while Hunt was on a mission to locate local commando leader Commandant Viljoen. Witton was a dairy farmer from Warrnambool who had joined the Victorian Imperial Bushmen as a corporal and had risen to the rank of sergeant major while serving in South Africa and was then commissioned as lieutenant in the Bushveldt Carbineers by Major Lenehan.

Witton never met his commanding officer, as Percy Hunt was killed attempting a surprise attack with seventeen troopers on a farm at Duiwelskloof where a group of some 36 Boer commandos were believed to be gathered. The Reverend Reuter, a local missionary, had reported to Hunt that Veldcornet Barend Viljoen's commandos had been 'harassing local non-combatant farmers' and had made threats against the mission station. When a Bushveldt Carbineer patrol was ambushed near the Medingen Mission Station, Hunt's patrol departed Fort Edward on 2 August, accompanied by Tony Schiel, a defector from the Boer commandos working as an 'intelligence scout' for Captain Taylor, with the intention of ambushing the Viljoen commando force. In effect Schiel's task was to 'raise the natives' to attack Boer farms and he commanded some 400 'irregular' troops from the local Lobedu people.

Although Hunt was warned not to attack the farm at night without Schiel's support and normal reconnaissance, he did so and found the Boers had more numbers than he expected. The Boers were able to drive off their attackers, killing Hunt and another trooper in the process. At least two Boers, including Viljoen, were also killed.

When news of the failed attack reached Morant, he assumed command but was visibly distressed to the point of being unable to address the men. Morant always claimed that he and Hunt were best friends, were engaged to two sisters back in Devon, and had joined the Bushveldt Carbineers in order to fight as brothers in arms. He led the mounted group to Sweetwaters, 2 kilometres (1.2 miles) away, where Taylor addressed them, emphasising that no quarter should be given in avenging their captain's death.

Morant's group met up with the survivors of Hunt's patrol an hour after they had buried Hunt. Morant visited the grave before pursuing the Boers and finally located them camped in a native kraal. Morant, apparently grief stricken and angered by reports that Hunt's body had been mutilated at Duiwelskloof, attacked hastily and lost the element of surprise. All the Boers fled except one named Visser, who had been wounded in the foot and could not walk.

Visser had in his possession an old British army coat and trousers, which Morant claimed were Hunt's. In spite of pleas and protests from Lieutenant Witton, Morant had Visser shot by firing squad the next day. As he was too badly wounded to stand, he was shot while seated on the ground. After all the men in the firing squad fired, he was still alive and Lieutenant Picton shot him in the head at close range. The trousers were later found to not be Hunt's and the mutilation, which was also apparent on the bodies of the dead Boers at Duiwelskloof, was thought by many to be the result of a local witchdoctor's ritual performed on the corpses of white men.

On 22 August, a report reached Fort Edward that eight prisoners were being brought in by a patrol. A detailed account of the events that followed were later written by Lieutenant Witton:

A patrol subsequently set out, consisting of Lieutenants Morant, Handcock, and myself, Sergeant-Major Hammett . . . and two troopers. We first called at the office of Captain Taylor. Morant dismounted and had a private interview with that officer; I was not informed as to the nature of it . . .

We went on, and Morant said that it was his intention to have the prisoners shot. Both myself and Sergeant-Major Hammett asked Morant if he was sure he was doing right. He replied that he was quite justified in shooting the Boers; he had his orders, and he would rely upon us to obey him. I also afterwards remonstrated with him for having the prisoners brought in and shot so close to the fort, but he said it was a matter of indifference where they were shot.

We met the patrol with the prisoners about ten kilometres out. Morant at once took charge, and instructed the escort to go on ahead as advance guard . . . I rode on in front of the waggon, and I did not see any civilian speak to the prisoners as we were passing the mission hospital. When we had trekked on about five kilometres Morant stopped the waggon, called the men off the road, and questioned them. Upon his asking, 'Have you any more information to give?' they were shot. One of them, a big, powerful Dutchman, made a rush at me and seized the end of my rifle, with the intention of taking it and shooting me, but I simplified matters by pulling the trigger and shooting him. I never had any qualms of conscience for having done so . . . By just escaping death in this tragedy I was afterwards sentenced to suffer death.

While Morant and some troopers buried the Boers, Witton returned to the fort with the wagons, the dead men's belongings and the oxen, and handed everything to Taylor. Not long after Morant returned, a German missionary, Reverend Carl Heese, who had been seen talking to the prisoners when the convoy stopped at the mission hospital, was seen passing the fort in his buggy, on his way to Pietersburg.

Morant rode out and spoke to him, returned to the fort and told Witton that he'd advised the man to wait till he could be escorted on the dangerous road, but the missionary had a permit to travel signed by Taylor and went on alone. Morant then went to Sweetwaters and talked with Taylor. According to Witton, Morant came back and talked to Lieutenant Handcock who 'had his breakfast, and . . . went away again'.

Almost a week later the missionary's body was found some distance off the road, 25 kilometres (16 miles) from the fort, where he had been shot through the chest. Morant said he had warned him not to travel alone and the Boers must have shot him. It has always been assumed, however, that Morant and Taylor discussed the matter and sent Handcock to shoot Heese to prevent him reaching Pietersburg and informing the British authorities of the Carbineers' activities.

Lenehan arrived at Fort Edward on 7 September 1901, the same day Roelf van Staden and his sons Roelf and Christiaan were coming in to surrender and get medical treatment for fourteen-year-old Christiaan, who was suffering from fever. Morant, Handcock and two others met them and shot them near Sweetwaters Farm. It was alleged that the three were made to dig their own graves before being shot. It was also later alleged that Lenehan was aware of this incident and failed to report it to Hall.

While staying at Fort Edward, Lenehan gave permission for a patrol of 30 men led by Morant and Witton to attempt to capture Tom Kelly, a local Boer guerrilla leader who had fled the district when the Carbineers arrived in May and was now rumoured to be returning with artillery. Lenehan insisted, however, that Kelly be brought in alive, and he was, on 22 September. Morant had patiently conducted an excellent and successful operation.

Witton, who was full of praise for Morant's tactics, leadership and *sangfroid*, told the following anecdote about the long wait for dawn as they lay in ambush, surrounding Kelly's camp:

> The night was intensely cold, but we lay there within 50 metres of them until the first streak of dawn. During the night a dog scented us and started to bark; a Boer got up and gave it a kick to quieten it, at which Morant remarked, 'A man never knows his luck in South Africa.'

Morant was congratulated by Colonel Hall and, as it seemed the Bushveldt Carbineers now had the district under control, he was granted fourteen days' leave, which he spent in Pretoria making arrangements for Percy Hunt's belongings to be sent home and sorting out his dead friend's finances and affairs.

When he returned to Pietersburg from leave, however, Morant was arrested and placed in solitary confinement. Fort Edward was abandoned and the detachment ordered back to Pietersburg where Lenehan, Handcock and Witton were all placed under arrest on 23 October. After a Court of Inquiry in November, they were informed of the charges against them and, in December, they were told they would be tried by court martial. Colonel Hall was transferred to India and the Bushveldt Carbineers were disbanded and the unit recommissioned as the Pietersburg Light Horse. The men were held in solitary confinement for three months and refused permission to advise the Australian government of their position.

On 15 January 1902, the men were shown the charges against them and Major James Thomas, a solicitor of Tenterfield, New South Wales, was appointed to defend them. Thomas had commanded A Squadron New South Wales Citizens' Bushmen at the siege of Elands River post; he had no experience in criminal or military courts.

Five Australians, Major Lenehan and lieutenants Morant, Handcock, Witton and Hannam, three British officers, Captains Taylor and Robertson and Lieutenant Picton, and Sergeant Major Morrison had charges made against them. Put in simple terms, the following six charges were made:

1. On 2 July six Boers captured and shot. (Robertson, Taylor and Sergeant Major Morrison charged with 'murder while on active service'.)

2. On 4 July Trooper van Buuren shot. (Handcock charged with murder. Lenehan charged with 'culpable neglect failing to make a report which it was his duty to make'.)

3. A prisoner named Visser was captured, court-martialled and shot. (Morant, Handcock, Witton and Picton were charged with 'the offense of murder'.)

4. On 3 August, eight Boers surrendered and were shot. (Morant, Handcock and Witton charged with 'the offense of murder'.) Reverend Heese shot. (Morant and Handcock charged with 'the offense of murder'.)

5. On 5 September, Lieutenant Hannam ordered his men to shoot into three wagons and 250 rounds were fired, two little boys were killed and one little girl wounded. (No charges were filed.)

6. On 7 September, Morant had two Boers and a boy aged fourteen taken prisoner and shot. (Lenehan charged with 'culpable neglect failing to make a report which it was his duty to make'. Morant and Handcock charged with 'the offense of murder'.)

The evidence had been gathered over several months, much of it by British intelligence officers, led by de Bertodano who was evidently attempting to build a case against Taylor and had informed Kitchener of the death of Heese, who was travelling in a buggy lent to him by de Bertodano when he was killed. The killing of Boers was one thing, but murdering a German citizen, who was also a Lutheran missionary, was another matter and was bound to bring official protests from Germany, which it did.

Many researchers believe that it was the death of Heese that triggered the inquiry and the courts martial, and that Kitchener then reluctantly approved the building of a case against Taylor and the Bushveldt Carbineer officers.

There was a letter, signed by fifteen Bushveldt Carbineer troopers and given to Colonel Hall, which was written by a mysterious character named Robert Cochrane, an English-born trooper who had been a mining engineer and Justice of the Peace in Western Australia who was also a journalist. Written in very formal language, the letter called for 'a full and exhaustive inquiry' into 'the following disgraceful incidents which have occurred in the Spelonken district'. It then listed in detail the six incidents that later became the formal charges.

Cochrane wrote:

> Sir, many of us are Australians who have fought throughout nearly the whole war ... We cannot return home with the stigma of these crimes attached to our names therefore we humbly pray that a full and exhaustive inquiry may be made by impartial Imperial officers in order that the truth may be elicited and justice done.

There are three 'odd' things about the letter, apart from its formal language and thoroughness of detail. Firstly, only two of the fifteen troopers who signed it were Australian; secondly, Cochrane had never served at Fort Edward; and, lastly, only one of the men who signed it was called to give evidence against Morant, Handcock and Witton. Two others gave evidence against Taylor.

It would seem that British Intelligence, in collusion with Cochrane, sought out witnesses, built a case against Taylor and the other men, and arranged for the letter to be written. Lenehan's visit to Fort Edward in September was also part of this plan; he was there to gather information about the shooting of the Boer prisoners and Heese, probably under orders from de Bertodano.

While the trial was underway, Boer commandos launched a surprise attack on Pietersburg. The prisoners were released from their cells and armed then fought bravely, in the direct line of fire, to help defeat the Boers. Major Thomas filed for clemency because of this, but the court dismissed his request.

Upon being cross-examined, witnesses stated that Captain Hunt had given them orders not to take prisoners, and they had been reprimanded for bringing them in.

Morant stated that under Captain Hunt, he had been 'clearing the northern district of Boers'. He said he believed Captain Hunt acted on orders from Pretoria to clear the Spelonken district and take no prisoners. He stated that Captain Hunt told him that Colonel Hamilton, military secretary, had given him the orders at Lord Kitchener's private house just before his departure to take charge at Fort Edward.

Morant also stated in his defence that it was known that other units, notably the Canadian regiment, Strathcona's Horse, and other brigades of Kitchener's, had acted in exactly the same manner. Morant stated that he had 'never questioned the validity of the orders, he was certain they were correct'.

When questioned as to whether his open-air court martial and summary execution of Visser had been constituted under the King's regulations, Morant famously replied:

> No; it was not quite so handsome. As to rules and sections, we had no Red Book, and knew nothing about them. We were out fighting the Boers, not sitting comfortably behind barb-wire entanglements; we got them and shot them under Rule 303.

The verdicts and outcomes varied considerably.

Lieutenant Hannam was not even brought to trial on the fifth charge as there was some evidence that he was unaware children were present in the wagons and some of those on the wagons had run when called on to surrender. Picton was simply cashiered from the army. Morrison was not convicted.

Captain Taylor, who had resigned his commission when arrested, stood accused of 'ordering the massacre of six unarmed men and boys on 2 July 1901 and the theft of their money and livestock, and the murder of an unarmed native'. All charges against him were dismissed.

Captain Robertson, having been forced to resign his commission in July, turned prosecution witness and charges against him were dropped. He gave evidence against Taylor.

Morant, Handcock and Witton were petitioned by the prosecution to do the same, and testify against Taylor, but all three refused and stuck fast, insisting that they had been ordered to take no prisoners and had been told that Boer prisoners wearing items of British uniform could be shot after a summary court martial in the field. They believed that those orders came from Kitchener via Colonel Hamilton via Hunt to them. Morant was acquitted of murdering Heese, but Morant, Handcock and Witton were found guilty of the murder of the eight Boers and all other charges.

I believe that Morant, Handcock and Witton, in refusing to testify for the prosecution against Taylor, metaphorically 'signed their own death warrants'.

All three were sentenced to death but Witton's sentence was commuted to penal servitude for life. He was imprisoned in Britain and there was strong pressure from Australia for his release, including legal advice from Sir Isaac Isaacs, who would later be Australia's governor-general.

Witton was released in August 1904, but not pardoned. He returned to Australia and was a dairy farmer in Victoria and later in Queensland until his death from a heart attack in 1941.

When Andrew Fisher famously pledged, at the start of WWI, that Australia would defend Britain to our 'last man and last shilling', Witton commented sarcastically that he would be 'that last man'. He is buried in Lutwyche Cemetery in Brisbane, which is, ironically, situated on Kitchener Road.

Lenehan appeared before the court martial on charges of failing to report two incidents, the shooting of two men and a boy, and the shooting of Trooper van Buuren. He was found guilty of 'when on active service by culpable neglect failing to make a report which it was his duty to make' in the case of the shooting of van Buuren. He was found not guilty of the other charge and was 'reprimanded', which was the lightest possible sentence, imprisoned at Cape Town and deported on the SS *Aberdeen*.

It was only after the ship docked in Melbourne on 25 March 1902 that Prime Minister Edmund Barton and parliament learned that two Australian officers, Morant and Handcock, had been executed and another, Witton, had a death sentence commuted to penal servitude for life.

At first Lenehan was not transferred from the New South Wales Colonial Military list to the Australian Military Forces—but was placed on the 'retired list'. He continued to seek justice, insisting that he verbally reported both incidents to Hall, who was not called as a witness as he was in India.

After Labor won government in 1904, Prime Minister Chris Watson took up the case, requested that the British War Office provide a copy of the court-martial proceedings and asked if there was any further evidence against Lenehan. When the War Office replied that there was not, Lenehan was placed on the active military list, backdated in seniority to 1 July 1903, and commanded the No. 1 Battery, Australian Field Artillery, until appointed to command the 4th Field Artillery Brigade with the rank of lieutenant colonel. During WWI he was on full-time duty commanding the military camp at Menangle until late in 1917, when he was named as co-respondent in a very public divorce case. He was relieved of his position at Menangle camp and later placed on the retired list in August 1918. He died in Sydney in 1922 of cirrhosis of the liver.

On 27 February 1902, Morant and Handcock were shot by a firing squad of Cameron Highlanders.

There is certainly a case to be made that Morant and Handcock were victims of Kitchener's attempts to tone down the savagery of the campaign against Boer civilians and appease the Boers and the Germans, as well as responding in some tokenistic way to the voices of criticism at home in Britain.

British welfare campaigner Emily Hobhouse published a report on the concentration camps in June 1901 that led David Lloyd George to accuse the government of 'a policy of extermination against the Boer population'. Liberal opposition party leader Henry Campbell-Bannerman asked in parliament, 'When is a war not a war?' and gave the answer, 'When it is carried on by methods of barbarism in South Africa.'

Labour peer, Thomas Pakenham, described Kitchener's 'scorched earth' plan as:

> . . . organised like a sporting shoot, with success defined in a weekly 'bag' of killed, captured and wounded, and to sweep the country bare of everything that could give sustenance to the guerrillas, including women and children . . .

It was the clearance of civilians that dominated the last phase of the war. Thirty thousand Boer farms were destroyed by the British, and Afrikaner men were hanged outside their houses. The plan included the systematic destruction of crops, the slaughtering or removal of livestock, and the burning down of homesteads and farms to prevent the Boers from returning to the fight.

The concentration camp system saw whole regions depopulated— 45 'tent city' concentration camps were built for Boer internees and there were another 64 for black Africans. Of the 28,000 Boer men taken as prisoners of war, 25,500 were sent overseas. The overwhelming majority of Boers remaining in the local camps were women and children. Women whose husbands had not surrendered were given less rations than those whose husbands had been killed or transported to POW camps in distant parts of the empire, so they could not rejoin the fight.

The official combatant death toll from the Second South African War is an odd statistic. Official British army losses were around 22,000 men and Boer army losses around 4000. However, it is estimated that between 26,000 and 28,000 people (a quarter of the 115,000 internees, almost all women and children) died in concentration camps of disease and starvation.

Banjo Paterson, as a war correspondent, was appalled at the acts of brutality carried out by British troops against Boer civilians:

> Come, let us join in the bloodthirsty shriek,
> Hooray for Lord Kitchener's 'bag'!
> Tho' fireman's torch and hangman's cord—
> They are hung on the English Flag!
>
> In the front of our brave old army! Whoop!
> The farmhouse blazes bright.
> And their women weep and their children die—
> How dare they presume to fight!
>
> And none of them dress in a uniform,
> The same as by rights they ought.
> They're fighting in rags and in naked feet,
> Like Wallace's Scotchmen fought!
>
> They clothe themselves from our captured troops—
> And they're catching them every week;
> But they don't hang them, that shame is ours,
> But we cover the shame with a shriek!

Morant and Handcock, as volunteers, were, perhaps, not *au fait* with the subtleties of regular army 'methods'. Hunt made several attempts to make Morant understand that 'no prisoners' meant 'shoot them before they surrender'. Morant was admonished for bringing in prisoners and made the mistake of taking prisoners and then killing them.

Kitchener needed to make some effort to appease the Boers, Germany and those who opposed his 'all-out war' policy at home, and executing two 'war criminals' from the wild frontier territory was one way to do it. Kitchener was said to have left headquarters so he couldn't receive the telegram asking for clemency that was sent by *all* members of the court martial! It seems Kitchener also went to great pains to distance himself from his previous support of Taylor's activities. Many other British troops also believed there was an unwritten 'no prisoners' order.

Morant himself wrote, the evening before he died:

'It really ain't the place nor time
To reel off rhyming diction—
But yet we'll write a final rhyme
Whilst waiting cru-ci-fi-xion! . . .

But we bequeath a parting tip
For sound advice of such men,
Who come across in transport ship
To polish off the Dutchmen!

If you encounter any Boers
You really must not loot 'em!
And if you wish to leave these shores,
For pity's sake, DON'T SHOOT 'EM!!

And if you'd earn a D.S.O.,
Why every British sinner
Should know the proper way to go is:
'Ask The Boer To Dinner!'

Morant's last words are often claimed to have been, 'Shoot straight, you bastards, don't make a mess of it.' A letter written by a prison warder who witnessed the execution, however, states they were, 'Be sure and make a good job of it.'

Afterword

Colonel J. St Claire, who observed the court proceedings, summed up the official British army position in a confidential report to the War Office:

I agree generally with the views expressed by the Court of Inquiry . . .
The idea that no prisoners were to be taken in the Spelonken area
appears to have been started by the late Captain Hunt & after his death
continued by orders given personally by Captain Taylor . . . Lieut
Morant acquiesced in the illegal execution of the wounded Boer Visser
& took a personal part in the massacre of the 8 surrendered Boers on

23 August . . . After the murder of Van Buuren the officers seem to have exercised a reign of terror in the District, which hindered their men from reporting their illegal acts & even prevented their objecting to assist in the crime.

The first published account of the incidents surrounding the case appeared as early as 1902, the same year Morant and Handcock were executed. It was a little book titled, *Bushman and Buccaneer: a memoir of Harry Morant—His 'Ventures and Verses'*, written by Australian journalist Frank Fox, under the pen-name Frank Renar, with a cover drawing by Norman Lindsay. Fox wrote for *The Bulletin* and edited the *Lone Hand* magazine and later worked on British newspapers as a political and military commentator, served with distinction in WWI and was knighted.

In 1907 the other man originally sentenced to death, Lieutenant George Witton, published his account of the affair, *Scapegoats of the Empire.*

The South African Wars were neglected by historians and almost forgotten for a time once WWI began and it was decades later, in 1959, after two world wars, that Rayne Kruger's book, *Goodbye Dolly Gray*, aroused some interest and reopened some debate.

Prior to the reawakened interest in the case in Australia, brought about by the Bruce Beresford film in 1980, there was *Breaker Morant, A Horseman Who Made History*, by Frederic Cutlack, in 1962; *The Breaker—A Novel*, by Kit Denton, in 1973; and *In Search of Breaker Morant*, by Margaret Carnegie and Frank Shields in 1979.

Bruce Beresford's film, *Breaker Morant*, was actually based on a play by Kenneth Ross, who successfully sued Angus & Robertson, the publisher of Denton's novel, for publicising that book as the source material for the film.

Since that time, more books have been written, all attempting to uncover the truth behind the only execution by British firing squad of soldiers fighting for Britain in the Second South African War: *Breaker Morant and the Bushveldt Carbineers*, by Arthur Davey (1987); *The Bushveldt Carbineers and the Pietersburg Light Horse*, by Bill Woolmore (2002); *Shoot Straight, You Bastards*, by Nick Bleszynski (2003); *Breaker Morant: The Final Roundup*, by Joe West and Roger Roper (2016); and *Ready, aim, fire: Major James Francis Thomas, the fourth victim in the execution of Lieutenant Harry 'Breaker' Morant*, by James Unkles (2018).

In 2009, James William Unkles, a naval reserve commander and barrister, sent petitions for pardons for Morant, Handcock and Witton to both the queen and the Petitions Committee of the Australian parliament. In November 2010, the UK Ministry of Defence replied:

> After detailed historical and legal consideration, the Secretary of State has concluded that no new primary evidence has come to light which supports the petition to overturn the original courts-martial verdicts and sentences.

In 2012, the Australian Attorney-General's Department announced that it would not seek a pardon for Morant from the British government, as 'a pardon for a Commonwealth offence would generally only be granted where the offender is both morally and technically innocent of the offence'.

As Edwin Murrant, alias Harry Harbord Morant, alias 'The Breaker', once whispered in the dark to George Witton, 'A man never knows his luck in South Africa.'

THE FIRST AND THE LAST

If you are inclined to be pedantic, and who among us is not from time to time, the first military action ever fought by 'Australians' occurred at Wolvekuil Kopjes, 32 kilometres (20 miles) north of Philipstown in the Cape Colony on Valentine's Day 1901, during the guerrilla phase of the Second South African (Anglo-Boer) War.

It was an attempt by the British to capture the 1400 men of a Boer commando force led by General Christiaan de Wet that had crossed the border into central Cape Colony from the Orange Free State two days previously and attempted a daring raid on Philipstown, in order to obtain food and supplies.

When the raid failed, de Wet and his troops found themselves pursued by a column of 1100 mounted British troops, made up mostly of New Zealanders, and Australians from Queensland, Tasmania, Victoria and Western Australia, who had gone to South Africa as colonial troops. As Australia had become a nation 45 days previously, these men were now also citizens of Australia.

Led by Brigadier General Herbert Plumer, the British force had been sent south from the Transvaal to deal with the incursion and capture the Boers.

Torrential rain helped them to overtake and force the Boers to fight a rear-guard action at the Wolvekuil Kopjes two days later, during which the first wave of British assault, an attack by two squadrons of the King's Dragoon Guards, failed dismally and resulted in the capture of the attacking British soldiers by the Boers.

The Australians and New Zealanders, led by Lieutenant Colonel Cradock, then made what was described as 'a very dashing assault', outflanking the enemy and causing de Wet to abandon the position and hurriedly retreat.

Heavy rainstorms hindered the British effort to capture the Boers and Cradock's force suffered 23 casualties in the fighting.

———

Eleven months later, on 4 January 1902, at Onverwacht, in south-eastern Transvaal, about 30 kilometres (19 miles) east of Ermelo, Plumer was once again in charge of British troops in an action designed as a pincer movement in which Plumer's force was supposed to trap the enemy, a 750-man force led by the Boer Commander in Chief, General Louis Botha, between Plumer's men and another British column operating along the border with Swaziland.

The action began badly. On 3 January the New Zealanders forming the advance guard were surprised by the enemy and suffered 28 men captured. Next day 300 Boers ambushed part of Plumer's column led by Major J.M. Vallentin, comprising 110 men of the 5th Queensland Imperial Bushmen under Major Frederick Toll, as well as British mounted troops.

The Boers, who had been concealed in a deep hollow, pursued Vallentin's men back to Onverwacht ridge and forced them to fight. The Boers, now reinforced to a strength of 500, wanted to capture the Maxim quick-fire (pom-pom) gun that the British troops were guarding, and shot the horses pulling it. The Queenslanders, aided by the Hampshire Mounted Infantry, pushed the gun into a gully and attempted to defend it, but were forced to retreat and make a last stand on a small ridge with no cover until the 70 left standing had no choice but to surrender.

The Boers then took all the weapons, clothing, boots and equipment they could carry from the prisoners and the dead troops, and used 30 captured horses to carry away their booty, as well as their dead and wounded, leaving their captives unharmed.

The pom-pom gun was retrieved by men of the 5th Victorian Mounted Rifles who arrived on the scene soon after and, although pursuit was mounted by Western Australian Major Harry Vialls, the Boers, who had lost nine men killed including their leader Commandant Oppermann, were not seen again.

British casualties were 29 dead and 45 wounded, with Major Vallentin among the dead. The Queenslanders lost thirteen men killed and seventeen wounded and, despite the humiliation, Plumer was satisfied that no blame was attached to them. He commended Toll for his leadership and recommended several Australians for gallantry awards.

This rather ignominious engagement was the last significant action fought by Australians in the Second South African (Anglo-Boer) War.

THE LAST PARADE

A.B. 'Banjo' Paterson

An estimated 300,000 horses died in the Boer War. Quarantine regulations ensured that those taken from Australia which did survive the war could not return home.

> With never a sound of trumpet,
> With never a flag displayed,
> The last of the old campaigners
> Lined up for the last parade.
>
> Weary they were and battered,
> Shoeless, and knocked about;
> From under their ragged forelocks
> Their hungry eyes looked out.
>
> And they watched as the old commander
> Read out, to the cheering men,
> The Nation's thanks and the orders
> To carry them home again.
>
> And the last of the old campaigners,
> Sinewy, lean, and spare—
> He spoke for his hungry comrades:
> 'Have we not done our share?

'Starving and tired and thirsty
We limped on the blazing plain;
And after a long night's picket
You saddled us up again.

'We froze on the windswept kopjes
When the frost lay snowy white.
Never a halt in the daytime,
Never a rest at night!

'We knew when the rifles rattled
From the hillside bare and brown,
And over our weary shoulders
We felt warm blood run down.

'As we turned for the stretching gallop,
Crushed to the earth with weight;
But we carried our riders through it—
Carried them p'raps too late.

'Steel! We were steel to stand it—
We that have lasted through,
We that are old campaigners
Pitiful, poor, and few.

'Over the sea you brought us,
Over the leagues of foam:
Now we have served you fairly
Will you not take us home?

'Home to the Hunter River,
To the flats where the lucerne grows;
Home where the Murrumbidgee
Runs white with the melted snows.

'This is a small thing, surely!
Will not you give command
That the last of the old campaigners
Go back to their native land?'

They looked at the grim commander,
But never a sign he made.
'Dismiss!' and the old campaigners
Moved off from their last parade.

PART II
FIGHTING THE KAISER

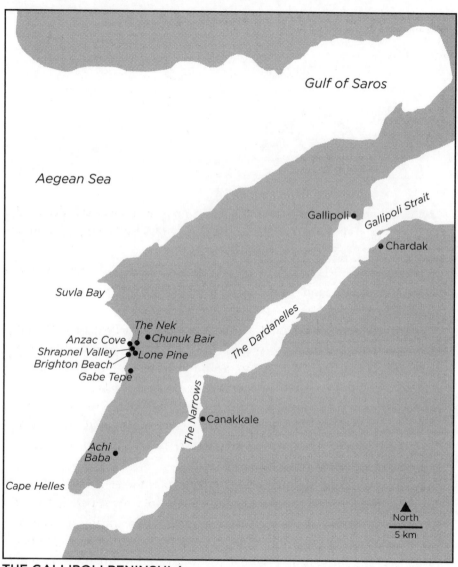

THE GALLIPOLI PENINSULA

ANSWERING THE CALL

A ustralia's population was about five million when war was declared in 1914 and 39 per cent of the males aged 18 to 40 enlisted voluntarily in WWI—a staggering 420,000.

There were several reasons why so many Australian men responded so eagerly to the call to join up and fight a war in Europe.

One was the weather.

There was a severe drought across Australia from 1911 to 1916 and many men living in rural areas had little to do. Grazing properties were largely unstocked, there were fewer crops to harvest and work was scarce in the bush. There were drought-producing *El Niño* events in 1911, 1913 and 1914, which led to prolonged drought until well into 1916. The ending of the drought varied around the continent but it wasn't until there were heavy rains and flooding across south-eastern Australia in December 1916 that the drought was over.

Other reasons for the large volunteer enlistment were cultural.

Cadet training in schools had been compulsory for Australian boys over the age of twelve from 1910. This meant that nearly all Aussie boys had been trained in rudimentary military procedure, had shot a rifle, camped in tents and worn army uniform. So, army life was not a mystery to them and many enjoyed playing soldiers. The teachers in charge of cadets had been trained by the army and most encouraged the boys to join up when war was declared.

Australia was 'more British than Britain' back then. Jingoism and a rather naive, sycophantic attitude to 'king and country' (and 'empire') were promoted by the Anglican Church and the establishment generally.

On the whole Australians believed Britain had every right to rule the empire and could do no wrong. Men joined up unthinkingly to defend what they perceived to be 'right' against 'wrong'.

Then again, many men openly admitted they joined up to 'see the world' and others, as Banjo Paterson put it, 'for the sake of a fight'.

Whatever the reason, when Britain called, 420,000 Aussies answered.

The response was almost too much. Training facilities were stretched to breaking point and new camps were being established hastily through-out 1915 and 1916. Recruitment procedure, training, logistics and organisation were often slapdash and shoddy.

It seems that the Australian army, only fifteen years on from being a separate group of colonial militia, had no idea how to organise and train large numbers of recruits for a proper war. The recruits were treated more like cadets or colonial militiamen than professional soldiers about to serve in a very serious international war.

Many were country boys and just eighteen years of age. Many lied about their age. The youngest known member of the 1st AIF was James Martin, from Tocumwal on the Murray River, who enlisted at fourteen years and three months claiming he was eighteen. He died of typhoid at Gallipoli aged fourteen years and nine months.

We know of more than twenty Australians who died in World War I before they were eighteen years of age. We will never know how many minors actually joined and served.

RECRUITED

Thomas Barkla

Phillis, your method of raising recruits
Smacks of the press-gang a trifle
Here I am wearing impossible boots
And marching about with a rifle
Because you have said we can never be wed
Until I am carried home, wounded or dead.

Now I've a number instead of a name
The cut of my clothes is atrocious
Daily I'm drilled until aching and lame
By officers young and precocious
Who force me to lie on my tummy to try
And shoot an imaginary bull in the eye.

Please do not think I'm unwilling to go
I have no intention of quitting;
But Phillis, there's one thing I really must know.
For whom is that muffler you're knitting?
I don't care a lot, if by Germans I'm shot;
But if that is for me—I'll desert on the spot!

FIRST BLOOD

The eastern part of Papua New Guinea was unexplored by Europeans until a Russian anthropologist spent time there in the 1870s.

In 1883, Queensland, as a colony, tried to annex the southern half of eastern New Guinea, but the British government did not approve. However, when Germany began settlements in the north a British protectorate was proclaimed in 1884 over the southern coast of New Guinea and its adjacent islands. British New Guinea was annexed outright on 4 September 1888 and placed under the authority of the Commonwealth of Australia in 1902. Following the passing of the *Papua Act* in 1905, British New Guinea became the Territory of Papua, and formal Australian administration began in 1906.

In 1884, Germany took possession of the north-east quarter of the island and put its administration in the hands of a chartered trading company, the German New Guinea Company. The German Imperial Government charter gave the company sovereign rights over the territory and other 'unoccupied' lands in the name of the government in May 1885. In 1899, the German Imperial Government assumed direct control of the territory, thereafter known as German New Guinea. The island that had been named New Britain by William Dampier in 1700 was renamed Neupommern (New Pomerania).

For the Germans, New Guinea was basically a business venture. Thousands of local workers were hired as cheap labour on cocoa and copra plantations. In 1899, the German government took control of the colony from the New Guinea Company of Berlin. Education was in the hands of missionaries.

At the outbreak of war in 1914 the British were worried that the East Asia Squadron of the Imperial German Navy, commanded by Vice Admiral von Spee and based in Tsingtao in China, could use German territories in the Pacific as bases and radio stations. The squadron was made up of the armoured cruisers SMS *Scharnhorst* and *Gneisenau*, and the light cruisers SMS *Emden, Nürnberg, Koenigsberg* and *Leipzig*.

The War Office asked the Royal Australian Navy (RAN) to help seize German territories in the Pacific and, in late August 1914, HMAS *Australia* and *Melbourne*, with HMS *Psyche, Philomel* and *Pyramus*, and the French cruiser *Montcalm*, took 1400 New Zealand troops to German Samoa. The colony surrendered without a fight. HMAS *Melbourne* then went to the German territory of Nauru, where the German administrator was arrested and the wireless station destroyed.

During August a volunteer force known as the ANMEF (Australian Naval and Military Expeditionary Force), consisting of a battalion of 1000 infantry and 500 naval reservists, was assembled to invade the German colonies in New Guinea. This force was given strong naval support, as the location of the German battleships was not known.

The flotilla—made up of HMAS *Australia, Sydney, Melbourne, Encounter, Parramatta, Warrego* and *Yarra, AE1, AE2*, a store-ship, three colliers, and the transport *Berrima*—sailed for New Britain (Neupommern), where two enemy wireless stations were operating. The first landing took place at Kabakaul at dawn on 11 September. A party of 25 sailors, led by Lieutenant Rowland Bowen, made their way inland on a side track to the back of Bitapaka wireless station and encountered three Germans and some local Melanesians preparing an ambush. The Germans ran, but one was shot and wounded and the others captured. The locals were ordered to surrender.

The captives were marched towards the main settlement and ordered to tell the garrison to surrender. Meanwhile, Lieutenant Bowen called for reinforcement and, at 10 am, Lieutenant G.A. Hill, RNR (Royal Naval Reserve) of HMAS *Yarra* and 59 men armed with rifles, pistols and swords, arrived and tried to outflank the enemy trenches on the main road in front of the wireless station. In the conflict Bowen was hit by a sniper's bullet and Hill took over and called for more reinforcements, which arrived at 1 pm with Lieutenant Commander Charles Elwell, RN (Royal Navy), who took command but was killed leading a bayonet charge on the German trenches. Hill continued the attack until Lieutenant Gillam,

RANR (Royal Australian Naval Reserve), arrived with more reinforcements and the Germans surrendered.

Lieutenant Commander Charles Elwell was a lieutenant on the HMAS *Melbourne* and gunnery instructor from RAN College in Geelong, who had volunteered for the ANMEF. The German who bayonetted Elwell was killed by Signaller Bert Reed. In a letter to his parents, Reed wrote: 'You may have read in the papers that Lieutenant Commander Elwell was run through with a bayonet. Well, I am very pleased to know that I shot the man who killed him. I was the signalman of No. 2 Company, and was with Lieutenant Commander Elwell at the time. I used my rifle and pistol a lot, but how many others I killed or wounded I do not know.'

After the defenders surrendered, Lieutenant Bond, RANR, advanced to secure the wireless station and became the first Australian decorated in World War I, receiving the Distinguished Service Order. One German and about 30 local Melanesian police were killed in the fighting.

Next day, after a naval bombardment, the port of Rabaul and Herbertshöhe wireless station were taken without opposition, and all German forces surrendered. Within a few weeks most of the German territories were occupied and all their merchant ships in the area were captured by RAN vessels. The five German cruisers, however, were still at large somewhere in the Pacific or Indian ocean.

After the war the plantations of the seized German possessions were given to Australian war veterans and, in 1921, the League of Nations gave Australia a trusteeship over New Guinea.

THE *AE1*

The *AE1* was the first of two 'E' Class submarines built by Vickers Ltd at Barrow-in-Furness for the Australian navy. Construction began in 1911 and she was launched in May 1913 and commissioned at Portsmouth on 28 February 1914. She was 55 metres long, 7 metres wide, and had a draught of 3.8 metres. Rather than champagne, an axe was used to ceremoniously launch both the *AE1* and her sister boat, the *AE2*. Now in a private collection, the head of the axe is engraved with the words:

> With this axe Mr H Wharton successfully launched submarines AE1 and AE2 from the Works of Vickers Ltd. Barrow, 22/5 and 18/6 1913.

AE1 had no guns and her four torpedo tubes faced forward, rearward, port and starboard. The crew of 34 was led by Lieutenant Commander Thomas Fleming Besant, RN, and her officers were Royal Navy men, while her crew came from the Royal Navy and the Royal Australian Navy.

With her sister boat, the *AE2*, launched a month later and commanded by Lieutenant Commander Henry Stoker, *AE1* left Portsmouth on 2 March 1914 and arrived in Sydney 83 days later, on 24 May. At the time this was the longest journey undertaken by any submarine, although the two boats were each towed for about half the trip.

The journey was planned in three stages. For the first stage, to Colombo, the Royal Navy cruiser HMS *Eclipse* escorted them and alternately towed the boats to reduce wear on their diesel engines. Submarines were still rather experimental vessels in 1914. Design was primitive and steering was erratic—*AE1* and *AE2* were basically two rather large tin cans which could submerge to 30 metres safely and 60 metres 'maybe', and travel at a top speed of 5 knots under water.

Not long after leaving Portsmouth *AE2* lost a propeller blade, which was replaced at Gibraltar. The slow journey then continued via Malta, the Suez Canal and Port Said until *AE2* lost a second propeller blade just out of Aden. A new blade was fitted in a two-day operation undertaken at sea by divers, after the submarine's rear end was hoisted up by chains from HMS *Eclipse*.

These mishaps did not bode well for the two submarines' chances of operating efficiently during times of conflict and another 'problem' became apparent as they made their way across the Red Sea. Lacking insulation the 'tin cans' were either freezing cold or boiling hot. Crossing the Red Sea the temperature inside the boats reached well over 100 degrees Fahrenheit (38 degrees Celsius) and, during the five days spent in Colombo in early April, the *AE2* was painted white to reflect the heat of the tropical sun.

From Colombo to Singapore the HMS *Yarmouth* provided the escort and towing duties. In Singapore the cruiser HMAS *Sydney* was waiting to take over for the final leg of the 20,800-kilometre (13,000-mile voyage). The submarines arrived in Sydney, after 60 days at sea, 83 days after leaving Portsmouth.

When WWI began in August 1914, the two submarines left Sydney with the ANMEF (Australian Naval and Military Expeditionary Force) and headed to German New Guinea in order to capture the German colonies for Australia.

Following the German surrender the British flag was hoisted at Rabaul on 13 September 1914, all the German New Guinea territories were surrendered to the ANMEF on 22 September 1914.

In between these two dates the submarines were assigned to patrol St George's Channel, between New Britain and New Ireland, and protect the RAN fleet from any danger posed by enemy ships. On 14 September 1914, *AE1* left Rabaul's harbour to patrol the area around Cape Gazelle and, when the destroyer HMAS *Parramatta* ceased her night patrol off Raluana Point at 7 am, she proceeded slowly towards Cape Gazelle to rendezvous with *AE1* and conduct another patrol. The vessels met at 8 am, exchanged signals and headed to Cape Gazelle, arriving at 9 am. *Parramatta* then headed south and *AE1* went north-east.

At 12.30 pm *Parramatta* turned back to meet *AE1* and, at 2.30, the submarine was visible and signalled: 'What is the distance of visibility?' *Parramatta* replied, 'About 5 miles.' When *Parramatta* lost sight of the submarine at 3.20 pm, she altered course to look for her, fully aware that the submarines were not as reliable as warships and needed 'looking after'. Finding no sign of *AE1*, *Parramatta*'s captain assumed she had returned to Rabaul.

By 8 pm, however, the submarine had not returned and HMAS *Parramatta* and *Yarra* went looking for her. HMAS *Sydney*, *Encounter* and *Warrego* joined the search, but no trace of *AE1* was found.

The loss of *AE1* and her three officers and 32 crew was Australia's first major loss of World War I and it was a blow to morale at home. Searches were conducted at the end of the war and again in 1976 to find her; but none was successful.

Finally, in December 2017, the search vessel *Fugro Equator* located the wreck of *AE1* in 300 metres of water near the Duke of York Islands. The Australian government announced, on 21 December, that the location of the wreck, now an official war grave, would not be made public.

The loss of *AE1* is commemorated in a poem by a wonderful Australian, Madoline 'Nina' Murdoch, who was also known by her married name, Madoline Brown, her pen name, 'Manin', and her 'radio' name 'Pat'.

She was born in Melbourne but her family moved to New South Wales and she attended Sydney Girls High School, where she began writing. Best known for her biographies, poetry and travel writings, more than 80 of her poems were published by *The Bulletin* and she was also a radio broadcaster and teacher. One of her greatest achievements was the creation of the famous ABC children's radio program *The Argonauts*.

She married fellow teacher and journalist James Brown in 1917 but remained an independent woman and travelled the world in the 1920s before becoming a journalist in Melbourne. When she, and other married female journalists, lost their jobs on the Melbourne *Herald* in the Depression, Nina began to give radio talks on her travels on the new medium of 'the wireless' and, when the Australian Broadcasting Commission was founded in 1932, she began 'Children's Corner' on station 3LO. She formulated the idea for, and as 'Pat' began running, the Argonauts' Club, a novel children's program that introduced cultural content to an area previously dominated by bunnies, kookaburras and birthday calls. Its pledge epitomised her style: 'I vow to stand faithfully by all that is brave and beautiful; to seek adventure, and having discovered aught of wonder or delight, of merriment or loveliness, to share it freely with my comrades.'

When husband, James, moved to Adelaide to work for News Limited in 1934, Nina left the ABC and followed him. The Argonauts' Club ceased, but was revived in 1941 and continued until 1972.

Nina Murdoch's poem about the *AE1* was written for the women who worked at Royal Naval House in Sydney. Originally named 'Goodenough House', Royal Naval House was a naval headquarters and sailors' refuge which was opened by Lord Carrington in 1890. It was a large establishment with many buildings; sailors ashore from ships in Sydney Harbour could have board and lodging overnight in the main building, known affectionately as 'Johnnies'. Wives and children of serving naval men lived in the complex, much of which was lost in the building of the Sydney Harbour Bridge approaches in the 1920s. Today, only the facade of the main building remains.

During World War I, many sailors' wives lived and worked at Royal Naval House, often performing clerical and domestic work. The navy presented a beautiful silver and blue enamel medal, in the form of a brooch, to the nearest female relative of every man serving in the RAN in the war. It featured an anchor and the inscription, 'Royal Australian Navy To Women Of Australia For Duty Done'. The women living and working at Royal Naval House also started wearing coloured bows to signify the vessels their men served on. Nina Murdoch wrote this poem for them, after the loss of the *AE1*.

COLOURED BOWS

Nina Murdoch

The cruisers and destroyers have borne our men away;
Perhaps ten thousand miles divide our men from us to-day.
They may be in the North Sea, they may be near at hand,
We only know for certain that we wish them safe on land.

O it's red for the Australia,
   The little Penguin's blue,
It's white for the Encounter,
   And the Sydney's purple hue;

But it's black, plain black if your husband or your son
Went out of Sydney Harbour on the AE1.

We're not afraid of hardships, and we're not the sort to shirk,
If the pay we get is not enough, we simply look for work;
And some have gone to service to raise an extra pound
To put towards a cottage or perhaps a piece of ground.

So it's not the fear of struggling with hunger at the door,
And it isn't that we're lonely—we've been through that before!
But it breaks a woman's spirit when there's trouble for her mate,
And for her the helpless knowledge she can only work and wait.

O it's red for the Australia,
  The little Penguin's blue,
It's white for the Encounter,
  And the Sydney's purple hue;

But it's black, plain black if your husband or your son
Went out of Sydney Harbour on the AE1.

VICTORY AT SEA

Throughout October 1914, transport ships in harbours around Australia and New Zealand were taking on troops in preparation for the voyage across the Indian Ocean to fight in Europe. But there was concern about the whereabouts of the German East Asia Squadron warships, especially the light cruisers *Emden* and *Koenigsberg*, which were somewhere west of Australia. The *Emden*, commanded by Captain von Müller, had been responsible for the loss of 100,000 tonnes of Allied merchant shipping. She had also sunk a Russian light cruiser, *Zemtchung*, and a French destroyer, the *Mosquet*, in a raid on Penang Harbour and had destroyed port installations and fuel tanks at Madras.

So, when the first ANZAC convoy left Albany, on 1 November 1914, the 38 transports heading for the Middle East were given plenty of protection. Four battlecruisers accompanied the convoy. HMS *Minotaur* led the way with HMAS *Melbourne* at the rear, HMAS *Sydney* guarded one flank and the Japanese battlecruiser *Ibuki* the other.

Allied warships hunting the *Emden* in the Indian Ocean at this time included the Japanese *Yahagi* and *Chikuma*, the Russian *Askold*, and the British ships HMS *Hampshire*, *Yarmouth*, *Weymouth*, *Gloucester*, *Empress of Russia* and *Empress of Asia*, while other Japanese warships were moving down towards the waters of the Malay Archipelago to join the search.

In a strange twist of fate, however, at 6.30 am on 9 November, when the ANZAC convoy just happened to be in the vicinity of the Cocos Islands, distress signals from the radio station on Direction Island were picked up by the cruisers and several of the transports. The message indicated that a 'strange warship' was approaching the islands. The message, repeated with an 'S.O.S.', was followed by messages picked up in Australia, that a three-funnelled warship was off the island and it was landing a party of men on the beach.

The convoy was proceeding cautiously at the time, attempting to keep all ships in formation and close, with speed limited to 10 knots (the fastest speed possible by the slowest of the horse transports). It was important for the ships to stay close as the convoy was now without any rear-guard protection. HMS *Minotaur* had been called away urgently the day before, to provide support for the campaign in South Africa after German warships had destroyed the British squadron protecting the convoys there.

HMAS *Melbourne* had replaced the *Minotaur* at the head of the convoy and her captain, Mortimer L'Estrange Silver, RN, was now in command.

As soon as he'd received and understood the message, Silver increased speed and veered west with the intention of proceeding to confront the German warship. No sooner had he done this than he re-evaluated the situation and, realising his duty was to the convoy, he slackened speed, returned to his station at the head of the convoy and radioed *Sydney*, the cruiser closest to the threatened island, to proceed and answer the call for help.

HMAS *Sydney*, under the command of Captain John Glossop, RN, immediately detached from the convoy to investigate and, within a few hours, sighted the German light cruiser *Emden* close to Cocos Island.

Von Müller, who had no idea that the ANZAC convoy was so far north, was taken by surprise when the *Sydney* appeared over the horizon. At first he assumed it was *Emden*'s German support collier *Buresk*. As the *Sydney* approached at 20 knots, however, he realised he was in trouble and would have to fight. Abandoning the shore party, which had landed in order to disable the wireless station and destroy the international cable connection between Australia, India and Africa, he headed out to sea to find room to manoeuvre and fight the *Sydney*.

Meanwhile, on board the Australian cruiser, Captain Glossop assessed the vessel he was about to fight and correctly assumed her armaments were 100-mm (4-inch) guns. He proceeded to close to 9500 yards (8.7 kilometres), where he knew his 150-mm (6-inch) guns could reach the enemy ship, assuming he would be out of her range. What he didn't know was that the *Emden*'s gun elevation mountings had been modified, which extended the range of her guns. To Glossop's surprise the first shells from the *Emden* hit the *Sydney* at around 9.45 am, when she was still 10,500 yards (9.6 kilometres) away. After one salvo overshot and landed beyond the *Sydney*, von Müller quickly corrected the range and the *Emden*'s guns, firing a salvo every sixteen seconds, and scoring fifteen hits on the Australian cruiser.

As soon as Glossop realised the *Emden*'s gun had a greater range than he thought, he used the *Sydney*'s superior speed (27 knots as opposed to the *Emden*'s 17 knots) to remove his ship from danger. In the first ten minutes of the battle, the *Sydney*'s range finders were damaged and four of her crew were killed and twelve wounded.

From then on, however, the battle became a very one-sided affair as the *Sydney* out-manoeuvred, out-sped and out-gunned the German raider. The *Emden* was hit by more than 100 of Sydney's 150-mm, 45-kilogram shells and, although she had one gun still functional at 11 am, the *Emden* was by then a shattered wreck, her hull full of holes, her superstructure and decks a blazing mess and her steering gone. At 11.15 am her captain ran her ashore on North Keeling Island in an attempt to save the lives of what was left of his crew. The *Sydney* then went after the *Emden*'s support collier the *Buresk*, and boarded her just after midday, only to find that her crew had opened the seacocks and she was sinking fast, so the Australian cruiser could not take her as a prize of war.

The *Sydney* returned to the wreck of the *Emden* at 4 pm to find her still flying her colours. Captured German officers from the *Buresk* told Glossop that von Müller would not surrender while the flag flew. After replying in Morse to Glossop's signal 'Will you surrender?' with 'What signal?' and 'No signal books', the *Emden* refused to answer the repeated signals, 'Do you surrender?' and 'Have you received my signal?' Glossop, worried that the *Emden* might still be capable of firing torpedoes or be planning resistance with small arms fire, stood off 3.2 kilometres (2 miles) and ordered two more salvos to be fired at her mainmast, where the flag was flying. A man was then seen to climb up to strike the flag and, finally, a white sheet was displayed on the quarterdeck.

Unsure of the whereabouts of the *Koenigsberg*, the other German cruiser known to be in the Indian Ocean, and worried about the situation at the wireless station, Glossop returned to rescue some of the Chinese crew of the *Buresk*, who had been left afloat in the ship's boats. He then sent the boats with the *Buresk* crewmen on board to the *Emden* with a message that he would return with help the next day.

On 10 November, after checking that the *Koenigsberg* was not lurking around the islands, Glossop investigated the situation on Direction Island, sending a boat ashore under a white flag, expecting to find 50 Germans in charge.

When he found that the landing party had left with the island's schooner, Glossop assessed the situation on the island and returned to the *Emden*, taking with him the doctor and the medical staff from the Direction Island cable station.

The scene on the wreck was horrific. Of the *Emden*'s crew of 316, 134 were dead and about 70 seriously wounded. Glossop was sickened and shocked at the results of his victory:

> My God, what a sight! Her captain had been out of action 10 minutes after the fight started from lyddite fumes, and everybody on board was demented . . . by shock, by fumes, and the roar of shells bursting among them. She was a shambles. Blood, guts, flesh, and uniforms were all scattered about. One of our shells had landed behind a gun shield, and had blown the whole gun crew into one pulp. You couldn't even tell how many men there had been. They had 40 minutes of hell on that ship and the survivors were practically mad men.

It was an unusual situation. Usually, after a battle at sea is decided, the wounded men go down with the sinking ship, but the *Emden* had been run ashore and the wounded survived. Transferring them to the *Sydney* was a nightmare, made worse by heavy surf. With the prisoners and wounded from the *Emden* on board, as well as those from the *Buresk*, the *Sydney* was overcrowded and her resources stretched.

The *Sydney*'s two surgeons, officers Darby and Todd, along with Dr Ollerhead from the cable station and the *Emden*'s surgeon, Dr Luther, worked for 40 hours without sleep, operating on the severely wounded. The worst cases from the *Emden* were given precedence over the twelve wounded crewmen from the *Sydney*.

Three days after the battle, as the *Sydney* headed for Colombo, she was met by the auxiliary cruiser HMS *Empress of Russia* and the prisoners who could be moved were transferred to that ship. When the *Sydney* was reunited with the ANZAC convoy in Colombo Harbour, Glossop sent a message to the fleet requesting that the men on the convoy ships refrain from cheering to welcome her, as a sign of respect for the many wounded men lying on her decks.

In replying to criticism of the way Glossop dealt with the defeated *Emden*, the official war history stated:

> If the *Sydney* had had no enemy but the *Emden* to deal with, she could have rendered expeditious and full assistance before the day of the fight was over; but she had the *Buresk* to chase, Direction Island to relieve, and the *Koenigsberg* to guard against.

The offices and crew of the *Sydney* were drawn from both the Royal Navy and Royal Australian Navy, and Glossop was full of praise for all of them. He was especially proud of the 60 Australian boys from the training ship *Tingira*, many of whom were only sixteen years old. Another RN officer wrote, just after the fight, 'Our men behaved splendidly; this was especially noticeable in the case of the young boys, many of them only 16 years old and just out of the training-ship.'

The HMAS *Tingira* was an old sailing ship, previously known as the *Sobraon*, she was moored off Cockatoo Island and used as a reform school ship for wayward boys under the control of the New South Wales State Welfare Department until taken over by the RAN in 1911 as a training ship for boys from fourteen years of age.

The *Emden's* widely reported successes and daring exploits had made the ship quite famous and her destruction was a big news item. The RAN enjoyed favourable publicity, and people celebrated the new navy's fighting prowess. The *Emden's* sinking brought an end to the operations to rid the Pacific and Indian oceans of German warships and made it safer for vessels to cross between the Middle East and Australia.

The ANZAC convoy proceeded peacefully from Colombo to Alexandria in the Mediterranean, arriving on 3 December 1914.

The *Emden's* landing party that had gone ashore to destroy the Direction Island wireless station escaped in the island's schooner *Ayesha*, sailed to the coast of Arabia and eventually made it home to Germany.

THE BATTLE OF BROKEN HILL

Four months before the landing at Gallipoli, on 1 January 1915, the first act of official, international war on Australian soil occurred— at Broken Hill. It was also the first act of international Islamic terrorism to be perpetrated in the nation of Australia.

The enemy, who were two in number, turned out to be a halal butcher and an ice-cream salesman who managed to kill four people and wound seven more, before being killed by a posse of police, army and locals.

The two-man army consisted of Badsha Mohammed Gool, a former camel driver who operated an ice-cream cart, and Mullah Mohammed Abdullah, the local imam and halal butcher.

Australia was, at that time, officially at war with the nation of Turkey (more correctly the Ottoman Empire), which was one of the Central Powers and, although neither of them was Turkish, the two men fought under a Turkish flag, which they flew proudly from their official military vehicle, Gool's ice-cream cart.

Gool was a member of the Pashtun tribe, from Afghanistan, and Abdullah was from what would today be Pakistan. He had arrived in Broken Hill around 1898 and had also worked as a cameleer before becoming the local mullah whose job included killing and preparing animals according to halal Islamic custom. Several days before the attack, Mullah Abdullah was convicted by the local chief sanitary officer of oper- ating an abattoir without a licence, when he was caught killing sheep at his home.

In the union-controlled town of Broken Hill, the Butchers Trade Union and the local abattoir had a 'union only' employment rule. It was, therefore, impossible for the non-union Abdullah to legally prepare halal meat for the Muslim community.

On New Year's Day each year, the local Manchester Unity Order of Oddfellows held a community picnic at Silverton, 26 kilometres west of Broken Hill.

Due to an odd quirk of history, the rail line which ran from Broken Hill, in New South Wales, to Cockburn, on the South Australian border, operated on the South Australian narrow 3 foot 6 inch gauge and was privately owned. All New South Wales railways were standard gauge and had to be owned by the government. To get around this, the company that owned and operated the 58-kilometre line was called the Silverton Tramway Company.

In 1915 the 'picnic train' from Broken Hill to Silverton was crowded with 1200 people in 40 open carriages. Gool and Abdullah hid behind an embankment three kilometres from town and ambushed the train with two rifles. Seventeen-year-old Alma Cowie and William Shaw, a sanitary department foreman, were shot dead, and William Shaw's daughter, Lucy, was injured, along with six other people on the train.

The two desperadoes then retreated towards the cameleers' camp where they lived. On the way they killed Alfred Millard who had taken shelter in his hut.

The train pulled into a siding and the police were telephoned and they contacted the local army base. Soon afterwards, the police, local militia and an army unit set out in pursuit.

A 90-minute shoot-out ensued at a place known as Cable Hill. A policeman was wounded before the shooting from the hill became sporadic and misdirected, which led the police to assume, correctly, that Abdullah was dead and Gool was wounded.

The unfortunate fourth fatality at the hands of Abdullah and Gool was 69-year-old local man James Craig, who lived 500 metres away. He ignored his daughter's warning about chopping wood during a gun battle and was hit by a stray bullet and killed.

At one o'clock the forces of righteous retribution rushed the enemy stronghold. One eyewitness stated that Gool stood with his hands raised and a white rag tied to his rifle, but he was shot down and later found to have sixteen bullet wounds. Both bodies were disposed of secretly later that day by the police.

Both men left letters saying that what they did was an act of war for the Ottoman Empire against the British Empire. Gool had a letter tucked in his belt, which stated that he was a subject of the Ottoman Sultan and ended, 'I must kill you and give my life for my faith, *Allāhu Akbar*.' Abdullah stated in his letter that he was also dying for his faith and in obedience to the sultan's orders, but added a rather poignant and pathetic statement that, 'owing to my grudge against Chief Sanitary Inspector Brosnan it was my intention to kill him first'.

Sadly, however, it seems that Abdullah shot the wrong sanitary official.

That night a lynch mob tried to march to the 'Afghan camp', but was stopped by the police.

Oddly, after this event there was no further hostility towards the Muslim community in Broken Hill during the war, but the German Club was burnt to the ground by an unruly mob and the firemen who came to fight the blaze had their hoses cut to prevent them putting out the fire. The next day the mining companies in Broken Hill fired all employees who qualified as 'enemy aliens' under the *War Precautions Act* and six Austrians, four Germans and a Turk were ordered out of town by the mob.

War, as we all know, often brings out the best in people. It can also bring out the worst.

THE DARDANELLES CAMPAIGN

In 1908 a group of students and military officers known as the Young Turks led a revolt against Sultan Abdulhamit and then ruled the Ottoman Empire using his brother, Mehmet V, as a puppet sultan. Not long after World War I began, the Ottoman Empire was lured into an alliance with the Central Powers, partly through the ruling committee's leader, Enver Pasha, having a German background and sympathies, and partly due to Russia being the Ottoman Empire's old and obvious enemy.

The Germans convinced the Ottomans to close the Dardanelles, the waterway between the Aegean Sea and the Black Sea, thereby blocking the sea route to southern Russia and preventing Allied arms and supplies being sent to the Eastern Front. An appeal by the Russian government to the British War Office and High Command prompted the Allied decision to attack the Dardanelles. Russian troops were being hard-pressed in the Caucasus and the Allies hoped that a British attack might cause the Ottomans to withdraw. They also hoped to open a supply route to Russia by 'forcing the Dardanelles'.

It is generally acknowledged that the fall of Constantinople would have been a foregone conclusion had the Allied fleet passed through The Narrows. Winston Churchill, First Lord of the Admiralty, believed the invasion would give the British a clear sea route to their ally Russia and persuade one or all of the neutral states of Greece, Bulgaria and Romania to join the Allies. The failure of the campaign led to his resignation from parliament and was to haunt him for the rest of his political career.

French and British warships attacked Turkish forts at Cape Helles and along the straits in February and March 1915. They encountered underwater mines, torpedoes and spirited defence and artillery bombardment from the Turkish forts along the shores of the Dardanelles at The Narrows, near the Turkish town of Canakkale.

On 18 March 1915 the British and French fleets attempting to force the straits suffered a humiliating defeat, losing six battleships. British losses were the *Irresistible* and the *Ocean* sunk in The Narrows, and the *Inflexible* crippled and run ashore at Tenedos. The French lost the *Bouvet*, sunk in The Narrows, the *Gaulois*, beached on a tiny island back towards Lemnos, and the *Suffren*, badly damaged and retired.

After this naval attack on the Dardanelles failed, Churchill decided that a naval action would not succeed without an invasion in force by infantry. Plans were immediately made for a massive invasion to try to seize the Gallipoli Peninsula.

At the time, the arrival at Gallipoli was the largest military landing in history. It involved about 75,000 men from the United Kingdom, France, Australia, New Zealand, Nepal and India. After several postponements due both to poor weather and to some of the supply ships being wrongly loaded and having to be reloaded, the huge flotilla sailed from the Allied base on the island of Lemnos on 24 April 1915. The landings began to take place before dawn the following day.

The main Allied force, consisting of British and French troops, landed at five different locations at Cape Helles, on the tip of the peninsula.

———

The Australian and New Zealand Army Corps (ANZAC) was a combined force of Australian and New Zealand volunteer soldiers. The corps was formed in Egypt during 1914 and was led by the British General William Birdwood. This force of about 30,000 men was to be landed at Gaba Tepe, more than 16 kilometres (10 miles) north of Helles.

The Anzacs actually landed even further north, in an area later called Anzac Cove. On the first day, 16,000 Anzac troops went ashore, the majority of them going into battle for the first time.

The Allied forces suffered severe casualties during the landings. The Allied naval attacks in the area had alerted the Ottoman and German commanders and they had strengthened their military defences on the peninsula. The Allied forces that landed were never able to penetrate past the ridges that run along the centre of the peninsula and mostly were dug in no more than a few kilometres inland for the entire campaign.

The first day of fighting saw the Anzacs attack the heights in small disjointed groups, due to confusion caused by the landings not occurring where planned and the troops becoming separated from their officers and battalions. They had been landed in a hilly, scrubby tangle of ravines and steep sandy gullies. Yet, amid the confusion and lack of artillery support and leadership, groups of Anzacs attacked and briefly captured key points on the peaks of the range that commands the centre of the narrow peninsula.

By the afternoon of the first day, with no supply lines opened and insufficient organised reinforcements, the Anzacs were unable to hold the positions they had gained.

No covering artillery had been available as the British warships were busy supporting the other landings. Few field guns were landed to give artillery support, as it was feared they would be lost as the forces retreated. So the Anzacs were driven back and forced to dig in along a line that would become the firing line they would hold and defend, with little change, throughout the whole campaign. The geography of the region and the limited size of supporting forces available prevented the Allied troops from advancing more than two or three kilometres beyond the positions they originally commanded both at Anzac Cove and Cape Helles.

The landings at the much better defended beaches at Helles resulted in heavy casualties and the British foothold there consisted of an area stretching approximately 8 kilometres (5 miles) from the toe of the peninsula to the foot of a range of hills called Achi Baba, at a point where the peninsula is also about 8 kilometres across. Efforts to take the hilltops failed time and again and many lives were wasted. Some Anzacs were sent to bolster the forces at Helles, the 2nd Australian Brigade and the 2nd New Zealand Brigade. They took part in the second battle of Krithia, which consisted of charges across open ground into machine-gun-defended territory. These attacks were ordered on three successive days, 6, 7 and 8 May 1915.

The Anzacs suffered terrible losses at Krithia. There is a photograph of some 27 men who were all that were left standing of a brigade of more than 700 after the Battle of Krithia. The hill was never taken and the campaign at Helles ground to a stalemate until forces were finally evacuated in January 1916. Those British soldiers were the last Allied troops to leave the peninsula. The battle-hardened 29th Division of the British army fought bravely at Helles and more than half of them were killed or wounded.

Having consolidated their hold on the narrow strip of beaches and hills at Anzac Cove, the Australian and New Zealand troops settled down to what really became a siege. The Ottoman forces controlled the heights and the key artillery positions on the southern shore. From the sea the British naval guns provided cover and protection for the Allied forces located on the northern side of the peninsula.

The infantry on both sides were entrenched along a front stretching for approximately 5 kilometres (3 miles) and curving in an arc from near Hell Spit up into the ranges and back down to North Beach. The distance between the Anzac and Ottoman trenches varied from a few metres to several hundred metres.

After the initial consolidation and digging in, the situation was stable for almost a month. Then, in mid-May, the Ottoman forces launched a fierce series of counter-attacks. On the night of 19 May, 40,000 Ottoman troops were thrown at the Anzac front line, which was made up of 12,000 men.

The Anzacs held the line against overwhelming odds and the horrific losses on the Ottoman side led to a request for an armistice to bury the dead. This was granted on 24 May. Losses along the central area of the Anzac line were estimated as 160 Allied soldiers and more than 4000 Ottoman dead.

The next real development occurred in August when a new invasion was undertaken at Suvla Bay to the north of Anzac Cove. This force of some 15,000 men was to land at Suvla on 6 August and advance across a dry salt lake and hilly open plain towards the Anafurta Range, Hill 971 and Chunuk Bair. Attacks by all forces on the peninsula were planned to divert Ottoman attention from the landing and enable this new force to become an important part of a pincer movement against the heights.

These invasion forces were all newcomers to war and were poorly led. The command was given to Sir Frederick Stopford, who had been retired since 1909, was 61 years old, and had never commanded men in battle.

Whatever the reason—unclear orders, poor morale after a botched landing, heat and difficult terrain, heavy Turkish resistance, or simply poor and hesitant leadership—the forces which landed at Suvla on 6 and 7 August failed to advance as expected.

Meanwhile, the Anzacs attacked according to plan. The Australians charged the Ottoman trenches at Lone Pine and captured them, the Light

Horse charged into the face of machine-gun fire and died at The Nek, and the New Zealanders charged up Rhododendron Ridge and took Chunuk Bair.

At Cape Helles the 29th Division made yet another futile and tragic attack on Krithia.

Allied losses all round were devastating. Australian casualties at Lone Pine were 2277. On the other side, losses were even worse; more than 5000 Ottoman troops died defending Lone Pine.

Ottoman troops under Mustafa Kemal recaptured the heights from the New Zealanders and Ghurkas on 10 August. The Anzacs held Lone Pine until the evacuation and the Allies effectively held most of the Suvla Bay area and Anafurta Plains after another concerted push with reinforcements finally allowed the forces at Anzac to link up with the forces at Suvla on 27 August.

After this time another stalemate eventuated; not one inch of territory was won or conceded by the Anzac forces from the end of August until they were evacuated in December.

By the end of August more than 80 per cent of the Allied troops were suffering from dysentery. Winter brought snow and many soldiers died from exposure or suffered frostbite.

The Allied troops at Anzac Cove and Suvla Bay were withdrawn in December 1915.

Unlike the landings and the eight-month siege campaign, the evacuation was a masterpiece of military strategy and coordination. Troops were evacuated steadily from 11 December and the final 20,000 left furtively and completely undetected on 18 and 19 December.

A rear-guard of 1500 men occupied the trenches and fired rifles, made noises and set timers on guns and booby traps to make it appear that the trenches were occupied as normal. On a given signal the rear-guard ran to the deserted beach and were taken off under cover of darkness. Only two lives were lost during the whole process of evacuation.

———

Gallipoli established the fighting reputation of the Anzacs and passed into Australian legend.

A total of 5482 Australian soldiers were killed in action during the Gallipoli campaign. A further 2012 soldiers died of wounds and 665 of diseases, bringing Australian battle losses to 8159. In all, 19,441 Australian soldiers were wounded, and 2721 New Zealanders were killed and 4752 were wounded.

Figures for the British were 21,255 dead and 52,230 wounded casualties. The French count wasn't accurate but was approximately 10,000 dead and 17,000 wounded.

Ottoman losses were 86,692 dead, 164,617 wounded and approximately 20,000 who died from disease.

We have no accurate record of the numbers on the Allied side who died from disease but about 150 soldiers a day were evacuated with illness from June onwards.

It is safe to say that around 150,000 men died during the Gallipoli campaign and twice that number were wounded. As the objective of the campaign was not realised, it was a futile exercise for the Allies. The Ottoman army lost more than a quarter of a million men in total and eventually lost the war as well.

THE TWENTY-FIFTH OF APRIL

Roderic Quinn

This day is Anzac Day!
Made sacred by the memory
Of those who fought and died, and fought and live,
And gave the best that men may give
For love of Land. It dawns once more,
And, though on alien sea and shore
The guns are silent all,
Yet with pride we recall
The deeds which gave immortality.

Great deeds are deathless things!
And doer dies, but not the deed,
And, when upon that fateful April day
Our Anzacs, throwing all but love away,
Gave life and limb for Honour's sake,
With Freedom tremblingly at stake
They lit a beacon-light
Imperishable, bright,
That evermore the Nation's soul shall heed.

Not Peace, not Peace alone
Can make a nation great and good
And bring it that full statute, strength, and grace
That fit it for an age-enduring place
In men's regard. Through storm and strife
It runs to sweet and noble life;

For through its veins there runs
The valour of great sons
Who died to give it stately nationhood.

This day is Anzac Day!
Made sacred by the thrilling thought
Of those who proved their souls, it reappears;
And thus 'twill dawn, and dawn through future years
Till Time our petty deeds efface,
And others, dwelling in our place,
Tell o'er, with tongue and pen,
The glorious tale again
Of how on beach and crags the Anzacs fought.

RED GALLIPOLI

H.W. Cavill

We were roused before 6 am by the rattle of the anchor cable, and, by the time we had scrambled on deck, we were gliding down the placid waters of Mudros Bay. We could hardly believe our luck. After eight strenuous months' training, we were at last on the move and, before many hours, should realise to the full what war meant.

Winding our way through the throng of ships, we quickly approached the mouth of the Bay—passing, as we steamed out, the monster battle-ships *Queen Elizabeth*, *London*, *Prince of Wales* and *Queen*, while sleek, business-like destroyers darted hither and thither.

Passing the heads and the peaceful-looking little lighthouse, we steamed slowly round the island and dropped anchor again in a small cove on the opposite side. Here business began in earnest; iron rations were distributed; arms and equipment inspected; in fact, everything possible to secure success was attended to.

My! Didn't I grin when I saw the ship's grindstone. The boys were afraid their bayonets would not be sharp enough, so there they were, gathered around waiting eagerly their turn to get at the stone. By the time we left the ship it was gouged and worn to such an extent that it was fit for nothing but a kellick stone.

As I sit up here on the boat-deck writing these lines, it is hard to believe that within a few hours we shall be in the midst of slaughter and suffering. As I sit and look around, all is peace and beauty. The setting sun floods the dancing water and casts its rays over the beautiful green hills of Lemnos, the quaint little windmills completing a sweet picture. But it is work that has to be accomplished, so we look to Him who has been our help in ages past.

The boys were entirely unconcerned; they lay about the decks absorbed in cards, reading, and so forth. Evening found them in the same good spirits, and a happy, rollicking time was spent. One thing, only, pointed to the fact that something unusual was happening. Before retiring, every man packed his valise with extra care; poised his rifle to an electric light and had a final squint through; then finally lay down, still in jocular mood.

I do not profess to know if it is the correct thing to sleep blissfully on the eve of a battle, especially such a battle as we were faced with, but this I do know, what within half an hour the ship was filled with the harmonious melody of a multitude of contented sleepers.

I was still enjoying that blissful period that comes on one just before fully waking. Events were taking shape in my mind; I had just become aware, by the even throb of the engines and the motion of the ship, that we were moving, when to my ears came a sound of distant thunder that swelled louder and louder, in a mighty crescendo, punctuated by terrific crashes as if the very heavens were falling.

You can easily guess I was fully awake by this time, and shouting 'We are there' I flew up the companion-way and on to deck. Already there were a few on deck, but there was little to be seen. The morning mist shrouded everything, and one could only judge the position of the land by the flash of the shore batteries as they returned the fire of the fleet.

Steadily we continued our way, passing battleships in action every few minutes. One after another they would loom up out of the impenetrable grey, deafen us with their mighty guns, and then, as we steamed on, disappear like phantom ships into the gloom. At last we dropped anchor close to two of our ships that could only be located by the flash of their guns.

It was a queer sight—on every hand these darting flames, followed by ear-splitting explosions, while every moment the leaden-coloured water would rise in a mighty column, like some magnificent fountain, as the shells from the shore plunged in.

Slowly the mist of the early morn lifted, and there before our eyes lay a scene such as I never dare hope to witness a second time in this life. I could hardly drag myself away to dress; but, at last, slipping into my clothes and putting the last touches to my equipment, I quickly got into a position where I could watch the mighty effort of the Fleet.

We occupied the extreme left of the position. Round about us lay scores of troopships, trawlers, destroyers, and warships. Standing out prominently among the latter was the old HMS *Euryalus*, so well known in Australia a few years ago as our navy's flagship. She was right inshore, and engaged at point-blank range the formidable Gaba Tepe battery, which had been doing serious damage, enfilading the beach.

The terrific duel that ensued made everything else appear trivial. The water about the *Euryalus* was churned into foam, and flew up in great columns, but the old ship doggedly hung to her position, while her gunners simply drove us into a frenzy of cheering, as, with marvellous exactness, they dropped shell after shell on to the position.

For over twenty minutes the scrap continued; till finally this piece of landscape lost all shape, the battery was silenced, and the forces no doubt retreated, for the guns were trained to throw the shells, first over the headland, then right up and over the first gradient.

One could hardly believe that at any moment the boys were under fire of the shore batteries. They filled the rigging and decks, and at every salvo from the warships a mighty cheer would rend the air, and then the ship would ring with laughter. No, there were no long faces, but rather a joyous, reckless fearlessness that boded ill for their foes.

The spasmodic crackle of rifle fire now grew into one continuous roll, like the beating of a thousand kettledrums; the 3rd Brigade were getting busy. But, hark!

'Fall in, A and B Companies.'

Swiftly, the eager waiters stepped into their places, and then just as quickly slipped over the ship's side and down the rope ladders, entirely forgetful of the seventy-odd pounds load of equipment they carried.

The crews of the destroyers on each side of the ship worked like Trojans, packing the men in like the proverbial sardines, while we of C and D Companies, who were to go by the second tow, wriggled out of portholes at the risk of cracking our necks, and shouted, 'Jack, I say, Jack, how'd things ashore? How did the boys go?'

Thus they rattled on in disjointed conversation, just as the pressure of business would allow.

At last, after what seemed an eternity, our turn came and with the eagerness of school children off for a picnic, we scrambled down the ladders and into the destroyer *Usk*. Scarcely had we left the *Derfflinger* than we heard a high whining noise.

A land battery had opened fire on her, and shell after shell came screaming overhead and plunged all round our recent home.

It was a nerve-trying time. Our destroyer raced toward the beach, escaping in a miraculous manner the storm of shrapnel. Within a few hundred yards of the shore the destroyer eased down; quickly we jumped into the ship's boats that were being towed alongside; and, with a hearty hurrah, gave way and rowed through the curtain of fire that enveloped the beach.

The question has been asked many times, 'What did you feel like when first under fire?'

I have already described our feelings when leaving the ship; but, as we drew nearer the shore, lips were set, faces grew stern and thoughtful, rifles were gripped more firmly, hands stole quietly round and loosened bayonets, and then—then nothing else to do, and being 'Real Australians', the lads once again joked and laughed, yes actually laughed.

As the keel of the boat grated on the rocky bottom, one and all jumped waist deep into the sea and waded ashore, still quite merry, in spite of the hail of shrapnel that bespattered the beach.

No sooner had we gained the shore than the first man was killed. Not five yards from where I stood a C Company man was struck in the head by a splinter of a shell that burst right in our midst; fortunately nobody else was hit.

We were now in the thick of business. Immediately the 1st, 2nd and 3rd Battalions were ordered to advance to support the covering party.

Dropping our packs, the 2nd Battalion rushed at once to the left flank, where a handful of the covering party were hotly engaged. Then came a toilsome scramble over the high bluffs, carrying, in addition to our equipment, picks, shovels, and boxes of ammunition.

Reaching the top of the first ridge, we came to a Turkish trench, in which lay those Turks who had stayed too long to dispute possession with the 3rd Brigade. Stooping low, we doubled across a plateau over which the sharp-nosed bullets flew, meowing like motherless kittens. A constant stream of wounded men—still quite cheerful—passed us on the way to the beach, saying, 'It's hot as hell up there'—and it was.

All down through Shrapnel Valley, thick with mines and pitfalls, infested with snipers, and torn with shrapnel—from whence it earned its name—hairbreadth escapes were now becoming so frequent that one scarcely stopped to notice them.

We commenced fighting our way up the third hill which, per-sonally, I think was the worst of the lot. Never again do I expect to see such superhuman efforts. Dragging the ammunition and entrenching implements, the men struggled up this almost perpendicular, crumbling, scrub-covered cliff in the face of a withering fire.

One exposed knoll, which the snipers were paying particular attention to, we were compelled to rush over singly. As it came to my turn, I bolted, pick in one hand and rifle in the other, as hard as my legs would carry me. One had simply to claw one's way up the soft, yielding bank. No sooner had I reached the top than a dozen bullets kicked up the dirt all around me. An officer who followed me said, 'What's the matter, laddie?'

'Drop,' I shouted.

He did so, only just in time to miss a perfect fusillade of snipers' bullets.

Side by side we wriggled over the knoll, slid down the opposite side, regained our feet, and put up a record sprint to where the rugged hill afforded some little cover.

At the top of the hill we were in the full blast of the enemy's fire. It was a perfect inferno. A score of machine-guns filled the air with their rat-a-tat; just like a hundred noisy motor bicycles; while the Turkish artillery threw a curtain of shrapnel along the ridge that looked as if it would stop any further effort to advance. But, knowing that our only safety lay in victory, one had to forget self and fight like the very devil.

Many of the boys never passed that shrapnel-swept ridge. One wounded lad, who was bleeding badly over the shoulder, propped himself up as we passed, and grinning hideously with his shattered mouth, he wheezed, 'Got it where the chicken got the axe,' then fainted.

Right and left men were being hit, and a fellow had to just clench his teeth and keep going, with the vague thought somewhere in the back of your cranium that you might be the next. It was just here that my chum, Howard Proctor, was killed.

A shrapnel burst right in the midst of the platoon in front of me; it cut the haversack from the side of Corporal Turton, and splashed two or three others, but poor Proctor was struck with a piece of the shell, which inflicted a fatal wound. The lads close at hand, after shaking hands with him, offered a few words of cheer, and then had to advance.

A few minutes later, when my platoon advanced, I knelt by his side, but he was going fast; I tried to cheer him, but somehow I got a big lump in my throat, my eyes were dimmed, and after a few incoherent words I was silent. Then, in spite of the fact that he was paralysed by his wound, and almost at his last gasp, his face brightened, and with a smile he said, 'Don't worry about me, Cav; I feel quite satisfied; I feel I have done my bit; take my glasses and try and return them to my mother.' And so brave Proctor passed away.

Can you wonder, reader, that we old boys of the 1st Brigade reverence the very name of Anzac?

When we remember the number of our hero chums that sleep the long sleep on the bleak, forbidding hills above Anzac Cove, well have they been named 'The Glorious Dead'.

Can we ever forget the unselfish spirit of soldiers like Pte. W. Penton. Mortally wounded, face downward he lay. Yet, with his last effort, and his last breath, he raised himself, and turning to a mate, said, 'Good-bye, Warrington, old boy; I'm going; but tell Albert he will find plenty of cigarettes in my pack.'

Upon uttering those words, poor Penton fell forward and he was gone. His parents weep and mourn, but we who knew him will ever cherish the memory of such a great, unselfish soul. No words are there more true than those of Souter, when he said:

We need no costly monument,
To keep their memory fast.

I trust I shall be forgiven if I tell of the heroism of yet another before I pick up the thread of my story.

It is the story of Sgt. Larkin, M.L.A. He lay wounded and dying and yet when the stretcher-bearers came to carry him in, he waved them on, saying, 'There's plenty worse than me out there.' Later, they found him—dead.

Can anyone feel surprised when we get in a rage at the sight of ham and beef shops branded 'ANZAC'?

The splendid courage of our officers compelled admiration. Separated from their own men—for in the wild fighting over the hills the 1st Brigade was quite mixed up—they gathered all the men in sight, and, with commendable courage, charged the enemy's position with the bayonet.

It was in this way that I was separated from my own Company, and fought throughout the day alongside of Major B. I. Swannell, who, with his Company, had got mixed up with our Battalion.

Never shall I forget the look on his face when we first got within striking distance of the enemy.

'Fix bayonets! Charge!' rang out his order.

There was a flash of steel, a wild hurrah, and the boys dashed straight at the wall of fire, heedless of the frightful slaughter. They were not to be stopped.

It was in this charge that Major Swannell was killed. He had seized a rifle, and with dauntless courage was leading his men, when a Turkish bullet, penetrating his forehead, ended his career, thus depriving the 1st Brigade of one of its bravest officers.

The few remaining hours of daylight were spent in such fierce, unequal fighting that I remembered little else until, about an hour before dusk, something hit me.

I thought at first that I had been struck by a shell. After picking myself up, and regaining a sitting position, I put my hand down to feel if my leg was still there; I was really scared to look, for fear it had gone. Feeling that that really useful member was still attached to my body, I started to discover the extent of the damage. Whipping off my puttee and slashing the seam of my breeches with my clasp knife, I reached my knee, to find a small, quite respectable looking puncture close alongside the knee-cap, from which oozed a thin stream of blood.

The bullet—for such it was—had gone right through, coming out behind the knee, severing, en route, some of the important nerves of the leg, thus paralysing the leg. This was temporarily useful, as it saved me any intense pain.

It was just at this stage that the Turks, heavily reinforced, counter-attacked, and compelled our sadly diminished force to fall back. I knew that if I jumped to my feet to retire I would only collapse, as my leg was as useless as though there was no bone in it.

The only thing to avoid capture was to crawl, and crawl pretty quickly.

So, on one knee and two hands, I started, faced with a three-mile journey over as rough country as it would be possible to find.

How I accomplished the distance safely I shall never know. At least a dozen snipers wasted a cartridge on me—the bullets clipping twigs in front of my nose, whistling through my hair, and kicking the dirt up in my face.

On one occasion a platoon of Australians passed on their way to the firing line. One man, dropping out, half carried me back about a hundred yards, and, with a sincere, 'Good luck, mate, I'm needed up above,' he raced away to assist the hard-pressed, exhausted men in the firing line.

So again I started off, crawling as hard as possible. While lying on my back, resting in one place, eight or nine shells burst in quick succession right over my head—one bursting so close that the black soot, like burnt powder, fell on my chest. The shrubs were torn and the earth scarred by the hail of shrapnel bullets, but again I got off without a scratch.

I came to the hurried conclusion, however, that there were many healthier places about, and made off again.

I had gone only a short distance when I came upon a touching spectacle. I was crossing a narrow road on the summit of a hill when I saw an officer sitting upright on the roadside, with his back to the shrubs that grew on either side.

I approached, but he did not speak or move, so I crawled up close, and found to my surprise that he was dead. He had just been in the act of writing when a bullet through the heart caused instantaneous death. He had never moved an inch; his notebook was still in the left hand; while the right still held a pencil poised in a natural position over the book. He was a colonel, past middle age, grey-haired, and wearing a breast full of service ribbons.

In a shallow trench close by another pathetic incident occurred. Lying in a trench was an Australian, who had been badly hit. His eyes opened slowly, his lips moved, and faintly he murmured, 'Mafeesh', the Arabic for 'finished', and more slowly, 'Take money-belt—missus and kids—dirty swap dirty . . .' Then a strange thing happened. Dying, shattered beyond recognition, he rose to his knees and dragged his rifle to the parapet. With a weak finger he took shaky aim and fired his last shot, then collapsed in the bottom of the trench.

A little later I had another very narrow escape. I was crawling along, dragging a rifle which I had picked up in case I met any stray Turks, when right before me, at no distance, I spotted a rifle poking through a shrub, and behind it a New Zealander in the act of pulling the trigger. 'Don't fire; I'm wounded,' I yelled and immediately a New Zealand officer jumped out from behind the bush. He was just rushing a company of infantry to reinforce the line.

'Where's the firing line?' he asked.

'Straight on, over a mile ahead of you,' I answered.

With a 'Sorry you're hurt, my boy!' he rushed his men on.

After escapes innumerable, and a struggle that I never expected to accomplish, I reached the ridge of the first hill in company with a New

Zealander, who was also wounded. Together we hopped and stumbled, with our arms about one another's neck, finally rolling over the brow of the hill into a hole that afforded some little amount of shelter.

We settled down there for a short spell before continuing to the dressing station on the beach. The wounded still passed in apparently endless procession. They were wonderfully cheerful and full of information. But here our peace was short-lived.

Gradually the enemy's range lengthened, and shells crept nearer and nearer; machine-gun and rifle fire commenced to whisk about us again; then suddenly through the scrub broke the head remnant of the firing line.

Slowly they came, disputing every inch and reluctantly yielding the ground which they had so gloriously occupied during the earlier hours of the day.

The Turks evidently intended to drive them into the sea by sheer weight of numbers, but they were determined to die rather than surrender the position dearly won. Having retired some little distance in an orderly manner, they concentrated on the ring of hills commanding the beach, and, hastily entrenching, prepared to meet the massed infantry that were being hurled forward.

They had not long to wait, for very soon the whole ridge was black with Turks. On they came, evidently thinking that very soon they would sweep the remnant of our little force from their shores. But they were sadly mistaken.

When they were within easy range, a storm of rifle and machine-gun fire tore lanes through their massed ranks, while the *Queen Elizabeth*, which had been unable to support us during the afternoon, opened fire with her fifteen-inch guns, causing fearful losses.

The Turks were stunned by such a reception, and retired over the hill, giving the boys time to further consolidate the position; but they came again and again, meeting with the same withering fire each time.

Eventually they retired for the night, leaving the gallant survivors in peace, and in possession of the joyful thought that they had come through the severest fighting, and 'had done their bit'.

Thus ended the memorable 25 April 1915, 'The Day' . . . on which 16,000 Anzacs won for Australasia an 'Imperishable Record' and a 'Name among all the Nations'.

SONG OF THE DARDANELLES

Henry Lawson

From the southern hills and the city lanes,
From the coastal towns and the Blacksoil Plains;
Australia's finest—there they stood,
To fight for the King as we knew they would.
    Knew they would—
    Knew they would;
To fight for the King as we knew they would.

They trained in the dust of an old dead land
Long months' of drill in the scorching sand;
But they knew in their hearts it was for their good,
And they saw it through as we knew they would.
    Knew they would—
    Knew they would;
And they saw it through as we knew they would.

They were shipped like sheep when the dawn was grey;
And as the ships left Mudros Bay
They squatted and perched where'er they could,
And they laughed and swore as we knew they would.
    Knew they would—
    Knew they would;
They laughed and swore as we knew they would.

The wireless tells and the cable tells
How our boys behaved by the Dardanelles.
Some thought in their hearts, 'Will our boys make good?'
We knew them of old and we knew they would!
    Knew they would—
    Knew they would;
They were mates of old and we knew they would.

The sea was hell and the shore was hell,
With mine, entanglement, shrapnel and shell,
But they stormed the heights as Australians should,
And they fought and they died as we knew they would.
    Knew they would—
    Knew they would;
They fought and they died as we knew they would.

THE FIRST DAY

Sir William Birdwood

At 3.30 am the battleships hove to, and the tows went ahead. It was very dark, and the tows got a mile or so farther north than had been intended; and some tows crossed one another. The enemy, entrenched on the shore to the number of about 900, with machine guns, did not suspect our approach till we were quite close, when they opened heavy fire on the boats and inflicted many casualties.

Meanwhile, as soon as this advance guard of 1500 had started off, the remainder of the covering force trans-shipped from their transports into eight destroyers; these followed closely, until the men were taken off by returning tows. All this worked entirely 'according to plan'. The boy midshipmen in command of small boats earned, and ever afterwards retained, the deep admiration of all my Anzac men.

Hardly waiting for the keels to touch the shore, men leaped into the water and raced ashore, dashing straight with the bayonet upon the Turks and driving them through the thick undergrowth.

This landing farther north than was intended naturally caused some temporary difficulties; for these I must take the blame, for they were caused by my insistence on landing before daylight. But the error brought great compensations also. The original spot chosen for the landing was on fairly open ground not far from Gaba Tepe, and troops landing there must have suffered heavily from machine–gun and other fire from the trenches in that locality, which had clearly been dug and wired in anticipation of an attack thereabouts. But though, by this accident, our right avoided this danger, our left came in for bad trouble farther north, beyond Ari Burnu.

On the open beach near the fishermen's huts we suffered heavy losses; some boats drifted off full of dead with no one in control. The centre landing, in the neighbourhood of what was later known as Anzac Cove, was more fortunate. The country here was very broken and difficult, and the Turks had evidently not expected an attack, for they were only lightly entrenched and were soon driven off by the impetuous Australians.

But the crossing of the tows in the dark was to cause great confusion and, for a time, dismay. Battalions had got hopelessly mixed up, and for a considerable time it was impossible to sort them out. My extreme right was being badly enfiladed by machine guns from Gaba Tepe, till the *Bacchante* (Captain Boyle) steamed right in, almost putting her bows on shore, and poured in welcome broadsides which silenced the enemy there—a gallant deed which the Australians never forgot.

Gradually the Turks were driven back through this very difficult country, which is covered with high scrub and in places quite precipitous. The day was very hot, and no water was available. It was a wonderful feat, therefore, that the Australians had performed—and they were nearly all young soldiers receiving their baptism of fire. Thanks to the first-rate naval arrangements, Bridges' entire Division (less guns) of 12,000 men was ashore by 10 am, and Godley's Division followed later.

As soon as I could, I went ashore to see the progress made, and clambered around as much as possible of the front line on the heights. Owing to the thick scrub I could see very little, but from a point later known as Walker's Top I got a fairly good idea of the situation, realising for the first time that a large valley separated the New Zealanders there from the Australians on a ridge to the east.

The men were naturally very exhausted after so hard a day—and inclined to be despondent, too. Small groups would tell me that they were all that was left of their respective battalions—'all the others cut up'!

On such occasions I would promptly tell them not to be damned fools: that the rest of the battalion was not far distant, having simply been separated in the tows. This always had an encouraging effect, though I must confess that I might not yet have seen 'the rest'.

Another factor, which did much to restore our men's confidence, was the landing of the two Indian Mountain Batteries (Numbers 1 and 6) for which I had so earnestly petitioned Lord Kitchener. Thanks to their great handiness and mobility we were able to get them, but no other guns, ashore on the twenty-fifth. Before their landing, the infantry were naturally perturbed by the fact that they were being continuously shelled, while no reply could be sent from our side.

The very first shot from one of our mountain guns (very hurriedly rushed up on the ridge over the landing place) had an electrifying effect upon our troops, who felt they could now hold their own.

The first brilliant advance was now checked, for the Turks had been able to bring up guns and there was a constant hail of shrapnel all the afternoon. In the scrub it was impossible to keep men together, and many stragglers found their way down gullies to the beach. Later we found that our casualties numbered some 5000 all told: in round figures, 500 killed, 2500 wounded and 2000 missing, although many of the 'missing' came in later.

Some, I am sorry to say, had in their impetuosity, advanced so fast, and with so little regard for their supports or troops on their flanks, that they had disappeared right into the enemy's position.

The heavy rate of casualties gives some indication how bitter and unceasing the fighting had been. By the superb efforts of Neville Howse, my D.M.S., the wounded were got away to the ships as fast as they could be collected.

Nevertheless, the situation ashore seemed fairly satisfactory when, in the evening, I returned to my headquarters on the *Queen* after discussing matters with Bridges and Godley. I was therefore horrified, about an hour later, to receive a message from Bridges asking me to return at once, as the position was now critical.

I went ashore again and was met by Bridges and Godley, with several of their senior officers. They told me that their men were so exhausted after all they had gone through, and so unnerved by constant shellfire after their wonderfully gallant work, that they feared a fiasco if a heavy attack should be launched against us next morning.

I was told that numbers had already dribbled back through the scrub, and the two divisional commanders urged me most strongly to make immediate arrangements for re-embarkation.

At first I refused to take any action. I argued that Turkish demoralisation was in all probability considerably greater than ours, and that in any case I would rather die there in the morning than withdraw now.

But, on thinking things over, I felt myself bound to place the position before Sir Ian Hamilton, if only because every report I had sent him so far (and these reports had been largely based on what Bridges himself had told me) had been entirely optimistic.

Sir Ian had little idea of the extent of our casualties at Anzac, though we knew that the 29th Division had suffered very badly indeed at Helles. It struck me, therefore, that, in view of the losses sustained by both forces, he might consider it advisable to abandon one landing or the other and concentrate all his strength either at Helles or at Anzac.

His reply came as an almost incredible relief to me, telling us to 'hang on and dig' as we were now through the most difficult part of the business. He also gave us the cheering news that the Australian submarine *AE2* had got through the narrows and torpedoed a gunship—a feat which opened up a new vista in the problem of checking Turkish reinforcements.

And so ended a day which will always stand out in my life: a day of great strain and of sharply contrasting emotions. I recall my feelings of confidence but natural anxiety as the troops entered the tows at 2.30 am; my elation and pride when I knew that great numbers of troops had landed on a broad front and with less opposition than we had feared; my growing satisfaction as cheering reports of progress continued to reach me; and then, at night, the sudden cold fear of threatened disaster.

But directly I got Sir Ian's reply, which accorded so well with my own wishes, I felt a load lifted from me. I longed for the daylight, so I could get round to the troops.

THE *AE2*

His Majesty's Australian submarine *AE2*, the second of two identical 'E' Class submarines built for the RAN, was launched in the yard of Vickers Ltd at Barrow-in-Furness on 18 June 1913 and commissioned at Portsmouth on 28 February 1914. Her crew of 35 were drawn from both the Royal Navy and Royal Australian Navy and her captain was a very interesting character—Lieutenant Commander Henry Hugh Gordon Dacre Stoker, RN.

Henry Stoker served as a naval officer in both world wars and was also a stage and screen actor, author, dramatist, theatre manager, prisoner of war for three and a half years, escapologist and an excellent polo, rugby, tennis, croquet and hurling player. He helped establish the submarine station at Gibraltar, competed at the Wimbledon tennis tournament, had character roles in more than twenty feature films, wrote and acted in many radio and television dramas, and became the Croquet Champion of Ireland in 1962 at the age of 77.

Henry was born in 1885 into an eminent Dublin family of literary, theatrical and medical men. His cousin Abraham (Bram) was personal secretary to famous theatre owner and actor, Sir Henry Irving, and wrote many plays and novels, including *Dracula*. Another cousin, William, was a baronet and President of the Royal College of Surgeons in Ireland. Henry's father was also a physician but Henry chose a naval career, joined the Royal Navy training ship HMS *Britannia* as a fourteen-year-old cadet in 1900 and proved to be an average student, although he excelled at sport, particularly rugby and tennis. He served as midshipman on the Channel Fleet, was promoted to lieutenant and selected for submarine training in 1906.

In 1908 Henry married Olive Leacock, a Bengal Cavalry colonel's daughter, and the following year was given command of the submarine HMS *A10*. In 1910, in command of HMS *B8*, he helped establish the first RN submarine base outside of Britain at Gibraltar. Expressing a desire to play polo in Australia, in 1913 he volunteered to serve on loan with the RAN, and was given command of HMAS *AE2*.

After her trip to Australia, during which she lost two propeller blades and was painted white as an experiment to reduce temperature inside the 'tin can', *AE2* served with the Australian Naval and Military Expeditionary Force (ANMEF) in New Guinea and then went to Suva with HMAS *Australia*, *Sydney*, *Encounter* and *Warrego* and the French light cruiser, *Montcalm*, to counter any threat to Fiji from the German cruisers *Scharnhorst* and *Gneisenau*.

AE2 returned to Sydney and joined the second convoy taking AIF troops from Albany, Western Australia, to Egypt in December. By February 1915 she was based on the island of Tenedos in the Aegean Sea, waiting to play her part in the Dardanelles campaign.

The failed attempt by the British and French navies to force a passage through the 'straits impregnable' and reach Constantinople gave the Turks victory at the Battle of Canakkale on 18 March. The Allied fleet had lost three battleships and three more had been badly damaged and a plan was formulated to land an army on the other side of the peninsula to cross the ranges and knock out the forts guarding the Dardanelles—this became the 'Gallipoli Campaign'.

Meanwhile, Henry Stoker had plans of his own. He presented to Vice Admiral de Robeck, Commander in Chief of the Eastern Mediterranean Fleet, a plan for a submarine to attempt a passage through the heavily mined 56-kilometre (35-mile) long Dardanelles Strait and enter the Sea of Marmara. This would restrict the enemy's ability to reinforce and supply troops defending the Dardanelles.

Several submarine attempts to pass through the strait had been made and had failed, largely due to minefields—but *AE2* had been modified in Malta and defensive wires had been welded to the submarine to prevent the mooring cables of mines from catching.

Admiral de Robeck approved the idea, commenting that there would be 'no calculating the result it will cause' were it to succeed. So *AE2* set out early on 24 April and made it 12 kilometres (7 miles) into the strait before part of her underwater steering failed and she had to retreat back to base on the surface.

Mechanics worked feverishly to complete the repairs and, while the troopships slid silently towards the beaches on the other side of the peninsula, *AE2* set off early on 25 April to try again to enter the strait.

'Having proceeded from the anchorage off Tenedos,' Stoker wrote later, 'I lay at the entrance off the Dardanelles until moonset and, at about 2:30 am on 25th April, entered the straits at 8 knots. Weather calm and clear.'

Although there were searchlight crews active on both shores and Stoker's intention was not to hide but to 'run amok' and cause panic by travelling on the surface, it was 4.30 am before the submarine was spotted and Turkish artillery opened fire from the northern shore.

Then *AE2* dived and entered the minefields. The crew could hear the wires tethering the mines scraping along the boat's sides. Stoker surfaced twice in the minefield to get his bearings and, at around 6 am, found that they were just 3.2 kilometres (two miles) short of The Narrows near the town of Canakkale. *AE2* was proceeding through a calm smooth sea, submerged at periscope depth, when she was spotted and forts on both shores opened fire. At the same time, Stoker, at the periscope, saw several ships approaching and decided to target what looked like a light cruiser. He also saw a torpedo boat destroyer closing fast in an attempt to ram *AE2* on her port side.

Stoker gave two orders almost simultaneously. One was to fire *AE2*'s bow torpedo and the other was 'descend to 70 feet [21 metres]'. As *AE2* descended, the torpedo boat destroyer passed overhead and an explosion was heard as the torpedo hit the cruiser.

Worried that the cruiser would sink on top of them, Stoker altered course a point to starboard and, understandably unsure of his position in the narrowest part of the strait in the midst of battle, waited four minutes and then resumed the original course, ordering *AE2* back up to 20 feet (6 metres), but it was too late. *AE2* hit the southern shore and slid 10 feet (3 metres) up onto the mud with most of her conning tower out of the water, immediately under Fort Anatoli Medjidieh.

Stoker later wrote:

An eternity of time seemed to pass . . . In reality it was only five minutes before the boat began to move; but it is inconceivable how, even in this time, the conning tower or, at any rate, the periscope pedestals were not hit. I afterwards learned that the guns of the fort could not be depressed sufficiently to bear on us, but surely the other forts and ships must have made very bad shooting to miss this standing target.

Shells fell all around until *AE2*'s engines finally gathered some reverse momentum and she slid back into the safety of deep water. The current was running fast in The Narrows and, in a rather comical overreaction to her narrow escape from one shore, *AE2* ran aground on the other side of the strait:

> The efforts which eventually proved successful in sliding the submarine down the bank left her pointing down the Strait. At a depth of seventy feet we went ahead on the port propeller, helm hard a-port, with the object of turning as quickly as possible into the centre of the Strait. A few minutes passed ... and then, swinging rapidly to our proper course, we went ahead on the starboard propeller.
>
> Bump! From a depth of seventy feet, if you please, we slid gracefully to a miserable eight feet. Where on earth were we now? Through the periscope I observed that *AE2*, with an apparent liking for forts, had chosen one on the western shore under which to run. The cursed current, which had swept us across to this point, for a moment relented and gave us its aid by swinging the boat's stern round to port ... In this position we remained for 5 minutes.
>
> As my vessel was lying with inclination down by the bows I went full speed ahead. Shortly afterwards she began to move down the bank, gave a slight bump, gathered way and then bumped very heavily. She, however, continued to descend and at 80 feet I dived off the bank. The last bump was calculated to considerably injure the vessel, and probably impaired the fighting efficiency, but as I considered my chief duty was to prove the passage through the Straits to be possible, I decided to continue on course.
>
> In connection with these two groundings, I have to report that the behaviour of the crew was exemplary. In these two highly dangerous situations it was only their cool and intelligent performance of their duties which enabled the vessel to be refloated.

Having resumed what he thought to be the correct course, Stoker kept the now seriously damaged *AE2* submerged and headed towards the Sea of Marmara. When he surfaced in order to check his position, he saw he was surrounded by pursuit craft, so he bottomed the submarine in 80 feet (24 metres) of water near the southern shore while Turkish warships searched above—and waited.

Around 9 pm, after more than sixteen hours on the seabed, *AE2* surfaced in a deserted stretch of calm moonlit water and recharged her batteries.

The boat's 22-year-old Victorian telegraphist, William Wolseley Falconer, tapped out a message telling of their successful mission, but received no reply and assumed the radio was not working and the message had not been received.

Stoker later recollected:

Now, too, we could signal to the Fleet. A dramatic moment this, while one watched the damp aerial wire throwing purply blue sparks as the longs and shorts of the call sign were flashed. But—myriads of maledictions—the answering call never came. Obviously there was something the matter with our receiving instruments, and possibly with the sending too.

When functional, the *AE2*'s wireless had a limited range of 48–160 kilo-metres (30–100 miles), depending on local topography, so the destroyer HMS *Jed* was stationed in the Gulf of Saros to wait for messages at set times.

As the message was being sent, a council of war was taking place on the flagship HMS *Queen Elizabeth* off the coast of the peninsula. Commander in Chief Sir Ian Hamilton had just received a message from General Birdwood who had conferred with his two divisional commanders ashore and was reluctantly recommending evacuation, the entire ANZAC landing force having been pushed back onto the beach at Anzac Cove.

When the message from *AE2* was received on HMAS *Jed*, it was relayed to *Queen Elizabeth* and the council of war was interrupted. An aide handed a copy of the message to Commodore Roger Keyes, who announced, 'Tell them [the troops on the shore] this. It is an omen. An Australian submarine has done the finest feat in submarine history and is going to torpedo all the ships bringing reinforcements, supplies and ammunition into Gallipoli.'

In response to Birdwood, Hamilton then wrote, 'Your news is indeed serious. But there is nothing for it but to dig yourselves right in and stick it out. It would take at least two days to re-embark you . . . Meanwhile, the Australian submarine has got up through the narrows and has torpedoed a gunboat . . . Make a personal appeal to your men . . . to make a supreme effort to hold their ground. P.S. You have got through the difficult business, now you have only to dig, dig, dig until you are safe.'

Many believe that the message from *AE2* influenced Hamilton's decision and resulted in the ANZAC troops staying to fight on. Stoker, who did not know until after the war that the message got through, wrote:

> Years afterwards I learnt from Admiral Keyes that our signal was received, and delivered to him at a critical moment during a Council of War on board the *Queen Elizabeth*. The council was discussing the question whether the troops could hold on shore or must be evacuated—this less than twenty-four hours after the Landing—and had almost decided for evacuation, when receipt of the news that a submarine had got through altered the whole tide of the discussion, and it was decided to hold on.

A little after 3 am, not long after the *AE2* started again moving eastward, she encountered three warships, fired a torpedo and missed. At 7 am she passed the town of Gelibulu ('Gallipoli' in English, after which the peninsula is named), dived to 70 feet (21 metres) and entered the Sea of Marmara.

In spite of being seriously damaged, *AE2* survived five days in the Sea of Marmara, causing panic, firing torpedoes at Turkish ships and disrupting supply convoys headed to the war zone. On the afternoon of 29 April she rendezvoused with HMS *E14*, which had followed her example and became the second Allied submarine to successfully make the passage through the 'straits impregnable'.

On the way to a second meeting with *E14* next morning at 10 am, Stoker sighted a torpedo boat approaching and dived to escape. The damaged submarine's diving mechanism then failed and at 10.30 am she rose, nose-first, and broke the surface clearly in view of the torpedo boat.

The torpedo boat was very close, and now a gunboat and destroyer were also approaching, but *AE2* could not be made to submerge. Stoker ordered a forward tank to be flooded and *AE2* suddenly tipped forward and dived rapidly, out of control, well beyond her depth gauge level of

100 feet (30 metres). Stoker ordered full speed astern and blew the main ballast—and *AE2* shot back up and broke the surface stern first.

She found herself surrounded by Turkish warships. Stoker reported:

> Within a few seconds the engine room was hit, and holed in three places. Owing to the great inclination down by the bow, it was impossible to see the torpedo boat through the periscope and I considered that any attempt to ram would be useless. I therefore blew main ballast and ordered all hands on deck. Assisted by Lieutenant Haggard, I then opened the tanks to flood and went on deck. The boat sank in a few minutes in about 55 fathoms, in approximate position 4 degrees north of Kara Burnu Point at 10:45 am. All hands were picked up by the torpedo boat and no lives lost.

Petty Officer Henry Kinder later recalled *AE2*'s final moments:

> *AE2* looked a proper wreck with everything in disorder. The captain had been collecting ship's papers and destroying charts ... I stood by the conning tower to warn the captain (who was still in the boat shutting off the air and opening up the Kingston valves to make sure that *AE2* would sink fast). He just got on deck when she took her final dive. For a few seconds I could see her moving through the water like a big, wounded fish, gradually disappearing from sight. I felt sorry to see *AE2* come to such an end but she had died fighting.

Stoker's second in command, Lieutenant Haggard, had been keen to fight on, but Stoker realised that could only mean the slaughter of the crew and had ordered a white tablecloth to be waved at the closest Turkish warship, which then blew her sirens to make the other ships cease fire. While his men abandoned ship one at a time through the conning tower, Stoker had time to ensure *AE2* would sink.

The crew of *AE2* became prisoners of war, four died in captivity and the rest were released following the armistice. Stoker spent the time in various prisons and internment camps and complained that he was treated badly, being forced to live in disgusting conditions in 'normal prisons' with Turkish criminals. In March 1916, he escaped for eighteen days before being recaptured.

Repatriated to England in December 1918, and promoted to

commander, Stoker was awarded the Distinguished Service Order: 'In recognition of his gallantry in making the passage of the Dardanelles in command of HM Australian Submarine *AE2* on 25 April 1915.'

In 1919 Stoker was divorced and he retired from the navy in 1920 and then built a successful career as an actor, writer and theatre director. In 1925 his autobiography, *Straws in the Wind*, was published and he married Dorothie 'Peg' Pidcock, a young actress. By the end of the 1920s Stoker was a regular and popular performer in West End plays. In 1932 he commenced radio broadcasts of his short dramatic stories, and a year later he made his first cinema appearance in the movie *Channel Crossing*. Stoker appeared in eight feature films between 1933 and 1948, and was also the business manager of the Apollo Theatre.

When war broke out in 1939, Stoker was recalled to the Royal Navy. In October, with the rank of Acting Captain, he became the Chief of Staff to Rear Admiral R.M. King, RN, and in 1940 he was given command of the coastal forces base HMS *Minos* at Lowestoft. In 1942 he was posted to the Press Division within the admiralty, and as public relations officer he provided updates to ships' crews on the progress of the war. Stoker became a staff officer in April 1944, working in the Supreme Headquarters Allied Expeditionary Force.

Retiring from the navy at age 60, in 1945, he returned to his life as an actor and playwright. He became involved in early television dramas in the 1950s and continued to play golf, tennis and croquet. Stoker died in London on his 81st birthday in 1966.

Footnote:
In June 1998 Mr Selçuk Kolay, director of the Rahmi Koç Museum in Istanbul, discovered *AE2*'s wreck lying in 72 metres of water in an area of dangerous currents near busy shipping lanes in the Sea of Marmara. In 2014 a team of Australian engineers and scientists led by retired submarine commander, Rear Admiral Peter Briggs, joined Turkish experts in a high-tech expedition to explore and photograph the wreck. Chief scientist on the expedition, Roger Neill, called the photos 'unbelievable' and 'incredible' and said they had 'learnt a huge amount' about the *AE2*.

ANZACS

Edgar Wallace

The children unborn shall acclaim
The standard the Anzacs unfurled,
When they made Australasia's fame
The wonder and pride of the world.
Some of you got a V.C.,
Some 'the Gallipoli trot',
Some had a grave by the sea,
And all of you got it damned hot,

And I see you go limping through town
In the faded old hospital blue,
And driving abroad—lying down,
And Lord! but I wish I were you!
I envy you beggars I meet,
From the dirty old hats on your head
To the rusty old boots on your feet—
I envy you living or dead.

A knighthood is fine in its way,
A peerage gives splendour and fame,
But I'd rather have tacked any day
That word to the end of my name.

I'd count it the greatest reward
That ever a man could attain;
I'd sooner be 'Anzac' than 'lord',
I'd sooner be 'Anzac' than 'thane'.

Here's a bar to the medal you'll wear,
There's word that will glitter and glow,
And an honour a king cannot share
When you're back in the cities you know.
The children unborn shall acclaim
The standard the Anzacs unfurled,
When they made Australasia's fame
The wonder and pride of the world.

THE NURSES' DIARIES I

Until the ABC Television series Anzac Girls *dramatised the story of the Anzac nurses in 2014, most Australians never realised there were Australian women serving at Gallipoli. This is a section of the script of the play for voices, 'We Were There', which contains extracts from diaries and letters home by various Australian nurses including Matron Wilson, Sisters Ella Tucker, Lydia king, Daisy Richmond and others.*

The wounded who could walk or be carried were taken out to the hospital ships lying off Anzac Cove. There were fifteen hospital ships operating at Gallipoli.

Over the next nine months one ship, the *Gascon*, took over 8000 sick and wounded men from the Gallipoli Peninsula to the hospitals on Imbros, Lemnos and Malta . . . or to Alexandria or England.

It was a few hours before the men wounded in the initial dawn assault started to make their way back to the hospital ships. The boats and barges that had been used to take them ashore were not available to bring them back until all the troops had been landed.

The ship's wards were soon full and wounded men lined the decks. The average time taken to put a man on board the ship after being wounded at Gallipoli was between nine and ten hours.

Most of the wounded had just simple field dressings, which were soaked through with blood, or none at all. Each of us had an orderly whose job was simply to cut off the field dressings and the patient's clothes so that we could start with new dressings. Each nurse had 70 to 100 patients to care for and that first day I worked from 9 am till 2 am the next morning.

There is certainly no honour or glory in this war as far as I can see. By the end of the first week I was in charge of five wards when on duty and had over 250 men to care for—and one orderly to help.

Every night there were two or three deaths, sometimes five or six.

There was a feeling of hopelessness on night duty. I tried to comfort men in the dim flickering lights and shut out the moans of the seriously wounded and dying. There was a real dread of what the dawn would bring and what each morning's death toll would be. Most men died from fractured skulls due to shrapnel wounds or abdominal wounds and loss of blood. It is best to not even attempt to describe the wounds caused by bullets and shrapnel—they are beyond imagining.

THE RED CROSS NURSE

Tom Skeyhill

When the bugle sounds advance, and it's time to take your chance
When the bullets fly and men are being shot
Though she's never held a gun, we all know that she's the one
Who has the very worst job of the lot.
Red Cross Nurse—she'll ease your pain and thirst
She'll tend you and pretend she doesn't hear you swear and curse
She'll say you're getting better when you know you're getting
    worse
But you love her like a mother—Red Cross Nurse.

When you're lying in your bed, with a buzzing in your head,
And a pain across your chest that's far from nice,
She moves about the place, with a sweet angelic grace,
That makes you think the dingy ward is paradise.
She's dressed in red and grey, and she doesn't get much pay,
Yet she never seems to worry or complain.
She's Australian through and through, with a heart that's big
    and true,
And when she's near, the deepest wound forgets to pain.

With her hand upon your head, she remains beside your bed,
Until your worries and your pains begin to go,
Then with fingers true and light, she will bind your wounds up
    tight,
And when she leaves you're sleeping fast and breathing low.

When the ward is sleeping sound, she begins her nightly round,
With eyes that share your sorrows and your joys.
With a heart so full of love, she beseeches Him above
To watch and care for all her darling soldier boys.

There is something in her face, that can hold your tongue in place,
When you'd curse because your wounds refuse to heal.
But if once you get her cross, you will find out to your loss,
The velvet scabbard holds the tempered sword of steel.
When you're once again yourself, and they pull you off the shelf,
And send you back again to do the fighting trick,
You'll just grip her by the hand, with a look she'll understand.
While you stand and curse your wound for healing quick.

Though she hasn't got a gun and she hasn't killed a Hun,
Still she fights as hard as veterans at the front.
When the Allies start to drive and the wounded boys arrive,
It's always she who has to bear the battle's brunt.
She's a queen without a throne, and her sceptre is her own
True woman's smile and sympathy so sweet.
So when guns no longer shoot, I'll spring to the salute
Every time I pass a sister in the street.

THE REJECT

In 1859 Queensland became a separate colony and, fifteen years later, as British forces were withdrawn from Australia in the 1870s, the colony had to take responsibility for its own defence. Volunteer 'Independent Rifle Companies' and mounted infantry units were raised. In 1886, in the North Military Region (comprising the area named after the explorer Edmund Kennedy, now the federal electorate of Kennedy), four of these companies joined to form the 3rd Queensland (Kennedy) Regiment. This militia unit was originally based in Townsville, and was made up of two rifle companies from that town, one from Charters Towers and one from Ravenswood. A few years later, another company was raised at Mackay.

The company at Mackay was converted to a mounted infantry unit in 1899 and the regiment was made up of six companies: one each at Townsville, Ravenshoe and Cairns, and three at Charters Towers, now the battalion headquarters. Some of its members volunteered and fought under their regimental banner in the Boer War and, when the Queensland Defence Force was disbanded in 1903, colonial units were transferred as militia to the Commonwealth Military Force. In 1912, when national compulsory military service was introduced, the name was changed to the 2nd Infantry Battalion, Kennedy Regiment.

With the outbreak of World War I in August 1914, the Kennedy Regiment was the first Australian military unit mobilised when more than 500 of its men volunteered for overseas service. The Kennedy Regiment had been told that their duty, should war break out, was to garrison Thursday Island, as a safeguard against any German military action in the Pacific.

By 8 August, only four days after the declaration of war, some enthusiastic part-time officers of the regiment had assembled more than 500 equally enthusiastic volunteer militiamen at Townsville, all ready and keen to take on any Germans that happened to be on or near Thursday Island.

The problem was, how to get them there.

It seems that one of the officers, using typical Queensland ingenuity, practicality and clear thinking, had turned to the fine print of the *Commonwealth Defence Act*, and discovered that merchant ships could be requisitioned for military purposes in times of war.

The SS *Kanowna*, of 6993 tonnes, was built in 1902 by W. Denny & Brothers of Dumbarton, Scotland, and serviced the towns and cities along Australia's coast for the Australian United Steam Navigation Company. She could accommodate 270 passengers, and carry 7000 tonnes of cargo. And she happened to be in Townsville Harbour on 8 August 1914.

Hastily requisitioned by the Kennedy Regiment, without the crew being consulted, *Kanowna* dutifully deposited them on Thursday Island to protect the wireless station and guard the Torres Strait from marauding German battleships.

The enthusiastic Queenslanders had, however, 'jumped the gun'. They had gone to war without realising that, during August, an official volunteer force, the ANMEF (Australian Naval and Military Expeditionary Force), was being assembled to invade the German colonies in New Guinea.

At first Colonel William Holmes, in charge of the infantry battalion of the ANMEF and responsible for the whole campaign, was pleased to hear that a Queensland regiment was already on Thursday Island. But he was soon to change his mind.

When they heard about the ANMEF, the bulk of the regiment on Thursday Island decided they should be part of it, and they re-embarked on the *Kanowna* and ordered that she head to Port Moresby, to rendezvous with the rest of the ANMEF convoy.

This caused mutterings of discontent among the crew of *Kanowna* who had, up to this point, been relatively happy to perform their duty as loyal citizens in a time of war. They had not, however, signed up to be part of any invasion of foreign territory. Nevertheless, they reluctantly agreed to follow their captain's orders to comply with the wishes of the part-time soldiers.

However, when they arrived in Port Moresby, on 4 September, Colonel Holmes inspected both the ship and the troops on board and he was not pleased. He quickly came to the conclusion that the Kennedy Regiment would be more of a hindrance than an asset to his campaign.

The overwhelming majority of the troops were young trainees aged eighteen to twenty, with very little military training and woefully ill-equipped for tropical warfare. Their part-time officers were mostly middle-aged civilians with little or no military experience. The regiment had no tents, no mosquito nets, no hammocks, and no reserve supplies of clothing, boots or food.

Holmes also quickly became aware that the crew, who had not volunteered for active service, were unhappy about being shanghaied and made to go to war. *Kanowna* was not equipped as a troopship and her crew were, at best, very reluctant participants in the whole business.

The convoy, however, needed to press on and do what it was created to do, so after consulting with his naval colleagues, Holmes decided *Kanowna* must depart with them in order to have the protection of the ANMEF warships. There was even talk of using the Kennedy Regiment on garrison duty in captured territory—though their fate had not been decided when the convoy steamed out of Port Moresby on 7 September to rendezvous with the last of the transports that would make up the invasion fleet.

The fleet, comprising three battlecruisers, three destroyers, two submarines and two supply ships, steamed across the rolling ocean, but it was soon noticed that the *Kanowna* was falling behind, dawdling and wandering erratically in the wake of the flotilla.

When *Kanowna* hoisted the flag signal 'Out of control', HMAS *Sydney* and one of the destroyers, assuming she was in trouble, steamed back to help, only to be informed by her captain, John Lewis Ward, that the firemen stoking her boilers had mutinied and were now 'on strike' until they were assured that the ship was going back home, and not going to war! The enthusiastic young men of the Kennedy Regiment, he reported, were already shovelling coal into the furnaces in order to enable the *Kanowna* to remain with the invasion fleet!

Captain Glossop, on the *Sydney*, ordered that the rebellious stokers 'be restrained' and commanded the *Kanowna* to return to Australia. The disappointed trainees then stoked the ship back to Townsville.

In his official report, Glossop, obviously relieved to be rid of the Queensland regiment and the *Kanowna*, attempted some degree of diplomacy and common sense:

It was only the firemen who mutinied; there were volunteers from the troops to do the stoking. I suggest the trainees being disbanded and, if more troops are required, seasoned men that have passed medical tests be employed.

Colonel Holmes, who would later be promoted to major general and then lose his life fighting with the AIF at Messines in Belgium in 1917, supported Glossop's evaluation:

I consider the *Kanowna* detachment . . . unfit for immediate service . . . and recommend disbandment.

Using unenlisted volunteers to conduct a war outside Australia, as was the case with the ANMEF, was merely a stop-gap measure that was used only until the AIF (Australian Infantry Forces) could be constitutionally formed by volunteer enlistment.

Some of the Queensland regiment rejects joined the AIF and became part of the 15th Battalion that landed at Gallipoli. One of them was a 26-year-old accountant from Charters Towers, who was the light heavyweight boxing champion of North Queensland and a captain in the Kennedy Regiment.

The young captain led his company, C Company, ashore on 26 April and they were employed in digging a communication trench up Monash Valley until 29 April, when he was ordered to hold a position at the top of the valley, where the cliffs rose abruptly 150 feet (46 metres) above the valley floor. This position formed the apex of the front-line triangle, with its base at Anzac Cove, and was the key to protecting the main supply route from the beach. It was the most forward, dangerous and exposed position held by the Australian troops. Both sides and the rear of the position were open to enemy fire, and in places the Turkish front line was only 10 yards (9 metres) away.

As the forward limit of the position could only be manned at night, when the Turkish observers could not see it clearly, the Turks, who had superior artillery positions and plentiful supplies of grenades, attacked, unsuccessfully, many times and the young captain constantly pleaded for more supplies of grenades and periscopes to defend the position. After a massive attack was repelled on 1 May, he was promoted to major.

In the early hours of 29 May 1915 the Turks, who'd been tunnelling, blew their way in and occupied part of the position's trenches. The young captain, who had spent his 27th birthday three weeks previously fighting off Turkish attacks, decided to lead a counter-attack at dawn. After preparing to send his men over the top twice and changing his mind due to his uncertainty about the Turkish numbers, he decided to go ahead alone through the trenches to reconnoitre before committing his men to a charge—and he was shot dead. His men then charged and took back the position.

The young Queenslander's name was Hugh Quinn, and the position he commanded has ever since been regarded as one of the most proudly remembered iconic names in Australian military history—Quinn's Post.

Footnote:

There's more to this tale. After the *Kanowna* debacle, the ship returned briefly to her trade along the Australian coast, but her firemen protested their innocence and demanded an inquiry into the alleged mutiny. The official verdict of the subsequent report was that no mutiny had occurred, and Captain Ward had 'acted hastily and without judgment in dealing with the situation'.

By the time this verdict was delivered, the same week that Quinn's death was reported, the *Kanowna*, rather ironically, had once again, this time officially, been requisitioned as a troopship and was again doing her part for the war effort. Now under the command of Captain William Smith, she left Australia at the beginning of July 1915 to carry troops to Egypt to reinforce the Anzacs. She then steamed to England and was converted into a hospital ship, designated 'No2 Hospital Ship, HMAT (His Majesty's Australian Transport) *Kanowna*'.

By a poignant quirk of fate, Major Hugh Quinn's kit bag and possessions were brought back later in the war, to be returned to his family, on one of the support vessels returning to Australia—the HMAT *Kanowna*.

AN ENGAGEMENT IN MAY— QUINN'S POST

E.F. Hanman

Stationed at Quinn's Post was the 4th Infantry Brigade, which comprised the bulk of the 2nd Australian Contingent. They had landed in early May and were commanded by General Monash. These men were put to the supreme test early on the morning of 19 May, when the Turks attacked in huge numbers.

E.C. Buley

The storming of the hillside like the brightest stars will shine,
But the grandest feat of all of them was The Holding of the Line.

Tom Skeyhill

About two o'clock one afternoon the foe opened fire on us again. By now, we knew his music only too well, but, thanks to our trenches, which we were ever improving, none of us were hit. We simply crouched well down, awaiting a happier mood.

Two or three times the enemy could be seen advancing in numbers. Our machine gun, and several others along the line, was a continual source of nuisance to them. They evidently spotted where ours was concealed, for the gunner put his hand to his head and slid gently down to the bottom of the trench. We placed him up behind us and left him until a burial party should make his last bed.

Shell after shell whizzed close to us. They were not shrapnel, but small high explosive missiles. One of them hit the machine-gun square, knocked the gun section off their feet, took the parapet clean away, and continued on its way. Strange to relate, it did not explode. The men who had been taken off their feet jumped up, laughing boisterously. They thoroughly enjoyed the fun, and as they were in no way injured, the affair was a huge joke. A new gun was quickly mounted, and as quickly in action.

The afternoon dragged slowly away, the shells were still screaming and hissing overhead, but we had become callous. Let them shoot away at us as much as they desired!

We were not very hungry, though we had not eaten a meal for two whole days, but our officer advised us to make the most of our time and take something to eat, as we might not now be feeling hungry, but we should become faint later on and unable to continue our duties, if we did not do as he asked us. So we opened beef tins and jam tins, and set to work on our ample supply of biscuits. More water was smuggled up to us, so we were perfectly content with our lot.

The sun shone down, bright and hot. We were very sleepy, but it was impossible to think of that, as every man might be required at a moment's notice. We did think that perhaps we might be able to snatch a wink at night, but we little knew what was before us Tuesday evening.

Darkness visited the earth, accompanied by rain. By this time we presented a sorry picture. Knees and elbows were worn through. We were covered with dust; it was down our necks, in our hair, in our ears. We were all unshaven and unwashed. The rain fell gently and lightly, turning the caked dust and dirt on us into slimy mud. It was all we could manage to keep our weapons in good working order. The mud clogged in the rifle bolts and prevented them from sliding freely.

We were dog-tired. How sleepy we were, no one would ever realise! Our heads ached and swam—our senses were dulled. It was a horrible nightmare. Nothing seemed real. As we gazed with heavy stupid eyes in front of us, the earth seemed to swim around us. We found our heads nodding, and as we were just on the point of falling to the ground, our senses would reassert themselves with a sickening, sudden jar.

This was awful; it could not last, if something did not happen to excite us and keep us at fever heat. We longed for the Turks to attack. Let us charge! Let them charge! Anything would be preferable to this state of affairs!

Of course, sentries were posted, and they stood the picture of forlorn desolation, the folds of their overcoats wrapped round their rifles to protect them from the cold, drizzling rain. Their uniforms were stained a red patchy colour where they had been in contact with the slimy sodden soil. Boots were wet, feet became numb and frozen, ears tingled, teeth chattered, and we stood and shivered, thinking of soft pillows and warm dry beds.

And all the while, the rain trickled down, augmenting our abject misery. Oh! For something to happen!

What was that?

To our right front, a bright light bursts into view. What is it?

Dim figures, jet black and weird, could be seen flitting about and around the lurid red flame. Evidently, it was some sort of a signalling apparatus the enemy was employing. It looked a very clumsy affair. The machine-gunners chuckled and turned their gun in that direction. It was laughable to see that light disappear so quickly, and cries of 'Allah! Allah!' reached our ears.

> Heavy bombardment from Hill 700, and from the top of the ridge where enemy artillery and machine-guns were concentrated, kept Australian heads down. Then the Turks dashed bravely through the scrub, heedless of the field guns and howitzers of the Australians, which were concentrated on them with deadly effect.
>
> E.C. Buley

We were wide awake now. Surely an attack was meditated. Yes! The enemy was advancing in mass formation. Our fellows had received orders to allow the Turks to come within ten paces, and then to pour the lead into them. Our rifles hold eleven cartridges, and are, in every way, very formidable little weapons.

'Allah! Allah! Allah!'

They are coming with leaps and bounds, their dismal, howling cry rending the night. Closer and closer, they are almost upon us! 'Fire!' yells an officer.

We comply willingly; rifles crack and rattle all down our line, the high-pitched music of machine guns being audible above the din.

What a withering hail of lead met those dusky warriors. They hesitate, rally, and then, throwing courage to the winds, they turned and fled, trampling under foot their dead and dying. The air is filled with moans and cries. 'Allah! Allah! Allah!'

A bugle sounds a long-drawn, dreary note. They are coming again. 'Allah! Allah! Allah!' We can easily distinguish their officers' voices, haranguing them, encouraging.

With a very determined rush, they come again. The darkness is illuminated by thousands of tiny spitting flashes—the rattle and roar is terrific. Our dark-hued foe melts before our well-directed fire. They stagger, stumble and fall like so many skittles. Then, again, they eventually turn and flee, as if possessed.

Again, and again, they came at us, determined to dishearten and dislodge us. We had come to stay. Undaunted, the wounded were removed, all the while under a veritable rain of shot. We turned to face them once more.

The Turk wearied first. He gave up the attempt as hopeless that night. He had learned a lesson. The scrubby hills were littered with dark huddled forms. The cries and groans of the terrified wounded wretches were appalling. We, too, had not escaped unscathed. There were many sad vacancies. We had witnessed our comrades' heads severed from their bodies, huge gaping wounds had appeared about our pals' limbs. They had been dragged away, cursing and crying to be allowed to remain to deal sudden death to the oncoming wave of Turks.

Others, too badly hurt for speech, were limp and inert, lying white and bloodstained, clawing at the ground. Others writhed in their death agony, calling upon us in piteous tones to shoot them and put an end to their sufferings. The din of battle never diminished. Oaths and curses could be heard on all sides. Faces and figures stood out distinct and red, red, like labouring demons, habitants of the lower regions. They disappeared and reappeared as the rifles flashed and flickered.

The enemy thought to trick us. They tried to blow our charge, thinking thus to draw us from our lair. We knew, though, that we had no bugles with us. All our orders were given by whistle. They played every call they knew—some of them we could not distinguish at all, but when the strains of 'Cook-house door' went echoing through the hills, we all roared with laughter. It was too ludicrous! 'Cook-house door'!! In the midst of all this butchering and slaughter! It is not necessary to relate that this ruse was not successful.

At last we could breathe, at last we could with safety throw ourselves down and rest, even though sleep was not allowed us. In fact, we no longer wished to sleep; we were too busy discussing the result of the attacks. Dawn found us still watching and waiting. How bitterly cold it was! A fierce, piercing wind was blowing, the icy-cold rain had penetrated our clothing, and we were wet through.

It was rumoured that we were to be relieved shortly. We became, all at once, jubilant and delighted. We had glorious visions of hot coffee and steaming stew. What a blessing would be a warm, dry shirt, and a good wash!

The relieving party crawled up without being perceived by the enemy. The morning was dull, and the light bad, so this was no wonderful feat. Out we scrambled, stiff and stumbling from being so many hours in awkward positions.

We made our way as quickly as circumstances permitted, past our reserve trenches. Here we saw lines of grinning, joking men, asking us what we thought of the night's attack. Snipers were exceptionally busy. Little spurts of mud close at our feet warned us that we had better hurry. Down the ranges we went, taking flying leaps, being torn by brambles, tripping and falling over stumps and holes in the half-light.

'Crack, crack, crack!'

'Run for it, boys! Come on!'

Round bends, over ridges, through slimy puddles, we kept to our mad pace. The beach presented a very inviting appearance. There were hundreds of men, all war-worn and battered, muffled up to their eyes in coats and scarves, sitting round little smokeless fires, cooking hot sizzling rashers of bacon. Its smell was to us famished chaps, simply heavenly. Then we felt safe, we had a respite. It did not take us long to make up more fires and do likewise.

How we did enjoy that early morning meal! When we had satisfied our appetites, we lay down in little groups and awaited the rising of the sun. Up he rose, bright and golden, despite the cold, damp night, it gave every promise of being a hot day.

Our hopes were fulfilled, it became very warm. The next best thing to do would be to have a wash. Here was the gently rolling ocean, water to spare, why not have a bathe? Bullets kept falling, making plopping sounds as they sent up little spouts of water. No one seemed to take any notice of these. It was well worth the risk to have a clean skin.

One of our section, who like ourselves, had come through the awful night safely, was stripped, and just in the act of diving into foam. A dull, resounding thud made us turn in his direction. We were just in time to see him reel and pitch face forward, blood issuing from his mouth. In less than a minute, we were forced to cover his face, and there he lay, a grim warning to others. There were nearly as many casualties down on the beach as in the first line of trenches.

The roll was called. We noticed the many silences as name after name remained unanswered. Every battalion was collected and drawn up in the usual manner. There were many who would never again call 'Here!' as his name was read from the roll. We said nothing, but we felt the loss of every man. Every silence was like a knife. Not till now had we realised how much our comrades were to us! We had lived with them, eaten with them, slept with them, fought with them! Now we knew their worth, now we were cognisant of the fact that they were gone. It could not be realised. Why, only yesterday, even this morning, early, we had spoken with them!

As our company commander listened, tears filled his eyes. He was, for several moments, unable to speak. We could see him swallowing hard, and we turned away so as not to embarrass him.

SARI BAHR

Frederick Loch

If you should step it out afar
To the pebbly beach of Sari Bahr
Full many rude graves you'll find there are,
By the road the sappers drove there.

Crooked the cross, and brief the prayer,
Close they lie by the hillside bare,
Captain and private, pair by pair,
Looking back on the days they strove there.

There still they lie, their work all done,
Resting at ease in the soil well won
And listening hard for Gabriel's gun,
To spring up and salute, as behove there.

PEACEABLE-LOOKING MEN

Joseph Beeston

On 23 May anyone looking down the coast could see a man on Gaba Tepe waving a white flag. He was soon joined by another occupied in a like manner.

Some officers came into the Ambulance and asked for the loan of some towels; we gave them two, which were pinned together with safety pins. White flags don't form part of the equipment of Australia's army.

Seven mounted men had been observed coming down Gaba Tepe, and they were joined on the beach by our four. The upshot was that one was brought in blindfolded to General Birdwood. Shortly after, we heard it announced that a truce had been arranged for the following day in order to bury the dead.

Next morning Major Millard and I started from our right and walked up and across the battlefield. It was a stretch of country between our lines and those of the Turks, and was designated no-man's land. At the extreme right there was a small farm; the owner's house occupied part of it, and was just as the man had left it. Our guns had knocked it about a good deal.

In close proximity was a field of wheat, in which there were scores of dead Turks. As these had been dead anything from a fortnight to three weeks their condition may be better imagined than described.

One body I saw was lying with the leg shattered. He had crawled into a depression in the ground and lay with his greatcoat rolled up for a pillow; the stains on the ground showed that he had bled to death, and it can only be conjectured how long he lay there before death relieved him of his sufferings.

Scores of the bodies were simply riddled with bullets. Midway between the trenches a line of Turkish sentries were posted. Each was in a natty blue uniform with gold braid, and top boots, and all were done 'up to the nines'. Each stood by a white flag on a pole stuck in the ground. We buried all the dead on our side of this line and they performed a similar office for those on their side.

Stretchers were used to carry the bodies, which were all placed in large trenches. The stench was awful, and many of our men wore handkerchiefs over their mouths in their endeavour to escape it. I counted 2000 dead Turks. One I judged to be an officer of rank, for the bearers carried him shoulder-high down a gully to the rear.

The ground was absolutely covered with rifles and equipment of all kinds, shell-cases and caps, and ammunition clips. The rifles were all collected and the bolts removed to prevent their being used again. Some of the Turks were lying right on our trenches, almost in some of them.

The Turkish sentries were peaceable-looking men, stolid in type and of the peasant class mostly. We fraternised with them and gave them cigarettes and tobacco.

Some Germans were there, but they viewed us with malignant eyes. When I talked to Colonel Pope about it afterwards he said the Germans were a mean lot of beggars.

'Why,' said he most indignantly, 'they came and had a look into my trenches.'

I asked, 'What did you do?'

He replied, 'Well, I had a look at theirs.'

MY LITTLE WET HOME IN THE TRENCH

Tom Skeyhill

I've a Little Wet Home in the Trench,
Which the rain storms continually drench.
Blue sky overhead, mud and sand for a bed,
And a stone that we use for a bench.

Bully beef and hard biscuit we chew,
It seems years since we tasted a stew,
Shells crackle and scare, there's no place can compare
With My Little Wet Home in the Trench.

Our friends in the trench o'er the way
Seem to know that we've come here to stay.
They rush and they shout, but they can't get us out,
Though there's no dirty trick they won't play.

They rushed us a few nights ago,
But we don't like intruders, and so,
Some departed quite sore, others sleep evermore,
Near My Little Wet Home in the Trench.

There's a Little Wet Home in the Trench,
Which the raindrops continually drench,
There's a dead Turk close by, with his toes to the sky,
Who causes a terrible stench.

There are snipers who keep on the go,
So we all keep our heads pretty low,
But with shells dropping there, there's no place can compare,
With My Little Wet Home in the Trench.

IN THE SWIM AT ANZAC COVE

Joseph Beeston

One thing that was really good in Anzac was the swimming. At first we used to dive off the barges; then the Engineers built Watson's Pier, at the end of which the water was fifteen feet deep and as clear as crystal, so that one could see every pebble at the bottom. At times the water was very cold, but always invigorating.

General Birdwood was an enthusiastic swimmer, but he always caused me a lot of anxiety. That pier was well covered by Beachy Bill, and one never knew when he might choose to give it his attention. This did not deter the General. He came down most regularly, sauntered out to the end, went through a lot of Sandow exercises and finally jumped in. He then swam out to a buoy moored about a quarter of a mile away. On his return he was most leisurely in drying himself. Had anything happened to him I don't know what the men would have done, for he was adored by everyone.

Swimming was popular with all hands. Early in the campaign we had a Turkish attack one morning; it was over by midday, and an hour later most of the men were in swimming.

I think it not unlikely that some of the 'missing' men were due to this habit. They would come to the beach and leave their clothes and identity discs ashore, and sometimes they were killed in the water. In this case there was no possibility of ascertaining their names. It often struck me that this might account for some whose whereabouts were unknown.

While swimming, the opportunity was taken by a good many to soak their pants and shirt, inside which there was, very often, more than the owner himself. I saw one man fish his pants out; after examining the seams, he said to his pal, 'They're not dead yet.'

His pal replied, 'Never mind, you gave them a hell of a fright.'

These insects were a great pest, and I would counsel friends sending parcels to the soldiers to include a tin of insecticide; it was invaluable when it could be obtained.

I got a fright myself one night. A lot of things were doing the Melbourne Cup inside my blanket. The horrible thought suggested itself that I had got 'them' too, but a light revealed the presence of fleas. These were very large able-bodied animals and became our constant companions at night-time; in fact one could only get to sleep after dosing the blanket with insecticide.

LAMENT

Lance Corporal Saxon

It ain't the work and it ain't the Turk
That causes us to swear,
It's having to fight at dark midnight
With the things in our underwear.

They're black and grey and brindle and white
And red and big and small
And they steeplechase around our knees
And we cannot sleep at all.

Today there's a score, tomorrow lots more
Of the rotters, it ain't too nice
To sit, skin bare in the morning air,
Looking for blooming lice!

'PRAISE GOD FROM WHOM ALL BLESSINGS FLOW'

Joseph Beeston

Joseph Beeston was born in Newcastle in 1859, studied medicine in London and later attended the Dublin College of Surgeons.

Beeston practised medicine in Newcastle and was honorary surgeon at Newcastle Hospital. He was also president of the Newcastle School of Arts and the Newcastle Agricultural and Horticultural Society. In 1908 he was appointed a lifetime Liberal member to the NSW Parliamentary Upper House.

He served as honorary captain in the Army Medical Staff Corps from 1891 and enlisted on the outbreak of war in September 1914. As lieutenant colonel he was officer in charge of the 4th Field Ambulance at Gallipoli and was awarded the C.M.G. and V.D. He contracted malaria and returned to Australia in 1916. He died in 1921.

This story by him is particularly amusing because Beeston was very short, only just over five feet.

No account of the war would be complete without some mention of the good work of the chaplains. They did their work nobly, and gave the greatest assistance to the bearers in getting the wounded down. I came into contact chiefly with those belonging to our own Brigade—Colonel Green, Colonel Wray, and Captain Gillitson, who was killed while trying to get to one of our men who had been wounded.

Services were held whenever possible, and sometimes under very peculiar circumstances.

Once service was being conducted in the gully when a platoon was observed coming down the opposite hill in a position exposed to rifle fire.

The thoughts of the audience were at once distracted from what the Padre was expounding by the risk the platoon was running; and members of the congregation pointed out the folly of such conduct, emphasising their remarks by all the adjectives in the Australian vocabulary.

Suddenly a shell burst over the platoon and killed a few men. After the wounded had been cared for, the Padre regained the attention of his congregation and gave out the last verse of 'Praise God from Whom all blessings flow'.

There was one man for whom I had a great admiration—a clergyman in civil life but a stretcher-bearer on the Peninsula—Private Greig McGregor. He belonged to the 1st Field Ambulance, and I frequently saw him. He always had a stretcher, either carrying a man or going for one, and in his odd moments he cared for the graves of those who were buried on Hell Spit. The neatness of many of them was due to his kindly thought. He gained the D.C.M., and richly deserved it.

All the graves were looked after by the departed one's chum. Each was adorned with the Corps' emblems: thus the Artillery used shell caps, the Army Medical Corps a Red Cross in stone, etc.

There were very few horses on the Peninsula, and those few belonged to the Artillery. But at the time I speak of we had one attached to the New Zealand and Australian Headquarters, to be used by the despatch rider.

Anzac, the Headquarters of General Birdwood, was about two and a half miles away; and, being a true Australian, the despatch-carrier declined to walk when he could ride, so he rode every day with despatches. Part of the journey had to be made across a position open to fire from Walker's Ridge.

We used to watch for the man every day, and make bets whether he would be hit. Directly he entered the fire zone, he started as if he were riding in the Melbourne Cup, sitting low in the saddle, while the bullets kicked up dust all round him.

One day the horse returned alone, and everyone thought the man had been hit at last; but in about an hour's time he walked in. The saddle had slipped, and he came off and rolled into a sap, whence he made his way to us on foot.

When going through the trenches it is not a disadvantage to be small of stature. It is not good form to put one's head over the sandbags; the Turks invariably objected, and even entered their protest against periscopes, which are very small in size. Numbers of observers were cut about the face and a few lost their eyes through the mirror at the top being smashed by a bullet.

On one occasion I was in a trench which the men were making deeper. A rise in the bottom of the trench just enabled me, by standing on it, to peer through the loophole.

On commending the man for leaving this lump in the floor of the trench, he replied, 'That's a dead Turk, sir!'

ARCADIA

H.E. Shell

I've dwelt in many a town and shire from Cairns to Wangaratta;
I've dropped into the Brisbane Show and Bundaberg Regatta,
But now I've struck the ideal spot where pleasure never cloys,
Just list' to the advantages this choice retreat enjoys—
The scenery is glorious, the sunsets are cyclonic;
The atmosphere's so full of iron, it acts as quite a tonic!

No parsons ever preach the Word or take up a collection;
While politicians don't exist, nor any by-election.
No scandal ever hovers here to sear our simple lives;
And married men are always true to absent, loving wives.
And should you doubt if there can be a spot which so excels,
Let me whisper—it is ANZAC! Anzac by the Dardanelles.

LONE PINE

William Baylebridge

In August a new force of some 15,000 men was to land at Suvla Bay and advance forward with a view to stretching a cordon across the peninsula and crumpling up the right wing of the Turkish army. Attacks by all forces on the peninsula were planned to divert enemy attention from the landing.

The Anzacs attacked according to plan. But due to a mis-timed artillery barrage, the Light Horse charged into the face of machine-gun fire and died at The Nek.

The New Zealanders charged up Rhododendron Ridge and took Chunuk Bair. And the Australian infantry charged the trenches at Lone Pine and captured them.

Whatever the reason, however—untrained troops, poor morale, difficult terrain, heavy Turkish resistance or simply poor leadership—the forces that landed at Suvla did not advance and the plan failed.

Of all those battles fought by our troops at Anzac, none was more fierce, and few were more bloody, than that waged at Lone Pine.

Shut too long in their trenches, with little room to pass beyond them and taking death, night and day, from the shells the Turks hurled into their lines, our troops' only desire was to be out and upon the move. Not only did Australian bayonets bring it through to a right end, but such things as were done there put Australian courage forever past doubt.

Lone Pine stood against the centre of our line. It was high land and so strong was the Turks' position there, both in defence-works and men, that any soldier, skilled in his trade, would have thought it impossible to be taken at all. The Turkish front trenches were roofed in with heavy logs, which were covered up with earth. Shelling, from our guns and ships, had little effect there.

Machine guns were set into the Turkish front line and room had been made there for snipers and for those who threw bombs out. In front of all these traps lay an ugly tangle of barbed wire. The open land further out was swept clean by rifle fire from both ends of the ridge, for the Turks controlled a dozen positions further north, and also many to the south. Turkish artillery had the accurate range of this country to a hair.

On the afternoon of the sixth day of August, a great bombardment of shellfire, from our ships behind us and our batteries on land, was poured into the wire and the Turkish back trenches at Lone Pine. These back trenches were not covered up and great numbers of Turks had been gathered there to defend that position. Those back trenches were soon choked up with dead and wounded.

While this was going on the Turkish gunners, shooting as often as they might, gave back something of what they got. With the roaring of guns, and the screech of that flying shell, there was little peace that afternoon. But then, all at once, our guns ceased firing and the charge was blown. Like hounds loosed from a leash, off raced our men: with bayonets fixed, up and over the parapet they leapt, and charged.

That charge might well have stirred the blood in any man! Those men raced towards the enemy trenches, spat upon by rifle fire from every loophole, cut down by machine guns, torn through by a rain of shrapnel, and not one hesitated. Thick they fell but they cared not. Believe me, it was not hard, later, to see the way they had gone, so heavy-sown it was with men dead.

Thinned out, but with Australian hearts yet, those who could swept on, pushed through the twisted wire, and swarmed at last up the parapet of the Turks. Once up and on that parapet, did these Australians wait? No, they tore up the roof from those front trenches and leapt down into a darkness ripe with death.

Then was there bloody work! In and home went their steel; it had a thirst in it for the blood of those Turks. Then did they fight like the men they were, now thrusting, now holding off, now twisting, now turning, now wrenching out their bayonets from this crush of flesh, now dropping down with their limbs shattered, with their bowels slit and torn out by the foe.

Along through those trenches, dark and stinking, men fought hand to hand. Many, with clubbed rifle, spilt out the brains of others, trodden soon to mud on the floor there. Bombs, knives, whatever came next to hand, both foe and friend brought into use. The bombs, bursting in little room, did great hurt: many a press of tough men they tore up, limb away from limb, making a right sickening mess.

Here and there the Turks got together in knots so that they might better hold out; but the steel of Australia ploughed a passage through those trenches. Little then did it help those Turks to know every corner, each turn and short cut, of that place; little then did their valour help them. As the two sides fought on in the heat and choking stench of that darkness, the dead lay thick under foot, here two-deep, three-deep there, and there four-deep.

Now, you have heard how these men of Australia, that tore the roof up and off those trenches, got *their* part done. While all this was doing, there were others who took those Turks in the rear. These men had charged on over the roofed trenches and struck out for the trenches behind. Coming up to these trenches—filled now with the death our guns had dealt—they pushed in, and sealed up behind them the passages that linked the back trenches with the front lines, so that the Turks could by no means get out.

Thus, taking the foe both in front and upon the rear, our steel drove them in and back upon themselves, and slew them like sheep in some accursed shambles. Too many of our own men as well were slain there! Neither friend nor foe escaped and the trenches were choked up with dead men and dying.

So thick lay the dead that we later piled them to the height of a tall man, and had to prop them up behind logs, and hold them up out of the trench with ropes, so that one side of the passage might be kept clear. Never, surely, was there a battle fought more fiercely hand to hand!

Our men, at last, got the better of those Turks. Those still alive and stirring, we drove up out of the ground and fell upon. Some we slew fighting; some, making off as they best might through the open, we caught with our machine guns; some we pushed up into saps where they were glad to give over.

As for their counter-attacks, the Turks made many, and in fine style; but, though these attacks cost us many good men, they cost the foe more, and were but lost labour.

Three days and three nights this battle lasted. The loss upon our side was a hard loss—we buried above 2000 slain.

As for the men who fought in this battle, all were infantry. There were men of the 1st Brigade in the first attack and, in the relief and making good the victory, men of the 2nd Brigade.

Footnote:
Seven Victoria Crosses were awarded for Lone Pine.

THOUGHTS OF HOME

Rowley Clark

'Tis springtime now in the Goulburn Valley
And the wheat grows high in the distant Mallee,
And at Widgiewa 'tis the lambing tally
And we're not there.

On the Clarence banks they're cutting the cane
On the Bowen Downs, time for milking again,
And the weights are out for the Spring campaign
And we're not there.

On the Diamantina the cattle are lowing,
At Narrabeen now the waratah's growing
Out on the Lachlan the billabong's flowing
And we're not there.

THE NURSES' DIARIES II

The 3rd Australian General Hospital, AIF, was set up in response to a request from the British War Office.

In May 1915, the new unit sailed from Circular Quay, Sydney, with a number of Australian Army nurses. On 8 August, after travelling via Plymouth and Alexandria, forty of us were landed at the new site on Lemnos.

There was, as yet, no hospital and no accommodation—just a site pegged out on the ground and a few tents. The previous day the August offensive had begun with massive battles at Lone Pine, Rhododendron Ridge and The Nek.

Before breakfast on 9 August, more than 200 wounded arrived from Gallipoli. Four days later, there were more than 800 patients.

On 10 August a convoy of wounded arrived at night and the next day another 400 seriously wounded stretcher cases were left on the beach, most of them horribly shattered and many dying. Matron Wilson wrote:

'. . . we found only a bare piece of ground with wounded men in pain, still in filthy, bloodstained clothes, lying amid stones and thistles. As we lacked tents, beds or medicines, we could do little for most of our patients'

We had no equipment and no water to give them a drink. We could only feed them and dress their wounds; many died. The store ship didn't arrive until 20 August. There was no medical equipment whatever and no water to drink or wash. The wounded were just laid on the ground on blankets or on the floors of tents.

Even after the stores arrived conditions were awful. The travelling kitchens would burn on windy days.

The weather was terrible, bitterly cold, with wind and rain. We nearly froze, even in our balaclavas, mufflers, mittens, cardigans, raincoats and

Wellingtons. We had no fruit or vegetables and butter and eggs only once a month.

The men got dysentery from the local bread and there were scorpions and centipedes everywhere and thistles and burrs, most girls cut their hair short to save trouble. We didn't even have a bath tent.

Night after night, in the high wind, the tents would shake and flap. We lay awake waiting for them to collapse. Hardly a night passed that a tent didn't collapse.

As for the poor wounded soldiers who arrived in hundreds, the scenes were too awful to describe. It would be better for these men to be killed outright.

Footnote:
Surgeon-General Neville Howse VC, director of the AIF's medical services, and later Minister for Defence in the Scullin government, called the treatment of the ANZAC wounded 'criminal negligence'.

SHRAPNEL

Tom Skeyhill

I was sittin' in me dug-out and was feelin' dinkum good,
Chewin' Queensland bully beef and biscuits hard as wood.
When, 'boom!' I nearly choked meself, I spilt me bloomin' tea,
I saw about a million stars and me dug-out fell on me!
They dug me out with picks and spades, I felt an awful wreck,
By that bloomin' Turkish shrapnel I was buried to the neck,
Me mouth was full of bully beef, me eyes were full of dust,
I rose up to me bloomin' feet and shook me fist and cussed.

The Sergeant says, 'You're lucky, lad, it might have got your head,
You ought to thank your lucky stars!' I says, 'Well, strike me
    dead!'
It smashed me bloomin' dug-out, it buried all me kit,
Spoilt me tea and bully beef . . . I'll revenge that little bit!

I was walkin' to the water barge along the busy shore,
Listenin' to the Maxims bark and our Big Lizzie roar,
When I heard a loud explosion above me bloomin' head,
And a bloke, not ten yards distant, flopped sudden down . . . stone
    dead.

I crawled out from the debris and lay pantin' on the sand,
I cussed that Turkish shrap and every Turk upon the land.
We cussed it when it busted a yard or two outside,
We cussed it when it missed us, a hundred yards out wide.

It's always bloomin' shrapnel, wherever you may be,
Sittin' in your dug-out, or bathin' in the sea.
At Shrapnel Valley, Deadman's Gully, Courtney's Post and
    Quinn's,
At Pope's Hill and Johnson's Jolly . . . that deadly shrapnel spins.

I don't mind bombs and rifles, and I like a bayonet charge,
But I'm hangin' out the white flag when shrapnel is at large.
When I get back to Australia and I hear a whistlin' train,
It's the nearest pub for shelter from that shrapnel once again!

THE ANZAC VCs

Oliver Hogue

Wounded or hale . . . home from war
Or yonder by the Lone Pine laid,
Give him his due, for evermore—
The bravest thing God ever made.

Will Ogilvie (Inspired by a British officer's summation of the ANZACs)

Our first Australian V.C. was Jacka of the 4th Brigade. He was young and didn't have the splendid tall physique of most of the Australians, but he was greased lightning with the bayonet. It all happened on Courtney's Post. The Turks had been sapping in towards the front trench, and after a shower of bombs they swarmed in and captured the trench. Lance Corporal Jacka, posted behind the traverse in the fire trench, blocked their advance. An officer and a few men hurried up and volunteers were immediately ready to eject the intruders.

Then, while the officer and three men engaged in a bombing exchange with the enemy, Albert Jacka jumped from the front trench into the communication trench behind, ran round and took the Turks in the rear. He shot five of them and bayoneted two. The officer's party then charged and shot the four remaining Turks who tried to escape. They found Jacka leaning up against the side of the trench with flushed face, a bloody bayonet in the end of his rifle and an unlighted cigarette in his mouth.

The boys who took Lone Pine in that fine charge, amid a shower of lead and shrapnel such as the war had not previously seen, got no V.C. for their valour. But the lads who held the hard-won post against all the subsequent counter-attacks did manage to secure a few. One of these was Captain Shout. But he never lived to wear the cross. For three long days and longer nights he participated in the furious hand-to-hand fighting in Lone Pine.

Captain Shout with his bombing gang was ubiquitous. Laughing and cheering them on he time and again drove the Turks back, and then when he reached a point where the final sandbag barrier was to be erected, he tried to light three bombs at once and throw them amongst the crowding Turks. To throw a single bomb is a risky job. To throw three bombs simultaneously was a desperate expedient. One exploded prematurely, shattered both his hands, laid open his cheek and destroyed an eye, besides minor injuries. Conscious and still cheerful he was carried away. But he died shortly afterwards.

Lance Corporal Keyzor was one of a band of heroes who did wonders in the hell-zone at the south-eastern corner of Lone Pine. It was a murder hole and after much slaughter we found that we could not hold the outer trench, while the enemy found that he also was unable to hold it. Finally it was abandoned as No Man's land.

As a bomb-thrower, Keyzor was pre-eminent. He was one of those who repeatedly caught the enemy's bombs and hurled them back before they could explode. It was here that Colonel Scobie was killed shortly afterwards, and here it was that for days and nights Keyzor moved amongst the showers of bombs with dead and dying all around, and threw bombs till every muscle ached and he could not lift his arm.

John Hamilton was very young, just nineteen. It was at Lone Pine, where the 3rd Battalion was defending a section of the line against the repeated attacks of the Turks, that young Hamilton climbed on to the top of the parapet and with a few sandbags as a precarious shield against bombs and bullets he stayed there for five solid hours sniping merrily, potting off any stray Turks that showed up, and giving warning to the officer below each time the enemy started out to attack. There was plenty of shrapnel flying and the zip of bullets into the sandbags grew monotonous. But young Hamilton hung on.

It was away on the left of our line at Hill 60 that Lieutenant Throssell of the 10th Light Horse performed his great act of valour. There was one section of the enemy's line that obstinately defied the Australasian attack but it had to be taken

Lieutenant Throssell, in charge of the digging party, shot half a dozen Turks and a fresh barricade was immediately erected. Early in the afternoon Throssell was wounded in the shoulder. But he kept on. At four o'clock he got another bullet in the neck, but still he kept on. Just after nightfall relief came and his superior officer sent him back to the field hospital.

There were other Australians who gained the V.C. and scores of the boys did big things that in lesser wars would have won distinction. Here they just were numbered with the unknown heroes. Every man on Lone Pine deserved special honour.

If they had been Germans they would have been covered with Iron Crosses. As it is they are just satisfied that they were able to do their job. Anyhow, Australia won't forget Lone Pine.

WHAT PRICE A VC?

Peter Mace

On 24 July 2006 the medals awarded to Captain Alfred Shout were auctioned in Sydney. Captain Shout was the most highly decorated Australian soldier during the Gallipoli campaign, winning the Military Cross during the initial attack and the Victoria Cross during the August offensive at Lone Pine. The auction set a world record for a medal. The winning bidder, who had wished to remain anonymous, was, however, later identified as Mr Kerry Stokes. The collection, including the last Gallipoli VC still in private hands, has been donated to the Australian War Memorial.

The auctioneer resplendent in white gloves and black bow tie,
Now calls the room to order with anticipation high.
'I thank you for your patience, but I'm sure it's worth the wait,
For now we've come to offer, lot ten-seventy-eight.'

The polished custom case is then put on display,
The cameras flash the press take notes, the auction's underway.
'You are bidding here tonight, for this collection that you see
A once in a lifetime chance I'm sure you will agree.

'For before us here the medals won by Captain Alfred Shout.
A unique opportunity of that there is no doubt.
For one lucky bidder to own a piece of history,
The highlight is of course, the last Gallipoli VC.'

In the centre was the dull bronze cross, its ribbon crimson red,
With 'for Valor' etched upon it, embossed crown and lion's head.
Beside it, the military cross with ribbon blue and white,
A testament to this soldier and his willingness to fight.

'One last thing I must mention,' the auctioneer did say.
'Before we start the bidding and the sale gets underway.
Because of its importance and to this country's laws,
This collection is forbidden to leave Australia's shores.'

'How much am I bid for it?' a white placard held on high,
The bid three hundred thousand, five hundred the reply.
The room then stunned to silence, a bid made on the phone
From a prominent, proud Australian, identity unknown.

'I have one million dollars, going once then twice then—sold.'
An auction record for a medal has been set, the room was told.
Who was this brave young ANZAC that the fuss is all about,
Pray tell me what's the story of this captain Alfred Shout.

———

A Kiwi army regular in the fight against the Boers,
Enlisted with the Aussies for the war to end all wars.
With the first battalion AIF, landed on that fateful day,
And there amongst the chaos the Turks sure made them pay.

For each foothold, ridge and stretch, of barren rocky shore.
But Shout there proved his worth, the slouch hat he proudly wore.
Bayonet charged machine guns, at Gaba Tepe—second day,
'The bravest thing I ever saw,' Private Thompson's heard to say.

On his feet for the first two days then a bullet in the arm.
Still carried back the wounded, a dozen saved from harm.
'I am with you to the finish,' Shout roared out in the fray.
But when he could no longer stand, they carried him away.

A month on board the hospital ship, discharged himself then
    back
Fighting in the trenches, till the orders came—attack
We're going to hit the Turks at The Nek and then Lone Pine
That rocky stretch of scrub that in time became a shrine.

Shout took aside young Ross McQueen, the night starless and
    black
'We'll make a name for Australia, and ourselves tomorrow, Mac.'
The fighting raged the next five days, trenches won then lost
Till Shout and Captain Sasse advanced—heedless of the cost.

Shout tossing homemade bombs, Sasse firing through the stench.
Sandbags used to fortify each foot of captured trench.
Armed with the last three jam tin bombs one last attack is
    planned
Two were hurled; the third went off, before it left his hand.

Aboard the ship *Neuralia* this hero lost the fight
A simple burial at sea, in the morning's pale half-light
He followed many others that the doctors could not save
Destined now, forever, to have no known grave.

I've stood before the monument at Lone Pine on ANZAC Day
And read the lists of fallen, this debt we can't repay
And recalled the words then spoken as the bugle starts to sing
'No braver man has ever worn the uniform of the King'.

So now back to the auction, and the million dollars bid,
A fair price to pay for the exploits that he did.
The price that all those heroes paid is one that makes me weep
A million for Shout's medals? Mate, I reckon that was cheap.

'BIG MAC'

William McKenzie was born in 1869 in Lanarkshire, Scotland, the first of seven sons of a farm labourer who migrated with his family, when William was fifteen, to Bundaberg and bought a sugar cane farm.

Raised a Presbyterian on 'catechism and porridge', William worked on farms as a teenager and was known as a hard worker and bareknuckle fighter until, aged eighteen, he attended a Salvation Army meeting and was converted. He went to train in Melbourne, served as a Salvation Army officer in Newcastle, Maitland, Sydney, New Zealand, Brisbane, Tasmania and Bendigo, and married in 1899. William joined the AIF as chaplain in September 1914 and sailed with the Australian Naval and Military Expeditionary Force (ANMEF) convoy in October.

One of the first ashore at Gallipoli, the tall 17-stone (108-kilogram) 46-year-old worked tirelessly as stretcher-bearer and water carrier, conducted services, buried the dead, and gained a reputation as a soldier as well as a chaplain.

So many myths and legends circulated about 'Big Mac' that it is hard to establish the facts. He apparently did work alone at night with a shovel to build a set of stairs up to the firing line to help the water carriers, he was never beaten in boxing matches against much younger soldiers, he sang songs, told stories, had the loudest voice at Anzac Cove, and regularly displayed extreme bravery under fire and lack of concern for his own safety to rescue the wounded. The Anzacs loved him.

The story about him leading the charge at Lone Pine swinging a shovel is, however, just a myth, as is the story that he led the soldiers from Mena camp to destroy the brothels of the Wazza, in Cairo. He did, however, most certainly deserve the Military Cross he was awarded for bravery under fire for returning time and time again into the fighting to bring out the wounded during the battle for Lone Pine.

It is rare for a non-combatant, especially a chaplain, to be decorated for bravery and it is also an accepted convention that chaplains accept only one military award. Legend has it that William McKenzie, who was in the thick of the front-line fighting on the Western Front at the battles of Pozières, Bullecourt, Mouquet Farm, Polygon Wood and Passchendaele, was recommended three times for a Victoria Cross, although none was ever awarded.

Between the Gallipoli landing in April 1915 and the bitter winter of 1916–17 in the Somme Valley, Big Mac had lost 5 stone (32 kilograms) and, late in 1917, aged 48, it was obvious his health was breaking down and army doctors recommended that he be sent home. The 4th Battalion gave him an official farewell and more than 7000 people attended his official 'welcome home' at the Melbourne Exhibition Building.

McKenzie admitted being 'completely unstrung and unnerved' by the war. 'I had seen so many fine chaps killed,' he wrote, 'and I had buried so many, too . . . that I had to ask myself again and again, is it worthwhile living?'

Once he had recovered some degree of health, he returned to Salvation Army work and, in 1926, led the church's mission in China during the four-year famine that saw millions die from starvation. In 1930 he was placed in charge of the 'southern territory' of the Salvation Army, which comprised Victoria, Tasmania, South Australia and Western Australia. Then, from 1932 to 1939, he was commander of the 'eastern territory' made up of New South Wales and Queensland.

Probably the most popular Australian soldier of World War I, Big Mac was given an OBE in 1935, quietly retired in 1940 and died in 1947.

'BULL' RYRIE

Granville de Laune 'Bull' Ryrie was born in 1865 at Michelago, on the Southern Tablelands of New South Wales. His father, Alexander Ryrie, was a grazier and member of the New South Wales parliament from 1880 to 1909.

Granville was educated at The King's School, Parramatta, worked as a jackeroo, was twice runner-up in the New South Wales amateur heavyweight championship, and was an excellent horseman and an expert shot with a rifle. Unusually for the time, he also took a close interest in Aboriginal culture and could speak an Aboriginal language. In 1898 he was commissioned second lieutenant and then served in the South African War as a captain, with the 6th New South Wales Imperial Bushmen, where he was severely wounded and promoted to honorary major.

Back home, promoted to lieutenant colonel in 1904, he took command of the 3rd Light Horse Brigade. Ryrie was elected to the Legislative Assembly as member for Queanbeyan in April 1906 and, in 1911, entered federal parliament as member for North Sydney.

In September 1914 Ryrie was given command of the 2nd Light Horse Brigade, AIF, as brigadier general. His horse, Plain Bill, was reputed to be the finest horse in the army.

The Light Horse remained in Egypt until May 1915, when Ryrie volunteered his brigade as dismounted reinforcements and, on 19 May, his regiments landed at Anzac Cove and joined the 1st Division. His brigade was allotted the southernmost section of the Anzac position and his courage, good humour and willingness to stand up for his troops earned him their respect and admiration. He twice successfully challenged orders given to attack by divisional headquarters when he was sure that men would be lost needlessly. He was twice wounded and, on the second occasion, refused to leave his command until the conflict was over. His troops held their position until the evacuation in December and even dug an extension, a new position on the front line, which they named 'Ryrie's Post'.

When Chauvel's Anzac Mounted Division was formed in March 1916, Ryrie's brigade joined and, with Ryrie absent attending an Empire Parliamentary Conference in London, his men fought in the crucial victory at Romani. He was back for the attack on Gaza where his 5th Regiment fought its way into the town by nightfall but were then unbelievably ordered to withdraw, due to a complete strategic stuff-up. Ryrie refused to move back until every man of his brigade had been collected.

Ryrie's troops took part in the battle for Beersheba on 31 October 1917, and also in the capture of Amman and the surrender of 5000 Turks at Ziza on 29 September 1918. On that occasion Ryrie's regiments famously camped with the Turks, who Ryrie allowed to retain their weapons in order to save themselves from being massacred by hostile Arab tribesmen keen on revenge. When the New Zealand Brigade arrived next day to take them all prisoner, the Turks surrendered their weapons.

Made a Companion of the Order of St Michael and St George in 1916 and a Companion of the Order of the Bath in 1917, Ryrie was Mentioned in Despatches five times and awarded the Order of the Nile by Sultan Hussein Kamel of Egypt. In April 1919 he took over from Chauvel as commander of the AIF in Egypt and was knighted later that year.

Back home Ryrie resumed his political career. Giving up his safe seat of North Sydney to Billy Hughes in 1922, he won the seat of Warringah and was chairman of committees in the House of Representatives, and chairman of the Joint Committee on Public Accounts. He also served as commander of the 1st Cavalry Division from 1921 to 1927 and retired that same year to take the post of High Commissioner in London.

He represented Australia at the League of Nations in Geneva, where his 'no nonsense' approach to complex matters was legendary. One such remark, in blunt colourful Aussie language, was translated into French during a debate and caused the French Prime Minister Aristide Briand to collapse into tears of laughter and shout, '*Magnifique, Australie*'.

'Bull' Ryrie returned to Australia in 1932 and died of cardiac failure in Sydney in 1937. Two portraits of him, by Charles Wheeler and Henry Woolcott, are in the Australian War Memorial.

THE MAN WITH THE DONKEY

When I was a kid in primary school we would all be mustered, on the last school day before the Anzac Day holiday, into the largest classroom, which was actually two classrooms with a dividing wall that could be opened. There we would be told the same story every year. After a prelude about the landing at Anzac Cove and the gallant charge up the hills in the face of the murderous Turkish barrage of gunfire, we were told the story of Simpson and his donkey.

As far as I was concerned as a kid, there was no one else at Gallipoli who had a name or a story, just Simpson . . . and the donkey. It seemed to all us kids that Simpson was the bravest man who ever lived. We were never told about the nine Australians who won the Victoria Cross at Gallipoli, or the Light Horsemen who charged the machine guns and died bravely and needlessly at the battle of The Nek, or the adventures of the submarine *AE2*—it was always Simpson and his donkey.

I was surprised to learn, later in my life, that Simpson only saw action for 25 days at Gallipoli. I was disappointed to learn, later still, that he was a 'deserter', from the merchant navy, a 'Pommie' who had 'jumped ship' in Newcastle, New South Wales, and later used his mother's maiden name to enlist in the AIF because he was technically still 'on the run'. I was further surprised to learn that he probably only enlisted to get a free passage back to his homeland to see his mum and sister, and he was disappointed when the AIF were sent directly to Egypt to train, rather than England, as had been originally planned.

He became one of the AIF's best-known soldiers, although his 'legend' was created only after his death.

Simpson, whose real name was Kirkpatrick, was born on 6 July 1892 at Shields in County Durham. He'd joined the merchant navy when his father, also a merchant seaman, died in 1909. John was seventeen when he signed up and he deserted just before his eighteenth birthday.

He travelled to Sydney, worked as a coalminer at Coledale, Corrimal and Mount Kembla and, by 1911, was on the Yilgarn goldfield in Western Australia. He travelled Australia for four years, sometimes carrying a swag and camping in the bush, and worked as a deckhand, stoker and steward on coastal trading vessels and as a cane-cutter and farmhand before enlisting in the AIF on 25 August 1914, at Blackboy Hill Camp, near Perth. He told his mother in a letter that the itinerant bush life was 'about the best life that a fellow could wish for'.

Posted to the 3rd Field Ambulance, Simpson was among those who landed at Gallipoli on 25 April 1915. Always a loner, he was, apparently, left to work solo, without being bothered with orders from Field Ambulance officers, and he did a wonderful job and saved many lives. When I researched his brief life I realised that the story we were told as kids was mostly true; he was indeed a rare and unusual, and extremely brave, young man.

The story we were told should, however, have been called 'Simpson and his *Donkeys*', for he certainly had more than one, probably three. They were called Abdul, Murphy and Duffy, though the names seemed to be interchangeable at will. The story we were told also said that he 'rounded up' stray donkeys that were wandering the hills at Anzac Cove, but I tend to think he 'procured them' from among those the Indian troops at Gallipoli used to carry water from the beach to the firing line. He certainly camped with the Indian troops, who had a few donkeys among the mule teams that were used for transporting goods from ship to shore along the jetty and carrying guns and goods up and down the beach and the gullies.

Simpson built a little 'donkey cart ambulance' to make his frequent trips from the front line to the beach easier. He often made that 5-kilometre (3-mile) journey more than fifteen times a day—over sandy trails exposed to artillery and sniper fire.

Because of his donkeys and 'donkey cart ambulance', and his non-chalant bravery and the fact that he was 'a character', Simpson was liked and remembered and talked about after his death on 19 May. He was known by most at Anzac as 'the bloke with the donk'. Some, who knew little of British accents, called him 'Scottie', due to his north country accent, while those who knew his name called him 'Simmie' or 'Simmo'.

As the campaign dragged on and men were killed, wounded or lost to disease, there was a desperate need for more men to enlist. Australians, however, continued to refuse to vote for conscription and there was a slowing enlistment rate.

The newspapers at home were full of pleas for men to enlist. Employers patriotically listed off the names of employees they had sponsored to join the AIF—and jingoistic posters, many drawn by Norman Lindsay, called for able-bodied men to come to the aid of their mates at the Dardanelles.

Stories of heroism and tragedy, especially those that featured a colourful Aussie character of some kind, were all part of the campaign to convince men to join up out of a sense of pride, shame or adventure. Simpson's was one of the stories used for a range of propaganda and political purposes, as insufficient numbers of new recruits loomed as a threat to the AIF's fighting ability. As the war went on, the story proved popular and was used more and more. Frills were added to the story, like the supposed meeting between Simpson and General Bridges, shot by a sniper on 15 May 1915. The bullet severed an artery in Bridges' leg and he died three days later.

In this version, often added to the 'man with the donkey' legend, General Bridges, mortally wounded, refuses to be carried back to the beach during the battle because the stretcher-bearers will be easy targets for the Turkish snipers. Simpson replies, 'I hope you'll be alright, Digger. I wish they'd let me take you down to the beach.' General Bridges, proud to be called 'Digger' by an Aussie private, and comforted by the humble gesture of mateship, dies peacefully.

The anecdote is, of course, pure nonsense. Although General Bridges *was* taken down to the beach and died three days later on a hospital ship. Also, had the conversation actually taken place, the 'Aussie' comments would have been delivered in a thick Durham accent (described as 'part Geordie, part Teeside').

On 19 May Simpson was shot during the massive Turkish counter-attack known as the May Offensive. One version says he was machine-gunned from behind and another says he was shot through the heart in Monash Valley by a sniper. He is buried in the small 'Commonwealth Graves' cemetery above the beach at Hell Spit and his grave is quite easy to find.

He received no bravery award but he was mentioned in orders of the day and in despatches.

As the 'story' developed after his death and was told and retold as part of the WWI propaganda machine, it took on a mythical, even iconic, status and 'Simpson and his donkey' became a legendary symbol of all that was selfless, heroic and 'Australian' about the Gallipoli campaign. John Simpson (Kirkpatrick) became the best-known and most famous Anzac of them all. There were even attempts made by various groups between the wars to have him awarded a posthumous Victoria Cross. Petitions were signed and angry letters written to the editors of newspapers. Some even, hilariously, accused the British of discriminating against him by refusing him a medal because he was just a 'fair dinkum common Aussie digger', which he, of course, was not.

Simpson did, however, have many commendable and admirable character traits that would have endeared him to Aussie troops, and Aussies generally. He was independent, witty, warm-hearted, happy-go-lucky, dressed carelessly and cared little for authority. He was devoted to his widowed mother and his sister and wrote to them constantly, sending them the bulk of the money he earned from his various jobs in Australia.

He was also, obviously, incredibly brave.

Life-sized bronze statues of 'The man with the donkey' stand at the Shrine of Remembrance in Melbourne, in Angas Gardens at North Adelaide, and at the entrance to the Australian War Memorial in Canberra.

BILLY SING—'THE ASSASSIN'

William Edward Sing was born in 1886 in Clermont in Queensland, and grew up with his parents and two sisters on the family farm at Proserpine. His father, John Sing, was from Shanghai in China and his mother, MaryAnn, was a nurse from Staffordshire in England. During his school days Billy developed a reputation for being an excellent rifle shot, both as a kangaroo shooter and a member of the Proserpine Rifle Club. He was also an excellent cricketer and did well at school before leaving to work as a timber getter, stockman and cane-cutter.

When Billy enlisted two months after the outbreak of war, as a trooper in 'Bull' Ryrie's 5th Light Horse Regiment, his height was given as 5 feet 5 inches (165 centimetres) and he weighed 10 stone (63.5 kilograms). In spite of the *Defence Act 1909*, which enabled military doctors to refuse enlistment to non-Europeans, Billy appears to have been readily accepted and there is no evidence that his ethnicity was ever a problem during his time in the AIF.

When his regiment, without their horses, were sent as reinforcements to Gallipoli in May 1915, Billy was immediately recruited as a sniper, due to his obvious skill as a marksman. It seems that Billy had the ability to see enemy soldiers merely as targets and he was a coldly efficient killer. He was said, however, to never shoot at stretcher-bearers or those attempting to rescue their wounded comrades. He was also known to kill severely wounded men rather than leaving them to die in agony.

Sniping played a major role in the conflict on the Gallipoli Peninsula, where the terrain was well suited to that particular tactic, and it was used constantly by both sides throughout the campaign.

Billy Sing was undoubtedly the most successful practitioner of the deadly art on either side of the conflict. His official tally was 150 but General Birdwood himself issued an order complimenting Billy on reaching 201 unofficial 'kills' and even acted as his spotter on one occasion in order to see how he operated.

Billy's likely total was estimated by Major Stephen Midgley, the officer who brought Billy to the attention of General Birdwood, to be around 300 but, to be an 'official kill', the spotter, who worked with the sniper, had to see the victim fall and this explains the discrepancy in the estimation of Billy's total kills.

Billy's first spotter was Ion Idriess, who would go on to be one of Australia's most prolific and popular authors. Idriess described Billy as 'a picturesque looking man-killer . . . a little chap, very dark, with a jet-black moustache and goatee beard'.

Later Idriess was replaced as Billy's spotter by Tom Sheehan and the only time that Billy was injured during the Gallipoli campaign was during the August offensive when a Turkish sniper, who had probably noticed a flash or two as Sheehan's telescope reflected the sunlight, scored a direct hit that shattered the telescope and injured Sheehan's face and hands. The bullet deflected into Billy's shoulder and he was out of action for a month recovering from the wound. Sheehan, although severely wounded, survived and was shipped home to Australia.

At Gallipoli snipers were given nicknames and talked about in much the same way as fighter pilots were on the Western Front. Evidently the Turks gave Billy the title of 'The Murderer', though he was more generally known as 'The Assassin'. There was a much-feared Turkish sniper, known to the Australian troops as 'Abdul the Terrible', who was given the task of eliminating Billy and almost succeeded. He had managed to locate Billy and Tom Sheehan at one of their most favoured positions of conceal-ment, a hill near Chatham's Post. Unfortunately for 'Abdul the Terrible', Tom spotted him as he moved to take aim from his position across the valley and so he, too, became a victim of 'The Assassin', Billy Sing. The Turks then directed an artillery barrage at Billy's position, but he and Tom had wisely vacated the spot immediately after killing 'Abdul'.

Billy suffered from poor health during the Gallipoli campaign and he was hospitalised several times with influenza, myalgia, parotitis and mumps. In November 1915 he was hospitalised on Malta and later in Egypt and did not rejoin his unit until March 1916. He was transferred to the 31st Infantry Battalion in July of that year and, after some training in England, entered the conflict on the Western Front in January 1917 where, two months later, he was severely wounded in the left leg. He spent time recovering in Scotland, where he met and married a waitress, Elizabeth Stewart.

Back in the action in September 1917, Billy led a patrol which successfully eliminated enemy gun positions during the Battle of Polygon Wood and was recognised for his bravery by being awarded the Belgian 'Croix de Guerre' (the *Oologskruis*), to add to the Distinguished Conduct Medal he was given for 'conspicuous gallantry from May to September, 1915, at Anzac, as sniper'.

In November 1917 Billy was again hospitalised due to recurring problems with his wounded leg. He returned to the front in early 1918, but was soon back in hospital due to a bullet wound in his back and lung disease as a result of exposure to poison gas. This time the war was over for Billy Sing. He was medically discharged and sent home in July 1918.

Back home in Queensland Billy tried his hand at sheep farming and gold prospecting, without much success. His wife never joined him in Australia although she did, apparently, migrate to Sydney with another partner and two children in 1924.

Billy Sing never really recovered from his wartime injuries. He moved to Brisbane in 1942 and found work as a labourer but died from a heart attack, in May 1943, in a boarding house in the Brisbane suburb of West End.

A SILENT GETAWAY

Oliver Hogue

Then like a bomb came word that in very surety we were going to evacuate. In the House of Commons members had asked in an airy way why the troops were not withdrawn from Suvla and Anzac.

To them, in their ignorance, it was merely a matter of embarking again and returning to Egypt or Salonica or France. So simple it seemed to those armchair strategists. They did not know that the beach at Anzac, our main depots, and our headquarters were within a thousand yards of the main Turkish line; that the beach had been constantly shelled by 'Beachy Bill' and other batteries for eight solid months on end.

However, the powers that be had so ordained it and that was sufficient. The Australians had talked about 'never retreating', but that was only a manifestation of the unconquerable spirit that animated them. They might talk, but they never yet disobeyed an order. It nearly broke their hearts to leave the spot where so many thousand gallant young Australians had found heroes' graves; but they knew how to obey orders. The only kick was for the honour of being the last to leave. So many wanted to be amongst the 'diehards'.

It was to be a silent 'get-away'. Absolute secrecy was essential for its success. It sounds just like a wild bit of fiction. Just imagine the possibility of withdrawing an army of 90,000 men with artillery, stores, field hospitals, mules and horses, and all the vast impedimenta of war, right from under the nose of an active enemy, and all on a clear moonlit night. One single traitor could have queered the whole pitch. But British, Indians, New Zealanders and Australians were loyal to the core.

The final attack of the Turks on the right of our line had been repulsed by the 2nd Light Horse Brigade, though the enemy in determined fashion had pushed forward with sandbags right to within a few yards of our trenches.

There were half a dozen spots in the Anzac firing line where we and the Turks could hear each other talking: Quinn's Post, Lone Pine, The Neck [sic], Apex, Turkish Despair, Chatham's Post. It would be fine fun sticking it out here while the army made its get-away. Men clamoured for the honour of being the last to leave . . .

It is the night of 19 December; the fatal night which will see the evacuation of Anzac. Men talked cheerily, but thought hard. Had the Turks any idea of our projected departure? Two nights ago, a little after midnight, there was an unrehearsed incident. A fire broke out in a depot near North Beach. Soon the whole sky was reddened with the glare and the rugged outline of Anzac was brightly illuminated. Bully beef and biscuits blazed merrily. Oil drums burst with terrific force.

Then we wondered if the Turks would deduce anything from this. Would they guess it was a preliminary to the 'get-away'? It was hardly likely. The 'fool English' would never burn the stores till the last minute. So the accidental fire did no harm. Maybe it did good. For during the past month the Anzacs had tried by all manner of tricks and subterfuges to induce Abdul to attack. But Abdul knew how costly a business it was attacking the Australians, and after a few abortive attempts he remained on the defensive . . .

Now all was normal. Down at Helles the British had, during the afternoon, made a big demonstration. The warships had joined in the fray and the bombardment of the Turkish lines was terrific. But on this last night there was nothing untoward happening.

General Birdwood during the day had gone the rounds of the trenches and the boys yarned with him as of old. It was a good thing for us to have had a General like that—one who understood the devil-may-care Australian character. That's why the boys called him the 'idol of Anzac'.

Now and then there was a round of shrapnel sent by Beachy Bill on to the southern depot at Brighton Beach. This clearly showed that the enemy suspected nothing. Yet it is bright moonlight . . . It is midnight, and nearly all the men have embarked save the thin khaki line of 'diehards' in the trenches.

An odd bomb or two is thrown by the Turks. Then from the Apex, after a final volley, streaked the first batch of the skeleton rear-guard. There is a breach in the brave Anzac line at last. But Abdul does not know it yet. Soon the daredevils at Quinn's Post heave a few bombs, then silently slink back, down the precipitous hillside, and along the gully to the beach.

From Courtney's and The Neck and the Pimple and Ryrie's Post and Chatham's all along the line came the 'diehards', full lick to the beach. But to their unutterable surprise there is no attack. They are not followed. The trenches that for eight long months defied the Turkish attacks are now open, not a solitary soldier left. But Abdul does not know it. There is still an intermittent fire from the Turkish trenches. They think our silence is some trick . . .

At half past three on the morning of 20 December there was a burst of red flame and a roar like distant thunder. This was repeated shortly afterwards, and our two big mines on The Neck blew up. It was our last slap at the Turk. We cannot say what harm it did, but thinking the explosions were a prelude to attack the Turkish line all round Anzac burst into spiteful protest. There was a wild fusillade at our empty trenches, and on the transports the Australians smiled grimly.

Shortly afterwards the Light Horsemen on the extreme right—Ryrie's lucky 2nd Brigade rear-guard—entered the waiting cutters on Brighton Beach. Then the stores—such as we could not take away—burst into flame. Only two men were wounded.

Before dawn word came that the whole force had been safely taken off, together with many of the mules and horses and guns, which it was thought, would have to be abandoned. At dawn the Turkish batteries opened a wild bombardment of our trenches, all along the line. Marvellous to relate, the enemy had not yet ascertained what had happened. But the silence soon told them the truth. Then they charged in irregular lines over the skyline at our empty trenches.

The warships fired a few salvoes at the enemy swarming over the hills, and they hurriedly took cover in our old trenches. These were the last shots fired over Anzac at the Turks. Then the flotilla turned its back on Gallipoli and swung slowly and sadly westward.

RIVERS OF BLOOD

Frederick Loch

Come, lay down the sword and the rifle
Whether you're ANZAC or Turk
And we'll sail away across Imbros Bay,
And leave all the worms to their work.

The moon will still ride through the night, friend,
The sun will still brighten the day:
Let the dead rest below where wildflowers grow
While the rivers of blood flow away.

Come, loosen the belt and the tunic,
And take off those heavy boots, too.
Leave the mess-tins to rust, let the guns choke with dust!
There are better things for men to do.

The harvest is heavy and waiting.
The eyes of our women are red;
There'll soon come an hour, when the hills burst in flower,
As the grasses climb over our dead.

Come, give me your hand for a moment
And let us be friends by and bye!
Let the rest of us live, not forget . . . but forgive,
When the rivers of blood have run dry.

OUR SONS AS WELL

For both Australia and New Zealand the Gallipoli campaign was the event that would stamp them as independent nations, both at war and in more general terms on the world stage. Even more significant, perhaps, was the effect the campaign had at home on the self-perception of both nations as independent entities with their own unique characteristics which were reflected in the character of their own fighting force.

The Anzacs represented a breed of men whose character, appearance, speech and attitude to life differed from that of their British ancestors and the other British troops at Gallipoli—and it is amazing to think that it was only a chance organisational move, a decision made while the troops were encamped in Egypt, that saw the Australian and New Zealand troops even fight as a combined entity. They could have easily been spread throughout the other British forces as they had been in South Africa.

The way the forces were organised at Gallipoli actually made it possible for the Anzacs to be seen as separate from the other British forces. Thus their differences and characteristics were able to be perceived by all and sundry, including their allies, their enemies, and those at home.

For the modern Turkish nation the events surrounding the Gallipoli campaign represent significant milestones on the path to emerging Turkish nationalism. The Ottoman Empire was crumbling and the Turkish nation would rise like a phoenix from its ashes.

There are three elements that, in retrospect, make the Gallipoli campaign a very Turkish victory, rather than an Ottoman one: the defeat of the British and French fleet at The Narrows on 18 March 1915; the holding of the peninsula against the three-pronged Allied invasion at

Helles, Anzac and Suvla; and the fact that Turkey's greatest national hero, Kemal Ataturk, rose to fame as a result of his involvement at Gallipoli.

Turks refer to the Gallipoli campaign as 'The Battle of Canakkale' and the significant date for them is 18 March, not 25 April. The eighteenth of March was the day the British and French fleet was defeated and turned back from its attempt to force the Straits by Turkish guns, mines and torpedoes. As a national day in Turkey, it is a celebration of Turkish nationhood—not a celebration of an old Ottoman victory.

The holding of the peninsula against the Allied forces is also generally seen by Turks as one of the first acts of a Turkish nation. Yet, Turks made up only a part of the Ottoman army, just as the Anzacs made up only a part of the Allied army. In fact, two-thirds of the forces commanded by Mustafa Kemal on 25 April at Gallipoli were Arab regiments, not Turkish ones.

For Turks, perhaps the most important element of the campaign is that it saw the emergence of their greatest national hero and the father of their nation, Mustafa Kemal, later known as Kemal Ataturk. Ataturk was elected Turkey's first president and instituted sweeping social changes and reforms.

When you begin to consider these elements of the Gallipoli experience, the seemingly strange bond between old enemies becomes a little easier to fathom.

———

These days Turkey is still a poor nation by European standards. Many Turks have migrated over the past decades, one and a half million in fact. The bulk of these have relocated on a temporary basis as 'migrant workers' in European nations, especially Germany.

Turkish migration to Australia, however, has for the most part been by families wanting to settle permanently. Government-assisted migration to Australia began in 1968 and the early intake was of unskilled labourers and peasant families with little English. Since the 1980s this has changed and permanent visas are given only to highly skilled Turks and those qualifying under family reunion regulations. There are now an estimated 200,000 Turkish-Australians.

———

In 1972 a Turkish migrant and former Turkish heavyweight wrestling champion, Kemal Dover, decided to march with six other Turks in

Sydney's Anzac Day March under a banner that read 'Turkish–Australian Friendship Will Never Die'. Their participation was apparently completely unofficial but well received by the crowd.

When official requests were made by Turkish groups to be involved in Anzac Day in the early 1980s, they were denied. Victorian RSL president Bruce Ruxton famously stated, 'Anyone that was shooting us doesn't get in.'

The Turkish attitude to their old foe, the Anzacs, has always been generous, forgiving and understanding. When our official Australian War Historian, Charles Bean, returned to the peninsula in 1919 to document and photograph the battlefields and the graves, he was received with courtesy and respect. Similar cooperation was afforded to the Commonwealth War Graves Commission, which was assisted by the Turks in setting up the many beautifully laid out and cared for Allied graveyards on the peninsula.

Even though the Ottoman army lost more than 86,000 men at Gallipoli, compared to 11,000 Anzacs and 31,000 British and French, there is really only one Ottoman cemetery on the peninsula. It is a combined cemetery, mosque and memorial to the 57th Regiment.

The 57th was one of those under the command of Kemal Ataturk. An all-Turkish regiment, it happened to be on the parade ground ready for exercises when news of the landing came on the morning of 25 April. It was the regiment to which Kemal issued the famous order-of-the-day:

> I don't order you to attack, I order you to die. In the time it takes us
> to die, other troops and commanders can come and take our places.

In buying time to allow reinforcements to be brought up into place on 25 April 1915, the 57th Regiment was completely wiped out.

The Turks did build other monuments at various places on the battlefields at Anzac Cove and Cape Helles. There is a gigantic statue of Kemal Ataturk on the spot where he turned the tide of the battle at Chunuk Bair. It stands beside the enormous monolithic memorial to the New Zealanders who died defending the hill.

There are a few isolated Turkish graves and other Turkish memorials and statues on the peninsula, including the statue of a brave Turkish soldier who carried a wounded British officer back to his trench during the fighting on 25 April. The bulk of the memorials and graveyards, however, are those of the invaders, not the defenders.

In 1934 Kemal Ataturk summed up many Turks' sentiments about the experience of 1915 when he wrote the words now enshrined on an enormous concrete tablet above Anzac Cove:

To those heroes that shed their blood and lost their lives . . .

You are now lying in the soil of a friendly country, therefore rest in peace.

There is no difference between the Johnnies and the Mehemets to us where they lie side by side here in this country of ours.

You, the mothers who sent your sons from far away countries . . .

Wipe away your tears; your sons are now lying in our bosom and are in peace. After having lost their lives on this land they have become our sons as well.

————

In 1973 the Turkish government designated 330 square kilometres of the peninsula as the Gallipoli Peninsula Historical National Park. In 1997 this became a Peace Park with a rehabilitation plan organised by the International Union of Architects.

From the late 1980s there has been Turkish representation in Anzac Day marches in Australia and, in 1985, a small group of Anzac veterans returned to Gallipoli on Anzac Day as invited guests of the Turkish government. At the same time Turkey officially renamed Ari Burnu Cove 'Anzac Cove', 'Anzak Koyu' in Turkish.

A larger group of Gallipoli veterans was there for the Dawn Service in 1990 to mark the 75th anniversary of Anzac Day, along with 10,000 others, including then Australian Prime Minister Bob Hawke and political leaders from Turkey, New Zealand and the United Kingdom.

Since that time the pilgrimage to Gallipoli for Anzac Day has grown to the point where new roads are having to be built to deal with the convoys of buses bringing in more than 20,000 travellers each Anzac Day. What is even more significant is that the crowd consists, to a large degree, of young Australian and New Zealand backpackers and school groups. The interest and involvement displayed by young people in the Anzac Day celebrations is fascinating and gives a true indication of the campaign's place in Australia's history, national pride and self-perception.

In my youth the conventional wisdom of the day was that Anzac would be forgotten as the veterans passed away. Despite the usual primary school lessons every April, as a young man I had little interest in the Gallipoli legend. My grandfathers fought at the Somme and in the Balkans as members of the British army, not at Gallipoli.

It wasn't until I stood at Ari Burnu point, where the first boats touched the shore, with the water lapping my shoes and tears running down my face, that I fully realised how much the Gallipoli experience is a part of the Australian psyche. I was rather glad the battlefields and beaches were virtually deserted when I was there.

I am sure many Turks feel the same about the 'Battle of Canakkale'.

Former New South Wales RSL president Rusty Priest once said, 'Australia and Turkey are perhaps the only two countries in the world that have a strong friendship born out of a war.' He meant, of course, a war in which the two countries were enemies.

Footnote:

Traveller Halt (Dur Yolcu)
Necmettin Halil Onan

This poem is carved into the hillside opposite Canakkale in Turkish—it applies to all who fought at Gallipoli.

Traveller, halt on this quiet mound.
This soil you thus tread, unaware,
Is where a generation ended . . . Listen,
The heart of a nation is beating there.

WE'RE ALL AUSTRALIANS NOW

A.B. 'Banjo' Paterson
(Published as an open letter to the troops, 1915)

Australia takes her pen in hand,
To write a line to you,
To let you fellows understand,
How proud we are of you.

From shearing shed and cattle run,
From Broome to Hobson's Bay,
Each native-born Australian son,
Stands straighter up today.

The man who used to 'hump his drum',
On far-out Queensland runs,
Is fighting side by side with some
Tasmanian farmer's sons.

The fisher-boys dropped sail and oar
To grimly stand the test,
Along that storm-swept Turkish shore,
With miners from the west.

The old state jealousies of yore
Are dead as Pharaoh's sow,
We're not State children any more
We're all Australians now!

Our six-starred flag that used to fly,
Half-shyly to the breeze,
Unknown where older nations ply
Their trade on foreign seas,

Flies out to meet the morning blue
With Vict'ry at the prow;
For that's the flag the *Sydney* flew,
The wide seas know it now!

The mettle that a race can show,
Is proved with shot and steel,
And now we know what nations know
And feel what nations feel.

The honoured graves beneath the crest
Of Gaba Tepe hill,
May hold our bravest and our best,
But we have brave men still.

With all our petty quarrels done,
Dissensions overthrown,
We have, through what you boys have done,
A history of our own.

Our old world diff'rences are dead,
Like weeds beneath the plough,
For English, Scotch, and Irish-bred,
They're all Australians now!

So now we'll toast the Third Brigade,
That led Australia's van,
For never shall their glory fade
In minds Australian.

Fight on, fight on, unflinchingly,
Till right and justice reign.
Fight on, fight on, till Victory
Shall send you home again.

And with Australia's flag shall fly
A spray of wattle bough,
To symbolise our unity,
We're all Australians now.

THE VALENTINE'S DAY MUTINY

F ew Australians know that, one day during World War I, 15,000 Australian soldiers mutinied, defied orders, marched into Liverpool, took over the town and wrecked the hotels. Many then took the trains into Sydney and terrorised the city until ten o'clock at night. The police called in 500 reinforcements from the suburbs. The army mobilised 1500 regular soldiers at Victoria Barracks and the showground, and a battle occurred at Central Railway in which seven men were shot and a man was killed.

The date was 14 February 1916.

This event never gets a mention in any lists of important events in our nation's history, yet the results were far-reaching. Hundreds of soldiers were sent to prison, 37 men were found guilty of various offences in civil courts, 280 were court-martialled and 'dismissed with ignominy' from the AIF and the whole system of housing and training army recruits was overhauled.

Four months after the day of the riot, the citizens of New South Wales voted overwhelmingly to close all pubs at 6 pm.

———

In February 1916 the war was in its second year and the 'Little Digger', Prime Minister Billy Hughes, was calling for conscription and urging men to join up—and they were! Conditions in the camps, however, were still makeshift and facilities were stretched to the point where living conditions were barely tolerable.

There were training facilities in Sydney at Randwick and Kensington racetracks and the showground, and a regular army facility at Victoria

Barracks. But the main training camp for the Commonwealth forces was at Liverpool, on the western edge of Sydney. Established in 1903, it became inadequate due to heavy enlistment once war was declared. A new camp was set up in 1914, just a mile away at Casula, to train men for the Light Horse.

These camps drew a lot of young men to the area to enlist. Infrastructure in the camps had not been extended and enlarged quickly enough to cope with the intake of recruits. Many men in the camp at Casula thought they and their fellow recruits were getting a raw deal and deserved better conditions. They had joined up to fight and die, but didn't have mattresses to sleep on or access to a beer after a day's training. They wanted better basic facilities and flexible leave, and they complained about excessive discipline and overwork.

There was no 'wet' canteen at Casula, which meant the men, who were drilling and training 36 hours a week, could not have a beer unless they had leave to visit Liverpool.

To make matters worse, the recruits were aware that conditions at the nearby internment camp for enemy aliens at Holsworthy were better than those they had to endure at Liverpool and Casula training camps. Anti-German sentiment was running high and jingoism and discontent were easily aroused among the recruits when exaggerated rumours of the better conditions at Holsworthy were spread around the camps.

Thus the scene was set for mutiny.

The tipping point came when it was decided, at the highest military level, that more drilling and route marching were required to prepare men for the Western Front. A new training syllabus was prepared, to be implemented at all AIF training camps on 14 February 1916.

When the men at Casula were told, on morning parade that day, that they would be required to train 40.5 hours in future, resentment spilled over into action.

The men rioted.

Well, the rioting actually came a little later. The men 'went on strike', although what occurred was later called a 'protest', a 'march', a 'demonstration', a 'rally', a 'mutiny' and a 'riot', as well as a 'strike'—take your pick.

What transpired after the morning parade was a call to join a protest march, along the lines of a 'union strike'. Men were invited to join in the protest action, or coerced into joining in, by a group of ringleaders. There were conflicting accounts about who these ringleaders were and just how the organisation and process of arranging the mutiny was achieved.

Evidently a deputation or representatives of the trainees delivered an ultimatum to Camp Commandant, Colonel Miller. According to the *Sydney Morning Herald*, Colonel Miller 'told the men frankly that their grievances would be inquired into, and that during the inquiry the old syllabus would be reverted to'.

Apparently this was not enough for the disgruntled troops.

The *Sydney Morning Herald* reported next day:

At breakfast-time yesterday about 5000 troops of the Australian Imperial Forces, camped at Casula, near Liverpool, refused duty and demanded the retraction of a new training syllabus which had been issued that morning. When it was explained to them that the new syllabus was a camp order issued from headquarters, and could not be treated in that cavalier fashion, almost the whole body of men marched out of the camp and on to the town of Liverpool.

Arriving at Liverpool, the principal training camp of the Commonwealth, the men called to their colleagues there, and within a few minutes about 15,000 soldiers were on strike.

A group of 'protesters' (estimated to be as many as 7000 by the police, 5000 by the *Sydney Morning Herald*, and as few as 2500 by officers at the camp) marched from Casula to Liverpool camp and urged the recruits there to join them. The enlarged mob then marched into Liverpool and the 'rioting' began.

Liverpool Council and the NSW Police Department had been warning the army for almost a year that something like the Valentine's Day Riot was inevitable—and this wasn't the first time that men from the Liverpool and Casula camps had 'rioted' in Liverpool.

As early as July 1915 the municipal council had asked for more police officers to be stationed at Liverpool, as about 6000 men were being trained in the district. By September 1915 Sergeant Coates, stationed at Liverpool, reported that there were discipline problems at the military camps and pointed out that numbers at the camps had increased to 17,000 men. On Sundays an extra 15,000 visiting family members were also in Liverpool.

On Friday 26 November 1915 there was a skirmish between sentries and men attempting to leave the camp at Casula without leave passes, to have a drink in Liverpool.

The following evening there were ugly scenes of civil disorder in the streets of central Sydney when a crowd estimated at 1500, led by about 400 soldiers on leave from camps, attacked and damaged the two 'German' clubs in the CBD as well as the building that housed the Socialist Club and (hilariously) a retail outlet of the Frankfurt Sausage Company, a British-owned smallgoods firm that had a contract to supply the Department of Defence with foodstuff!

The soldiers assembled around 8 pm outside the Deutscher Club in Phillip Street and twelve windows were smashed. The police dispersed the crowd but not long afterwards the soldiers marched down George Street and stopped at the Frankfurt Sausage Company shop, where one soldier kicked in the window and goods were stolen.

Police apprehended the window smasher but the crowd intervened and he got away. As the crowd moved away towards Circular Quay, police arrested three soldiers and not long after another fifteen soldiers and two civilians were arrested when the crowd moved up Elizabeth Street and started throwing stones at the Concordia Club.

The crowd then followed the police and the arrested men to Central Police Station where a huge mob demanded the release of the prisoners and threatened to attack the station. Police made a baton charge into the crowd, which dispersed. Some of the mob proceeded to the building in Bathurst Street that housed the Socialist Club, and several windows of the building were smashed. Two police were injured in the disturbances.

On Monday 29 November, three days after the trouble at the camp, 36 hours after the soldier-led mob violence in the CBD, and five months after an official request from Liverpool Council for more police, 1000 soldiers took over several hotels and caroused drunkenly in the streets of Liverpool. In effect they took over the town and behaved in an openly lawless, 'riotous' manner.

When Police Inspector Musgrave and thirteen police officers arrived from Parramatta at 9.30 pm, to deal with the problem, they found groups of men were roaming the streets, laughing and singing and drinking from bottles stolen from several hotels. The scene at the Commercial Hotel was chaotic with drunken soldiers doing as they pleased, taking whatever they liked and passing the pub's supply of liquor to others in the street.

At the Railway Hotel windows were smashed and the Golden Fleece Hotel had been invaded and casks of beer stolen and taken into the street to be opened and their contents shared around. Also smashed were the windows of a shop owned by a Greek family and the windows of the last train leaving Liverpool for Sydney that evening.

Musgrave wisely avoided a direct standoff between his small band of police and the 1000 drunken soldiers and called the military to come and control their recruits. It took army officers one and a half hours to convince the soldiers to return to camp.

In a report to the Chief Secretary and the Premier's Department next day, James Mitchell, Inspector General of Police, warned NSW state administrators at the highest level that:

> As the resources of the Police Department are wholly inadequate to contend with hundreds of military men, many of them armed, I would strongly urge that the matter be at once brought officially under the notice of the military authorities.

He concluded the report by suggesting that the New South Wales government contact the army and officially:

> ... request that immediate steps be taken both to prevent destruction of the property of law abiding citizens and to ensure law and order being maintained by military men in our public thoroughfares.

A royal commission was finally established and investigated the complaints about the camp conditions at Liverpool and Casula then made recommendations in a report. State Army Commandant, Colonel Ramaciotti, inspected the camps and promised better conditions and proper barracks, instead of tents. He also promised to heed the soldiers' complaints about the difficulty of obtaining leave and the availability of rail tickets.

The report, released in December 1915, noted that 53 soldiers had died at the camp in the first nine months of 1915; 48 from measles, meningitis and pneumonia, and the other five from accidents and violence. One former commandant had refused to let 1500 men use straw to fill their mattress covers because he said it made the camp 'untidy'. The commandant at the German Concentration Camp at nearby Holsworthy agreed his prisoners were better clothed, housed and fed than regular army recruits. As a result of the report, the federal defence department decided to decentralise Liverpool and Casula camps.

Promises and plans were made, but little was done in the short term. There was more riotous and anti-social behaviour involving army recruits in Sydney over the New Year weekend.

The royal commission report proved accurate but the colonel's promises were not acted upon promptly and a far worse riot occurred less than three months after the Liverpool rioting, just as James Mitchell had warned it might. Law and order broke down in Liverpool and in the city of Sydney, much public and private property was damaged, seven men were shot and a man was killed.

The Valentine's Day Riot might have begun as some form of 'protest' or 'strike' but it soon developed along the same lines as the 'riotous' behaviour of 29 November, except that the drinking and pillaging began around 11 am. There was a whole day for the rioting to spread and grow—and travel into the heart of downtown Sydney. Also, there were many more soldiers involved this time, somewhere in the vicinity of 15,000, although levels of involvement and types of behaviour varied.

The thousands who marched into Liverpool eventually separated themselves in several groups.

A large number stayed in Liverpool and rioted, ransacking the local pubs in a far more serious and violent way than had occurred in the previous 'riot' of 29 November. Their 'spree' lasted until around 6 pm and once again poor Inspector Musgrave did his best to reason with and restrain the men, with the help of a small band of about twenty police from Parramatta, Auburn and Lidcombe and an army chaplain. But they were ignored and, at one point, violently pushed aside by rioters.

The official police report indicates that the rioting in Liverpool continued unchecked from around 11 am until 5 pm. Inspector Musgrave reported:

> On arrival I found the main streets thronged with men in military uniform, the majority of them more or less intoxicated. They had complete charge of the Commercial Hotel ... intoxicated men were looting the liquor. The bar was wrecked and everything in it smashed and windows broken ...
>
> Previous to my arrival, Rafferty's Hotel had been looted ...

Several attempts were then made to break into the Golden Fleece Hotel which the police were for a time able to prevent but being at last overwhelmed the rioters obtained an entrance and looted the contents.

The rioters next turned their attention to Penny's Hotel but by this time twenty additional police had arrived from Sydney, and with their assistance the attempt to break into this hotel was prevented, and also a raid on the Warwick Farm Hotel.

Some of the soldiers parading the streets climbed over the fence into a bakery and commenced throwing loaves of bread into the street to their comrades. The loaves were broken up and the crusts thrown at all and sundry, including Captain Smith who came up with another officer on horseback and tried to restrain the men . . .

About 5 pm a considerable number of the soldiers having left for their camps an opportunity arose for arresting four of the most aggressive of the rioters. Immediately an arrest was made the police were rushed and a struggle took place, bottles, blue metal were thrown, and several of the police had narrow escapes.

After a great deal of exertion the prisoners were lodged in the lockup. Shortly after Inspector Barry arrived from Sydney with twenty police. The arrival had the effect of preventing any further trouble, and the rioters gradually melted away.

Leaving behind those whose only idea of a 'protest' was to ransack the local pubs in Liverpool and drink them dry, many of the men made for Liverpool Railway Station and boarded the trains to Sydney. Most of the men who left the rioting at Liverpool to cause trouble in the city travelled between 1 pm and 4 pm.

There were obviously some on board the trains who were motivated by the politics of the situation and genuinely wanted to protest about the situation at the camps. It seems the plan was to march from Central Railway through the city to the Domain and conduct a 'rally' with speeches, and perhaps to take their concerns to Macquarie Street or some 'official' building.

Unfortunately their chances of achieving this goal were hindered by the fact that most of those who went 'along for the ride' were already quite inebriated and had little interest in the politics of the situation or the fairness or otherwise of what they were expected to do as army recruits.

The *Sydney Morning Herald* described the scene on 17 February:

Among the train-load of soldiers, were some of the rowdy type, and as usual on occasions of lawlessness, these asserted themselves on the journey down. Windows were smashed, and, notwithstanding the presence of women and children on the train, some of the men behaved like hoodlums . . .

Arrived at Sydney, the soldiers formed up in a rough column of fours, and, headed by some men carrying flags, set off for the city, to the accompaniment of the discordant noise of trumpets and scraps of songs. Each succeeding train, as it arrived at Sydney, was crammed with soldiers, many semi-drunk, and nearly all very noisy. One man nonchalantly sauntering along with two liquor measures, one under each arm, was arrested by some of the policemen on duty at the station and taken to No 2 Police Station, where he was charged.

It seems the 'official' march formed up before 2.30 pm and marched around the block via George Street, Hay Street and Elizabeth Street and back to Central Railway where others joined in.

Photos taken on the day show at least two groups marching behind flags. One group has several Union Jacks, battalion colours and a sign that reads 'Strike—We won't drill 40½ hours'. Another group were photographed marching behind a Union Jack flying from a sapling clothes prop with a small triangular flag above the British flag.

Reading the *Sydney Morning Herald*'s version of events published on 15 February, it is easy to see how discipline broke down quite early and those attempting to 'organise' the chaos into a true protest march had an impossible task:

The last train from Liverpool prior to the cancellation of the service to the camp town was packed with soldiers. These, evidently under someone's leadership, quickly formed up in fours on the assembly platform. At the head of the long line were two buglers and two 'standard-bearers', one of the latter carrying the green and purple colours of the 5th Reinforcements of the 2nd Battalion, and the other holding aloft on a clothes prop the Union Jack, surmounted by a small red flag . . .

In a very short time the men had marched off the station down Pitt-street and into Hay-street. Here they made a really fine picture, and, keeping good time, the fours properly dressed, the men marched as if on parade. With this exception—they were very noisy . . .

Near one of the Elizabeth-street approaches to the station was the 'Pomona' fruit stall. One of the soldiers made for it, another followed, and in a few seconds the stall was surrounded by a surging mass of riotous soldiery. All the fruit was taken—and the soldiers spared nothing of the vehicle to get it. The men started to pelt the big crowd that was watching the proceedings from the balcony of the station and one of the tramway bridges. Oranges, peaches, bananas, all flew about, but misses were more frequent than hits.

The soldiers, still in fours, then proceeded to the fruit stalls at the other end of the station. One soldier made to help himself to the contents of a barrow, but he was so fiercely attacked by the boyish-looking proprietor that he was driven off. Then an AMC non-commissioned man jumped up on to a barrow and started to harangue the men. He exhorted them to play the game, to give the barrowmen a chance, and to get going again. His words had effect. The stalls were left alone, the men formed up and re-commenced their 'protest' march.

Some of the men started to commandeer different vehicles. Motor cars, motor bicycles, lorries, drays, on all of these the men deposited themselves without as much as 'with your leave'. However, in the majority of cases, it was tolerated.

Before the trains were cancelled, every arrival from Liverpool carried more drunken trainees. Police estimated the number in the original marching group to be 3000. After the march split, one section went west, towards Chinatown, Grace Brothers store, Broadway and Tooth's Brewery. The other marched down George Street and back up Pitt Street via Elizabeth and Macquarie Streets and then started to break up. Some men went east towards Hyde Park and Oxford Street.

Although there were two 'main' marches, the groups were constantly splitting with smaller groups breaking away. The police report and the newspaper reports seem to contradict each other at times about which group was the 'official' one, and what route it took through the city.

All pubs were targets. Men simply invaded and took over the bars. Those publicans who tried to close their doors had them smashed open. One group marched to Tooth's Brewery on Broadway and another ransacked the Queen Victoria Markets. The Regent Street Police Station,

Grace Brothers store in West George Street, the *Evening News* offices in Market Street and the Manly ferry wharf at Circular Quay were all attacked during the afternoon. The sheer weight of numbers meant that police were powerless to stop most of the rioting.

The *Sydney Morning Herald* report suggests that the main march reached Circular Quay and headed up Macquarie Street, while the police report states that this group marched down George Street and back up Pitt Street to near the railway.

Most agree that this group heading back south towards the railway appears to have heralded the end of any 'official march'. The whole event apparently then descended into uncoordinated riotous behaviour, drinking and destruction of property.

Meanwhile, the men from the second marching group were rioting near Chinatown and Broadway, in the vicinity of Tooth's Brewery. According to the *Sydney Morning Herald*:

> In Castlereagh-street the men took charge of a waggo [sic] belonging to Starkey's Aerated Waters Co., and emptied it of all its contents. The bottles and syphons, after they had drunk their contents, were then thrown about the street and at inoffensive people passing. The next victim was a Chinaman, whose handcart was promptly captured and the contents were strewn along the streets.
>
> In Rawson-place the rioters again raided the street fruiterers, and in a few moments the contents of the carts were being fought for amongst themselves. From a brewer's cart a barrel of beer was seized.
>
> One soldier, waving a broom over his head, and hitting out wildly, was arrested at the Broadway and taken to the lock-up. Some of his comrades, who still retained the bottles stolen from Starkey's, then threw them at the police, one hitting Constable Gordon and wounding him to such an extent as to necessitate his removal to the hospital.

At first the police believed the riotous behaviour had been confined to Liverpool. They were surprised to hear the first reports of the trouble in the city of Sydney and, realising what was happening, ordered the cancellation of train services from Liverpool at around 4.30 pm.

Once the police realised what had happened, coordination of services was reasonably prompt and efficient. The NSW Labor Premier, William Holman, called an emergency cabinet meeting and was kept informed of developments as the afternoon wore on. He had also given police the use of state government vehicles to travel quickly around the city to trouble spots and told the chief magistrate to order the closure of all hotels in the city of Sydney and the council areas of Redfern, Glebe, Paddington and Newtown. This was done by 7.30 pm and all pubs were shut by 8 pm.

By 5 pm around 500 more police had been summoned to the city from suburban stations and by 6 pm the army had 1500 troops ready for action. By 8 pm 500 armed soldiers had been sent to help the police from the camp at the showground. State Army Commandant, Colonel Ramaciotti, issued an order forbidding the selling of firearms or explosives in the County of Cumberland, which meant the entire suburban area of Greater Sydney.

By now many of the trainees who lived in and around Sydney had started 'melting away'. Those remaining were now mostly in groups of several hundred or less and some civilians, most of them 'larrikins' and troublemakers, had joined them. These groups were slowly gravitating back towards Central Railway Station.

For many of the men there was no alternative but to attempt to return to Liverpool and Casula camps.

Just after 8 pm one group, estimated at 100 soldiers and 300 civilians, attacked Kliesdorff's tobacconist at the corner of Hunter and Castlereagh streets, smashed the shopfront windows and stole cigars. Police arrested the 'ringleader' and the mob moved on to the German Club in Phillip Street and smashed some windows. When dispersed by police, they moved south towards Hyde Park.

The official police report states:

> Between this time and 10 pm a number of minor disturbances caused by scattered bodies of soldiers took place in the city.

The report then turns to events at Central Railway Station:

> From 6 pm an armed guard had been on duty at the Central Railway Station near the eastern entrance.

This 'guard' was a detachment of regular soldiers sent as a picket to maintain order as men started to congregate back at the station; they had, in fact, arrived at Central Station after 8 pm.

The police report tells what transpired in a very brief and matter-of-fact manner:

> About 10.40 pm this guard was attacked by a mob of 500 Liverpool
> soldiers throwing bottles and stones and turning the fire hose on them
> A revolver is also said to have been fired at the guard. Ultimately the
> guard fired into the mob with the result that one soldier was killed
> and six wounded. The leader of the affray was arrested by the military.

The man killed was 26-year-old Private Keefe, of the 6th Australian Light Horse being trained at Casula. The autopsy showed that a bullet entered his right cheek, fractured the lower jaw, tore the jugular vein, and then entered the left shoulder, the collarbone and the shoulder blade.

Lieutenant Colonel Marcus Logan, in command of the military police picket at Central Railway Station, said it was his understanding that Keefe came down from Liverpool with the main body of mutineers in the morning, returned to Liverpool during the afternoon and came back to town again about 5 pm. Logan stated that the approach taken by the picket, acting as military police, was one of 'cajolery' and said he told his 150 men to remember that the mutineers were still their comrades.

The rioters outnumbered the picket about four to one and started to push them back. Logan ordered his men to charge the rioters using only rifle butts. The few police in attendance used batons. A fire hose was then turned on the picket by the rioters, men in the picket were knocked down and then shots were fired by someone in the mob.

There was also a mob of some 1200 civilians outside the station entrance, which included troublemakers. Police Constable Rupert John Bailey gave evidence that:

> The crowd were calling the pickets 'scabs' and 'blacklegs', and inviting
> them to join them. Stones and bottles were thrown. The crowd broke
> through the eastern archway. The conduct of the crowd was riotous . . .
> The hose was then taken by three men and fixed to a hydrant. When
> the order was given for the picket to line up one of the crowd said,
> 'Don't be frightened, boys; it's only blank cartridges they have.'

Logan admitted he did not warn the crowd the picket was about to fire as it was 'not his intention there should be any shooting. The picket fired in self-defence.' He also stated that the *Riot Act* was not read on the station. He said that he made all men with fixed bayonets fall back away from the action to avoid injuring the men in the mob. He also testified that he did not actually see Keefe fire the pistol. He said in his evidence that:

> The mob behaved in a menacing way. A large stone was thrown at me, and hit one of my men in the back. The mutineers were pressing the pickets back gradually, and were using bad language and making threats . . . and I said, 'I will give you while I count three to get off the platform and will give the word charge.' They took no notice and used filthy language. I then gave the word 'charge, and use the butts not the bayonets'. We had not got them fixed at the time.
>
> There were a number of civilians urging the soldiers on, so we bowled over some of them. They threw missiles at us, building material, sand and stones which they obtained from the railway, bottles and pickets wrenched off the fence . . . Three of my men had been knocked insensible by bottles, and one was kicked by a civilian . . . It appeared that we would be driven into the assembly hall, and the whole station wrecked, if they regained possession of the firehose. It was then I gave the order to the pickets to load. I followed with the command, 'Keep your muzzles up, and if you have to fire, fire low.'
>
> My idea in giving these directions was that by firing low, we would not kill anyone, but hit their legs, and that only one or two shots would be required to intimidate them . . . The pickets saw a man on one knee firing. It was Keefe that was firing. The picket in self-defence fired. We fired about 25 shots, and the crowd cleared out.

Police Constable William Andrews gave evidence that he distinctly heard the order 'Fire, clear' given by a man in the picket before they opened fire. Constable Bailey stated that he saw Keefe fall and went and picked him up and carried him to the refreshment room, where he died. It seems apparent that Keefe was very drunk and belligerent. He certainly helped turn the fire hose on the picket and was in possession of a pistol, although the weapon was never found. The coroner found that:

> The deceased, Ernest William Keefe, died from the effects of a bullet wound in the head, justifiably inflicted upon him by a military picket,

then in the lawful execution of their duty in maintaining the public peace and suppressing a riot of mutinous soldiers and civilians.

During the Valentine's Day Riot more than 100 men were taken into custody and 37 arrested and charged by police subsequently went to court. The army court-martialled 280 men. Private Jack Sutcliffe and Private Frederick Short were accused of leading the parade from Casula. The official charge was 'joining in a mutiny' and they were tried before a General Court Martial on 27 March 1916. Sutcliffe was found guilty and 'discharged with ignominy' from the army. Sentenced to three years' prison, he served one year, in Long Bay and Goulburn gaols, before being released.

Private Frederick Short turned out to be sixteen-year-old Frederick Nathaniel James, who had enlisted under a false name and lied about his age. He gave evidence that 'a big crowd . . . nearly all the camp . . . was going from tent to tent pulling people out'. He said they ordered him to 'come with us'.

The *Sydney Morning Herald*, on 15 February, reflected his claim:

It is perhaps only fair to point out that thousands of the men were absolutely dragooned into the meeting, and realised their position soon after reaching Sydney. Thousands of them retired quietly to their homes in the afternoon, and returned quietly to camp at night.

In spite of his evidence, James was found guilty and sentenced to 60 days' detention.

Another sixteen-year-old, Private William Roy Heaton, was tried at Sydney Quarter Sessions on 2 March 1916 and found guilty of 'maliciously injuring a plate glass window at the Grace Bros department store worth £10'. He was sentenced to six months with hard labour.

The Mirror of Australia newspaper took up Heaton's case after their court reporter heard his evidence. Heaton was an orphan who supported his younger sister from his army pay. Although Heaton was sentenced to six months' in Goulburn Gaol, the newspaper's campaign saw him released on special licence after ten weeks.

Heaton wrote to *The Mirror*:

Dear Mr Editor,—I am not much of a scholar, so you must not mind if this letter is short. I have to thank 'The Mirror' for taking up my case, and securing my release, and I hope now that I shall be allowed to re-join the Light Horse and get to the front. That is where I want to be, with the boys in the trenches.

Heaton, however, had been 'discharged with ignominy' from the AIF upon his release from gaol on 26 March. So, on 30 June 1916, he re-enlisted as 'William Westacott', served throughout the remainder of the war and only confessed his real identity when he felt it 'safe' to do so, in February 1918.

Many of the men sentenced and 'discharged with ignominy' did the same. Men such as Cecil Madden, who was found guilty of riot at the Central Police Court and sentenced to three months' at the Darling-hurst Detention Barracks. He was discharged on his release in May 1916, but re-enlisted five months later, in November 1916, and was killed in action in France in 1918.

At least the army acted quickly for once in the wake of the riot. A mere ten days after it reported on the riot, the *Sydney Morning Herald* informed its readers on 25 February that:

> The Premier was informed yesterday by the State Commandant that by March 9 next the number of men in camp at Liverpool would be reduced to 6000. The number there at the time of the recent riot was 14,000. The Commandant also said that the despatch of men overseas and to the various country camps was proceeding actively.

The most far-reaching result of the riot was felt a few months later, on 10 June 1916.

Back on 30 November 1915 James Mitchell, Inspector General of Police, wrote in his official report of the 'disturbances' at Liverpool the previous day:

> It is suggested by the local Police that steps be taken to close the hotels at Liverpool at 6.00 o'clock pm while the war continues. This matter comes directly within the province of the military authorities and no doubt will receive their earnest consideration.

After the Valentine's Day Riot there was no need to wait for the military authorities to act. When the residents of New South Wales had the chance to make the decision four months later, on 10 June 1916, they overwhelmingly voted to close the pubs at 6 pm.

Although there were six choices, each hour from 6 pm to 11 pm, and despite the liquor industry heavily campaigning to reduce the hours by two per day and asking people to vote for 9 pm, a stunning 63 per cent voted for six o'clock! Thus, New South Wales was condemned to 40 years of the wretched social consequences of the 'six o'clock swill'. It was a terrible price to pay for the social disorder caused by a few thousand disgruntled would-be servicemen who had no straw for their mattresses and wanted a drink.

Footnote:

Some men stationed at the Casula camp were able to avoid the whole event.

Those lucky enough to have an officer like Patrick Gordon Taylor could be grateful that they were kept right out of the affair. Second Lieutenant Taylor, always known as 'Bill' and nineteen years old at the time, took his men on a route march along the Holsworthy Road and into the bush.

Years later he recalled:

I didn't want my chaps swept up into this shambles. So I lined them up on the parade . . . and told them what I thought was going to happen. I then told them we were going to march out immediately into the country on a skirmishing exercise, and that any man who wanted to stay and join the mutiny must fall out now and leave the company. There were a few sideways glances, but not a man moved.

Taylor's company thus avoided the whole incident. Later in the war Bill Taylor joined the Flying Corps. After the war he became an aviation pioneer and was the man who walked out on the wings of the *Southern Cross* several times, to transfer oil from the one 'good' engine to the one that was overheating during the 'Jubilee Flight' across the Tasman in 1935 with Charles Kingsford Smith, thus saving the lives of all three men on board. He was knighted in 1954.

THE RAGTIME ARMY

Anonymous

We are the ragtime army, the A.N.Z.A.C.,
We cannot shoot, we won't salute,
What bloody good are we?
And when we get to Berlin Old Kaiser Bill says he:
'Hoch, hoch, mein Gott, what a lousy rotten lot,
Are the A.N.Z.A.C.'

FROMELLES

This battle, fought in Northern France through July and August 1916, introduced the Australian troops of the 5th Division to the horrors of the Western Front.

It occurred near the village of Fromelles, about 10 kilometres (6 miles) south of the Belgian border and the French town of Armentières, and was fought for strategic reasons in the grand chess game conducted in the mud of the Western Front. It was not even a battle that the British General Headquarters cared much about winning or losing, The attack was conducted in order to make the Germans think that the next major push in the Battle of the Somme would take place 80 kilometres (50 miles) further north than was really intended.

The purpose of the attack, carried out by the British 61st Division and the Australian 5th Division, was to take a German stronghold known as The Sugarloaf, situated on a hilltop in front of the Aubers Ridge.

The attack, which was preceded by a massive seven-hour artillery bombardment of the German positions, began at 6 pm on 19 July, which meant that there were still almost three hours of summer daylight before the cover of darkness would have given the advancing troops a better chance of success.

Three Australian brigades, led by Major General James M'Cay, attacked from the north, while the British 61st Division, on the right of the Australians, attacked from the west. The Australian 8th and 14th Brigades crossed the waterlogged ground towards The Sugarloaf with difficulty, but their spirited attack resulted in them capturing a kilo-metre of German trenches. In front of the 15th Brigade, however, the massive seven-hour barrage had been virtually ineffective and, when the men of the 15th emerged from a ruined orchard, they found the Germans well positioned and prepared and they were mowed down by machine-gun fire. This resulted in the right flank of the 14th Brigade being exposed and finally resulted in the Australians being unable to hold the territory that they had gained.

The inexperienced men of the 61st Division encountered fierce machine-gun and artillery fire and entered German-held territory at only a few isolated points. The German 6th Bavarian Division counter-attacked and the 8th Brigade was forced to retire across no-man's land and give up all the territory they had won. Eventually the 14th Brigade was also ordered to withdraw.

The 'operational diversionary tactical' that was the 'Battle of Fromelles' had resulted in the greatest loss of Australian lives in a single 24-hour period in our military history.

Tactically, the battle was also a failure, the limited nature of the attack, and the troops used, quickly made it obvious to the Germans that this was nothing more than an attempt to draw attention away from operations further south on the Somme.

The reasons for, and the nature of, the Battle of Fromelles, along with the shock of the huge Australian losses, led to doubts about the judgement of British GHQ in the minds of Australian officers and troops, and certainly damaged relations between the AIF and the British army at the highest level.

The performance on the field of the inexperienced British troops, when compared to that of the Australian men of the 5th Division, who were responsible for more than 75 per cent of German losses, led to further doubts and discontent, as talk about the unreliability of British troops spread in the Australian infantry units.

Neither the British nor the Aussie troops were prepared for battle. The 5th Australian Division had arrived in France only days before the planned attack to relieve the 4th Australian Division on the right flank of the Second Army, and the 5th Division artillery had no experience of tactics and conditions on the Western Front. As the more experienced men of the 4th Division, who had been on the Western Front since March, prepared to move south to the Somme, a considerable shuffling of divisions had taken place, which hampered preparations and readiness for the attack.

The British 61st Division were also woefully unprepared having arrived in France in late May 1916. Delays in training, caused by shortages and lack of equipment, meant that they didn't enter the war zone until June. Their introduction to 'action' was an exhausting 'cleaning up' operation. On 15 July a failed British gas attack, known as a 'discharge', had been stopped after it had begun, due to a wind change. This meant that every one of the men of the 61st Division had spent the four days in the battlefield painstakingly removing 470 poison gas cylinders from the British front line. The work was only stopped on 19 July, and that afternoon those exhausted British soldiers were then sent straight into the Battle of Fromelles.

A German assessment of the battle, made ten days later, after interviews with captured officers, reported that the Australians made a basic error in trying to hold the German second-line trenches, instead of consolidating and falling back to the front-line trenches. Once the 15th Australian Brigade was trapped in no-man's land, the entire Australian attack broke down and was vulnerable from the right, enabling German counter-attacking troops to regain the first trench and isolate the Australian troops further forward.

In another report of 16 December 1916, the Germans called the attack 'operationally and tactically senseless' and assessed the Australian troops as 'physically imposing with virtually no military discipline' and 'no interest in soldiering as it was understood in Europe'.

While lack of experience of Western Front conditions certainly contributed to the defeat, the Australians were angered by a British GHQ media statement that read:

> Yesterday evening, south of Armentières, we carried out some important raids on a front of two miles in which Australian troops took part. About 140 German prisoners were captured.

This attitude seemed rather disrespectful to the 5th Division, which suffered 5533 casualties at Fromelles, including 400 men taken prisoner, and remained virtually inoperative until October. A number of senior Australian officers were removed after the defeat and M'Cay was criticised for not consolidating the initial gains and for the ineffective artillery support.

The British 61st Division lost 1547 in the battle and German casualties were around 1000, including the 140 captured, all by the Australians.

Brigadier General Harold 'Pompey' Elliott, who led the 15th Brigade at Fromelles, gave a fitting summation of the involvement of the AIF in the battle, when he said:

Practically all my best officers, the Anzac men who helped to build up my Brigade, are dead. I presume there was some plan at the back of the attack but it is difficult to know what it was.

THE DIGGER

Anonymous

He went over to London and straight away strode,
Into army headquarters, in Horseferry Road.
And he saw all the bludgers who dodge all the strafe,
By getting soft jobs on the headquarters' staff.

A lousy lance-corporal said, 'Pardon me please,
You've mud on your tunic and blood on your sleeve!
You look so disgraceful that people will laugh!'
Said the lousy lance-corporal on headquarters' staff.

The Digger then shot him a murderous glance;
He said, 'I've come back from that balls-up in France,
Where bullets are flying and comforts are few,
And good men are dying for bastards like you!

'We're shelled from the left and we're shelled from the right,
We're bombed all the day and we're bombed all the night,
And if something don't happen, and that pretty soon,
There'll be nobody left in the bloody platoon!'

The story soon got to the ears of Lord Gort,
Who gave the whole matter a great deal of thought,
And awarded the Digger a VC and two bars,
For giving that corporal a kick up the arse.

Now, when this war's over and we're out of here,
You'll see him in Sydney town, begging for beer.
He'll ask for a deener to buy a small glass . . .
But all that he'll get is a kick up the arse!

PRIVATE LEAK—THE LARRIKIN

The National Archives of Australia show that a man calling himself John Leak enlisted as a private in 9th Battalion, 3rd Brigade, 1st Division of the AIF, on 28 January 1915 in Rockhampton, Queensland. The 9th Battalion was recruited almost exclusively from Queensland. His army records show that he was born in Portsmouth, England, in 1892 and came to Australia sometime before the war began. His file shows that his parents were dead and his next of kin was listed as a brother living in Canada. His profession is given as 'teamster': in other words he was a bullock driver. There were still many teams of bullocks carting freight in that part of Queensland in 1915.

Private Leak embarked with the 5th Reinforcements for the 9th Battalion on the transport HMAT *Kyarra A55*, arrived at Gallipoli and joined his unit on 22 June 1915. He served there until the evacuation on 19 December. After the withdrawal from Gallipoli, the battalion returned to Egypt, was brought up to strength with reinforcements, sailed for France in March 1916, disembarked at Marseilles and headed to northern France to engage in the Somme offensive in July on the Western Front.

The 9th Battalion spearheaded the attack as the 1st Australian Division, flanked by British divisions, moved towards Pozières on 22 July 1916. Pozières, situated on a ridge overlooking the Somme, was a vital objective for the Allies and was taken after four days of savage fighting.

Private Leak survived the fighting at Pozières, but was severely wounded at the Battle of Mouquet Farm one month later on 21 August 1916.

The Battle of Mouquet Farm was fought just 1.5 kilometres (1 mile) north-west of Pozières. The purpose of the operation was to extend

British control of the strategic ridge that extended from Pozières to the ruined town of Thiepval by capturing a relatively small area of farmland.

The Australian divisions that fought in this battle were the three which had served at Gallipoli, the 1st, 2nd and 4th.

During the second week of August the 4th Division led the attack and managed to gain a small amount of territory on the fringe of the farm. This small gain cost the 4th Division 4649 casualties, mostly due to the fact that the German artillery had well-entrenched positions within range of the farm and the shelling was constant.

The 1st Division replaced the 4th and took up the attack in the third week of August. Having lost one-third of its men during the Battle of Pozières a month earlier, the 4th Division made little progress and, in one week of fighting, lost another 2650 men killed and wounded. One of the wounded was Private John Leak.

The 2nd Division, led by Major General Gordon Legge, then took over. In a dawn attack on 26 August, they actually succeeded in reaching the farm, only to discover well-entrenched shelters, which had been reinforced by troops of the German Guard Reserve Corps.

The Australians were forced to retreat and suffered another 1268 casualties. The 4th Division was then brought back into the fray and captured the farm again on 29 August, but could not hold it against German counter-attacks. The Australians recaptured the farm on 3 September but were again forced to retreat in the face of German artillery fire and counter-attacks.

These two operations cost the 4th Division a further 2405 casualties. The farm remained an island of German resistance after the Australian divisions were withdrawn on 5 September and was not captured until British forces swept past and completely surrounded it some three weeks later.

In the futile attempt to capture Mouquet Farm, 11,000 Australian casualties were sustained. In the first six weeks of the Somme offensive, the three Anzac divisions of the Australian army had suffered casualties of 23,000. Of these 6741 had been killed. This figure is roughly comparable to the fatalities suffered by these divisions during the eight months of fighting at Gallipoli, when 5833 men were killed in action and a further 1985 died later from wounds.

Leak was hospitalised from the wounds he received in the fighting at Mouquet Farm and then repatriated to London for further treatment and recovery. He did not rejoin the 9th Battalion until 15 October 1917 then continued fighting with them until 7 March 1918, when he was severely gassed in Belgium and was again hospitalised. During the time between his two bouts in hospital, he was constantly found to be in breach of army regulations and was punished on a number of occasions.

John Leak was a larrikin; throughout his army career he appears to have been a repeat offender when it came to such crimes as insolence, disobedience and going absent without leave. A look at his official record 'charge sheet' reveals a long list of offences and there is plenty of evidence to mark him out as what we might call 'an habitual offender'.

The most common of his crimes was 'absent without leave', but his service record shows a long list of offences under the heading 'CRIME', which is written in bold capitals.

The entries include 'Entering sergeants' mess & demanding drink', 'Neglecting to obey RSM [regimental sergeant major] in that he refused to leave Sergeant's Mess when ordered to by the RSM' (for which he served fourteen days' detention) and, in 1917 alone, being 'absent without leave on at least six occasions'.

The punishments handed out to Private Leak varied from forfeiting his pay on three occasions, to detention in military prison on three other occasions.

Finally, in November 1917, after Leak was absent without leave from 1 to 6 November, he was called in to face his commanding officer, who told him that he was sick of handing out punishment after punishment and was passing the problem on to a higher authority—John Leak was to be court-martialled as a deserter.

Within days Private Leak went before a Field General Court Martial charged with being a deserter. He was found guilty and sentenced to 'Penal Servitude for Life'. Had John Leak served in the ranks of the land of his birth, the British army, he would almost certainly have been shot by firing squad. As it was, he served less than a month of the life sentence. Within days of the verdict being handed down, the sentence was commuted to two years and, soon after that, it was suspended and Leak rejoined his battalion in the trenches.

In his defence Private Leak gave his side of the story, which was that he and a mate, having been gassed in action, had requested permission from the company commander to seek medical treatment. Not only was this request denied but also, according to Leak's testimony, the two men were accused of malingering.

Leak went on to say that, as he feared that his mate's eyesight had been permanently impaired, they both went to find the medical help that they desperately needed.

It does appear that the court martial was, perhaps, an attempt to scare the 25-year-old soldier into mending his ways. The most likely explanation is that Leak's commanding officers were fed up with his behaviour and, when their patience ran out, decided to change what would probably have been another 'absent without leave' charge into something more serious. So the charge was upgraded to 'desertion', in order to teach him a lesson.

If that is the case, the plan failed. On 25 April 1918, Leak went absent without leave again, deserting from hospital without permission and turning up again four days later.

(This particular desertion occurred, coincidentally, on the third anniversary of Anzac Day. That day may have marked the low point in the military career of John Leak, but it also happens to be the day that Australian troops recaptured the French village of Villers-Bretonneux and stopped the advance of the German army once and for all, an action that was, perhaps, the crowning glory of the AIF in World War I.)

This time the punishment handed out to Private Leak was the forfeiture of eleven days' pay, but it was like water off a duck's back to the bullock driver from Rockhampton. In June 1918, less than two months later, and within days of returning from hospital where he had been recoveing from being gassed at Hollebeke, he was in trouble again, serving seven days' field punishment for 'insolence to an NCO'.

In spite of his clashes with army authority, John Leak served until the end of the war and survived the conflict, having been wounded three times, gassed three times and disciplined for breaches of army regulations on more than a dozen occasions. On 9 February 1919 he embarked for Australia on a troopship and was officially discharged from the AIF in Queensland on 31 May.

Leak then picked up the threads of his life in Australia. He returned briefly to Rockhampton before spending two years on the Southern Darling Downs, where he took up a soldier-settler's block near the small village of Berat, north of Warwick.

After two years there he abandoned the block he had been given and moved south to New South Wales where he applied, unsuccessfully, to be given another soldier-settler's block. He appears to have drifted from place to place and job to job for two years before moving briefly to South Australia and then on to Esperance in Western Australia where he worked as a mechanic and ran a garage.

On 12 January 1927, using the name William J.E. Leak, he married Ada Victoria Bood-Smith. The couple reportedly lived in a tent and had either seven or eight children before moving to South Australia where John worked drilling for water in rural areas before retiring to Crafers in the Adelaide Hills, where he died, aged 80, in 1972.

This marriage to Ada is rather odd and surprising for, on 30 December 1918, less than six weeks before his departure from England by troopship, he had married Beatrice May Chapman in the Parish Church of St John The Baptist, in Cardiff, Wales. The couple were never divorced and Beatrice May Chapman was still very much alive, and recorded on the census.

An article in the *Cardiff Times* gave a report of the wedding, complete with background details about the happy couple, on 4 January 1919.

It appears that Beatrice, commonly known as 'May', was possibly the motivation, at least in part, for Private Leak's frequent absences without leave. He was certainly in a relationship with her as early as 1916, when she was nineteen years of age.

There is a photograph, taken on 30 December 1916 and reproduced in the *Cardiff Times* article, of him holding her hand, surrounded by her family, outside Buckingham Palace and, at some point during the war, he changed his next of kin on his official army record to 'Miss May Chapman of 62 Bridge Street, Cardiff'. When he enlisted he had given his next of kin as his brother George of Saskatchewan in Canada.

One version of the story, gleaned from comments made by Leak in a previous article published in the *Cardiff Times*, suggests that he first met Beatrice May Chapman when her father was helping him to trace his family during a visit the young soldier made to Wales early in 1916.

This article suggests that John Leak was born in Queensland, although his parents were both Welsh. The article quite specifically states that he believed his father was from Brynmawr and his mother was from Mountain Ash, both of which are in South Wales.

This information is, of course, in conflict with the information given by Leak on his enlistment, which states that he was born in Portsmouth and implies that his parents were English and migrated to Australia at some unknown time before the war. It is also in conflict with the information, given on his second marriage certificate, which states that he was born at Peak Hill, in Canada.

John 'William' Leak was, and still is, a 'man of mystery'.

He gave his age as 23 on enlistment in 1915. Twelve years later, on his second marriage certificate, his age was given as 28. Perhaps this seven-year discrepancy indicates that, like many other young men, he lied about his age in order to enlist, and was just sixteen at the time.

On the other hand, he may have lied about his age, as well as his first name, on the Western Australian marriage certificate in order to disguise the fact that the marriage was, in fact, bigamous and therefore illegal.

Those who have investigated the life of John Leak as thoroughly as possible, using all the military and public records available, have been unable to find any record of him being born anywhere at any time. There is no record of his birth in Wales, Canada, Australia or at Portsmouth, and the best estimate of his date of birth that can be gained from circumstantial evidence is 'sometime between 1892 and 1899'.

Tom McVeigh, former National Party Member for Darling Downs in federal parliament, and a member of the Malcolm Fraser ministry, spent many years researching the life of John Leak and co-wrote a book about him.

McVeigh is of the opinion that Leak certainly lied when he claimed to be a 'teamster from Emerald' on the day he enlisted. Even at the age of 23, according to McVeigh, the Englishman would not have had the experience to lead a team of bullocks.

It could be that the young man lied about his age and profession as well as the name of the town he came from, choosing Emerald simply because it was far enough away from Rockhampton for the information he gave to not be easily checked, yet not so far away as to arouse suspicion about why he was enlisting at Rockhampton.

Another possibility to consider is, of course, that the young man also lied about his name.

On his first marriage certificate he gave his father's name as James Leak; no mother's name was required. He was consistent on the second marriage certificate, again giving his father's name as James Leak but this time his mother's name as Sarah Wilson.

There is, however, no evidence yet found in census records or birth and marriage registrations of these two people being born or married or living in Britain; nor is there any evidence, in shipping or migration records, of them ever leaving Britain or arriving in Australia or Canada.

Tom McVeigh was born at Allora, close to Berat where John Leak lived for two years after the war. Tom spent his life farming in the district and had heard stories about John Leak from people of his parents' generation, although he himself was not born until almost a decade after the World War I veteran had left the district.

Evidently the returned soldier was made welcome in the district at first and invited to many Sunday dinners. However, he soon proved to be shiftless and untrustworthy and, according to Tom, 'after about two years he just shot through, owing money all around the town'.

Tom's research also seems to indicate that John Leak 'pulled a variety of lurks' in the various towns he lived in briefly in New South Wales, after he shot through from Berat.

What Tom found particularly frustrating in his search for the truth was the fact that John Leak gave different accounts of his birth and background in different interviews over the years. It appears that he and his second 'wife' had eight children and seven of those survived their father. Unfortunately, his children's stories about their father's origins were also 'inconsistent and unsupported'.

It is true, of course, that, if you are bigamist, you have every reason to lie about your past, but it is also not beyond the realms of possibility that the man we know as John Leak did not know where his parents came from. It seems significant to me that the first thing he did when he arrived in Britain in early 1916 was to go to Wales and enlist the help of William Chapman, his first wife's father, to trace his Welsh heritage.

It is also interesting that the article in the *Cardiff Times* specifically mentions the fact that he could not find anyone who knew his parents in either of the two towns in which he thought they had lived. Anyone who knows anything about towns in Wales will know how ludicrously impossible it is that anyone could live in those towns for any length of time and not be known and remembered.

There is, at least, some possibility that the man who called himself John Leak didn't actually know who he was.

In an interview the year before he died, the enigmatic war veteran indicated that his only wish on returning to Australia in 1919 was to forget the war and have nothing to do with the army or the memory of the conflict in which he'd served.

He told a story about arriving by train in Rockhampton, seeing a flag-waving welcoming party waiting for him on the station platform, and immediately jumping on a southbound train to escape the fuss. He claimed that he never returned to Rockhampton.

Leak never joined the RSL and he never marched on Anzac Day. In fact, he went so far as to say, 'I don't believe in war.'

The more cynical among us might be tempted to point out that the man who didn't believe in war was still happy to accept a soldier-settler's block of land in Queensland and apply for another in New South Wales.

Further evidence that he did not entirely turn his back on his military past is the fact that, in 1951, he wrote to the army seeking payment of certain entitlements that he had not bothered to claim in 1919. The army received the letter but took no action for, unfortunately, although it contained his service number and details of his service, it did not contain a return address. It was filed away as 'no address supplied' and the army made no attempt to track him down.

Although there does seem to be ample evidence that John Leak was a shiftless, unreliable, self-serving and dishonest opportunist, the more sympathetic readers of this story may find some excuses, or at least alleviating circumstances, for his behaviour.

He did at least make an honest woman of Beatrice May Chapman before leaving Britain and there is circumstantial evidence to suggest that there was an understanding that he would arrange her passage to Australia. Perhaps there was insufficient time to do this between the date of their marriage and his embarkation home.

Whatever the reason, however, the Australian government did not fund her passage and it seems certain that her husband could not afford to at the time, or at any time in the decade after he left her behind. She stayed in Wales and lived with her parents until at least 1935 when she was recorded on the census under her maiden name. After that, there is no record of her at all and she's not mentioned in her father's funeral notice in 1955, although the rest of the family are.

The lies and confusion that John Leak perpetrated about his past may not all be related to the fact that he was a bigamist, or often 'moved on' when he owed money. There is, at least, some evidence that he himself did not know much about his origins and heritage.

It is also true that he had been through the horrors of war and been wounded three times and gassed three times. He certainly suffered from emphysema and continual bouts of bronchitis in later life and, like so many World War I veterans, probably also suffered from untreated 'post-traumatic stress disorder' or 'shellshock', as it was known then.

There is no doubt that private John Leak had experienced the distress and horror of war at first hand. Which brings us, finally, to the whole point of this story.

Perhaps the inquisitive reader has wondered by now why we are bothering to talk about this enigmatic lay-about at all. Some of you may be wondering why he seemed to get off so lightly so many times when he flouted army rules so blatantly. Others among you might even have wondered how he came to be photographed outside Buckingham Palace with his girlfriend's family, and why a newspaper like the *Cardiff Times* took so much interest in an Australian infantry private.

Well, for those of you who don't already know, I'll tell you.

For actions performed in the heat of battle at Pozières on 23 July 1916, a month before he was severely wounded at the Battle of Mouquet Farm, Private John Leak became the first Queenslander, and the only member of the 9th Battalion in WWI, to be awarded the Victoria Cross for bravery.

The full citation reads:

He was one of a party which finally captured an enemy strong point. At one assault, when the enemy's bombs were outranging ours, Private Leak jumped out of the trench, ran forward under heavy machine-gun fire at close range, and threw three bombs into the enemy's bombing post. He then jumped into the post and bayoneted three unwounded enemy bombers.

Later, when the enemy in overwhelming numbers was driving his party back, he was always the last to withdraw at each stage, and kept on throwing bombs. His courage and energy had such an effect on the enemy that, on the arrival of reinforcements, the whole trench was recaptured.

While many acts of selfless heroism in war have been performed by men who were model soldiers—obedient, disciplined, well-trained men who put duty and service before self-preservation—not all acts of bravery are performed by such men. Some are, as Tom McVeigh has noted, 'the actions of a loner, a courageous individual who has no great regard for life'.

It is, perhaps, possible to reconcile some of the more unsavoury and less socially acceptable elements of John Leak's character with his amazing and admirable act of bravery that occurred that day on the Western Front, and in who knows how many other similar instances in other battles he fought.

As Tom McVeigh says:

When he'd see a challenge he'd just respond to it, not thinking about the implications of what that action might be or anything you'd done previously.

Bravery comes in many forms.

SONG OF A SOCK

Anonymous

(Found in a pair of socks sent to troops in France in a Red Cross parcel)

Knitted in the tram-car, knitted in the street,
Knitted by the fireside, knitted in the heat;
Knitted in Australia, where the wattle grows,
Sent to you in France dear, just to warm your toes.
Knitted by the seaside, knitted in the train,
Knitted in the sunshine, knitted in the rain.
Knitted here and knitted there with the glad refrain,
'May the one who wears them come back to us again.'

POZIÈRES

The Battle of the Somme began on 1 July with a massive British attack along the entire German front line in the Somme Valley. General Sir Henry Rawlinson, leading the British Fourth Army, was the overseer of a complete British disaster, losing 57,000 men, including 8000 taken prisoner, in the first three days.

Throughout the summer of 1916, Field Marshal Sir Douglas Haig, commanding the British army on the Western Front, stuck doggedly to the strategy of pushing the troops of the British Fourth Army forward step by step eastward along the valley of the Somme, against well-entrenched German positions, behind a massive artillery barrage. There is no better example of this tactic than the Battle of Bazentin Ridge, fought just 5 kilometres (3 miles) east of Pozières on 14 July, when a two-day preparatory bombardment of more than 375,000 shells preceded a five-minute 'intensive hurricane' bombardment before the leading British attackers, waiting within 100 yards of enemy lines, stormed into the German position and took 1400 prisoners. The Germans suffered 2200 casualties.

Between 13 and 17 July, the Fourth Army made four attacks against the German stronghold in the village of Pozières, but made no progress and suffered high casualty rates. In this four-day period the village, a quite substantial community with public buildings and streets lined with sturdy stone houses, was pounded until it was transformed into a vast field of rubble, but the advancing British infantry could not penetrate beyond a German defensive line, known as the 'Pozières trench', that skirted the south-western edge of the village.

Another attack, involving six divisions, was planned as Haig rearranged his generals and swapped and replaced divisions like chess pieces. Lieutenant General Hubert Gough was put in charge of the attack on Pozières and three divisions of 1 Anzac Corps joined the battle on 23 July. The Australian 1st Division, led by Englishman Major General Harold Walker, had arrived on 18 July and Gough, who had a reputation for being rather 'gung-ho', told him he was to attack Pozières the following day. Walker refused to attack unprepared and the battle was delayed. It began, in line with other attacks conducted by the Fourth Army, on the night of 22–23 July.

After the mandatory massive artillery bombardment of German positions, the 1st and 3rd Brigades of the 1st Division attacked, took the first line of German trenches, the 'Pozières trench', and pushed on to rout the German garrison and take the ruined town. Massive enemy counterattacks were repelled and the 2nd Brigade moved up the following day and secured the positions taken.

The 1st Division's victory at Pozières was the only success along the British line, but it came at a huge cost, as all German artillery within range now took aim at the Australian positions and pounded them mercilessly. Sergeant Archie Barwick wrote:

All day the ground rocked and swayed from the concussion ... we were all nearly in a state of silliness and half dazed, but still the Australians refused to give ground.

Casualties in three days amounted to 5285 and the shattered 1st Division was replaced, on 27 July, by the 2nd Australian Division under Major General Gordon Legge.

Gough was keen to press home the advantage gained by the Australians in order to assist the stalled British attacks to the north and he asked Legge to attempt to take the high ground behind the village. The 2nd Division gained some ground but suffered shocking casualties and were pushed back. Despite losing 3500 men, Legge requested permission to attack again and, on 4 August, three brigades of the 2nd Division surprised the Germans in a swift advance, following an artillery bombardment, and took their trenches. Once again the Australian troops were subjected to concentrated artillery attacks until they handed over the position to their comrades of the 4th Division on 6 August. The 2nd Division losses totalled 6848.

Just before dawn on 7 August, after a night of heavy shelling, the Germans launched a massive counter-attack on a 400-yard front and overran the outer Australian positions on the 'Old German' lines, where some Australians were occupying the former German dugouts.

One of the dugouts was occupied by ten Australians, including Lieutenant Albert Jacka who, as a corporal, had won a Victoria Cross at Gallipoli. A bomb was thrown into the dugout and killed two of his men. The Germans then moved past and advanced towards Pozières. Emerging from the dugout with the seven men left alive, Jacka saw a group of Germans holding 40 Australians prisoner and he and his seven comrades charged and engaged the Germans in hand-to-hand fighting. The Australian prisoners then turned on their captors as more Germans joined the action but, as support arrived from further along the Australian line, the Australians rallied, gained the advantage, repelled the counter-attack and captured most of the surviving Germans.

Jacka is credited variously with killing between twelve and twenty of the Germans. Every member of his platoon was wounded, including Jacka himself seven times. A bullet passed through his body under his right shoulder, and he had two serious head wounds.

Jacka was awarded the Military Cross for his leadership and bravery at Pozières, though many believed he deserved a second VC. After he returned home, Jacka established a successful electrical goods firm and became Mayor of St Kilda, but never really recovered from his war wounds and died in 1931, aged 39.

No more German attempts were made to retake Pozières.

Once the 4th Division had consolidated the territory gained at Pozières, it was then decided the Australians should attack the German stronghold at Mouquet Farm, in order to threaten the enemy positions at Thiepval, where the British had been stuck for weeks.

The Australians surrounded the German position and stubbornly held on. It was the German artillery that stopped them attaining a final victory. After the 4th Division had lost 4649 men, they were replaced by the 1st Division, who lost another 2650 men before handing over to the 2nd Division, who actually took the position on 26 August but could not hold it and withdrew, having lost another 1268 men. The 4th Division then returned to the battle and they, too, took the farm, on 29 August, but were driven back by German counter-attacks and lost another 2409 men.

The Australian efforts meant that Mouquet Farm was now isolated and it was finally taken by British troops three weeks later, after the 1 Anzac Corps had left the Somme front.

Pozières and Mouquet Farm were simply hell for infantrymen. The battlefield was the focus of massive artillery bombardment from both sides. Men attacked, waited for the counter-attack, held or retreated, and then did it again. The fighting was savage, hand to hand and, as soon as the fighting stopped, artillery barrages resumed, tearing up the ground, collapsing trenches and blowing away men and defences.

The three Australian divisions made sixteen night-time attacks and three in daylight. Each division took two turns at attacking or holding Pozières and Mouquet Farm and all three suffered huge losses. The 1st Division lost 7700 men, the 2nd Division 8100, and the 4th 7100 men. Total Australian casualties were more than 23,000 men, of whom 6741 were killed.

These battles pushed men to the very edge of human physical and mental endurance. Sergeant Baldwin, who fought with the 2nd Division, 27th Battalion, wrote:

> We went in and relieved the first division on the night of August 1, six days ago. I saw some awful things although I never got a mark, we are all on the edge, all our nerves are wrecked.

What an infantryman needed to survive at Pozières was a lot of luck and the ability to endure a living hell. Courage was mostly irrelevant, but five Victoria Crosses were won. One of them was awarded posthumously to a New Zealander, 35-year-old Corporal Tom Cooke, a married man with three kids who had migrated with his family to Australia in 1912. A carpenter by trade and an enthusiastic cornet player in civilian life, Cooke was ordered to take his Lewis gun team to defend recently captured ground that was the target of enemy counter-attacks.

Although the rest of his crew were killed, Cooke kept firing and was found dead at his gun the following morning as the fighting raged all around. His body was lost in the mud and, like many others, he has no known grave.

At Pozières the destructive power of artillery dominated the battlefield. Shrapnel tore you to pieces, high explosive shells blew you to bits, and fumes and gas shrouded the muddy, stinking ground. Gas was used by both sides and stretcher-bearers, working in the mud, exposed to artillery and rifle fire, were often blown to pieces while carrying men to field hospitals behind the lines.

Finally, in early September, the Australian divisions were taken out of the main battle and sent back to Flanders to recover and rebuild their strength.

IN PICARDY

Sergeant Major Geddes

Have you seen them march to battle,
In Picardy?
Heedless of the rifles' rattle,
In Picardy?
Have you seen them leaping, crashing,
(Muscles taut and good steel flashing)
Through the leaden Hell, and dashing
'Gainst the foe in Picardy?

Have you heard the great guns crashing,
In Picardy?
Shrapnel hail the air a-lashing,
In Picardy?
Have you seen the aircraft winging,
Through the sky, and swiftly flinging,
Devil's playthings, ever bringing,
Hell and death in Picardy?

Have you heard the south wind calling,
In Picardy?
Have you seen the red leaves falling,
In Picardy?

Have you heard the elm trees sighing
Requiem for dead and dying
On the cold white earth low lying,
Anzacs slain in Picardy?

Have you seen the poppies waving
In Picardy?
Blood red poppies dew a'laving,
In Picardy?
Have you seen them at the dawning
Droop their heads to make an awning
Guarding 'gainst the mists of morning
Anzac graves in Picardy?

TURNING THE TIDE

Sometime around the year 1030 Canute, King of England, Denmark and Norway, apparently had his throne carried down to the seashore and ordered his courtiers to watch as he attempted to turn back the tide. The point that Canute was trying to make, evidently, was that mortal men cannot achieve the impossible, there are some things that even a king cannot do.

We don't know exactly when this happened, because the story was first told a hundred years after Canute's death, by the historian Henry of Huntingdon, who may well have made up the whole thing.

There have, however, been times in history when men have turned the tide of events against all odds and achieved the seemingly impossible. On several occasions in the 20th century, this was done by Australian soldiers.

In World War II the first 'defeat' suffered by the German army was at Tobruk and the first Japanese 'defeat' was at Milne Bay, and both of those defeats were inflicted by Australian troops.

When I say 'defeat' what I really mean is that, in each case, the relentless advance of the two enemy powers was halted for the first time in the war.

At Tobruk, in April 1941, Rommel employed the 'Blitzkrieg' tactic that had not failed since the war began in September 1939. He attacked with 50 tanks, which were repulsed by infantrymen of the Australian 9th Division, ably assisted by the British Royal Horse Artillery Division.

Rommel was forced to leave the fortified enclave to be an isolated pocket of resistance for more than eight months.

Holding Tobruk was only possible for two reasons. Firstly, it could be supplied by sea and, secondly, the Australian 9th Division happened to be there when it was cut off by Rommel's advance.

But it proved to be a costly exercise. Twenty-two Allied ships, all part of what became known as 'the Tobruk Ferry', were lost in the hazardous exercise of getting convoys through in the face of constant attacks by the Luftwaffe and German U-boats.

While holding Tobruk, 832 Australians died, another 941 were captured and 2177 were wounded. British artillery casualties were more than 2000 and, in the end, Tobruk finally fell to Rommel's forces, but only after the Australian troops had been withdrawn.

At Milne Bay in August 1942 the Japanese suffered their first defeat of WWII when an invasion force of 2000 men was completely crushed by the Australian 25th and 61st Battalions, assisted by the 46th Engineers Regiment and the 43rd US Engineers, and by Australian artillery and the RAAF.

What makes that engagement even more commendable is that many of the Allied troops at Milne Bay were not crack infantry troops, they were there building an airfield.

I mention these two highly significant victories of World War II merely to point out that achieving unexpected victories, which prove to be the turning points in world wars, is something that Australian fighting forces seem to be rather good at.

All that is, however, really only a patriotic preamble to the story of what many believe to be Australia's greatest military achievement, stopping the German army at Villers-Bretonneux on two occasions and turning the tide of World War I irrevocably in the Allies' favour. This occurred during what is commonly known as the Battle of Amiens, in April 1918.

On 24 April 1918 Australia's official war historian, Charles Bean, made an entry in his diary which referred to the planned pincer movement to be made that night by the Australian 13th and 15th Brigades, in an effort to recapture the town of Villers-Bretonneux. It reads:

I don't believe they have a chance. Went to bed thoroughly depressed . . . feeling certain that this hurried attack would fail hopelessly.

Next morning, when the sun rose on the third anniversary of Anzac Day, Villers-Bretonneux was safely in Allied hands, the massive German offensive known as the *Kaiserschlacht* had been stopped in its tracks, the strategic cathedral city of Amiens was safe, and the tide of war had been turned. The German army was in retreat from that moment until the end of the war.

The *Kaiserschlacht*, or 'Kaiser's Battle', was a series of strategic attacks along the Western Front, part of the final German major offensive of the war, known as 'Operation Michael'. The aim of this offensive was to win the war before the massive manpower and military resources of the United States could be mobilised and brought to bear against the Central Powers.

The United States had declared war on Germany almost a year previously, in April 1917, and the German High Command realised that the full force of the US war effort would be felt on the Western Front sometime in 1918.

The signing of the Treaty of Brest-Litovsk by the new Soviet Russian government and the Central Powers, on 3 March 1918, ended Russia's involvement in the war and freed up more than 40 divisions, which could now be used against the Allied forces on the Western Front.

Operation Michael began with the Spring Offensive on 21 March 1918. The plan was for a massive German army, reinforced by the divisions from the Eastern Front, to push due west along the British front north of the River Somme, thus separating the French and British armies, pushing the British into the sea and capturing the channel ports.

The most important strategic target of the offensive was the cathedral city of Amiens, which had actually been taken by German forces in the very early days of the war but had subsequently been retaken by the French.

Amiens was the central hub of rail and road networks in northern France. It was a communication centre, supply base and headquarters for the Allies. The main north–south railway line ran through Amiens. If Amiens fell, the British could no longer move troops and supplies by rail, ensuring victory on the Western Front would go to Germany.

Sixteen kilometres (10 miles) to the east of Amiens, the town of Villers-Bretonneux sits on a ridge overlooking the valley of the Somme. The ridge was strategically important to the German offensive for, in order to win the *Kaiserschlacht*, they needed to establish safe artillery positions from which the shelling of Amiens could begin. This would have allowed their infantry to then sweep across the Somme Valley, the aims of Operation Michael would be achieved and a German victory on the Western Front would be assured.

Both the *Kaiserschlacht* and Operation Michael, however, ended at Villers-Bretonneux.

On 29 March the 9th Brigade of the 3rd Australian Division was sent to Villers-Bretonneux to prevent the Germans from driving a wedge between the remnants of the British 5th Army and the French 1st Army to the south.

The first encounters with the German forces occurred the following day. Four battalions of the Australian 9th Brigade were sent to defend Villers-Bretonneux. One battalion, the 35th, was protecting the eastern front of the village while three other battalions lay in support behind, on the western side.

On 4 April the full force of the German operation was brought to bear against the villages of Hamel and Villers-Bretonneux and other strategic locations in the district.

The British 18th Division, fighting around Villers-Bretonneux, held fast, but the British 14th Division was overwhelmed and the village of Hamel, 5 kilometres (3 miles) north of Villers-Bretonneux, fell to the Germans. This forced the Australian 35th Battalion to swing back to the left to prevent being surrounded.

Meanwhile, down in the valley, the 15th Brigade of the 5th Australian Division, commanded by Brigadier General Harold 'Pompey' Elliott, was guarding the bridges across the River Somme.

Harold 'Pompey' Elliott was a Victorian farmer's son who served with the Victorian Contingent in South Africa in 1900–02, was awarded the Distinguished Conduct Medal and Mentioned in Despatches before returning to university where he attained two degrees and was a champion athlete and footballer. At Gallipoli he led a battalion that won four Victoria Crosses at Lone Pine and he served in most of the great AIF battles on the Western Front. He was awarded the Distinguished Service Order, the Order of St Michael and St George, the Russian Order of St Anne and the *Croix de Guerre* and was Mentioned in Despatches seven times.

Elliott, who cried openly when he saw how few of his men had survived the Battle of Fromelles, was extremely proud of the bravery of the Australians he led and their stoic acceptance of seemingly hopeless situations. There is a story that he was once leading his men towards the enemy as a group of French women, whose homes had been destroyed, fled past them. Some of the women, noticing the men were Australian, stopped and cried, '*Vive l'Australie!*'

A gruff Australian voice from the ranks yelled back, in mangled French, '*Fini retreat madame, beaucoup Australiens ici.*'

Relating the story later Elliott said, 'I was never so proud of being an Australian.'

When large numbers of retreating British troops began arriving at his position on 4 April 1918, it became apparent to Elliott that things were desperate up on the ridge and, later that afternoon, he sent his brigade's two reserve battalions across the Somme to hold the strategically important high ground to the west of Hamel.

Meanwhile, a new German thrust against the British 18th Division brought the enemy front line to the outskirts of Villers-Bretonneux and the town seemed certain to fall.

Just as the Germans seemed certain to capture the town, they were surprised to see hundreds of Allied troops emerge from the woods to the south-west and run towards them with fixed bayonets. This courageous charge was led by the 9th Brigade's 36th Battalion, which had been lying in wait behind the village. They were joined by a company of the 35th Battalion and some men from the British 7th Battalion of the Queen's Regiment.

There was a space of some 400 metres between the opposing forces and at first the Germans held their ground and inflicted heavy casualties on the advancing troops. Finally, however, the audacious action achieved its goal. The Germans hesitated and then broke ranks and retreated into the woods. Villers-Bretonneux was saved.

Soon afterwards British troops, along with the Australian 33rd and 34th Battalions, secured the Allied line to the north of the town and the crisis was over.

Australia's 9th Brigade of the 3rd Division suffered 665 casualties in the battle.

Elsewhere, Operation Michael was going quite well for the Germans. They had taken the town of Hamel and established secure positions around the strategically vital Hill 104. If the Germans could take Hill 104, the bombardment of Amiens by their heavy artillery could begin.

Further along the line, to the north-west, the Germans pressed on through Armentières, and the Portuguese divisions holding the front at the Lys River were also forced to retreat.

Two weeks after the defence of Villers-Bretonneux, it was obvious that the only thing left for the Germans to do, in order to achieve victory, was to capture Amiens. To do this, they needed to secure Hill 104 and, in order to do that, they needed to take Villers-Bretonneux from the Allies.

On 24 April a huge German force, led by fifteen tanks, launched a massive attack against the British forces that were now defending the town. The tanks pushed through the British ranks and, in a savage and hard-fought battle, the town fell to the Germans.

This battle is famous for being the first in which tanks fought against tanks. In a field to the south of the town, three British tanks successfully attacked three German tanks, one of which was destroyed while the other two retreated.

The situation was now desperate. If the Germans could secure the district and safely install artillery on Hill 104, Amiens would be an easy target. Villers-Bretonneux had to be retaken.

Within hours two Australian brigades were rushed forward and a daring and unconventional plan was put into action. The 15th Brigade of the 5th Australian Division, led by 'Pompey' Elliott, swept around the north of the town and the 13th Brigade of the 4th Australian Division attacked from the south. Meanwhile, the 14th Brigade of the 5th Australian Division, already holding the line to the north-east, in a forested area known as Vaire Wood, moved forward to cover the left flank on the advance.

Charles Bean had every reason to be pessimistic about the outcome of this operation. In a break with conventional military wisdom of the day, it was decided that there would be no preliminary artillery barrage prior to the Australians advancing. This preliminary tactic, which was standard procedure in World War I, was designed to knock out or disrupt enemy defences in order to make an attack more likely to be successful.

In the case of Villers-Bretonneux it was thought that the only chance of success lay in surprise. It was hoped that the Germans would not expect such a sudden retaliation and therefore no artillery cover was given to the Australian battalions as they advanced in the dark on the night of 24 April 1918.

The 13th Brigade of the 4th Australian Division, led by Brigadier General William Glasgow, had just arrived after marching 13 kilometres (8 miles) to reach the battle zone. They set off at 10 pm. Glasgow had been assured by the British that they had knocked out enemy resistance in D'Arquenne Wood, through which his men had to advance. As the 13th Brigade advanced, however, machine guns in the woods opened fire and inflicted heavy casualties and progress became impossible.

Two Western Australians, Lieutenant Cliff Sadlier and Sergeant Charlie Stokes, led a small band of six volunteers into the woods and managed to locate and destroy six German machine-gun nests. Sadlier, who was wounded twice, was awarded the Victoria Cross and Stokes the Distinguished Conduct Medal.

Glasgow's brigade encountered barbed wire, came under shellfire and was targeted by other machine-gun posts before they finally reached their objective and joined the battle. Although they did not connect up with Elliott's brigade as intended, they ended up close enough to ensure success.

The departure of the 15th Brigade was delayed when one company became lost in the dark when told to make a detour around a gassed area and were late arriving at the assembly point. As a result, the brigade set off almost two hours late but actually reached the road north of the town before Glasgow's men.

The 15th Brigade stopped to regroup just outside the town and was detected by the enemy who sent up flares. A German machine gun opened fire but the Australians waited until 23-year-old Captain Eric Young, a bookkeeper from St Kilda, gave the order to charge.

The Australians, who knew that it was now officially 25 April and the third anniversary of Anzac Day, charged forward with an ear-splitting roar. The noise, Lieutenant Colonel Jack Scanlan wrote later, was 'sufficient to make the enemy's blood run cold'.

The surprised Germans were swiftly overwhelmed and the northern part of the pincer movement was successful, although some Germans escaped to the east of the town through a narrow gap that the Australians had not managed to close up. By dawn on 25 April, the town was surrounded and the remaining Germans were trapped.

By mid-morning the German army was evacuating D'Arquenne Wood and relinquishing its positions around Villers-Bretonneux. The German garrison trapped in Villers-Bretonneux had all been killed or captured by the morning of 26 April.

The German threat to Amiens was over. Australian casualties were more than 2400, while the British lost 9500 men, most of whom were captured on 24 April in the German advance. Including prisoners taken, German losses were about 10,000.

Villers-Bretonneux today is an unremarkable place. There are no ancient monuments or lovely old medieval churches for tourists to look at.

In fact, it looks like every building in the town was built after 1920, which it was, because the town was pretty much completely demolished by artillery in WWI. There is a war museum, however, and, if you're looking for those quirky, amusing, touristy photos, you can take a selfie beside the street sign in the main street, which is named 'Rue de Melbourne'.

Oh, and there is the 'Kangaroo Restaurant' and the 'Victoria School', the town's only school, which was paid for with money donated by the school children of Victoria. There are quaint old plaques in every classroom which read, *'N'oublions jamais l'Australie'* (Never forget Australia) and painted in huge letters in English across a building in the playground are the words 'DO NOT FORGET AUSTRALIA'.

Just out of town at Hill 104 is the main Australian War Cemetery and Memorial for the Western Front. Most of the 1200 Australians who died saving the village in 1918 are buried there. The town has never forgotten them.

Legendary Australian General John Monash was not involved in the 1st or 2nd Battles of Villers-Bretonneux, but the man who is credited with being instrumental in the Allied victory on the Western Front later said:

> In my opinion, this counter-attack, at night, without artillery support, is the finest thing yet done in the war, by Australians or any other troops.

If you ever doubt that there *can* be some honour in war, or believe that Australia has little to be proud of in world affairs, apart from sporting success, visit a small, rather dull-looking French town, population 5000, in the Nord-Pas-de-Calais-Picardie Region, Departement de la Somme, L'arrondisement d'Amiens, Le canton de Corbie—it's called Villers-Bretonneux (that's *Vee-yers Bre-tonn-oh*).

Footnote:
'Pompey' Elliott stood for the Senate in 1919 and topped the Victorian poll. He harboured many grievances about his lack of promotion in WWI and, after being hospitalised for blood pressure, he took his own life in March 1931 and was buried with full military honours in Burwood (Melbourne) cemetery. He was 52 years old.

BOOTS

A.B. 'Banjo' Paterson

We've travelled per Joe Gardiner, a humping of our swag
In the country of the Gidgee and Belar.
We've swum the Di'mantina with our raiment in a bag,
And we've travelled per superior motor car,
But when we went to Germany we hadn't any choice,
No matter what our training or pursuits,
For they gave us no selection 'twixt a Ford or Rolls de Royce
So we did it in our good Australian boots.

They called us 'mad Australians'; they couldn't understand
How officers and men could fraternise,
They said that we were 'reckless', we were 'wild, and out of hand',
With nothing great or sacred to our eyes.
But on one thing you could gamble, in the thickest of the fray,
Though they called us volunteers and raw recruits,
You could track us past the shell holes, and the tracks were all one way
Of the good Australian ammunition boots.

The Highlanders were next of kin, the Irish were a treat,
The Yankees knew it all and had to learn,
The Frenchmen kept it going, both in vict'ry and defeat,
Fighting grimly till the tide was on the turn.
And our army kept beside 'em, did its bit and took its chance,
And I hailed our newborn nation and its fruits,
As I listened to the clatter on the cobblestones of France
Of the good Australian military boots.

GOOD FORTUNE COMES FROM VALOUR

Fighting began in the Sinai-Palestine campaign when the German Colonel Kress von Kressenstein led a large Ottoman force to invade what was then part of the British Protectorate of Egypt and raid the Suez Canal, which was obviously strategically vital to the Allied cause.

Australia's involvement in the desert campaign against the Ottoman Empire began in 1916 when Australian troops took part in what began as the defence of the Suez Canal and then developed into a campaign to take back the Sinai Desert. The following year our troops were part of the British push into Palestine that eventually captured Gaza and Jerusalem, occupied Lebanon and Syria, and were approaching Damascus, in October 1918, when the Turks sued for peace.

The Australian Light Horse and Imperial Camel Corps fought in desert heat over harsh terrain. Often the locals, as well as the Turks, were hostile, and there were water shortages and poor supply lines. In spite of all this, casualties in this campaign, 1394 Australians killed or wounded over three years of fighting, seem remarkably light compared to those suffered in the Dardanelles campaign and on the Western Front.

The precursors to the Australian Light Horse regiments were formed during the colonial era as militia. They were not true cavalry units and were often called 'mounted infantry'. During World War I the Light Horse usually fought dismounted, the role of their horses being to get them into battle and get them away again. One man in every four during an engagement was given the task of holding the horses while the rest of the regiment were fighting.

On the other hand, the Light Horse were not exactly true mounted infantry, either. They were organised along cavalry rather than infantry lines and also operated as traditional cavalry at times, being used in mounted roles such as scouting and reconnaissance. Some regiments were issued with sabres and fought as cavalry during the advance on Damascus. Although each regiment was equivalent to an infantry battalion in terms of organisation and command, it contained only 25 officers and 400 men, while an infantry battalion consisted of 1000 men.

As infantry the Light Horse are best remembered for their role in the Gallipoli campaign, when they left their horses behind in Egypt and, from May to December 1915, established themselves as part of the Anzac legend, holding the line at Ryrie's Post and other positions on the front line and dying needlessly as they charged suicidally and bravely into a barrage of Turkish machine-gun fire at the Battle of The Nek.

Most Australians, I'm sure, think of the Light Horse as cavalry, because of the famous charge of the 4th and 12th Light Horse Regiments at Beersheba. Often considered to be the last great cavalry charge in history, this was a truly remarkable feat made even more remarkable by the fact that the men who made it were not cavalry and had never been trained to operate as such. The fact that they were simply exceptionally brave Australian horsemen obeying orders is probably the reason that the charge was so successful.

It was decided not to issue the men who made this charge with swords, as they had no experience of using them. Instead, they were ordered to charge with bayonets held in their hands, as it was thought that controlling a horse would be too difficult if the bayonets were fixed to rifles. Divisional armourers quickly sharpened all the regiment's bayonets before the charge.

Fifteen Light Horse regiments were raised during WWI, and formed into five brigades. It may seem odd to readers a century later, but the 1st Regiment was raised in Sydney. Of course many of the men came from country areas in New South Wales but it is also true that many city boys owned horses and were quite skilful horsemen. Oliver Hogue, a trooper in the 6th Regiment, who later wrote two books about his experiences at Ryrie's Post, grew up in Glebe in inner Sydney and was educated at Forest Lodge Public School, yet he was a skilled horseman and rifle-shot.

The 2nd Light Horse Regiment was formed at Enoggera in Queensland, although many of the men were from northern New South Wales. The

3rd Light Horse Regiment was raised in Adelaide. Two of its squad-
rons were made up of South Australian men, while the third were all
Tasmanians. These three regiments formed the 1st Brigade of the Light
Horse.

The 2nd Brigade was made up of the 5th Regiment, who were all
Queenslanders, and the 6th and 7th Regiments, which were both raised
in New South Wales.

The 3rd Brigade consisted of the 8th Regiment, all Victorians; the 9th,
South Australians who trained in Melbourne; and the 10th, all Western
Australian men.

The 4th Brigade contained the 4th Regiment, who had originally
enlisted in Melbourne at the very beginning of the war as 'divisional
cavalry' for the 1st AIF. As recruitment evolved rapidly at the start of
the war these men, about a quarter of whom were city-dwellers, became
part of this brigade, along with another Victorian regiment, the 13th, and
the 12th from New South Wales. It was the 4th Brigade that made the
glorious charge at Beersheba. However, by then the 13th Regiment had
been separated from the brigade and sent to France as a divisional cavalry
regiment for I Anzac Corps, where they carried out traffic control, rear
area security and prisoner escort tasks, and, when the tactical situation
permitted, the more traditional cavalry role of reconnaissance.

The 14th Light Horse Regiment was formed in Palestine in June 1918.
It was made up of the Australian companies of the disbanded Imperial
Camel Corps, which was no longer an effective fighting unit as the
campaign moved out of desert areas. Many of these troops had joined
the Camel Corps from the Light Horse earlier in the war, though some
had been recruited from the infantry. The 15th Light Horse Regiment,
the last formed during the conflict, was also made up of Australian
troops from the Camel Corps but, strangely, also included a regiment of
French colonial cavalry that served proudly at the Battle of Megiddo, on
19 September 1918, as part of the famous Australian Light Horse.

Footnote:
'*Virtutis fortuna comes*' was the motto of the 12th Light Horse Regiment that charged
at Beersheba. They borrowed it from the Duke of Wellington—it translates as 'Good
Fortune Comes From Valour'.

CHAUVEL AT ROMANI

Henry (Harry) Chauvel was born in 1865 and grew up on a cattle property at Tabulam, in the Clarence Valley, northern New South Wales. His family had a strong military connection with the British army and, after attending Sydney Grammar School and Toowoomba Grammar, he was commissioned in the Upper Clarence Light Horse, a volunteer regiment raised by his father.

In 1888 the family moved to the Darling Downs where Harry managed cattle properties and joined the Queensland Mounted Infantry in 1890. In 1896 he became a captain in the Queensland Permanent Military Force, went to England with the Queensland Jubilee Contingent in 1897 and spent a year training with the British army.

Already showing an aptitude for tactics, Chauvel served with distinction in the South African War as a major in the 1st Queensland Mounted Infantry and, when the war ended in 1901, post Federation, he was commander of the 7th Australian Commonwealth Horse, with the rank of lieutenant colonel. Back home he developed a reputation as an excellent trainer of troops, both infantry and cavalry, and was instrumental in the creation and organisation of the compulsory training systems in schools and citizens' militia, which began in 1910. He designed the system of training officers in volunteer regiments.

As a member of the Military Board from 1911, he helped Brigadier General Sir William Bridges set up the Royal Military College at Duntroon and, in 1914, he was sent to London as the Australian representative on the Imperial General Staff. When he reached England, however, Europe was at war and Australia was raising an army. Chauvel was chosen to command the 1st Light Horse Brigade. There were only two regular Australian army officers given commands in the original Australian Imperial Force—Harry Chauvel was one and the man who appointed him, William Bridges, was the other.

As well as advocating citizen military training and designing the training programs for civilian militia officers in the lead-up to WWI, Chauvel changed the course of Australian military history in other ways. While in England in 1914, he visited Salisbury Plain, the proposed training ground for the AIF, and, after deciding it was inadequate for the purpose, convinced Sir George Reid, Australian high commissioner in London, to use his influence to have the plan changed—leading to the decision to disembark the AIF for training in Egypt.

When the three Light Horse brigades remaining in Egypt were needed as reinforcements for the infantry at Gallipoli, it was Chauvel who insisted that they be sent as complete units, and not scattered among the infantry units. He himself landed at Anzac Cove on 12 May and commanded the vital sector around Pope's, Quinn's and Courtney's posts. He took command of the 1st Division on 6 November. He led it through the evacuation in December and the subsequent expansion of the AIF in Egypt. In December he was promoted to major general and was offered posts on the Western Front, but chose to remain with the Light Horse as commander of the newly formed Australian and New Zealand Mounted Division.

Chauvel's greatest moments as a commander and tactician came at Gaza and Beersheba, but his victory at Romani was one of the finest in the desert war.

Romani was a desert outpost 35 kilometres (22 miles) east of Suez on the old caravan route to Palestine. It was part of the British defensive line protecting the Suez Canal from the German-led Turkish army.

Since April 1916, Romani had been occupied by the British 52nd Lowland Infantry Division and the Australian Anzac Mounted Division, which was made up of two brigades of the Australian Light Horse, under the command of Chauvel. The mounted troops undertook patrols in the area in an attempt to keep the enemy away from this approach to the Suez Canal.

At the beginning of July 1916 the Turks began raiding and attacking British outposts in the area, attempting to take the fortifications by surprise attack. Aerial reconnaissance flights were routinely flown over the area and, on 18 July, four large columns of Turkish troops were detected a few days' march away from the line of British outposts.

Some hostile contact was made with enemy forces and skirmishes occurred. Some of the Turkish prisoners taken by patrols were interrogated and it was established that a Turkish force of some 15,000 men, led by the German general Kress von Kressenstein, was approaching the defensive line, with the intention of knocking out or capturing the British bases and forcing an access to the Suez Canal.

By 2 August the Turks had advanced to Katia, just 8 kilometres (5 miles) south-east of Romani, and it appeared certain that attack was imminent. The obvious plan of attack was to surround the southern end of the defences at Romani and then attack the camps and the railway line, which were behind the main defences.

Chauvel had only one brigade available, as the other was out on patrol, so he divided the brigade into small groups and placed them so that they covered an 8-kilometre front to the south of the positions taken up by the British infantry of the 52nd Division.

As the Turks were forming up for the attack, they unexpectedly encountered the Australians around midnight on 3 August and attacked within the hour. The 500 rifles of the 1st Brigade Australian Light Horse were positioned in out posts ahead of Romani, where they came under attack from 8000 Turkish troops.

The Light Horsemen were forced back just before dawn when the Turks commenced an outflanking movement, which was a fairly obvious manoeuvre, given they outnumbered the Australians by about fifteen to one. Chauvel was, however, able to bring in the 2nd Brigade, which had returned from patrol, to extend his right flank. So, as the Turks attempted to outflank the Australians to the south, Chauvel kept moving troops from the left of the line to extend the right flank and the 52nd Division took up the posts relinquished by the Australians. This tactic was successful to a degree but by 7 am the enemy had gained the tactical outpost known as Wellington Ridge, an enormous sand hill that flanked the camp. The Australians were pushed back onto another enormous sand hill, known as Mount Royston.

Just after 7 am the New Zealand Mounted Rifles and a brigade of British infantry, which had been sent forward from posts closer to the Suez Canal, were ordered into action on the Turkish exposed flank. A counter-attack from Mount Royston was finally made at 2 pm and the battle continued throughout the afternoon. When a brigade of the 42nd Lancashire Division joined the battle, at around 6 pm, it was all but over.

By then the Turks were surrendering in large numbers, while Chauvel's brigades had maintained their positions but were too exhausted to counter-attack.

Before dawn on 5 August the Light Horse brigades and the supporting infantry began advancing in a mass charge, which pushed the Turks off Wellington Ridge. The Turkish flank was now annihilated and Chauvel gave orders to pursue the enemy using all his available mounted troops, including the 3rd Brigade of his division, which had recently arrived from the canal. This brigade had a major victory south of Katia when they rushed a Turkish stronghold and captured 425 of the enemy and seven machine guns.

Other parts of the Turkish front line resisted all the attacks and Katia itself remained in Turkish hands. Due to lack of water for the horses in the searing midsummer heat, the British forces were compelled to consolidate the losses and withdraw.

The threat to Romani had been eliminated, although the failure of the British to completely defeat the Turkish advance somewhat lessened the impact of the Australian victory.

The battle of Romani was a proud moment for the Anzac Mounted Division which lost more than 900 men in the fighting, including 202 killed in action. Turkish casualties were not accurately known but estimated to be 9000. The Turkish death toll is not known, but the Allies buried 1200 dead Turkish soldiers and more than 400 Turks were taken prisoner.

After the war Chauvel was appointed inspector general of troops and a member of the Council of Defence and served as the Australian Chief of Staff from 1923 to 1930. In the lead-up to WWII he warned the government constantly about Australia's strategic weakness owing to the decline of Britain as a sea power, questioned the idea of using Singapore as the main naval defence for Australia, and argued that a strong army was essential to our national defence—but few, if any, listened.

When war did come and the Volunteer Defence Corps was set up in June 1940, Chauvel was its Inspector in Chief, at the age of 75. When Sir Cyril Brudenell White, the army Chief of Staff, was killed with three federal cabinet ministers in an air crash in Canberra in August 1940,

Prime Minister Menzies consulted with Chauvel before choosing his successor, Lieutenant General Vernon Sturdee.

Chauvel died in Melbourne on 4 March 1945, after suffering failing health for some time, and was given a state funeral.

WHEN AUSSIE SOLDIERS GOT THE HUMP

What do you do with insubordinate unruly colonial soldiers who won't salute, obey orders or follow the established and necessary rules of military discipline and engagement?

One thing you can do is to match them up with beasts of burden that have a similar attitude problem and reputation for surliness, nastiness and refusal to obey commands.

The Imperial Camel Corps was one of the oddest fighting forces in World War I. It was originally formed in early 1916, in response to an uprising of tribesmen in Egypt's Western Desert. The rebels were men of the Senussi tribe, who were sympathetic to the Turkish cause.

Most of the 'cameleers' were recruited from the Australian infantry and Light Horse battalions who were back in Egypt recuperating after the Gallipoli campaign. Some were also recruited from infantry units.

Eventually there were four battalions of Camel Corps and the 1st and 3rd were entirely Australian. The 2nd was British, and the 4th was a mix of Australians and New Zealanders.

The Camel Corps also had a machine-gun unit, and a battery of light artillery manned by recruits from Hong Kong and Singapore.

The operations of the corps against the rebels were characterised by long desert patrols and surprise attacks, ambushes and skirmishes.

Late in 1916 the Camel Corps transferred to the Sinai Desert to fight against the Turkish army alongside the Australian Light Horse. They served with distinction at Romani, Magdhaba and Rafa, and remained an integral part of the British and dominion force during the advance north through Palestine in 1917 and 1918.

The corps suffered heavy casualties and losses at the Second Battle of Gaza on 19 April 1917, and in the battles fought in November as part of the campaign to destroy the Turkish desert defences and capture Beersheba.

The Camel Corps had a tough reputation. Not only were the camels cantankerous and feared by other troops, their riders were, too!

There was a good reason for this.

When the corps was originally formed, the Australian battalion commanders saw an opportunity to offload some of the more difficult, unruly and insubordinate members of their battalions.

It was common practice for British headquarters to warn other British officers if the Camel Corps were to be stationed nearby. In 1917 officers commanding the supply dump at Rafa were warned to double their guards as the Camel Corps was going to be camped nearby.

The cameleers were tough, resourceful and effective fighting men, but they were a law unto themselves when it came to discipline and rules of engagement. While defending a hill called Musallabeh in April 1918, they ran out of hand grenades so they simply set to and loosened all the nearby rocks and boulders and began heaving and rolling them down upon the attacking Turks. The plan worked, the Turks retreated and the hill became known as the 'Camel's Hump'.

As the fighting moved into the more fertile country of northern Palestine, horses could move much faster and so this odd fighting force was disbanded in June 1918. The Australian 'cameleers' swapped their camels for horses and became the 14th and 15th Light Horse Regiments.

PALESTINE AND POETS

Anonymous

Where the tracks are hard and dreary,
The tracks are long and dry,
The tropic sun is beating down
From out a cloudless sky;
There's naught to see but sand
And now and then you'll see a clump
Of palm trees . . . it's no wonder
That the camel's got the hump.

Never-ending sands that stretch
To where the sky and land
Meet in a line of blue and brown . . .
And poets say it's grand!
But poets stay at home in ease
And travel not afar,
To where the way is lighted
By a 'pale unwavering star'.

Poets never rise at dawn
And feed a blinking horse,
And poets never eat our grub,
Plain bully-beef, of course.
They never scorch or swelter,
At the desert never swear,
The reason why's not hard to find;
They never have been there!

Now, when you hear the poet rave
Of 'vast encircling sands
Whose magnitude is circumscribed
By cloudless azure bands
Of Heaven's vault' (his poesy's
Imagination grows)
Just think of all these scorching sands . . .
And bash him on the nose!

BEERSHEBA

Chris Coulthard-Clark

The most famous mounted charge involving Australians was carried out by lighthorsemen against Turkish fixed defences at Beersheba in Palestine on 31 October 1917. After two previous British failures that year to take the strategic coastal city of Gaza, preparations were made for a third attempt by the newly appointed commander-in-chief of the Egyptian Expeditionary Force, General Sir Edmund Allenby. The plan he devised entailed turning the left flank of the Turkish defensive line which rested on Beersheba, a small town situated in the desert about 43 kilometres south-east of Gaza.

To this end British infantry corps were to make frontal attacks against both ends of the Turkish line simultaneously, while the Desert Mounted Corps (commanded by Australian Lieutenant General Harry Chauvel) made a wide circling movement to approach Beersheba in the rear, from the east and north.

On 27 October the 15,000 Australian and New Zealand horsemen in the two divisions of the Desert Mounted Corps available to Chauvel embarked on a series of night marches which took them east, to concentration areas at the water-points of Khelasa and Asluj more than 10 kilometres south of Beersheba. Three days later they were positioned in readiness for the 25,000 men of the British 20th Corps to begin their assault on Beersheba from the west and south-west at dawn on 31 October. Chauvel's first assigned objective was to capture enemy positions beside the Hebron road behind the town, thereby completing its encirclement.

Stubborn resistance was overcome to take these posts by 3 pm, by which stage the seizure of the town itself was becoming critical because of the attackers' need for water. With only two hours remaining before nightfall Chauvel decided to send in Brigadier General William Grant's 4th Light Horse Brigade, which so far had been hardly involved in the day's fighting; 'Put Grant straight at it' was his terse instruction.

Although the conventional use of Light Horse units was as mounted infantry only, the urgency of the situation prompted Grant to adopt the hazardous cavalry-style tactic of an open charge. Concealed behind a ridge some 8 kilometres south-east of the objective, the two leading regiments of Grant's brigade—the 4th from Victoria on the right, and the 12th from New South Wales on the left—were drawn up in three lines 300–500 metres apart, with 5 metres spacing between men. As neither unit was equipped with the normal shock action cavalry weapons of lance or sabre, the troops were ordered to carry their long bayonets in their hands.

At 4.30 pm, just on sunset, the attack force moved off at the trot with Grant initially at its head. The 400–500 horsemen were already at the gallop when they crested the ridge and came into Turkish view, but the speed and momentum of their charge quickly carried them through the curtain of fire from enemy field guns, machine guns and rifles.

The Turkish positions—unprotected by wire—were breached without difficulty by the leading ranks, who leapt their horses over the trenches before dismounting and engaging the defenders in brutal hand-to-hand combat. Two squadrons of the 12th Regiment raced on into the town, in time to prevent the destruction of all but two of seventeen wells by the fleeing Turks. Within an hour of the charge's commencement all resistance collapsed, as those defenders who could made a rush for the safety of hills to the north and north-west. Nine guns and more than 1000 prisoners were taken from the reinforced 27th Division occupying the town, and the commander of the Turkish 3rd Corps himself barely escaped capture. All this at a cost to the Australians of only 31 killed and 36 wounded.

The dramatic fall of Beersheba opened the way for the whole Turkish defensive line to be outflanked and rolled up from east to west. After further heavy fighting, the Turks abandoned Gaza on 6 November and began a northerly retreat deeper into Palestine. The charge was a truly memorable and heroic feat of arms, fully deserving of the epic status it has subsequently achieved. The absence of the sort of casualties which might have been expected from an assault across nearly 6000 metres of open ground swept by automatic weapons owed much to the speed of the unexpected attack. This was later discovered to have caused many Turks to forget to make range adjustments on their weapon sights, with the result that during the final stages of the charge much of the defenders' fire had passed harmlessly over the Australians' heads.

TOO DARK FOR THE LIGHT HORSE

During World War I many ethnically non-European Australians enlisted and served in the AIF without any apparent impediment or objection. Many others, however, particularly full-blood Indigenous men, were prevented from enlisting, rejected on the grounds of race, physique, or not having a long enough 'association with white people'.

Others were accepted into the AIF only to be later discharged on the grounds of having been 'irregularly enlisted' or being of an 'unsuitable physique'. Some of these men had fully signed and validated enlistment papers and were photographed in uniform, only to later have their enlistment papers stamped 'Discharged before leaving Australia'.

The cause of this inconsistent approach towards the enlistment of non-European Australians was the way in which the *Australian Defence Act of 1909* was interpreted by various enlistment agencies and individuals. Parts of the *Defence Act* were influenced by the *Immigration Restriction Act of 1901*, the act that created the White Australia Policy and attempted to restrict immigration to people of European ethnicity.

The *Defence Act of 1909* did not state who could be *prevented* from joining the military forces, nor did it state the grounds by which anyone could be rejected as unsuitable to serve in times of war. What the Act did state, quite clearly, was just who *could be forced* to join the militia and train during times of peace—and who was exempt. It was one of the exemptions to this part of the Act that was used to discriminate against non-Europeans and prevent them from enlisting in the AIF.

The act divided the male population into five classes. Each of these classes could be legally forced to join the militia and train as soldiers under different circumstances. Class I included all men who were unmarried or childless widowers between the ages of 18 and 35. Class II was the same group up to age 45. Class III was all married men and widowers aged 18 to 35; Class IV the same group up to age 45; while Class V was all men 45 to 60 years old. (All schoolboys were likewise required to train, providing there were schoolmasters available who had been trained by the army to give the correct instruction.)

Part XIII—section 138 (1) (*a*) and (*b*) of the *Defence Act* stated who 'shall be exempt from the training'. Both of these exemptions were to be judged by medical authorities: (*a*) was those medically 'unfit for any naval or military service whatever'; while (*b*) exempted 'Those who are not substantially of European origin or descent, of which the medical authorities appointed in that behalf under the regulations shall be the judges'.

This exemption from compulsory military training was widely interpreted as a reason to prevent those who fell into this category from enlisting in the AIF, thus prohibiting men from non-European backgrounds from serving their country. Later changes to enlistment regulations by the AIF in 1917—one of which was to accept men with one parent of European descent—only served to ratify the notion that the exemption from compulsory training clause in the *Defence Act* could be used to prevent enlistment.

Many who would only have qualified under the later 'new' regulations of 1917 had already joined as early as 1914, as had many with no European ethnicity at all.

At least 30 Aboriginal men were accepted into the AIF in 1914, and the inconsistency in accepting or rejecting non-Europeans is glaringly obvious in the case of South Australia, where men from Point Pearce and Point McLeay missions were readily accepted, while men attempting to enlist from Koonibba mission were uniformly rejected on the grounds of 'physique not good enough for military service', a euphemism it would seem for 'Aboriginal'. Edmund Bilney, described as 'half caste' on enlistment in June 1917, joined B Company at Mitcham AIF Training Camp in South Australia but was discharged two weeks later after the medical board reconsidered and decided he was of 'deficient physique, half cast Aboriginal, too full blood for the AIF'.

So, the power to discriminate was assumed to be inherent or implied in the exemption provisions of the *Defence Act*.

One of the worst examples of the use of this power occurred in Queensland in May 1917 when seventeen Aboriginal men from

Barambah Aboriginal Mission (which later became known as Cherbourg Mission), about 100 kilometres (62 miles) inland from Noosa Heads, joined up during a recruiting drive organised by the Queensland Recruiting Committee.

Two weeks later, at a special ceremony in Brisbane, conducted in conjunction with the Queensland Light Horse, the recruiting officer responsible for signing up the men, Lieutenant Colonel Garland, an army chaplain, delivered a stirring patriotic speech. This was followed by a well-rehearsed piece of regimental military theatre, which involved a slow parade of seventeen mounted Light Horsemen, each of whom was leading a riderless horse, saddled and ready for battle.

The seventeen new recruits then solemnly mounted the riderless horses and all 34 men paraded along Queen Street in front of a cheering crowd. The symbolism of the ceremony was hard to miss, but the irony of what happened next was far more poignant.

On Wednesday 13 June 1917, a month after the ceremony, all of the Barambah Mission recruits were discharged for 'having been irregularly enlisted'. As an additional indignity, the men were taken back to the mission under escort. They received no payment, no benefits and no discharge documents. Their enlistment papers were stamped 'Discharged Prior To Leaving Australia'.

When asked for an official explanation, those responsible at AIF headquarters replied that 'a coloured man must have been associated with white people for some time prior to enlistment'. It was also noted that full-blood Indigenous men 'would not make soldiers'.

Well, a good many did.

In many cases non-European men were simply accepted by recruiting officers along with anyone else. Perhaps the recruiting officers felt that the *Defence Act* exemption clause did not apply to enlistment in time of war, or perhaps they simply overlooked it, chose to ignore it, or had no idea that it existed. It was certainly no impediment to Billy Sing, who was half Chinese, enlisting in 1914. It has been established that there were at least 56 Aboriginal soldiers among the 60,000 who served in the Gallipoli campaign.

Aboriginal men such as Harry Thorpe, who came from Lake Tyers Mission in Eastern Victoria, simply joined and served like many thousands of others. Harry enlisted at Sale in February 1916, and joined the 7th Battalion in France in July of that year. He was wounded at Pozières in 1916 and again at Bullecourt in 1917. Harry was awarded the Military

Medal and promoted to corporal for 'displaying conspicuous courage and leadership' in an engagement near Ypres, in Belgium, in October 1917. He died in August 1918, after being shot in the stomach in a battle at Lihons Wood, near Vauvillers in Western France, and is buried at Harbonnières Cemetery close to his friend William Rawlings, another Aboriginal Military Medal winner, who was killed on the same day.

There were many Aboriginal troopers in the Light Horse. We will never know the exact number as many changed their names to make it easier for recruiting officers to overlook their obvious Aboriginality, and often the recruiting officers deliberately neglected to mention their ethnicity on their enlistment papers, to prevent them being discharged on account of it.

Historian Jonathan King noted that, 'Indigenous troopers were considered to be equal by the other troopers because they were all riding horses and surviving in the desert, eating at the same campfires . . . when the Indigenous troopers came back to Australia . . . they couldn't eat in the same restaurants; they couldn't go into the same pubs. They were relegated to the status they had before world war one.'

They also went from equal pay in the army back to much lower, unregulated wages at home.

We know there were Indigenous troopers involved in the famous charge at Beersheba. Research done by Pastor Ray Minniecon, a Kabi Kabi man from Queensland, shows that the Light Horse had the highest number of Indigenous soldiers of any section of the 1st AIF. One of them was his grandfather, James Lingwoodock, who grew up working on cattle stations and was an excellent horseman.

One trooper from the Barambah Aboriginal Settlement who did finally get to serve overseas with the Light Horse was Trooper Frank Fisher. He enlisted in Brisbane in August 1917 with the 11th Light Horse Regiment reinforcements, sailed from Sydney on the troopship *A38* in December 1917, trained in Egypt, and served from April 1918 until July 1919.

Fisher was a well-known rugby league player whose nickname was 'King' Fisher and he represented Wide Bay District in 1932 and 1936 against the British touring teams. Perhaps few outside of the Wide Bay district have ever heard of Frank 'King' Fisher, but his sporting genes apparently passed down a couple of generations. His great-granddaughter could run pretty fast—her name is Cathy Freeman.

UP, UP AND AWAY

World War I began almost exactly twenty years after Lawrence Hargrave lifted himself from the beach at Stanwell Park, just south of Sydney, in a four-box-kite construction he had invented. Hargrave, who opposed the idea of patents and believed in sharing discoveries and ideas, did not patent or copyright his inventions and designs, but allowed others, like the Wright brothers in the United States and Alberto Santos-Dumont, Gabriel and Charles Voisin and Louis Blériot in France, to use them freely. Octave Chanute, the man who wrote the definitive history of early heavier-than-air flight, said of Hargrave:

> He has now constructed with his own hands no less than 18 flying machines of increasing size, all of which fly, and as a result of his many experiments he is now regarded by many, including Santos-Dumont, Voisin, Bleriot and other European aviation pioneers, as the father of powered flight.

The Wright brothers, who claimed the first powered flight in 1903, used Hargrave's ideas, and even patented some of them, and never acknowledged him. Blériot crossed the Channel in 1909, the same year that the Royal Aircraft Factory was established at Farnborough, 60 kilometres (37 miles) south-west of London. With war in mind the factory developed new planes so quickly that the various, ever-evolving aircraft designs and models were named 'BE', which stood for 'British Experimentals', followed by letters of the alphabet and numerals ('B.E.a1', 'B.E.2' etc.). As these aircraft changed and developed, they became the fighters and bombers that were used once the war began. The men who flew them called them 'Bloody Emergencies'.

Compared to the millions of infantry who died in WWI, aviation losses, which amounted to 9400 on the Allied side and 8200 German flyers, seem almost trifling but, in fact, the opposite is true. The mortality rate among pilots and aircrew, looked at as a percentage, was shocking. In some squadrons long-term casualty rates reached 98 per cent. The rate for the entire war averaged 50 per cent and the life expectancy of a new pilot over the Western Front was five weeks.

Aerial combat was a completely new concept at the start of the war and the role of the fighter pilot took some time to develop. Originally the role of aircraft was aerial reconnaissance and officer and dispatch transport, while pilots were seen as scouts or chauffeurs for photographers and high-ranking officers.

Inevitably someone in a plane shot at someone in another, or on the ground, with a pistol or rifle, and someone else used a machine gun. The first recorded machine-gun killing was on 5 October 1914 when French corporal Louis Quenault, observer in a French Voisin, shot a German Aviatik scout in the sky over the French city of Rheims.

Shooting machine guns in planes was often more dangerous to those on board than those being targeted and, incredibly, a system was developed by which machine guns could be synchronised to fire through the path of the aircraft's propellers without hitting and shattering the wooden blades. Bombers, which started out as planes dropping heavy debris and deadly little steel arrows, called *flechettes*, onto ground troops, or even onto other planes, had developed, by the end of the war, into specialised heavier aircraft that were used to drop bombs.

Many of the young men who enlisted in the army in WWI saw the chance to join the Flying Corps as a wonderful piece of luck. They would never have had the chance to learn to fly back home on the farm or in their city jobs. The majority of them, however, died, in training, in battle, or just in the normal course of flying. The few who survived had mostly joined the Flying Corps towards the end of the war, and nearly all of them wanted the chance to keep flying as civilians after the war.

Back home in Australia this small group became the foundation of our early aviation industry. They begged and borrowed money to purchase or lease surplus army planes after the war. They badgered governments for sponsorship. They dreamed of flying home instead of a slow return by troopship. Kingsford Smith, Charles Ulm, the Smith brothers, Hudson Fysh and Bert Hinkler all learned to fly during the war. The Australian government had an inkling of the future possibilities when it offered a £10,000 reward for the fastest flight back to Australia. The incentive worked.

Mail routes, charter flights, flying schools, air shows, aerodromes and workshops all sprang up thanks to these returned servicemen-aviators. Few of them got rich, but mostly they earned enough to keep flying. Kingsford Smith spent much of his time chasing money to finance his next long-distance flight.

Australia's military aviation history had begun in December 1911, when the Commonwealth Department of Defence advertised for 'two competent mechanists and aviators' to set up a training school which would lead to the establishment of an Australian Flying Corps.

Although the advertising was done in the United Kingdom, one of the two men chosen was an Australian, Eric Harrison, the other was an English solicitor, Henry Aloysius Petre, who had been so impressed by the French aviator Blériot's historic crossing of the English Channel in 1909 that he quit practising law and began building his own aeroplanes.

The Department of Defence had wanted the flying school to be situated at Duntroon, the military training establishment near Canberra, but Petre chose a far more suitable site at Point Cook, on the shores of Port Phillip Bay, just 20 kilometres (12 miles) south-west of Melbourne, where the Commonwealth had purchased 300 hectares of land for possible military use in 1912.

The Central Flying School was set up with Petre and Harrison, now commissioned as lieutenants in the Australian Military Forces, as instructors, four mechanics and three support staff. The five aircraft purchased were a Bristol Boxkite, two French monoplanes and two B.E.2 'British Experimental' biplanes, from the Royal Aircraft Factory.

Thursday 1 March 1914 was an historic day for the Central Flying School. On the morning of that day Eric Harrison made history when he completed Australia's first military flight in the Bristol Boxkite. On the afternoon of the day Henry Petre also made history when he crashed a Deperdussin monoplane, after the aircraft's tail hit telephone wires, and thus survived the Central Flying School's first official accident.

The instructors and students became known as the Australian Flying Corps and the Central Flying School commenced its first flying course on 17 August 1914, two weeks after the outbreak of World War I. The first four students trained were Captain Thomas White and lieutenants George Merz, Richard Williams and David Manwell. By May 1915 only four officers had been trained to fly and Australia still didn't have any combat aircraft or enough manpower to make up a squadron.

The Australian Flying Corps' first foray into combat occurred when it was posted to Mesopotamia in response to a call for help from the Indian Flying Corps to support them against the Turks in their attempt to capture Baghdad.

At the start of the war the meagre Allied aviation resources, the available aircraft and pilots, were used on the Western Front, which meant that the Indian army had no air support as they fought the Ottoman army in Mesopotamia. In February 1915 the Australian government received a request from the British government in India for air assistance in the campaign in Mesopotamia, but the Australian Flying Corps could only provide enough aircrews and ground staff for what became known as the 'Mesopotamian Half-Flight', or Australian Half-Flight, with Henry Petre, now a captain, appointed commander.

The unit consisted of four officers and 41 enlisted personnel and, as no British military aircraft were available, three obsolete Maurice Farman biplanes were procured by the Indian army. Because the propeller, situated behind the cockpit, faced backwards in these aircraft, they were known as 'pushers' and they were not suitable for the desert flying. They had a top speed of 80 km/h (50 mph), and the desert winds often reached 130 km/h (80 mph), so the Rajah of Gwalior bought two old Caudron aircraft for the Australians to use. Their early work with the Indian army was reconnaissance. Finally, in August 1915, the Half-Flight received four more modern Martynside aircraft. The Half-Flight was made part of the Royal Flying Corps' No. 30 Squadron in August and began flying reconnaissance in preparation for a strike on Baghdad.

Australia's first air combat casualty occurred when the two Caudrons of the Half-Flight were returning from a reconnaissance operation in high winds on 29 July 1915. The Caudron flown by Indian Flying Corps pilot Captain Reilly landed near a village among friendly Arabs. The Caudron of Lieutenant Merz and New Zealand Lieutenant Burns was forced down with engine trouble 32 kilometres (20 miles) from the refilling station and Merz and Burns were killed after a gun battle with hostile Arabs. Friendly Arabs reported that the pair fought a running battle of 8 kilometres

(5 miles) in which they killed one Arab and wounded five others before being killed. Lieutenant Thomas White led a group to find the Arabs who shot Merz and Burns and burned the village of a local sheik, where the killers were reported to be hiding. Merz, a medical graduate aged 23, was returning to Basra after helping out at the hospital at Nasiriyah.

The Indian army was forced back into the fortress at Kut on 4 December and Captain Henry Petre, the last remaining Australian airman in Meso-potamia, flew the only remaining Maurice Farman biplane to Egypt on 7 December. Kut surrendered after a five-month siege, nine Australian ground staff were taken prisoner and only two of them survived captivity. The Mesopotamian Half-Flight was officially disbanded in October 1916. Of the nine pilots who flew with the unit, two were killed and six were taken prisoner.

One of those taken prisoner was Thomas Walter White. Born in North Melbourne in 1888, the son of a hardware merchant, White had been an excellent athlete as a teenager, competing successfully in athletics, cycling and boxing, while at the same time becoming a bugler in the Citizens Military Force. He was commissioned into the 5th Australian Regiment in 1911 and, in 1914, was selected for the Australian Flying Corps and became one of the first batch of officers to be trained at the Central Flying School at Point Cook. While there he helped found the Australian Aero Club and, in April 1915, he was promoted to captain and attached to the Mesopotamian Half-Flight.

In the desert campaign White quickly developed a reputation for being the most daring and competent of all reconnaissance pilots. On one mission in October 1915 he and his observer, a British captain named Yeats-Brown, were well behind enemy lines when their Maurice Farman developed engine trouble and they were forced to land. Keeping in mind the fate of George Merz, White had no desire to wait until hostile Arabs, having seen the aircraft land, were attracted to the scene.

He managed to start the engine but had insufficient power to take off so, with Yeats-Brown standing facing backwards with his rifle at the ready, the 27-year-old Captain White taxied the aircraft most of the 24 kilometres (15 miles) back to the Australian airfield at Aziziyah. At one point, the aircraft sped past Turkish infantry who were too surprised and astounded to realise what was happening until the aircraft was well past. Near the end of the long journey, the engine returned to full power and they were able to fly the last few kilometres.

Just two weeks later Major General Kimball, Chief of General Staff in Mesopotamia, was stranded when his seaplane was forced to land due to engine failure and White flew a solo mission in his Maurice Farman to attempt to find him. He caught sight of the seaplane on the bank of a river quite close to an Arab camp. Flying low over the stranded aircraft, White could see that the general and his pilot were alive. He could also see a group of hostile Arabs approaching, and soon they began firing, scoring hits on the Maurice Farman's wing and propeller. White landed about a kilometre from the stranded seaplane and began yelling commands in a loud voice to make the Arabs think there were other troops following him on foot.

Having put some doubt into the minds of the hesitant Arabs by yelling at his imaginary comrades, White ran to the seaplane, where he found the general and the pilot both alive. Having room for only one passenger, White and the general ran back to the Maurice Farman and, with the general holding off the angry Arabs with rifle fire, they managed to take off and flew to safety. Just then an Indian cavalry unit, which had seen White's aircraft landing, came to the rescue and saved the seaplane's pilot.

On 13 November, in order to wreck the Turkish communication system, it was deemed necessary to cut the telegraph line between Baghdad and Constantinople. White and Yeats-Brown volunteered for the task. They flew to within 12 kilometres (7 miles) of Baghdad, chose a spot and attempted to land. Unfortunately the plane collided with a telegraph post on landing, they became stranded and were once again attacked by hostile Arabs. Yeats-Brown managed to blow up the telegraph line but, after a gun battle, the two airmen were cornered by the Arabs who began beating them and would no doubt have killed them had not Turkish troops intervened.

The men were taken to Baghdad and later imprisoned at Mosul for two and a half years. Captain White's wartime adventures were far from over, however. In July 1918 while he was being sent to Constantinople by train, he managed to escape during a stoppage caused by a railway accident and, disguising himself as a Turk, procured a fake Russian passport and stowed away on a ship to Odessa where he joined the Bolshevik army and secured passage on a Ukrainian hospital ship, which took him back into Allied territory the week the armistice was signed. He was awarded the Distinguished Flying Cross.

Many prisoners of war, including most of the Australian ground crew who had surrendered at Kut, died on long route marches from

Mesopotamia to Turkey or in Turkish prisons. Thomas White remained critical and contemptuous of his former enemies for the rest of his life. The book he wrote about his experiences as a prisoner of war was titled *Guests of the Unspeakable.*

Thomas Walter White served in the RAAF and RAF in World War II with a rank of wing commander and, having been elected to federal parliament in 1929, became the Minister for Trade and Customs in the cabinet of Prime Minister Joseph Lyons before World War II, and Minister for Civil Aviation in Robert Menzies' government after the war. He was knighted in 1956 and died in 1957.

Of course, most of the focus in World War I was on the Western Front, and the Australian Flying Corps eventually sent three squadrons there, to be absorbed into the British Royal Flying Corps.

On 20 March 1917, another product of the Central Flying School at Point Cook, Lieutenant Frank McNamara, became the first Australian airman to win a Victoria Cross. Born in 1894, McNamara, a schoolteacher, enlisted in the AIF at the start of the war and became an instructor at the Broadmeadows Training Depot. Promoted to lieutenant in July 1915, he volunteered for the Australian Flying Corps, took his first solo flight in August of that year and graduated as a pilot in October. He received further training in England and was seconded to the Royal Flying Corps, stationed in Egypt.

On 20 March 1917, McNamara, now a captain, was flying as one of four No. 1 Squadron pilots attacking a Turkish railway junction near Gaza. His Martinsyde was armed with six specially modified 4.5-inch artillery shells. He had dropped three of them when one exploded prematurely, and his leg was badly wounded by shrapnel.

As he attempted to fly back to base, he spotted his comrade Captain Douglas Rutherford, on the ground beside his crashed B.E.2. Although severely wounded, McNamara landed his Martynside single-seater in the desert to attempt a rescue. The citation reads:

> For most conspicuous bravery and devotion to duty during an aerial bomb attack upon a hostile construction train, when one of our pilots was forced to land behind the enemy's lines. Lieutenant McNamara, observing this pilot's predicament and the fact that hostile cavalry were approaching, descended to his rescue. He did this under heavy rifle fire and in spite of the fact that he himself had been severely wounded in

the thigh. He landed about 200 yards from the damaged machine, the pilot of which climbed on to Lieutenant McNamara's machine, and an attempt was made to rise. Owing, however, to his disabled leg, Lieutenant McNamara was unable to keep his machine straight, and it turned over. The two officers, having extricated themselves, immediately set fire to the machine and made their way across to the damaged machine, which they succeeded in starting. Finally Lieutenant McNamara, although weak from loss of blood, flew this machine back to the aerodrome, a distance of seventy miles, and thus completed his comrade's rescue.

After the war, Frank McNamara became Air Liaison Officer at Australia House in London and, promoted to Air Commodore, served in various capacities in Britain in WWII and later became Deputy Director of Education for the British Zone in the Occupation of Germany.

THE TUMULT AND THE SHOUTING

Charles Kingsford Smith

> The tumult and the shouting dies,
> The captains and the kings depart . . .
> Lord, god of hosts, be with us yet,
> Lest we forget, lest we forget.
>
> Rudyard Kipling

There comes a time in the lives of most young men when they have to make decisions—I mean decisions which will affect the future course of their lives.

Some of us are born to the humdrum, placid existence of city life; some are born wanderers; others are impatient of the yoke and are a law unto themselves, and some are content to drift along in the path that leads nowhere.

I do not know in which category to place myself. I think perhaps that my future was determined on that day in 1915, my eighteenth birthday, when I presented myself at the Recruiting Office in Sydney Town Hall and enlisted in the Signal Engineers A.I.F.

Not that there was anything special about that. Everyone was joining up in those hectic days, but from that hall in Australia to France and England in war time was a short cut. That, in itself, meant a violent change in one's life.

Until then, I had been an Australian schoolboy, 'messing about' with electric gadgets and interested in engines of all kinds, and consequently apprenticed by my parents to the electrical engineering trade.

Most men look back to their war days with disgust and horror. So do I, but I must confess that I didn't dislike it at the time. The war meant to me a change of scene, a plunge into a big adventure, a new life, new countries. But first there were early days of training as a soldier in the Australian army, in my first unit, the 19th Battery A.I.F. Somehow or other, guns did not appeal to me, so I got a transfer to the Signal Corps, and it was with the Signallers that I found myself in Egypt and thereafter in Gallipoli, where we remained until the evacuation.

That was certainly an exciting enough adventure for most of us who were still in our teens, but it was hardly the sort of adventure we had visualised in our hot young dreams.

From Gallipoli to France via Egypt was but a step, a step that led to another change for me, from the Signal Corps to the motor-cycle despatch riders, a more interesting occupation for one whose thoughts were largely centred on speed, and on gadgets devised to produce it.

I might have been a despatch rider for the 'duration'; returning when demobbed to Australia, like many thousands of my cobbers, to the humdrum life of peace. But there came a day in 1916 when an opportunity offered itself to become, if not an airman, at least to have the chance of training for a commission in the then Royal Flying Corps.

It was the chance of a lifetime; it proved to be the chance of my flying life, and it was a decision I made without a moment's hesitation. I was not peculiar in this respect. There were hundreds, thousands situated like me, each of whom would have given their soul cases to have been selected for the R.F.C. But although many were called, few were chosen, and those of us who were selected left for our new life, envied by our fellow Diggers whom we left behind.

The story of the 'War Birds' over France in those hectic days of 1917 and 1918 has been told by many. I will not linger over them myself, except to remark, in passing, that they were great days. There were giants in the sky then—Albert Ball, Jimmy McCudden, Mannock, Bishop and the Frenchmen Nungesser, Guynemer, Garros and others.

And on 'the other side' there were foemen worthy of our steel, and of our Lewis-Vickers guns; such as Immelmann of 'The Turn', the slickest and quickest method of doubling in one's track, Richtofen and his circus and others.

The names of these great fighting pilots stand out, but there are hundreds of others of equal calibre whose names are unknown except to their own comrades and to those in their immediate circle who knew of their deeds, and their exploits with the flying gun.

And the machines we flew!

The old names recur to me like wraiths from the past. Maurice Farman, the B.E.'s, the Martinsydes, the D.H.2, Camels and Pups, the wonderful S.E.5, noted for its speed, and last but not least, the machines with which my own squadron, the 23rd, was equipped—the famous French 'Spads'. And on 'the other side', the Rumplers, Albatross and Fokkers, whose machine-guns were timed to fire ahead through the propellers.

Queer old antediluvian craft they seem now, looking back across the years, but what tricks we performed in them, what feats of daring were accomplished.

I came into the world of flying at its dawn, and what a glorious dawn! There was barely a glimpse of dawn in those dark drear days of 1914 when the sole idea in air warfare was that the machines were designed, and the men were trained, for reconnaissance only.

They were to be scouts, the eyes of the army. But long before Armistice Day arrived, the flying forces of all the combatants had reached a pitch of development in design, speed, fighting power which, two years earlier, had hardly been dreamt of.

Everything was in a state of flux, so rapid were the developments taking place almost from day to day. And among the pilots was a keen and friendly rivalry to outdo each other, which nothing could dampen.

When we were not dodging the German 'Archies' we were on patrol, or loosing off drums of Lewis or Vickers bullets, or engaged in performing terrific stunts in fighting aviation known as the 'zoom' or the ''oll', or the 'dive'.

Our planes flew and fought at 15,000 feet, a tremendous ceiling in those days; the Spads had a top speed even then (and that was nearly twenty years ago) of 130 m.p.h. and a ceiling of 20,000 feet.

Sometimes our squadrons would sweep the sky in bands twenty strong, looking for trouble in the shape of the Hun machines, and generally finding it. We flew low over enemy aerodromes and trenches, ground strafing and attacking anything in sight with our drums of Lewis fire.

At other times we flew high, waiting at 15,000 feet to pounce on our enemies, and there were exciting and adventurous occasions when we deliberately cultivated a spinning nose dive in an effort to avoid attack, or with nonchalant abandon rolled carefree.

But, underneath this youthful impetuosity and superficial gaiety, there was a deadly concentration of purpose and superb nervous stability. You hardly ever heard of an airman having a nervous breakdown in those days, though how we managed to avoid them with all that immense output of energy, I do not know.

I expect it was just youth living on its nerves. Another memory of those days comes to me—of the long summer evenings of 1918 over the famous old Salient; there is, too, still in my nostrils the unmistakable odour of the German tracer bullets as they streamed past like a jet from a hose, and I recall the joy of battle when one first 'bagged one's own bird' and had the inexpressible relief of seeing the enemy going down to disaster.

Julian Grenfell, in his poem 'Into Battle', expressed the thoughts of the fighting airmen of the Western Front, though he died not knowing of the tremendous developments that were to take place in the air.

> The naked earth is warm with spring,
> And with green grass and bursting trees
> Leans to the sun's gaze glorying,
> And quivers in the sunny breeze;
> And life is colour and warmth and light,
> And a striving evermore for these;
> And he is dead who will not fight;
> And who dies fighting has increase.
>
> The fighting man shall from the sun
> Take warmth, and life from the glowing earth;
> Speed with the light-foot winds to run,
> And with the trees to newer birth;
> And find, when fighting shall be done,
> Great rest, and fullness after dearth . . .
>
> And when the burning moment breaks,
> And all things else are out of mind,
> And only joy of battle takes
> Him by the throat, and makes him blind,
>
> Through joy and blindness he shall know
> Not caring much to know, that still
> Nor lead nor steel shall reach him, so
> That it be not the Destined Will.

The thundering line of battle stands,
And in the air death moans and sings;
But Day shall clasp him with strong hands,
And Night shall fold him in soft wings.

But why linger over those hectic days on the Western Front? In our funny old machines, prodigious feats were performed by 'intrepid airmen' in things tied up with bits of string, and when it was not unknown for the *London Gazette* to announce that a packet of Military Crosses had been handed out to as many young subalterns and airmen for 'distinguished service'.

I managed to shoot down a few 'Huns', as we called them in those good old days, and I managed to get wounded and shot down myself. It was service all right, though I doubt whether it was very distinguished, but all the time we were youngsters learning a lot. We were imbibing an immense store of flying experience and technical knowledge, and we were learning something which to my mind is far more valuable—the capacity to look after yourself, the instinct to do or to die, the desire for action, without thought of the risks and dangers.

For one thing, you had to be wounded, and I duly received my 'Blighty', a fact which enabled me to take further and more advanced courses in flying, with the result that by the summer of 1918, when I was barely twenty-one, I became an Instructor.

It might seem a little presumptuous to many people that a youth not yet twenty-one should take upon himself the style, title and dignity of 'Instructor R.A.F.'.

The truth was that I, and many more like me, felt in those days that we could instruct anybody in anything. We thought we knew everything, from how to win the war down to the stripping and re-assembly of any aero engine you liked to place in front of us.

We were a care-free, cigarette-smoking, leave-seeking lot of young devils who feared nothing; except being brought down behind the enemy lines.

Looking back on that slap-dash, careless, nonchalant time, we seem to have been coldly efficient. We did our job to the best of our ability in what seem to be the craziest old antiquarian contraptions imaginable—the machines of the Royal Flying Corps. And we were up against an enemy that was ahead of us in aircraft design, and certainly not our inferiors in courage, elan and dash. And then suddenly it was all over.

The tumult and the shouting died, and there was I, with the remains of a war wound, a war gratuity and a war decoration, and with the wide world before me.

SMITHY

In 1906 Lyster Ormsby, of the 'Bondi Surf Bathers Club', had an idea for a device to enable safer rescue operations at the beach and built a model from a cotton reel and two bobby pins of a portable horizontal reel for the rope. The first full-size reel was built by Sergeant John Bond of Victoria Barracks in Paddington; and was improved on in the same year by Sydney coachbuilder G.H. Olding whose final design was used until 1993.

The reel allowed a lifesaver wearing a belt with a rope attached to reach a distressed swimmer. The crew on the beach could then pull them back to the beach. It required discipline and control to carry this out efficiently. The first surf life-saving reel in the world was demonstrated at Bondi Beach on 23 December 1906.

Several weeks later the reel was used for a rescue for the first time. The *Sydney Morning Herald* reported the event as, 'ANOTHER SENSATION AT BONDI—A NARROW ESCAPE OF TWO BOYS'.

The surf bathers at Bondi had another exciting experience yesterday afternoon, when two lads, Rupert Swallow, a resident of Darlinghurst and Chas. Smith living at McMahon's Point, narrowly escaped losing their lives.

About 3 o'clock a number of people on the beach noticed that the boys, both of whom were about 9 years old, had been carried out by the undertow, and that they were unable to make any headway towards the beach. The alarm was given, and immediately many willing hands were ready to grasp the lifeline and go to the assistance of the struggling boys. James McLeod, a resident of Park Parade

Waverley, and Wm. Burns, of Mill Hill Road, Waverley, succeeded in bringing Swallow into safety; while James McCarthy, of Rowe Street, Darlington and Warwick Wilce, of Croydon, rescued Smith.

When brought to the shore Smith was in a bad way, having lost consciousness, but Nurse Sweeney, of Quirindi, who happened to be on the scene, applied restorative measures, and shortly after both lads were able to return to their homes.

Little Chas. Smith was indeed nine years old, he would celebrate his tenth birthday a month later and go on to become Sir Charles Kingsford Smith, war hero, pioneer aviator, Australian legend, and the first person ever rescued by Lyster Ormsby's new-fangled life-saving reel!

Smithy was one of seven children of William Smith and his wife, Catherine Kingsford, whose father had been mayor of Brisbane. William went into real estate in Canada in 1903 and worked as a clerk with the Canadian Pacific Railways before the family returned to live in Sydney at the end of 1906.

It was not long after the family returned to Australia that Smithy, aged nine, became the first person to be rescued using the new life-saving reel, at Bondi Beach. Charles was partly educated in Vancouver, at St Andrew's Cathedral Choir School, Sydney, and at Sydney Technical High School. At sixteen he was apprenticed to the Colonial Sugar Refining Co. Ltd.

He was at home in the United States and Canada, having lived there as a boy, and his record-breaking flight across the Pacific was, in fact, mostly an American-funded venture and the *Southern Cross* was an American-registered aircraft.

Smith served in the first AIF at Gallipoli and on the Western Front as a dispatch rider, before joining the fledgling Australian Flying Corps. Serving on the Western Front with the Royal Flying Corps (RFC), he brought down four German planes before he was shot down himself in a dogfight with several German aircraft. He had several toes shot off and was awarded the Military Cross 'for conspicuous gallantry and devotion to duty'.

Writing about the incident later, Smithy recalled:

I blasted those Jerries with everything I had, and I was sure I could account for at least one of them when I felt a sharp pain searing up my left leg . . . I had no way of knowing how badly I had been hit, but quite suddenly the whole sky seems to be turning upside down and flashes of light struck at my brain. Somehow I was able to break off the fight and head for our landing field. All the while I flew I felt myself becoming weaker, and my left boot felt filled with blood. I could barely feel my foot.

On being lifted from his plane unconscious, it was discovered that two of the toes on his left foot had been shot off. The ground crew counted 165 bullet holes in his aircraft.

Promoted to lieutenant Smithy served as an RFC instructor until the war ended and then went to the United States to fly and perform stunts in a 'flying circus' and in early Hollywood movies.

Smithy returned to Australia and flew in Western Australia where he formed a partnership in 1924 with fellow pilot Keith Anderson to form a trucking and aviation business.

Smithy was a restless soul and, when the business struggled, he started raising money for the historic flight across the Pacific. The NSW government helped and so did the Jewish businessman Sidney Myer, but the US oil magnate G.A. Hancock provided most of the money.

With Charles Ulm and two Americans, Harry Lyon and Jim Warner, Smithy took off from Oakland, California, on 31 May 1928 and flew via Hawaii and Suva to Brisbane, completing the historic crossing in 83 hours and 38 minutes of flying time. The flyers received subscriptions of more than £20,000 and Smithy was awarded the Air Force Cross and appointed an honorary squadron leader of the Royal Australian Air Force.

Smithy was a controversial figure. Anderson, no longer a partner, sued unsuccessfully for part of the prize-money from the flight across the Pacific. Smithy caused a scandal by divorcing and remarrying. His aviation company went broke when the *Southern Cloud* crashed taking mail to Melbourne. He was accused of costing the lives of two mates who died during a search for his plane, which he had crash-landed on a deserted beach in Western Australia; some in the press said it was a publicity stunt to raise money for his flights.

His fame did not stop his life from being troubled and full of financial worries and he was forced to keep breaking records to raise funds.

He and Tom Pethybridge left England on 6 November 1935 attempting to break the record to Australia in the *Lady Southern Cross*, a Lockheed Altair single-engined aircraft. Smithy had not been well for some time and suffered severe headaches during the two-day flight to Allahabad. The next day Jim Melrose, who was engaged in an attempt to break the solo Britain to Australia record, sighted the *Lady Southern Cross* over the Bay of Bengal.

'I could see jets of flame spurting from Smithy's plane's exhaust pipe,' Melrose said, 'and I was overcome by an eerie sensation as I watched.'

Despite a huge search at the time, which lasted ten days and involved planes from the Royal Air Force, three aircraft chartered by the Australian government, another flown by old friends Bill Taylor and John Stannage and the one flown by Jim Melrose, who aborted his own record attempt to join the search, no trace of the two men or their aircraft was found. The search was called off and Smithy and Pethybridge were assumed dead.

Eighteen months later fishermen found a landing wheel from the *Lady Southern Cross*, with its tyre still inflated, attached to part of an undercarriage leg, washed ashore on an island in the Gulf of Martaban, 3 kilometres (1.9 miles) off the south coast of Burma (Myanmar).

That piece of wreckage is now in the Powerhouse Museum in Sydney.

KINGSFORD SMITH

Winifred Tennant

Ask the sun; it has watched him pass—
A shadow mirrored on seas of glass;
Ask the stars that he knew so well
If they beheld where a bird-man fell.
Ask the wind that has blown with him
Over the edge of the ocean's rim,
Far from the charted haunts of men,
To the utmost limits and back again.
Ask the clouds on the mountain height,
The echoes that followed him in his flight,
The thunder that prowls the midnight sky,
If a silvered 'plane went riding by.

If the birds could talk, would they tell of the fall
Of a god who winged above them all?
Of an eagle-man, by the world's decrees,
King of the blue immensities.

THE RED BARON'S AUSSIE SEND-OFF

I t is fairly certain that Australian gunners were responsible for ending the career and life of Baron Manfred Albrecht Freiherr von Richthofen, the WWI German flying ace known as the 'Red Baron' on 21 April 1918. He was certainly buried with full military honours by the Australian forces.

Private Alfred Fowler, a soldier with the 40th Australian Battalion, witnessed the Red Baron's death. He recalls delivering a message to a gunner at the 11th Battalion, who opened fire on von Richthofen's plane and claims to have seen the bullets pierce the cockpit. Running to the wreckage, Fowler himself saw the bullet wounds in von Richthofen's chest, and was convinced he had been killed by the Aussie gunners, although surgeons who conducted von Richthofen's autopsy formed the opinion that the angle and nature of the bullet wounds ruled out being shot from the ground, and concluded that his injuries were probably caused by bullets from the guns of Canadian pilot, Roy Brown.

In hindsight it appears more than likely that Australian Lewis guns on the ground killed von Richthofen.

The last surviving member of the Australian Flying Corps, Howard Edwards, who passed away in 1998, was certain it was Australian 3rd Squadron field guns that killed the Red Baron.

Here is his story:

We used to see the Red Baron's three-decker plane, and there was a deal of 'scare' attached to him because he had the name of being a successful aeronaut. He certainly was a force to be reckoned with. But he had an umbrella, as I call it, of other aeroplanes all around him.

He'd have eight to ten other planes making a great circus—we used to call it the Red Baron's Circus. Not infrequently he would be up very early in the morning. At daybreak you'd find this circus up in the air waiting for some of our people to come out, and then they'd just sink down onto them and surround this one plane and let the Baron have the pleasure of shooting him down.

We felt it wasn't fair sportsmanship. What it was, was war, and as they say, 'all is fair in love and war'. We were more than delighted when we heard Richthofen had been brought down.

As I understand it, he was following one of our aeroplanes down. Our fellow dived to get away and he was following. When they got down near the ground he levelled off. He had flown some half a mile, or a mile, on the level, a few hundred feet above the ground, when he was brought down. He couldn't have done that if he'd been shot from above, but he was shot by ground forces while he was on the parallel, chasing our aeroplane.

Our squadron was commissioned to go out and collect his crashed machine. When they got out to the scene of the crash (it was in no-man's land and under pretty close observance by the enemy) it was felt that it was not wise to attempt to bring in the plane under the circumstances, so they decided to wait until night. But in the meantime they wanted to get the body of Richthofen out, so one of our corporals, Corporal Collins if I remember rightly, went out with a rope and put it around the Baron's body so that by pulling the rope they could pull him out. Then they pulled the Baron's body to their cover and brought him back and Scotty Melville and I were deputed to take it in two-hour turns to guard the body in one of our hangars until the authorities had verified the authenticity of it being the Red Baron.

Richthofen was very poorly dressed. He didn't have any sort of coat on, just what I considered to be a rather shabby kind of shirt and an undershirt, a singlet. I was rather amazed that one in his position could be so poorly dressed.

He had a stern, set face it seemed to me and there were several marks, indentations and wounds. I could touch four or five on his face, but I didn't think any of them were bullet wounds. I felt they were wounds from the crash. What brought him down, undoubtedly, was a bullet that went through his right side, right underarm, and came out just in front of the left arm, just below the heart.

New South Wales Bushmen Contingent heading for the Second Boer War
camped at Kensington Racecourse, Sydney, early 1900.

2nd South Australian Mounted Rifles.
Harry Morant is third from left on a grey horse.

Nevile Howse VC.

The Boers: Afrikaner Commandos.

Major Robert Lenehan, commander of the Bushveldt Carbineers.

(L–R) Peter Handcock, Harry Morant, unknown, Percy Hunt, unknown,
Alfred 'Bulala' Taylor, Transvaal, 1901.

Colonel Granville 'Bull' Ryrie in front of a Bristol Boxkite, 1914.

The *AE2* in Sydney Harbour.

Commander Henry Stoker of the *AE2*, 1919.

The Women's RAN medal, World War I.

The first HMAS *Sydney*, 1914.

The boarding party approaches the wreck of the *Emden*,
aground on North Keeling Island, 10 November 1914.

Anzac Cove, 1915.

Private John 'Simpson' Kirkpatrick and his donkey cart at Gallipoli, May 1915.

Mesopotamian Half-Flight pilots (L–R): Henry Petre, Tom White,
George Merz, H.R. Reilly and friend at Basra, June 1915.

Billy Sing 'The Assassin'.

Valentine's Day Mutiny March, Sydney, 1916.

Light Horse on the move near Esdoud (Tel Ashdod), Palestine, 1916.

The Light Horse charging at Beersheba, 31 October 1917.

Lone Pine, Gallipoli.

2nd Australian Imperial Force troops depart Sydney, 1940.

In World War II, women joined the services in unprecedented numbers.

Field Marshall Erwin Rommel.

The grave of Corporal
Jack Edmondson VC, Tobruk.

Aussie troops at Tobruk.

The crew of the second HMAS *Sydney*.

HMAS *Sydney* leaves Sydney Harbour, August 1941.

Scrapped tanks at El Alamein.

Australian and New Zealand war graves at Suda Bay, Crete.

Nancy Wake in the uniform of the British First Aid Nursing Yeomanry.

US marines and sailors parade through Brisbane, 1941.

Bruce Kingsbury VC.

Milne Bay airstrip, September 1942.

Milne Bay airstrip from above.

Raising *M-14*, Sydney Harbour, June 1942.

The sinking of the hospital ship *Centaur* and the deaths of eleven staff nurses on board affected Australians deeply.

Sister Ellen Savage GM.

Private Rowe assists Corporal Hall
DCM at Shaggy Ridge,
27 December 1943.

A wounded Australian carried
out of Shaggy Ridge.

Cowra prisoner of war camp.

General Adachi surrenders to Major General Robertson at Wewak, 13 September 1945.

No. 77 Squadron Meteors in flight over Korea.

Aussie troops celebrate Christmas in Korea, 1952.

Bruce Fletcher's 1970 painting 'The Battle of Long Tan'.
(*Australian War Memorial*)

Vietnam War memorial, Adelaide.

Statue of Cameron Baird VC,
Currumbin RSL, Queensland.

After Scotty Melville and I had been looking after the body, we heard that the autopsy had revealed that Richthofen had been carrying 2000 francs in French money, in case he was brought down, to buy his way out. Scotty said he wished he'd known; he would have helped himself. When I told him what I thought of that, he wanted to fight me.

He said, 'if you feel that way about me, come back at four o'clock'.

I did, and blow me if he wasn't there standing waiting for me. I had to peel off and hop into him. That's the only fight I ever had.

When he saw a bit of blood from his own nose he didn't like it, because my arms were a bit longer than his.

Harold was an instrument fitter and he was ordered to engrave the name-plate for von Richthofen's coffin. He commented:

You do what you are told when you are in the Army or the Air Force. So I made up little engravers from bits of wire from the aeroplane's steel wires, polished them up and cut them suitably, then did the engraving.

When the results of an exhaustive investigation into the death of von Richthofen were published in 1997 in *The Red Baron's Last Flight* by Norman Franks and Alan Bennett, they seemed to prove that the bullet that killed the flying ace could not have come from Brown's plane but had to have been fired by Australians on the ground.

Von Richthofen was buried on 22 April 1918 in the small village of Bertangles. British and Australian troops gave him full military honours. A British pilot dropped a note in German territory containing the news. Germany went into deep mourning.

In 1925, Manfred von Richthofen's younger brother Bolko recovered the body and Baron Manfred von Richthofen had the largest funeral ever seen in Berlin.

However, there is a strange twist to the tale. Some years later author and historian P.J. Carisella reopened the grave in search of the coffin plaque made by Harold Edwards. He found the well-preserved bones of the Red Baron, all intact . . . except for the skull.

He didn't find the plaque.

THE RIGHT MAN—CAPTAIN ROSS SMITH

There was probably no better example of what a fighting airman should be like than the Australian, Ross Smith. Like many of the successful airmen of the Australian Flying Corps, Ross Smith came from the Australian Light Horse.

Official Australian War History

Captain Ross Macpherson Smith—Knight Commander of the Order of the British Empire, Air Force Cross (twice), Military Cross (twice), Distinguished Flying Cross (three times)—was born in Adelaide, in 1892.

A gifted athlete and horseman, he enlisted as a trooper in the 3rd Australian Light Horse at the outbreak of war in 1914. All eleven members of the school cricket team, which Ross had captained, enlisted. Five were killed, including his younger brother, Colin, and another five were wounded.

Ross's elder brother, Keith, was rejected by the AIF because he had varicose veins, so he had them surgically removed, made his way to Britain and joined the Royal Flying Corps.

Ross Smith served at Gallipoli and was promoted to regimental sergeant major in August 1915 and commissioned as a second lieutenant in September, just as he was evacuated from Gallipoli with enteric fever. He spent six months recovering, then was given command of a machine-gun section in Egypt in early 1916, fought at the decisive Battle of Romani, and decided to join the Australian Flying Corps.

Ross began training in Cairo in October 1916 and received his observer's wings in January 1917 then his pilot's wings in July.

Despite starting so late and spending most of his time with No. 1 Squadron, which was a bomber and reconnaissance unit, he finished the war as Australia's 10th top pilot for confirmed 'kills' in air combat and was decorated for gallantry five times between January 1917 and November 1918.

> The watcher on the tower yelled 'Aeroplane up!' One enemy two-seater and three scouts were coming . . . Ross Smith, with his observer, climbed like a cat up the sky . . . fastened on the big one, and, after five minutes of sharp machine gun rattle, the German dived suddenly towards the railway line . . . Five minutes later Ross Smith was back. Our sausages were still hot; we ate them and drank tea. Ross Smith wished he might stay forever on this Arab front with an enemy every half hour.
>
> T.E. Lawrence, *The Seven Pillars of Wisdom*

Ross flew Lawrence of Arabia on secret missions into the desert and gained expertise with all kinds of aircraft including Bristol Fighters, various prototypes called 'British Experimentals' (christened 'Bloody Emergencies' because of their unreliability), and the lumbering HP100 heavy bomber, made by Handley Page.

His experience with the HP100, which could carry a tonne of bombs over long distances, was to change his life and turn him into a legend. After the armistice, Ross Smith made the first ever flight from Cairo to Calcutta in the HP100, with Brigadier Borton and sergeants Wally Shiers and Jim Bennett. They intended to fly on to Australia and travelled as far as Timor by ship to check for landing places and talk to the Dutch colonial authorities. Meanwhile, the HP100 was flown to the north-west frontier to deal with an Afghan uprising and crashed in a storm.

They had abandoned the idea of flying to Australia, when a chance acquaintance showed them the first Australian newspaper they had seen in five years. On the front page was an offer from Prime Minister Billy Hughes of £10,000 to the first Australian aircrew to fly a British aircraft from England to Australia in less than 30 days.

Hundreds of Australians attempted to enter the race and the Australian government recruited the Royal Aero Club as arbiters and organisers. The rules were strict in order to avoid the government being criticised for putting lives in danger.

The aircraft entered had to be airworthy. This meant in effect that only an aircraft entered by a manufacturer was acceptable. Most would-be entrants could not afford new machines.

Each crew had to have a navigator, which eliminated the entry put up by Charles Kingsford Smith, and solo entries were forbidden by the regulations, so Lieutenant Bert Hinkler's entry in a Sopwith Dove was also eliminated.

Ross Smith knew somebody who really could navigate and who could also share the burden of flying the machine—his own brother, Keith, an RFC and RAF flying instructor who was still based in Britain and available to take part in the venture.

Altogether six Australian crews, five of them backed by the cream of the British aircraft industry—Sopwith, Vickers, Blackburn, Alliance and Martinsyde—took part in the race. The sixth crew, lieutenants Ray Parer and John McIntosh, after months of setbacks and failed schemes, were backed by Scots whisky magnate Peter Dawson and had entered a war surplus De Havilland DH.9 which they named '*PD*' in his honour.

There was also an unofficial 'seventh' entry. French flyer, Etienne Poulet and his mechanic, Jean Benoist, flying a tiny Caudron biplane, set off from Paris on 14 October 1919. Not being Australian, they were ineligible for the cash prize, but they were determined to win the race, and the glory, for France. They were to lead the race for more than half the distance.

Of the seven entrants, only two would reach Australia. The Vimy, with its crew of the Smiths and mechanics Shiers and Bennett, took off from Hounslow Heath at 9.05 am on 12 November 1919. It had the British identification G-EAOU in huge letters across the wing top and the crew used the identification letters to name their craft *God 'Elp All Of Us*.

They flew up to ten hours each day, then Shiers and Bennett would work on the Rolls-Royce engines while Ross and Keith refuelled, straining petrol through a chamois leather filter. They followed this routine for 27 days.

Of the other entrants, two crashed fatally: the Alliance Endeavour, flown by Douglas and Ross, just after taking off from Hounslow, and the Martinsyde, flown by fighter ace Cedric Howell and George Fraser, when it ditched off Corfu in the Adriatic Sea after a navigation error during the night.

The Blackburn Kangaroo of Captain Sir Hubert Wilkins was forced to turn back to Crete with engine trouble and crashed on landing, while George Matthews and Tom Kay in the Sopwith Wallaby so nearly made it but crashed in a banana plantation in Bali.

Etienne Poulet in his tiny Caudron G4 biplane just kept plugging away and led the field as far as Rangoon before he, too, was eliminated with engine trouble.

The astonishingly determined Parer and McIntosh limped from one near-disaster to another in their single-engined DH.9 eventually arriving in Darwin eight months after leaving London. Their flight was the first to Australia in a single-engined plane.

The biggest problem for the competitors was that there were no landing grounds between India and Darwin. There wasn't even a landing ground at Darwin. The Dutch had set up a couple of flying schools in Indonesia and constructed rudimentary airstrips during 1919, but elsewhere most 'airfields' consisted of racecourses like those at Rangoon and Singapore or clearings in the jungle with a stockpile of fuel.

Ross Smith later wrote:

I made the first aerial voyage from London to Australia largely due to the experiences gained piloting a Handley-Page aeroplane towards the end of the war . . . The trip itself was first suggested in a joke.

Brigadier-General Borton invited me to join him in a flight to link up the forces in Palestine with the army in Mesopotamia. After reaching Baghdad, we would find a route to India, 'to see,' he jocularly remarked, 'the Viceroy's Cup run in Calcutta'.

'Then, after that,' I replied sarcastically, 'let's fly on to Australia and see the Melbourne Cup!' . . . It took just three weeks to pioneer a route to India, where we arrived, on December 10, 1918, scarcely a month after the signing of the Armistice . . . This was the longest flight that had been made up to this time, and it convinced me that a well-equipped and serviced plane was capable of flying anywhere, given suitable landing grounds.

In India, General Borton chartered a steamer, the R.I.M.S Sphinx, intending to explore the route to Australia, arrange suitable landing grounds, return to India, and fly to Australia over the established course. I accompanied him.

We sailed from Calcutta on February 10, 1919, with stores and equipment and 7,000 gallons of petrol. We intended to dump 200 gallons of petrol at each suitable landing place along the anticipated flight route . . . at our first port of call, the Sphinx caught fire and blew up. We lost everything but . . . the Indian Government generously lent us another vessel . . . Our three month expedition visited Burma, the Federated Malay States, the Netherlands Indies, Borneo and Siam but on our return we found that our machine had been crashed in a storm in the North of India.

Then we learned that the Australian Commonwealth Government had offered a prize of £10,000 for the first machine, manned by Australians, to fly from London to Australia in 30 days.

In England my brother Keith was awaiting repatriation to Australia. He had been flying with the Royal Air Force and had gained extensive and varied air experience. He signed up as assistant pilot and navigator. Sergeants Bennett and Shiers agreed to accompany us as air mechanics, making a crew of four.

Shell agreed to have petrol supplies at the required depots and Wakefield Ltd. undertook to arrange oils. From Darwin the Defense [sic] Department of Australia had made all necessary arrangements.

The challenge was to reach Australia.

The Vickers Vimy touched down on the specially built Fannie Bay airstrip near Darwin at 3.40 pm on 10 December. Her tanks were almost empty. 'We almost fell into Darwin,' Wally Shiers recalled many years later. The journey had taken 27 days and 20 hours.

Waiting to greet them were a customs officer and quarantine official and Ross Smith's old friend from the 1st Squadron Australian Flying Corps, Hudson Fysh, who had built the airfield at Darwin and surveyed the air route from Darwin to Brisbane, in case anyone got that far.

It was this survey that convinced Fysh that air travel was the answer to Australia's vast distances and led directly to the formation of Qantas.

Brigadier Borton called the flight 'the most magnificent pioneer undertaking of the age' and British Prime Minister Lloyd George telegrammed: 'Your flight shows how the inventions of war can advance the progress of peace.'

WHY WE SHALL PREVAIL

F.J. Leigh

(A private in the 4th Field Ambulance of the 4th Infantry Division)

> Not because our hearts are stouter;
> Or that we are better men;
> Not because we mock the doubter,
> Fighting battles with his pen.
>
> Not because our arms are stronger;
> Or that we are better born;
> But that we can hang on longer,
> Even when we're spent and worn.
>
> Not because our Navy's greater
> Or our store of shells is more;
> Not because our guns are 'later',
> Guns alone don't win a war;
>
> Not because our Empire's peerless;
> Or that we have got more 'tin';
> But, because, when things look cheerless,
> We can set our teeth and grin.

PART III
FIGHTING THE FÜHRER

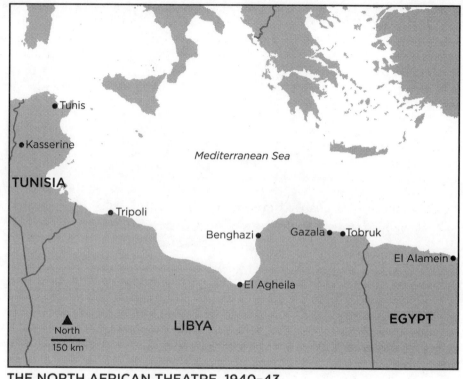

THE NORTH AFRICAN THEATRE, 1940–43

AUSTRALIA'S WORLD WAR II

World War II changed everything about Australia. For a young nation it was the most defining period of change in our history.

The young men who left our shores to fight in the defence of Australia, the British Empire and the free world, between 1939 and 1945, returned to a very different Australia than the one they left.

WWII was the catalyst for major changes in Australia's economic and social structure, as well as military and foreign policy.

From a military point of view, we entered the war as a subsidiary of the British Armed Forces and ended the war with the fourth largest air force in the world, a regular standing army for the first time in our history and an efficient navy designed to protect our own shores. A direct result of the war was the development of much larger, regular peacetime military forces. We effectively had no regular army before WWII; the Citizens' Military Force, the CMF Militia, *was* the army, and we raised expeditionary forces in times of war, as in WWI, and disbanded them when the conflict ended. The regular Australian army was born out of WWII.

When Germany's aggressive expansionist policies of the 1930s finally led to a threat to invade Poland in 1939, Britain and France warned that they would declare war if that occurred. Germany invaded on 1 September. Britain and France, after demanding a withdrawal from Germany that was ignored, declared war on 3 September 1939.

At this point in history, Australians still thought of themselves as 'British'. It came as no surprise when Prime Minister Robert Menzies announced that, 'as a consequence' of Britain's declaration, Australia was also at war.

At first, the whole focus of Australia's war effort was aimed at supporting Britain. The Royal Australian Navy (RAN) was put under the control of the British and large numbers of Royal Australian Air Force (RAAF) recruits were sent to Britain as bomber and fighter crews.

The Great Depression had curtailed Australia's defence spending, leading to a decline in the size and effectiveness of the armed forces during the late 1920s and early 1930s. Defence spending represented a mere 2 per cent of the national budget in 1937 and 1938. This would rise to 37 per cent in 1942 and 1943.

In 1939, the navy was the best prepared of the three armed forces. Even so, it was woefully under-equipped to fight a war, with just two heavy cruisers, four light cruisers, five destroyers, three sloops and the usual variety of support and ancillary craft. The destroyers were antiquated but the cruisers were relatively modern. The total number of naval personnel in 1939 was 5010. This would increase to almost 40,000 during WWII.

The RAAF, at the start of the war, had nine under-strength squadrons and about 3500 officers and crew for 246 mostly antiquated aircraft. Half of the aircraft were 'gifts' from the British RAF and were pretty much obsolete.

When war was declared, 450 Australian pilots were already serving with the British air force and men from RAAF No. 10 Squadron were about to take delivery of nine Sunderland flying boats in Britain. These remained in Britain for the duration of the war as part of RAF Coastal Command. A flight to Tunisia on 10 October 1939 was the first official RAAF action of the war.

Recruiting for the RAAF began immediately when war was declared. The Menzies government at one stage proposed sending the entire RAAF overseas in defence of Britain, but the main focus eventually was to train aircrews for the defence of Britain under the Empire Air Training Scheme (EATS). Basic training was done at home and 40 training schools were set up around the country for this purpose.

It wasn't until November 1940 that the first crews graduated from these RAAF Service Flying Training Schools, but eventually more than 37,000 Australians served as RAAF and RAF aircrew and almost 30,000 of those were trained under the EATS. Almost 16,000 Australians flew in Britain with the RAF, while the remaining 11,000 became part of the RAAF campaign against the Japanese.

In Europe, RAAF personnel were mostly involved in RAF Bomber Command. Although they represented only 2 per cent of all RAAF personnel during the war, they accounted for 23 per cent of the total number killed in action. An illustration of this tragic statistic is the Australian manned No. 460 Squadron, which had an official establishment of about 200 aircrew but suffered 1018 combat deaths. In effect, the squadron was wiped out five times during the war.

The Australian army, in 1939, consisted of 3000 regular soldiers and 80,000 part-time members of the Citizens' Military Force. Australia effectively had two armies throughout WWII. (This is the subject of the story, *Two Armies*, later in this collection.)

When the war ended, there were 225,000 Australian troops in Asia and the Pacific; 20,000 in Europe and the Mediterranean; and the total in uniform in all the armed services (army, navy and air force) was more than 600,000.

Almost one million Australians served in WWII and the death toll among all Australian armed services was almost 40,000, of whom 30,000 were killed in action. Military wounded amounted to almost 24,000. Civilian deaths were around 800.

While a significant number served, and the war was a traumatic time for the whole nation, Australia was to a certain extent removed from the major theatres of war and our allies and enemies generally fared much worse.

Military deaths for Britain totalled more than 300,000 and the United States lost more than 400,000 men. More than half of Russia's armed servicemen died (11 million) and that nation lost 14 million of its civilian population.

Of our two major enemies, German losses were 3.25 million servicemen and 2.5 million civilians. Japanese losses were 1.75 million military personnel killed and civilian deaths amounted to 400,000.

During the war, Australia shifted the focus of its foreign policy from the United Kingdom to the United States. The dilemma facing our politicians and decision-makers in the early years of WWII was that Japan was looming as an obvious threat to the north, while Britain demanded more and more support in Europe and North Africa. While Churchill and others assured Australians that they would be adequately defended if Japan entered the war, there were concerns that Britain might not be able to fulfil its pledge to defend Singapore in the event of a Japanese invasion.

These doubts proved to be well founded and, after the defeat of the Fadden government in October 1941 and the attack on Pearl Harbor in December, the new Labor Prime Minister, John Curtin, took a much firmer stand against British demands to use Australia's troops to defend British interests in Europe, Africa and Burma.

Upon becoming prime minister on 7 October 1941, Curtin insisted that the Australian 9th Division return to Australia and, on 27 December, within three weeks of the Japanese attack on Pearl Harbor, he made his famous pronouncement as part of his New Year message for 1942, printed in the *Melbourne Herald*:

> Without any inhibitions of any kind I make it quite clear that Australia looks to America, free from any pangs as to our traditional links or kinship with the United Kingdom.
>
> We know the problems that the United Kingdom faces. We know the constant threat of invasion. We know the dangers of dispersal of strength, but we know, too, that Australia can go and Britain can still hold on.
>
> We are, therefore, determined that Australia shall not go, and we shall devote all our energies towards the shaping of a plan, with the United States as its keystone, which will give to our country some confidence of being able to hold out until the tide of battle swings against our enemy.

The fall of Singapore on 15 February 1942 vindicated Curtin's policy of looking to America and drawing a line in the sand with Churchill about Australian troops defending Australia first and Britain second. When Churchill ordered the diversion of the Australian 7th Division to Burma while the troops were crossing the Indian Ocean just a day later, Curtin defied him, saying it was 'quite impossible to reverse a decision which we have made with the utmost care' and the troops returned to Australia.

After Singapore there was a feeling that the mother country had let Australia down and failed to recognise that it was a nation and not a colony. Australia was no longer happy to jeopardise her own safety in order to defend the land of her forefathers.

The situation of the 9th Division remaining in North Africa was used as a bargaining tool by Curtin when, in a secret cable on 30 July 1942, he demanded Churchill's support in Washington and the delivery of planes to defend Australia. Unlike Menzies, who tried in vain to balance Australia's needs with those of Britain in the early years of WWII as a member of Churchill's War Cabinet, Curtin was blunt and undiplomatic in his attitude. Curtin's cable read, in part:

Australia has been critically threatened on two occasions—firstly following the fall of the Malay Barrier, and secondly following the threatened advance through the Coral Sea. Japan is now consolidating her position in New Guinea and the Solomon Islands and has made a landing in Papua which threatens our important advanced base at Port Moresby . . . It is imperative . . . that the Commander-in-Chief, South-West Pacific Area, shall have at his disposal for the defence of his base and for offensive operations in the Pacific all the Australian forces it can place at his disposal . . . For the reasons stated, it is impossible for us to do more than agree to an extension of the period for the temporary retention of the 9th Division in the Middle East.

Australia's relationship with the mother country was never the same after the fall of Singapore. The nation had a much greater sense of independence and pride in the achievements of our troops in the defence of our own shores. The alliance with the United States had also made us more aware of ourselves as 'Australian' rather than 'British' subjects. Australian citizenship, with our own passports and identity separate from 'British', was introduced not long after WWII ended, in 1948.

The stimulus provided by the war effort was the final factor in conquering the effects of the Great Depression in Australia. The war effort stimulated the economy as the government borrowed and spent.

Unemployment fell as men joined the armed forces and women, for the first time in Australia's short history as a nation, joined the workforce in truly significant numbers. Restrictions on availability of consumer goods and rationing meant that many people had increased savings. This aided the post-war 'boom'.

In the short term, the effect of the war effort on the Australian lifestyle was very restrictive. Not since the convict era had there been more restrictions on the population than there were during WWII.

A list of the most obvious restrictions serves as a reminder of just how intrusive the war was in the life of ordinary Australians. It must be remembered that Australians, far more so than Europeans, were not used to such restrictions and interventions in their everyday lives.

- Leisure time and leisure activities were curtailed. The Christmas and New Year holiday period was reduced to three days. Many sporting events and competitions were suspended 'for the duration'. Racecourses were closed or used as military camps and some of these, like Victoria Park in Sydney, never opened again as public racetracks.

- Daylight saving was introduced and blackouts were common. Clothing, footwear, tea, butter and sugar were rationed. Home building and renovations were restricted.

- Men of eligible age were called up into the militia or, conversely, were not allowed to join the forces if they worked in certain industries. Identity cards were introduced.

- Political parties opposed to the war (the Communist Party and Australia First) were banned. Striking workers were drafted into the army or into labour gangs. More than 1000 conscientious objectors were prosecuted and some were gaoled. 'Aliens' of a nationality linked to the enemy (mostly Italians) were interned.

- The government decided whether your job was 'essential' and also what jobs you could and could not take, or leave. Although a referendum to increase federal powers over organised marketing of primary produce, social services and industrial employment was lost in 1944, many restrictions on employment and production were in place under Labor during the war and were opposed by many as draconian and unnecessary.

On the 'positive' side, social changes precipitated by the war were the catalyst for change and the social evolution that led to the modern, cosmopolitan, multicultural nation we live in today.

The role of women in Australian society was changed dramatically during WWII. The long-term effect of these changes in the workforce and in society was a big step towards equality for women.

The increased enlistment of women into the auxiliary forces and the formation of the Australian Women's Land Army (AWLA) meant that women were seen as being a genuine part of the war effort, and encouraged women to work in rural industries as well as in munitions production.

Although their roles were mostly supportive and non-combat, nurses and auxiliary staff were perceived by the public as being on the front line against the enemy. This was highlighted when, on 12 May 1943, the news of the sinking of the hospital ship *Centaur* and the death of eleven of the twelve staff nurses on board was heard. This tragic story affected Australians deeply, as did the sinking of the *Vyner Brooke* and the machine-gun massacre of 21 female survivors by Japanese soldiers on Banka Island on 12 February 1942, with the sole survivor Vivian Bulwinkel eventually returning to Australia.

Another huge factor in the move towards equality was the setting of some women's pay rates at near-male levels. The Labor government set women's wage rates as high as 90 per cent for munitions workers. These increased wages were an incentive to get women to shift into work while caring for their families. These wages, however, were dropped back once the men came back from war. Probably the most common new experience of Australian women during the war was gaining financial responsibility of the household.

The war also fostered the development of a more diverse and cosmopolitan Australian society. There were several reasons for this.

Many Australian troops served in Europe and North Africa and many of our airmen spent the war in Britain. This gave them exposure to a different lifestyle and a more sophisticated and diverse culture and lifestyle than they had known at home. A very good example was the acceptance of the large numbers of Greek migrants into Australian society after the war. This was partly made possible due to the great respect and gratitude that developed among Aussie troops for the people of Greece and Crete during the failed campaigns of 1941.

Similarly, large numbers of Australians were, for the first time, exposed to the lifestyles and cultures of the nations to our north, which improved levels of understanding of the nations and people of Asia and the Pacific and was a major factor in Australia's move towards taking a greater political and defensive role in these regions after the war. It also meant that the Australian public perception of 'Asia' and 'the islands' changed significantly.

This exposure of Australian troops to other lifestyles in Asia and the Pacific led to a diminution of the old imperialist attitude of superiority towards non-European races. An obvious example of this is the great respect and publicity given to the role played by the people of Papua New Guinea who assisted and escorted Australian troops down through the treacherous Kokoda Track and Timor, affectionately named the 'Fuzzy Wuzzy Angels' by grateful troops.

A similar sense of affection and gratitude fed into the outrage that grew around the political situation in East Timor through the 1970s and into the 1990s. This sentiment was partly driven by a feeling that we had let down people who had stood by our men when they needed help during WWII.

As well as our troops being exposed to other cultures overseas, the reverse situation occurred with prisoners of war here in Australia. The 17,000 Italian prisoners of war captured in North Africa and transported to Australian POW camps were sent to work on Australian farms and rural properties. Many of these men returned as sponsored migrants after the war, often sponsored by the people they had worked for during the war, and their presence in rural communities had a big effect on Australians' acceptance of Italian culture, diet and lifestyle after the war.

The desperate times even heralded changes for Indigenous Australians, many of whom were evacuated from the north to urban areas in the south and entered the workforce for the first time. The federal government even eased the existing paternalistic and racist regulations to allow Aborigines to serve in the 2nd AIF, and more than 3000 did so. (At first, only those with a European parent were allowed to serve!)

Other refugees from Europe made their way to Australia in large numbers after the war to escape the collapse of their communities in their homeland and brought with them their culture and sophisticated social attitudes. Many of these people became teachers in our schools and universities, taking the lead in the artistic, cultural and culinary life of our cities. Generations of Australians after the war have been educated and influenced by these 'New Australians'.

Another consequence of Australia being a base for US troops was that Australians were forced to confront some serious racial issues. It is a sad fact that the Australian government, still steeped in the culture of the 'White Australia Policy', only reluctantly agreed to accept black US troops into Australia. Many of the Americans stationed here were black and they were segregated and treated differently from the white US soldiers. This led to a variety of opposing reactions from the Australian public.

In Brisbane there were demands by many residents for these black US soldiers to be segregated to 'south of the river'. This reaction was consistent with the poor attitude of many Australians to their own Indigenous people, who were seen to be 'primitive', lower class 'non-citizens' without any political or social rights.

There may also have been a reaction to the white American racist attitudes and anti-black propaganda that was common at that time in the United States and no doubt spread here by some white American soldiers. To stem any backlash from the Australian public, the US Military Police set boundaries for the black troops, which restricted their 'exposure' to Brisbane's residents and to many parts of the city.

On the other side, many Australians were appalled by the segregation of American troops. Their attitude was that all those fighting to save Australia should be treated equally. It has even been argued in some quarters that the 'Battle of Brisbane' was partly brought about by Aussie troops protesting the harsh treatment and segregation of black American troops. This is probably a case of retrospective history, imposing 21st century sensibilities on mid-20th century history.

As a result, these factors played a part in forcing Australians to confront their own attitudes towards, and treatment of, Aboriginal Australians. While black American troops were discriminated against, they had more civil rights than Australia's own Indigenous people.

It is impossible to over-emphasise the effect of WWII on Australian society and the Aussie lifestyle. Those of us who grew up in the afterglow of 'The War' were very different people from our parents and grand-parents. The post-war 'baby boom', the economic security and expansion of the 1950s, and the changing of attitudes regarding social equality all contributed to a dramatically different social and political landscape for Australia after WWII.

INFANTRY MARCHING SONG

Anonymous

(To the tune of 'Colonel Bogey')

> Hitler . . . has only one big ball,
> Goering . . . has two, but they are small,
> Himmler . . . has something sim'lar,
> But poor old Goebbels has no balls at all!

HITLER'S FIRST DEFEAT

In early 1941 the war was going very badly for the Allies. Italy had declared war on France and Britain on 10 June 1940, France had fallen in June 1940 and 'Fortress Europe' was in the hands of the Axis forces. Also, British cities had suffered nightly bombing raids for more than six months with the Battle of Britain at its height in late 1940 and early 1941.

Most of the 'good news' in the twelve months between June 1940 and June 1941 came via major victories against the Italians. British naval victories over the Italian fleet occurred in the Battle of Calabria in July 1940, the Battle of Taranto in November 1940 and the Battle of Matapan off the coast of Crete in March 1941. The Italian fleet was never an offensive threat after these British victories, although they harassed British naval convoys and supply lines continuously and effectively in the Mediterranean with the aid of German air support and U-boats.

On land, things were even worse for the Italians. The ill-fated decision to invade Greece was made by Mussolini in a fit of pique after he learned that Hitler had invaded Romania without consultation. Much to Hitler's annoyance, and without his prior knowledge, Italian troops invaded Greece on 28 October 1940.

The Greeks had defeated the Italians and driven them out of Greece within three weeks, an Italian counter-attack failed in March 1941 and Germany had to come to the aid of her Italian ally.

In North Africa, an Italian offensive from their colony of Libya into the neighbouring British Protectorate of Egypt had led, in December 1940, to 'Operation Compass', a British and Commonwealth offensive. The Italian army had a million men in Libya and 200,000 were involved in the offensive against Egypt. There were 36,000 British troops in Egypt defending the oil fields and the Suez Canal.

Operation Compass pushed the Italians back 800 kilometres (497 miles), virtually destroyed the Italian Tenth Army and captured huge numbers of guns, vehicles and tanks.

It was during this campaign that the Australian 6th Division, led by Major General Mackay, helped capture the Mediterranean fortress port of Tobruk, on 22 January 1941. Twenty-five thousand Italian prisoners were taken and 208 guns, 23 tanks and 200 vehicles were captured. Australian losses were 49 killed and 306 wounded.

The Italians officially asked for German help in Libya on 10 February 1941. In order to prevent a total Axis defeat in North Africa, Hitler had decided, in January 1941, to make plans to send a new tank-based force, the *Deutsches Afrikakorps*, to North Africa. It was to be led by Field Marshal Erwin Rommel, who had commanded the Panzer Tank Divisions through the Blitzkrieg campaign that gave Hitler his 'Fortress Europe'.

Elsewhere things were going from bad to worse for the Italian army, which was defeated in East Africa and Ethiopia by British and South African forces during the first three months of 1941.

However, by June 1941, victories over the Italian army and navy were all in the past and the stark reality of the situation in Europe was clear. The Germans controlled 'Fortress Europe', Romania, Greece, Yugoslavia and Crete had fallen, Britain was under siege and Rommel was on the rampage in North Africa.

Against this background of defeat for the Allied forces, the deeds of the 'Rats of Tobruk' shone like a beacon of hope in a hellish world.

If you look at a map of the Mediterranean as it is today, you will see Libya and Egypt with borders unchanged from 1940 when the Italian colony of Libya was divided almost equally into a western province, Tripolitania, and an eastern province, Cyrenaica. Tripoli, the capital of Tripolitania, is directly below Italy and was the base and main port of the Axis campaign. Between the toe of Italy and the coast on North Africa lies the island of Malta, the critically strategic British base during the war in the Mediterranean.

The towns and cities of Cyrenaica, however, were the critical stepping-stones, which charted the fortunes of the two sides in the desert war, which ebbed and flowed east/west/east/west/east/west from 1940 to 1943.

The desert war in North Africa began in September 1940 when the Italian army advanced eastward from bases in Cyrenaica into Egypt.

Repeatedly taken and lost by both sides in Cyrenaica over the following three years were places along the coastline such as Bardia, Tobruk, Gazala, Derna, Benghazi and El Agheila.

All these places were Italian garrisons at the start of the war; all were taken by the British Commonwealth forces as they pushed the Italians west. All but Tobruk were retaken by the Axis forces under Rommel as they moved east to the Egyptian border and all were retaken again by the British Eighth Army, which drove Rommel back to El Agheila at the end of 1941.

In 1942 Rommel again took Cyrenaica and moved into Egypt until defeated at El Alamein and driven back westward to final defeat in 1943, leaving the towns and cities of Cyrenaica in Allied hands.

The exception to this predictable east/west/east/west/east/west ebb and flow was Tobruk, which resisted the Axis forces for eight months in 1941. Supplied from the sea and defended heroically, by Australian infantry troops and Brtish artillery, the Tobruk garrison defied the odds and the predictable changes of fortune of the two opposing armies and its defence became a legend for stubborn resistance and heroism.

Tobruk defied the logic and arithmetic of the various Allied and Axis campaigns by changing hands a mere three times during the war, whereas all other places mentioned in Cyrenaica changed hands five times!

Tobruk's strength as a fortress was the fact that the harbour is surrounded by a flat plateau with ancient defences built in a rough semi-circle running from the coast 13 kilometres (8 miles) east of the harbour, into the desert and back to the coast again 14.5 kilometres (9 miles) west of it. There were many defence posts around the perimeter, which were protected, in 1941, by barbed wire, minefields and anti-tank ditches. Beyond the defences the ground was a perfectly flat desert plateau with no cover for attacking forces.

When Mussolini declared war on Britain on 10 June 1941, Marshal Graziani was appointed governor of Libya and Commander in Chief of Italian forces in North Africa on 1 July 1940. In a letter dated 11 August 1940, Mussolini told Graziani to be ready to attack Egypt as soon as German troops landed on British soil, which he said had been 'decided on . . . and may take place within a week or a month'.

The invasion of Britain never occurred and, on 11 September 1940, Graziani's Italian troops commenced the offensive against Egypt, crossing the border on 13 September, occupying the town of Sidi Barrani on 15 September.

They halted in front of the main British defences at Mersa Matruh and, rather inexplicably, waited there for almost three months. Although heavily outnumbered, Major General Wavell, in command of two Commonwealth Divisions, one Indian and one British, decided to counter-attack against the seven Italian divisions on 9 December.

In the surprise attack, four Italian divisions were completely wiped out. Thirty-eight thousand prisoners were taken, including four generals, and 240 guns, 73 tanks and more than 1000 trucks were captured. The Italians were pushed out of Egypt in three days.

The British and Indian troops moved along the coast taking back all Egyptian towns by the end of December. Reinforcements were constantly arriving at Alexandria and the Australian 6th Division replaced the Indian 4th Division in the front line and helped capture the Italian fortress of Bardia on 5 January 1941. On 22 January, the 6th Division captured Tobruk.

On the day Tobruk fell to Australian troops, General Wavell was ordered to prepare to help Greece repel the expected German invasion. This meant diverting troops from North Africa to the Greek mainland and Crete.

In full retreat from the province of Cyrenaica, the Italians lost Derna and Benghazi to British troops in the first week of February. A large portion of the retreating army was encircled near Benghazi and the Italians lost 80 tanks attempting to break out. Italian troops surrendered by the thousands and General Graziani asked to be replaced on 8 February 1941.

The eastern half of Libya (Cyrenaica) was in British hands and the Italian army was in disarray. The Commonwealth force of 31,000 men, reinforced during the campaign by Australian, Indian and Free French divisions, had accomplished the amazing feat of advancing 800 kilometres (497 miles) in two months, totally destroying the Italian Tenth Army.

The Italians had lost 150,000 men (20,000 dead, 130,000 prisoners), 850 guns, 400 tanks and thousands of vehicles. British losses were 500 dead and 1400 wounded.

The British army had reached the border town of El Agheila on 9 February and the western half of Libya (Tripolitania) waited to be taken, but two factors halted the advance.

The first was that plans to send troops to Greece meant the North African campaign needed to be reassessed. The second was that the Afrika Korps was on its way to Tripoli.

Hitler evidently made the decision to send the *Deutsches Afrikakorps* to North Africa in January. Rommel arrived in Tripoli on 12 February 1941, just four days after General Graziani, Commander in Chief of the Italian forces, wrote to Mussolini asking to be replaced. The first contingents of the Afrika Korps disembarked at Tripoli on 14 February.

The first encounter with German troops occurred on 27 February and Rommel mounted his first attack on 24 March, taking El Agheila in a lightning move and moving east on 30 March in a three-pronged attack that cut British lines of communication. The British forces, with their most experienced troops and commanders on their way to Greece, were in retreat. Benghazi was evacuated on 3 April and Derna fell to Axis forces on 7 April.

The Australian 6th Division, which was heading to Greece, had been replaced by the 9th Division, commanded by Gallipoli veteran Major General Leslie Morshead, in the second week of March. The 9th Division withdrew from near Benghazi to Derna and finally to Tobruk on 10 April. The 18th Brigade of the Australian 7th Division was already there, along with various British troops and armoured divisions. Australians made up two-thirds of the 31,000 troops at Tobruk during the siege.

Rommel launched his first sudden violent attack on the fortress of Tobruk the day after the retreating 9th Division arrived in the town. On 11 April, the Italian Trento and Brescia Divisions attacked along the coast and the German 5th Armoured Division attacked from the south-west without success. Axis forces then swept eastward past Tobruk, leaving the fortress under siege. Rommel took Bardia on the following day, 12 April, and consolidated his front line near the Egyptian border at Sollum.

When Lieutenant General Neame was captured during the withdrawal, Major General John Lavarack, commander of the Australian 7th Division, was appointed temporary military commander of Cyrenaica by Wavell, who gave him written orders to hold Tobruk for 'about two months' and reminded him, ominously, '. . . there is nothing between you and Cairo'.

Lavarack organised the defence of the fortress but returned to his division in Egypt on 14 April when General Morshead, commanding the 9th Division, took over.

The Germans launched the first serious attempt to break the siege on Tobruk late on the night of Easter Sunday, 13 April 1941. Many hours before dawn broke on Easter Monday, 50 German tanks used the familiar

Blitzkrieg tactics, using tanks to break through the opposing forces and an infantry follow-up, in an attempt to breach the southern defences. These tactics had never failed—until Tobruk.

A German advance party established two field guns, a mortar and eight machine guns inside the perimeter, but was wiped out by a small party of seven men of the 20th Brigade of the Australian 9th Division in a grenade and bayonet charge. The German tanks were let through and the Australian and British troops silently waited until the German infantry appeared and engaged them, leaving the German tanks to advance without the support they had expected. Seventeen tanks were destroyed, most by the British Royal Horse Artillery. German losses were 150 dead and 250 captured. Australian losses were 26 killed and 64 wounded.

In this battle Corporal Jack Edmondson, from Wagga Wagga, became the first Australian to win a Victoria Cross in WWII when he saved his wounded platoon commander's life, despite being mortally wounded himself, and managed to shoot or bayonet at least three of the enemy.

In response to this defeat, Rommel strengthened the siege and Tobruk was subjected to heavy bombing and air attacks with the supply lines being specially targeted. Ships on their way to Tobruk with supplies, returning with wounded, or in the harbour, were constantly pummelled from the air and raided by German U-boats.

The supply line became known as the 'Tobruk Ferry'. Made up mostly of old warships, the fleet included the Australian destroyers *Napier*, *Nizam*, *Nestor* and *Vendetta*. Like all British supply lines into the Mediterranean, the staging posts were Gibraltar and Malta and losses were high. After enemy propagandists on Radio Berlin called the supply-line ships 'a pile of scrap iron', Australian troops christened them 'The Scrap Iron Fleet'.

Lost on the supply run in the eight months of the siege were two destroyers, three escort sloops and 21 other vessels. Australian ships lost were the destroyer HMAS *Waterhen* on 30 June 1941 (making her the first Australian naval vessel lost in WWII) and the support vessel HMAS *Parramatta*, on which 141 of the crew of 161 died when it was torpedoed on 2 December 1941.

Inside the garrison the policy was one of night raids and patrols. These were either to capture supplies and gather abandoned equipment or to harass the enemy with surprise attacks. One of the most memorable of these occurred on 16 April 1941 when the 2/48th Battalion, without loss except for two men wounded, captured 803 prisoners, including a complete battalion of the Italian Trento Division.

Rommel attacked again, from the west, on 30 April 1941. After prolonged dive-bombing and an artillery barrage, the Germans disarmed a minefield and broke through the perimeter barbed wire at Hill 209, the best observation point within the perimeter, so called because it was 209 metres above sea level.

The Germans managed to take fifteen defence posts, punching a hole 5 kilometres (3 miles) wide in the perimeter and gaining 5 kilometres of territory before minefields and British tanks stopped their advance.

The exercise ended with a counter-attack on the night of 3 May 1941, which recaptured one defence post and halted the German advance. One of the most celebrated actions of the siege occurred that night when Lieutenant William Noyes led a patrol, which stalked and destroyed three German light tanks, killed or wounded seven machine-gun crews, destroyed eleven artillery positions and their infantry supports, damaged a German heavy tank, and killed and wounded 130 enemy troops in taking a German garrison. This was mostly achieved in the initial bayonet charge and without loss. Noyes was awarded the Military Cross and knighted after the war.

A new perimeter was now established and the Axis forces had lost about 30 tanks and gained a semicircular piece of desert roughly 20 square kilometres (8 square miles) in size at a cost of 954 lives. Losses inside the garrison were almost equally severe, with 800 lives lost.

A huge convoy carrying 240 tanks and 40 Hurricane fighters reached Alexandria on 12 May and subsequently Wavell attempted to raise the siege by attacking from the east while Rommel's forces were engaged at Tobruk.

The first of these attempts, on 15 May, was codenamed 'Brevity'. It failed to recapture territory around the Egyptian border but did result in Rommel being ordered, by German Chief of Staff, Marshal Franz Halder, to leave the siege of Tobruk to the Italians and concentrate his efforts on engaging the British forces further east. This ensured a stalemate at Tobruk and renewed patrols and harassment during June succeeded in regaining about half of the territory lost in May.

Wavell's second attempt to bridge the 100-kilometre (62-mile) gap between the front line in Egypt and Tobruk was codenamed 'Battleaxe' and began on 15 June. After heavy fighting and fierce battles around Sollum and Fort Capuzzo and in the desert further south along the Egyptian–Libyan border, Rommel won the tactical struggle and the British were defeated at the Battle of Halfaya Pass on 17 June.

On 21 June, Churchill, having decided a fresh approach was needed for the campaign, replaced Wavell as Commander in Chief in the Middle East with Major General Sir Claude Auchinleck, previously Commander in Chief in India. It was a straight 'swap' with Wavell again taking up his previous post as Commander in Chief in India.

As midsummer approached Rommel noted in letters that thirst would win him Tobruk. Rations were low and each man received only half a litre of water per day. The Germans concentrated on attacking supply lines in an effort to starve the garrison into submission. To counter this, the garrison was reduced to 22,000 men.

Morshead made one final attempt to restore the perimeter on 2 August 1941. This was basically an artillery battle with 60 guns being used against German positions, which responded with heavy artillery fire, inflicting heavy losses on the Australians.

As a result of this action, which was effectively the last battle of the siege, Major General Morshead and General Blamey, commander of the AIF, made representations to the Australian War Cabinet and the new Labor Prime Minister John Curtin to strengthen requests to the British government that Australian troops at Tobruk be relieved.

Despite protests from Churchill that these requests would delay British plans to retake Libya, the 18th Brigade 7th Division was withdrawn in August to join the rest of the 7th Division in Syria. They were replaced by the Polish Carpathian Brigade.

Finally, after six months of sustained siege and constant fighting and bombardment, the 9th Division was withdrawn through September and October and replaced by the 70th British Division. The 9th was sent to re-equip in Syria, but they were to meet Rommel's army yet again a year later—at the second battle of El Alamein.

The last Aussies to leave Tobruk were the men of the 2/13th Battalion, whose convoy was forced to turn back during the relief operation due to an air attack. These men were still in Tobruk in the final weeks of November, when the third operation to break through from Egypt, codenamed 'Crusader', took place.

Major General Auchinleck had reorganised the North African campaign and the 'Western Desert Force' was transformed into the

Eighth Army, commanded by Lieutenant General Sir Alan Cunningham, in September 1941.

Operation Crusader was launched on 18 November 1941 and heavy engagement occurred on 20 November as British forces moved into Libya. The following day forces in the garrison began an operation to break out to the east and join up with the British forces moving westward. This meant Rommel was forced to fight on two fronts. Fighting was ferocious in the final week of November and losses of lives and tanks on both sides were heavy.

The 2/13th Battalion was called upon to regain lost ground at El Duda with a bayonet charge on 30 November and captured 167 prisoners at a cost of two men killed and five wounded.

Rommel re-established the blockade at the old perimeter on 1 December but the tide was turning as the British moved west. After one last failed attempt to take Tobruk in a massive attack on 4 December, Rommel withdrew his troops from the eastern side of the town. A British flanking move caused him to withdraw from the western perimeter and the whole area from Tobruk to Egypt on 7 December. The siege was over and the town was officially relieved on 10 December 1941.

On 16 December, the remaining men of the 2/13th Battalion finally left Tobruk by road to join their division in Syria. The eight-month siege had cost 832 Australian lives, with 941 Aussies taken prisoner and another 2177 wounded.

During the time that Tobruk was under siege, Greece and Crete fell to Hitler, Russia had been invaded and the Japanese had attacked Pearl Harbor. But, for the first time in the war, the German army had suffered a defeat, thanks to the 'Rats of Tobruk'.

WOUNDED FROM TOBRUK

'Tip' Kelaher

You come limping down the gangplank, or you're carried down
    instead,
Covered by a blanket, with a boot beneath your head,
And you all look lean and hungry underneath that Aussie grin,
Sick of bully beef and biscuits, but the sort that won't give in.

And you're smiled at by the bearer, who is muscular and big,
Fishing fags out of his pocket with a, 'Have a cigger, Dig?'
And you hold it while he lights it and you give the old, wry grin
And make little of your troubles, but there's no one taken in.

For we know what you've been through and there's nothing much
    to say,
You're a 'base job' or a 'Blighty' and they'll help you on your way;
For the sky was thick with 'zoomers' and the sandbags near you
    shook,
Like the beach 'neath Bondi boomers, when you blocked 'em at
    Tobruk.

And I'm proud that I'm Australian when I look at men like these,
They are men who marched beside me back at Ingleburn in
    threes,
In the days when life was rosy, full of laughter, leave and beer,
And I never thought I'd see them carried down the gangplank
    here.

Well, they've done their best for 'Blighty' and they've done their
    best for 'home',
And the girls they left behind them and the pals who could not
    come;
And may 'Aussie' not forget them, when they're invalided back,
Nor leave them poor and jobless on the dole queue or 'the track'.

THE LEGEND OF THE 'RATS'

When the siege of Tobruk ended in December 1941, the war in North Africa still had a year and a half to run. Many changes of fortune would take place before the decisive second battle of El Alamein, in October and early November of 1942, and the invasion of Tunisia by the British First Army and US forces under General Eisenhower. The eventual collapse of the Axis forces in Africa led to their final surrender in May 1943. Tobruk would change hands twice again before then.

The siege of Tobruk was a very 'Australian' affair. Almost two-thirds of the troops defending the garrison were Australians. There were about 15,000 Aussies and they provided virtually the whole of the infantry at Tobruk with the 12,000 British troops making up four artillery brigades.

It was a matter of great pride back home in Australia that Hitler's first defeat was suffered at the hands of Australian soldiers. An Australian, Major General John Lavarack, was in charge of the garrison defence at first and Major General Leslie Morshead, who succeeded him as garrison commander and led the 9th Division at Tobruk and El Alamein, is considered to be one of the two greatest generals Australia ever produced, ranked alongside Monash.

The name 'Rats of Tobruk' was taken from phrases used in the German propaganda radio broadcasts. These broadcasts were generically known as 'Lord Haw Haw' if broadcast by a male voice on medium wave from Hamburg into Britain. The two main broadcasters were the British-educated German, Wolf Mittler, and William Joyce, a British fascist who became a German citizen and was later captured and hanged after the war. Mittler also broadcast into North Africa as part of Radio

Berlin's 'Axis Sally' programs, which were fronted by the American Mildred Gillars.

In a propaganda move that backfired, Lord Haw Haw had referred to the garrison troops as 'poor desert rats of Tobruk' during radio broadcasts. The name was appropriate as the troops defending the garrison dug extensive tunnel networks and shelters to supplement their trenches. These were used as protection from air raids and also to launch surprise attacks. Patrols gathered equipment as soon as the enemy retreated. Huge amounts of mostly Italian vehicles and arms and equipment were taken by the Commonwealth troops in the early part of the campaign and the scavenging, salvaging and re-using of Italian and German arms and equipment was a feature of the Allied campaign in Libya and Egypt.

These factors no doubt led to the name 'Rats' being applied to the troops defending the garrison at Tobruk. Radio Berlin also described the Australians as 'caught like rats in a trap' during the siege.

What the German propaganda machine didn't realise, and perhaps could never understand, was the characteristic Australian affection for the underdog and the Aussie penchant for self-deprecating and ironic humour. The Australians troops gave themselves the nickname 'Rats of Tobruk' and wore the title as a badge of pride.

With typical Australian ironic wit, the men of the 9th Division removed metal from a German bomber, one they had shot down with a salvaged German gun, and made their own unofficial medal with a rat emblem. The 9th Division was also officially allowed to have all their badges and flashes shaped in the form of a 'T' after the siege of Tobruk.

The Australian media and general public loved the 'Rats of Tobruk'. The siege helped Australians at home to feel that the nation was playing a vital role in the war effort against Nazism. The resilience and risk-taking cheekiness of the 'Rats', in the face of overwhelming odds, gave a nation hope in the darkest hours of war. Their dry wit and unmistakable 'Australianness' were a source of pride and inspiration.

Here are the 'official' Rules of Cricket for a game played between Australia's 20th Brigade and Britain's 107 Royal Horse Artillery at Tobruk on 30 July 1941:

- **Rule 2.** Play to be continuous until 18:00 hours, except by interference by air raids. Play will NOT, repeat NOT cease during shellfire.

- **Rule 4.** Shirts, shorts, long socks, sand shoes if available. Helmets will not be worn or any other fancy headgear. Umpires will wear white coat (if available) and will carry loaded rifle with fixed bayonet.
- **Rule 6.** All players to be searched for concealed weapons before start of play, and all weapons found, other than ST grenades, Mills bombs, and revolvers will be confiscated. (This does not apply to umpires.)
- **Rule 8.** Manager will make medical arrangements and have ambulance in attendance.

I have no idea what happened to rules 1, 3, 5 and 7!

The 'Rats of Tobruk' held an almost sacred place within the ranks of returned servicemen in Australia and are remembered with almost the same reverence as the original Anzacs and traditionally received the loudest cheer at every Anzac Day march. There is the Rats of Tobruk Memorial in Canberra and the international Rats of Tobruk Association was responsible for official memorial services and the erection of numerous other monuments in Australia and the United Kingdom. The association also organised with the Royal Mint of Australia the striking of a 50-year anniversary medallion in 1991. *The Rats of Tobruk* movie, starring Peter Finch and Chips Rafferty and directed by Charles Chauvel, was a 1944 film that played a big part in establishing the legend in Australian hearts and minds.

In April 2007, the *Melbourne Age* reported that the Victorian contingent of the Rats of Tobruk Association reluctantly decided that it could no longer afford the upkeep of Tobruk House, the inner-city Melbourne meeting hall purchased by the association in the 1950s, when the Victorian branch had 2000 members.

By 2007, the 80 'Rats' who were left, all aged in their 80s and 90s, decided they had to sell the hall. From the sale, they hoped to raise $1.5 million to be used for research at the Royal Children's Hospital, Melbourne, where there is a Rats of Tobruk Neuroscience Ward.

Bill Gibbins, who made his wealth out of trucking, had seen reports of the 'Rats' deciding it was time to sell the Victoria Avenue property and felt it was a shame they should lose the home they had bought in the 1950s. At the auction he beat off four other bidders for the hall, but had to pay $400,000 above what anyone expected. He then told the veterans they could keep the hall as long as they liked.

Gibbins, whose father served for three years in the Middle East, but not at Tobruk, said, 'I went down there, shot my hand up and paid more than I ever intended, as you do at auctions . . . but everyone in Australia would have a feeling they should retain this place.'

TOBRUK

Anonymous

There's places that I've been in
That I didn't like too well;
Scotland's far too bloody cold
And Cairo's hot as hell.
English beer is always warm,
Each place has something crook.
But each is perfect when compared
To the place they call Tobruk.

I've seen some dust storms back at home
That made poor housewives work,
But there's enough inside our shirts
To smother all of Bourke.
Two diggers cleaned their dug-out,
Their blankets out they shook;
Two colonels perished in the dust,
In this place they call Tobruk.

There's centipedes like pythons,
And there's countless hordes of fleas;
As big as poodle dogs they are,
All snapping round your knees,
And scorpions like lobsters
Come round to have a look,
There's lots of bloody livestock
In this place they call Tobruk.

Now there's militant teetotallers,
Who abhor all kinds of drink.
There's wives who break good bottles
And pour grog down the sink.
This place would suit them to the ground,
We've searched in every nook,
But booze is scarce as hen's teeth
In this place they call Tobruk.

The shelling's nice and frequent,
They whistle overhead.
You go into your dug-out
And find shrapnel in your bed;
And when the stukas dive on us
We never stop to look,
We go down our holes like rabbits
In this place they call Tobruk.

Sometimes we go in swimming
And we float about at ease,
The water's clear as crystal,
There's a lovely ocean breeze,
Then down comes bloody Herman
And we have to sling our hook;
We dive right to the bottom
In this place they call Tobruk.

I really do not think this place
Was made for me and you,
Let's leave it to the Arab,
And he knows what he can do.
We'll leave this god-forsaken place
Without one backward look,
We've called it lots of other names,
This place they call Tobruk.

HERE WE BLOODY WELL ARE . . .

The occupation of historic Thermopylae Pass by men of the Anzac Corps lasted four days and ended with the Battle of Thermopylae on 24 April 1941.

It may not be as famous as the defence of the same pass against the Persians by Leonidas and his Spartans for three days in September 480 BC, but it was, nonetheless, a proud moment in Australasian military history.

Men of the 19th Brigade of the 6th Division AIF, commanded by Brigadier George Vasey, and the 6th Brigade of New Zealand's 2nd Infantry, led by Brigadier Harold Barrowclough, held the pass long enough to save the lives of thousands of Greek and Allied troops.

The year 1941 was a very bad one for the Allies. France had fallen, 'Fortress Europe' was in the hands of the Axis forces, British cities suffered nightly bombing raids, and Field Marshal Erwin Rommel's Panzer Tank Divisions had pushed the British Commonwealth forces back into Egypt.

In spite of British naval victories over the Italian fleet at the Battle of Calabria in July 1940 and the Battle of Taranto in November 1940, the Italian fleet attacked British naval convoys with the aid of German air support and U-boats.

Germany had mastery of the skies and seemed invincible on land with better equipment, technology, strategic skills and ruthlessness in all areas of warfare than the British and their allies.

The decision to invade Greece was made by Mussolini in a fit of pique after Hitler had invaded Romania without consultation.

An ultimatum, sent by Italian dictator Benito Mussolini and presented to the Greek prime minister, the dictator Ioannis Metaxas, by the Italian ambassador around 3 am on 28 October 1940 (after a party in the Italian embassy), was that Greece allow Axis forces to enter Greek territory and occupy strategic locations—or face war.

According to Greek legend, Metaxas allegedly answered with 'όχι'* (No) . . . or a simple short reply that implied the same thing.

His actual reply is reported to have been delivered in the diplomatic *lingua Franca* used between statesmen who did not share a common language—and it was, '*Alors, c'est la guerre.*' (Then, it's war.)

The point is that the reply was simple, stoic and laconic—in the true manner of Greek heroes**. Once it was known that Metaxas had said 'no', 'Όχι' became a rallying cry to all Greeks.

Much to Hitler's annoyance, and without his prior knowledge, Italian troops invaded Greece, crossing the border from Albania at 5 am that same day, 28 October. As soon as the news was known, the Greek population took to the streets, irrespective of their political affiliations, shouting, 'Όχι.'

From 1942 onwards, 28 October was celebrated as 'Όχι Day', at first among members of the Greek resistance and then by all Greeks world-wide. After World War II it became a public holiday in Greece and Cyprus. Many Greek towns and cities have an 'Όχι Square' or 'Όχι Park', much like we have 'Anzac' parks, roads, etc.

In 1939 Britain had agreed to assist Greece and Romania in the event of threats to their independence. Under this agreement Britain provided RAF squadrons in November 1940 in response to the invasion and the Greeks counter-attacked on 4 November. By 8 November the Italian troops were a retreating rabble, being pushed back over the border and, by 15 November, the Greek Third Army was well inside Albania.

(The Greek advance was so swift that one French town on the Riviera, Menton, near the Italian border, erected signs in Greek saying, 'This is French territory, Greeks. Do not advance any further.' I assume it was meant as a joke!)

With the consent of the Greek government, British forces were also dispatched to Crete on 31 October to guard the deepwater port of Souda Bay. This enabled the Greek government to redeploy the 5th Cretan Division to the mainland campaign (a move that would cause great tragedy and suffering when Hitler's paratroop divisions invaded Crete in May 1941).

The British navy also began laying mines in Greek waters to prepare themselves for an Italian naval invasion. But the Greeks had defeated the

Italians and driven them out of Greece within three weeks, before Britain could provide any other military help.

A stalemate between the Greek and Italian troops had the Greek forces occupying much of Albania, with no power changes until an Italian counter-attack failed in March 1941 and Germany again came to the aid of her Italian ally.

Greek Prime Minister Metaxas proposed to the British a joint offensive in the Balkans using the Greek strongholds in South Albania as the base of the operations. The British were reluctant because the deployment of the necessary troops would seriously weaken their position in North Africa.

The Greeks decided not to push further into Albania, instead they set about capturing strategic ports. Metaxas, who was keen to avoid Germany becoming involved, died after a short illness on 29 January 1941, and his successor Alexandros Koryzis accepted British help in the form of an expeditionary force.

So, at a meeting in Athens in February 1941, the British agreed to send a Commonwealth expeditionary force to Greece and more than 60,000 Commonwealth troops (British, Australians and New Zealanders) were sent to Greece from North Africa, including two-thirds of the Australian 6th Division.

Hitler's invasion of Hungary and Romania, 'Operation Marita', had begun in December 1940 with 24 divisions dispatched through Hungary toward Romania and the Balkans. As early as January, Hitler had 'asked' King Boris of Bulgaria to open his borders with Greece for German troops and, on 6 April 1941, German troops invaded Greece from Bulgaria. On the first day, the Germans made a devastating air attack on the Athenian port at Piraeus. Yugoslavia fell within days and the supply route to Greek forces on the Italian front in Albania was cut. This effectively split the Allied and Greek forces and left both armies vulnerable to the advance of the German Second and Twelfth Armies.

Despite the Greek and British earlier victories over Italian troops at the end of 1940, they had no real chance against the Germans as the campaign fought by the Greek army and the Commonwealth expeditionary forces was ill-planned and the outcome was inevitable and disastrous for the Allies.

The British, Australian and New Zealand troops, under the command of the British General Sir Henry Maitland Wilson, supported Greek forces against the Axis powers, but the Allied troops were vastly outnumbered.

The Greek army and almost 60,000 Commonwealth troops, including the Australian 6th Division under the command of Major General Iven Mackay, were transported from Africa in the first week of April 1941. They faced two German armies: the Twelfth, consisting of thirteen divisions, and the Second, with fifteen divisions, including four armoured divisions within each brigade.

Winston Churchill had attempted to improve the odds by making Turkey an ally but was unable to secure Turkish support for an Allied Balkan front against the Axis army.

Prime Minister Robert Menzies was uneasy about the operation and sought, unsuccessfully, to have it reassessed. The Australian and New Zealand governments, who provided most of the troops, were not privy to the planning of the operation.

The campaign was hindered by several factors: poor communications between the Greek and British commanders; the primitive road and rail system in Greece; the difficult terrain; and the speed and success of the German advance.

This is how Lieutenant General John Coates summed up the campaign:

> In almost every Allied campaign in the early part of the war, the bravery, fighting qualities and sheer dogged determination of the troops moderated the worst mistakes of the politicians and strategists. Greece was no exception.

On 6 April the German air attack, which practically destroyed the Athenian port of Piraeus, along with Yugoslavia's rapid capitulation and the cutting off of the Greek supply route to Greek forces in Albania, meant the Allies lost the initiative and never regained it.

Greece's second largest city, Thessaloniki, fell on 8 April and General Maitland Wilson, mindful of British losses at Dunkirk when France fell, ordered a retreat on 10 April.

Australian and New Zealand troops undertook some very successful local fighting, mostly notably at Vevi Pass near Mount Olympus, Tempe Gorge, near the town of Larissa, and Bralos Pass, near Thermopylae. These three battles were rear-guard actions fought in mountainous terrain to defend passes and hold the line against the advancing German troops and tanks while an orderly retreat was made to Athens.

The establishment of a defensive line between Mount Olympus and the Aliakmon River was part of the British withdrawal strategy. It became apparent, however, that a stoic resistance was necessary to ensure this plan worked in order to stop the obliteration of Greek troops in the Florina Valley.

A force of Australian infantry, with a New Zealand motorised battalion and a British armoured brigade, was hastily assembled under General Iven Mackay, commander of the Australian 6th Division. The whole force was known as 'Mackay Force'. This diverse combination was given the task of shoring up the left flank of the defensive line to prevent a Blitzkrieg-style advance by the elite German troops, which would have led to the breakdown of the orderly retreat. The Australian and New Zealand infantry brigades were called 'the Anzac Corps'.

At the Battle of Vevi (also known as the Battle of Klidi Pass) on 11 and 12 April, Brigadier George Vasey, commanding the Australian 19th Brigade, distinguished himself with brilliant placement of available troops and armour, which held up the advance of the elite SS Leibstandarte 'Adolph Hitler' Division for more than two days.

In near blizzard conditions, the defence was conducted with Vasey's own troops, a New Zealand machine-gun battalion and the British Motorised 1st Armoured Brigade, known as the 1st Rangers.

Despite the withdrawal of the 1st Rangers without Vasey's knowledge due to poorly established communication during a confused battle, a successful defence of Klidi Pass enabled an orderly southward movement of the defending forces, which prevented a complete collapse of the retreat and a rout of the Greek and Commonwealth armies.

Following the successful delaying tactic and rear-guard action at Vevi, a further action was required as German troops followed the retreating Commonwealth forces towards Larissa. At Tempe Gorge, the Australian 16th Brigade, under Brigadier Arthur Allen, defended a narrow valley long enough to prevent all British units to the north being cut off by advancing German mountain troops. This was achieved in a massive battle fought without any time to built weapon pits, earth mounds or a defendable headquarters. The 16th Brigade lost 80 men and 120 were taken prisoner.

With the coastal route blocked by New Zealanders and the 17th Australian Brigade blocking the western flank across the mountains, Vasey's brigade, aided by the New Zealand infantry's 6th Brigade, held

Bralos Pass for four days and bought time, once again, for a successful retreat to Athens. Vasey's famous 'order of the day' on 20 April was very Australian. It read: 'Here we bloody well are and here we bloody well stay.'

And the 19th Brigade did stay, along with the New Zealand 2nd Infantry 6th Brigade led by Brigadier Harold Barrowclough; defending the pass from massive onslaughts and fighting a pitched battle on 24 April until all units withdrew successfully on the eve of Anzac Day 1941.

The Australians and New Zealanders held out all day, destroyed fifteen German tanks and inflicted many casualties. The rear-guard then retreated towards the next defensive position at Thebes.

These battles prevented a rout and enabled the retreat of Allied troops down to Athens and south to the Peloponnese. The evacuation began on 24 April and more than 50,000 troops were removed in a massive naval operation over five successive nights from five embarkation points at Kalamata, Monemvasia and Nauplia on the Peloponnese, and Rafina and Porto Rafti to the east of Athens. During the evacuation the Luftwaffe sank 26 heavily laden troopships.

More than 26,000 weary Allied troops landed on Crete in the last week of April 1941. A number of small, isolated groups and individual Allied soldiers, who had been cut off from the retreat, were left behind in mainland Greece. Many of these escaped, largely due to the bravery and assistance of the Greek people.

The Greek Prime Minister, Alexandros Koryzis, had committed suicide on 18 April and, in an attempt to keep the Italians out of the occupation, the Greek forces surrendered to Germany in Macedonia, without any authority from Athens, on 21 April. Mussolini was furious and demanded the surrender be repeated two days later with Italian involvement.

The Italian and German forces joined up on their southward march on 24 April, after the Italians took the Perati Bridge across the Gulf of Corinth. Athens fell on 27 April.

The Allied expeditionary force losses were 3800 dead and more than 9000 taken prisoner. Virtually all equipment, ammunition, vehicles, armour and supplies were lost.

German losses amounted to 2200 dead or missing, and 3700 wounded.

Greek losses were 15,700 dead and 300,000 taken prisoner. More than 450,000 Greeks and Cretans would die during the next four years of German occupation, nearly 25,000 of them executed for assisting the Allies.

The Italians lost 28,800 dead or missing, and more than 50,000 wounded. A poignant statistic of the campaign for Italy was that 12,400 Italian soldiers were severely frostbitten.

Although the Northern Greek Army had already officially capitulated on 9 April, and General Zolakoglu surrendered in Western Macedonia on 21 April, some Greek units were still retreating south with Mackay Force and did fight in the actions around Vevi and Larissa, though none took part in the Battle of Thermopylae.

After the war, Aris Velouchiotis, leader of the People's Liberation Army, said it was an 'eternal shame' that the Greek army didn't defend Thermopylae.

Most of the Commonwealth troops evacuated would remain on the island of Crete for just a month before the next sad chapter in the saga unfolded. But that is another story.

Footnotes:
* 'όχι' is pronounced with short 'o' and gutteral 'ch' ('o—kee').
** When Philip of Macedon was conquering the Greek mainland in 345 BC, only the state of Laconia with its capital city of Sparta remained independent. Philip sent a message: 'You are advised to submit without further delay, for if my army defeats you, I will destroy your farms, slay your people, and raze your city to the ground.' The Spartan reply was one word: 'If'.

Philip and his son, Alexander the Great, both chose to leave Sparta alone. It is from the name Laconia that we get the word 'laconic'.

CRETE

The battle for Crete began with 'Operation Mercury', the first major airborne invasion in military history, by Hitler's crack paratroop brigades, on the morning of 20 May 1941. On the first day the Germans suffered dreadful losses, due in part to the Allies breaking the German secretive Enigma Code and discovering what the German plans were, although they failed to respond strongly enough to prevent the airfield at Maleme, in western Crete, falling into German hands on the second day. This enabled the Germans to fly in reinforcements and defeat the unprepared Allied forces in a battle that lasted just over a week. Once the Germans gained control of the airports, the battle for Crete was a formality.

The British had naval superiority and control of the deepwater base at Souda Bay. The Allies also had more troops on the island than the Germans. The island's garrison numbered 14,000 men and the battle-weary troops evacuated from the mainland numbered 25,000, and were poorly organised into hastily formed units. Cretan troops were mostly militia left behind when the island's best divisions were sent to fight on the mainland.

The Allied troops were under the command of the British-born New Zealand general, Bernard Freyberg VC, a hero of WWI and an inspirational leader who would later become governor-general of New Zealand and a lord. The forces at his command included the Cretan police force and remnants of the 12th and 20th Hellenic Army Divisions, who had escaped to Crete and were under British command, the New Zealand 2nd Division minus headquarters staff, the 19th Brigade of the Australian

6th Division, who had fought so valiantly at Vevi and Bralos Pass, the British 14th Infantry, and a composite Australian artillery battery.

Freyberg lacked heavy equipment, ammunition and armour, most of which had been lost in the evacuation of the mainland. He also had about 10,000 troops lacking any weapons or real purpose. He asked for these troops to be evacuated from Crete before the battle, but this had not been done when the invasion took place.

The Germans had air superiority, better equipment, elite trained troops (paratroopers and mountain divisions), and greater mobility with tanks and armoured cars. They also had a good leader in General Kurt Student and gained control of the airports early in the battle.

Freyberg knew the basic German battle plan and based his strategy on defence of the airfields along the north coast. He knew in advance that he had insufficient artillery for a defence and proposed making the airfields unusable in advance of the attack, in order to prevent the Germans landing heavy equipment and large numbers of troops. This, however, was vetoed by the British High Command who believed the invasion would fail.

Freyberg's lack of equipment and lack of detail in the intelligence he received meant his troops were as lightly armed as the German para-troopers and often in the wrong place to muster effective resistance.

The German troops had new lightweight machine guns and artillery to use against the Allies' standard Lee–Enfield rifles, Bren and Vickers machine guns and antique Greek rifles. There were only 25 outdated tanks on the island, many of which were non-operational, one anti-aircraft battery and very few trucks.

The Battle of Crete was also the first time invading German troops encountered mass resistance from civilians in WWII. Many German troops were bludgeoned to death with axes and spades as they landed or were shot as they descended. Casualties were so high among these elite forces that Hitler banned any further such operations.

The first German paratroopers landed at Canea (Chania/Xania), the second largest city in Crete, and at Maleme airfield, just to the west. The New Zealand battalions defending Maleme inflicted heavy casualties within the first hours of the invasion. One German battalion of the 1st Assault Regiment had 400 of its 600 men killed before the end of the first day. Many of the gliders following the paratroops were hit by mortars as they landed and the paratroopers were shot as they landed by the New

Zealand and Greek defenders. At first the Germans failed to take the airfield, but eventually they dug in and established defensible positions.

The second German wave arrived in the afternoon, attacking the towns of Retimo (Rethymno/Rethimno) and Iraklion (Irakleio/Heraklion/ Candia). As before, at Maleme and Canea, defenders were waiting for them and inflicted heavy casualties.

When night fell, the Germans had failed to achieve any of their objectives. Indeed, the plan to use surprise attacks in four places had caused huge losses and the universal and brutal civilian resistance had surprised and confounded the Germans.

The Cretans were renowned for their bravery and savagery through many centuries of fighting invading Phoenicians, Greeks, Romans, Turks and Venetians, as well as each other in tribal feuds. They engaged the German troops with ancient rifles last used against the Turks or whatever they could find in kitchens and barns. Many German parachutists were knifed or clubbed to death and the civilian population joined the Greek and Allied forces as a very effective militia.

The Germans responded with equal ferocity once they realised what they were up against. As far as the invading forces were concerned, civilian militias were not protected by the Geneva Convention. The occupation of Crete was a brutal and inhuman experience.

Late at night on 20 May 1941, the Germans attacked the strategic position overlooking Maleme airfield. Poor communication by the Allies led to the New Zealand infantry battalion defending the position being mistakenly withdrawn at night, giving the Germans control of the airfield just as a sea landing took place nearby, and the Axis commanders decided to concentrate their efforts on the Maleme sector.

By the afternoon of day two, units of the German 5th Mountain Division were being landed at Maleme. The German plan was for these troops to outflank the Allied troops through the rugged mountains south of the coast, while the paratroop divisions attacked eastward along the coast road. Iraklion was heavily bombed to prepare for the German push eastward.

Meanwhile, the British navy was attempting to repel German invasion forces that were sailing to the island from the port of Piraeus. These flotillas consisted of Italian warships and fleets of wooden *caïques* loaded with German troops and supplies. One flotilla was attacked by the British navy's D-Force and suffered huge losses, while another was forced to turn back by Admiral King's C-Force.

Although the invading forces were forced to turn back, C-Force suffered huge losses as it withdrew to Alexandria. Attacking from the air, German Junkers and Stukas sank two of the three cruisers and one of the four destroyers with huge loss of life; 722 men died on the cruiser HMS *Gloucester* alone.

The 5th British Destroyer Flotilla, consisting of five ships commanded by Lord Louis Mountbatten, sailed from Malta on 21 May to help defend Crete. These five small warships were to pick up survivors from the cruisers HMS *Gloucester* and HMS *Fiji* but were diverted to shell the Germans at Maleme and attack another invading flotilla of *caïques* off the north coast.

Three of the five destroyers then headed back to Alexandria but came under heavy air attack from 24 Stuka dive-bombers as they rounded the western side of Crete. HMS *Kashmir* sank in two minutes and HMS *Kelly* turned over and sank soon after. HMS *Kipling* survived 83 bombs, picked up 279 survivors from the other two ships and escaped. Noel Coward's famous wartime film, *In Which We Serve*, was based on this incident.

By 23 May the Allies began a series of defensive actions as the Germans gained control of the coastal roads. Australian troops were in action in the Souda Bay/Canea area and the 2/4th Battalion fought at Iraklion and killed 90 German paratroopers for the loss of just three men, but the most famous action from an Australian perspective was the Battle for Retimo.

Brigadier George Vasey had command of the central sector of defence based around Retimo. He had four battalions of the 19th Brigade (the 6th Division) and three Greek battalions at his command. At Retimo airfield he placed the 2/1st and 2/11th Battalions with the Greeks, under the command of Lieutenant Colonel Ian Campbell. These troops fought bravely and prevented the capture of the airfield, although they could not retain control of the roads into Retimo from the east and west. After Maleme fell, they were gradually isolated and continued to fight until eventually cut off.

In a famous and ferocious bayonet charge against the German 141st Mountain Regiment on the morning of 27 May, the New Zealand 28th (Maori) Battalion and the Aussie 2/7th and 2/8th Battalions cleared a section of road between Souda and Canea which enabled safe passage for some Allied troops to the south.

On the same day the British High Command in London decided Crete was lost and ordered Major General Freyberg to begin withdrawing all available troops to the south coast to be evacuated to Egypt. The order to withdraw failed to reach Lieutenant Colonel Campbell at Retimo. Unaware of the withdrawal, his Aussie and Greek troops continued fighting, mounting a huge, but unsuccessful, push to clear the roads on the night of 28 May after the bulk of the Allies had already been withdrawn. They were surrounded and surrendered on 30 May.

Some troops were evacuated from Iraklion and Souda Bay but the majority left from the south coast town of Sphakia. The troops retreated down the rugged mountain passes while the 8th Greek Regiment, composed of young Cretan recruits, gendarmes and cadets, poorly equipped and only 850 strong, protected their line of retreat. Fortunately, German intelligence overestimated the strength of the resistance and air strikes were being aimed at Retimo and Iraklion, allowing Allied troops to retreat down the mountain roads in relative safety.

Between 28 May and 1 June, 16,000 troops were evacuated to Egypt by a task force, which was constantly attacked en route by the Luftwaffe. The cruiser HMS *Calcutta* and the destroyers HMS *Greyhound*, *Hereward* and *Imperial* were lost during the evacuation. The Australian cruiser HMAS *Perth* was also hit and damaged.

More than 9000 Anzacs and thousands of Greeks were left behind to defend the remaining territory as best they could. They fought on until they were surrounded. The Germans took the cities of Iraklion and Retimo in the following days. Most British heavy equipment was destroyed in order to keep it from falling into enemy hands, but many troops, feeling they had let down their brave Greek allies, gave their guns and ammunition to the Cretans to help fight the Germans.

Late on 1 June most of the remaining 5000 troops at Sphakia surrendered. Many others took to the hills and harassed the German occupation force for years. An estimated 500 British Commonwealth troops remained at large over the next four years, along with many Greeks, who easily blended in with the Cretan population. British Intelligence officers landed secretly on Crete's south coast throughout the war and helped organise resistance. Most famously they organised the abduction of the German commander on Crete, General Kreipe. On 26 April 1944, he was kidnapped in his staff car from his headquarters and spirited away into the mountains. Three weeks later he was successfully taken off the island to Egypt and interrogated. He remained a prisoner of war in Canada until the war ended.

The Germans paid a high price for their victory: 4465 Germans are buried at Maleme Cemetery and, in total, 6600 German troops died on Crete. The Allies lost 3500 soldiers: 1751 dead, with an equal number wounded, as well as 12,254 Commonwealth and 5255 Greek captured. There were also 1828 dead and 183 wounded among the Royal Navy. After the war, the Allied graves were all moved to the Souda Bay War Cemetery.

The consequences of the invasion for the island population were horrific. Many Cretans were killed during the invasion and many more were shot by the Germans in reprisals, during the ten-day battle and in the occupation that followed. Official German records say 3474 Cretans were executed by firing squad. More than 1000 civilians were killed in massacres late in 1944 as the war was ending. Cretan sources put the number killed by German action at 6593 men, 1113 women and 869 children. Up to 13,000 homes were destroyed and another 12,000 partially destroyed.

Allied commanders were worried about the Germans using Crete as a springboard to attack Egypt, Malta and Cyprus. However, the huge losses sustained in capturing the island, along with the attack on Russia (Operation Barbarossa began on 22 June 1941), meant that German operations on Crete were confined to using the airfields and were largely defensive.

The huge losses among the German paratroops led Hitler to eliminate this strategy from his future planning. The failure of the British and Commonwealth army units to protect the airfield at Maleme led to the formation, in February 1942, of the RAF (Royal Air Force) Regiment, which was given responsibility for defending its own bases from ground and air attack.

Greece and Crete were costly operations for Australia. Almost 40 per cent of the Australian troops in Greece on 6 April 1941 were either killed, wounded or became prisoners of war. Australian Prime Minister Menzies had sought unsuccessfully to have the plan reassessed and the Australian and New Zealand governments, who provided most of the troops, had no part in planning the operation. It seemed like Gallipoli all over again, this time with the familiar face of Churchill in the background, and was a factor in the change of government, with Menzies losing government to Curtin and the Australian Labor Party.

There was a certain bitterness back home about the way Aussies and New Zealanders were used as cannon fodder in Europe, which was later exacerbated after Pearl Harbor in December 1941 and the fall of Singapore in February 1942. The public feeling that our troops should be defending home soil, expressed in the Australian media at the time, probably helped the new Labor Prime Minister, John Curtin, stick to his guns and win his famous battle to have the 6th and 7th Divisions returned to Australia when Churchill tried to divert them to Burma to protect British interests there.

Many Australian soldiers felt we let the Greeks down and many others felt they owed their lives to the brave Greeks who fought beside them and kept them out of German hands at great risk to themselves during the occupation. The respect and friendship that developed between our troops and their Greek comrades probably helped establish some acceptance for the large migrant intake of Greeks into Australia after WWII. Today the Greek community is a much loved and well-respected part of our Australian society.

The Greek campaign was a harsh and bitter one for Australians and New Zealanders, as a visit to Souda Bay War Cemetery will attest. Not only was it a lost cause and a failure, it was a campaign of which our own generals had disapproved.

The brutal experiences of the German occupation left generations of Cretans emotionally scarred, and led to widespread and enduring hatred of the Germans, that still lingers today. In 2004 a Cretan taxi driver told me that when a German couple occupied a holiday house in his village the previous summer, he and his family, along with others, had moved out of the village until the Germans left.

THE 68-YEAR MYSTERY OF HMAS *SYDNEY*

The second HMAS *Sydney* was a modified Leander class light cruiser, although she was more often called a Perth class. She was built at Wallsend-on-Tyne in the United Kingdom in 1933 as HMS *Phaeton*. In 1934, before launching, she was purchased by the Australian government and renamed in memory of the earlier HMAS *Sydney*.

Her armaments included four twin-mounted 150-mm (6-inch) guns, four 100-mm (4-inch) anti-aircraft guns, three Vickers machine-gun nests and eight torpedo tubes. She also carried a catapult-launched seaplane. These light cruisers were designed for speed and long campaigns at sea, and many experts felt they were inadequately armoured to engage in battles with ships carrying substantial weaponry.

HMAS *Sydney*'s design had a number of problems: her guns did not have shields, her anti-aircraft guns lacked firepower and her main guns could not be aimed effectively if power was lost. In 1938, a report to the Australian Commonwealth Navy Board stated that *Sydney*'s gun systems were extremely vulnerable to gunfire and bombs, even of small calibre. These problems were fixed on the sister ship HMAS *Hobart* but not on *Sydney*.

In October 1935, HMAS *Sydney* sailed for Australia but was diverted to help enforce the League of Nations' blockade against Italy until January 1936. She finally arrived in Australia in August 1936. Her initial WWII duties consisted of Indian Ocean escorts but when Italy joined the war, she was sent to join the 7th British Cruiser Squadron based at Alexandria in Egypt. On 21 June 1940, *Sydney* took part in the bombardment of Bardia and is also credited with the sinking of the Italian destroyer *Espero* when a large British convoy heading for Alexandria came across a smaller Italian convoy on 28 June.

Less than a month later, on 19 July 1940, at the Battle of Cape Spada, HMAS *Sydney* engaged the Italian light cruisers *Bartolomeo Colleoni* and *Giovanni dalle Bande Nere*. The *Bartolomeo Colleoni* was crippled by *Sydney* and then finished off by torpedoes from British destroyers HMS *Hyperion* and *Ilex*.

In this action, HMAS *Sydney* received the only damage of her Mediterranean campaign, when a shell penetrated one of her funnels. This strategically important battle gave the British navy control of the Aegean and Eastern Mediterranean. On 27 July 1940, *Sydney* was involved in the sinking of the tanker *Ermioni*, which was carrying fuel to an Italian garrison in the Aegean and, on the night of 11 November, she and three other destroyers attacked an Italian convoy, drove off the escorting battleships and sank all of the four merchant ships in the Battle of the Strait of Otranto.

HMAS *Sydney* returned to Australia and, after a stopover in Fremantle, reached Sydney Harbour. School children were given a holiday to see the crew of their city's namesake parade through the city on 27 February 1941. Captain John Collins, who had commanded the ship through the Mediterranean campaign, handed over command of the vessel to Captain Joseph Burnett, a senior naval officer who had never commanded a battleship in wartime, and the refitted HMAS *Sydney* left in May for its new base in Fremantle, to carry out patrol and escort duties in the Indian Ocean.

On 11 November 1941, HMAS *Sydney* left Fremantle to escort the troopship *Zealandia* part of the way to Singapore. On 17 November, near Sunda Strait, *Sydney* handed over the escort job to HMAS *Durban* and turned back to Fremantle.

At about 4 pm on 19 November, somewhere west of Shark Bay, about 250 kilometres (155 miles) south-west of Carnarvon, HMAS *Sydney* sighted a vessel sailing north at a distance of about 20 kilometres (12 miles). Captain Burnett needed to investigate all shipping in the area and, when the strange ship was seen making a significant change in course, he ordered action stations and altered course to close in on her.

The vessel they had sighted was the disguised German raider *Kormoran*. This ship was capable of 'posing' as many vessels and, at the time she was spotted by HMAS *Sydney*, her disguise was that of a Dutch freighter, the *Straat Malakka*.

Kormoran was built in 1938 as the merchant ship *Steiermark*. Renamed *Schiff 41* for operational purposes and named *Kormoran* by her new captain, Theodor Detmers, she was refitted, in October 1940, as a *hilfskreuzer* or 'auxiliary cruiser', also known as a 'disguised freighter'. *Schiff 41/Kormoran* was the largest of the eleven German raiders used in this fashion by Hitler's navy in WWII. She sailed under a number of disguises, choosing to model herself on different ships from each area in which she operated.

Captain Theodor Detmers was a very able and battle-hardened German naval officer. At 39 years of age, he was the youngest of the German raider captains and had visited Australia as an officer on the German training cruiser *Koln* in 1932 and had great regard and affection for Australians. The captain celebrated his 39th birthday at sea, in August 1941, by issuing rum to the Australian crew members of the freighter *Mareeba*, who were prisoners aboard *Kormoran* after their vessel was sunk by her several weeks earlier. Later that day he had appeared in person with more rum, chatted and drank with the Australians and conducted an impromptu concert.

Schiff 41/Kormoran's hidden armaments included six 150-mm (6-inch) guns; six anti-aircraft guns, six torpedo tubes and two seaplanes, but she lacked the armoured protection, fire safety systems and speed of a proper warship. Between December 1940 and May 1941 *Schiff 41/Kormoran* had sunk seven Allied merchant ships in the South Atlantic and captured another that was sent to occupied France as a prize.

The raider then moved into the Indian Ocean, where she sank three ships between April and November 1941. She was cruising off the west coast of Australia, disguised as the Dutch freighter *Straat Malakka*, before heading for a planned move to the South Pacific, when she was sighted by HMAS *Sydney*.

Realising he was in trouble, and no match for a battlecruiser, Detmers knew he had to rely on disguise. He had groups of sailors walk the decks in civilian clothing, altered course to present his stern to the oncoming cruiser, and slightly increased his speed. Detmers later claimed to have not understood the normal signal *N.N.J.* ('show your identification letters') which was repeatedly flashed in Morse code from the cruiser. This may have been true as the signal was normally a flag signal and, when used in Morse, needed a prefix, which was not used on this occasion by *Sydney*'s signalmen.

When HMAS *Sydney* flashed 'what ship?', Detmers replied by flag signals, rather than Morse. He did this deliberately, realising the more confusion his flag signals created and the longer he took to respond to the enemy's signals, the fewer awkward questions he would have to answer. He replied to the 'what ship?' demand by hoisting the signal-code pennant halfway, meaning, 'I can see your signal, but I can't make out what it is.' When the signal was repeated *Kormoran* replied, very slowly, first with one flag missing, and then with several tangled flags, that she now understood. This was followed, a little later, by a recognition signal.

Sydney, now 12 kilometres (7 miles) away, flashed a further signal asking 'port of destination?' Detmers, who couldn't understand why the enemy ship was maintaining radio silence and why he hadn't yet been asked to heave to, replied 'Batavia' (now Jakarta).

The cruiser continued to close in on the *Kormoran*, while flashing another signal, 'nature of cargo?' The answer, 'piece goods', was signalled so inefficiently and slowly that it was probably incomprehensible.

To add to the confusion, at about 5 pm, Detmers raised the Dutch flag and transmitted a '*QQQ Straat Malakka*' ('suspicious ship approaching') distress signal.

This message, sent twice, was a ruse designed to be picked up by the HMAS *Sydney*, as it no doubt was. The message was picked up at several places on the Western Australian mainland and was acknowledged by the Perth station.

Officers on the bridge of the *Kormoran* were amazed at *Sydney*'s lack of caution in approaching an unidentified ship. They waited for the cruiser to call their bluff by requesting their secret call sign letters, which, of course, Detmers did not know.

Finally the request came and Detmers hoisted the letters 'IK', which he had correctly guessed was part of *Straat Malakka*'s four-letter secret call sign. The cruiser was so close that the Germans could see members of her crew leaning on the rails staring at this strange 'Dutch' freighter. The cruiser repeated the demand for the secret letters to be clearly shown. HMAS *Sydney* was now sailing directly abeam of the *Kormoran* at a greatly reduced speed and at a range of less than 1000 metres (3280 feet).

At that point, exactly 5.30 pm, Commander Detmers struck the Dutch flag, ran up the German colours, removed his camouflage and opened fire with all six of the *Kormoran*'s 150-mm (6-inch) guns. This was all achieved in less than ten seconds. Because HMAS *Sydney* was so close, Detmers was also able to use his anti-aircraft guns and torpedoes at the same time. The first salvo from the *Kormoran* took out *Sydney*'s bridge and gun control tower and destroyed her seaplane before it could be launched. As the raider's second salvo was fired, the cruiser opened up with a full eight-gun broadside but, due to her being so close, *Sydney*'s return fire passed harmlessly high over the *Kormoran*'s stern.

The second salvo from the German raider knocked out the Australian battlecruiser's forward guns, while a torpedo hit her just forward of amidships, right underneath the disabled forward-gun turrets. The *Kormoran* then fired eight salvos in succession, at six-second intervals, without any fire coming back, due to the damage done to the enemy's fire-control centre. It was virtually impossible for the German gunners to miss, with shell after shell scoring direct hits. The *Kormoran*'s anti-aircraft guns pumped shells into the cruiser's bridge and German machine-gun fire swept *Sydney*'s upper decks, preventing her crew from manning anti-aircraft weapons and torpedo batteries.

When *Sydney*'s rear-gun turrets finally came into action, she returned fast and accurate fire, hitting the *Kormoran*'s funnel, starting a fire below decks and disabling her engine room. With the *Sydney*'s bow low in the water and the *Kormoran*'s engines failing, the Australian ship made an attempt to ram and destroy the German vessel, but passed just astern and headed off to the south after firing four torpedoes that all missed their target. Detmers fired one last torpedo at the crippled cruiser, which missed, and continued to fire on her until she was 10 kilometres (6 miles) away.

The *Kormoran* had fired more than 450 shells and scored at least 50 direct hits. The crippled and battered HMAS *Sydney* disappeared over the horizon with her forward midship section ablaze. It seems she sank suddenly when her severely damaged bow broke off in heavy seas, 23 kilometres (14 miles) south of the *Kormoran*.

At 6.30 pm the German raider ceased firing at the stricken cruiser, and realising the serious state of his ruined vessel, Detmers ordered the crew to abandon ship.

The *Kormoran* was carrying more than 300 mines to be laid in enemy waters. With the fire in the engine room and below decks out of control, Detmers knew the ship was a floating time bomb. Sixty of the raider's crew of 397 died in the battle, mostly in the fire which engulfed her control room and engine room. The rest of the crew, along with prisoners and others on board at the time, all abandoned ship in an orderly fashion and took to rafts and lifeboats by around 9 pm.

Several officers stayed on board to make sure the boat was damaged enough to ensure it would sink when the mines exploded. They then set scuttling charges as they had done many times before on ships they had captured and sunk. Detmers was last to leave the ship at around 11.45 pm. Just after midnight the *Kormoran* exploded spectacularly, showering the sea around the lifeboats and rafts with metal fragments and sending a gigantic sheet of flame a thousand feet into the night sky. Her bow lifted into the air and she slid slowly backwards into the sea.

Of the crew and prisoners who left *Kormoran*, 40 perished when their overcrowded raft capsized, 103 reached Carnarvon by lifeboat, and 212 were rescued by various vessels that were in the area at the time, or that later joined the search for the HMAS *Sydney*. Among these rescue vessels were the freighters HMAS *Trocas* and HMAS *Centaur* (later requisitioned by the Australian navy, converted to a hospital ship and infamously sunk by a Japanese submarine), the troopship *Aquitania* (once the world's premier Cunard liner), the Australian government vessel *Koolinda* and the HMAS *Yandra*. There were 315 survivors from the *Kormoran*.

Nine days after the battle, a Carley lifefloat, clearly damaged by shrapnel, was discovered by HMAS *Heros*, which had joined the search. In February 1942, another Carley float from HMAS *Sydney*, containing an unidentifiable body, washed ashore on Christmas Island, which was then under Japanese occupation.

Nothing else was found of the HMAS *Sydney*, or her crew of 645, for another 67 years.

––––––

Theories abounded over the years about the way HMAS *Sydney* was lost, from lurking submarines (both German and Japanese—although Japan had not entered the war at that point) to a second German raider. All these are fanciful at best. But one question remains, why did Captain Burnett put his warship in such a vulnerable position?

Some military historians believe Captain Burnett mistook the disguised raider for an unarmed German supply ship.

HMAS *Sydney*, like all warships, carried a book of information on enemy warships, supplied by naval intelligence. It contained a photo of the *Schiff41/Kormoran*, also known to the Allies as '*Raider G*'. The photo was taken, however, prior to her conversion to a 'disguised freighter' or 'auxiliary cruiser'. It was a photo of her when she was the *Steiermark*.

Also, it was not a good photo. It showed the ship riding high in the water, where the *Kormoran* sat low. It showed the wrong number of Sampson poles and a stern that looked like a half counter-half cruiser, not the full cruiser stern the *Kormoran* actually had in 1941. Perhaps the photo caused the officers on HMAS *Sydney* to think the *Kormoran* was actually a supply ship they knew was working in the area out of a base in Japan, supplying U-boats and raiders.

This ship was the *Kulmerland*, a very similar ship to the *Kormoran* with a full cruiser stern. More importantly, the *Kulmerland* was known to be unarmed and was known to operate in Australian waters, usually disguised as the Japanese steamer *Tokyo Maru*.

The *Kulmerland* was *Kormoran*'s Indian Ocean 'mother ship'. Less than a month previously, the two vessels had rendezvoused west of Cape Leeuwin and spent a week resupplying the *Kormoran* at sea. Detmers had also transferred a large number of prisoners, survivors of the ships they had sunk, to the *Kulmerland*, to be taken to Germany.

Information gained from survivors after the sinking of another German raider, the *Pinguin*, in May 1941, by HMS *Cornwall*, caused British Naval Intelligence Service to issue an intelligence report on German raiders, on 30 May 1941. This report outlined the tactics of the 'auxiliary cruisers' and their methods of communication, and it also described each ship, giving her original identity, alternative names, known disguises and appearance.

While descriptions of most of the raiders were quite comprehensive, the report gave little information on '*Raider G*', the *Schiff 41/Kormoran*. In fact, she was quite wrongly described as having a '*squat funnel in the centre of a rather high superstructure*', with a '*half-cruiser, half-counter*' stern. She was, in fact, specifically reported to resemble 'a modified *Kulmerland*'. Perhaps the faulty photo and misleading description caused the *Kormoran* to be misidentified as the *Kulmerland*, the unarmed German supply ship. If Captain Burnett, whom it is assumed had read the intelligence report of 30 May, believed *Kormoran* was the *Kulmerland*, the whole tragic scenario is explicable.

The pretence about identity and the unreadable signal would have been logical. It would have been a quite normal and expected ploy to gain time to scuttle the ship and prevent her falling into enemy hands, which was a common practice. It also explains HMAS *Sydney*'s haste to get to the *Kormoran*, to prevent her being scuttled and take her as a prize. And it also explains why the warship came along broadside to the raider; this would have been the normal practice when sending a boarding party. It even explains why *Sydney*'s first salvo missed completely, as her guns would have been set to miss in order to scare an unarmed enemy ship into surrendering and not attempting to scuttle. As there were no officially reported messages from *Sydney* at all, it will never be known what Captain Burnett believed

However, there is nothing to disprove this theory. Indeed, an unsubstantiated claim, made by Chief Petty Officer Robert Mason, that a signal *was* received from the HMAS *Sydney* at the Naval Communications Station HMAS *Harman* in Canberra, would seem to add credence to the theory. Mason claimed that the message from HMAS *Sydney* said that she had 'bailed up a queer fellow in the Indian Ocean'. Subsequent searches of archives years later have failed to find any record of this message. However, given the secrecy and cover-up that occurred in the weeks following *Sydney*'s disappearance, and the huge number of messages flowing through the radio station at the time, there is no real evidence to say that Mason was lying.

A handwritten air force intelligence file also appeared to give substance to Mason's claims. It reported that a message alleged to be from HMAS *Sydney* was heard on short-wave radio at the Esplanade Hotel in Geraldton in Western Australia. These notes are claimed to have been seen by a Mr Gordon Laffer on an official file that 'was allegedly sent to Canberra after the war' and lost.

We can only assume that the *Kormoran*'s first salvo destroyed HMAS *Sydney*'s wireless communications and, therefore, any false assumptions about the identity of *Sydney*'s nemesis, or indeed her fate, could never be substantiated.

The aftermath

As news of the *Sydney*'s fate filtered through from the German survivors picked up by various vessels, official reactions appear to have been confused and disbelieving. The shock and sense of bewilderment is reflected in the fact that, for twelve days, the government maintained the strictest secrecy, issuing eleven censorship notices preventing the publication of information about the disappearance of the cruiser.

Three radio stations had their broadcasting licences suspended for contravening a 48-hour ban on broadcasting the known details and the prime minister's public statement on 1 December 1941 did little more than confirm the widely circulating rumours that HMAS *Sydney* had been sunk. In a message to his minister on the same day, the Secretary of the Department of the Navy advised that the number of survivors from the *Kormoran* should not be published 'in view of the effect on next of kin, relatives and friends of personnel of HMAS *Sydney*'. When no explanation was given as to how HMAS *Sydney* and her full complement had disappeared, virtually without trace, while 315 men from the *Kormoran* survived, conspiracy theories and anti-German sentiment began to grow via the media and public debate raged all through the war years and beyond.

Despite this ongoing interest, the official reaction was silence. A Navy Office investigation of the *Sydney*'s loss concluded in early 1942 and, apart from two brief public statements by the prime minister on 1 and 3 December 1941, two weeks after the sinking, no further information was officially released until publication in 1957 of the official history of the Royal Australian Navy in World War II.

The official history did little to satisfy those seeking answers to a number of questions. How was it that more than 300 survivors of the German raider were rescued, while all 645 men on board HMAS *Sydney* were lost? How could the HMAS *Sydney*, with such superior firepower and armour, have been sunk by the *Kormoran*? Why did the *Sydney* send no distress signal? Why did the *Sydney*'s captain seemingly expose his ship to danger by approaching the *Kormoran* at such close quarters? Why did *Sydney* not launch her aircraft? With all *Sydney*'s guns and torpedoes trained on the *Kormoran*, how did the raider have time to remove her camouflage, hoist the German flag and still fire the first shot?

The issue of the surviving German crew was a very sensitive one and four months after HMAS *Sydney*'s disappearance, a War Cabinet meeting referred officially to the '200 German survivors', when there were in fact 315, all of whom had been interrogated.

In spite of the German accounts being seemingly honest and accurate to the best of the survivors' knowledge, the official records and public opinion show a reluctance to accept the facts as offered up by crew of the *Kormoran*. Conspiracy theories about a second ship, Japanese submarines and Detmers not following the rules of fair combat abounded until the discovery of the wreck in 2008 and the report that followed in 2009.

The surviving members of the *Kormoran*'s crew were interned in Australia for more than five years, during which time Detmers was promoted to the rank of *Kapitän zur See* (the most senior of officer ranks of the German navy) in absentia and awarded the Nazi decoration of the Knight's Cross. The survivors, including Detmers, were interrogated separately in Perth and later taken to POW Camp 13, at Dhurringile near Murchison, in Victoria. On the night of 10 January 1945, Detmers led nineteen others in an escape from Dhurringile camp through a 120-metre (394-foot) tunnel they excavated from the camp's music room. Detmers was among the last of the group recaptured at Shepparton a week later.

Detmers was obviously a resolute leader and appears to have had a strong sense of fair play. Seven days after his recapture, while still in punitive detention, he was granted an interview with the Swiss consul during which he complained about his accommodation, the lack of light in his cell, and the refusal of his request for a daily issue of fresh fruit.

There is no record of the *Kormoran* ever firing unnecessarily on ships or abandoning the survivors of ships she sank. Indeed, the opposite appears to be the case, prisoners were well treated aboard the *Kormoran* and all efforts to save lives were made before ships were sunk. Having said that, the *Kormoran* had never before encountered such a fearsome foe as HMAS *Sydney*. Nevertheless, no charges were ever brought against Detmers in relation to his action against HMAS *Sydney*, despite some obvious media and public suspicion and accusations about possible 'foul play'. There is even an account of the interned crew of *Kormoran* attempting to donate money to the family of one of the crew of *Sydney* after reading about their distressed state in the local press. The offer was refused by military prison authorities. (There is also an account of the family of one of those lost on HMAS *Sydney* tending to the grave of a *Kormoran* crew member who died after being rescued and was buried at Geraldton.)

The crew of the *Kormoran* were the last prisoners of war to be released from internment in Australia and, when the Australian government finally released Detmers and his crew on 21 January 1947, it was nearly seventeen months after the end of the war. Many think this prolonged internment was a form of revenge. Detmers' health never fully recovered from his internment, during which he suffered two minor strokes. On his return to Germany he was declared unsuitable for service in the post-war *Bundesmarine*. Partially disabled by the strokes, Detmers lived out the rest of his life in Hamburg, wrote a book about his wartime experiences, *The Raider Kormoran*, and died, aged 74, in 1976.

At least one *Kormoran* survivor, Austrian Bill Elmecker, returned to live in rural Victoria with his wife after the war and was still alive, aged 85, when the wrecks were found in 2008.

The loss of HMAS *Sydney* with all hands accounted for more than 35 per cent of the RAN's servicemen killed in action between 1939 and 1945. With such a relatively small population in Australia at that time, the personal tragedy suffered by the families and friends of the crew was felt by the whole nation: almost everyone knew someone who knew someone on HMAS *Sydney*.

Because of the fame of HMAS *Sydney*'s predecessor and its feats in the Mediterranean during WWI, she held a special place in the nation's heart and this public sentiment was reflected at the highest levels. In a meeting of the War Cabinet, the official note-taker recorded one minister commenting, 'There'll always be a *Sydney*.'

During and after the war, there were rumours and claims of incompetence and cover-ups. Were messages sent by HMAS *Sydney* not heard due to laziness and poor practice? Chief Petty Officer Mason, who was working at HMAS *Harman* at the time, claimed later that 'there certainly was another and last message and indeed a number of people actually heard it at a distance as the headsets lay on the desk— the operator had briefly left the ship–shore channel unmonitored, with both headsets lying on the desk—three or four people including a couple of WRANS heard a short message being transmitted but being several yards away could not recognise it'. As operators leaving their headsets was a serious breach of operations room protocol, the staff, according to this theory, were sworn to secrecy. Subsequent attempts to locate the signal log for HMAS *Harman* for the relevant period, in the National Archives of Australia, the Australian War Memorial, the Naval Historical Section in the Department of Defence and the archives of HMAS *Harman*, have failed. The whereabouts of the records remains unknown.

Why were records of supposed messages received and official statements made at the time 'lost' after the war? Why was there no official court of inquiry? Was her captain, a senior officer with no battle experience, simply incompetent? Was Captain Detmers a liar and a cheat? Debate about the mystery of the *Sydney*'s loss continued unabated after the war. A beautiful memorial and information centre set up near Geraldton has become a must-see experience for Australians touring Western Australia and many books and articles have been written attempting to make sense of the incident.

As technology improved in the 1980s and famous wrecks such as that of the *Titanic* and *Bismarck* were discovered, speculation about solving the mystery of HMAS *Sydney* began to grow once more. As early as 1981, the Western Australian Museum and the Royal Australian Navy had begun examining magnetic anomalies off the coast near Zuytdorp Cliffs, just north of the mouth of the Murchison River at Kalbarri.

In November 1991, the 50th anniversary of the ship's loss, the museum conducted a seminar designed to see if HMAS *Sydney* could be located. While the position of the battle given by Detmers meant that the wreck of the *Kormoran* was a relatively easy target for discovery with new technology, doubt existed as to the whereabouts of HMAS *Sydney*. This meant any search area would be so big as to be impractical and costly to cover.

Although the evidence given by German survivors of the battle was more or less consistent, it was also varied and confused to a certain extent. This was due to the different experiences and positions of the crew members of *Kormoran* after the battle and the sinking of their own ship and also, no doubt, to the fallible memory and honesty of each survivor. Since 1941 various theories had existed. One was that the damaged cruiser had tried to get to the nearest dry dock in Surabaya, another that it had tried to make for the coast or headed towards the nearest port facilities at Geraldton. Some German accounts stated HMAS *Sydney* had sunk while they rowed towards its burning hulk after they abandoned ship; others said that it had disappeared into the night on a south-easterly course.

In 1997, as a result of pressure from the newly formed HMAS *Sydney* Foundation Trust and many politicians, a parliamentary inquiry was held. It took submissions from hundreds of parties and made a number of findings and recommendations. The inquiry concluded the following:

- No documents had been maliciously destroyed.
- The *Kormoran*'s torpedoes were an important factor in the battle.
- It was common practice at the time to close in on unknown ships to prevent their crews from scuttling them.
- There was no evidence of Japanese involvement.
- Attempts should be made using DNA to identify the unknown sailor on Christmas Island.

And, most importantly:

- The newly formed HMAS *Sydney* Foundation Trust should coordinate a search for the wrecks centring on the position identified by the Western Australian Museum's seminar in 1991.

Although a navy seminar in 2001 examined the conflicting evidence and advised against conducting a search, the HMAS *Sydney* Search Pty Ltd organisation planned an attempt to locate the wrecks in conjunction with successful deepwater wreck hunter David Mearns, the man who had found the wreck of the HMS *Hood*, the pride of the Royal Navy in the early period of WWII.

In spite of theories that the sinkings may have occurred much further south, or even west of the Abrolhos Islands, money for the official search was provided by the federal government, the states of Western Australia and New South Wales, and private funding and, on 12 March 2008, the wreck of *Kormoran* was found approximately where Detmers had said it would be. On 16 March 2008, the wreck of HMAS *Sydney* was found 12 nautical miles (22 kilometres) away from that of the *Kormoran*, approximately 100 nautical miles (185 kilometres) west of the coast at a depth of 2469 metres (8100 feet). Both wrecks were immediately protected under the *Historic Shipwrecks Act 1976* and the site of the HMAS *Sydney* was declared a war grave.

A Commission of Inquiry into the loss of HMAS *Sydney* was held following the finding of the wrecks, since no formal Board of Inquiry or Commission of Inquiry had previously been held. In a report released on 12 August 2009, the commission concluded that *Sydney* had been lost because Captain Joseph Burnett made an error in judgement and ordered the cruiser to approach *Kormoran* under the protocols for approaching 'innocent' ships instead of those for 'suspicious' ships and without going to action stations.

In spite of this conclusion, the commission did not find Burnett to be negligent and it also found that German accounts of the battle were accurate and confirmed by observations of the wrecks. The commission also stated that there was no evidence to support the conspiracy theories surrounding the ship's loss. This finally put to rest any suggestion that Detmers had committed a war crime by opening fire while still displaying a false flag.

LOST WITH ALL HANDS

Peter Mace

Her hull was laid down on a far distant shore,
When the threat to world peace was too great to ignore,
Designed for a purpose, and that purpose was war,
The dockyards were building the *Sydney*.

Launched when the great depression held sway,
In action to keep the Italians at bay,
By blockading the ports in the Med, far away,
From her namesake, the city of Sydney.

With the world now at war the real work has begun,
Against Germany now, soon Japan's rising sun,
The *Bartolomeo* felt her twin six-inch guns,
The day she was sunk by the *Sydney*.

Steaming down south to the west of Shark Bay,
A freighter is seen at the close of the day,
With the flag of the Dutch flying there on display,
But a raider is stalking the *Sydney*.

The Captain approached what he thought was a friend,
But the one thousand yards is too close to defend,
Then the flag of the Reich on the mast did ascend,
And all hell breaks loose on the *Sydney*.

Taking water and burning she turns on the hun,
Returning her fire, 'These colours won't run',
Determined to finish what she has begun,
She fought to the end did the *Sydney*.

The battle is over, both ships drift in haze,
The *Kormoran* scuttled and *Sydney* ablaze.
The painful conclusion, made after six days,
All hands have gone down on the *Sydney*.

————

The bronze woman stands gazing, grief etched on her face,
Symbolizing the mothers and wives who, with grace,
Had waited for news on the last resting place,
Of their loved ones who served on the *Sydney*.

————

It was just a dark smudge on a video screen,
But the hunters were cheering for what they had seen,
Then the thoughtful reflection on what it may mean
Had they found the wreck of the *Sydney*?

A nation had waited sixty-seven long years,
Long after the loved ones had shed all their tears,
Then a shadowy shape on the sonar appears
And reveals the wreck of the *Sydney*.

A cold watery grave for captain and crew.
No one will ever know what they went through,
When the *Kormoran*'s guns and torpedoes flew,
Straight into the heart of the *Sydney*.

The fate of six hundred and forty-five men
Remembered in silence by the Navy, and when
The wreaths were cast out, the priest whispered, 'Amen,'
And they prayed for the souls of the *Sydney*.

The wreaths were cast out, the priest whispered, 'Amen',
And they prayed for the souls of the *Sydney*.

THE FIRST BATTLE OF EL ALAMEIN

Once 'Fortress Europe' had been established by the Axis powers, the conflict in North Africa became the focal point of the war for Britain. By the end of 1941 Axis forces controlled Europe from the English Channel in the west to the Russian border and beyond in the east, and from Scandinavia in the north to the coast of Africa in the south.

The only Allied bases in the Mediterranean were Gibraltar and Malta. Once Hitler had attacked Russia, in June 1941, the war in Europe was actually being fought on two fronts 'outside' Western Europe: deep inside Russia and in North Africa.

The war in North Africa swept from east to west and back again in a series of campaigns across Libya. The Axis forces relied on supply lines from Tunis and Tripoli in the west, supplied from Italy. The British forces were reliant on supply lines from Alexandria and Cairo in the east, supplied via convoys coming in stages from Malta and Gibraltar, or via the Suez Canal, or by air.

Whichever army controlled the various coastal forts and cities, like Benghazi, Tobruk and El Alamein, could be supplied from the sea, while whoever controlled the air space and the airfields could obviously supply their troops, and attack the enemy, from the air.

The war was going very badly on all fronts for the Allies in early 1942, with the exception of victories against the Italians in East Africa and short-lived 'moral victories' like the holding of Tobruk. The Japanese had attacked Pearl Harbor in December 1941 and Singapore fell in February 1942, placing more pressure on Australian politicians to lobby for the return of our troops to the Pacific area.

The Russians were retreating and seven million Russians were dead. Rommel, determined to remove all obstacles to a clean sweep of the Western Desert and cut off any Allied rear-guard supply lines, took Tobruk once again on 21 June 1942. The week before Tobruk fell to Rommel, the British attempted to make Malta safe, with 'Operation Harpoon' from Gibraltar and 'Operation Vigorous' from Alexandria, ending in disaster with nine vessels sunk, nine seriously damaged and none making it through after the Battle of Pantellaria.

U-boats were having a major effect on Britain in the Atlantic and the Germans controlled mainland Europe. Therefore, the war in the desert of North Africa was pivotal. If Rommel reached the Suez Canal, the only alternative supply route for the Allies would be via South Africa—and Germany would have access to the oil in the Middle East.

The British High Command in Cairo was prepared for defeat and even began destroying documents. Major General Sir Claude Auchinleck, who headed the British troops during the siege of Tobruk, believed there was a possibility that Rommel might again outmanoeuvre him at El Alamein and planned for the possibility of a further retreat by preparing defensive positions west of Alexandria and on the approaches to Cairo. As a further precaution, considerable areas in the Nile delta were flooded. The Axis leaders believed that the capture of Egypt was imminent—Mussolini, sensing an historic moment, flew to Libya to prepare for his triumphal entry to Cairo.

El Alamein was the last stand for the Allies in North Africa.

During the initial North African campaign by joint Axis forces, Rommel and his Afrika Korps were technically under the command of the Italians. This campaign was actually the second stage of the war in the Western Desert, after the Italians had been routed and pushed back into western Libya and the Germans came to their aid.

In August 1941, the German High Command created a larger command structure in Africa called Panzer Group Africa (*Panzergruppe Afrika*). Rommel was in overall command while General Cruwell took charge of the Afrika Korps. Some additional German units were sent to Africa, as well as two corps of Italian troops. The original Panzer Group Africa was made up of the German Afrika Korps, the Italian XXI Corps and the German 15th Panzer (Tank) Division. The Italian 10th Corps, 55th Division, *Savona*, 155th Armoured Division, *Littorio*, and 20th Motorised Corps, along with the German 90th Light Africa

Division, were added during the successful push east, before the first battle of El Alamein.

After Rommel was forced to abandon his siege of Tobruk in April 1941, he retreated during December as far west as El Agheila, a coastal city in Libya. The situation was back to where it had been in March 1942. Rommel was, however, aware that British supply lines were overextended and, after he obtained reinforcements from Tripoli, he launched a counter-attack. It was once again the turn of the British to retreat.

The critical event in the campaign that followed was the Battle of Gazala in June 1942. The British had established a defensive line running south from Gazala, 48 kilometres (30 miles) west of Tobruk. In a series of tactically brilliant flanking moves, Rommel defeated the British Eighth Army and returned to Tobruk and took the port on 21 June 1942, capturing significant amounts of military equipment and 35,000 British Commonwealth troops, including almost the entire South African 2nd Division. It was the second largest British surrender of the war after Singapore.

The Axis forces then pushed on into Egypt, threatening Britain's control of the Suez Canal. General Auchinleck responded by withdrawing the Eighth Army to a line about 90 kilometres (56 miles) west of Alexandria. He chose to defend a line running north–south, just west of El Alamein, at a point where the landscape provided a natural barrier and the Qattara Depression comes to within 65 kilometres (40 miles) of El Alamein on the coast. This gave the defenders a relatively short front to defend and secure flanks, because tanks could not traverse the rugged desert valley of the Qattara Depression.

El Alamein itself was an insignificant railway station on the coast. Some 20 kilometres (12 miles) to the south lay the Ruweisat Ridge, which gave excellent observation posts over the surrounding desert. Thirty-five kilometres (22 miles) south of that lay the Qattara Depression. The line the British chose to defend stretched between the sea and the Qattara Depression, which meant that Rommel could only outflank it by taking a significant detour to the south and crossing the Sahara Desert. Between the Mediterranean and the Qattara Depression was a defendable bottleneck where Rommel could not use his famous outflanking tactics.

The battle begins

The first battle of El Alamein began on 1 July 1942 but, while preparing the El Alamein positions, Major General Auchinleck fought strong delaying actions, first at Mersa Matruh, roughly 160 kilometres (100 miles) from the Egyptian border, on 26 and 27 June and then at Fuka on 28 June. In these exchanges a late change of orders resulted in some confusion and poor coordination between front-line units.

This confusion was caused by the conflicting need to inflict maximum damage and delay Rommel's progress without getting cut off as the Eighth Army retreated to the prepared defences behind the minefields of the El Alamein front.

Casualties were heavy and the 10th Indian Division sustained heavy losses, including the destruction of the Indian 29th Infantry Brigade at Fuka. Axis forces captured more than 6000 prisoners, in addition to 40 tanks and an enormous quantity of supplies, and Auchinleck's general-ship was questioned.

On 30 June Rommel's Panzer Group Africa approached the El Alamein position. They were exhausted and under-strength but Rommel hoped that, if he struck quickly before the Eighth Army had time to settle, his momentum would take him through the El Alamein defences and he could then advance to the Nile with little further opposition.

Supplies remained a problem for Rommel. Axis headquarters had estimated they needed six weeks after the capture of Tobruk to resupply Rommel's army. Captured supplies had been a bonus for Rommel, but water, ammunition and transport were lacking.

The battle began at 3 am on 1 July 1942. German infantry advanced east but strayed too far north and ran into the 1st South African Div-ision's defences and became pinned down. The Allies had placed a huge number of landmines south of El Alamein. The Panzer tanks were severely depleted by these and those remaining were held up and became sitting targets for Allied fighter planes. It seemed the Afrika Korps would be wiped out. Rommel ordered his tanks north and a sandstorm blew up, giving his tanks much needed cover. When the sandstorm cleared, Rommel's force was hit by more Allied bombers.

Rommel called the Afrika Korps to abandon its planned sweep south-ward and instead join the effort to break through to the coast road by attacking east towards Ruweisat Ridge. The British defence managed to hold Ruweisat Ridge, reinforcing it during the night of 2 July, while the RAF bombarded the Axis forces, flying 780 sorties on 3 July and 900 on 4 July, the same day that the Australian 9th Division entered the battle and Rommel ordered the Axis forces to go on the defensive. Rommel had just 36 Panzers left and his overextended supply lines were being constantly battered from the air.

Tel el Eisa

Auchinleck turned his attention to securing the northern sector—the coastal railway line and the low ridges at Tel el Eisa, the next station west of El Alamein. Following a bombardment, which started at 3.30 am on 10 July 1942, the 26th Australian Brigade launched an attack against the ridge north of Tel el Eisa station. The bombardment was the heaviest barrage yet experienced in North Africa and created panic among the inexperienced soldiers of the Italian Sabratha Division.

The Australian attack took more than 1500 prisoners, routed an Italian Division and overran the German Signals Intercept Company, which had been intercepting British radio communications. Now this priceless source of intelligence was lost to Rommel.

Later that afternoon and evening, tanks from the 15th Panzer Division and the Italian Trieste Division launched counter-attacks against the Australian positions, which failed in the face of overwhelming artillery and Australian anti-tank guns. Rommel was determined to drive through to the north and the Australian defenders were gradually forced back by German counter-attacks, suffering nearly 50 per cent casualties between 10 and 17 July. After seven days of fierce fighting around Tel el Eisa, the 9th Australian Division estimated at least 2000 Axis troops had been killed and more than 3700 prisoners of war taken in the battle.

As the Axis forces dug in, Auchinleck, knowing the Tel el Eisa fighting had drawn a number of German units to the coastal sector, attempted to break the Axis line at Ruweisat Ridge with a concerted attack on the Italian Pavia and Brescia Divisions. Despite some poor communications this plan succeeded, with exceptional bravery shown by New Zealand and Indian troops. Seeing the Italians under pressure, Rommel rushed German troops to Ruweisat Ridge. In three days of fighting the Allies captured more than 2000 Axis prisoners of war, but the New Zealand division suffered 1405 casualties.

Knowing the Germans had sent troops and tanks south to help relieve pressure on Ruweisat Ridge, Auchinleck ordered the 9th Australian Division to make another attack from the north. With strong fighter cover from the air, the Australians attacked Miteirya Ridge, which became known among them as 'Ruin Ridge'.

The initial night attack succeeded, the Australians made a bayonet charge and 740 prisoners were taken, but the 50th Royal Tank Regiment supporting the Australians was having difficulty locating the minefield gaps made by 2/24th Australian Battalion. They failed to get through and were caught by heavy fire and lost thirteen tanks. As a result, the unsupported 2/28th Australian Battalion on Miteirya Ridge was cut off and overrun by hastily assembled German and Italian units, with Axis tanks attacking from three sides. Twenty-two British tanks were destroyed attempting to reach them and Australian commander, Lieutenant Colonel McCarter, surrendered rather than see all his men killed. Sixty-five Australians died in the failed attack and 490 were taken prisoner.

Auchinleck's Eighth Army enjoyed a massive superiority in material over the Axis forces, yet it faltered badly at the second battle of Ruweisat Ridge. Poor communications, indecision and lack of knowledge about minefields led to the 23rd Armoured Brigade being destroyed, with the loss of 87 tanks. A counter-attack by the 5th and 8th Panzer Regiments overran the New Zealand infantry, which had been left in the open without support, inflicting more than 900 casualties on the New Zealanders. Entire Indian brigades were lost during confused and fruitless night attacks.

To the north, the Australian 9th Division continued its attacks. Early on 22 July, the 26th Australian Brigade attacked Tel el Eisa again. The fighting was costly, but by the afternoon the Australians controlled the position. It was here that Private Stan Gurney secured a victory when his company was pinned down by machine-gun crossfire. He charged the nearest machine-gun post, bayoneting three of the crew. He then rushed a second post and killed two Germans before a grenade knocked him down. Picking himself up, he charged a third post and disappeared from view. He cleared the way for his company to advance; as they did they found and recovered his body. He was posthumously awarded the Victoria Cross.

Further south the 24th Australian Brigade attacked Tel el Makh Khad with the tanks of 50th Royal Tank Regiment in support. The tank unit had not been trained in infantry support, failed to coordinate with the Australian infantry and lost 23 tanks.

Rommel launched an immediate counter-attack against the exhausted Eighth Army and, on 31 July, Major General Auchinleck ordered an end to offensive operations with a view to rebuilding the army's strength.

The battle was a stalemate: it had halted the Axis advance but the Eighth Army had suffered more than 13,000 casualties with massive losses to New Zealand and Indian divisions.

The Australian 9th Division had suffered 2552 battle casualties but had taken 7000 prisoners and inflicted heavy damage on the Axis army. Axis losses were 7000 men, 1000 of whom were Germans, but Rommel could afford the losses to a much lesser degree than the Allies.

A LITTLE SPRIG OF WATTLE

A.H. Scott

My mother's letter came to-day,
And now my thoughts are far away,
For in between its pages lay
A little sprig of wattle.

'The old home now looks at its best,'
The message ran; 'the country's dressed
In spring's gay cloak, and I have pressed
A little sprig of wattle.'

I almost see that glimpse of spring:
The very air here seems to ring
With joyful notes of birds that sing
Among the sprigs of wattle.

The old home snug amidst the pines,
The trickling creek that twists and twines
Round tall gum roots and undermines,
Is all ablaze with wattle.

THE 'SILENT 7TH'

The 7th Division was formed in February 1940. Its 17,000 men were under the command of Major General John Lavarack and received some training prior to embarking for the Middle East in October 1940 for further training in Egypt and Palestine. There was some swapping of brigades between the 7th and 9th Divisions but, by February 1941, the 7th Division was made up of the 18th, 21st and 25th Brigades of the 2nd AIF.

In March 1941 the 18th Brigade fought with distinction in the Allied victory at the Siege of Giarabub, in the desert south of Tobruk. The Australians attacked the stronghold on 17 March and the Italians surrendered on 20 March. The 18th Brigade then continued to serve in the North African campaign, famously defending the port of Tobruk with men of the 9th Australian Division and the British Royal Horse Artillery, from May to August 1941.

The other two brigades of the 7th Division fought in one of the most successful campaigns of WWII in Syria and Lebanon.

After WWI the Ottoman Empire was broken up and France was given the 'mandate' over Syria and Lebanon, which became French administered territories. These territories were also known generally as 'the Levant'.

After France surrendered to Germany in June 1940, the Vichy government, under Marshal Petain, ruled the 'Free Zone' in the south of France and technically governed all of France, as long as its laws did not conflict with those of Germany.

So the Vichy French directly controlled the mandate of Lebanon while Syria, which had achieved partial self-government in 1936 and had two French air bases, came back under Vichy French control in June 1940.

Nearby Iraq had achieved self-government from Britain in 1932 but a pro-German government, installed in a coup on 1 May 1941, led Britain to declare war on Iraq the next day. The same month the Vichy French gave Germany permission to use Syrian bases and British air strikes against Axis planes began. Germany began moving troops through Syria into Iraq through Vichy French territory, which led to quite justifiable fears by the British that these territories would be used as bases to open a second front against Egypt.

The first encounters were with German and Italian aircraft stationed in Syria. British aircraft destroyed six Axis planes between mid May and mid June. By the end of May, the pro-German 'revolution' in Iraq had collapsed and the British had regained control and could move against the Vichy French.

The combatants who fought in the campaign through June and into July 1941 were described as a 'mixed force': they were certainly an odd assortment. The Vichy French were led by the High Commissioner of the Levant, General Dentz, who was also Commander in Chief of the French armed forces. Dentz had at his disposal 45,000 troops made up from seven regular French army infantry divisions, including the 6th Regiment of the Foreign Legion. He also had eleven 'special' divisions of Syrian and Lebanese troops and 5000 cavalry, some mounted and some motorised. Air power was a vital element of this campaign and Dentz had 90 aircraft available in May, but this was increased to 289 by mid June.

On the Allied side General Maitland Wilson, fresh from the evacuation of Greece and now 'General Officer Commanding the military in Palestine and Trans Jordan', had a force built around the Australian 7th Division (except for the 18th Brigade, which was at Tobruk), plus the 17th Brigade of the Australian 6th Division. Fighting with the Australians was 'Gentforce', named after its commander, Major General Paul Louis Le Gentilhomme, which comprised two Free French brigades, including the 13th Foreign Legion, and the 5th Indian Infantry Brigade, plus engineers and artillery.

Added to this already polyglot army was Lieutenant General Quinlan's Iraqi army, made up of the entire 10th Indian Infantry Division, a force of motorised armoured British artillery (still oddly called 'cavalry'), the 11th British Commando Unit, an Arab battalion known as 'Habforce', and a Jewish unit from Palestine called 'Palmach', which included the future Israeli general Moshe Dayan, who lost an eye during the campaign.

The Australians were led by Major General John Lavarack until his promotion to commander of all Australian front-line forces on 18 June; they were then led by Major General 'Tubby' Allen.

Maitland Wilson had squadrons of both the RAF and RAAF at his disposal and both sides had naval support during the coastal parts of the campaign.

It was a short but savage campaign fought by two rather odd, conglomerate armies, each made up of a collection of very disparate troop formations. Free French soldiers opposed the Vichy French and various elements of the French Foreign Legion fought on both sides!

The 7th Division advanced from Palestine and fought the Battle of Litani River on 9 June 1941. This was an unusual battle in that Australian artillery had to fight off naval attacks from Vichy French destroyers while infantry crossed the river in canvas boats to help the commandos, arriving by sea, to capture the Vichy positions.

The following day the Australian advance was halted near Djezzine. Private James Gordon was later awarded a Victoria Cross for his single-handed bayonet attack here, which took out an enemy machine-gun nest and killed four enemy soldiers. Gordon survived the war, saw action in New Guinea, suffered from Malaria, and lived till 1986. His portrait, painted by William Dargie, won the Archibald Prize in 1942.

Between 19 and 24 June, troops of the 6th and 7th Australian Divisions held a pass at the Battle of Merdjayoun and prevented the enemy from gaining the initiative and attacking Palestine.

During this battle Lieutenant Arthur Roden Cutler of the 2/5th Australian Field Regiment repaired telegraph wires and repeatedly engaged enemy tanks, anti-tank guns, machine-gun posts and infantry with a 25-pounder field gun, an anti-tank rifle, a Bren gun and a .303 rifle. He was badly wounded on 6 July and waited 26 hours to be rescued. His leg was amputated and he was awarded the VC. Cutler later became Governor of New South Wales and is the only Australian artilleryman to have ever been awarded the Victoria Cross.

The campaign lasted a mere five weeks. The Free French entered Damascus on 21 June and the Australians were about to enter Beirut when Dentz sought an armistice on 12 June.

The Vichy French lost approximately 1000 killed and 5000 wounded. The 38,000 Vichy French prisoners of war were given the choice of being repatriated to France or joining de Gaulle's Free French Army—5668 men chose to join de Gaulle; the rest returned to France in eight convoys in August and September 1941.

Dentz and 29 of his most senior officers were held until all British prisoners were returned to Syria and General Catroux was placed in charge of Syria and Lebanon and recognised its independence in the name of the Free French movement.

Total casualties on the Allied side were about 4000, of which 416 Australians were killed and 1136 wounded.

The RAAF—especially No. 3 Squadron—played a major role in the campaign. Aircraft losses on the Allied side were 27, compared to 179 on the enemy side.

In September the 18th Brigade joined the other two brigades of the 7th Division in Palestine, where they were given the task of defending the city of Aleppo from an anticipated German attack that never eventuated.

When Singapore fell to the Japanese on 15 February 1942, the 7th Division was on its way home, in response to Prime Minister Curtin's demand that they return to defend Australia. Churchill, however, ordered that the troopships be diverted to Burma but this order was famously defied by Curtin's cablegram of 23 February, stating that it was 'quite impossible to reverse' the decision to return home. The 7th then served with distinction in the defeat of the Japanese invading forces in New Guinea, on the Kokoda Track and at Milne Bay, and later in Borneo.

The 7th Division gave themselves the nickname the 'Silent 7th' due to the fact that their wartime efforts appeared to go unrecognised.

Perhaps it's because they were fighting the French, not the Germans, that their exploits in the Middle East get lost in the big picture of WWII; or perhaps it was because the campaign was not seen as central to the struggle against the Axis powers for European and Mediterranean supremacy.

MIDDLE EAST SONG

Anonymous

Oh they took us out to Egypt, that god-forsaken land,
It's filled with bloody nothing and covered up with sand.
They fed us on stale biscuits, camel piss and stew,
And we wandered round in circles with bugger-all to do.

The generals that they sent us had not a bloody clue,
They ought to round the bastards up and put them in a zoo.
They said, 'Keep your eye on Rommel, don't let the bastard pass.'
But he'd sneak around behind them and kick them in the arse!

Then out came Montgomery, his prayerbook in his hand.
He said, 'Now men, the time has come to make a bloody stand.
We've got the Lord on our side and Rommel's cupboard's bare.
Now then men, down on your knees and say a bloody prayer!'

And we prayed, 'Oh Jesus save us, 'tis not the Hun we fear,
Save us from the crazy bastards Churchill sends out here!'

THE SECOND BATTLE OF EL ALAMEIN

In August 1942, Winston Churchill faced the prospect of a vote of no confidence in the House of Commons and was desperate for a victory to boost morale at home. He visited Cairo and replaced Major General Auchinleck as Commander in Chief of the Middle East with Major General Sir Harold Alexander. Lieutenant General Gott was to command the Eighth Army. Gott died, however, when the Luftwaffe shot down his transport plane and Lieutenant General Bernard Montgomery became Eighth Army commander by default.

'Monty' was clever, ruthless and popular with the troops. He put a great deal of emphasis on organisation and morale, often addressing the troops and attempting to restore confidence. He knew that he needed to hold El Alamein at all costs.

Rommel planned to hit the Allies in the south. Montgomery had guessed that this would be Rommel's plan, and it was also backed up by intelligence coming from the Enigma decoding team working at Bletchley Park, the United Kingdom's main decryption centre, who had got hold of Rommel's battle plan and deciphered it. Montgomery also knew the supply lines Rommel was going to be using and worked with his troops to diminish these supplies. By August 1942, only about one-third of the supplies that Rommel needed were getting through to him.

While Rommel was short of fuel and slowly being starved of supplies, the Allied supply lines via Suez and the Mediterranean were working well. Rommel decided to attack quickly despite not being well equipped.

He decided to attempt a flanking move around the southern end of the Eighth Army's minefields and make a thrust to Alam el Halfa Ridge.

This position was well behind the front-line defences and was defended by the 44th Home Counties Division.

On the night of 30 August 1942, the Panzers attacked, but found the southern minefield more of an obstacle than expected. By dawn, on 31 August, the Germans had advanced only 12 kilometres (7 miles) past the mines and came under fire from the artillery of the 22nd Armoured Brigade, and were held up by the New Zealanders, considered the best desert infantry on the front line, and 7th Armoured Division.

However, the recently modified Panzer MK IV tanks took a heavy toll on the British Grant tanks and it was only a furious charge by the Scots Greys, a famous cavalry regiment which had exchanged its horses for Stuart Tanks in 1941, that stopped them breaking through. Under the light of flares the RAF bombed the Germans all night, forcing them to withdraw.

Although the Desert Air Force played a major role in halting the German advance, it was Rommel's lack of petrol which reduced the attack on Alam el Halfa Ridge on 1 September 1942 to a small-scale affair. For the Australians, the most important element of this battle was a diversionary raid carried out on 1 September. In this operation, officially called 'Operation Bulimba' but also known as the 'Raid on Tel el Eisa', the Australian 2/15th Battalion crossed a minefield and captured the Axis fort known as West Point 23, 3 kilometres (1.9 miles) from Tel el Eisa. A tank regiment was to follow and the plan was to cut Rommel's coastal supply line. But a strong counter-attack forced the plan to be abandoned, leaving the Australians to fight their way out and withdraw. They did this under heavy fire with losses of 40 dead, 110 wounded and 25 missing. German losses were 150 dead and 140 taken prisoner.

By the end of September 1942, Montgomery was ready to sustain a long campaign. Knowing the Axis forces could not do the same due to dwindling supplies, he merely waited for Rommel to act. Montgomery was also waiting for the arrival of 300 US-made Sherman tanks with 75-mm (3-inch) guns that could shoot a 2.7-kilogram (6-pound) shell that could penetrate a Panzer at 2000 metres. When Montgomery was woken up to be told that the second battle of El Alamein had begun on the evening of 23 October, he is said to have replied 'Excellent', and gone back to sleep.

The Eighth Army had 220,000 men and 1100 tanks, while the Axis had 110,000 men and 500 tanks. But the factors that had favoured the Eighth

Army's defensive plan in the first battle of El Alamein, the short front line and the secure flanks, now favoured the Axis. Rommel had plenty of time to prepare his defensive positions and lay 500,000 mines and barbed wire in patterns which suited his battle plan and funnelled all attacks towards his fortified positions.

Rommel knew he could not win against a larger and better-supplied army unless his defences held. He could not let the British armour break out into the open because he had neither the strength of numbers nor the fuel to match them in a battle of manoeuvre. His plan was to destroy the Eighth Army as it battered itself against his defensive line and attempted to break through his defences.

Any chance of an Axis victory relied on Rommel's minefields and defensive plan. The only other hope in Rommel's mind was that German forces would win the Battle of Stalingrad that had been raging since 17 July 1942, and then threaten Persia and the Middle East. A German victory such as this would require large numbers of British Commonwealth forces to be sent from the Egyptian front to reinforce British forces in Persia, and perhaps postpone any offensive against Rommel's army. If this occurred, Rommel hoped to convince the German High Command to reinforce his forces for the eventual link-up between *Panzerarmee Afrika* and the German armies in southern Russia, enabling them to finally defeat the British in the Middle East. In the meantime, Axis forces dug in and waited for the eventual attack by the Eighth Army.

Montgomery's plan was to use his superior numbers and better supply lines to batter and break the Axis defences and then exploit the break-through and destroy *Panzerarmee Afrika*. This is why he waited until he had a vastly superior army to use, although he knew that every day he waited, the Axis defences improved.

In all the previous swings of the pendulum in the Western Desert, neither side ever had the resources or supply lines to exploit victory decisively: the losing side had always been able to withdraw and regroup closer to their main supply bases. Montgomery knew he had to not only win the battle; he had to win the war in North Africa.

Critics who say Montgomery only won the battle due to force of numbers at El Alamein fail to understand the nature of the battle and the goals set by Montgomery for the Eighth Army. It is also true to say that Montgomery used his infantry as 'bait' to draw the Axis forces away from areas of battle where he needed more time to penetrate defences. The main infantry to suffer from this tactic were the Australian 9th Division and the New Zealanders.

Montgomery planned to cut two corridors through the Axis minefields in the north around Miteirya Ridge. Through the corridor to the south, the New Zealand Division would advance, while the 9th Australian and 51st (Highland) Divisions would attack through the second corridor, which passed 3.2 kilometres (2 miles) north of Miteirya Ridge. British tanks would then pass through and defeat the inferior Axis armour. Diversionary attacks at Ruweisat Ridge and further south would keep the rest of the Axis forces from moving northwards.

In the weeks before the battle Montgomery instituted a number of famous deceptions, codenamed 'Operation Bertram', to confuse the Axis Intelligence. A dummy pipeline was built to the south and dummy tanks, consisting of plywood frames placed over jeeps, were built and deployed in the south, while the tanks destined for battle in the north were disguised as supply lorries by placing removable plywood frames over them.

In an even more cunning move, dummy supply dumps of waste materials, discarded packing cases and debris were placed under camouflage nets in the northern sector. These were designed to look like 'fake' ammunition and ration dumps. The Axis noticed these but, as no offensive action followed and the dumps never changed in appearance, they were assumed to be a ploy and were ignored. This allowed the Eighth Army to replace the rubbish with ammunition, petrol or rations at night and build up supplies in the forward area.

Montgomery planned for a twelve-day battle in three stages: the break-in, the dogfight, and the final breaking of the enemy. What actually occurred can be divided into five phases (plus a 'breathing space') and took thirteen days. These phases consisted of 'Operation Lightfoot', 23–25 October; Montgomery's rethink, 25–26 October; Rommel's counter-attack, 27–28 October; then a 'breathing space' on 29–31 October; followed by 'Operation Supercharge', 2–3 November; and the breakout, 3–6 November.

Phase One: Operation Lightfoot, 23–25 October

This operation began with a diversion by the 24th Australian Brigade, which engaged the 15th Panzer Division with heavy fire for a few minutes just after 9 pm on 23 October. At 9.40 pm, the first rounds fired by all 882 guns from the field batteries landed across the entire 60-kilometre

(37-mile) front. After twenty minutes of heavy general bombardment, the guns switched to precision targets in support of the advancing infantry. The shelling plan continued for five and a half hours, by the end of which each gun had fired about 600 rounds.

It was named 'Operation Lightfoot' because infantry had to attack first. Most anti-tank mines would not be tripped by soldiers running over them. As the infantry advanced, engineers had to clear a path for the tanks coming behind. Each stretch of land cleared of mines was just wide enough to get tanks through in single file. The engineers had to clear an 8-kilometre (5-mile) path through Rommel's complex double minefields known as the Devil's Gardens. It was a difficult task as one mine was interconnected with others via wires and if one mine was set off, many others could be. The plan to get the tanks through in one night failed due to the depth of the Axis minefields and the second night of the attack was also largely unsuccessful. Montgomery blamed his Chief of Tanks, General Lumsden, and Operation Lightfoot was called off and the tanks withdrawn. When he received the news, Churchill was furious.

By 25 October, the Allies had advanced through the minefields in the west to make a 10-kilometre (6-mile) wide by 8-kilometre deep inroad north of Miteirya Ridge, which they had also captured, but Axis forces were firmly entrenched in most of their original battle positions and the battle was at a standstill.

What had been achieved had been made possible by a massive air attack on German positions; the RAF flew more than 1000 sorties on 24 October alone. There had been huge losses of Allied troops and tanks and, for the most part, the Axis minefields had proven to be too deep to be cleared fast enough for Montgomery's plan to work. More time was needed to clear the minefields. So Monty changed his plans.

On the Axis side there was even worse news. Rommel, who was ill and recuperating at a sanatorium in Italy, was ordered back to the front. His replacement, General Stumme, had gone to see the front-line positions on the morning of 24 October and suffered a heart attack and died when his armoured car came under attack. On 25 October, RAF Beaufort Torpedo Bombers sank the tanker *Proserpina*, full of petrol and supplies for the Axis army, in Tobruk Harbour. The other last hope for supplies to the Axis forces, the tanker *Luisiano*, was sunk off the coast by a Wellington Bomber and the Axis forces were down to just 350 tanks after the savage defensive battles of the two previous nights.

Phase Two: Montgomery's rethink (The Crumbling), 25–26 October

Montgomery decided that the planned advance south from Miteirya Ridge by the New Zealanders would be too costly. He needed to buy time for the minefields to be cleared, consolidate the gains made around Miteirya Ridge and draw the Axis forces away from the ground gained there. So, once again, the 9th Australian Division was called on to take the brunt of the battle and strike northwards towards the coast and Tel el Eisa until a breakthrough occurred further south. The 1st Armoured Division, on the left of the advancing Australians' column, supported by the 51st Highlanders of the British Infantry Division, was to continue to attack west and north-west, but activity to the south on both these fronts would be confined to patrolling and containment.

When night fell, the plan was put into operation. The 51st Highlanders Division launched three attacks, but chaos and carnage ensued, leaving 500 dead and only one officer left among the attacking forces. Meanwhile the Australians attacked and captured Point 29, an Axis artillery observation post south-west of Tel el Eisa. They then attempted to push through and surround the Axis coastal positions containing the German 164th Light Division and large numbers of Italian infantry. Fierce fighting continued in this area for the next week, as the Axis tried to recover the vital defensive position and prevent their troops from being surrounded.

To the south, however, the British failed to take advantage of the missing tanks sent north. Each time they tried to move forward, anti-tank guns would stop them and the Allied offensive was stalled. It was at this point that Churchill famously asked the British High Command, 'Is it really impossible to find a general who can win a battle?'

Making use of the 1st Armoured Division's path through the minefield north of Miteirya Ridge, Montgomery planned a double thrust, on 26 October, to capture two high points of terrain to the west known as Snipe and Woodcock while Axis forces were busy defending positions against the Australians further north.

Over the next two days, Montgomery thinned out his front line to create a reserve to restore his momentum. This included the New Zealand Division with three British armoured units: the 9th Armoured Brigade, led by Brigadier John Currie, the 10th Armoured Division and the 7th Armoured Division.

Phase Three: Rommel's counter-attack, 27–28 October

On Rommel's return to North Africa, he was informed that the Italian *Trento* Division had lost half its infantry and most of its artillery, the 164th Light Division had lost two battalions, and the 15th Panzer and *Littorio* Divisions, which had held off the Allied armour, had suffered huge losses. Most other units were under-strength, all men were on half rations, a large number were sick, and the Axis army had only enough fuel for three days.

Convinced that the main assault was coming from the Australians near the coast, Rommel immediately ordered counter-attacks by the 15th Panzer, 164th Light Divisions and elements of the Italian XX Corps on 27 October, but these failed due to stoic resistance from the Australians and air attacks by the RAF. When Rommel heard that the British had broken out west of Miteirya Ridge, he decided to make two major counter-attacks using his last fresh troops. The German 90th Light Division was to make a renewed attempt to capture Point 29 from the Australians and the 21st Panzer was to target Snipe.

At Snipe, German and Italian tanks moved forward against the British Rifle Brigade and 239th Anti-Tank Battery, who had twenty anti-tank guns. Although on the point of being overrun more than once, the British famously and bravely held their ground, destroying 22 German and ten Italian tanks.

So, the momentum swung slightly in Montgomery's favour; however, attempts to hold the two hilltops, Snipe and Woodcock, faltered due to poor communications and errors in map reading. The positions were actually left undefended by mistake on 28 October and, by the time troops were rushed back to the position, Montgomery's plan was in disarray and he ordered formations in the Woodcock–Snipe area to go over to defence while he focused his army's attack further to the north.

On the night of 28 October, the 9th Australian Division was ordered to push north-west with tank support and take the Axis-held railway line and coast road in a move that would outflank and surround the Axis troop positions on the coast. The 20th Brigade took its objectives with little trouble, but the 26th Brigade lost touch with the 46th Royal Tank Regiment in minefields and came face to face with the German 125th Panzer Grenadier Regiment and a battalion of the Italian anti-tank 7th *Bersaglieri* Regiment sent to reinforce the sector. The Italians fought fiercely and were all killed, except for twenty wounded men who were captured the following morning. The Australians suffered 27 killed and 290 wounded.

The operation had to be called off when daylight came, leaving no time for the various brigades to close the cordon and achieve their goal. However, by forcing Rommel to counter-attack on two fronts and rush troops north and south, Montgomery had achieved his objective of holding a short breathing space to reorganise his forces, cross minefields and focus his attack on the weaker points of Rommel's defensive line.

Breathing space: 29–31 October

Montgomery always acknowledged that the Australian 9th Division gave him victory at El Alamein. He knew that the gains made by the Australians to the north had forced Rommel to commit his reserves to the coastal sector. Montgomery knew that Rommel expected the next major Eighth Army offensive to come in this sector and reorganised his battle lines so the attack would take place further south, on a 4-kilometre (2.5-mile) front south of Point 29. The attack was originally planned for the night of 31 October, but was postponed by 24 hours while reserves were organised.

To keep Rommel's attention on the coast, Montgomery ordered the renewal of the Australian 9th Division's operation on the night of 30 October. This time four battalions of the 9th Division reached the sea and turned west to cut off the troops in the Axis coastal positions. A desperate and ferocious concerted thrust by the 21st Panzer Division, before the 9th Division could establish positions, prevented this from happening. The Australians suffered dreadful casualties in this fighting. The 2/48th Battalion, for example, was reduced from 690 men to 40 men in one week. Only exceptional bravery by the troops and brilliant leadership from General Morshead prevented defeat in the face of Rommel's concerted attacks.

Meanwhile, RAF night bombers dropped 115 tonnes of bombs on selected targets in the battlefield and 14 tonnes on the Axis air base at Sidi Haneish, 35 kilometres (22 miles) east-south-east from Marsa Matruh, while fighters flew constant strafing patrols over the Axis troop positions and landing strips. At this point Rommel, whose previous requests for permission to withdraw had been denied by Hitler, told his commanders, 'It will be quite impossible for us to disengage from the enemy. There is no gasoline left for us to retreat. We have only one choice and that is to fight to the end at Alamein.'

Phase Four: Operation Supercharge, 2–3 November

This operation, designed to destroy enemy armour, forced Rommel to use any supplies and reserves he might have left, and force Axis troops into the open, started with a seven-hour aerial bombardment of Axis positions and known supply depots, followed by a four-and-a-half-hour barrage of 360 guns firing 15,000 shells at the Axis defensive line. Two assault brigades, made up of the 2nd New Zealand Division and various British infantry, advanced to clear a path through the mines for the British 9th Armoured Division and the 8th and 50th Royal Tank Regiments, while the 7th Armoured Division was in reserve, ready to join the battle from the south of Ruweisat Ridge. The Axis defence was a massive artillery line running north–south.

The ground attack started at 1.05 am on 2 November and most objectives were gained on schedule with only moderate losses. The 28th Maori Battalion captured positions to protect the right flank of the newly formed front line and New Zealand engineers cleared five lines through the mines, allowing armoured car regiments to slip out into the open and begin attacking Axis communication posts.

Currie's 9th Armoured Brigade left El Alamein railway station with 130 tanks and arrived at its start line with 94 tanks fit for action. Just before dawn the brigade advanced towards the Axis gun line. In the next half hour 35 guns were destroyed and several hundred prisoners taken, but the British 9th Armoured Brigade's 94 tanks were reduced to only 24, while 230 men of the 400 tank crew involved in the attack were killed, wounded or captured. After the brigade's action, Brigadier Gentry of 6th New Zealand Brigade found Brigadier Currie, commander of the British 9th Armoured Division, asleep on a stretcher. 'Sorry to wake you, John,' Gentry began, 'but I need to know where your tanks are?'

Currie, who had complained that his brigade had been asked to achieve an impossible task and had predicted 50 per cent casualties, waved his hand at a small group of tanks and said, 'There they are.'

When Gentry said, 'Not your headquarters tanks, where are your armoured regiments?' Currie replied, 'They are my armoured regiments.'

The 9th Brigade had been sacrificed on the Axis gun line but had failed to create the gap for the British 1st Armoured Division to pass through. In spite of this, the 1st Armoured Division joined the battle and the remains of the 9th Armoured Brigade dug in and was able to set up a screen of anti-tank guns and artillery, with the help of intensive air support.

At 11 am on 2 November, the remains of 15th Panzer, 21st Panzer and *Littorio* Armoured Divisions launched a massive counter-attack, which failed under a barrage of shells and bombs and resulted in the loss of some 100 tanks.

Although Operation Supercharge failed in its attempt to create a full breakout, it had succeeded in its objective of finding and destroying enemy tanks. Tank losses were approximately equal, but British losses represented only a portion of total British armour, while the Panzer Corps General von Thoma's report to Rommel that night said he would have at most 35 tanks available to fight the next day and his artillery and anti-tank weapons had been reduced to one-third of their strength.

Phase Five: The Breakout, 3–6 November

Late on the evening of 2 November, Rommel decided he must start a retreat to the planned withdrawal position at Fuka to prevent the destruction of his army. He let Hitler know that his army 'was not now capable of offering any effective opposition to the enemy's next break-through attempt . . . With our great shortage of vehicles an orderly withdrawal is impossible.'

Hitler replied at 1.30 pm on 3 November: 'there can be no other thought but to stand fast, yield not a yard of ground and throw every gun and every man into the battle . . . As to your troops, you can show them no other road than that to victory or death.'

Rommel said later, 'I was completely stunned, and for the first time in the African campaign I did not know what to do. A kind of apathy took hold . . .'

Rommel decided to compromise: the 10th and 21st Italian Corps and 90th Light Division would stand firm, while the Afrika Korps would withdraw during the night of 3 November with the 20th Italian Corps and the *Ariete* Division moving back to hold their positions. He then told Hitler he was determined to hold the battlefield. Meanwhile, the RAF continued to apply huge pressure. In what was its biggest day of the battle, it flew more than 1200 sorties and dropped 400 tonnes of bombs on 3 November.

On the night of 3 November, Montgomery launched his reserve brigades in a pre-planned attack on the Axis line of retreat, the Rahman track, which led back west from the Axis positions and from which connecting roads led north towards the main coast road into Libya.

On 4 November, the British Eighth Army's plan for pursuit was set in motion at dawn. There were no fresh units available for the chase, so the 1st and 7th Armoured Divisions were to swing northward towards the coastal road to pursue the Axis units.

On the morning of 4 November, Rommel reported his situation: 'powerful enemy armoured forces . . . had burst a 12-mile hole in our front, through which strong bodies of tanks were moving to the west . . . our forces in the north were threatened with encirclement by enemy formations twenty times their number in tanks . . . With our front broken and the fully motorised enemy streaming into our rear, superior orders could no longer count.'

However, the 7th Armoured Division was held up by the Italian *Ariete* Armoured Division. They surrounded the *Ariete* and *Trento* Divisions who battled to hold off the offensive attack. This enabled the remaining Axis troops to retreat safely. At 5.30 pm, unable to wait any longer for a reply from Hitler, Rommel gave orders to retreat along the coast to the north-west.

Due to Hitler's and Mussolini's insistence that Rommel hold his ground, obliging him to keep the unmotorised Italian infantry in the field, and because of insufficient transportation, most of the Italian infantry formations were abandoned and left to their fate. In addition to the *Ariete* and *Trento* Divisions, this day also saw the destruction of the *Littorio* Armoured Division.

The remaining *Bologna* Infantry Division, which had taken the brunt of the Allied armoured attacks, and what was left of the *Trento* Division fought their way out of El Alamein and marched into the desert without water, food or transport, eventually surrendering, exhausted and dying from dehydration. When Colonel Dall'Olio, commanding *Bologna* Division, surrendered, he stated, 'We have ceased firing not because we haven't the desire but because we have fired every round.'

Montgomery attempted to finish the Axis army off with armoured thrusts westward. The 7th Armoured Division were ordered across country to intercept the coastal road 100 kilometres (62 miles) west of the Rahman track, while the 1st Armoured Division were ordered to take a wide detour through the desert to a point 130 kilometres (81 miles) west of the Rahman track and then swing up to cut the road at Mersa Matruh. Neither move succeeded, the 7th Armoured finished the day 51 kilometres (32 miles) short of its objective and the 1st Armoured, attempting to make up time with a night march, lost their support vehicles and ran out of fuel at dawn on 6 November, 26 kilometres (16 miles) short of their goal.

At midday on 6 November, heavy rain started to fall in the desert and the pursuit became bogged down. There were several skirmishes and battles during which 21st Panzer Division lost sixteen tanks, numerous guns and narrowly escaped encirclement, before escaping in trucks into Mersa Matruh. The United States had entered the North African conflict in August and, on 6 November, US heavy bombers attacked Tobruk and Benghazi, sinking several Axis supply ships.

On 7 November poor ground conditions after the rain and lack of fuel saw the British 1st and 7th Armoured Divisions grounded. The 10th Armoured Division, working on the coastal road with ample fuel supplies, pushed its tanks on to Mersa Matruh while its infantry mopped up.

Rommel intended to fight a delaying action at Sidi Barrani, 130 kilometres (81 miles) west of Mersa Matruh, to give his retreating forces time to get through escarpment passes at Halfaya and Sollum. The Axis rear-guard left Mersa Matruh early on 8 November, but was only able to hold Sidi Barrani until the evening of 9 November. On the morning of 11 October, the 5th New Zealand Infantry Brigade stormed Halfaya Pass, taking 600 Italian prisoners. By that evening the Egyptian border area was clear.

In the second battle of El Alamein, 37,000 Germans and Italians had been killed or wounded; 13,500 Allied troops of the Eighth Army were killed, wounded or missing, one-fifth were Australian. The 9th Division, for whom the battle ended on 4 November, suffered losses of 620 killed, 1944 wounded and 130 taken prisoner.

The aftermath

Winston Churchill famously said, 'Before Alamein we never had a victory. After Alamein we never had a defeat.'

Including those taken prisoner, Rommel's army lost 75,000 men in North Africa. He had also lost 1000 guns and 500 tanks. He hastened westward across Libya, fighting a brilliant rear-guard delaying campaign until he had the remnants of his army safe in Tunisia. It was a textbook retreat, equipment and infrastructure destroyed, and minefields and booby traps laid to slow the advance of the Eighth Army.

Montgomery's victory at El Alamein was comprehensive. Axis casualties of 37,000 amounted to one-third of their total force. Allied casualties of 13,560 were small by comparison at around 6 per cent.

The Eighth Army did not successfully exploit the victory and failed to cut off Rommel at Fuka and Mersa Matruh. It is fair to say that Rommel 'won the retreat'. He held up the Eighth Army's advance at El Agheila for three weeks and was eventually outflanked and forced to retreat from El Agheila, Sirte, Buerat and Tripoli. The New Zealand infantry were in the vanguard of these actions and Allied forces entered and took Tripoli on 23 January 1943.

Montgomery, as usual, was cautious and conservative. What he managed to do that was quite remarkable was to conduct a huge engineering program to reconstruct roads, ports and railways to supply the Eighth Army with the 2400 tonnes of supply it needed daily.

Although the railway line between El Alamein and Fort Capuzzo had been blown up in more than 200 places, it was quickly repaired and carried 133,000 tonnes of supplies in the month after the victory. The port at Benghazi was handling 3000 tonnes of cargo a day by the end of December, although Montgomery had been told its capacity would be 800 tonnes maximum.

Montgomery was in no hurry: he paused in front of the Axis line for three weeks at El Agheila to concentrate his strung-out forces and prepare for the assault, which would drive Rommel west beyond Tripoli. Rommel was caught between the Eighth Army to the east and the multinational First Army, led by General Eisenhower, which had invaded Morocco and Tunisia in the days just following Montgomery's victory at El Alamein.

Axis forces in North Africa faced Allied armies east and west and, as Vichy French governments changed sides in Morocco and Algeria, German troops were needed to oppose two well-equipped Allied forces in North Africa as well as the French Resistance. Rommel finally retreated beyond the German-held Mareth Line into Tunisia on 4 March and joined up with General von Arnim's army. The resupplied German–Italian Panzer Army was re-designated the Italian First Army while Rommel assumed command of the new Army Group Africa, responsible for fighting the Allies on both fronts.

On 6 March, Rommel attacked the Eighth Army at Medenine in Tunisia with the largest concentration of Axis armour ever assembled in North Africa. The Eighth Army withstood Rommel's onslaught and, in the final week of March 1943, using the RAF and flanking manoeuvres, Montgomery broke through and again turned the tide of battle. The two Allied armies in North Africa met 200 kilometres (124 miles) south of

Tunis on 7 April and the Axis forces in North Africa officially surrendered on 12 May.

The way was now clear to liberate Europe from the south.

El Alamein further enhanced the legendary status of the 9th Division and the famous Rats of Tobruk had again held the line and shown extreme courage and stoicism, taking the main brunt of the Axis attack while other elements of the British Eighth Army fumbled and stumbled their way to victory further south. It also established the reputation of Major General Morshead, who had led his courageous troops to hard-won victory.

In spite of his battle experience, Morshead, a reservist officer in peacetime, had been passed over as Commander of the 30th Corps in favour of General Leese, a British regular officer, who was junior to him and had never commanded a division in action. This caused resentment among the Australian troops and the media at home. To his credit, after the Aussies punched a massive dent in German and Italian positions and forced Rommel to retreat, Leese sought out Morshead to praise his generalship.

'I am quite certain,' Leese told Morshead, 'that this breakout was made possible by the Homeric fighting of your division.'

For his part in the famous victory, Morshead was created a Knight Commander of the Order of the Bath (KCB).

During the entire El Alamein campaign, the 9th Division suffered 22 per cent of the British Eighth Army's casualties: 1177 Australians were killed, while 3629 were wounded, 795 were captured and 193 were missing.

As soon as it was obvious that the battle was won at El Alamein, General Montgomery made his way to 9th Division Headquarters to thank Morshead for the Australian role in the victory. This acknowledgement of the troops' bravery made Australia inordinately and justifiably proud of their famous 9th Division, who would continue to fight in New Guinea and Borneo before the war ended.

Perhaps the ultimate tribute came on D-Day, by which time the 9th Division had fought a campaign against the Japanese in New Guinea. Legend has it that just before the Allies landed in Normandy, Montgomery, now Viscount Field Marshal Montgomery, asked his Chief of Staff, Major General Francis de Guingand, what he thought of the prospects for victory. 'I only wish,' the general replied, 'we had the Australian 9th Division with us this morning.'

EL ALAMEIN

John Jarmain

There are flowers now, they say, at Alamein;
Yes, flowers in the minefields now.
So those that come to view that vacant scene
Where death remains and agony has been
Will find the lilies grow—
Flowers, and nothing that we know.

So they rang the bells for us and Alamein,
Bells which we could not hear:
And to those who heard the bells what could it mean,
That name of loss and pride, El Alamein?
Not the murk and harm of war,
But their hope, their own warm prayer.

It will become a staid historic name,
That crazy sea of sand!
Like Troy or Agincourt its single fame
Will be the garland for our brow, our claim,
On us a fleck of glory to the end:
And there our dead will keep their holy ground.

And this is not the place that we recall,
The crowded desert crossed with foaming tracks.
The one blotched building, lacking half a wall,
The grey-faced men, sand powdered over all;

The tanks, the guns, the trucks,
The black, dark-smoking wrecks.

So be it: none but us has known that land:
El Alamein will still be only ours
And those ten days of chaos in the sand.
Others will come who cannot understand,
Will halt beside the rusty minefield wires
And find there—flowers.

NANCY, ANDRÉE, HÉLÈNE, *UND DIE WEISSE MAUS*

I don't see why we women should just wave our men a proud goodbye and then knit them balaclavas.

Nancy Wake

Nancy Wake was born in Wellington, New Zealand. Before she was two years old the family moved to Australia and she was raised and educated in North Sydney. Her father returned home to New Zealand shortly after the family's arrival in Australia and the six children were raised by their mother.

Nancy attended the North Sydney Household Arts School, which later became North Sydney Technical High School. She was always a feisty and independent individual and, at the age of sixteen, she ran away from home and became a nurse in the country town of Mudgee for two years.

When she returned to Sydney, Nancy worked in a shipping office and lived independently until an aunt in New Zealand bequeathed her enough money to travel to New York and London and become a journalist. She worked for the Hearst newspaper group and as a foreign correspondent. She lived in Paris, travelled around Europe and was a witness to the rise of the Nazi Party in Vienna. She was horrified by what she saw.

Nancy, whose great-grandmother was one of the first Maori women to marry a white man, was a very attractive, vivacious character, with a strong personality to match her beauty. She was a fast learner, practical, adventurous and fearless. She was known throughout her life for saying exactly what she thought, sticking to her beliefs and always acting according to her principles and her own sense of justice.

While living in France in 1937 she met Henri Fiocca, a wealthy French industrialist from Marseille, and the couple married in 1939. When the war began Nancy became an ambulance driver and, after the fall of France in 1940, she began working for the Resistance as a courier.

Under the French Vichy regime in southern France, she was able to help set up and run an escape network, which was so successful that Nancy, who was fluent in French, quick-witted and well acquainted with many people in the region, became the Gestapo's prime target, with a price of one million francs on her head. Her Resistance codename was Andrée but, due to her elusive nature and their inability to track her down or trap her, the Gestapo codenamed her *Die Weisse Maus*—The White Mouse.

In 1942 the Nazis occupied southern France, replacing the puppet Vichy government, and Resistance work became much more difficult and dangerous. There were betrayals within the network and Nancy made the decision to flee and continue her work from outside France. The train on which she was travelling, however, was stopped at Toulouse and Nancy was arrested on suspicion of being a spy. She was saved by a quick-thinking male Resistance colleague, who claimed that she was hiding her identity because she was his married mistress and they were running away from her husband.

After several failed attempts, Nancy crossed the Pyrenees and made it into Spain, where she was again arrested. This time a large bribe arranged by the British Embassy led to her release and she made it back to Britain, where she joined the SOE—Special Operations Executive—and was trained in espionage, sabotage and commando combat tactics. Her official rank during the war was captain.

It was decided that Nancy should rejoin the Resistance in the central French province of Auvergne, and she parachuted in on 1 March 1944 to join Captain Henri Tardivat and led what became the most successful resistance movement of the entire war.

The group they led, which had more than 7000 members, destroyed railway lines and bridges and attacked enemy convoys. Nancy communicated by wireless with London and coordinated parachute drops of supplies onto dozens of farms in the area. She also monitored and arranged the distribution of supplies, arms and ammunition to the network of Resistance fighters. When the group's wireless communications failed, she bicycled 300 kilometres (186 miles), bluffing her way through Nazi checkpoints, to make contact with another Resistance group in order to let London know the problem.

Nancy, whose official SOE codename was Hélène, was unquestionably the most successful Resistance leader of World War II. Her group was responsible for killing about 1500 German soldiers and, in spite of the Nazis sending an army of 22,000 men to hunt down the group, only about 100 of the Auvergne Resistance fighters died at the hands of the Nazis. The Auvergne Resistance are credited with being responsible for more than 70 per cent of the German deaths during the occupation of France.

As the Resistance leader Hélène, Nancy Wake was successful because she was ruthless, determined and exceptionally brave. She was a good shot and was known to have killed more than one German sentry with her bare hands. Once, when she learned that a young female traitor had been captured by some of her group, Nancy ordered that she be shot in cold blood. When the order was not carried out, due to the group's familiarity with and sympathy for the girl, Nancy said she would come and do it herself. The order was then carried out.

After the war, Nancy discovered that the Gestapo, in their attempts to track her down, had tortured her husband to death in 1943, but he had not betrayed her. She always blamed herself for his death.

Nancy worked in the intelligence section of the British embassies in Paris and Prague, post-war, before returning to Australia where she stood as a candidate for the Liberal Party against the Labor stalwart and Deputy Prime Minister Dr H.V. Evatt, in the 1949 federal election. Although she did not win, Nancy recorded a 13 per cent swing to the Liberals in the safe Labor-held seat. The Curtin Labor government lost the election and Robert Menzies became prime minister.

Nancy ran against Evatt again in 1951, and came within 250 votes of taking one of Australia's safest Labor electorates, Barton, for the Liberals. She then went to live in England and worked as an intelligence officer for the Air Ministry in Whitehall. In 1957 she married John Forward, an officer in the RAF, and the couple came to Australia several years later and settled in Sydney. Nancy stood unsuccessfully at the federal election in 1966, in the safe Labor seat of Kingsford Smith, and achieved a 7 per cent swing against the sitting Labor member.

Nancy was famous for her bluntness and quotable quotes. When she parachuted into France in 1944 and first met her fellow Resistance captain, Henri Tardivat, she was hanging from the branches of a tree by her parachute. He looked up and remarked that he hoped all the trees would bear such beautiful fruit that year. Nancy replied, 'Don't give me that French shit, get me down.'

After the war Nancy was not awarded any Australian medals, as she had been a French and British agent. Many Australians thought this was wrong and it became a political issue. Nancy was fed up with the debate and refused to accept any Australian honours. After decades of feisty argument and disagreements over government policy with both major parties, she told a reporter who brought up the subject, 'The last time there was a suggestion of that, I told the government they could stick their medals where the monkey stuck his nuts . . . They can bugger off!'

At the end of the war, Nancy had been awarded the British George Medal, the US Medal of Freedom and the French *Médaille de la Résistance*, as well as the *Croix de Guerre* . . . three times, to go with her four British service and campaign medals. In 1970 she became a chevalier of *la Légion d'Honneur* and, in 1988, she was awarded France's highest honour and made an officer of the order.

She finally graciously accepted Australia's highest honour in 2004, at the age of 92 and became a Companion of the Order of Australia. The Returned Services Association in the land of her birth, New Zealand, gave her its highest honour, the RSA Badge in Gold, in 2006.

After the death of her husband in 1997, Nancy decided to return to Britain, which she did in 2001. She lived for two years, as a guest of the management, at one of her favourite places, the Stafford Hotel in St James's Place, which had been an Allied Forces Club run by her friend Louis Burdet, another Resistance fighter, at the end of the war. In 2003 she moved to the Royal Star and Garter Home for Disabled Ex Service Men and Women, where she was well looked after until her death, aged 98, in 2011.

In accordance with her wishes, Nancy's ashes were scattered in the woods in the countryside outside Montluçon, the town where she led her Resistance fighters in a successful raid on Gestapo Headquarters in 1944.

IN THE WAKE OF NANCY

Martin Rossleigh

> If a German came at me I'd kick him in the three-piece service and
> chop him in the side of the neck.
>
> Nancy Wake

I came to know Nancy Wake as a result of her wonderful generosity of
spirit in doing something very special for me.

I was a teacher for many years at Sydney Grammar School. Each year
I had a new class of primary school boys and one thing I used to teach
was 'how to write a letter'. I was inspired to become involved in primary
school education because of my amazing Year 6 teacher, who made each
day enjoyable. Consequently, when I started my teaching career, I endeav-
oured to make my students' school days as memorable as possible.

One year, to make letter writing more interesting, I decided to tell the
class about a friend who had complained about never receiving any mail.
Our job was to put a smile on his face when he next went to check his
letterbox. The mission was successful! After twenty-four letters tumbled
out of his letterbox, he was both amused and gracious enough to reply.

So, each year, I went through the same routine. Friends, family, even
my future wife, were recipients of the dreaded envelopes. As every student
had to finish the letter with a joke, I hoped that our 'victim' would finish
his or her reading with a smile.

After a decade, my list of friends and family had been seriously
diminished and I needed to think of a different angle. In 1995, I told my
class of ten and eleven year olds that I thought it would be a wonderful
idea if we could find someone special, a person who was connected

to the events of World War II, it being the fiftieth anniversary of its conclusion.

I had always been fascinated by the story of Nancy Wake, The White Mouse, so I told my class her story. I explained what a brave and heroic lady she was, how she travelled to Europe in the 1930s as a young journalist, discovered the horrors of Nazism and worked for the French Resistance.

With my own interest re-aroused, I made it my mission to find out where she lived and off I went to the local library. All I needed to find was a copy of *Who's Who*, which did not take long. I looked up the 'W' entries and there she was—'Nancy Wake 5/82 William St, Port Macquarie'.

Next day, full of enthusiasm, I informed the boys that I had a postal address for our project. We were on our way.

As always, it began as a formal letter-writing exercise. The boys explained why they were writing to her; they talked about school, their families and interests. The most interesting part, though, were the questions that they were formulating to ask her. Responses to these would make the exercise special.

The letters and accompanying illustrations were sent off before the school holidays. Little did we know that individual replies would be waiting for us all when we returned to our classroom a fortnight later.

The Nazis had killed Nancy's first husband, Frenchman Henri Fiocca, during the war and, in 1957, she married John Forward, an English RAF officer. Consequently, her letter to me was signed 'Nancy Forward'. Interestingly, however, her individual replies to the boys were all signed 'Nancy Wake'.

Nancy's letter to me was dated Wednesday 5 July 1995:

Thank you so much for sending me your students' letters—some of them made me laugh, as did their sketches. I made a terrific effort and answered each one—my husband was very helpful and typed them. Please don't tell any more students about me!!

I'm off to France early next month to celebrate the end of World War II with my old friends in the Auvergne.

I am enclosing three paperbacks of 'The White Mouse'. Do what you like with them.

I hope you are having an enjoyable holiday.

Yours sincerely,

Nancy Forward

The boys were very excited to hear back from Nancy—but to receive individual replies, and so soon, was completely unexpected.

Her responses to their statements and questions were full of detail and her personality and character really shone through.

Among her sometimes humorous and kind answers about childhood pets and experiences, she wrote answers to questions about what it was like living through a war and why she risked her life for others, when she could have been 'safe at home':

> You ask what it is like to live through a war. If one believes in what one is fighting for it is fairly easy. I was fighting for freedom and because of my loathing and hatred of Hitler and his Nazi Party.
>
> I joined the French Resistance early in 1941 simply because I believed in freedom and hated and despised the Nazi Germans and all they stood for.
>
> As a young cadet journalist visiting Vienna soon after Hitler was becoming powerful, I saw the stormtroopers whipping and kicking Jews. I was horrified and vowed there and then that if I could ever do anything against the Nazis I would do so.
>
> The most difficult and dangerous task was to pretend to be an innocent citizen whilst carrying out subversive work.

One boy wrote, 'We have researched heroes such as yourself who put their lives at risk for others.'

Nancy replied, 'I am very old-fashioned. I do not consider myself to be a hero. As I am a female, I think heroine would be a better word.'

Several boys were interested in her medals and asked how it felt to own them and where they were now.

She replied:

> I am very proud of my medals—they were all given to me with affection, gratefulness and respect. The RSL bought my medals and donated them to the Australian War Memorial Museum. I still have my miniatures, which I wear on official occasions.

Asked by one boy if she was scared when she parachuted into France, she replied, 'No, I was not scared when I jumped into France—just thankful the parachute opened.'

Quite a few of the boys saw Nancy as a sort of swashbuckling female James Bond. One typical question was, 'I would like to ask you if you were a double spy and how did you like travelling and parachuting?'

Nancy replied matter-of-factly to these inquiries:

I was not a spy. I was sent to France with an Englishman and our duty was to arm the Maquisards in the Auvergne region, train them and teach them the finer points of sabotage.

Obviously we did not do this on our own—we had lots of assistance. We had seventeen fields on which to receive the parachute drops and had to man the fields from 10 pm to 4 am every night during the full moon period. The containers were filled with arms, ammunition and trousers, shirts, boots and socks.

The most memorable and useful thing I did was to get through the German lines on my bicycle and re-establish contact with England.

For your information I have never ridden a bicycle since.

Hiding did not cause too many problems—I had lived in France for several years before the war and had many friends scattered all over the country. I enjoyed any exploit as long as it hampered the enemy. I was never afraid and only hoped that if I was captured, I would keep my mouth shut when they tortured me.

I am not quite sure why the Germans called me The White Mouse. We think that perhaps I was like a little field mouse wiggling in and out of things! I got caught when the Germans surrounded a train and ended up in Toulouse but Patrick O'Leary bluffed the police and I was released.

I was also in a Spanish prison for a few days but the British paid the Spanish Head of Police a thousand pounds sterling and a gold bracelet and I was released.

Another boy, who was reading Nancy's autobiography, was more concerned with her personal welfare. He wrote, 'My favourite part so far in your book is when you parachute into France and a young Frenchman wouldn't let you bury your parachute. It kept you warm for nights to come.'

Nancy replied:

The young Frenchman who would not let me bury my parachute (which we were supposed to do) became one of my very best friends and I was sad when he died several years ago. His name was Henri Tardivat. His daughter is named Nancy after me and I am her Godmother.

———

I kept in touch with Nancy over the next couple of years and in January 1998 my wife and I, with our three young children, headed off to Port Macquarie for a family holiday. Before we left, I rang Nancy to ask her if we could take her and her husband out for dinner one night. I was unaware that John, sadly, had passed away a few months earlier. Nancy said that she would love to go out with one proviso—'Can you please make it a Wednesday?' she asked. 'That is when I get my hair done.'

That evening was memorable in many ways. Nancy loved a Gordon's gin to start, and quite a lot of Mateus Rose to follow; they were her favourites. She was very relaxed and a true raconteur.

When I dropped Nancy back to her flat there was a problem; she could not find her key.

I stood watching her rifle through her handbag. After several minutes I asked if I could help. Her response was priceless. 'You won't be able to find it because I was a secret agent and it's hidden,' she whispered.

When she finally gave me permission to assist in the search, she repeated the comment. I looked in vain until she suddenly said, 'Oh, I know where it is!' She grabbed the handbag back from me and exclaimed, 'Here it is! I told you!'

To this day I still do not know where in that handbag she had hidden her key.

We visited Nancy the next day, to see how she was and thank her for her company the night before. We were struck by the fact that, on the walls of a very unremarkable flat, on the mid-north coast of New South Wales, were framed awards for remarkable bravery from the French, British and United States governments.

I continued to check up on Nancy now and then, to see how she was getting along. She was in her mid to late eighties, living on her own, and I was concerned to make sure that she was healthy and happy. She appreciated our chats over the phone and would often refer to the letters that she had received from my class.

'If you are ever in Sydney,' I always concluded, 'we would love to see you.'

During a chat in 2000, amazed that I hadn't thought of it much earlier, I asked what I would need to do to get her to Sydney, to speak at the school.

Her reply was very succinct; 'Just fly me down and put me into a hotel.' And that is what we did!

I was quite anxious when the day arrived. Nancy was now in her 88th year and my fear was that her memory could be failing. This concern, however, vanished as soon as I met her at the airport. Her mind was as sharp and active as ever and I knew that this would be a special event.

All the Year 5 and Year 6 students had prepared questions to ask Nancy and that part of the visit went particularly well. Small groups of pupils sat around her and engaged in some great conversations.

The editor of the local newspaper sent a journalist to write a story on the visit, which appeared in the following week's edition.

After school, the Year 5 boys who had written the letters in 1995, and were now in Year 10, were invited to a memorable afternoon tea, one of the highlights of which was the plate of 'White Mouse' meringues.

It was wonderful to see the looks on their faces when they met Nancy and realised she was a real person, not just someone they had written to five years earlier as a class exercise.

The next morning, at a special assembly attended by every pupil from Kindergarten to Year 6, our music teacher played a stirring rendition of *La Marseillaise* on the piano. Nancy waved her walking stick to the beat of the music, on her way to her seat at the front of the hall.

Her speech was memorable in many ways. However, what the teachers who were there remember to this day is a comment Nancy made about her work in the Resistance. She said that, as far as she was concerned, 'the only good German was a dead German.'

Although it was said 'in context', it was perhaps unfortunate that sitting in the front row was a Year 3 boy whose parents were German. It could have been a very awkward moment but, happily, it wasn't—though it was the part that many of the staff still remember.

In January 2002, I received a short letter from Nancy. I was well aware that she wanted to move to the United Kingdom and one day, when she left this earth, to have her ashes scattered in France. This is what she wrote:

I have left Australia for good and now live at the above address.
I often think of you and the school children and yours as well.
I do hope you are all well and thriving.
Love from Nancy

The address to which she was referring was the Stafford Hotel in London. There are different theories as to who was paying for her comfortable retirement accommodation, but one thing is certain; it wasn't Nancy.

Not long after this, poor health meant that she was relocated to the Royal Star and Garter War Veterans' Home. I was pleased that I was able to pass on an email message from Nancy, via her nurse, wishing the Year 5 letter writers all the best at their farewell dinner, when they were finishing school as Year 12 students.

In November 2009 her nurse emailed.

> Thank you for your message. Nancy receives all the good wishes that you send her. Unfortunately, it is not possible for her to acknowledge them personally, but she is always pleased to hear from you with news of your family and the boys at school. She remains particularly interested in news about young men, and whilst she is now a very good age with a memory that is not what it was once, her personality and sense of mischief remain intact.

When word came through in 2011 that Nancy had died just three weeks short of her 99th birthday, there was much sadness at our school, but also many smiles when memories of her visit were recalled.

She was an amazing woman.

THE REWARD

Anonymous

In later days some child with careless whim,
Will gather flowers where now the dead are piled.
He will not know, this careless little child,
What thing it was made bright those flowers for him.

PART IV

FIGHTING THE EMPEROR

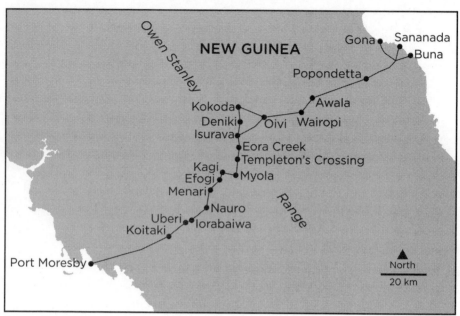

THE KOKODA TRACK

TWO ARMIES

Australia effectively had no regular army before World War II; the Citizens' Military Force, the CMF Militia, *was* the army. We raised expeditionary forces in times of war, as in WWI and the Boer Wars, and disbanded them when the conflict ended. The regular Australian army was born out of WWII.

The Australian army, in 1939, consisted of 3000 regular soldiers and 80,000 part-time members of the Citizens' Military Force (CMF).

Prime Minister Menzies announced the formation of the 2nd Australian Imperial Force (AIF) for overseas service on 15 September 1939. As the CMF was legally restricted to service only in Australia and its territories, this had to be done by raising new units rather than transferring CMF units, giving Australia two separate armies throughout WWII.

Recruitment for the 2nd AIF was slow at first, probably due to Menzies announcing, in October 1939, that compulsory conscription of all men of eligible age into the CMF militia would begin on 1 January 1940. Conscription had been a divisive issue in WWI and no Australian government was willing to conscript men for overseas service, although many in the Menzies government advocated such a plan.

The initial AIF recruitment intake of 20,000 men, along with CMF militiamen who transferred to the 2nd AIF during October and November 1939, was organised into an infantry division, which became the 6th Division, the first division of the 2nd AIF to be formed. It was intended that the 6th Division would fight in France and they embarked for the Middle East to complete training in February and March 1940.

The British evacuation from Dunkirk in May 1940 had a big effect on the future of Australia's involvement in WWII, sharply increasing the rate of enlistment into the AIF with men volunteering out of a sense of duty to defend Australia and the British Empire. Approximately one in six Australians of military age enlisted before the British evacuation from Dunkirk in May 1940. After Dunkirk, with Britain under serious threat, there was a big increase in the rate of volunteers.

The other effect of the fall of France, however, was that the plan for the 6th Division to fight in France was scrapped and Australia's part in the war against Germany and Italy shifted, with the 6th Division seeing action in not only North Africa in 1940 against Italian forces but also in Greece and Crete in April 1941 and later in New Guinea, including the Kokoda Track between July 1942 and January 1943.

The 7th, 8th and 9th Divisions of the 2nd AIF were organised from recruitment in 1940 and were deployed overseas during 1940 and 1941.

The 7th Division fought against the Vichy French in Syria and Lebanon with the British, and in North Africa where the 18th Brigade (a brigade of the 7th Division) were part of the defensive role in the Siege of Tobruk. They later served in Java and New Guinea in December 1941.

The 8th Division were sent to fight in Malaya and the islands to the north and were mostly taken prisoner during the Fall of Singapore in 1942 and at Ambon and Rabaul, and many suffered horribly in Japanese prison camps.

The famous 9th Division became the 'Rats of Tobruk' and the heroes of El Alamein in 1942. They later served with distinction in the New Guinea campaign and in Borneo in 1944.

The 10th Division was formed in 1942 but was disbanded later that year when it was realised that losses of 7000 men a month meant that other divisions needed the men as reserves. The 7th, 8th and 9th Divisions lost men and gained replacements constantly. An entire tank corps, the 1st Armoured Division, was one of the first raised, but never left Australia and was disbanded when the threat of invasion from Japan faded in 1943.

The 2nd AIF was the Australian army's main combat force throughout the war and more than 200,000 of the 265,000 CMF militiamen transferred to the AIF during the war, although the Menzies government attempted to limit the number of transfers in order to build defences at home.

Because the AIF was serving overseas initially, the defence of Australia was the responsibility of the Australian Military Force (AMF). The AMF was made up of units of conscripted and volunteer militiamen (CMF) and some units of specialist permanent soldiers, such as ordnance (army stores) personnel, coastal artillerymen and fortress engineers.

At first, there were obvious differences in uniform and status between the two armies. The AIF, as an expeditionary force, had higher status, better equipment and smarter uniforms. As the war went on, however, practical differences between the AIF and AMF disappeared. By 1943 they were eating the same food and carrying the same weapons and wearing the same blackened General Service Badges (Rising Sun).

Only the AIF wore the 'AUSTRALIA' metal shoulder badge, which was introduced for 1st AIF overseas contingents in WWI. This badge signified to the public that the member had volunteered and had been accepted for voluntary active service overseas in defence of Australia and the empire.

The differences between Australia's two armies were to come into play when the AMF and AIF served together in the defence of the Kokoda Track in 1942, where there was evidence that certain members of the military hierarchy held prejudicial views about the CMF conscripts.

The fact that the CMF was a part-time force and the 2nd AIF drew from the traditions of the 1st AIF in WWI, meant that there were always tensions between the two because of the different nature of the forces. The militia were called 'chocolate soldiers' or 'chocos'; the AIF men were called 'five bob a day tourists'.

Many Australians had their doubts about the British capacity to defend Australia and, after the attack on Pearl Harbor in December 1941, the newly elected Labor Prime Minister, John Curtin, demanded Australia's troops be sent home rather than being used to defend British interests in Europe, Africa and Burma.

After the Fall of Singapore on 15 February 1942, Curtin defied Churchill and demanded the return home of the Australian 7th Division, which was headed to Burma. Curtin telegraphed Churchill saying it was 'quite impossible to reverse a decision which we have made with the utmost care' and the troopships changed course in the Indian Ocean and the men came home to Australia.

Once the AIF divisions returned home, animosity deepened between the two different Australian 'armies'. The men in the militia units, the 'chocolate soldiers', were accused of melting away when the going was hot, and suffered scornful criticism from certain elements of the public and the media, as well as from the 'regulars' of the AIF. This was in spite of the fact that many of the militiamen had volunteered for overseas service and were not allowed to go.

As New Guinea was an Australian protectorate, classified as 'home', militia divisions saw service there on the Kokoda Track and at Milne Bay, Gona and Sanananda.

In 1943, the law was changed to allow the transfer of militia units to join the AIF if 65 per cent of their members had volunteered for overseas service. Further controversial changes to the *Defence Act* meant that militia units were able to serve anywhere south of the equator.

During October and November 1942 there had been articles in US and British newspapers criticising Australia's war effort. At this time the AMF totalled 262,333 men and the AIF 171,246. In response to this, and with an election looming, Prime Minister Curtin, who had been imprisoned for his anti-conscription stance in WWI, managed to convince the Labor Party to accept legislation that meant AMF troops could be sent to serve in an area 'bounded by the equator and 110th and 159th meridians of longitude, for the duration of the war and up to six months of Australia ceasing to be involved in hostilities' or 'such other territories in the South-West Pacific Area as the Governor-General proclaims as being territories associated with the defence of Australia'. This policy was passed by parliament on Australia Day, 26 January 1943.

Militia units saw action against Japanese forces from early 1942 and 32 militia infantry battalions, organised into three militia divisions, saw service over much of the south-west Pacific.

Until early 1944, Australian infantry forces played a key role in the Pacific providing the majority of troops in the south-west Pacific. From the middle of 1944, due to American strategy, Australian troops were more or less used in secondary operations against the Japanese.

When the war ended, there were 225,000 Australian troops in Asia and the Pacific, and 20,000 in Europe and the Mediterranean.

So, Australia had two separate armies during the period of the war—the Citizen's Military Force and the 2nd AIF. The CMF militia, restricted to service in Australia and her territories, took no part in the war against the Axis forces in Europe, North Africa and the Middle East.

The two armies finally joined forces in New Guinea, coming together to defend Port Moresby from the massive Japanese overland assault on the Kokoda Track. But that's another story—told elsewhere in this section.

THE FALL OF RABAUL

The small Australian garrison at Rabaul, the peacetime capital of the Australian Mandated Territory of New Guinea, had been strengthened in March 1941, due to the impending threat of Japan entering the war. By May 1941 this garrison consisted of 900 men and 40 officers of the 2/22nd Battalion of the 8th Division with anti-tank and anti-aircraft regiments, known as Lark Force, most of whom had arrived at Rabaul on Anzac Day 1941.

By December, Lark Force had increased to about 1400 troops, including a headquarters group, infantry, and anti-tank and coastal artillery battery crews. These troops had not been trained for jungle warfare or fighting in tropical war zones. The battalion had been specially trained for mobile warfare in open country. Their main task was to protect the Vunakanau airfield near Rabaul and the flying boat anchorage in Simpson Harbour.

Also part of Lark Force were the local militiamen of the New Guinea Volunteer Rifles, many of whom were teenagers, and, oddly enough, a field ambulance detachment, the 2/10th Field Ambulance, which was recruited entirely from the Salvation Army and included six nurses of the Australian Army Nursing Service (AANS). The aircraft based at Rabaul were four light Hudson bombers, all used for surveillance, and ten Wirraway fighter planes, all from No. 24 Squadron RAAF.

Rabaul was just 1250 kilometres (780 miles) due south of the major Japanese base at Truk Lagoon, on the island of Truk (or Chuuk) in the Caroline Island Group on the other side of the equator. Rabaul was the obvious stepping-stone for the Japanese, the perfect location to establish a base to protect Truk and provide a headquarters from which to orchestrate the conquest of New Guinea and the Solomon Islands.

The Caroline Islands, to the east of the Philippines, had come under Spanish colonial rule in 1885, and were governed and administered from Manila until after the Spanish American War of 1898, when they were sold to Germany for £1 million under the German–Spanish Treaty of 1899. Japan, fighting as part of the Allied Powers against Germany in WWI, invaded the islands in 1914 and was granted sovereignty by a League of Nations Mandate in 1920.

On 12 December 1941, five days after the attack on Pearl Harbor, the Australian War Cabinet consulted the military Chiefs of Staff about whether to withdraw the troops from Rabaul or reinforce the garrison. On being advised that reinforcement would be difficult and possibly futile, the decision was made to evacuate women and children and leave the troops in place. This decision was made in full knowledge that they would not be able to hold out against a strong Japanese force.

With the Japanese invasion of the Philippines well underway to the north-west, and Japanese forces moving inexorably down the Malay Peninsula to the west, the first Japanese bombs fell on Rabaul on 4 January 1942. Bombing raids were then regular events until 21 January, when a massive air raid by 109 carrier-based Japanese planes was a prelude to the arrival of a 5000-strong Japanese invasion force.

The coastal artillery was destroyed in the air raid and the invasion force, known as South Seas Force and commanded by Major General Tomitaro Horii, landed on New Britain on 23 January. The Japanese had taken the main town of Kavieng on the nearby island of New Ireland unopposed on the previous day.

At midnight, Japanese ships entered Rabaul's harbour and troops were landed at Blanche Bay. Lark Force, fighting with a few anti-tank guns, mortars and Vickers machine guns, were overwhelmed in just a few hours.

More Japanese troops landed unopposed at Rabaul at around 3 pm. By nightfall Lieutenant Colonel Scanlan, commander of Lark Force, gave the order 'every man for himself' and his troops dispersed and retreated south and west into the jungle. There was stiff resistance at Vulcan Beach from a company-sized group of the 2/22nd Battalion, augmented by a small number of artillerymen, engineers and New Guinea Volunteer Rifles personnel. They held off the Japanese until daybreak when their situation became hopeless.

Squadron leader John Lerew, who famously signalled to the RAAF headquarters with the Roman gladiators' motto, *morituri te salutamus* (we who are about to die, salute you), had sent his eight available Wirraways out against the Japanese planes during the air attack the day before the invasion. The Wirraways attacked and three were shot down, two crash-landed and another was damaged. Six Australian aircrew died in the battle and five were wounded. One Japanese bomber was shot down by anti-aircraft crews. Lerew, in defiance of orders, had also prearranged an airlift and his staff were evacuated, which undoubtedly saved their lives.

The army, however, had no escape plan and only the fittest, most determined and luckiest troops and civilians survived the long withdrawal through the jungle across New Britain.

About 450 of the military personnel and civilians who dispersed into the jungle were later rescued by boat and seaplane. HMAS *Laurabada*, a yacht converted to a patrol boat, and the schooner *Lokotai* evacuated 368 survivors from the south coast of New Britain between March and May 1942. Some had spent more than three months in the jungle, evading the Japanese.

Most of Lark Force, some 1100 men, were captured and, in one of WWII's worst atrocities, 130 of these men were tied up and bayoneted to death in the infamous Tol Plantation massacre, and another 35 were tied up and shot. After the war, the man responsible for these crimes, Colonel Kusunose, committed suicide by starvation rather than face a War Crimes trial.

In a further tragic twist of fate, more than 1000 soldiers and civilian prisoners of war from Rabaul died on 1 July 1942, when the *Montevideo Maru*, carrying them to slave labour camps in Japan, was sunk by the submarine USS *Sturgeon*. The Australian officers, the nurses and several civilians who were left behind at Rabaul were later transported to Japan on the *Natuno Maru*, and remained there until liberated in September 1945, but only four of the civilian prisoners from Rabaul were alive at the end of the war.

The 2/22nd Battalion lost more than 600 men in WWII. There was no recruitment to replace them—the battalion simply ceased to exist.

A few Lark Force members remained in the jungles of New Britain and helped locals in guerrilla operations against the Japanese. Rabaul became the centre of Japanese operations in New Guinea and, although US troops invaded to take back Rabaul in December 1944, scattered Japanese forces were active on New Britain until the surrender in August 1945.

GULLS AND SPARROWS

Gull Force and Sparrow Force were part of the 8th Division 2nd AIF forces. Along with Lark Force, they made up the three relatively small units put together in early 1941 to defend the islands of New Britain, Ambon and Timor, to Australia's north, from possible Japanese invasion. Their tasks were to protect airfields and prepare the bases for larger forces of defenders who were destined never to arrive. All three forces were woefully inadequate, both in numbers and preparedness, for the tasks assigned to them in the face of massive Japanese military superiority.

The reliance on the 'Fortress Singapore' strategy was partly to blame for this inadequate response to the Japanese threat. However, the truth is that Australia's military resources were stretched to breaking point with the AIF fighting in North Africa and the Middle East. The doomed 8th Division's resources had to be thinly spread across the probable battle areas of Malaya, Singapore, Ambon, Timor and New Britain. Once the Japanese had established bases in Indo-China in 1940, and invaded the Philippines in December 1941, it was merely a matter of time before disaster befell the men of the 8th Division.

Ambon: Gull Force

The island of Ambon, in what was then the Dutch East Indies, was correctly seen to be a perfect site for an enemy air base, so two flights of RAAF light bombers were sent to the island, to provide support to the Dutch and US aircraft stationed there. The island's garrison, which consisted of 2800 Indonesian troops commanded by Dutch officers, was reinforced on 17 December 1941 by Gull Force, comprising 1131 men of the 8th Division's 2/21st Battalion, commanded by Lieutenant Colonel Leonard Roach, plus artillery and support units.

The Japanese began bombing Ambon on 6 January 1942 and, when Roach demanded more troops and guns, he was replaced by Lieutenant Colonel John Scott on 14 January.

In the mistaken belief that the southern part of the island was not suitable for landings, Allied forces were concentrated in the north. On 30 January, a Japanese invasion fleet, which included the strike force of two aircraft carriers, arrived and more than 5000 Japanese troops invaded the island from the south. With massive air support, and naval and field artillery, the Japanese easily overwhelmed the Dutch forces, which surrendered within a day.

Two hundred and ninety men of Gull Force were sent to defend the airstrip at Laha, on the western side of the island, and fought bravely against a Japanese invasion force that eventually numbered more than 20,000. Forty-seven men died defending Laha before all of Gull Force surrendered on 3 February.

In one of the worst military atrocities suffered by Australian troops, more than 300 Australians who surrendered near Laha Airstrip were executed over the following weeks, some were publicly beheaded. The bulk of Gull Force surrendered on the other side of the island, after seven Australians died in action against the invasion force there. Two hundred and sixty-seven men of Gull Force were sent to the island of Hainan, where 86 died as prisoners of war. Another 582 Australians spent the war as prisoners on Ambon, where 405 of them died from malnutrition, disease and as a result of brutal bashings and executions. Only 302 of the 1131 men of Gull Force survived the war.

Timor: Sparrow Force

In 1941, Australia's closest neighbour, Timor, was divided between two colonial powers, with the Dutch in possession of the western half and the Portuguese in control of the eastern half of the island. The Australian and Dutch governments had agreed to be allies if Japan entered the war and the ABDA Force, which opposed the Japanese, comprised American, British, Dutch and Australian forces.

Australia agreed to provide a force to complement the 650 Dutch East Indies troops on Timor. The 1400 men, known as Sparrow Force, arrived on 12 December 1941 and set up defensive positions around the

West Timorese capital of Koepang and Penfui aerodrome, where twelve RAAF Hudson medium bombers from No. 2 Squadron were stationed. Sparrow Force was made up of the mostly Tasmanian 2/40th Battalion of the 8th Division AIF infantry, plus the British 79th Anti-Aircraft Battery and artillery, signals, medical and headquarters units. Significantly, these troops were joined by the 2/2nd Independent Company, a commando unit made up of Western Australians.

Although Portugal was neutral, and opposed to any Dutch or Australian troops on its territory for fear of antagonising the Japanese, part of the 2/2nd commando unit and some Dutch East Indies troops landed near Dili in Portuguese territory on 17 December. There was no resistance from the Portuguese garrison and the rest of the 2/2nd Independent Company had joined them by 22 December.

Allied command knew Sparrow Force could not hold the island; these units (Lark, Gull and Sparrow) were always intended to be forward units to prepare defences and protect airstrips. Japanese air attacks on Koepang begun on 26 January 1942 and Allied reinforcements, which embarked from Darwin, turned back due to lack of air support and the threat of Japanese air attacks on 18 February.

On 19 February the Japanese 228th Regiment began landing at Dili, in Portuguese Timor, and on the same day the RAAF force was withdrawn from Penfui to Australia after heavy air attacks. The bombing was followed by Japanese landings on the undefended south side of the island. Enemy tanks and infantry advanced in a two-pronged attack, which divided the Allied forces and cut off their line of retreat. The 2/40th Battalion attempted to move east to Champlong after destroying the airfield but found a force of Japanese paratroops, estimated at between 300 and 500, had been dropped in their path.

The Allies killed all but 78 of the paratroop force, but were overtaken by the main Japanese force. With ammunition almost gone, 84 men dead and 130 seriously wounded, Lieutenant Colonel William Leggatt, commanding the 2/40th Battalion, accepted a Japanese invitation to surrender on 23 February.

Brigadier William Veale, however, led the Sparrow Force headquarters staff plus some members of the 2/40th and about 200 Dutch East Indies troops eastward across the border and joined the 2/2nd Independent Company commandos at Dili, in Portuguese Timor. The Australians already there had mistaken the Japanese troops arriving in the dark on 19 February for Portuguese troops until they were almost upon their positions. In a fierce all-night fight, eighteen men of the 2/2nd Independent Company, led by Lieutenant McKenzie, held the airfield at Dili against a massive Japanese force and killed an estimated 200 Japanese before damaging the airfield with explosives and retreating into the jungle. McKenzie and four others successfully ambushed the Japanese troops as they followed.

After the surrender on 23 February, nothing was heard from Sparrow Force for two months and it was assumed they were all dead or captured. On 19 April contact was made with Darwin on a radio built from recycled and stolen parts, and supplies were soon air-dropped to the guerrilla force in the jungle. The radio was nicknamed 'Winnie the War Winner'.

An entire Japanese division was kept busy attempting to find and destroy what was left of Sparrow Force, now led by Major Geoff Laidlaw. The Japanese High Command even sent an expert in jungle warfare, a Japanese major known as the 'Singapore Tiger', to Timor to solve the problem. He was killed when he rode his white horse into a Sparrow Force ambush not long after his arrival.

Sparrow Force, reinforced by another commando unit known as Lancer Force (the 2/4th Independent Company), continued to harass the Japanese for the remainder of 1942 until they were successfully evacuated in December.

Many of the men who surrendered on Timor were executed and many others died in prison camps. However, the death toll among the Timorese people was far worse—it is estimated to have been around 50,000.

The doggedness and fighting spirit of the commandos of Sparrow Force was a small ray of hope and rallying point for Australians during the darkest days of the war against Japan. Filmmaker Damien Parer travelled to Timor to film the Australians in action in late 1942. His amazing documentary *Men of Timor* is as fresh today as it was when it was made, and it can be viewed on YouTube by anyone curious enough to look for it.

SINGAPORE

During the 1920s and 1930s, as Japanese militarism began to dominate in areas to the north, Australia developed an Asian defence plan based on a subservient, pro-British notion called the 'Singapore Strategy'. This revolved around the construction of a major British naval base and garrison at Singapore that would be home to a modern, well-equipped British fleet able to act as a strike force anywhere in Asia from what was known as 'Fortress Singapore'. This pro-British strategy suited Australian governments at a time when defence spending was not a high priority—something to be avoided if possible. The idea of Britain as the mother country was still part of the Australian psyche until well after WWII. Australians were all considered British citizens—there was no separate Australian citizenship or passport until three years after WWII—and politically conservative governments were subservient to British policies on defence.

Singapore Island was fortified and equipped with huge firepower in the form of massive gun emplacements—all of which were positioned to defend the garrison from attack from the open sea to the south. When the invasion came, it came from across the narrow straits separating Singapore from the Malay Peninsula to the north. The guns facing the sea could not be moved and were never fired. The Japanese invaded French Indo-China (Vietnam) in September 1940 and had air bases capable of attacking not only Singapore, but also other British, Dutch and Australian territories.

With most of Australia's military force committed to defending Britain and fighting in the Mediterranean and North Africa, it was left to the 8th Division to join with British and Indian forces in Malaya as a precaution against a Japanese move on Singapore from the north. This concentration on defending the British territory in Malaya, and the British fortress of Singapore, left other areas, closer to Australia's north, especially Papua New Guinea, poorly defended.

When the Japanese entered the war in December 1941, two-thirds of the Australian 8th Division were stationed in southern Malaya with orders to defend the Johore region. Australia also had four RAAF squadrons and eight warships in the area. The remaining brigade of the 8th Division had been sent, at the request of the Dutch government, to defend the islands of Ambon and Timor, which were strategically important stepping-stones between the Dutch East Indies (Indonesia) and Australian territories. There was also a small garrison established at Rabaul on the island of New Britain, north of Papua New Guinea.

When the various well-prepared Japanese invasion fleets sailed for the Philippines, the Dutch East Indies, the Solomons, the Celebes, Rabaul and other destinations in late 1941 and early 1942, the inadequate and unrealistic nature of the 'Singapore Strategy' was exposed with tragic consequences for the 8th Division.

The two British battleships, HMS *Prince of Wales* and HMS *Repulse*, that were to be the core of the Singapore naval defence named 'Taskforce Z' were summarily sunk by a massive Japanese air attack on 10 December 1941. This gave the Japanese unfettered control of the sea and the ability to send convoys of invading troops wherever they wished. After taking Thailand with minimal resistance, the Japanese began their successful landings on both the east and west coast of the Malay Peninsula and moved steadily south.

In mid-January 1942, the Japanese 25th Army reached the state of Johore and engaged the men of the 8th Division. The Australian in charge of the defence of Malaya was Major General Gordon Bennett. He was facing a near impossible task as the Japanese continued to land south of British-held areas and outflank the defending troops. The geography of the narrow peninsula meant the Japanese could land to the east or west of British positions and easily outflank the defences set up by the Commonwealth troops. As in other areas of the Pacific and South-East Asia, the British had completely underestimated the size and the efficiency of the forces Japan had gathered for the invasion. Bennett made some errors in judgement and deployment, but cannot possibly be blamed for losing what was a very uneven contest as the three Japanese infantry divisions, well trained, well equipped and led brilliantly by General Yamashita, poured down the Malay Peninsula towards Singapore. At the battles of Muar and Bakri, fought between 15 and 22 January 1942, Bennett's poor troop deployment led to tragic losses. He placed the raw and inexperienced Indian troops of the 45th Brigade in the path of the veterans of the Japanese Imperial Guard at the Muar River on Malaya's west coast. It was left to two battalions of the 8th Division (the 2/19th and 2/29th) to redeploy and attempt to block the Japanese advance at Bakri, in an attempt to save the Indian 45th Brigade.

In this action Lieutenant Colonel Charles Anderson of the 2/19th Battalion took command of the Indian and Australian troops when all superior officers were killed. Anderson attempted to wait for the retreating Indian troops and led a number of heroic and valiant attacks against the encircling Japanese, who had landed more troops and outflanked the Commonwealth positions. Finally surrounded and out of ammunition, Anderson ordered his men to destroy their vehicles and disperse to the east in small groups to attempt to regain the British line. More than 400 men made it back to the British defensive position, 25 kilometres (16 miles) away at Yong Peng. The Japanese murdered the 150 wounded Indian and Australian troops who remained behind.

The Commonwealth forces in Johore did achieve some minor victories and fought some successful actions, but the whole campaign was essentially about a tactical withdrawal with delaying actions being fought against a superior force. The most successful battles of this nature were the two ambush battles fought at Gemas and Jemaluang.

Shortly before 4 pm on 14 January 1942, Captain Des Duffy and his men of the 2/30th Battalion set an ambush at Gemencheh Bridge, ten kilometres (6 miles) west of Gemas, where a wooden bridge over the creek on the main road was booby-trapped ahead of the Japanese invasion column. After allowing the advance group of 200 Japanese troops on bicycles to pass over the bridge, the explosives were set off and it is estimated that about 1000 Japanese, trapped on the road in a narrow ravine, were machine-gunned to death.

The highly successful action ended badly for the Aussies when a dead telephone line caused a loss of communication with artillery units ahead of the bridge. Unable to call for artillery cover against the main body of Japanese tanks and infantry advancing upon them, the 2/30th

Battalion had to hold the road to the south with anti-tank guns and conduct a retreat. Six tanks were destroyed before a tactical withdrawal was affected through thick jungle. Australian losses at Gemencheh Creek were 81 killed, wounded or missing.

Bloodiest of all the actions in Malaya was that fought by the 2/18th Battalion of the 22nd Brigade of the 8th Australian Division at Jemalu-ang, on the east coast of the Malay Peninsula, on the night of Australia Day, 26 January 1942. The 22nd Brigade was defending the Mersing area when reports were received from the RAAF that a Japanese invasion convoy was approaching the coast nearby. Two air raids were mounted on the convoy, but large numbers of Japanese troops were disembarked to join up with other troops in the area and a major Japanese infantry force was ready to move southward. As the 22nd Brigade withdrew, the 2/18th Battalion, commanded by Lieutenant Colonel Varley, set up an ambush south of Mersing, between rubber plantations at the village of Jemaluang. The plan was to place two rifle companies on either side of the road and allow the Japanese to pass between them. Another force with machine guns and mortars, plus the artillery of the 2/10th Field Regiment, blocked the road ahead. A further force of two companies, deployed in hiding to the north of the rifle companies, was to allow the bulk of the Japanese to pass and then close the trap behind them.

The Japanese column appeared after dark on the night of 26 January and more than a battalion of Japanese troops passed the Australian pos-itions and marched into the trap. They halted in front of the Australian road-block and waited, assessing the situation for several hours before they began attacking the flanks of the Australian forward position around 2 am. Varley waited an hour and then sprang the trap. Artillery, mortar, machine-gun and rifle fire rained down on the Japanese from three sides and the back of the trap was closed by the two companies of infantry who had been hidden to the north. In this very successful action, which delayed the Japanese advance by several days and enabled troops and civilians further south time to withdraw, Japanese losses were substantial.

When Varley received orders from headquarters to withdraw to the south at 8 am, he was forced to leave the two companies who had closed the trap from the north to fight their way out without artillery support. The bulk of the 98 Australians who died at Jemaluang were in those two companies, and after savage hand-to-hand fighting there were only enough men left to form one platoon.

In spite of actions like these, and heavy losses, the 8th Division could do no more than slow the inevitable Japanese advance. After being outmanoeuvred by more troop landings and superior military strategy, all Commonwealth units withdrew to the island of Singapore on the night of 30 January 1942. By that time most of the 8th Division units were at half-strength.

By 1 February, the population of Singapore Island had swollen from its normal half a million to a million civilians and 85,000 troops, as refugees from Malaya fled from the advancing Japanese. Severe food and water shortages and frequent bombing raids by the Japanese made the situation desperate.

Lieutenant General Percival, the British commander of Singapore, was convinced the Japanese would cross the strait and land on the north-east coast of the island. With this in mind, he placed the near full-strength British 18th Division to the east and the under-strength Australian 8th Division to the west. The first Japanese landings took place in the Australian sector, where the straits are narrowest, on 8 February, after a massive air attack and ferocious bombardment by artillery. The Japanese pushed back the 22nd Brigade of the 8th Division and a Chinese company, establishing a base on the shore of the island by the afternoon of 9 February.

The following day the 27th Brigade of the 8th Division failed to repel another landing of elite troops further east near Kranji. The Australians were then forced from their positions after two days of heavy fighting and withdrew back towards the centre of the island, fighting rear-guard actions against Japanese tanks. General Yamashita called on Percival to surrender on 11 February, but the British general was desperate to hang on.

On the morning of 12 February, the Australians managed to turn back a tank attack aimed at the city, but the end was near and all vessels were ordered to sail at once with nursing staff and medical personnel. Percival withdrew all Commonwealth troops on the island to form a cordon 40 kilometres (25 miles) long around the city in the hope of buying time to evacuate. Many troops and officers escaped in the confused evacuation, including General Bennett, and many ships leaving Singapore were sunk by Japanese air strikes. With water supplies dwindling and his troops in disarray, Percival, who had been advised to surrender two days earlier by his senior officers, sought a meeting with General Yamashita on 15 February and formally surrendered the island at 5.15 pm that day.

Hostilities ceased at 8.30 pm and all military and civilian equipment and supplies were handed over intact to the Japanese.

Australian troops made up only 14 per cent of the fighting force on the Malay Peninsula and at Singapore, but they accounted for 73 per cent of the total deaths during the Japanese invasion. Following the surrender, almost 15,000 Australians were taken prisoner and dispatched, with some British troops, to a series of prisoner-of-war camps constructed over 25 square kilometres (10 square miles) on the far eastern end of Singapore Island. These camps were to be forever burned into the pages of Australian history as the infamous Changi POW camps.

After their success at Singapore, the Japanese had virtual control of the Bay of Bengal and turned their attention towards Ceylon (Sri Lanka) in order to press home their military superiority over the British. The Japanese carrier fleet headed towards Colombo and pursued the British fleet for a while, bombing the port at Trincomalee and successfully sinking two British cruisers and the carrier HMS *Hermes*, as well as two destroyers, including the Australian vessel HMAS *Vampire* in air strikes. Three smaller naval vessels and 23 merchant ships were also sunk in this sortie before the Japanese withdrew most of the carriers and other ships for duty in the Pacific.

The British naval operations in the wake of the defeat at Singapore were inept and poorly organised, and this reinforced the growing awareness of Japan's superior military and naval skills and tactics. Britain's false sense of superiority and outdated military organisation and attitudes were exposed for the world to see.

The Fall of Singapore on 15 February 1942 vindicated Prime Minister Curtin's decision to defy Churchill and bring our troops home. By the end of the war, Australia's attitude towards the mother country had changed significantly. The nation had a much greater sense of independence and pride in the achievements of our troops in the defence of our own shores.

Civilian inhabitants of Singapore suffered death and hardship at the hands of the Japanese, and British prestige in Asia would never recover from the surrender. After the war, General Yamashita was tried and hanged as a war criminal for atrocities committed by his troops in the Philippines before the invasion of Malaya.

Controversy still surrounds the Fall of Singapore to this day. Some British officers blamed Australian troops for the defeat; there were claims of cowardice and desertion and accounts of Australian soldiers forcing their way onto ships leaving the harbour. Major General Gordon Bennett was also accused of cowardice in deserting his men and taking a ship out of Singapore without Percival's knowledge. His excuse that he had to take valuable knowledge of Japanese tactics back to Australia seems rather flimsy in hindsight. It has been suggested that Bennett, who had criticised the British efforts in Malaya and was known to be ambitious, with a desire to lead the AIF, simply did not wish to spend the war as a prisoner. Prime Minister Curtin took the unusual step of publicly exonerating him from any wrong-doing when he arrived in Darwin, but he was effectively sidelined as commander of the militia unit responsible for the defence of Western Australia. There are no doubt elements of truth in all aspects of the debate. What is undeniable is that the 8th Division was virtually wiped out in Malaya and Singapore.

BIGGER THAN PEARL HARBOR

The grand Japanese plan for the Pacific and South-East Asia did not include the invasion of Australia. Although the Japanese High Command discussed the idea, it was decided that Japan's infantry forces and naval strength would be better used invading the islands to the north and east of Australia. There were plans to invade Fiji, Samoa and New Caledonia to the east and, by the end of January 1942, the Japanese were preparing to invade Timor and a plan had been formulated to capture Port Moresby.

As Darwin was the only base from which the Allies could launch a major counter-offensive to these Japanese operations, a pre-emptive strike was planned against what was seen as the only potential Allied stronghold on Australia's north coast. Darwin was a vital staging point for air reinforcements bound for Java. The Japanese planned to capture Timor, thus gaining an air base off the north coast of Australia, and the timing of the first and largest air raid on Darwin was due to the planned invasion of Timor the following day. The first Darwin bombing was not a sign of impending invasion, it was aimed at crippling an Allied base that posed a potential threat to the success of the Japanese invasion of Timor and New Guinea.

The two air raids against Darwin on 19 February 1942 were the first of 97 raids against Australia in WWII. These raids were not unexpected. On 16 December 1941, just nine days after the Japanese attack on Pearl Harbor, an official order to evacuate women and children from Darwin was issued by the Territory's administrator. This evacuation was carried out and effectively reduced Darwin's civilian population of near 5000 to about 2000. There were also some 15,000 Allied troops in Darwin at the time.

Air Raid Precautions (ARP) personnel were in charge of the evacuation. Assisted by local police and military staff, they organised for about 1100 women and 900 children to leave Darwin by sea for Fremantle and Brisbane, between 19 December 1941 and 15 February 1942. Many were evacuated on short notice and allowed little luggage. There was no direct railway link from Darwin to the south, but evacuation by road to Alice Springs and then train to Adelaide was possible. (Many troops arrived via the train to Alice Springs and then road to Darwin during WWII.)

Some families of military personnel and others left Darwin by plane, but the bulk of the evacuees made the trip on overcrowded ships with limited supplies of food and water. The ships were blacked out at night and a constant watch was made for enemy aircraft and mines.

Vessels taking part in the evacuation included the troop carrier *Zealandia*, which had helped take the 8th Division to Malaya, the Burns-Philp merchant vessel MV *Koolinda* and her sister ship MV *Koolama*, which was attacked by Japanese planes on 20 February, badly damaged by bombs and run aground by her captain between Derby and Wyndham west of Darwin at a place now called Koolama Bay. Most of the crew and passengers left the vessel and made their way to Wyndham overland. Later the *Koolama* managed to leave the bay and limp into port at Wyndham where she sank during another air raid on 2 March 1942. Amazingly all passengers and crew survived.

Despite the fact that an attack on Darwin was expected, and the evacuation had taken place, the town was woefully unprepared to defend itself and there was a general lack of vigilance and professionalism in both the military and civilian administrations in Darwin.

A cyclone had shut down the port from 2 to 10 February and the harbour was crammed with some 30 merchant ships waiting to unload. With the Japanese sweeping their way south, it seems incredible to realise that a strike by waterside workers had added to the congestion and armed US troops had been unloading cargo from the ships, which, because of the limited wharf capacity, could only be unloaded two at a time.

There were also US and Australian naval vessels in the port, including an Australian minesweeper group and a US seaplane tender and escorts. Ships were anchored so closely in the harbour, which had one jetty for unloading, that many were unable to move or separate to escape the bombing.

All of Australia's operational RAAF fighter squadrons were either in North Africa, Europe or the Middle East. The only modern fighter planes in Darwin were eleven US army Kittyhawks of the 33rd Pursuit Squadron, which were on their way to Java and were to fly as escort for an airlift of equipment to Timor. The Australian planes stationed in Darwin consisted of five unserviceable Wirraway training planes and six Hudson patrol aircraft.

Darwin had only light automatic anti-aircraft weapons and none larger than 20 mm, although there were quite a few batteries of these small guns in place. An experimental station for the new RADAR technology was being built but was not operational.

On the morning of 19 February, the approaching Japanese planes were spotted and reported by a coast watcher on Melville Island and also by Father John McGrath, a Catholic missionary on Bathurst Island who sent a message to the effect that 'an unusually large air formation' was approaching from the north-west.

Darwin received both warnings, at least twice by radio, between 9.15 and 9.37 am, but no action was taken. RAAF operations staff ignored the warning as they assumed the coast watcher and the priest had spotted the ten operational US Kittyhawks and a Liberator bomber, which had taken off earlier for Timor.

The information was passed on to Captain Edward Thomas, Naval Commander in Darwin. He was expecting just such an event, but failed to challenge the RAAF dismissal of the sightings and any chance the military had to make preparations for the attack was lost.

The two air raids on 19 February 1942 were planned and led by Japanese Naval Air Service Captain Mitsuo Fuchida, who also famously planned and led the attack on Pearl Harbor two months earlier.

The Darwin raids on 19 February were, however, larger than the Pearl Harbor raid and more bombs were dropped than at Pearl Harbor. It was the first time since European settlement that mainland Australia had been attacked by a foreign enemy. The operation has often been described by military historians in retrospect as 'using a sledgehammer to crack an egg' and even Fuchida himself said later in his report that the operation 'seemed hardly worthy' of his highly trained strike force.

Fuchida led the first group of 188 attack aircraft, which were launched from *Akagi*, *Kaga*, *Hiryū* and *Sōryū*, the four Japanese carriers of the First Carrier Fleet, commanded by Admiral Nagumo and stationed 350 kilometres (217 miles) from Darwin in the Arafura Sea near Timor.

In the first attack, which began at 9.58 am, heavy bombers pattern-bombed the harbour and town while dive-bombers and Zero fighters attacked shipping in the harbour and bombed the military and civil airfields. The first victim of the raid was a US Catalina flying boat near Bathurst Island, which was spotted and attacked by nine Zeroes. The pilot was Lieutenant Tom Moorer, who would survive to later become an admiral and eventually Chairman of the US Joint Chiefs of Staff. Moorer crash-landed into the sea and, although the passing freighter that rescued him, the *Florence D*, was later attacked and sunk, Moorer and most of the crew survived.

The Japanese also met the US Kittyhawks, which had aborted their mission to Timor due to a storm and heavy cloud and returned to Darwin. Some were refuelling and the rest were in the air. In the resulting air battle, Japanese fighters shot down all of the US planes, except one piloted by Lieutenant Robert Oestreicher who managed to survive the attack and claimed to have shot down two Japanese planes. The Kitty-hawks on the ground refuelling, along with Lieutenant Oestreicher's plane that he landed safely, were all destroyed, along with all the Allied planes. None managed to take off.

Once the pattern-bombing runs of the town and harbour were completed, 80 torpedo bombers attacked the ships in the harbour, while 70 dive-bombers, escorted by 36 Zeroes, attacked the RAAF bases, other airfields and public buildings, including a hospital.

Eight ships were sunk in Darwin Harbour including a large American troop carrier and the destroyer USS *Peary*, which lost 80 crew in the attack. The merchant ship SS *Zealandia*, which was being used as a troop trans-port, also sank. Not long after the raid was over, MV *Neptuna* exploded spectacularly when 200 depth charges she was transporting blew up as a result of fires caused by the bombing.

The HMAS *Mavie*, a patrol boat, was also sunk along with an American freighter, a British refuelling vessel and a coal transport ship. A loco-motive, which was on the pier, was blown into the harbour and the jetty was partly destroyed.

The seaplane tender USS *William B Preston* was badly damaged but managed to make a run to the open sea and was later repaired at Fre-mantle. The hospital ship *Manunda* was attacked and damaged in spite of her obvious white hospital colour and signage, and the minesweeper HMAS *Gunbar* was damaged by strafing as she left port. A crewman was killed and five others were wounded. Three ships were saved from sinking only by being beached after suffering severe damage and another ten were badly damaged in the raid.

Planes from the strike force found and sank the *Florence D* after it had gone to the rescue of another Filipino merchant ship, the *Don Isadore*, which was able to run aground on the Australian coast although severely damaged and sinking. Most of the crew of the *Florence D* made it to shore and the corvette HMAS *Warrnambool* rescued the survivors of both crews a few days later.

In total the air force hardware damage included all ten Kittyhawks, a B24 bomber and three transport planes. The US navy lost four flying boats and the RAAF lost all six Hudsons and the Wirraway training planes. Most civil and military facilities in Darwin, along with most essential services including water and electricity, were badly damaged or totally destroyed.

The attack lasted 40 minutes and was followed, an hour later, by the second wave—a twenty-minute attack on the RAAF base from high altitude by 54 land-based heavy bombers that had taken off from recently captured airfields at Ambon and Kendari.

Darwin was devastated and left in chaos, but the Japanese were dismissive of their easy target. Captain Fuchada noted derisively that 'a single pier and a few waterfront buildings appeared to be the only port installations. The airfield on the outskirts of the town . . . had no more than two or three small hangars, and twenty-odd planes of various types scattered about the field . . . were destroyed where they stood. Anti-aircraft fire was intense but largely ineffectual, and we quickly accomplished our objectives.'

The number of Japanese aircraft shot down during the air raid has always been a matter for conjecture. Two aircraft were acknowledged as lost by the Japanese, while Allied reports claimed five Japanese aircraft were definitely destroyed and probably another five shot down. One Japanese Zero pilot crash-landed on Melville Island and was captured by a local Tiwi Islander and handed over to the army to become the first prisoner of war captured on Australian soil.

The two raids on 19 February, the first of 64 that Darwin would suffer, claimed at least 243 lives and around 400 more people were badly wounded. Some estimates by rescue workers of up to 1100 dead have never been substantiated. Darwin Mayor Jack Burton estimated 900 people were killed, while the official government figure, given via the census as fifteen several days later in order to prevent panic, was obviously nonsense. The best official count possible after the war estimated the number at 292 to 297 dead.

Chaos reigned in Darwin after the air raids as rumours of an imminent invasion spread. There was widespread panic and about half of Darwin's remaining civilian population fled, believing the Japanese were about to land. Even worse, there were reports of soldiers looting and, according to official figures, 278 RAAF servicemen were considered to have deserted—as the panic in the town was repeated at the RAAF base.

There are explanations for these reports. The desertions among RAAF personnel were actually mostly the result of a verbal order from the RAAF Station Commander, Wing Commander Griffith, for all airmen to move half a mile down the main road and then half a mile inland, where a food station would be set up. This vague order was passed on by word of mouth and interpreted as an order for the general evacuation of the area in response to an impending Japanese invasion. Many men gathered their belongings and abandoned their stations; the looting had been interpreted as a further response to this every-man-for-himself misinterpretation of orders. Order was gradually restored to the town in the days following the raids, services and infrastructure were slowly restored, and the military defences were eventually rebuilt and strengthened.

Darwin remained an important base for the RAAF and the garrison was reinforced with infantry and artillery units, but the Royal Australian Navy (RAN) moved its operations to Fremantle and Queensland ports. Many civilians who fled either never returned and some who did return after the war claimed land they owned had been appropriated by government bodies or other residents in their absence.

Darwin was bombed 62 more times between March 1942 and November 1943. Most of these raids were small scale in comparison to the first and aimed at RAAF installations and airfields. Some of the heaviest attacks, however, targeted the harbour and fuel storage facilities and involved large numbers of planes. Up to 50 planes took part in many of these raids throughout April 1942. On 16 June, a large Japanese raid set fire to the oil storage tanks around the harbour and destroyed many of the vacant buildings in the town and the railway yards.

The attack enabled Prime Minister Curtin to apply pressure on Britain to provide planes and release RAAF squadrons to defend Australia.

Pressure was also brought to bear on Australia's US allies to realise the importance of protecting the north of Australia and using the area to attack Japanese bases.

In response to this call from Curtin, Allied air power in the region was gradually increased, there were several air bases within 100 kilometres (62 miles) of Darwin and they slowly built up squadron numbers and resistance capability. The US 49th Army Air Force group had three squadrons in the area by September 1942 and, in January 1943, three squadrons of Mark V Spitfires arrived from Britain and fighter aces such as Allan Walters and Clive 'Killer' Caldwell began to turn the tide of battle against Japan in the air. Darwin became an expensive target with the Spitfires accounting for an estimated 76 Japanese planes during 1943. Thirteen Spitfires were lost due to enemy action during that time, although another 40 were lost in accidents or as a result of damage and ditching.

Many other places in Australia's north suffered bombing raids. At Broome there were four major strikes between March and August 1942, the first of which managed to sink sixteen flying boats and kill more than 70 people, many of them refugees fleeing the Japanese invasion of the Dutch East Indies (Indonesia). The port at Wyndham was attacked twice and the air base at Horn Island was hit seven times. Derby, on the remote west coast, was bombed on 20 March 1942. Townsville, the site of the most important Allied air base in Australia, was bombed at night three times in the last week of July 1942. Katherine, inland in the Northern Territory, and Port Hedland, in Western Australia, were also bombed. Many of these incidents were substantial raids, while others involved one or two aircraft only.

By 1943 the Japanese had lost much of their strike capability and their carrier fleets were hit by growing Allied naval forces. The four carriers involved in the first Darwin bombings, *Akagi*, *Kaga*, *Hiryū* and *Sōryū*, were all sunk during the Battle of Midway in June 1942.

The truth about the bombings in the north and the successful Japanese devastation of Darwin was hidden from the public until 1945, but a Commission of Inquiry, led by Justice Lowe, issued two reports, on 27 March and 9 April 1942, which were scathing, pointing out the poor coordination between civilian and military authorities and the lack of leadership in the chaos that followed. Lowe found the RAAF's failure to act on warnings of the impending raids 'inexplicable' and was so concerned about Darwin's vulnerability that he telegraphed the Minister for Defence to tell him the town was 'vulnerable to any major attack' and it was 'absolutely imperative' that defences be strengthened.

Retrospective debate has raged in Australia since the war about the Darwin bombings, partly due to the suppression of the truth about the raids during the war. Lowe's reports, delivered within weeks of the event, provide a clear picture of the facts. Even Lowe was, however, accused of narrowing his report to cover some of the unpalatable truth.

On the Japanese side, there was also debate about the relative necessity of bombing Darwin. While Captain Fuchida's derogatory comments about Darwin as a target hardly worthy of his squadrons would seem to lend some credibility to the theory that the attacks were a waste of time, attack was seen as an essential tactic in the invasion of Timor and if it was a mistake it seems odd that the mistake was to be repeated another 62 times afterwards.

While the exact number killed in the raids remains unknown, partly due to the fact that the Aboriginal population was not accurately recorded at that time or even included in the census, the number of injured and hospitalised *is* known reasonably accurately and the figure of around 300 dead seems to make sense in light of the number injured.

To commemorate and remember the WWII attacks on Darwin, a memorial ceremony is held on 19 February every year at the Cenotaph in Darwin starting at 9.58 am, the exact time of the first attack.

THE BATTLES OF THE JAVA SEA AND SUNDA STRAIT

During January and February 1942, Japanese forces, using bases on Palau and in what is now Vietnam, took the Philippines and Borneo and spread south in a full-scale invasion of the Dutch East Indies (Indonesia). Darwin was bombed on 19 February in order to render it useless as a defensive base and Timor was invaded and taken in the next week.

Allied naval resistance was limited. The poorly equipped and poorly organised fleet opposing the Japanese was made up of mostly older WWI vessels fighting under a joint command as the ABDA (American, British, Dutch, Australian) Naval Command. This force put up some resistance to the Japanese navy at the battles of Makassar Strait (23 January) and Palembang (13 February) but the Japanese advance was rapid and resistance seemed futile. On 25 February, General Wavell left Java and the unified ABDA force was broken up and left in the hands of the Dutch, who were left to defend Java from the approaching Japanese invasion forces.

An ABDA fleet of the remaining ships was assembled at Surabaya in the last week of February to attempt to delay and inflict damage on the Japanese invasion convoys known to be crossing the Makassar Strait towards Java. The ABDA force was made up of five cruisers and nine destroyers under the command of the Dutch Rear Admiral Karel Doorman. Two of the cruisers were Dutch (HNLMS *Java* and *de Ruyter*), one British (HMS *Exeter*), one American (USS *Houston* under the command of Captain Albert Rooks) and one Australian (HMAS *Perth*, commanded by Captain Hector Waller). The destroyer squadron was made up of four American, three British and two Dutch ships.

The *Houston* had been the flagship of the US navy for part of 1938 and had served with distinction as the flagship of the Asiatic Fleet. Known as 'the galloping ghost of the Java coast', she had landed the Australian reinforcements on Timor earlier in February and defended them against a large Japanese air attack.

HMAS *Perth* began her career as a Leander class light cruiser named HMS *Amphion* in 1936, spending two years as flagship of the Africa station, based on the Cape of Good Hope. Following an agreement between the British and Australian governments and a refit at Portsmouth in the United Kingdom, she was recommissioned as HMAS *Perth* in June 1939 and performed escort duties in the Indian Ocean and Middle East, embarked troops to Greece from Alexandria, and played a minor role in the Battle of Cape Matapan in March 1941, before assisting in the evacuation of Crete in May. Returning to Alexandria with 1200 men from Crete, she was hit by a bomb that put her boiler room out of action and killed thirteen passengers and crew. She then took part in operations off Syria against Vichy French forces before returning to Sydney for a refit.

In late February 1942 she left for Batavia (Jakarta) and sailed for Surabaya to join Admiral Doorman's ABDA fleet on 25 February. Two days later at around 4 pm, 140 kilometres (87 miles) out of Surabaya, the ABDA fleet sighted the first of the Japanese convoys off the north coast of Java. Over the next seven hours, Rear Admiral Doorman attempted to manoeuvre his ships to reach the convoy and inflict damage on the troopships and supply transports.

The convoy was defended by a Japanese fleet of four modern cruisers and fourteen destroyers, under the command of Rear Admiral Nishimura. The Japanese cruisers had superior firepower, more torpedoes and superior range to those on the ABDA force.

ABDA force's ability to coordinate an attack was restricted due to poor weather, which neutralised their air reconnaissance superiority, and the fact that the Japanese jammed their radio communication, making cooperation between the four separate naval forces even more difficult than it was already.

The heavy cruisers HMS *Exeter* and USS *Houston* opened fire first. At 4.25 pm, HMAS *Perth* started firing as soon as she was within range and hit one of the enemy destroyers before the Japanese retired behind a smokescreen from where they counter-attacked with artillery, hitting and crippling *Exeter*, which was saved by a smokescreen laid between her and the enemy by *Perth*.

While Doorman persisted in attempts to get through and attack the convoy, one Dutch destroyer was sunk by torpedoes and a British destroyer was sunk by gunfire. A second British destroyer hit a mine and exploded, and HMS *Essex* managed to retire from the battle and limp back to Surabaya with a Dutch destroyer as escort. The other destroyers, having run out of ammunition and torpedoes, also returned to Surabaya.

With his force reduced to four cruisers, Doorman followed the convoy north and attempted to once again engage the Japanese. In this action both Dutch cruisers were hit by torpedoes and sank quickly, Admiral Doorman going down with HNLMS *de Ruyter*. With just the USS *Houston* and HMAS *Perth* facing a flotilla of Japanese warships, both ships headed at high speed to the port at Batavia.

The Battle of the Java Sea took more than 2300 Allied lives. Two cruisers and three destroyers were lost, but worse was to come in the next 36 hours. Next day the HMS *Exeter* and the two US destroyers escorting her to Colombo (Sri Lanka) were intercepted off the coast of Borneo and sunk by a Japanese force of eight warships.

HMAS *Perth* and USS *Houston* arrived at the Port of Tanjung Priok (in Jakarta) on 28 February while preparations were being made to evacuate the city and destroy all warehouses and harbour installations. The opportunity was taken to refuel and embark any stores that might prove useful. The day after escaping from the Battle of the Java Sea, *Perth* and *Houston* were ordered to sail for safe waters on Java's south coast. They were told there were no enemy ships in the area.

A separate Allied naval force, led by HMAS *Hobart*, had searched to the north-west for the Japanese convoy coming from Cam Ranh Bay, a deepwater bay in Vietnam, but failed to find any enemy ships at the western end of Java. As she returned to Batavia, *Hobart* was attacked from the air and damaged but reached port safely, refuelled and left via Sunda Strait for safety in Colombo.

HMAS *Perth* and USS *Houston* cast off at 7 pm and a course was set for Sunda Strait, the strait between the Indonesian islands of Java and Sumatra. At 11 pm, as they passed Bantam Bay and approached the entrance to Sunda Strait, they sailed headlong into the Japanese West Java invasion convoy's escort fleet of two aircraft carriers, five cruisers and twelve destroyers. The Japanese convoy of 50 transports and nineteen warships had arrived from Japanese Indo-Chinese bases in the north at the north-western tip of Java, near the Sunda Strait, just hours before Perth and Houston steamed into their midst.

The transports were mostly safe in Bantam Bay and the main part of the escort was patrolling to the north between Panjang and Babi islands. Just before 11 pm HMAS *Perth*, steaming ahead of USS *Houston*, was sighted by the Japanese destroyer *Fubuki*, which began following her, unseen. At 11.06 pm, *Perth* sighted a ship 8 kilometres (5 miles) ahead and, assuming it was an Australian corvette on patrol, signalled her to identify herself. This ship was, in fact, the Japanese destroyer *Harukaze*. With a battlecruiser approaching at speed, the *Harukaze* attempted to gain time by flashing an unintelligible signal in reply. The signal was the wrong colour and Captain Waller aboard the *Perth* realised his mistake when the destroyer began to make a smokescreen and attempted to retreat.

Swinging HMAS *Perth* to the north, Waller immediately ordered action stations and opened fire on the *Harukaze* with his forward turret guns. He thought he was chasing a lone patrolling Japanese destroyer. This manoeuvre brought HMAS *Perth* within sight of a group of Japanese destroyers to her north and Waller ordered his gun crews to fire at multiple targets as *Perth*, with *Houston* following a kilometre in her wake, continued swinging in a huge starboard arc westward and then south-ward and eastward to avoid the Japanese fleet.

As the two cruisers engaged in a running gun battle with the destroy-ers, they ran into Japanese fire from the ships on their port side that were protecting the Japanese convoy in Bantam Bay. The Allied cruisers fired at this convoy at anchor in Bantam Bay and sank one transport in deep water and three more in shallow water.

A destroyer squadron stood at the entrance to Sunda Strait, between the cruisers and their only means of retreat, and, with two Japanese heavy cruisers closing in fast, USS *Houston* and HMAS *Perth* could not withdraw. They were also heading directly towards the main force of Japanese cruisers and destroyers guarding the entrance to the Sunda Strait. It was not possible for the Allied cruisers to engage all the enemy vessels, which were coming at them from three sides. At midnight, with ammunition running out, Captain Waller attempted to force a passage through the Japanese war fleet to move into the Sunda Strait. Just as he altered course and ordered full speed ahead on a course for Toppers Island in Sunda Strait, HMAS *Perth* was hit on her starboard side by a torpedo from the *Fubuki*. Captain Waller gave the order to 'prepare to abandon ship' but another torpedo struck almost immediately, changing the order to 'abandon ship'.

As the crew were attempting to leave HMAS *Perth*, she was hit a third and fourth time by torpedoes. The first of these two hits came on her starboard side and sent her careening to starboard. The fourth torpedo, which hit on the port side, caused the ship to right herself and then heel over to port and sink. The explosions from the third and fourth torpedoes killed many of the men who were in the water close to the vessel and many others were dragged down as she sank. The HMAS *Perth* went down at 12.30 am on 1 March 1942.

During this time, USS *Houston* was still fighting, although badly on fire. Her gunners scored hits on three different destroyers, but the ship was then hit by three torpedoes that exploded in quick succession. *Houston*'s commander, Captain Rooks, was killed by a bursting shell just as the *Perth* went down and, as the ship lost power and Japanese destroyers moved in to machine-gun the decks, *Houston* rolled over and sank in relatively shallow water, 3 kilometres (1.9 miles) inshore from where the *Perth* lay.

While most of HMAS *Perth*'s crew managed to abandon ship before the third torpedo struck, there was not time between the torpedo strikes to launch her lifeboats and the cruiser was under heavy fire from several destroyers at close range as the crew left the vessel. Of the 680 men on board the Australian cruiser, 357 lost their lives, including Captain Waller. The USS *Houston* lost 693 of her crew of 1061.

With Japanese ships firing from all sides at the two Allied cruisers as they swung in a huge circle at sea, it is not surprising that the Japanese sustained some losses to 'friendly fire'. A minesweeper and a transport from the convoy were sunk when hit by torpedoes from the *Fubuki*. On board the seaplane transport *Ryujo Maru* in Bantam Bay was Lieutenant General Hitoshi Imamura, commander of the invasion force. He was forced to jump into the sea as the ship was hit and sunk. Imamura was picked up and rescued by a small boat and the *Ryujo Maru* was later refloated.

The naval defence of Java was a catastrophe for the Allies. The battles of the Java Sea and the Sunda Strait were crushing victories for the Japanese navy with the Allied fleet in the Dutch East Indies being almost totally destroyed. The Allies lost five cruisers, six destroyers, many smaller ships and thousands of lives. The only result was that the Japanese invasion of Java was delayed by one day. The Japanese did not lose one warship, and they effectively destroyed all opposition vessels in 48 hours. This gave the Japanese a free hand in the waters north of Australia and made the occupation of Java, Borneo, Sumatra and other islands an easy task. It also meant that Australian towns and airfields were soft targets for bombing raids for the next twelve months.

Of the 323 survivors of the HMAS *Perth*, four died ashore without being taken prisoner and another 106 men died in captivity, mostly at prison camps in Java and at the infamous Changi prison camp in Singapore and on the Burma Railway. Others died when Allied aircraft sank ships in which they were being transported—four sailors from *Perth* were saved in September 1944 when they were among prisoners of war rescued after the sinking of a Japanese transport. At the end of the war, 214 survivors of the sinking of HMAS *Perth* returned to Australia.

The full story of the Battle of Sunda Strait was not known for many months after the encounter, until accounts were finally collected from survivors and pieced together. Captain Waller was posthumously Mentioned in Despatches for his bravery; this was his third. Waller had been twice Mentioned in Despatches and awarded the DSO for his courage and devotion to duty while commanding destroyers in the Mediterranean earlier in WWII as part of the 'Scrap Iron Flotilla' and at the Battle of Matapan.

Captain Rooks was posthumously awarded the Medal of Honor for 'extraordinary heroism, outstanding courage, gallantry in action and distinguished service in the line of his profession as Commanding Officer of the USS *Houston* during the period of 4 to February 27, 1942, while in action with superior Japanese enemy aerial and surface forces'. In 1944 a US destroyer was named USS *Rooks*, in honour of the captain, and the US military maintain a park named in his honour in his home state of Washington.

The loss of the HMAS *Perth* ranks second only to the loss of HMAS *Sydney* as Australia's major naval tragedy of WWII. The fact that many of those who did survive suffered and died in the slave labour camps of the Burma Railway made the tragedy even more poignant for Australians. The failure of the combined Allied forces to even significantly delay the invasion, and the relentless and seemingly unstoppable movement of Japanese forces south, made Australians quite justifiably scared of the threat of invasion and also led to a certain amount of paranoia among politicians and the media. The 'Brisbane Line' debate, where suggestions were put forward about conceding territory to a possible Japanese invading force, was born out of this period of doom and gloom. The high regard given to the two brave cruisers HMAS *Perth* and USS *Houston* in their heroic stand against overwhelming odds did much, however, to strengthen US–Australian camaraderie and inspire public support for the war effort.

The wreck of HMAS *Perth* is now a dive destination. Much of the ship is intact and she sits on a sandy bottom in 36 metres (118 feet) of water with her 150-mm (6-inch) guns still mounted, providing a wonderful home for schools of large trevally and snapper and families of gropers. The ship's bell from HMAS *Perth* was recovered by an Indonesian diving team in 1974 and is now on display at the Australian War Memorial in Canberra.

There are memorials to the HMAS *Perth* at Perth Town Hall and overlooking the sea at Rockingham in Western Australia. The crews of the HMAS *Perth* and the USS *Houston* are honoured at the Shrine of Remembrance in Melbourne.

Three days after the Battle of Sunda Strait, in a footnote to the evacuation of Java, came the valiant action by the Australian sloop HMAS *Yarra*.

Escorting a small convoy of three ships to safety 500 kilometres (311 miles) south of Java, the tiny warship was confronted by three heavy cruisers and two destroyers of the Imperial Japanese Navy 2nd Fleet. HMAS *Yarra*'s captain, Lieutenant Commander Robert Rankin, placed his tiny ship between the convoy and the Japanese fleet and fought a futile action, firing on the Japanese warships for an hour and a half until his battered vessel finally sank under a barrage of gunfire and bombs dropped by the cruisers' aircraft.

Even after giving the order to abandon ship, Rankin stayed on the bridge, where he was killed by a direct hit, and gun crew members stayed aboard firing at the Japanese ships as the sloop went down. All three vessels in the convoy were sunk along with HMAS *Yarra*. Only thirteen of the *Yarra*'s crew of 151 survived to be picked up several days later by a Dutch submarine.

Many believe that these two naval battles, vastly different, but both featuring heroic actions by doomed ships commanded by brave men against overwhelming odds, were the finest Australian naval actions of WWII.

THE MOST CONFUSED BATTLE AREA IN WORLD HISTORY: THE BATTLE OF THE CORAL SEA

This is the amazing story of how Australia's fate and the outcome of the war in the Pacific hung in the balance while more than 60 warships and hundreds of aircraft played hide and seek in the ocean to the east of Queensland.

We remember the Battle of the Coral Sea as a defining moment in World War II and celebrate it each year because of its importance in our nation's history, but it was, in fact, a farcical series of events. Military historian Chris Coulthard-Clark described the battle as 'a series of confused and indecisive attempts by both sides to inflict serious damage on the other'. American military historian Admiral Duckworth went even further. He described Coral Sea on 7 May 1942 as 'the most confused battle area in world history'.

Maps attempting to show the movements of the various fleets from 4 to 8 May 1942 are so complex and indecipherable that they resemble more the crayon scrawlings of toddlers who have overdosed on red lollies than they do maps of any naval or military campaign.

In order to understand the importance of such an indecisive and shambolic series of encounters, which some military experts have said hardly deserves the name of a 'battle' of any kind, it is necessary to remind ourselves of the situation that Australia and the United States found themselves in as Japan speedily and successfully took control of East Asia and the islands to Australia's north.

Once the Japanese had established Rabaul as a secure military and naval base, in February 1942, they were free to attack and invade the north coast of New Guinea as well as the Solomon Islands. February 1942 saw the Fall of Singapore, the destruction of the port at Darwin, successful Japanese invasions on Timor and Ambon, and the destruction of the Allied fleet in the Battle of the Java Sea. These victories gave the Japanese virtual control of the entire region north of Australia, from Burma to Bougainville in New Guinea. The Japanese fleet, air force and various invasion forces were free to move and attack as they wished in this area.

On 8 March Japanese invasion forces established garrisons at Lae and Salamaua on Australian territory on the north coast of New Guinea. The only territory north of Australia left unoccupied by the Japanese was the eastern end of Papua New Guinea, where Port Moresby, on the southern coast, was the last strategically important bastion of Allied resistance.

To the east, the Japanese needed to gain control of the Solomon Island chain and then they intended to occupy Fiji and Samoa. As part of their war strategy, some of Japan's General Staff had suggested an invasion of Australia to prevent Australia becoming a base against their operations in the South Pacific. The idea was rejected on the grounds that Japan's forces and naval strength would be too thinly spread and could be better used elsewhere. The idea that *was* adopted was a four-part strategy that had been around since 1938 and called for the establishment of an air base at Tulagi Island, near Guadalcanal, the occupation of Port Moresby, an assault on Fiji, New Caledonia and Samoa, and the presence of a large naval carrier force in the Coral Sea, between the east coast of northern Australia and the Solomon Island chain. Control of this area would give Japan a free hand to attack Townsville and Cairns at will and would place the eastern seaboard of Australia at the mercy of the Japanese, whether they chose to invade or not.

This strategy was called 'Operation MO' and, early in 1942, Vice Admiral Inoue, commander of the Imperial Japanese 4th Fleet, also known as the 'South Seas Force', suggested it be implemented in May that year. Tulagi was to be invaded on 3 May and Port Moresby on 10 May. These two bases would then be used to strengthen the ring of defence around the main Japanese base at Rabaul and expand Japanese air and naval control further into the Pacific.

If Operation MO succeeded, Australia's northern ports and airfields would be within easy bomber range, then New Caledonia, Fiji and Samoa could be invaded and the Allied supply lines across the Pacific effectively cut. A secondary operation was also planned as part of Inoue's strategy; codenamed 'RY' this operation was to see the invasion of Nauru and Ocean Island and the capture of their valuable phosphate deposits.

In order to make Operation MO effective and successful, Inoue needed aircraft carrier support until the captured bases were established as airfields. He requested carriers from the Japanese Combined Fleet to provide the air power he needed.

Meanwhile, Naval Marshal General Yamamoto, Commander in Chief of the Japanese Combined Fleet, was working on a plan of his own. He needed to destroy, or render ineffective, the US carrier fleet, which had not been damaged in the attack on Pearl Harbor.

Yamamoto's plan was to draw the US carriers into a major sea and air engagement near Midway Atoll and use his superior strength and better-trained aircrews to put the US carriers out of action. Midway, as the name suggests, was a strategically vital base halfway between Hawaii and Japan in the Pacific. Yamamoto had built up his fleet with this objective in mind but, in response to the need for Operation MO to be successful under the command of Vice Admiral Inoue, he sent two fleet carriers, a light carrier, a cruiser division and two destroyer divisions to support the operation.

The Japanese planned to take Port Moresby in the same way that they had taken so many other places in South-East Asia. An invasion force embarked on twelve transport vessels at Rabaul in the first few days of May 1942. It departed on 6 May, bound for Port Moresby. Vice Admiral Inoue, based at Rabaul, was in charge of protecting this invasion force and the other which sailed on 2 May to occupy the Australian advanced operational base on Tulagi in the Solomons. Inoue had at his disposal no less than 51 warships, which were divided into six operational groups.

Allied vessels available to counter the Japanese fleet numbered about twenty, most of which were located south of Guadalcanal when the Japanese invasion convoy sailed from Rabaul. What the Japanese did not know was that the US navy had cracked their communication ciphers and codes and picked up references to Operation MO in March 1942. On 13 April, the British deciphered a message to Inoue that ships he needed were on their way. This made it clear to the Allied Forces that Port Moresby was the likely target for the Japanese operation.

Newly appointed commander of Allied Forces in the Pacific, Admiral Chester Nimitz, took charge of the situation and ordered all four US fleet carriers based in the Pacific to head to the Coral Sea. These would be organised into three task forces (TF), named as TF11, TF16 and TF17, in an effort to form a three-pronged attack to pre-empt the invasion by the Japanese fleet.

TF17, commanded by Rear Admiral Fletcher and centred around USS *Yorktown*, was already heading towards the Coral Sea; while TF11, under Rear Admiral Fitch, centred around USS *Lexington*, was between Fiji and New Caledonia. These two forces, which joined north of New Caledonia, comprised 27 ships (two carriers, nine cruisers, thirteen destroyers and three support vessels) and 128 aircraft. TF16, based around the carriers USS *Enterprise* and *Hornet*, was not ready, having just returned to base at Pearl Harbor. Although the Coral Sea was under the control of General MacArthur, the naval commanders of the three task forces were answerable to Nimitz, who was also based at Pearl Harbor.

A series of airborne naval engagements was fought between Inoue's fleet and the Allied ships, commanded by Rear Admiral Jack Fletcher, between 4 and 8 May 1942. This became known as the Battle of the Coral Sea. It was a confused series of engagements and near-misses but it affected the course of the war dramatically.

TF17 refuelled and headed north on 2 May. TF11 completed refuelling on 4 May and headed into the Coral Sea to rendezvous with TF44, a joint US–Australian force of three cruisers (HMAS *Hobart* and *Australia* and USS *Chicago*) and three destroyers—under the command of Australian Rear Admiral John Crace. TF44 was under General MacArthur's control. TF11 and TF44 joined up due east of Cape York, south-east of the tip of New Guinea, on 5 May.

The Japanese fleet supporting the invasion was in several groups. Some warships, under the command of Admiral Goto, accompanied the troopships from Rabaul while most left the base at the island of Truk, north-east of Bougainville. Some Japanese warships entered the Coral Sea from south of Bougainville to support the invasion fleet sailing from Rabaul. The main Japanese strike force, commanded by Admiral Takagi, with Admiral Hara in charge of air strikes, proceeded down the eastern side of the Solomon Islands. Some ships then supported the invasion of Tulagi, which was easily accomplished under the command of Admiral Shima on 3 May after the Australian reconnaissance force evacuated before the Japanese arrival. The main carrier fleet entered the Coral Sea from south of San Cristobal Island (now Makira), at the bottom of the Solomon Islands.

The Japanese had mistakenly assumed that only one US carrier was in the area. They also assumed that the Allied ships were to the east, when they were actually inside the Japanese area of operations, to the west.

Rear Admiral Fletcher was notified of a sighting of the Tulagi invasion force on 3 May. He changed course and launched air strikes against the Japanese ships and the forces attempting to build an airstrip and seaplane base on Tulagi on 4 May. These air strikes sank a destroyer and four mine-sweepers and destroyed four seaplanes; despite those losses, the Japanese were operating seaplanes from Tulagi by 6 May.

The Japanese force situated north of Tulagi sent planes to find the US carrier, but they searched to the east of the Solomon chain of islands and found nothing as the Allied ships were all to the west.

On 5 May the Allied task forces all joined up and refuelled 600 kilo-metres (373 miles) south of Guadalcanal and Rear Admiral Fletcher learned from Pearl Harbor that deciphered messages suggested the Port Moresby invasion fleet was due to arrive on 10 May. In response, Fletcher merged all the Allied ships into task force 17, which he then split into two groups called TF17 and TF17.3.

TF17.3 was the old TF44, Rear Admiral Crace's six warships. This group was sent north-west, without air support, to the south-east of Port Moresby in order to block the passage of the Japanese invasion fleet. TF17 then headed north-west where Fletcher believed he would find the Japanese warships.

Unbeknown to either side, after the Japanese force had rounded the southern tip of San Cristobal, entered the Coral Sea and moved south, the two main fleets were within 130 kilometres (81 miles) of each other. It was the closest they ever came to meeting. The Japanese assumed the Allied fleet was to the south-east and the Allies assumed the main Japanese force was in the vicinity of the transports heading to Port Moresby from the north.

On 6 May, a Japanese seaplane from Tulagi sighted TF17 about 550 kilometres (342 miles) south of Takagi's force that had moved north again. As the Japanese were refuelling and the distance range was at the extreme limit for their aircraft, they finished refuelling and then headed south to close the gap. As they were doing this, TF17 moved in a north-westerly direction.

7 May

At 7.22 am on 7 May, a Japanese reconnaissance plane from the main Japanese carrier fleet south of Fletcher's TF17 spotted the two support vessels, which had refuelled TF17 and headed south. He wrongly reported that he had found an American fleet and, in a major error of judgement due to his faulty reporting and the assumption that the Allied fleet was to the south-east, the Japanese Admirals Hara and Takagi sent the full weight of their air power, 78 fighters and bombers, to the south.

The aircraft were launched between 8 am and 8.15 am. At exactly 8.20 am, a Japanese aircraft flying out of Rabaul spotted the Allied TF17 to the north-west of the Japanese strike force and reported back to base. The message was passed on to Hara and Takagi who were confused and assumed that there were two Allied fleets operating in the Coral Sea. They decided not to recall the 78 aircraft they had dispatched five minutes earlier, sending their entire air strike force to attack a fuel oiler, USS *Neosho*, and a destroyer, USS *Sims*.

Just as the last aircraft departed from the Japanese carriers, a US aircraft from TF17 spotted the Japanese warships escorting the invasion task force to Port Moresby to the north of the Allied fleet. The pilot reported back in code that he had seen 'two carriers and four heavy cruisers' when he actually meant to say 'two cruisers and four destroyers'. Fletcher assumed that the main Japanese carrier force had been found and prepared his aircraft to attack.

All was ready two hours later when a flight of American B17s sighted and reported the same invasion convoy, 'ten transports and sixteen warships', just south of the first sighting. Although no large carriers were sighted, Fletcher took this sighting as confirmation that this was the main strike force.

All 93 available aircraft were ordered to attack and by 10.15 am they were gone to the north. At 10.19 am, the pilot who had made the first sighting landed back on the USS *Yorktown* and realised he had made a coding error. There were, in fact, no confirmed sightings of Japanese fleet carriers to the north.

The Japanese had mistakenly sent their full airborne firepower in the wrong direction, against the wrong target, and the Allies had done the same. The Japanese planes found the two support vessels and searched in vain for the main Allied fleet. Finally realising there had been a mistake, they reported back to Admiral Takagi who immediately understood that he had acted on the wrong report and the American fleet was now in between his ships and the invasion convoy. All aircraft were ordered back to the carriers except for 36 dive-bombers who were to attack the two American ships.

USS *Sims* was sunk and USS *Neosho* was crippled and drifted until found by the destroyer USS *Henley* on 11 May. The survivors of the *Neosho* and *Sims* were taken on board and *Neosho* was sunk by torpedoes. *Neosho* had sent a garbled message to Rear Admiral Fletcher saying they were sinking, but gave out the incorrect coordinates. Only fourteen men from *Sims* survived. One hundred and twenty of the *Neosho*'s crew were rescued. The death toll from the two ships was 180 men.

The American strike aircraft sighted the Japanese support force for the invasion fleet at 10.40 am. The light carrier *Shōhō* was the only aircraft carrier they could find, as she was the only one in the convoy. The *Shōhō* had only eight planes ready to launch in her own defence. *Shōhō* was a small aircraft carrier with a crew of 834 and, ironically, her other ten aircraft were below decks being prepared for an attack on TF17, whose general whereabouts was now known to the Japanese.

Although surrounded by the Japanese cruisers giving anti-aircraft support, *Shōhō* was hit by thirteen 1000-pound (454-kilogram) bombs and seven torpedoes and sank at 11.30 am. The Japanese support fleet withdrew to the north, hoping to get out of range of further attacks. Later that afternoon a Japanese destroyer was sent back to look for survivors from the *Shōhō*. Only 203 of her crew of 834 were found. The Americans lost three aircraft in the attack while all of *Shōhō*'s eighteen aircraft were lost.

The American aircraft had returned to USS *Yorktown* and *Lexington* by 2 pm and were re-armed by 2.30. Although Fletcher was tempted to attack the invasion convoy and the support fleet again, he was worried that there were other Japanese fleet carriers somewhere in the Coral Sea that he hadn't found yet. As the weather was overcast and his fleet screened by cloud, he decided to wait until scout aircraft found the main Japanese strike force before launching another attack. TF17 turned south-west.

After the loss of *Shōhō*, Inoue ordered the invasion convoy and its supporting warships to withdraw to the north and prepare for a sea battle with the Allied fleet, which he assumed was still headed north-west. The Japanese convoy was attacked by US army land-based B17s but not damaged.

Admiral Takagi was told to find and to destroy the Allied carrier fleet. However, a Japanese aircraft from Rabaul had sighted Admiral Grace's TF17.3 fleet of six warships, heading north to blockade Port Moresby, and made a mistaken report that it contained two carriers. Based on this report,

Takagi, whose aircraft had not returned from attacking USS *Neosho*, turned his fleet to the west at 1.30 pm and reported to Inoue that the Allied fleet was too distant for him to attack them that day. Two attacks were mounted against Admiral Crace's TF17.3 by aircraft based at Rabaul, but Crace's ships were undamaged and managed to shoot down four Japanese aircraft. A short time later, three US army B17s also bombed TF17.3, mistaking them for Japanese ships. Luckily they caused no damage.

Understandably fed up with being isolated from air support and running low on fuel, Admiral Crace radioed Fletcher that he was unable to reach the planned position. He then retired to a position 400 kilometres (249 miles) south-east of Port Moresby. This was a compromise designed to increase the distance between TF17.3 and Japanese carrier-based or land-based aircraft and yet still be close enough to intercept any Japanese convoy using the Jomard Passage or China Strait to reach Port Moresby. To add to the general confusion, Admiral Crace did not know that Admiral Fletcher was maintaining radio silence and consequently had no idea what was going on elsewhere in the Coral Sea.

At around 3 pm, a Japanese reconnaissance aircraft reported that Admiral Crace's TF17.3 had altered course, but the new bearing was wrongly reported as being south-easterly. Admiral Takagi made another major error. Based on the pilot's error about TF17.3's direction, and assuming that the aircraft had spotted the main Allied fleet, Takagi calculated that, on the course wrongly reported, the Allied ships would be within striking range of an air attack before dark. So, eight torpedo bombers were sent as scouts to search the sea to the west. Naturally, they did not find TF17 although they certainly flew past Fletcher's ships as they headed west.

At 4.15 pm twelve Japanese dive-bombers and fifteen torpedo bombers were launched to join the search for the Allied carrier fleet. This was a risky decision, as the planes would have to return to the carriers in darkness. As these planes flew towards a non-existent target, they were actually on a course that took them directly over the real target.

TF17 was now 370 kilometres (230 miles) to the west of the Japanese fleet under thick cloud and the American radar picked up the oncoming Japanese formation. At around 6 pm Fletcher launched eleven Wildcat fighters in a surprise attack against the Japanese planes. Eight of the twelve torpedo bombers and a dive-bomber were shot down, for the loss of three Wildcats.

The Japanese planes scattered and aborted their mission. They jettisoned their bombs and attempted to return to their fleet carriers. In a twist of fate that is almost comical, several Japanese planes found TF17 after dark and, mistaking the Allied fleet for their own, attempted to land on the American carriers until driven off by anti-aircraft fire from escorting destroyers.

The day ended with both sides preparing for extensive scouting flights at dawn next morning. Admiral Fletcher took TF17 to the west and Admiral Takagi decided to take the Japanese fleet north to be closer to the invasion convoy, which he assumed was about to engage in a sea battle with the Allied fleet.

US military historian Admiral Duckworth commented in 1972 after reading official Japanese reports of the time, 'Without a doubt, May 7 1942, vicinity of Coral Sea, was the most confused battle area in world history.' He may have been right.

8 May

Admiral Hara, in command of aircraft on Admiral Takagi's fleet, said he could never believe his bad luck on 7 May 1942 and felt like quitting the navy. On 8 May, however, luck was to turn against the Allies. To begin with, the cloud cover that had protected TF17 moved north and covered the Japanese fleet, leaving TF17 easily detectable under clear skies with visibility at 30 kilometres (19 miles).

An American plane from USS *Lexington* spotted the Japanese fleet through a break in the clouds at 8.20 am and a Japanese plane found TF17 two minutes later. The two fleets turned towards each other and launched their dive-bombers, torpedo planes and fighters almost simultaneously at 9.15 am. Sixty-nine Japanese planes headed south-west as 75 American planes headed north-east.

The planes from USS *Yorktown* found and attacked the Japanese carrier *Shōkaku* just before 11 am. Two 1000-pound (454-kilogram) bombs hit *Shōkaku* and caused massive damage to her forecastle and flight and hangar decks. The other Japanese carrier, *Zuikaku*, was hidden under a bank of low clouds in a tropical rainstorm.

Two of USS *Lexington*'s bombers found the *Shōkaku* at 11.30 am and she was hit with another 1000-pound bomb. Two other bombers found *Zuikaku* and attacked her without doing any damage, but the rest of USS *Lexington*'s dive-bombers could not find the Japanese ships in the low cloud. In the air-to-air battle two of the thirteen Japanese Zeroes protecting the fleet were shot down and five American planes were lost. *Shōkaku* was severely damaged and unable to land aircraft. With 223 of her crew dead, she withdrew from the battle and headed north-east, escorted by two destroyers, bound for Japan.

USS *Lexington* detected the Japanese aircraft approaching by radar at a distance of 126 kilometres (78 miles) and Wildcat fighter planes were launched to defend the US carriers. The savage air battle helped deflect the Japanese attack to a large extent, but two torpedoes hit *Lexington* and an armour-piercing bomb hit *Yorktown* and exploded four decks beneath her flight deck.

As aircraft from the two enemies returned to their fleets, they met in mid-air and another battle ensued in which two Japanese planes were shot down, including that of their flight commander, Kakuichi Takahashi. Forty-six of the 69 Japanese planes returned to land on *Zuikaku*, of which only 36 were able to fly again without repairs.

Admiral Takagi made another error when he reported to Inoue that two American carriers had been sunk. He also reported that, as his aircraft losses were heavy and he was low on fuel, he could not provide air cover for the invasion fleet. Admiral Inoue, aware of the presence of Admiral Crace's TF17.3, recalled the invasion convoy to Rabaul and ordered his warships to head north-east of the Solomons to prepare for the 'RY' operation against Nauru.

Meanwhile, Admiral Fletcher was assessing the damage to his strike force. Although both USS *Yorktown* and *Lexington* were badly damaged, they were still able to land the returning aircraft. The Allies lost 23 aircraft in the action and another eight during recovery. However, the worst was yet to come for Admiral Fletcher. *Lexington* had suffered damage to aviation fuel tanks in the bombing and petrol fumes had leaked through much of the ship. The first of a series of explosions, caused by sparks from unattended electric motors, rocked the vessel just before 1 pm, as planes were returning and landing. Further explosions between 2.45 and 3.45 pm resulted in a massive fire and the crew began to abandon ship around 5 pm.

With the fire out of control and the ship listing heavily, the destroyer USS *Phelps* was ordered to sink the carrier with torpedoes just after 7 pm. Thirty-six aircraft went down with the USS *Lexington*. Despite the sudden loss of the *Lexington*, only 216 out of a crew of 2951 died. Sadly, some of them died by jumping from the decks before it was really necessary to leave the ship.

Fletcher had already decided to take TF17 out of the Coral Sea before losing the USS *Lexington*. With the oiler USS *Neosho* sunk, he had no fuel supply, so he radioed General MacArthur suggesting an attack on the Japanese fleet by land-based army bombers. MacArthur radioed back that B17s had attacked the invasion convoy and it was retreating northwards. TF17 headed south then east to refuel at Tonga before the damaged USS *Yorktown* headed to Pearl Harbor for hasty repairs.

Meanwhile, Admiral Crace and his TF17.3 were unaware of any of the battles of 7 and 8 May. TF17.3 patrolled until 10 May and then returned to harbour in the Whitsundays on 11 May. At the time Crace had no way of knowing how important a part sighting of his fleet had played in creating errors of judgement and poor strategy by Japanese commanders.

Both sides claimed victory in the Battle of the Coral Sea. The sinking of USS *Lexington*, and the amount of bad luck involved in keeping the battle from being a major Japanese victory, gave the Japanese Imperial Navy a false sense of superiority and confirmed their poor opinion of Allied naval capability. They believed that future sea-to-air battles against the Allies would be easily won.

In simplistic terms, looking at the battle losses over the five days of conflict, the Japanese scored a major hit against the Allied fleet by sinking USS *Lexington*, one of only four American fleet carriers in the Pacific. They also sank a destroyer and a fuel oiler, while the Allied tally was a light aircraft carrier, a destroyer and four minesweepers. The Allies lost 70 aircraft, half of which went down on the USS *Lexington*, while the Japanese lost 92 aircraft. In terms of numbers killed, Japanese losses were 970 dead and the Allies lost 660 men.

The real results of the battle had nothing to do with numbers of ships or aircraft or lives lost.

Most importantly, the seaborne invasion of Port Moresby failed. For the first time a Japanese invasion force was made to turn back without achieving its objective. Subsequently, the Japanese made plans to invade the eastern end of New Guinea from the north and then attack overland and around the coast to capture Port Moresby. In order to mount an overland attack on Port Moresby, the Japanese needed to use the only available overland route, the narrow 100-kilometre (62-mile) pathway over the Owen Stanley Ranges known as the Kokoda Track.

The fact that Japan did not win a decisive victory in the Coral Sea meant that the threat to the supply lines between the United States and Australia was removed. This lifted morale among Allied forces, which had suffered a continuous series of defeats by the Japanese since Pearl Harbor.

The most important result of the Battle of the Coral Sea, however, was not apparent until after the Battle of Midway.

Shōkaku, *Zuikaku* and *Shōhō* were all scheduled to be part of General Yamamoto's planned showdown with the American carriers at Midway. Now all three were lost from his battle line-up. One was gone, one was being repaired and the other was waiting on new aircraft to replace those lost in the Coral Sea. *Shōkaku* required almost three months of repair in Japan. *Zuikaku* needed new crew and aircraft and was not considered for use at Midway by Yamamoto, although it has been suggested that surviving *Shōkaku* aircrews combined with *Zuikaku*'s aircrews could have seen her with sufficient air power to take some part in the battle.

Also, Yamamoto wrongly believed that two US carriers were lost in the Coral Sea. USS *Yorktown* was, in fact, still operational. She was sufficiently repaired at Pearl Harbor in late May to be able to take part in the Battle of Midway in the first week of June 1942, one month after the Coral Sea battle. *Yorktown*'s aircraft helped sink two Japanese fleet carriers at Midway and the patched-up carrier was a third target for Japanese aerial attacks, which meant the Japanese strike force was thinned out considerably rather than being concentrated on the other two American carriers. Historians and critics say that Yamamoto, having decided that the decisive naval battle was to take place at Midway, should never have diverted any of his fleet carriers to a secondary operation such as Operation MO.

Inoue and Yamamoto missed significant factors in the Coral Sea battle. The unexpected appearance of American carriers and planes in the right place was partly due to luck, but it was also due to the improving use of radar by the Allies. Also, although not as well trained and experienced as their Japanese counterparts, US aircrews demonstrated skill and bravery in the Coral Sea encounters. The United States was training men faster than Japan and had superior industrial strength to build ships and planes, which meant that, once the Japanese lost their numerical naval superiority, as they did at Midway, they could never regain it. Every Japanese aircraft, airman and ship lost was irreplaceable.

The Allies learned more from the Battle of the Coral Sea than the Japanese and these lessons would count at Midway where Japan lost four fleet carriers, the mainstay of her Pacific naval force. It was at Midway that Japan lost the initiative in the Pacific War. The Battle of the Coral Sea made victory at Midway achievable for the Allies and created a renewed mood of optimism about our alliance with the United States. The Coral Sea is off the coast of Australia. This battle, celebrated annually around Australia as one of the most important events of WWII, was 'at home'. The war was no longer being fought in strange foreign places with exotic names.

THE WAR COMES TO SYDNEY

M idget submarines had been part of Japanese naval strategy for many years and five were used at Pearl Harbor, of which two were sunk after being spotted and a third was captured the day after the attack when it was found drifting off the coast. The submarines were unreliable and the crews often lost control of the steering and buoyancy of the vessels. This happened to at least two of the submarines that invaded Sydney Harbour in 1942.

The attack on Sydney was one of two such attacks planned for that week. The other took place in Diego Suarez Harbour, Madagascar, and was aimed at sinking the battleship HMS *Ramillies*. The main target in Sydney was the US battleship *Chicago*.

The tactics in both submarine attacks were similar. A small floatplane from a mother submarine flew over the harbour to check out targets and the midget submarines were deployed some hours later. In Madagascar the floatplane was recognised as being an enemy spotter plane and the HMS *Ramillies* changed her anchorage in the harbour as a precaution. The battleship was hit by a torpedo, which caused minor damage, and a British tanker nearby was sunk. In Sydney there were two flights around the harbour by the Japanese floatplanes. The first was very early on 23 May 1942 and was picked up on newly installed radar and dismissed as a radar error.

The second flight, occurring very early on 30 May, was observed and reported to authorities as the plane flew around the USS *Chicago* moored on the western side of Garden Island, just to the east of where the Opera House is today. The plane was thought to be from a US warship and no action was taken until someone worked out that the only four planes of a similar nature were actually all on the USS *Chicago* and had been when the plane was observed. RAAF Wirraways were hurriedly sent to search for the plane but found nothing and no extra defence measures were taken.

These planes were from the Japanese submarines *I–21* and *I–29*, which were part of a fleet of five submarines from the Japanese naval base at Truk in the Caroline Islands. Two of this group were equipped to carry light aircraft and the other three carried midget submarines. This Special Attack Unit operated along the east coast of Australia under the command of Captain Hankyu Sasaki, who had also been in command of submarine attacks at Pearl Harbor. The two mother submarines from which the planes were launched (*I–21* and *I–29*) arrived off the east coast of Sydney in early May 1942 and were joined by three more (*I–22*, *I–24* and *I–27*), carrying midget submarines strapped to their decks, in the last week of May. The mother submarines were massive 120-metre (394-foot) long vessels with crews of 95 men. Although the two-man submarines are referred to as 'midget', they were 25 metres (82 feet) long and weighed almost 50 tonnes. Each carried two torpedoes.

The attacks on Sydney and Diego Suarez occurred within two hours of each other. In Sydney the three midget submarines were launched about 10 kilometres (6 miles) east of the heads at about 5.30 pm. The mother submarines waited off Port Hacking south of Sydney but there were contingency plans to rendezvous off Broken Bay, north of Sydney, if the midget submarines had problems.

At the time of the attack, Sydney's static harbour defences consisted of eight sensor loops (of which six were outside the harbour and two were inside, one between Sydney Heads and one near Middle Head). These defences relied on the production of an induced current in a stationary loop of wire when submarines, which had sufficient magnetism to produce a small current in the loop, moved overhead. There was also a partially completed submarine net between Middle Head and South Head. On 30 May the six loops outside the harbour were not in use due to lack of manpower and the loop between Sydney Heads had been often ignored since early 1940, as there was so much civilian traffic over it and it often gave faulty readings.

The Officer in Charge of Sydney Harbour was Admiral Muirhead-Gould, who had at his disposal the patrol boats HMAS *Yandra* and *Bingera* on anti-submarine duty, along with minesweepers HMAS *Goonambee* and *Samuel Benbow*. Converted pleasure craft armed with depth charges patrolled the shipping channels. These were the HMAS *Yarroma, Lolita, Steady Hour, Sea Mist, Marlean* and *Toomaree*. There were three heavy cruisers in the harbour, USS *Chicago* and the HMAS *Canberra* and *Adelaide*. Other naval vessels included a dozen or more destroyers and corvettes of the Australian, Indian and US navies and a Dutch submarine.

The first of the submarines, *M–14*, launched from *I–27*, entered Sydney Heads at 8 pm and was detected by the loop sensors and dismissed as civilian traffic. At 8.15 pm, a Maritime Services Board watchman saw the submarine as it passed the western end of the gap in the submarine net, collided with the pile light, then reversed and trapped its stern in the net. The watchman rowed out to investigate and then rowed to the nearby patrol boat HMAS *Yarroma* to report that it was a submarine. *Yarroma*'s attempts to pass on this information to Sydney Naval Headquarters did not succeed until 9.52 pm.

HMAS *Yarroma* and *Lolita* were then told to investigate and, after doing so, *Lolita* dropped two depth charges, which failed to explode due to the shallow water, and *Yarroma*'s commander requested orders from headquarters. At 10.35 pm, while *Yarroma* was waiting instructions, the crew of *M–14* activated the submarine's self-destruct charges, which killed the two men in it and destroyed the submarine's front section.

Meanwhile, Admiral Muirhead-Gould had been summoned from an official dinner. At first he failed to believe the reports and reprimanded patrol boat crews for acting hastily and endangering civilian harbour traffic. At 10.27 pm Muirhead-Gould ordered all ships to take anti-submarine measures as an enemy submarine might be in the harbour. He closed the harbour to external traffic but ordered all ferries and other internal traffic to continue in the belief that this would keep any enemy submarines from exposing themselves and attacking warships.

Midget submarine *M–24* (often also referred to as 'A') was the second to enter the harbour. *M–24* crossed the indicator loop undetected and followed a Manly ferry through the anti-submarine net at 10 pm. This submarine actually bumped against the store carrier HMAS *Falie* and the incident was reported but ignored. A searchlight operator on USS *Chicago* spotted *M–24* 500 metres (1640 feet) from the cruiser just before 10 pm and *Chicago* opened fire with a 125-mm (5-inch) gun. *M–24* was hit, along with Fort Denison and a few buildings in Cremorne, but not put out of action.

The corvettes HMAS *Geelong* and *Whyalla* also fired at *M–24* as it fled west towards the Harbour Bridge. The submarine escaped and returned to a position near Bradleys Head, 2 kilometres (1.2 miles) from USS *Chicago*, which could be seen, silhouetted against the construction flood-lights at Garden Island.

The third midget submarine *M–21*, launched from *I–22*, entered the harbour just before 11 pm and was spotted by the unarmed patrol boat HMAS *Lauriana*. The crew of *Lauriana* alerted the nearby anti-submarine vessel HMAS *Yandra*, which attempted to ram the submarine and then dropped six depth charges. *M–21* rested on the harbour floor until the patrol boats moved away.

At 11.15 pm, Muirhead-Gould ordered the harbour blacked out but the Garden Island floodlights remained on. They were finally turned off at 12.25 am, just as *M–24* was preparing to fire on USS *Chicago*. *M–24* fired her torpedoes a few minutes apart just after the lights went out. Both torpedoes missed *Chicago*, one passed underneath the Dutch sub-marine and the converted ferry HMAS *Kuttabul*, but then hit the seawall where *Kuttabul* was tied up and exploded beneath the ship. The explo-sion rocked nearby streets and damaged equipment on Garden Island, knocking out all the base's communications. *Kuttabul* broke in two and sank. Nineteen Australian and two British sailors asleep on board the converted ferry were killed and another ten were wounded. The second torpedo ran aground on Garden Island without detonating.

M–24 then dived and moved off to her secondary planned rendezvous position north of Sydney.

The active indicator loop recorded a vessel passing at 1.58 am. This was believed to be another midget submarine entering the harbour, but was most likely *M–24* leaving.

Ships were ordered to make for the open ocean. USS *Chicago* was the first to get underway at 2.15 am and, as she left the harbour at 3 am, her lookouts spotted a submarine periscope passing alongside. One minute later the indicator loop registered an inbound signal. It was *M–21* re-entering the harbour after lying low for four hours.

M–21 was spotted and fired at in Neutral Bay by HMAS *Kanimbla* just before 4 am and, at 4.40 am, HMAS *Canberra*, preparing to head to sea as ordered, reported that a Japanese submarine may have fired torpedoes at her. What lookouts on *Canberra* may have seen was a trail of compressed air bubbles rising from an attempted but abortive torpedo-firing by *M–21*.

At 5 am the patrol boats HMAS *Steady Hour*, *Sea Mist* and *Yarroma* tracked the submarine down in Taylors Bay, heading back the way she had come. *Sea Mist* passed over the submarine and dropped a depth charge, which hit *M–21* and caused her to rise to the surface upside down before sinking again. *Sea Mist* dropped a second depth charge, and *Steady Hour* and *Yarroma* dropped seventeen more depth charges over the next four hours as they tracked the submarine around the bay.

Around 7.30 am on 1 June, *Steady Hour*'s anchor chain was entangled in the submarine and a final depth charge was dropped which brought oil and air bubbles to the surface.

A diver investigated *M–21* later that day. Her engines were still running as she lay on the harbour floor with her two torpedoes jammed in their tubes. Some time after the first depth charge hit, the crew of *M–21*, Lieutenant Keiu Matsuo and Petty Officer Masao Tsuzuku, had shot themselves in the head with their revolvers. The submarine was brought ashore on 4 June and the damaged remains of *M–24* were found and salvaged on 8 June 1942.

The bombardment of Sydney and Newcastle

On 8 June, just after midnight, the submarine *I–24*, positioned about 6 kilometres (3.7 miles) offshore, fired ten rounds into the eastern suburbs of Sydney. The shells landed in Bondi, Rose Bay, Woollahra, Vaucluse and Bellevue Hill. Only four of the shells exploded on impact and only minor damage to buildings resulted. However, the incident added to the general panic and house prices fell in the eastern suburbs and rose in the Blue Mountains.

The same night, another submarine from the fleet of five, *I–21*, conducted a similar bombardment at Newcastle. This time 34 shells were fired from a point some 9 kilometres (5.6 miles) off Fort Scratchley. Only one shell exploded on impact but damage was caused to buildings and houses around the Fort Scratchley area. The guns at the fort replied with four rounds in the direction of the submarine.

The Federal Censor ordered total censorship of the events, issuing an official statement on the afternoon of 1 June reporting that the Allies had destroyed three submarines in Sydney Harbour, and described the loss of HMAS *Kuttabul* and the 21 deaths as the loss of 'one small harbour vessel of no military value'. When *Smith's Weekly* released much of the real story on 6 June, and followed up with more details the following week, the navy attempted to charge the newspaper with releasing classified defence information. The bodies of the 21 dead sailors from HMAS *Kuttabul* were recovered and they were buried on 3 June. The navy base at Garden Island was later renamed HMAS *Kuttabul* in memory of the ferry and the lives lost.

The competence of those in charge of defences was questioned. Admiral Muirhead-Gould was hosting a dinner party at which the captain of USS *Chicago*, Howard Bode, was present. Both men dismissed the reports at first and crew members of the patrol boats visited by Muirhead-Gould, along with junior officers on *Chicago*, described Muirhead-Gould and Bode as being drunk. More than two hours passed between the observation of *M–14* in the boom net and Muirhead-Gould's first anti-submarine orders. It was three hours before patrol boats were activated.

Communication systems were woefully inadequate. None of the auxiliary patrol craft in the harbour had radio communications; so all instructions and reports came from signal lights via the Port War Signal Station or Garden Island, or by launch. Telephone communications on Garden Island were unreliable and disabled completely by the torpedo explosion. The supposed need for information secrecy meant that the auxiliary patrol boat crews and indicator loop staff were not informed about any of the incidents prior to the attack or made aware of developments which might have made them more vigilant.

Although the almost identical midget submarine attack in Madagascar occurred on the morning of 31 May (Sydney time), no alert was sent to other command regions. In fact the Madagascar attack was believed to be the work of Vichy French forces. No official inquiry into the attacks was held, despite demands from some quarters. After Justice Lowe's scathing report after the Darwin bombing, it was felt that any inquiry would have a negative impact on morale.

The bodies of the four Japanese crewmen from the midget submarines were recovered and cremated at Sydney's Eastern Suburbs Crematorium with full naval honours on 9 June 1942. Rear Admiral Muirhead-Gould, along with the Swiss Consul-General and members of the press, attended the service. The decision to accord the enemy a military funeral was criticised by many Australians, but it was hoped that showing respect might help to improve the conditions of the many Australians in Japanese prisoner-of-war camps. It didn't. Prime Minister John Curtin even allowed the ex–Japanese Ambassador, Tatsuo Kawai, to take the ashes of the four submariners back to Japan via East Africa when an exchange of diplomatic staff, stranded in each of the two enemy countries at the start of the war, occurred in October 1942.

After the salvage operations, a composite submarine was constructed using the bow section of one submarine and the stern of the other. This was put on display at Bennelong Point and the public was charged a small fee to view it. Money raised went to the Royal Australian Navy Relief Fund and the King George Fund for Merchant Sailors. The composite submarine was then transported by truck around south-eastern Australia, raising further funds for almost a year, before being placed at the Australian War Memorial in Canberra, where it remains to this day. The submarine attacks led to a significant increase in enlistment into the AIF and volunteer defence organisations, and defences in Sydney Harbour and Port Newcastle were strengthened and communication systems updated.

For many years it was believed that *M–24* went south after leaving the harbour towards the five huge submarines waiting off Port Hacking. However, it is now apparent that the crew of *M–24*, Sub-Lieutenant Katsuhisa Ban and Petty Officer Mamoru Ashibe, decided on the northern rendezvous spot, north off Broken Bay, perhaps because they were wary of being followed and leading the Allies to the fleet of mother submarines to the south. One submarine did head north to check the alternative meeting place, but *M–24* never arrived. In 2006, *M–24* was located several kilometres out to sea off Bungan Head, near the Sydney suburb of Newport. The remains of the two crew and some unexploded weapons remain in the submarine, which is now a protected site. It will never be known exactly how the men died. Memorial ceremonies were held at the site with representatives of both nations and military personnel.

It would appear that Captain Sasaki missed a golden opportunity to prey on the Allied naval vessels as they headed to sea, scared out of the harbour by the three midget subs. USS *Chicago*, the destroyer USS *Perkins*, the Dutch submarine *K-IX*, HMAS *Whyalla* and *Canberra* and others all fled the harbour and could have been easy targets for the five mother submarines.

Captain Sasaki's plan at Pearl Harbor had been to use submarines to pick off fleeing vessels, although this had not eventuated. He had the perfect opportunity to do this in Sydney, but did not attempt to repeat the tactic. When the three midget subs failed to return to the fleet after two days, four of the five mother submarines reverted to their secondary function of destroying merchant shipping along the east coast. *I–21* patrolled north of Sydney and *I–24* south. *I–27* went further south to look for ships departing Melbourne, while *I–29* headed to Brisbane. *I–22* left the group to conduct reconnaissance missions in New Zealand and Fiji.

The four remaining submarines attacked at least seven merchant vessels between them, and *I–24* sank the *Iron Chieftain* on 3 June, *I–27* sank the *Iron Crown* on 4 June and *I–21* was responsible for sinking the *Guatemala* on 12 June. Fifty lives were lost in these sinkings and the attacks forced changes in merchant traffic. Shipping out of Melbourne was restricted until a system of escorted convoys was established. All the mother submarines left Australian waters at the end of June for their home base at Truk.

I–21 returned to Australian waters and sank three more merchant ships in January and February 1943, taking her tally to 44,000 tonnes of Allied shipping, which made her the most successful Japanese submarine to operate in Australian waters in WWII.

None of the Japanese mother submarines involved in the attack on Sydney Harbour survived the war. All except *I–27* were sunk by US navy ships in the Pacific between December 1942 and July 1944. *I–27* was sunk by two British destroyers, HMS *Paladin* and *Petard*, off the Maldive Islands in the Indian Ocean in February 1943.

The two main targets of the midget submarine attacks in Sydney Harbour also failed to see out the war. USS *Chicago* sank following the Battle of Rennell Island in January 1943 and HMAS *Canberra* was lost near Savo Island in August 1942.

INTO THE JUNGLE

The Japanese invaded Rabaul, the old capital of New Guinea, on the island of New Britain, on 23 January 1942. It was close enough to their massive naval base at Truk, in the Caroline Islands, to be the perfect base for the invasion of New Guinea.

February 1942 saw the Fall of Singapore, the destruction of the port at Darwin, successful Japanese invasions on Timor and Ambon, and the destruction of the Allied fleet in the Battle of the Java Sea on 27 February. In March, the Japanese established garrisons at Lae and Salamaua on Australian territory on the north coast of New Guinea.

Although these towns were taken unopposed, there was a successful raid on the garrison at Salamaua on 29 June 1942 in which 70 men of the 2/5th Commando Unit and New Guinea Volunteer Rifles, based at Wau, killed 100 Japanese and seriously damaged the airfield. The Australian casualties were three wounded, none seriously.

The only territory north of Australia left unoccupied by the Japanese was the eastern end of New Guinea, where Port Moresby, on the southern coast, was the last strategically important bastion of Allied resistance.

The Japanese decided to take Port Moresby in the same way they had taken so many other places in South-East Asia. An invasion force embarked on twelve transport vessels at Rabaul in the first few days of May 1942. It departed early on 6 May, bound for Port Moresby.

Vice Admiral Inoue, commanding the Japanese 4th Fleet at Rabaul, was in charge of protecting this invasion force and another fleet, which sailed on 2 May to occupy the Australian advanced operational base on the island of Tulagi in the Solomons. Inoue had at his disposal no less than 51 warships.

Allied vessels available to counter the Japanese fleet numbered about twenty. A series of airborne naval engagements was fought between Inoue's fleet and the Allied ships, commanded by Rear Admiral Jack Fletcher, between 4 and 8 May. As a result of these battles, the Japanese were forced to abort their invasion plans and the convoy heading for Port Moresby was forced to turn back to Rabaul. This series of air-to-sea engagements became known as the Battle of the Coral Sea.

With their planned seaborne invasion of Port Moresby thwarted, the Japanese made plans to invade the eastern end of New Guinea from the north and, subsequently, attack over land and come around the coast to capture Port Moresby. To do this, the Japanese forces needed to use the only available overland route, the narrow 100-kilometre (62-mile) pathway over the Owen Stanley Ranges. Their plan was to land a force at Buna and reconnoitre along what became known as the Kokoda Track and march towards Port Moresby while, at the same time, an amphibious landing force would attack and invade the Australian base at Milne Bay, on the very eastern tip of the island. This would give them access to Port Moresby from the east.

As a Japanese landing at Buna seemed a logical move, and there was an airstrip at Kokoda, General MacArthur asked General Blamey, Commander in Chief of Australian Military Forces (AMF), to make plans to strengthen and defend Buna and Kokoda.

A military unit, originally known as the 30th Brigade AMF, had been formed in December 1941 as a response to Japan's entry into the war. It comprised three militia battalions, the 49th (Queensland), 39th (Victoria) and 53rd (New South Wales). The 49th had actually been deployed to Port Moresby in March 1941 and the two other battalions joined them there in early January 1942. With the inclusion of the Papuan Infantry Battalion, the 30th Brigade became 'New Guinea Force' commanded by Major General Basil Morris.

On 21 June 1942, the 49th Battalion was assigned to remain in defence of Moresby and the rest of New Guinea Force (the Papuan Infantry Battalion and the 39th and 53rd Battalions—now known as 'Maroubra Force') began preparing to fortify and defend Kokoda with the aim of preparing it as a base for an Allied build-up along the north coast. In order to begin these preparations, the 100 men of B Company of the 39th Battalion travelled overland along the track to the village of Kokoda to secure the airstrip.

The rest of the 39th Battalion stayed south of the Owen Stanley Ranges, setting up lines of communication. B Company was securing positions north of Kokoda when news reached them of Japanese landings on the north coast on 21 July 1942.

The first Australian army unit to make contact with the Japanese on mainland New Guinea was a platoon of the Papuan Infantry Battalion (PIB) led by an Australian officer, Lieutenant John Chalk. The PIB was a force of 310 Indigenous Papuans, led by Australian officers. The PIB fought valiantly and bravely along the Kokoda Track and their local knowledge saved many Australian lives.

On 22 July, Chalk reported the arrival of the Japanese, who made successful landings at Gona, Buna and Sanananda. Lieutenant Chalk was told to engage the enemy. That night Chalk and 40 men ambushed a Japanese force from a hill overlooking the Gona road, doing as much damage as possible using the element of surprise, and then wisely retreating into the jungle.

B Company of the 39th Battalion had its first serious engagement with the Japanese when 60 men of 11th and 12th Platoons, along with some PIB soldiers commanded by Captain Sam Templeton, ambushed 500 Japanese troops at the village of Gorari on the afternoon of 25 July. The small group of militia and PIB soldiers then withdrew, pursued by 500 Japanese infantry, and dug in near Oivi that night.

Next morning two transport planes each landed fifteen reinforcements from Port Moresby at Kokoda airstrip and the first group made their way north and met up with the 60 men of B Company at Oivi, just as the Japanese attacked in force. This small group held off frontal and flanking attacks for six hours until 5 pm when Captain Templeton, unaware that the Japanese had surrounded them, went to find the missing fifteen reinforcements and was not seen again.

Templeton's fate was not known until 2010 when former Japanese soldier Kokichi Nishimura, the only man from his platoon to survive the campaign, revealed that he himself had buried Templeton, who had been captured and murdered by Japanese officers. Nishimura led a Kokoda Track tour operator to the gravesite.

With the track to Kokoda cut off, Lance Corporal Sanopa of the PIB led the Australian and Papuan troops, under the cover of darkness, along a jungle creek south-east around Kokoda to safety back at Deniki. At Deniki they met Lieutenant Colonel Owen and a small company of the

39th Battalion. Owen decided to attempt a defence of the Kokoda airstrip and radioed Port Moresby for reinforcements. Leaving 40 men at Deniki, he took the remaining 77 to the Kokoda airstrip.

Two transports carrying reinforcements did arrive next day but, fearing an attack while on the ground, the American pilots refused to land and returned to Port Moresby. That afternoon the airstrip came under heavy machine-gun fire and mortar attack. Lieutenant Colonel Owen was killed and Major Watson of the PIB took command.

On the afternoon of 29 July, Kokoda airstrip was overrun and captured by the Japanese. At the very last minute Major Watson ordered a retreat to Deniki and the Japanese, now in control of the airstrip, did not follow the Australians.

Japanese dispatches estimated the defending force at Kokoda to be 'at least 1200 men'. In fact, they had been fighting 77 poorly trained Australian militiamen and a dozen or so Papuan troops who had not slept for four days.

Major General Horii, originally based at Rabaul, had at his disposal the South Seas Force, a command of 10,000 well-trained troops. With Kokoda captured he ordered Colonel Tsukamoto, leading the troops in New Guinea, to capture Port Moresby.

The only serious impediment to Japanese attempts to build a base at their beachhead at Buna and push on to Kokoda and beyond was the combined Allied air force, which did a mighty job of making life hell for the invaders. One transport carrying more troops and equipment arrived safely on 25 July but, on 29 July, a Japanese transport vessel was sunk by the RAAF and another was forced to return to Rabaul. A major supply convoy was forced to turn back by Allied air attacks on 31 July, though two weeks later poor flying conditions and air support from Japanese Zero fighters enabled a major convoy to land 3000 enemy infantrymen and two divisions of naval construction units.

With the airstrip at Kokoda in Japanese hands, all troops had to reach the Australian front line at Deniki on foot along the Kokoda Track. Papuans carried supplies, previously flown in, and all wounded men were carried out the same way. The men who performed these life-saving tasks were nicknamed the 'Fuzzy Wuzzy Angels' by the Australians.

By the first week in August 1942, the rest of the 39th Infantry Battalion had arrived in Deniki. The Australian force at Deniki, under the command of Major Allan Cameron, comprised 480 officers and men along with ten Australian officers in charge of 47 native troops of the PIB and New Guinea administration.

An attempt to retake the Kokoda airfield was made on 8 August, using A, C and D Companies attacking along different tracks. B Company, having fought so bravely to defend it against a vastly superior force, were astoundingly accused by Cameron of 'lacking fighting spirit' and were left out of the plan.

The Citizens' Military Force (CMF) had become part of the AMF (Australian Military Force) after legislation to accept these men as a fighting force was passed in 1939, but there was still animosity between the two 'armies'. The AIF saw themselves as the elite Australian troops, and were fond of calling the militia 'koalas', a protected species that could not be exported or shot at, or 'chocolate soldiers' ('chocos'), implying they would melt as soon as they saw action. The militia soldiers countered by calling the AIF 'five bob a day tourists' or 'five bob a day murderers' because they signed up for steady wages after the Depression.

Prejudice against the militia in spite of their obvious bravery in the face of overwhelming odds, as displayed by Cameron, was to be a common theme during the Kokoda campaign, from as high up the command chain as the undiplomatic General Blamey.

A Company succeeded in reaching Kokoda and successfully retook the village. D Company ran into massive enemy resistance and was forced to fight its way out over the next two days. A large Japanese force ambushed C Company, their commanding officer was killed and they were unable to withdraw until nightfall. As they withdrew they were pursued by a large Japanese force, which attacked the base at Deniki for several hours before withdrawing.

Early the following day, Lance Corporal Sanopa of the PIB arrived at Deniki to tell Cameron that they had occupied Kokoda and were waiting for reinforcements and supplies. Cameron radioed for reinforcements but Port Moresby advised that none were available for at least 24 hours. Hand-to-hand fighting continued until the next morning and, when the promised reinforcements failed to land after aircrew could not establish that A Company controlled the airstrip, a fighting withdrawal towards Deniki was ordered.

Unable to break through the Japanese lines while carrying their wounded, A Company took shelter in the village of Naro and a villager ran to Deniki for help. Warrant Officer Wilkinson led a small patrol of native troops to Naro and led what remained of A Company past the Japanese lines and through the jungle to Isurava, rejoining the rest of 39th Battalion on 13 August.

On 12 August Deniki had been overrun and the 39th Battalion retreated to Isurava, where Lieutenant Colonel Honner ordered them to dig in and hold their positions. He left the 53rd Battalion at Alola, the first village south on the track from Isurava, to guard the parallel, alternative track south.

UP NORTH

David Campbell

Oh, Bill and Joe to the north have gone,
A green shirt on their back;
There are not many ewes and lambs
Along Kokoda track.

There are not many ewes and lambs,
But men in single file
Like sheep along a mountain pad
Walk mile on sweating mile;

And each half-hour they change the lead,
Though I have never read
Where any fat bell-wether was
Shot, in the mountains, dead.

The only sheep they muster there
Leap through the mind at night;
'Twould be as red as marking time
To change green shirt for white.

And though Bill dreams of droving now
On the drought-coloured plain,
There's little need to tap the glass
Or pray for it to rain.

They have no lack of water there
But there is a stinging tail,
For men lie dying in the grass
Along Kokoda trail.

THE BATTLE OF SAVO ISLAND

The Battle of Savo Island, 8 to 9 August 1942, was the first major naval engagement of the Guadalcanal campaign, the vital struggle for supremacy in the Pacific. Once the battles of the Coral Sea and Midway had been fought, the Japanese no longer had naval supremacy and General MacArthur could set about recapturing the islands occupied by the Japanese.

The process of island hopping would eventually be used to recapture the Philippines, the Dutch East Indies (Indonesia) and the islands between Hawaii and Japan in the North Pacific. But it began with the Solomon Islands and the battle of Guadalcanal. The campaign would last six months as the Allies recaptured the territory and established the bases they needed to use as starting points in a campaign to recapture the Solomons, isolate or capture the major Japanese base at Rabaul, and isolate and defeat the Japanese forces in New Guinea. It was important to attack before the Japanese could build airfields and establish secure bases on the southernmost islands of the Solomons group. In fact, the Japanese were only one week away from completing the airfield on Guadalcanal when 'Operation Watchtower', the first major US offensive operation since Pearl Harbor, began on 7 August 1942.

A task force of 75 ships, including transports, landing craft, aircraft carriers and a screening fleet of battleships, began landing 17,000 troops, mostly US Marines, on the Japanese-held south-eastern islands of the Solomons. The amphibious task force was the largest ever assembled at that time. The action centred around the north coast of Guadalcanal and the ring of islands to the north-east. The waters in between were to become known as 'Ironbottom Sound'.

The action began with massive bombardment of the selected landing places, and air strikes on Japanese positions, from the carrier fleet. Then, using amphibious craft and parachute regiments, the troops landed on Tulagi, Guadalcanal, Florida Island, Gavutu and Tanambogo. Resistance was fierce, especially on Tulagi and Guadalcanal. The Japanese troops fought to the death with no surrender. Nevertheless, all islands except Guadalcanal were in Allied hands by the following day.

Although taken by surprise, Japanese response by air and sea was remarkably swift. Japanese aircraft from Rabaul attacked the landing fleet on 8 August, sinking one transport and one destroyer. The Japanese lost 36 aircraft and the United States lost twenty aircraft from the supporting carriers, USS *Saratoga*, *Wasp* and *Enterprise*. The transport USS *George F. Elliot* was hit and abandoned and became a burning wreck.

In a remarkable counter-offensive action, Vice Admiral Mikawa led a task force of seven cruisers and a destroyer from Rabaul and bases in Bougainville down what was known as 'the Slot', the narrow passage of water between the islands of Choiseul and Santa Isabel, to the east and the Georgia Group to the west, to attack the Allied landing craft and the supporting fleet of warships on the night of 8 August.

Mikawa was commander of the newly formed Japanese 8th Fleet based at Rabaul, his new flagship was the *Chōkai*, a Takao class heavy cruiser. At first, the Japanese thought the Allied attack was a raid to sabotage the construction of the airfield on Guadalcanal, and Mikawa sent 500 naval troops on two transports towards Guadalcanal on the morning of 7 August.

However, when the Japanese learned more about the nature of the attack, Mikawa recalled the transports and quickly assembled all the available warships in the area. On the evening of 7 August, three cruisers and a destroyer from Rabaul and four heavy cruisers from the base at Kavieng to the north assembled east of Rabaul and headed east around the north tip of Bougainville before turning south towards Guadalcanal via the Slot. A series of farcical events led to the presence of Mikawa's fleet being completely missed by Allied command.

The 75 ships of the invading fleet were divided into three groups. Vice Admiral Fletcher, on the flagship USS *Saratoga*, was in total command, Rear Admiral Turner commanded the amphibious fleet, while the 'screening' or protective fleet of eight cruisers, fifteen destroyers and five minesweepers, was under the command of British Rear Admiral Crutchley, who had been awarded the Victoria Cross for his part in a raid on the U-boat bases at Zeebrugge in WWI. His flagship was the heavy cruiser HMAS *Australia*. Five cruisers and seven destroyers from this fleet were involved in the Battle of Savo Island, including the ill-fated HMAS *Perth*.

The Japanese ships were spotted twice by Australian Hudson reconnaissance aircraft flying out of the base at Milne Bay, New Guinea. The first Hudson misidentified them as 'three cruisers, three destroyers, and two seaplane tenders'. The Hudson's crew tried to report the sighting by radio but, receiving no acknowledgement, returned to Milne Bay to report at 1 pm. A second Hudson landed at Milne Bay at 3 pm and reported sighting 'two heavy cruisers, two light cruisers, and one unknown type'. These reports were not relayed to the Allied fleet off Guadalcanal until almost 7 pm. Admiral Turner had requested extra reconnaissance missions over the Slot in the afternoon of 8 August. But, for unexplained reasons, Admiral John McCain, commander of Allied air forces for the South Pacific area, did not order extra missions. Turner mistakenly believed that the Slot was under observation and planned his naval movements accordingly.

Admiral Crutchley divided his ships into three groups. One group of cruisers ('northern') patrolled between Savo Island and Tulagi, another ('southern') between Savo Island and Guadalcanal, while a third ('eastern') guarded the eastern entrances to the sound between Florida and Guadalcanal islands. Two radar-equipped destroyers, USS *Blue* and *Ralph Talbot*, patrolled the passage west of Savo Island. It was not known, at this stage, that early radar was made ineffective by nearby landmasses. Mikawa's ships sailed right between the two destroyers, unobserved. In fact, lookouts in Mikawa's ships spotted *Blue* about 9 kilometres (5.6 miles) ahead and changed course to pass north of Savo Island. Mikawa was trained in night warfare and ordered his ships to slow to 22 knots to reduce wakes that might make them visible to the patrolling destroyer.

Minutes later, Mikawa's lookouts spied USS *Ralph Talbot* about 15 kilometres (9 miles) away, so the convoy held its course with all guns pointing at USS *Blue* ready to fire. USS *Blue* reached the end of her patrol track less than 2 kilometres (1.2 miles) from the Japanese fleet and turned and steamed away, totally oblivious to the fleet of Japanese warships moving past her. Mikawa then returned to his intended course around Savo Island, increased speed to 30 knots and ordered, 'Every ship attack'.

Meanwhile, Admiral Crutchley had left in HMAS *Australia* to attend a conference on Turner's command ship off Guadalcanal to discuss the departure of Fletcher's carriers and the resulting withdrawal schedule for the transport ships. At this meeting, the mistaken reports of the 'seaplane tender' force reported by the Australian Hudson crew were discussed and it was decided there was no real threat, as seaplane tenders, ships whose role was to transport and service these 'spotter aircraft', did not normally engage in any surface action.

Crutchley was more concerned about possible submarine attacks and, before leaving for the meeting, positioned his remaining seven destroyers as close-in protection around the two transport anchorages and left Captain Bode of the cruiser USS *Chicago* in charge of the southern group of warships. Bode decided not to place his ship in the lead of the group as was customary, and went back to sleep. It appears there was an air of complacency engendered among the officers involved, due to the relative success of this particular operation and the size of the task force. The crews were tired and lethargic after two days on alert in the extremely hot and humid weather. While still running their patrol patterns, most of Crutchley's warships went to 'Condition 2' that night with half the crews on duty while the other half rested. There was a sense that their task of screening the landings had been achieved.

Mikawa's ships had launched three floatplanes just before midnight for a final reconnaissance. Several Allied ships heard and observed these planes, but none of them reported the presence of unknown aircraft in the area to Allied command. Crutchley decided not to return to his ships after the conference and, without informing the other Allied ship commanders, stationed HMAS *Australia* just outside the Guadalcanal transport anchorage.

At approximately 1.30 am Japanese lookouts sighted the southern force, now made up of the two cruisers HMAS *Canberra* and USS *Chicago* and two destroyers, USS *Patterson* and *Bagley*, silhouetted by the glow from the fires which were still burning on the transport *George F. Elliot*.

HMAS *Canberra* was a heavy cruiser of the Kent sub-class of County Class cruisers. She was built at Clydebank, Scotland, between September 1925 and May 1927 and commissioned in 1928. During the first nine months of the war, *Canberra* performed escort duty and, in 1940 and 1941, she was involved in the unsuccessful searches for the German raiders *Atlantis* and *Pinguin* and the German pocket battleship *Admiral Scheer*. HMAS *Canberra* was credited with having sunk the ex-Norwegian tanker *Ketty Brovig* while it was under Nazi command.

In 1942, HMAS *Canberra* underwent a three-month refit in Sydney and was one of the intended targets of the Japanese midget submarine attack in Sydney Harbour. In June 1942 she patrolled the Coral Sea before joining Operation Watchtower and becoming a prime target for Mikawa's attacking fleet at Savo Island.

The Japanese cruisers had just begun launching torpedoes at the Allied ships when lookouts on *Chōkai* spotted the ships of the Allied northern force about 15 kilometres (9 miles) away and the Japanese force then turned towards them. The crew of one of the two destroyers of southern force, USS *Patterson*, was still on full alert because her commander, Captain Francis T. Spellman, had taken the earlier reported sightings of Japanese warships and unknown aircraft seriously.

At 1.43 am USS *Patterson* spotted a Japanese warship at about 5 kilometres (3 miles) and immediately sent a message, 'Warning! Warning! Strange ships entering the harbor!' by both radio and signal lamp. Spellman increased his ship's speed, fired flares above the Japanese column and then opened fire. At the same time, the Japanese floatplanes dropped aerial flares directly over HMAS *Canberra* and USS *Chicago*. *Canberra* responded immediately, with an increase in speed and a change in course designed to keep the ship between the Japanese and the Allied transports, and bring her guns to bear on any targets that could be sighted.

As *Canberra*'s guns were taking aim at the Japanese, four of the Japanese cruisers opened fire on her and she took at least 25 hits within three minutes. This barrage killed *Canberra*'s gunnery officer and mortally wounded her captain, Frank Getting. Both boiler rooms were destroyed and she lost all power before she could open fire or radio a warning to other Allied ships.

She came to rest with a 10-degree list to starboard, unable to fight fires or pump out flooded compartments. All of the Japanese ships were on the port side of *Canberra*, so the serious damage to the ship's starboard side was either from shells entering low on the port side and exiting below the waterline on the starboard side, or from accidental hits from the US destroyer *Bagley*, which had fired torpedoes moments earlier. Alerted by the flares and the sudden turn made by *Canberra* in front of them, the crew of USS *Chicago* woke Captain Bode from 'a sound sleep' and attempted to fire star shells towards the Japanese column, but the shells did not function.

At 1.47 pm, four minutes after the USS *Patterson* had sighted the Japanese warships, a torpedo hit USS *Chicago*'s bow, causing damage to her main gun battery, and a shell hit the cruiser's mainmast, killing two crewmen. *Chicago* left the battle scene and steamed west for 40 minutes. Captain Bode issued no orders to the ships under his command and made no attempt to warn other Allied ships.

USS *Patterson* engaged the Japanese ships in an artillery battle and took a major hit, which caused moderate damage and killed ten of her crew. *Patterson* continued to pursue and fire at the Japanese ships as they steamed towards the ships of the northern force and may have hit one cruiser, the *Kinugasa*, causing moderate damage. USS *Bagley* circled to port and fired torpedoes in the direction of the disappearing Japanese ships. One or two of these torpedoes may have caused the starboard damage to HMAS *Canberra*. USS *Bagley* played no further role in the battle.

Mikawa's ships were already headed towards the Allied northern force as *Canberra* and *Chicago* were hit. Three of the Japanese ships veered westward, which meant the northern force was about to be attacked on two sides.

Meanwhile, the captains of the three US northern force cruisers, the USS *Astoria*, *Quincy* and *Vincennes*, were all asleep. The ships were steaming slowly with crews on 'Condition 2'. This meant that half the crew was on duty while the other half rested in their bunks or close to their battle stations. In spite of the USS *Patterson*'s warning and the fact that crewmen on all three ships observed flares and gunfire from the battle south of Savo Island, it took some time for the crews to go from 'Condition 2' to full alert and Japanese torpedoes had already been fired at them at 1.44 am. At 1.50, the Japanese aimed powerful searchlights at the three cruisers and opened fire.

USS *Astoria*'s gun crews spotted the Japanese cruisers and opened fire, but *Astoria*'s captain, waking up to find his ship in action, rushed to the bridge and ordered a ceasefire, fearing they were firing on other Allied ships. *Astoria* resumed firing a minute later once they realised the conditions they were facing, but Mikawa's flagship, *Chōkai*, quickly scored numerous hits on her, destroying the engine room and reducing the US cruiser to a crippled, burning wreck.

On USS *Quincy* the crew saw the flares and received USS *Patterson*'s warning, and general quarters had just sounded when the ship was caught in the Japanese searchlights. *Quincy* was immediately caught in the crossfire between the two Japanese columns, hit by gunfire and set on fire. Her captain ordered his cruiser to turn to engage the eastern Japanese column but two torpedoes hit his ship as she turned.

The *Quincy* managed to fire several salvos, one of which hit *Chōkai*'s chart room and killed or wounded 36 men. At 2.10 am, however, a direct hit killed most of *Quincy*'s bridge crew, including the captain. She was then hit by another torpedo, ceased firing and sank, bow first, at 2.38 am.

USS *Vincennes* also saw the flares and gunfire to the south but was slow to respond when hit by searchlights and gunfire at 1.50 am. She responded with her own gunfire at 1.53 am but was hit by two torpedoes from *Chōkai* at 1.55. It is calculated that the Japanese gunners hit *Vincennes* up to 74 times and, after another torpedo hit her just after 2 am, her captain ordered the crew to abandon ship and she sank at 2.50 am.

At 2.15, having decided not to risk attempting to sink the transports and encounter the rest of the Allied force in poor weather, Mikawa ceased fire and took the Japanese ships around the north side of Savo Island. Here they met the destroyer USS *Ralph Talbot* and hit her several times, but the destroyer managed to escape in a rain squall after suffering severe damage. The entire battle was carried out in rainy, squally weather conditions.

Mikawa knew that the Japanese navy could not replace any heavy cruisers he might lose to air attack the next day if he had to steam back to base in daylight. He had no way of knowing that the US carriers had withdrawn from the battle area and would not be a threat the next day. At 2.20 am Mikawa ordered his ships to return to their bases at Rabaul and Kavieng.

Around 4 am USS *Patterson* returned and attempted to assist fighting the fires on HMAS *Canberra*. Progress was made in putting out the fires but Admiral Turner intended to withdraw all Allied ships by 6.30 am and ordered *Canberra* scuttled if she could not steam by that time. After all survivors were removed, the US destroyers, *Selfridge* and *Ellet*, sank her with torpedoes and gunfire.

Later it was decided that more time was needed for supplies to be unloaded from the transports before they withdrew. Therefore Turner postponed the withdrawal of his ships until mid-afternoon. The crippled USS *Astoria*'s crew tried to save their ship in that time but the fires were out of control and she sank at 12.15 pm.

Mikawa's bold action was very risky but led to a stunning surprise attack and complete victory for the Japanese. His convoy of cruisers surprised the Allies and inflicted a major defeat, which caused serious Allied losses. Mikawa's action led to the loss of HMAS *Canberra* and three American battlecruisers without loss to the Japanese fleet.

However, on 10 August, one of the four cruisers returning to Kavieng, the *Kako*, was torpedoed and sunk by the US submarine *S44* 100 kilometres (62 miles) from her home port. The other three Kavieng-based cruisers picked up all but 71 of her crew. The remaining Allied warships and the amphibious force withdrew on 9 August, temporarily conceding control of the seas around Guadalcanal to the Japanese. The withdrawal of the fleet left the Allied ground forces that had landed on Guadalcanal and nearby islands in a precarious situation, with barely enough supplies, equipment and food to hold their beachhead.

Mikawa's failure to destroy the Allied invasion transports when he had the chance, however, would prove to be a crucial strategic mistake for the Japanese as it allowed the Allies to maintain their foothold on Guadalcanal and eventually emerge victorious from the campaign. After the Battle of Savo Island, all Allied supplies and reinforcements arrived in small convoys during daylight hours, with Allied aircraft flying covering missions. This slowed the campaign considerably and meant that forces on Guadalcanal received barely enough ammunition and provisions to withstand several serious Japanese attempts to retake the islands.

Despite their crushing naval defeat, the Allied warships did accomplish their mission to protect the vital transports from harm. Many of those same transports ferried crucial supplies and reinforcements to Guadalcanal over succeeding months.

The defeat at Savo Island and the loss of three US navy cruisers caused concern in the United States and questions were asked in the US media; especially controversial was the fact that US ships were under the command of a British admiral.

A retired US admiral, A.J. Hepburn, was selected in December 1942 to interview all relevant personnel and make a report. Hepburn visited Australia and talked to MacArthur, Crutchley and various Australian politicians before producing a very detailed report, which concluded that the primary cause of defeat was complete surprise achieved by the Japanese, and that the reasons for this were:

1. Inadequate condition of readiness on all ships to meet sudden night attack.

2. Failure to recognise the implication of the enemy planes in the vicinity prior to the attack.
3. Misplaced confidence in the capabilities of radar.
4. Failure in communications, which resulted in vital enemy contact information not being received and therefore led to the withdrawal of the carrier group the evening before the battle, leaving no force available to inflict damage on the withdrawing enemy.

An Australian Commonwealth Naval Board of Inquiry made two reports in August and September 1942. The second report found that HMAS *Canberra* was not torpedoed, but was hit by 24 Japanese shells. Rear Admiral Crutchley, however, disagreed with this finding, as did many witnesses. The officer of the watch that night was Mackenzie Gregory. He concluded, after a lifetime of research, 'I now believe we were hit in the starboard side by a torpedo which emanated from our destroyer escort USS *Bagley*.' Crutchley attributed the defeat to fatigue and lack of experience in night fighting, along with the absence of HMAS *Australia* and the fact that ships failed to receive the warning given by USS *Patterson*.

Although Hepburn was critical of many of those involved, he only recommended official censure for Captain Bode. When he learned that the report was critical of his actions, Captain Bode, then stationed in Panama, shot himself on 19 April 1943. He died the next day. The battle remains controversial and is often regarded as the worst US naval defeat in history.

Seventy-four of HMAS *Canberra*'s crew were killed in the action at Savo Island and a further ten, including Captain Frank Getting, died of wounds. Another 109 of her crew were wounded. The British government approved the transfer HMS *Shropshire* as a replacement and the ship was commissioned into the Royal Australian Navy as HMAS *Shropshire* in April 1943.

US President Roosevelt requested that an American heavy cruiser be renamed as a tribute to HMAS *Canberra* and a cruiser previously designated as USS *Pittsburgh* was renamed and launched as USS *Canberra* in April 1943. That ship is the only US warship to be named after a foreign city.

Since there was a policy not to duplicate names across the Allied fleets, plans to rename HMAS *Shropshire* as *Canberra* were not carried out. A memorial, incorporating an anchor, is located on the shore of Lake Burley

Griffin, in HMAS *Canberra*'s name city, and her wreck was discovered and examined in 1992, almost exactly 50 years after her scuttling. She lies upright on the ocean floor, in approximately 763 metres (2503 feet) of water, among many other wartime wrecks in Ironbottom Sound, the name given by Allied sailors to Savo Sound, between Guadalcanal, Savo Island and Florida Island in the Solomon Islands.

The Battle of Savo Island must be seen in light of the fact that the invasion of Guadalcanal was a success. Mikawa's Japanese force did not prevent Operation Watchtower from laying the foundation for a reversal of fortunes in the Pacific and the eventual defeat of the Japanese threat to Australia's freedom and way of life. It was the first time Australia had been involved in a major invasion with our US, as well as our British, allies. The bonds of friendship and general goodwill towards America, which were to alter Australian cultural orientation both politically and socially after WWII, were forged in operations like 'Watchtower'.

The actions of the captain and crew of the USS *Patterson* in bravely chasing the Japanese from the HMAS *Canberra* and returning to help attempt to save her was a great example of comradeship and a true working alliance under fire; and Roosevelt's gesture in naming a US battleship *Canberra* was, perhaps, as an apology of sorts as well as a tribute to a ship that performed to expectations when others around her did not.

On the other hand, there was resentment towards our American allies over the fate of HMAS *Canberra*. Why had her crew not been given extra time to save their ship, as the crew of USS *Astoria* had? Reports indicated that the fires were almost under control at around 5 am, but she was given no reprieve while the USS *Astoria* was given an extra six hours. Why had Bode allowed HMAS *Canberra* to continue to lead the group on patrol after he had taken command, when the role should have been the USS *Chicago*'s responsibility? Why did he leave the scene of the battle? Was his lack of leadership partly to blame for the USS *Bagley* inadvertently torpedoing HMAS *Canberra*? All these questions added to anti-American sentiment back home. This was just weeks before the infamous 'Battle of Brisbane' of 26 and 27 November 1942, where many Australian and American troops fought it out in the central business district of Brisbane, bringing anti-American feelings among servicemen and the general public to a head in Australia.

REAR-GUARD ACTION

After the defeat at the Battle of Isurava, the Japanese extended their supply lines and the men of the 39th and 2/14th Battalions were pushed relentlessly back towards Port Moresby.

Knowing that they were all that stood between the Japanese and Port Moresby, several attempts were made to mount a defence of the track and halt the advancing Japanese.

Problems with supply drops held up any chance of an Australian counter-offensive. Many of the drops were lost or ruined due to lack of parachutes. General MacArthur wanted airdrops used only in emergencies, but in Port Moresby General Rowell, in charge of the operation, knew there was no alternative to keep the men on the track fed and supplied.

General Allen, in Port Moresby, pressured Brigadier Potts to counter-attack, but Potts knew his supply lines were flimsy and his men outnumbered. Major battles were fought at Alola, Eora Creek and Templeton's Crossing, but the Japanese were victorious every time against a weary and ill-equipped Australian force, which was not being reinforced. General Allen, waiting for news of any action at Milne Bay, was reluctant to commit more men of the 7th Division to Kokoda until he was sure there was no threat to Port Moresby on other fronts.

As Australian casualties mounted and supplies ran low, Maroubra Force withdrew to the only defensible point to the south, Mission Ridge, near the village of Myola.

When he received news that the Japanese had been defeated at Milne Bay, on 4 September, 'Tubby' Allen released the 2/27th Battalion to join

Maroubra Force, which comprised the 39th and 53rd Battalions and the Papuan Infantry Battalion, at Mission Ridge.

Brigadier Potts ordered the 39th Battalion and the remnants of the 53rd back to Port Moresby. The famous 'bloody heroes' of the 39th Battalion would be thrown back into the battle for Kokoda later.

Now able to commit his entire brigade to the battle, Potts established defensive positions on the hill known as 'Brigade Hill', and waited for the Japanese advance.

On 8 September, 1000 Japanese launched a frontal attack on the Australian positions, while a force of around 5000 again used the tactic of outflanking and managed to cut the Australian brigade headquarters off from the three battalions.

With their headquarters about to be overrun, headquarters staff and the rear elements of Maroubra Force retreated back south to the village of Menari.

The 2/14th and 2/16th Battalions, with no rations and with almost no ammunition left, attempted to break through the Japanese lines, but it became clear that they were about to be surrounded and wiped out so all three battalions were ordered to 'go bush' and find their way back to Menari while B and D Companies of the 2/27th fought a rear-guard action to cover the retreat.

The 2/14th and 2/16th managed to reach 21st Brigade headquarters at Menari before the rest of the brigade was again forced to retreat, but the men of the 2/27th, along with the wounded from the other battalions, were forced to follow jungle paths parallel to the main track and rejoined the main Australian force at Jawarere.

Meanwhile, the rest of the men of Maroubra Force had reached Ioribaiwa and set up the final barrier of artillery and entrenchments at Imita Ridge.

The defeat of the 21st Brigade at Brigade Hill was a decisive victory for the Japanese. By 16 September they were within sight of Port Moresby and victory was within their grasp. However, to the bewilderment of many of his officers, the Japanese commander, Major General Horii, ordered his troops to dig in and wait.

The defeats on the Kokoda Track were a blow to morale among Aussie troops and to people back in Australia. Maroubra Force was relieved by the 25th Infantry Brigade at Imita Ridge and, on 10 September, Brigadier Potts was replaced as Maroubra Force commander with Brigadier

Porter. He was later also replaced as commander of the 21st Brigade on the orders of General Blamey.

As a result of the defeat at Mission Ridge, General MacArthur reported to his superiors that 'the Australians have proven themselves unable to match the enemy in jungle fighting. Aggressive leadership is lacking.'

Pressured by MacArthur, Prime Minister Curtin ordered General Blamey to go up to New Guinea and take charge of the situation, despite the fact that it was well known that Blamey was unpopular with the troops and among his superiors. Jack Beasley, Labor Cabinet member, famously said, 'Moresby is going to fall. Send Blamey up there and let him fall with it.'

Blamey took command in New Guinea on 23 September and famously insulted the men of the 21st Brigade when he addressed them at their camp on 22 October and commented, with typical lack of diplomacy, that 'it's the rabbit who runs who gets shot, not the man holding the gun'. The men, who had fought bravely against superior numbers on the Kokoda Track, never forgave Blamey for his unnecessary criticism.

Having taken up positions on the hills around Ioribaiwa, the Japanese seemed to have only one step left for inevitable victory: they could see the ocean by day and the lights of Port Moresby at night.

Major General Horii, occasionally riding through the encampments on his white horse to cheer and rally his elite troops, waited for the order from General Harukichi Hyakutake in Rabaul to advance and take Port Moresby.

THE BATTLE OF MILNE BAY

While the Australian infantry retreated along the Kokoda Track in August, the Japanese were putting into action the second part of the plan to ensure the capture of Port Moresby: a seaborne invasion around the eastern end of New Guinea to take over the safe anchorage and newly constructed airstrips at Milne Bay.

Invasion by sea was the forte of the Japanese Imperial Force. They had used it to take over all the islands of what was then the Dutch East Indies (now Indonesia) and the Philippines. They were quite skilled at land-based invasion also, having swept down the Malay and Indo-Chinese peninsulas in record time.

In fact, since Japan had entered WWII, no Japanese invasion force had ever been repelled or defeated—until Milne Bay.

Situated on the eastern tip of mainland Papua, Milne Bay was a strategic position for several reasons. It had a fine deepwater port, which commanded the sea-lanes to the south coast, and was also an excellent position from which to fly reconnaissance missions to the Coral Sea and the Solomon Islands.

In preparation for their landing, the Japanese had been regularly bombing the three Allied airstrips that were being built at Milne Bay since 4 August. During these raids, Japanese intelligence reports mistakenly indicated a small force of Allied infantry was constructing the three airfields at Milne Bay.

There were, in fact, almost 9000 Allied troops at Milne Bay. About half of these were infantry, the rest were made up of more than 1300 US engineering, construction and anti-aircraft troops, with RAAF personnel. The

Australian infantry stationed at Milne Bay included militia from the 7th Brigade and the 55th Battalion, along with the men of the 18th Brigade 7th Division 2nd AIF, who had famously served with the 9th Division at Tobruk.

On 24 August a force of some 2000 Japanese troops, including 850 from the elite Marine Landing Corps, left Rabaul on three transports escorted by two cruisers and three destroyers. Another smaller convoy, consisting of 350 marines led by Commander Tsukioka, left Buna to land further along the north coast and attack overland. Both convoys were spotted and subsequently attacked by the RAAF.

The RAAF effectively stranded the convoy from Buna on Goodenough Island by destroying the convoy's landing barges. The only Australian naval vessels in the deepwater bay when the Japanese convoy was sighted were a destroyer and a transport. Both were able to leave before the superior Japanese force arrived. Air strikes against the larger convoy inflicted little damage but forced the Japanese troops to land well away from the airstrips.

The Japanese landed 2000 marines and two tanks 11 kilometres (7 miles) east of their intended landing place. These troops faced a long march through swamp and jungle but made a concerted attack on one of the airfields after pushing Allied defenders westward. The tanks simply bogged in the heavy mud and dense landscape and Australian troops found them abandoned on 30 August. The Japanese then landed 800 more marines and the big attack came, with artillery support from the warships, on the night of 31 August 1942.

The Australian 25th and 61st Battalions, Australian 46th Engineers Regiment and Australian 2/5th Field Regiment, along with the 43rd US Engineers, took the brunt of this attack, which included three waves of frenzied Japanese troops attacking across open ground. The Allied troops held firm in a furious battle and the Japanese were forced to withdraw back to the east, only to be pursued along the peninsula back to their base and again defeated by the 2/12th and 2/9th Battalions on 4 September.

The Japanese managed to gain complete naval supremacy at Milne Bay and were able to move troops up and down the coast at night. The RAAF, however, had control of the air and were able to land and take off even when the airstrips were under heavy attack.

This situation, along with spirited resistance from Allied troops on land, produced a stalemate and eventually led to the Japanese retreating from Milne Bay after sinking a British merchant ship on 6 September. It was the first time the Japanese had been defeated in a land battle and forced to withdraw after attempting an amphibious landing.

By the end of this battle, 167 Australians had died at Milne Bay, along with fourteen men of the 43rd US Engineers. The RAAF were magnificent in their defence of the bay, taking off under fire and attacking Japanese ships and artillery without thought of their own safety.

Only half of the expeditionary forces landed by the Japanese managed to evacuate. About 750 were killed in the battles and the rest attempted to retreat overland to the Japanese base at Buna, only to be hunted down by Allied patrols.

Australian forces had inflicted the first defeat on the German army in WWII at Tobruk, and followed it up with the first defeat of Japanese forces—at Milne Bay.

THE TRACK WINDING BACK

B y September 1942 the tide of war was turning in the Pacific.
The result of the Battle of Midway in June meant the end of total
Japanese naval supremacy. Japanese invasion forces had been defeated
for the first time at Milne Bay and losses at Guadalcanal began to have a
telling strategic impact on Japanese operations in the Pacific. In Rabaul,
General Harukichi Hyakutake doubted Japan could achieve victory at
Guadalcanal and, at the same time, support the major ongoing offensive
in New Guinea.

Port Moresby was bombed more than 80 times before September
1942 but better defences and improved RAAF capability gradually made
the port safer. General MacArthur's visit on 4 October 1942 led to the
establishment of a Combined Operations Service Command led by Brigadier General Dwight F. Johns, an expert in air base construction, and
Deputy Commander, United States Army Services of Supply. His second
in command was Australian Brigadier Victor Secombe, who had been in
charge of rebuilding Tobruk in 1941.

The development of Port Moresby and Milne Bay as efficient air bases
was well advanced and, in October, the capacity of the harbour at Port
Moresby was more than doubled, allowing it to handle several large ships
at a time instead of only one.

Meanwhile, Major General Horii and the Japanese invasion force
waited on the ridges 51 kilometres (32 miles) from Port Moresby; from
here they could see the ocean in the distance.

However, Major General Horii knew something his officers didn't
know. The Japanese had suffered a massive defeat on 14 September

attempting to retake Guadalcanal. Eight hundred and fifty Japanese troops had been killed and headquarters staff in Rabaul doubted their ability to maintain two infantry campaigns in the South Pacific. All troops in reserve were needed at Guadalcanal. Horii had also stretched his supply lines to breaking point. No supplies had reached them for days and the Australians had deliberately contaminated the food they left behind at Myola. Many of the Japanese troops were suffering from dysentery and malaria, and all were in the early stages of starvation.

On 27 September, Australian patrols discovered that the Japanese had withdrawn from Imita Ridge the night before, and Ioribaiwa was recaptured on 28 September. Major General 'Tubby' Allen then took command of operations on the Kokoda Track as the counter-offensive began against Major General Horii's men.

With two full brigades at his disposal, the 25th and 16th, Allen took a conservative approach, moving forward cautiously in an attempt to lose as few men as possible. Conditions were appalling with deep mud and poor supply lines due to a scarcity of carriers. The withdrawing Japanese were starving to death and fought with suicidal resignation. Expecting to die rather than to be evacuated, the Japanese fought fierce delaying battles from behind heavily defended positions at Templeton's Crossing and Eora Creek, which slowed the Australian advance and caused heavy casualties.

At Eora Creek the terrain favoured defence. The 16th Brigade made slow progress as Papuan carriers fell sick or deserted. The brigade could not get enough food and the attack stalled. General MacArthur was not satisfied with the speed of the counter-attack, and Major General Allen was replaced by Major General George Vasey of the 6th Division AIF on 26 October 1942.

The 25th Brigade reoccupied Kokoda on 2 November and transport aircraft were soon flying in supplies and equipment. General Vasey assembled hundreds of Papuan carriers and thanked them and awarded service medals. The Papuans promptly returned to work and the 16th and 25th Brigades crossed the Kumusi River at Wairopi on 13 November.

When the Japanese retreated to Oivi, Vasey planned an encirclement operation by the 25th Brigade and the Japanese stronghold was captured. Some Japanese reached Buna but most died at Oivi or in the jungle. Major General Horii drowned while attempting to cross the Kumasi River near the sea on 23 November. When the current swept away his horse, Horii and two of his staff attempted to reach Buna by canoe to organise defences. The canoe was swept out to sea in a storm and all three were drowned.

The battle on the Kokoda Track was over; the 16th and 25th Brigades were down to one-third of their normal strength.

REMEMBER THE WALTZING

Jim Haynes

She was Tilly, the funny old lady,
She lived at the end of our street—
And I'd always stop
When I went to the shop
And she'd give me a smile and a treat.

One day we sat in her kitchen,
I asked why she lived alone.
That was when she
Showed his photo to me,
And read me his last letter home.

'Remember the Waltzing Matilda?
Remember the old one-two-three?
A Barndance and then a Varso Vienna,
Remember your arms around me?

'Remember the Waltzing Matilda?
And if this war ever should end,
The very first chance,
The first Town Hall Dance,
I'll waltz my Matilda again.'

He never returned from Kokoda
To dance in our little Town Hall.
She never went there,
She couldn't bear
To see his name up on the wall.

Tilly, the funny old lady,
She lived a lifetime alone—
Reading the page,
Watching them fade,
The words of his last letter home.

'Remember the Waltzing Matilda?
Remember the old one-two-three?
A Barndance and then a Varso Vienna,
Remember your arms around me?

'Remember the Waltzing Matilda?
And if this war ever should end,
The very first chance,
The first Town Hall Dance,
I'll waltz my Matilda again.'

FIGHTING OUR FRIENDS—
THE 'BATTLE OF BRISBANE'

This is the story of one of the strangest, and least savoury, events in Australia's 20th century history. World War II forced Australia out of isolation and also forced us to confront the puzzling dilemma of dealing with people of other nationalities, whose cultures and philosophies of life were remarkably different from ours.

The differences between our way of life and those of our enemy the Japanese were stark and obvious, especially when it came to the attitudes of soldiers towards the enemy. Australians struggle to understand the Japanese mentality and the common response was hatred and loathing, along with a certain level of paranoia, as invasion seemed imminent.

When Japan entered the war in December 1941, it had a well-prepared invasion force, or series of such forces, and a well-planned campaign to capture most of South-East Asia very quickly.

The Japanese plan proved to be a great success. Within weeks the Americans were driven out of the Philippines and the British out of Malaya as the Japanese tide moved south. By March 1942 the Dutch had surrendered the East Indies (Indonesia) and Papua New Guinea and the Solomons were being invaded.

It was in March that General MacArthur arrived in Australia after escaping from the Philippines with his headquarters' staff. He immediately assumed supreme command of Allied forces in the South-West Pacific Area (SWPA). All of Australia's military combat units in this area were part of SWPA forces and, consequently, they were placed under MacArthur's command. Douglas MacArthur replaced the Australian

Chiefs of Staff as the Australian government's main source of military advice and influence until the war ended in 1945.

The relationship with our allies the Americans was generally cordial and successful. On the surface, our lifestyles and philosophies of life appeared similar, and we had an understanding of the American way of life due to the invasive nature of Hollywood movies, American literature and popular songs, as well as a long history of visits from American entertainers of all kinds. We also, of course, shared a certain amount of history and culture from our common British backgrounds.

Just below the surface there were, however, major differences in Australian and American attitudes to life, social structures, economic development and opinions on how the war should be fought.

The USA was more modern, more developed and had an economy and population larger than ours. The clash of cultures and attitudes, although perhaps not as big a problem as it might have been, was still sufficient to cause some minor problems when certain single-minded American military leaders were imposed upon us, and almost one million testosterone-laden young American men of fighting age were forced to assimilate temporarily into our society.

Although General Blamey was appointed the Allied Land Force commander, he was not permitted by MacArthur to command American forces. MacArthur also rejected requests from his own superiors in the United States to appoint Australians to his General Headquarters senior positions. Later in the war, he would be accused of relegating Australian troops to minor mopping-up campaigns.

In spite of this, Prime Minister Curtin and General MacArthur developed a good relationship that proved very beneficial to Australia after 1942 and Curtin used MacArthur as a direct line of contact for Australian requests for assistance to the US government.

Close to one million US military personnel spent time in Australia during the war. US military bases for both the US air force and troop deployment were constructed in Australia during 1942 and 1943—mostly in Queensland—and Australia was the major supply base for US forces in the Pacific until the end of the war.

What must be said at the outset is that Australians and Americans, thrown together in large numbers for the first time during WWII, by and large found they had a similar outlook on life. Both were generally open and friendly and managed to get on quite well together. There was a feeling of gratitude towards the United States in Australian society during the war, and the Australian and American attitudes to life generally had more in common than they had differences.

However, at times there were difficulties between Australian commanders and their US counterparts, like the incidents surrounding the sinking of HMAS *Canberra*. These were mostly localised incidents, which were dealt with diplomatically in the long term.

Many in our military resented MacArthur's marginalising of Australian troops for use in 'unimportant' areas of war towards the end. It was felt that he wanted US troops to have the glory, but at least it was a change from our troops being used as 'lambs to the slaughter' by the British. MacArthur had a job to do and he did it well.

The impact and consequences of the US–Australian alliance were felt more keenly at home than on the battlefield. During WWII the Australian public had to undergo quite dramatic social changes due to the war effort. On top of this came the cultural clashes when large numbers of American troops arrived in Australia on their way to and from various theatres of war.

Even before the war, the Australian social tradition was for towns and cities to virtually shut down from noon on Saturday until Monday morning. The war had restricted entertainment and sporting activities even more. In Brisbane, for example, where the bulk of the Americans were stationed after MacArthur moved his headquarters there from Melbourne, only Doomben operated as a racetrack, while Albion Park and Eagle Farm had become army camps. With thousands of troops in capital cities, there was huge pressure on local authorities to change their policies, and to open hotels, theatres, nightclubs and restaurants longer and for more varied hours. This led to a boost in the local economy, and new tastes and fashions in entertainment and dining.

When MacArthur moved his headquarters to Brisbane, many buildings and areas around the city were taken over by the US military. Brisbane's population of 320,000 increased by more than 50 per cent during 1942. Almost 90,000 US servicemen were stationed in the city. Normal life was disrupted, some schools and other public services were closed, crime increased, the city's infrastructure was barely adequate and electricity often failed, causing 'blackouts' and 'brownouts'. In response to these changes, many families left Brisbane and moved inland or back to rural areas where they had relatives. These social upheavals, and the presence of large numbers of non-Australian young men, inevitably led to resentment and rivalry.

There was considerable resentment and jealousy due to the American troops being better paid and having access to consumer items in their military-based PX Stores. These were stores set up exclusively for American defence personnel serving overseas, giving them access to some of the items they were used to having at home. Australians who had possibly never seen them before and were also suffering the strict rationing of essentials considered many of these items luxuries.

Another feeling of strong resentment came from the belief among Australian men that 'the Yanks' often 'bought' the favours of Aussie girls with luxury items such as nylon stockings. While there is some truth in this, it must also be said that many women in Australia found the Americans to have a better attitude towards women than Australian men. Americans often had a more respectful, sophisticated and friendly approach to the opposite sex than was common in Australian society at the time.

As with many social problems in Australia's history, alcohol was a factor. The American PX Stores also sold cigarettes and alcohol at low prices. Australian servicemen were not allowed into American PX Stores. Beer was scarce and hotels had quotas and were only allowed to serve alcohol for restricted periods each day. This led to binge drinking and groups of servicemen roaming the streets in search of pubs serving beer, rushing from one hotel to the next and drinking as quickly as possible before it closed.

It was against this background of social upheaval and resentment that a number of clashes between Australian and American troops occurred. They occurred in Melbourne, Sydney, Rockhampton and Perth, but were probably most common in Brisbane where they climaxed in the infamous 'Battle of Brisbane'.

Just before 7 pm on 26 November 1942, Private James Stein of the 404th Signal Company of the US army apparently left the Australian canteen where he had been drinking (though some versions say he had been in a pub) to walk to the American PX canteen on the corner of Creek and Adelaide Streets. Stein was either chatting to or arguing with three Aussie soldiers when US military policeman (MP) Private Anthony O'Sullivan asked to see his leave pass and became impatient when the inebriated soldier couldn't find it. American MPs were not popular with the Australian soldiers, who traditionally disliked authority figures, and the three Australians told the MP to leave Stein alone. This started an altercation that attracted more Australian soldiers and a few civilians and more MPs from the American PX canteen. A fight ensued in which MP O'Sullivan was assaulted and his fellow MPs were forced to retreat into the PX canteen, carrying their wounded colleague.

A crowd gathered outside the PX, throwing bottles and rocks, and a parking sign was thrown through a window. By 7.15 pm there were about 100 Australian soldiers trying to break through a makeshift cordon of US MPs around the PX door. As the crowd grew, fights broke out along the street and the American Red Cross building diagonally opposite the PX building was also attacked.

Police Inspector Charles Price arrived on the scene and Queensland policemen and US MPs began barricading the doors to the PX canteen. By 8 pm a crowd estimated by some later at up to 5000 people, but probably around half that size in reality, was involved in the disturbance and more fights broke out in other streets in the city area.

Women working in the city area were told not to use the streets until they could be escorted from the area by soldiers with fixed bayonets, theatres were closed by the MPs, and service personnel were ordered back to their barracks or ships.

Rumours abounded in the days after the riot, including that Australian MPs removed their armbands and joined in the attack on the PX canteen and that the Brisbane Fire Brigade arrived but refused to use their hoses on the Aussie soldiers. Legend has it that, inside the PX canteen, a still inebriated Private Stein was searching the pockets of the unconscious MP O'Sullivan looking for his leave pass when he was handed a baton and told to help protect the building. There were also reports of an army truck being stopped by Aussie soldiers and Owen sub-machine guns, ammunition and hand grenades being 'requisitioned' and handed to rioters.

What is certain is that some of the MPs in the PX canteen armed themselves with 12-gauge pump-action shotguns and elbowed their way to the front of the PX in an attempt to stop the riot. The crowd reacted angrily to the sight of firearms and US Private Norbert Grant was jostled and grabbed by some of the men attacking the canteen in an attempt to take the gun from him. As Grant jabbed one Australian soldier in the chest with the shotgun, another soldier from the crowd grabbed the gun and yet another grabbed Grant around the neck.

The shotgun discharged three times. The first shot hit Private Edward Webster from the 2/2nd Australian Anti-Tank Regiment in the chest and killed him instantly. Two male civilians and five other Australian soldiers, all privates, received shotgun wounds.

As Private Grant fought his way back into the canteen, he clubbed another soldier and damaged the shotgun butt. One of the MPs guarding the PX canteen suffered a fractured skull.

The Americans fled to safety deeper in the building and by 10 pm the riot was over. The front area of the ground floor of the American PX Store was demolished by the mob.

Officially, the Military Censor's Office did a great job of killing the story: although the Brisbane *Courier-Mail* newspaper ran a heavily censored article about a disturbance in which a person was killed, there was no mention of the nature of the event or the nationalities involved. No mention of the riot ever appeared in the American press, so the censors obviously did their job on letters home as well.

While there was a successful cover-up by the censor, that didn't stop the rumours and the resentment growing. Word-of-mouth rumours quickly spread and exaggerated reports of the events appeared, such as fifteen Aussies being killed by American MPs with machine guns. These rumours fuelled the fires of resentment and prejudice against the US troops to the extent that the following evening was a low point in Australian military history for behaviour by soldiers. In a night of shameful thuggery and violence, mobs of Australian servicemen prowled the streets of Brisbane beating and kicking any Americans they found.

Where the mob anger had been directed at the authority figures of the unpopular military police on the first night, any American was a target on the second night. A crowd of Australian servicemen, estimated at between 500 and 600, formed three circles at the intersection of Queen and Adelaide streets and any passing American soldiers were pushed into the centre of the circles and then punched and kicked. Another crowd gathered outside General MacArthur's headquarters on the corner of Queen and Edward streets and shouted abuse at the building. MacArthur was in New Guinea at the time.

Brisbane identity 'Big Bill' Edwards was closing his pharmacy that night when an American officer and his Australian wife left a cinema nearby and were spotted by a group of a dozen Australian servicemen. Bill heard shouts of 'There's a bloody Yank—kill him' and 'Kick his brains out'. Bill saw the woman knocked to the ground twice. The couple scrambled into Bill's shop and he closed the wire security door to keep the mob out. When one of the soldiers said, 'Give us the bastard, Bill, he killed our mate', Bill evidently replied, 'He didn't kill anyone, and if you find the one who did, I'll kill him for you.' The mob then moved on.

More than twenty Americans, mostly MPs and officers, were seriously injured on the second night of the 'Battle of Brisbane' and more than half of those were hospitalised. The units involved in the disturbance were relocated out of Brisbane and the number of MPs patrolling Brisbane streets at night was increased. The American PX canteen was relocated, while the Australian canteen was closed permanently. The MP who held the shotgun, Private Norbert Grant, was subsequently court-martialled on a charge of manslaughter in February 1943. He was found not guilty on the grounds of self-defence. Five Australians were convicted of assault and one of them served a six-month gaol term.

The 'Battle of Brisbane' showed the duality of the Australian attitude towards the Americans who were stationed here in WWII. On one side, there was gratitude and relief that General MacArthur and the US troops and personnel were in Australia, supporting the Australians' involvement in the war. The paranoia and fear of a Japanese invasion generally overrode any animosity felt towards the American troops.

There is no doubt that the majority of Australians warmly welcomed the presence of the Americans. This is evidenced by the number of American names used as street names in the suburbs of Australian cities in the post-war expansion.

On the flipside, there were major cultural differences that made the presence of the Americans problematic at times. The differences were as simple as such things as smarter uniforms, access to luxury items, different manners and grooming. There were also major differences in social attitudes to such things as public affection between dating couples and the right to bear arms. Conservative Australia found public affection, kissing and 'smooching', offensive. Australian servicemen were also critical of the wearing of handguns and the use of firearms generally by Americans. Even today the attitude towards gun control is one of the defining differences between Australian and American societies.

It is easy to dismiss the 'Battle of Brisbane' as an isolated incident, but wartime authorities stated after the war that many similar incidents occurred. There are reports of an incident at Rockhampton when two troop trains stopped side by side. One was full of US troops heading south on leave and the other full of Aussies heading north to fight, and a full-scale battle developed. Censorship kept the truth of these incidents from being revealed at the time to the Australian public.

As a sign that the times had changed and perceptions had shifted slightly, after the war ended young Australians sought to emulate the American lifestyle and adopted the very habits that annoyed the more conservative elements of our society during WWII.

While the 'Battle of Brisbane' revealed some of the nastier elements of the Aussie character, it was largely the result of large numbers of young men from two different cultures, full of alcohol and testosterone, being forced into an alliance in a time of stress and difficulty.

To this day some of the cultural differences that led to this event are still apparent in our relationships with, and our feelings about, our American friends 'across the pond'.

A STUBBORN ENEMY

A common misconception is that all campaigns fought in New Guinea after Kokoda were merely difficult mopping-up exercises as the Japanese slowly withdrew. This is far from the truth. The Japanese attempted to reinforce their bases on the north coast of New Guinea and were partly successful in doing so. They had no intention of abandoning their aspirations to conquer New Guinea and the Solomons in late 1942. The three Japanese beachheads—Gona, Buna and Sanananda—could still be supplied by sea and the 500 surviving Japanese troops from the Kokoda campaign joined the garrison at Sanananda when they reached the coast.

The Allies' estimate of 1500 starving, mostly non-combatant troops defending the three bases was totally inaccurate. There were, in fact, 6000 troops still in place, many of them elite marine troops from Japan's special landing force.

American aircraft, engineers, supply and communications personnel had been involved in the Papua New Guinea campaign from the earliest Japanese invasions and US infantry were now to be deployed in force against the Japanese. On 12 October General MacArthur sent 1250 men of the 2nd Battalion of the 126th US Infantry across the Owen Stanley Ranges, to attack the enemy at Gona and Buna, via the Kapa Kapa–Jaure Trail, a goat track even worse than the Kokoda Track. They became the first Americans to cross the Owen Stanleys and the first white men across the track since 1917. The trek took 42 days and Allied troops had already engaged the enemy before they arrived.

Other troops crossed overland to the north coast from Milne Bay, making slow progress through jungle swamp and mountain passes. The

Australian 2/10th Battalion and American regiments were flown in to Wanigela (200 kilometres east of Kokoda) once an airstrip was built, and luggers were also used to transport troops along the north coast to the battle areas.

It was assumed these battles would be fought on swampy coastal ground, but the Japanese constructed intricate series of near-impenetrable bunkers on the higher, drier ground, cleverly designed to cover all approaches with crossfire. These bunkers held 30 men and were just above ground level with slits for machine guns. Allied troops had to work their way through the swamp to destroy them one by one while watching for snipers stationed in the trees.

On 16 November the 850 fit men of the 25th Brigade, who had survived the Kokoda Track, were given the task of capturing Gona, while the US troops of the 32nd Division attacked at Buna. Both attacks failed: the Japanese positions appeared to be unassailable. On 18 November, however, the Australian 16th Brigade took Popondetta, 20 kilometres (12 miles) inland from Gona, on the Kokoda Track, and construction of a landing strip began immediately.

By 23 November the Australians had suffered 25 per cent casualties at Gona, and the US troops had lost 400 at Buna. MacArthur offered a US division to reinforce the Australians at Gona, and Blamey took the opportunity to pay him back for his earlier criticism of Aussie troops by telling him he'd send what was left of the Australian 21st Brigade instead, because he 'knew they would fight'.

After Gona was heavily bombed by Allied aircraft on 24 November, the 25th Brigade, 21st Brigade, US 32nd Division and the remnants of Maroubra Force, including the 'ragged bloody heroes' of the 39th Battalion, made a series of attacks and finally defeated the Japanese on 8 December—530 Allied troops died taking Gona and 640 Japanese bodies were found, but only a handful of survivors.

Infuriated by the failure to take Buna, where the Japanese managed to land 1300 reinforcements, MacArthur blamed the poorly trained US troops of the 32nd Division, National Guardsmen from Michigan and Wisconsin, and ordered Major General Robert Eichelberger to 'take Buna or not come back alive'.

Eichelberger halted the fighting, replaced the regimental and battalion commanders, issued additional rations and medical supplies for the troops, and resumed the attack on 5 December. Reinforced by the

18th Brigade 7th Australian Division and the tanks of the 2/16 Armoured Division, the Allies broke through the Japanese coastal defences and surrounded and defeated the Japanese in ten days of fighting, which involved grenades being dropped by hand into bunker after bunker under heavy fire between 18 and 28 December, as the enemy fought to the death. Allied casualties were 2900. The 18th Brigade lost 306 killed and 500 more were wounded. Fewer than 50 Japanese prisoners were taken at Buna and 1400 bodies were counted, though many more died in collapsed bunkers.

At Sanananda the situation was similar. The Allies could not make headway against the entrenched Japanese positions. Through November, the Australian 16th Brigade tried and failed, followed by the US 126th Regiment and then the Australian 30th Brigade. After Gona fell to the Allies, the 39th Battalion reinforced the troops at Sanananda along with a fresh regiment of American soldiers. The Australians engaged the Japanese defending the road into Sanananda and lost three tanks and 100 men. The Americans, however, began to find empty bunkers, for 1200 Japanese troops had been evacuated by sea and another 1000 fled to the west, but at least 1500 Japanese died at Sanananda. Allied casualties, killed and wounded, totalled 2100. Almost 600 Australians died at Sanananda.

With Buna, Gona and Sanananda all lost at the start of 1943, the Japanese realised that the airstrip at Wau was a serious threat to their Salamaua, Mubo and Lae bases to the west. They planned to send a large force from Rabaul to capture the airfield, which became a base for guerrilla resistance after the 2/5th Australian Commando Unit was deployed there to join the local militiamen of the New Guinea Volunteer Rifles in May 1942. Known as 'Kanga Force', they were responsible for a highly successful raid on Salamaua in June 1942.

Allied command had broken Japanese codes and knew most of their plan to capture Wau and a race developed between the Japanese troops coming by sea and land, and the Allied troops being airlifted into the village, New Guinea's most dangerous landing place, under often-impossible flying conditions.

The large convoy that left Rabaul on 6 January was attacked by Allied bombers which sank one troopship, *Nichiryu Maru*, and disabled another. The Japanese also lost all their medical supplies and 70 aircraft in the air battle, while the Allies lost ten planes. Four thousand troops were landed at Lae and taken by barge to Salamaua. Japanese General Toru

Okabe decided to follow an old, seldom-used track to avoid detection and his troops become separated and arrived at Wau disorganised. Meanwhile, Australian reinforcements were being flown into Wau but, of the 28 Dakotas available in New Guinea, only ten could be spared and three crashed attempting to get troops of the 6th Division to Wau. Dakotas only carried 27 passengers and poor weather meant many flights had to return to Port Moresby and try again next day. Brigadier Murray Moten, who led the defence of Wau, took three trips before his plane was able to land.

The battle began on 28 January 1943, and on the next day the Australians were forced back to positions near the town and the airstrip was under attack. However, 52 new Dakotas had arrived in Australia the week before and 57 planeloads of troops and artillery were flown into Wau and unloaded under enemy fire as the Japanese came within range of the airstrip on 29 January.

Although a further 190 planeloads of men and supplies were flown in over the following three days, the Japanese reached the edge of the airfield on 30 January, but Beaufighters of the 30th RAAF Squadron attacked Japanese ground positions and, by 4 February, the Japanese began to withdraw. Japanese attempts to bomb the airstrip on 6 February were repelled by US fighter planes, which shot down 26 Japanese aircraft.

The body count of Japanese dead at Wau was more than 750, and 360 troops died when the troopship *Nichiryu Maru* was sunk. Combined Kanga Force losses were 350 killed.

In spite of a crushing defeat at Wau, the Japanese, who had already made a decision in late December to transport more than 100,000 troops from China to New Guinea, began building a road into Wau Valley from the north, and another huge convoy of troopships was assembled in Rabaul to reinforce Lae and Salamaua and attack Wau.

BEAUFIGHTERS OVER THE BISMARCK SEA

By the end of 1942 the Japanese needed to reinforce their bases in New Guinea in order to hold off the Allied advance. A convoy of eight troopships carrying 6500 Japanese troops, escorted by eight destroyers, left Rabaul on 28 February 1943. There were 100 fighter planes ready to give air support.

Allied reconnaissance had suggested that something was being planned but, due to tropical storms, the fleet was not detected and attacked until it had reached the south-west tip of New Britain on 2 March. Three Japanese transports were sunk on that day but two Japanese destroyers managed to rescue 800 men and take them ahead to disembark at Lae.

The following day, with better flying conditions, the RAAF 22nd, 30th and 100th Squadrons attacked the convoy, along with US B17s, B25s and A20s of the US 3rd Attack Group. At the same time as the 90 Allied planes attacked the convoy, RAAF Douglas Bostons attacked the Japanese fighter base at Lae to restrict air cover for the fleet.

The thirteen Beaufighters of No. 30 Squadron RAAF approached low to make the enemy believe they were Beauforts making a torpedo attack and the tactic worked. The Japanese convoy, under the impression that they were under torpedo attack, made the tactical error of turning their ships towards the Beaufighters, to present a smaller target for bombs and torpedoes. This allowed the Beaufighters to inflict severe damage on the ships' anti-aircraft guns, bridges and crews during strafing runs along the length of each ship with their four 20-mm (¾-inch) nose cannons and six wing-mounted 7.7-mm (.303-inch) machine guns. It also meant that the Japanese ships were then left exposed to mast-height bombing and 'skip' or 'bounce' bombing attacks by US bombers.

US airman Garrett Middlebrook, a co-pilot in one of the B25s, observed the Beaufighters in action:

> They went in and hit this troop ship. What I saw looked like little sticks, maybe a foot long or something like that, or splinters flying up off the deck of ship; they'd fly all around ... and twist crazily in the air and fall out in the water. Then I realized what I was watching were human beings. I was watching hundreds of those Japanese just blown off the deck by those machine guns. They just splintered around the air like sticks in a whirlwind and they'd fall in the water.

All the transports and four destroyers were sunk for the loss of five aircraft, including one Beaufighter. The battle was a decisive Allied victory and a disaster for Japan. The Japanese lost twenty planes and the Allies five and Allied patrol boats and planes later attacked and sank barges and rescue vessels carrying Japanese survivors towards their bases on the coast.

On board one of the Beaufighters, the famous cameraman Damien Parer filmed the attack and it was later shown in cinemas. The official RAAF media release stated that, 'Enemy crews were slain beside their guns, deck cargo burst into flame, superstructures toppled and burned.'

The fourteen US B25s involved in the battle claimed seventeen hits and, when the Beaufighters and B25s were out of ammunition, USAAF A20 Havocs of the 3rd Attack Group joined in, while B17s of the US 43rd Bombardment Group scored five hits from higher altitudes and USAAF B25s and Bostons, along with No. 22 Squadron RAAF, also flying American-made Douglas Boston bombers, continued the attack.

All of the transports were hit and sank about 100 kilometres (62 miles) south-east of Finschhafen and the destroyers *Shirayuki*, *Tokitsukaze* and *Arashio* also went down. Another destroyer, the *Asashio*, sank when a B17 hit her with a 500-pound (228-kilogram) bomb as she was trying to rescue survivors.

After the battle 2700 Japanese troops were taken from the water and returned to Rabaul on the remaining destroyers, only one of which, the *Yukikaze*, was undamaged. About 1000 survivors were left adrift on rafts to be attacked by US PT boats and US and RAAF planes to prevent any chance of them landing and returning to active service. Some saw this as justifiable retaliation for Japanese fighter planes shooting surviving Allied aircrew in the water during the battle.

One group of eighteen Japanese survivors was captured by *PT–114* after making it ashore on an island, and another group made it all the way to Guadalcanal, only to be killed by an American patrol.

Overall troop losses for Japan were huge. About half of the 6800 troops being transported died and the Japanese later cited the Allied attacks on survivors as justification for sinking the hospital ship ASH *Centaur* in May 1943. The truth was that Major General George Kenney, Air Commander of South-West Pacific Area (SWPA), ordered the attacks to prevent any reinforcements reaching the Japanese bases. Some RAAF aircrew were reportedly sickened at being ordered to machine-gun men on rafts.

After the Battle of the Bismarck Sea, the Australians advanced west towards the Japanese bases of Lae and Salamaua knowing that the US air force and RAAF had established air supremacy, which made it very hard for the Japanese to move large numbers of troops to the New Guinea mainland base at Lae. Despite this setback, however, the Japanese continued to reinforce and supply Wewak.

The Bristol Beaufighters of the RAAF 30th Squadron performed exceptionally well in the battle. As well as four cannons in the nose and six machine guns in the wings, each Beaufighter also carried bombs and rockets, making it the most heavily armed fighter plane in the world at that time.

The Beaufighter was a heavy fighter variant of the Beaufort bomber. It was built by the Bristol Aeroplane Company and extensively and successfully used in the war by the RAF (59 squadrons) and the Fleet Air Arm (fifteen squadrons), as well as the RAAF (seven squadrons).

When Australia came under threat from the Japanese movement towards the mainland in 1941, the RAAF had no fighter/bomber aircraft capable of defending the coastline. Beaufighters were chosen as the aircraft that best suited the task and Britain was able to supply them, although it was 1942 before the RAAF took possession of its first British-built Beaufighters.

Australian factories had successfully built 700 Beaufort bombers under licence and began to produce an Australian version of the Beaufighter in January 1943. The planes began flying in May 1944 and eventually 365 Australian Beaufighters were produced before the war ended, to add to the 5928 built in Britain.

There are currently only three Beaufighters left in museums in Australia.

HOMING BOMBERS

Jack Sorensen

We see them go on giant wings,
Dark in the aftermath of night,
To strike before a new sun flings
To Capricorn fresh gift of light.

And in noon's hush we wait to hear,
Faint and far in steel-blue dome,
A droning, sweet to anxious ear,
The song of bombers coming home.

They strike to save, and we who wait
Hard by a threatened northern shore,
Know that our fledgling nation's fate,
Lies in the hands of men she bore.

So strike, brave hands, strike hard and true
At tyranny across the foam,
And faint and far from out the blue,
Comes song of conquerors, coming home.

AHS *CENTAUR*

The *Centaur* was a trading vessel owned by the Ocean Steamship Company, a subsidiary of a shipping company known as the Blue Funnel Line. She was built in Scotland specifically for the Fremantle to Singapore trade route in 1923–24 and was designed to carry about 70 passengers and 450 cattle. She replaced an older vessel, the *Charon*, which had plied the coastal waters off Western Australia and the Dutch East Indies (Indonesia) for many years.

Centaur had some interesting features. Her hull was flat and reinforced in order to enable her to rest on coastal mud flats and access Western Australian ports, which were subject to huge tidal variations. She also had a distinctive 11-metre (36-foot) smokestack, in spite of the fact that she was among the earliest diesel-powered merchant ships.

Before being handed over to the Australian government for conversion to a hospital ship in 1943, *Centaur* was involved in two famous rescues. In November 1938 she picked up a distress signal from the Japanese whaling ship *Kyo Maru II* which was drifting towards the Abrolhos Islands off the coast of Western Australia with her engines disabled and was in grave danger of being wrecked on the reefs in the area, as had many other vessels in history. HMAS *Centaur* went to the rescue and towed *Kyo Maru II* into Geraldton.

On 26 November 1941, an aircraft looking for the missing Australian cruiser HMAS *Sydney* contacted *Centaur* and directed the ship to a crowded and damaged lifeboat. As an official British merchant navy vessel, *Centaur* had been fitted, in September 1939, with a 100-mm (4-inch) naval gun and two Vickers .303 machine guns as protection against Axis warships and aircraft. *Centaur*'s captain at that time was Walter Francis Dark. He was the survivor of two torpedo attacks that saw ships he commanded, HMAS *Titan* and HMAS *Ixion*, sunk by German U-boats. He had recently taken command of *Centaur* after the sinking of *Ixion* six months previously.

Captain Dark had nothing to fear from an unarmed lifeboat but he was not about to take any chances and, when the lifeboat was located, food was lowered and one man was allowed on board. At first he claimed to be a Norwegian merchant seaman but soon admitted to being the first officer of the German raider, *Kormoran*. The lifeboat contained 62 crew members of the German vessel who had been at sea for seven days since the battle between the *Kormoran* and HMAS *Sydney*. Among the survivors in the lifeboat was the *Kormoran*'s captain, Theodor Detmers.

HMAS *Centaur* took nine badly wounded men aboard and began towing the lifeboat towards Carnarvon. When it was swamped by heavy seas, two of HMAS *Centaur*'s lifeboats were lowered and the Germans were towed into Carnarvon in these. At Carnarvon, the Germans were placed in the *Centaur*'s cargo hold and taken to Fremantle, along with other *Kormoran* survivors and 40 Australian soldiers.

After Japan entered the war with the bombing of Pearl Harbor in December 1941, the HMAS *Centaur*'s normal activities were curtailed and she ventured no further north than Broome until October 1942, when she relocated to Queensland, where she was used to carry supplies to Allied troops and bases in New Guinea.

As Australian casualties mounted in the New Guinea campaign, it was realised that another hospital ship was required. HMAS *Centaur* was a perfect choice. Due to her flat hull and shallow draught, she could operate in coastal tropical waters, which none of the three existing hospital ships, AHS *Wanganella*, *Manunda* and *Oranje*, could do. Early in 1943, HMAS *Centaur* was handed over to the Department of Defence and converted to a hospital ship in Melbourne.

As hospitals in Queensland could not cope with the numbers of wounded arriving from the fighting in New Guinea and the Solomons, the ship had to be capable of taking the casualties directly to Sydney. When relaunched as the AHS *Centaur* in March 1943, the ship had an operating theatre, dispensary, two wards that could hold 250 patients and a dental surgery. There was accommodation for 75 crew and 65 medical staff. AHS *Centaur* was able to stay at sea for eighteen days without being resupplied.

During her conversion, *Centaur* was painted with the markings of a hospital ship as detailed in Article 5, section 10 of the 1907 Hague Convention. Her white hull had a green band interspersed by three red crosses on each flank of the hull. She had a white superstructure, multiple large red crosses visible from both sea and air, and the identification number 47 painted on her bows. Details of AHS *Centaur*'s new identifying markings and features were provided to International Red Cross and passed on to the Japanese in the first week of February 1943. These markings highlighted that she was a hospital ship and was protected from any attacks at sea as directed by the Hague and Geneva Conventions.

AHS *Centaur*'s first task as a hospital ship was transporting wounded servicemen to Brisbane from overcrowded hospitals in Townsville. She then delivered medical personnel to New Guinea and returned to Brisbane with Australian and American wounded as well as a number of wounded Japanese prisoners before returning to Sydney to be reprovisioned for another voyage to New Guinea.

She left Sydney on 12 May with 74 crew, 53 army officers and personnel, twelve female army nurses, 192 soldiers of the 2nd/12th Field Ambulance and one Torres Strait ship pilot. At approximately 4 am on 14 May 1943, AHS *Centaur* was torpedoed by an unseen submarine while travelling just north of Brisbane about 45 kilometres (28 miles) north-east of North Stradbroke Island. This was confirmed by the Japanese, many years later, to be KD7 class submarine *I77*, captained by Lieutenant Commander Hajime Nakagawa.

Although the ship was expected to sail in the normal merchant shipping lanes further out to sea, her master decided that a route closer to land was desirable. This decision meant she was a perfect target, with land to port and an island close by offering cover for submarines, alongside deep open sea, perfect for submarine operations, to starboard.

The torpedo hit a fuel tank 2 metres (6.5 feet) below the waterline, opening a huge hole in the vessel's side and causing an explosion which set the front part of the ship on fire and killed many on board instantly. Others were burned to death or drowned as AHS *Centaur* rolled over and sank in less than three minutes, too quickly for lifeboats to be put to use; also, as almost everyone was asleep on board at the time of the attack, most did not survive. It is estimated that about 200 of the 332 on board lived through the explosion and fire but only 64 survivors were rescued.

The survivors spent more than 36 hours in the water. Two damaged lifeboats had broken free as the ship went down and were used by some survivors, while others stayed afloat on wreckage and barrels.

Those left afloat were spread out over roughly 4 kilometres (2.5 miles) of ocean as they drifted almost 40 kilometres (25 miles) north on ocean currents. The survivors saw and heard several ships and planes during this time, but they were not sighted by any of them until the afternoon of 15 May when a lookout aboard the destroyer USS *Mugford*, which was escorting the New Zealand freighter *Sussex* out of Brisbane to New Zealand, reported an object on the horizon.

An RAAF Avro Anson on anti-submarine watch investigated and returned to the two ships to signal that there were shipwreck survivors in the water. USS *Mugford*'s captain, Lieutenant Commander H.J. Corey, ordered the Anson to accompany the *Sussex* while his vessel spent an hour and a half picking up the survivors as sailors on deck with rifles kept watch for sharks. He also radioed Brisbane with the news that AHS *Centaur* had been sunk and, after searching the area until dark, returned to Brisbane around midnight with the survivors. The USS *Helm* and HMAS *Lithgow* and four torpedo boats carried out further searches until 21 May, but no more survivors were found.

Of the medical staff aboard, only one doctor out of eighteen and one nurse out of twelve survived. Sister Ellen Savage was asleep in her bunk when the *Centaur* collapsed around her. She later told her story:

> Merle Morton and myself were awakened by two terrific explosions and practically thrown out of bed . . . I registered mentally that it was a torpedo explosion . . . In that instant the ship was in flames . . . we ran into Colonel Manson, our commanding officer, in full dress even to his cap and 'Mae West' life-jacket, who kindly said 'That's right girlies, jump for it now.' The first words I spoke was to say 'Will I have time to go back for my great-coat?' as we were only in our pyjamas. He said 'No' and with that climbed the deck and jumped and I followed . . . the ship was commencing to go down. It all happened in three minutes.

The suction of the sinking *Centaur* dragged Sister Savage down into a whirlpool of moving metal and wood. Here her ribs, nose and palate were broken, her ear drums perforated and she sustained multiple bruises. Then she was propelled to the surface in the middle of an oil slick. She found her way to a raft that was part of the *Centaur*'s wheel-house. During the 36 hours on this makeshift raft, Sister Savage gave whatever medical care she could to survivors despite being badly injured herself. For her courage and inspiring behaviour during this period, Sister Savage was awarded the George Medal. During the hours before their rescue, Sister Savage led the survivors in prayer and song and supervised the distribution of rations.

Three Japanese submarines were operating off Australia's east coast when AHS *Centaur* was torpedoed. Some of the survivors, afloat among the wreckage's debris and resulting oil slick, heard and vaguely saw what they thought was a submarine surface and then submerge. Francis Martin, the ship's cook, who was afloat on a hatch cover some distance from the main groups of survivors, clearly saw a submarine, which he later described to naval investigators.

Martin's descriptions perfectly matched a Japanese KD7 class submarine. After denying any involvement in the incident following official Australian protests via the Red Cross at the time, an official Japanese war history acknowledged, in 1979, that the Japanese KD7 class submarine *177*, captained by Lieutenant Commander Hajime Nakagawa, sank the AHS *Centaur*.

The sinking of the AHS *Centaur* outraged the Australian public and media. Prime Minister John Curtin called it 'an entirely inexcusable act, undertaken in violation of the convention to which Japan is a party and of all the principles of common humanity'. The US commander General MacArthur said it was an example of the 'limitless savagery' of the Japanese.

Curtin's public outrage was curtailed after some of his advisers suggested he stop condemning the sinking, for fear of reprisals against Australian prisoners of war held by the Japanese. The Australian government officially protested via the Red Cross and the Japanese denied any involvement in the incident, countering with claims of their hospital ships being attacked by Allied aircraft and naval vessels.

The incident became a propagandist's dream: it was used to fuel the war effort and silence any dissent at home. The government had posters printed showing the sinking and urging Australians to enlist in the armed services or purchase war bonds, with the slogan 'Avenge the Nurses'. A public fund was organised to replace the lost medical equipment and dockyard workers offered to work for free on a replacement vessel, while many other workers donated an hour's pay towards fitting out a replacement.

Rumours and conspiracy theories abounded about the AHS *Centaur* and her sinking. In spite of the xenophobic, anti-Japanese reaction to the sinking, one common rumour was that the ship was carrying ammunition and secret military personnel. This rumour has persisted over the decades, fuelled by unsubstantiated claims by some survivors in spite of denials and contradictions by other survivors, suggesting that the attack might have been a valid one.

While AHS *Centaur* was being loaded at Darling Harbour for her fatal voyage, the medical support troops, 149 men of the 2nd/12th Field Ambulance unit, arrived at the dock carrying rifles and ammunition. This amounted to a total of 52 rifles and 2000 rounds of ammunition. The Chief Medical Officer on board, Captain Hindmarsh, had raised concerns among the crew and wharf labourers that AHS *Centaur* would be transporting military supplies or commandos to New Guinea, and the rifles were not allowed on board until the *Centaur's* master received official reassurance that ambulance drivers were allowed to carry weapons under Article 8 of the Hague Convention, 'for the maintenance of order and the defence of the wounded'.

The civilian crew decided not to sail until they were satisfied about the clarity of this particular point and a union representative made a phone call to the union headquarters. An official of the Seamen's Union then made a thorough search of the cargo on the wharf and on the ship, finding nothing suspicious.

It was this incident that seems to have started most of the rumours and conspiracy theories. There are reports that an army file in the Australian Archives contains allegations made by a Red Cross representative that the AHS *Centaur* was carrying personnel and equipment in contravention of the Red Cross conventions, and that this information was known to the Japanese and gave them reason to consider the hospital ship a legitimate target, as carrying military supplies was a breach of wartime conventions.

In 1988, a magazine article claimed a member of the 2/15th Australian Field Engineers remembered soldiers 'working through the night' loading ammunition, rifles and machine guns onto the AHS *Centaur*. A member of the crew who survived the sinking made a statement many years later that some of the passengers were combat troops carrying automatic weapons

Sergeant Dick Metcalfe, a radiographer and part of the ship's medical staff, helped store weapons aboard the AHS *Centaur* and he had a very different memory: 'Captain Hindmarsh told me to put the rifles in the bottom of number one hold, between the mattresses, to avoid any chance of trouble,' Metcalfe said. He claimed he stored the .303 rifles and ammunition, permitted under the Geneva Convention and taken from the Field Ambulance troops, as ordered and was adamant there were 'no commandos, bombs or Bren guns'.

One very plausible conclusion is that Captain Nakagawa sank the *Centaur* in full knowledge that he was in breach of all the conventions of war. Nakagawa was a war criminal, convicted in 1948 of hideous crimes and sadistic cruelty to survivors of British merchant ships he torpedoed in the Indian Ocean while captain of another submarine, the *I–37*. He forced the captain of one vessel to watch as 54 survivors in lifeboats were machine-gunned to death. He was also convicted of ordering the killing of more than a hundred prisoners with pistols, samurai swords and hammers.

At his trial his only defence was that he had been following orders. He was convicted of the above crimes and sentenced to eight years' hard labour, of which he served six. He was also tried for the sinking of the AHS *Centaur*, but there was considered to be insufficient evidence to secure a conviction. Nakagawa never denied or confirmed any involvement in the incident and refused to talk to anyone about it. He died, aged 84, in 1986.

It is possible that Nakagawa interpreted secret orders issued in 1943 by the Japanese High Command to 'destroy enemy ships and cargoes and carry out the complete destruction of the crews of enemy ships' as meaning ALL enemy vessels, including hospital ships. It is also possible that the strike was in retaliation for similar attacks on Japanese ships. There were claims by the Japanese that the Allies had targeted Japanese hospital ships, particularly in the Battle of the Bismarck Sea during 2 and 4 March 1943, causing a high number of Japanese losses.

The sinking of AHS *Centaur* was one of the most significant incidents that helped engender and justify Australian hatred towards Japan during and after WWII. It confirmed the Australian public's distrust and loathing for the enemy. There were many reasons for Australians to hate the Japanese. From the December 1941 bombing of Pearl Harbor onwards, the Japanese were portrayed by the military and the media, often quite justifiably, as unprincipled, barbaric and cruel opponents. The murder and mistreatment of prisoners, cruelty towards the helpless, relentless bombing of Australia's northern towns and cities, and fanatical refusal to surrender when cornered, along with the obvious racial and cultural differences between the two opponents, led to the Japanese being seen as inhuman and immoral adversaries. This attitude lasted among many Australians for decades after the war.

The other result of the tragedy was that it played a part in the changing attitude towards women that occurred during WWII. The role played by Sister Savage, and the fact that eleven of the twelve staff nurses died, was huge news and affected Australians deeply, as did the sinking of the SS *Vyner Brooke* on 14 February 1942, carrying the last 65 Australian nurses from Singapore, and the Banka Island massacre by Japanese soldiers of the Aussie nurses who survived. The outrage and attention given to these events highlighted that women were a very real part of the military effort and brought to the public's attention the massive effort being made by women in all areas of the war effort, such as the 'Women's Land Army' and the other auxiliary services. This change in perception had a long-term impact on how Australia would view women in post-war society.

Several memorials have been created for AHS *Centaur*. From 1948 to 1979 the Centaur Memorial Fund for Nurses provided accommodation and a meeting place for nurses visiting Brisbane. In 1968, a memorial cairn was erected at the point on shore closest to where the survivors were located, at Caloundra, and in 1990 a large stained-glass window and a plaque listing the names of those lost was installed at Concord Repatriation Hospital in Sydney. In 1993, on the 50th anniversary of the tragedy, another memorial was unveiled at Point Danger, Coolangatta, in Queensland. The memorial is surrounded by a park with a boardwalk overlooking the sea, and there are also plaques for all other vessels lost during WWII. Some survivors of the tragedy attended the unveiling of this memorial, as did a contingent from the USS *Mugford*.

Many searches have been made for the wreck of AHS *Centaur*. She was reliably reported to have been 'found' several times, most notably in 1995 by a deep-sea recovery operator who was later convicted of fraud when photos proved the wreck he claimed to be the *Centaur* was actually another vessel lost in 1951. In 2008, following the discovery of the *Kormoran* and *Sydney*, the Australian federal and Queensland state governments formed a joint committee and contributed AU$2 million each towards a search for the *Centaur*. Using *Seahorse Spirit*, a private vessel operated by naval support company Defence Maritime Services,

David Mearns, who discovered the *Sydney* and *Kormoran*, was given 35 days to locate and film the wreck before funding dried up.

The search began in earnest on 15 December 2009 and six wrecks with similar dimensions to *Centaur* were located in the first three days. Further investigation followed before Mearns announced on 20 December that they had found *Centaur* 30 nautical miles (56 kilometres) east of Moreton Island, resting 2059 metres (6755 feet) below sea level in an underwater gully 150 metres (492 feet) wide. The first photographs, taken by remotely operated camera on 10 January 2010, showed the Red Cross identification number, the hospital ship markings and the ship's bell.

A memorial service was held on 12 January 2010 and a memorial plaque, with the names of all 268 men and women who perished when the *Centaur* was sunk, was placed on the foredeck of the wreck. A protection zone was declared around the site under the *Historic Shipwrecks Act 1976* to protect the wreck and the military and civilian graves.

THE BRISBANE LINE

Although the truth about the scale of the bombings in Darwin, which began on 19 February 1942, was suppressed for years, the paranoia and near-panic about Japanese presence was very palpable in the lead-up to the federal election in August 1943.

The population of Darwin acted as they did due to a very real belief that the Japanese army was about to invade. Three months later, when the midget submarines penetrated Sydney Harbour, many residents of the eastern suburbs thought the same way and real estate prices fell as many sold up and moved away. The bombings and presence of enemy submarines enabled politicians to play upon the paranoia, as Labor MP Eddie Ward did with the 'Brisbane Line' debate leading into the election of 1943. The Curtin Labor Cabinet had discussed a Brisbane Line–type strategy as a hypothetical while brainstorming ideas to cover worst-possible scenarios after the Japanese presence became seen as a very real threat to the Australian mainland.

The Darwin bombing and the continued attacks on bases and towns in the north inevitably led to discussions about policies that would enable Australia to resist in various ways should Japanese forces attempt to occupy all or part of the Australian continent.

This strategy was based on the assumption that Australia had too few army units to protect the whole continent, so a defensive line was drawn around the main areas of industry and population that were essential for the war effort. Militia units would take positions behind a defensive line around the south-east corner of the country, including Brisbane, Sydney, Melbourne and Adelaide. In the worst-case hypothetical scenario, this area would be defended at all costs and held until new developments led to a renewed fight to expel the Japanese. It was even suggested that this might not occur until future generations of Australians had grown to military age.

Eddie Ward, Curtin's Minister for Labour and National Service, accused the previous Menzies government of planning a different Brisbane Line strategy where a line was drawn east–west just north of Brisbane, allowing Japan to keep the more sparsely populated areas to the north. According to Ward, this pact would have resembled the one signed by the Vichy government with the Germans in France, acknowledging Japanese authority while maintaining self-government.

Ward's scaremongering accusations during the 1943 election campaign led to this simplistic version of the Brisbane Line being the one most remembered.

In June 1943, Justice Lowe was named Royal Commissioner to investigate Ward's allegations. Ward claimed the plans were missing from official files and continued to suggest the idea of a conspiracy theory in which Menzies had planned a Brisbane Line. However, Prime Minister John Curtin, fearful perhaps that his own Cabinet's discussions might come to light, denied that any files were missing.

Eddie Ward then claimed privilege and did not appear before the commission. Justice Lowe concluded that there was no substance in the charges.

Labor won the election convincingly.

PLANT AN ARUM LILY IF I DIE

Pilot Officer Michael Dicken was on a morning training flight when he died on 17 August 1943. The accident that took his life occurred 24 kilometres (15 miles) out from Mildura Airport, which was a pilot training centre during World War II. The crash took place near the village of Iraak in far north-western Victoria.

Pilot Officer Dicken was just twenty years of age.

The Wirraway aircraft in which he was flying was seen to pull out of a steep dive and one wing broke off, causing the plane to crash into the ground immediately. Pilot Officer Dicken and his instructor, Flight Officer Power, were both killed instantly.

Michael Dicken had a fascinating short life. His father was in the British Foreign Service and Micheal was born in Egypt and raised in Morocco. It was there that he developed a love of arum lilies, which grew in profusion around his childhood home.

When war came in 1939 it was thought safest to send Michael to far-off Australia to complete his education. North Africa was certainly not a safe place for a teenager during the war, nor was Britain during the 'Blitz', so young Michael was sent to finish his education at Melbourne Grammar School.

His father was posted to India soon after Michael left so, when he finished school during the darkest hours of the war, there was no real option for Michael of making his way to his parents' new home. Instead he enlisted in the Royal Australian Air Force and was sent to Deniliquin where he completed the first stage of his service flying training.

It was at Deniliquin that Michael met a local girl, Joan Gooch. Michael and Joan became sweethearts and he told her many stories of his childhood in the exotic lands of North Africa. One evening he told her that, if he died during the war, he would like her to plant an arum lily in his memory.

While Michael Dicken's background was uncommon, his fate was, sadly, not uncommon.

At the Number Two Operational Training Unit at Mildura alone, a total of 52 young men were killed in accidents while engaged in pilot training during the chaotic years of WWII.

Those 52 men were either training officers, repatriated from the war zones, or youngsters who never had the chance to fly in combat, their short lives ending abruptly before they had a chance to fight or serve.

That sort of thing happened all over Australia, of course. The difference is that, in Mildura, a genuine, long-term attempt to remember the sacrifice of so many young lives continues.

As well as the well-kept graveyard where the crash victims were laid to rest, and the memorial in the Number Two Operational Training Unit Museum at Mildura, there are now plaques at the various crash sites, each dedicated separately with a memorial service attended by the mayor of Mildura, a chaplain, local historian Ken Wright, and any friends or relatives who can be traced.

The land-owners on whose properties the crashes occurred are also often present to pay their respects. Indeed, in some cases the land-owners erected markers and memorials themselves and have kept the crash sites in order as memorials to the victims.

During the war the owner of Keera Station, 48 kilometres (30 miles) west of Mildura, was Tom Grace. When two Boomerang training aircraft collided over his property and crashed, he erected crosses and planted two tamarisk trees in memory of the airmen who died.

Tom Grace and the owner of nearby Lybra Station, where the second plane crashed after the collision, allowed the families of the two dead airmen, Flight Officers Syd Knapman and Roger Byrne, to place plaques at the sites. Subsequent owners of the properties continued to look after the sites. When the official plaques were unveiled more than 60 years later, friends and descendants of the property owners, along with friends and family of the two airmen, including Flight Officer Knapman's widow, attended the memorial service.

The official Memorial Plaques are the brainchild of Ken Wright OAM, who is one of only eight RAAF WWII flying veterans to still hold a pilot's licence. Ken is a past Mayor of Mildura and was also the driving force behind having the museum set up at Mildura, in the reconstructed headquarters of Number Two Operational Training Unit.

The granite memorials have bronze plates attached and it is no surprise to discover that 60 per cent of them will be located within the grounds of Mildura airport or close by.

Interestingly, the very first memorial erected is actually within the city boundaries and marks the spot where Pilot Officer McGowan crashed and died in a Kittyhawk. Three other fatalities occurred in the populated part of the city in January 1943 when two Wirraways collided over the streets of suburban Mildura and the two planes crashed into San Mateo Avenue and Etiwanda Avenue. Plaques now mark all these sites.

It is, perhaps, typical of the people of a rural area like Mildura to want to remember the past in this fashion. Civic pride has always been strong in the city which is proud of its unusual history as an independent, planned and regulated town. The Canadian Chaffey brothers founded the Mildura irrigation colony in 1887 and Mildura became an oasis in the desert, Australia's first irrigated colony.

Civic-minded individuals such as Ken Wright are determined to see to it that the 52 young flyers who died in training at Mildura are not forgotten. The sadness that their deaths engendered among their friends and families, and also among the people whose lives they touched while training in Mildura and on whose properties they crashed and lost their lives, will be remembered when passers-by stop to read the plaques.

On occasions such as Anzac Day and Remembrance Day, the plaques will serve as shrines and memorials to those men and many others like them who may not have died in battle, but who nonetheless gave their lives as a result of the call to duty and as a sacrifice to their country.

On 17 August 2004, on the roadside at Iraak, at a spot nearest to the crash site that it is possible for the public to access, Archdeacon Colin Tett dedicated a Memorial Plaque to Flight Officer Power and Pilot Officer Michael Dicken. Among those in attendance were the Mayor of Mildura, Peter Byrne, instigator of the Memorial Plaque scheme, Ken Wright, and Mrs Joan Ward of Canberra.

Sixty-one years previously, while living at Deniliquin where she grew up, Mrs Joan Ward had been the sweetheart of Michael Dicken and, after the ceremony, she planted an arum lily beside the memorial.

OPERATION POSTERN

By September 1943, the war in New Guinea was all about building airstrips and using the RAAF and US air force to assert supremacy, while pushing the Japanese north-west. By May 1943 troops of the 2/6th and 2/7th Battalions 6th Division, many of them veterans of the fighting in Greece, had advanced from Wau to within 20 kilometres (12 miles) of Salamaua and set up a base at Lababia Ridge, which was attacked by superior numbers of Japanese troops on 20 June. Strafing attacks by Beaufighters of the RAAF enabled the Australians, who only numbered 150 even after reinforcements arrived, to hold out against 1500 enemy troops for three days until the Japanese withdrew towards their bases at Lae and Salamaua. Australian losses were eleven dead and twelve wounded, while the Japanese lost 41 men with 172 wounded. The same day that the Japanese attacked at Lababia Ridge, the US 6th Army headquarters was established at Milne Bay.

In the first week of July, the US 162nd Regimental Combat Team established a beachhead unopposed 15 kilometres (9 miles) east of Salamaua, and the main body of US troops advanced along the coast. On 17 August, 47 American B24s and B17s and 80 fighter planes made two raids on Japanese bases at Wewak, Boram, But and Dogau. At Boram, 60 Japanese planes were destroyed on the ground, as their crews were warming them up. Only three US aircraft were lost in these two raids and more than 100 Japanese aircraft were destroyed. The Japanese Fourth Air Army was reduced to just 30 planes.

Through July and August, the Australian forces fought their way overland from Wau towards Salamaua until the Japanese were in danger of being encircled at Salamaua and withdrew to the north. The Australian 5th Division Militia occupied the town on 11 September.

In preparation for the 'pincer movement' attack on Lae, named 'Operation Postern', the US 871st Airborne Engineers had secretly constructed an airfield at Tsili-Tsili, south of Lae, in June 1943 and the first fighters were based at the airfield from late July. An attack was planned on the Japanese base at Lae. This time the plan was to stop a Japanese retreat by attacking from the sea to the east of the town and using an airborne invasion from the west to cut off any retreat through the Markham Valley.

On the night of 4 September, 7800 troops of the 9th Division, commanded by Major General George Wootten, made amphibious landings on two beaches east of Lae, supported by US destroyers providing artillery support. Next day 1700 US paratroops, along with an Australian artillery unit and eight 25-pounder guns, were parachuted into an area north-west of Lae, near Nadzab in the Markham Valley, by 302 aircraft flying out of Port Moresby and the Dobadura air base, which had been established just south of Buna.

General MacArthur and General Kenney, Commanding General of the Allied Air Forces in the South-West Pacific Area (SWPA), were present and observed the operation from B17s and MacArthur was reported to have 'jumped up and down like a kid' as the whole operation proceeded like clockwork.

By 6 September, an airfield had been constructed at Nadzab and troop carriers made their first landings, bringing in construction equipment and infantry of the Australian 7th Division, from Tsili-Tsili. By 14 September, 333 planeloads of invasion equipment, supplies, guns and troops had been shuttled in from Tsili-Tsili and another 90 planeloads of similar equipment had been flown in from Port Moresby. Nadzab had two parallel runways about 18 kilometres (11 miles) long and could handle 36 transport planes simultaneously.

In what became a race with the 9th Division, advancing from the east, the 7th Division fought their way down the Markham Valley from the north-west towards Lae, and its 25th Infantry Brigade entered the town on 15 September, just before the 9th Division's 24th Infantry Brigade arrived. Japanese losses at Lae were 1500 dead and 2000 taken prisoner. But Operation Postern had not 'shut the gate' and more than 7000 Japanese escaped north along the Saruwaged Range and had to be fought again later in the Huon Peninsula campaign.

To consolidate the Allied position in the Markham Valley and establish another airfield, a successful commando raid was carried out by 190 men of the 2/6th Australian Commandos at Kaiapit village, about 100 kilometres (62 miles) north of Nadzab, on 19 September. Two hundred and six Japanese were killed and the area was secured for a safe airfield. Twelve Australians died in the operation.

A total of 190 Australian troops died in the capture of Lae and the 7th Division suffered its worst casualties of the campaign at Port Moresby on 7 September, when a B24 Liberator bomber crashed on take-off, hitting five trucks carrying men of the 2/33rd Battalion, killing 59 and injuring another 92.

On 13 September, at Heath's Plantation just west of Lae, Private Richard Kelliher of the 2/25th Brigade 7th Division, whose platoon had come under heavy fire, saw his platoon leader, Corporal William Richards, shot down ahead of the platoon. Kelliher suddenly broke cover, ran 70 metres (230 feet) towards a Japanese machine-gun post and hurled two grenades at it; he then ran back, seized a Bren gun, returned to the enemy post and silenced it. He then asked permission to go out again to rescue Richards, which he did successfully under heavy fire from other enemy positions, undoubtedly saving the severely wounded corporal's life. Nine dead Japanese were later found in the machine-gun post. In an interesting twist to this heroic story, Kelliher, an Irishman by birth, had been court-martialled for cowardice in the face of the enemy during the battle for Gona. He had always claimed his platoon commander, who was killed in the action, had sent him back from the front line to obtain orders and information. After he was found guilty but later acquitted due to lack of evidence, Kelliher said he would prove one day that he was no coward. He did so at Heath's Plantation ten months later, and was awarded a Victoria Cross for bravery.

MEN IN GREEN

David Campbell

Oh, there were fifteen men in green,
Each with a tommy-gun,
Who leapt into my plane at dawn;
We rose to meet the sun.
We set our course towards the east
And climbed into the day
Till the ribbed jungle underneath
Like a giant fossil lay.

We climbed towards the distant range
Where two white paws of cloud
Clutched at the shoulders of the pass;
The green men laughed aloud.
They did not fear the ape-like cloud
That climbed the mountain crest
And hung from twisted ropes of air
With thunder in their breast.

They did not fear the summer's sun
In whose hot centre lie
A hundred hissing cannon shells
For the unwatchful eye.

And when on Dobodura's field
We landed, each man raised
His thumb towards the open sky;
But to their right I gazed.

For fifteen men in jungle green
Rose from the kunai grass
And came towards the plane. My men
In silence watched them pass;
It seemed they looked upon themselves
In Time's prophetic glass.
Oh, there were some leaned on a stick
And some on stretchers lay.

But few walked on their own two feet
In the early green of day.
They had not feared the ape-like cloud
That climbed the mountain crest;
They had not feared the summer's sun
With bullets for their breast.
Their eyes were bright, their looks were dull,
Their skin had turned to clay.

Nature had met them in the night
And stalked them in the day.
And I think still of men in green
On the Soputa track
With fifteen spitting tommy-guns
To keep a jungle back.

BY JUNGLE, COAST AND RIDGE

Once Lae was in Allied hands, the New Guinea campaign now moved further west. The Japanese were still strong in numbers at Wewak and Madang and to press home the advantage gained at Lae, the Allies could not allow the Japanese who escaped Operation Postern to regroup and threaten counter-attacks.

The 20th Brigade 9th Division, commanded by Brigadier Victor Windeyer, were sent ahead from Lae on 22 September 1943 and made an amphibious landing 10 kilometres (6 miles) north of Finschhafen, which the US 6th Army wanted as a base for the assault against Rabaul.

As the 20th Brigade fought their way south, taking the Finschhafen airfield and crossing the Bumi River, constant Japanese attacks from inland made it obvious there was an enemy base in the jungle and it turned out to be a garrison of 5000 Japanese troops at Sattelberg Mission, on a 9000-metre (29,500-foot) high ridge just 8 kilometres (5 miles) from where the Aussies had landed. The Australians lost 73 men taking the town of Finschhafen and again the Japanese evacuated, leaving the town to the men of the 20th Brigade and their comrades of the 22nd Battalion, who had marched eastward, along the coast from Lae.

To safely hold Finschhafen and continue to advance, the Japanese stronghold at Sattelberg had to be taken, but while Major General Wootten was preparing the attack on Sattelberg, both his headquarters at Langemak Bay south of the town and the beachhead at Scarlet Beach north of Finschhafen were subjected to massive counter-attacks by land and sea. These attacks were successfully repulsed by 16 October and 700 Japanese bodies were counted. Forty-nine Australians died in these counter-attacks.

Reinforcements and tanks arrived on 20 October and Wootten was able to send all three brigades of the 9th Division against Sattelberg in November. After constant bombing and strafing by the RAAF, the Japanese counter-attacked on 22 November, but the Australian 2/48th Battalion were dug in on the heights near Sattelberg on 24 November and, again, the Japanese abandoned their position and retreated to the north-west. The 9th Division casualties during the three-week campaign were 49 killed and just over 100 wounded. Japanese losses are not known.

While the 9th Division was attacking the Japanese garrison at Sattelberg, near the coast, further inland the 2/27th Battalion of the 7th Division had been flown into Kaiapit and their 21st Brigade fought a desperate battle at John's Knoll, in the foothills of the Finisterre Range in the Ramu Valley, where the last-minute arrival of ammunition by Papuan porters enabled them to force a Japanese retreat. The Japanese left 200 dead and the 21st Brigade lost seven men with 28 wounded.

As the 9th Division 2nd AIF and the 5th Division Militia moved along the coast throughout December and January, the 7th Division fought a sustained campaign along the ridges of the Finisterre Range to the south. This series of battles, which cleared the Ramu Valley of Japanese forces, became known as the 'Battle of Shaggy Ridge'. The ridge was named in honour of the commanding officer of A Company, 2/27th Battalion, Captain Robert 'Shaggy Bob' Clampett, who played a major role in defending the ridge from Japanese counter-attacks.

The battle began on 27 December 1943 with 3500 rounds of 25-pounder shells being fired at Japanese positions, which were then bombed and strafed by a squadron of Australian Boomerangs and American Kittyhawks. The 21st and 25th Brigades fought a series of hand-to-hand actions and captured the southern half of the ridge in early January 1944. The 15th and 18th Brigades relieved the 21st and 25th Brigades on 19 January and the 18th attacked on the morning of 20 January, after another artillery and airborne barrage against the entrenched enemy positions. Despite desperate close combat and counter-attacks, the Japanese were finally defeated and driven out of the valley by the end of the month. The 18th Brigade losses were 46 killed and 150 wounded, and 244 Japanese bodies were found.

Meanwhile, on the coast, the American 6th Army had made an amphibious landing at Saidor, ahead of the Australian coastal advance, and established a base there after heavy fighting. The Australian troops under General Wootten advanced along the coast of the Huon Peninsula, taking the town of Sio, where the Japanese from Lae had taken refuge, and linking up with the American forces at Saidor on 20 January. Pursuit of the enemy along the Finisterre Range in February and March was difficult but steady as the enemy was pushed back northward along the range towards the coast. The Australians took the coastal town of Bogadjim, where the Finisterre Range meets the coast, on 13 April 1944.

On 24 April Australian troops entered Madang. Two days later, units of the Australian 5th Division Militia took the stronghold of Alexishafen and the battle for the Huon Peninsula was over. Further to the west, the Americans had landed 84,000 troops at beachheads around Aitape and Hollandia on 22 April.

With the Huon Peninsula firmly in Allied hands, the 7th and 9th Divisions were withdrawn to Australia and the Americans took over the campaign in New Guinea. But Australia still had two important battles to fight before the job was done.

From 19 March to 5 April, 750 men of the 7th Brigade Militia fought a savage and decisive action against 2500 Japanese at Slater's Knoll, on Bougainville, which is politically part of New Guinea as well as being part of the Solomon Islands chain—189 Australians were killed or wounded. The suicidal ferocity of the Japanese is illustrated by their casualty figures in this battle—620 were killed at Slater's Knoll, more than 1000 were wounded and four were taken prisoner.

Back on the mainland of New Guinea, US forces had bypassed the Japanese base at Wewak by taking Aitape and developing a base there in April 1944. The task of taking the Japanese base at Wewak, which was isolated, short of supplies, and weakened by tropical diseases, was given to the 6th Division, commanded by Major General Jack Stevens. They started arriving at Aitape in October 1944 and in November began two parallel advances—one along the coast towards Wewak and the other into the Torricelli Mountains towards the Japanese supply base at Maprik. The Allied plan was to force the Japanese Eighteenth Army, based at Wewak and numbering some 35,000 men, inland where they would become ineffective as a fighting force.

Like most campaigns in New Guinea, this was a slow and tedious process. General Stevens hoped to limit casualties and take as few risks as possible and by March the Australians were within 40 kilometres (25 miles) of Wewak. Seaborne landings by two commando squadrons on 11 May 1945 were planned to coincide with an attack on the airfield by the 19th Brigade and fierce fighting ensued before the Australian troops secured the coastal region on 15 May. Although Wewak was in Australian hands in May, the Japanese continued to fight in pockets until General Adachi of the Japanese Eighteenth Army handed his sword to Major General Robertson on 13 September 1945, a month after the Japanese Emperor had announced the surrender.

The Wewak campaign cost the 6th Division 442 men killed and almost 1200 wounded. Japanese losses were around 9000 dead and 270 taken prisoner.

PLAYING THE OBOE FOR THE FINALE

B efore World War II, most of Borneo belonged to the Dutch East Indies (now Indonesia) while the north-west third of the island was British territory. The Japanese occupied Borneo in early 1942. As the tide of war turned in 1944, Australian Special Forces, known as 'Z' Force, arrived on the island and successfully organised local villagers in guerrilla warfare against the Japanese. About 2000 Japanese were killed in these operations.

The decision to invade Borneo in 1945 has been criticised as being largely unnecessary and political. With the main Allied thrust up through the Philippines cutting off the Japanese supply lines, Borneo was subjected to an Allied aerial and naval blockade much like the Japanese base was at Rabaul. There was no need to invade these bases; they could be left to 'wither on the vine' as the Japanese were defeated closer to home.

There were important airfields and oilfields on Borneo and Tarakan, but these had marginal strategic value by 1945 as the Japanese supply lines were cut.

US troops had effectively taken over the campaign in New Guinea from 1944 and General MacArthur, as Commander in Chief of Allied forces in the South-West Pacific Area (SWPA), had left Australian troops out of the main operations of the final stages of the war.

The RAN was involved in the push towards Japan, most significantly at the Battle of Lingayen Gulf where HMAS *Australia* was badly damaged, but the Australian infantry were seemingly sidelined by MacArthur.

Many believe MacArthur planned the Borneo campaign merely to alleviate Australian government complaints that our forces were being relegated to operational backwaters behind the front line, as in New

Guinea. MacArthur wanted US troops to win the campaign in the Philippines, which was a US territory, but he had to provide Australia with some of the 'glory of victory', so he devised the Borneo campaign, using the argument that the airfields would be vital if a campaign to return the island of Java to Dutch control should become necessary.

The campaign was codenamed 'Oboe' and six stages were originally planned: 'Oboe 1' was to be against the garrison at Tarakan, an island off the north-east coast, and 'Oboe 2' was aimed at Balikpapan on the south-east coast. 'Oboe 3', 'Oboe 4' and 'Oboe 5', against Banjarmasin, Surabaya and the eastern islands, were never put into operation. 'Oboe 6' was the operation against Labuan and Brunei, in the British territory of Sabah.

Oboe 1, Oboe 6 and Oboe 2 were put into effect, in that order, between May and July 1945. The 9th Division conducted Oboe 1 and Oboe 6, while the 7th Division undertook the Balikpapan campaign.

Tarakan

Air attacks began against the Japanese garrison and airfield on 11 April 1945 and continued until the landings on 1 May. These were carried out by the RAAF unit known as the 1st Tactical Air Force, based on the island of Morotai, which is part of the Moluccas group, between Borneo and New Guinea. Between 27 and 30 April minesweepers cleared the way for the landing craft and commandos set up guns on nearby Sadau Island in order to provide covering fire while engineers landed to clear the beach defences on 30 April.

The next day the men of the 2/23rd and 2/48th Battalions of the 26th Brigade, 9th Division, waded ashore and met little resistance. The Japanese retreated into the jungle and set up defensive positions in the hills. These two battalions, plus the 2/24th, the 2/7th Field Regiment and some commando, machine-gun and engineer regiments and support units, made up the 15,000-strong Allied force on Tarakan. They were led by Brigadier David Whitehead and vastly outnumbered the estimated 2200 Japanese on Tarakan.

Japanese resistance increased as the Australians moved towards the airfield, which was not secured until 5 May, and the pockets of resistance required heavy bombardment by air and field artillery before the island was declared 'secured' on 15 May. Japanese troops continued to harass the Australians and conduct counter-offensive actions until mid June.

The Tarakan airfield had been so heavily damaged by the RAAF that engineers of the RAAF Airfield Construction Squadrons did not have it operational until 28 June, far too late to be used to support the other Borneo landings. However, the airfield was used to support ground troops during the Oboe campaigns. Two hundred and twenty-five Australians died at Tarakan and almost 700 were wounded. Only 300 of the Japanese troops survived, with around 1500 killed in action.

Brunei

The task of securing the large bay between Labuan and the town Brunei, in the British territory on the north-west of Borneo, was given to the remaining brigades of the 9th Division, led by Major General George Wootten. Their objectives were to protect the rubber plantations and oilfields and to establish an Allied fleet base in the bay.

Twenty-nine thousand men of the 9th Division, with some US naval and ground support, were involved in this invasion. The 20th and 24th Brigades landed on three beaches on Labuan and the mainland on 10 June. The 2000 Japanese troops in the area were apparently expecting the attack to come further south. They offered little resistance to the landings and retreated southward. General MacArthur, who was present at the Brunei landings, on the battlecruiser USS *Boise*, was amazed at the lack of opposition and remarked that the landings were conducted in an atmosphere of 'peace and quiet'.

The town and airfield were secured by nightfall but, in the days that followed, the Japanese set up a defensive stronghold, called 'the pocket'; in an impenetrable mangrove swamp a mile west of the airfield. Here the Japanese troops withstood ten days of constant attacks. After five days of land-based artillery bombardment, the cruiser HMAS *Shropshire* was called in to shell the position and the RAAF added further bombing. Finally tanks equipped with flamethrowers were used to dislodge the entrenched Japanese troops.

On 16 June another landing was conducted to the north of the bay and the 2/32nd Battalion took the coastal town of Weston while the 2/43rd overcame strong resistance to take Beaufort, further inland. The 2/13th proceeded south to secure the coast and liberate the prisoner-of-war camp at Kuching.

Japanese resistance took the lives of 114 Australians at Brunei, with a further 221 wounded. Around 1300 Japanese died; only 130 were taken prisoner.

Balikpapan

Although the Australian Commander in Chief, General Sir Thomas Blamey, advised the Labor government to withdraw its support for the Oboe 2 operation against Balikpapan, the government supported General MacArthur, who claimed the landings were an essential part of the final phase of the war against Japan, and so the landings went ahead. Oboe 2 was the last major Australian offensive of WWII and the largest amphibious landing ever made by Australian troops. The purpose was to secure the port and the oilfields and refinery at Balikpapan on the south-east coast of Borneo.

Thirty-three thousand personnel were involved in the assault on Balikpapan. The bulk of these were 21,000 troops of three brigades of the 7th Division—the 18th, 21st and 25th Infantry Brigades—led by Major General Edward Milford. RAAF units, headquarters staff, engineers and support units, including some US and Dutch forces, made up the rest of the Oboe 2 expeditionary force.

Milford controversially decided to land two brigades at Klandasan, right in the main industrial area of the town. His reasoning was that this was better than landing out of town and fighting their way to the main Japanese defences. In order for this to be successful, a naval force of six cruisers, including the RAN vessels HMAS *Shropshire* and *Hobart*, commenced a bombardment of the town and industrial areas on 15 June 1945. This barrage lasted two weeks and more than 23,000 shells were fired.

On the morning of 1 July, a further 17,000 rounds of heavy artillery and rockets were fired at suspected Japanese positions before the landings, using Matilda tanks and infantry, took place, unopposed, at 9 am. The 18th Brigade secured the high ground behind Balikpapan and Klandasan by the afternoon. The only opposition was encountered by the 2/10th Adelaide Rifles Battalion, which suffered losses in a surprise encounter with a Japanese force that had remained behind. Mostly the Japanese tunnels and pillbox defences were abandoned but, as the 21st Brigade landed on the right and pushed towards the airfield at Sepinggang, the usual pattern of Japanese defence soon became evident; there was little resistance at first but the Australians encountered entrenched pockets of Japanese troops determined to fight to the death. The 21st Brigade overcame dogged resistance to take the airfield on 2 July and the 25th Brigade landed that same day and proceeded east towards Batuchamper, where it became involved in a fierce battle with an entrenched Japanese battalion.

By 4 July the port facilities were secured and coastal areas were all in Allied hands by 9 July. Japanese resistance in outlying areas continued until 21 July, when defensive positions were suddenly abandoned and the Japanese forces retreated into the hills.

Only 63 Japanese were taken prisoner during the fighting at Balikpapan; almost 1800 Japanese bodies were counted but many more died in the naval bombardment and were buried in the rubble. The stragglers came out of the hills to surrender gradually when the war ended three weeks later.

Australian losses in Oboe 2 were 229 killed and 634 wounded.

Though successful at a relatively minimal loss of lives, the Borneo campaign was controversial in that it was criticised for being unnecessary. Japanese resistance, as in other areas, was dogged and stoic and Australian lives were lost against a suicidal enemy. The people of Borneo were forced to suffer the chaos of an invasion rather than waiting for the Japanese to surrender, as they did just weeks later. It is true, however, that the military objectives of Oboe were achieved and many prisoners of war held in camps on Borneo were liberated earlier than they may have been otherwise.

Although MacArthur doubtless played politics in planning the final stages of the war in the South-West Pacific, he was criticised for not using Australian troops in the main push into Japan and for using Australian troops needlessly in relatively minor campaigns. On the other hand, this at least gave Australia a part to play in the final victory. MacArthur was the ultimate 'self-promoter', in many ways, but he conducted a very successful war in the South-West Pacific and managed to diplomatically balance his relationship with the Australian government while keeping the big picture of the war in perspective. He praised the 'skill and courage' of the Australians at Balikpapan, a campaign that had been fiercely opposed by his old political sparring partner Thomas Blamey, and he was present when Australian troops landed at Brunei.

The final-phase campaigns fought by the 7th and 9th Divisions in Borneo may have been largely unnecessary, but they gave Australia a sense of having been in the war till the end and prevented the final phases of the war against Japan from seeming anti-climactic for a nation that had waited six years for victory.

RINGED WITH MENACE

A WWII propaganda poster, designed to sell war bonds to raise money to build Beaufighters, claimed Australia was 'ringed with menace'. It was.

Although Japan had decided not to invade Australia as part of its wartime strategy, Australians did not know that in 1942. Indeed, all the evidence seemed to point to the opposite conclusion. Japan's plan was to establish military control in the Pacific, invade New Guinea and then take Fiji, Samoa and other Pacific islands. In short, to conquer the Pacific and separate us from our American allies, making an immediate invasion unnecessary.

To the west, a fleet of German raiders was operating in the Indian Ocean and one of them, the ship known as the *Schiff41/Kormoran*, had sunk the battlecruiser HMAS *Sydney*, which was lost with all 645 hands, in November 1941. The shock that the nation felt over the loss of the *Sydney* is hard to imagine 79 years after the event. When you add the devastating bombing of Darwin three months later and a major sea battle off the east coast three months later again, you begin to realise just how like an island under siege Australia felt to its citizens in 1942.

Although the Battle of the Coral Sea prevented the enemy invasion fleet from reaching Port Moresby, the Japanese already controlled the seas to our north and could use aircraft carriers operating in Australian waters to bomb Darwin and Port Moresby with impunity many times after February 1942. The Australian mainland was bombed on 97 separate occasions, Darwin more than 60 times. A different menace, however, lurked in a much more sinister and silent fashion, in waters all around Australia, including the heavily populated south-eastern corner of the continent.

Of more than 50 enemy vessels which operated in Australian waters between 1940 and 1945, six were German raiders (Hilfskreuzers or auxiliary cruisers which disguised themselves as merchant ships) and 28 were submarines.

During their stay in Australian waters, the German raiders laid extensive mine fields off the coasts of Tasmania, Victoria, New South Wales, South Australia and Western Australia, as well as in Bass Strait.

In 1940 the German raider *Schiff36/Orion* placed mines in the entrance to the port of Albany in Western Australia. In 1941 the German raider *Schiff33/Pinguin*, accompanied by a captured Norwegian tanker *Storstad*, which had been converted to an auxiliary minelayer and renamed *Passat*, sailed through Bass Strait and the two ships laid mines along the coast of Victoria, New South Wales and South Australia.

The *Schiff33/Pinguin* was the most successful of the Hilfskreuzers, or German raiders. She was responsible for capturing sixteen ships and sinking sixteen more between June 1940 and 8 May 1941, when she was blown apart by the cruiser HMS *Cornwall* near the Seychelles in the Indian Ocean.

The Hilfskreuzers were converted freighters armed mostly with WWI guns and torpedo tubes. They were given the official name 'Schiff' and a number. The captain of each vessel chose a name for his ship. Captain Kruder, in command of the *Schiff 33*, decided to call his vessel *Schiff 33/ Pinguin* when he was ordered to patrol the Southern Ocean after taking command in June 1940.

Most Hilfskreuzers could disguise themselves as several different merchant ships, depending on the area of the ocean in which they were operating. Their task was to capture or destroy merchant ships by guile, pretence, and force when necessary. They were, however, under orders to run up their true colours before taking any aggressive action.

On 7 October 1940 the *Schiff33/Pinguin* captured the 9000-tonne Norwegian motor-tanker *Storstad*, off Christmas Island. Loaded with 12,000 tonnes of diesel oil and 500 tonnes of heavy fuel oil, *Storstad* was on her way from British North Borneo to Melbourne. She was taken to a remote spot between Java and the north-west tip of Australia and converted into an auxiliary minelayer and renamed *Passat*. One hundred and ten mines were transferred to her from the *Schiff33/Pinguin*.

Passat/Storstad headed for the Banks Strait, off Tasmania, Bass Strait and the approaches to Melbourne, while the *Schiff33/Pinguin* headed for the ports of Sydney, Newcastle and Hobart, and later laid mines off Adelaide.

Between 28 October and 7 November, the two ships laid their mines without being detected and then rendezvoused in the Indian Ocean.

On 7 November 1940 the mines off Wilsons Promontory claimed the 11,000-tonne British refrigerated cargo liner *Cambridge*, which was making its 31st trip to Australia. Next day the MS *City of Rayville* struck a mine off Cape Otway and became the first US merchant ship sunk in WWII.

The United States had not entered the war when the *City of Rayville*, which had the stars and stripes painted on both sides of her hull, hit a German mine laid by *Passat/Storstad* between Cape Otway and Apollo Bay.

In a letter to Prime Minister Menzies, the 37 crewmen who survived the sinking of the *City of Rayville* wrote:

> Since the time of our rescue by the fishermen of Apollo Bay, through our stay at the Ballarat Hotel at Apollo Bay, and since our arrival in Melbourne, we have received every consideration and courtesy from our Australian friends. We cannot adequately express our deep appreciation of this kindness.

It was a portent of things to come—a friendship which would help save Australia in the years ahead.

A month later, on 5 December 1940, the Australian freighter MV *Nimbin* hit a mine laid by the *Schiff33/Pinguin* and sank off Norah Head, north of Sydney, with the loss of seven lives. Two days later the British freighter *Hertford* hit a mine at the entrance to Spencer Gulf but managed to limp into Port Lincoln for repairs which enabled her to be towed to Adelaide.

The trawler *Millimumal* hit one of *Schiff33/Pinguin*'s mines off Barrenjoey Head, just out of Sydney, in March 1941 and seven of her crew of twelve died.

Some of the mines washed up on the coast of South Australia and the first men killed on Australian soil as a result of enemy action were two members of an RMS (Rendering Mines Safe) patrol who responded to reports of a mine which a fisherman found floating in Rivoli Bay near Beachport, South Australia, and towed to shore on 12 July 1941.

Naval headquarters in Adelaide were advised and a party of one officer and two ratings arrived at Beachport the next day. Able Seamen Thomas Todd and William Danswan were killed when a wave picked up the mine and dropped it on the shore, causing it to detonate as they attempted to disarm it.

The damage done around our coast by German raiders was minor in the big scheme of things in WWII but the sense of vulnerability was something that scared Australians, so long used to living safely on their island nation at the bottom of the world.

The censor kept many of the facts hidden from the general public but Australians felt vulnerable, especially after the loss of the HMAS *Sydney*, sunk by another German raider, the *Schiff41/Kormoran*, off Western Australia in November 1941.

When Japan entered the war, Australia was exposed to a calculated onslaught on coastal shipping by Japanese submarines which, had all the facts been known at the time, would have added considerably to the justifiable paranoia felt by the nation.

At the start of the Pacific War, the Imperial Japanese Navy had 63 submarines. Most of them were the large 'I Class', massive 400-foot (122-metre) long vessels of 2900 tonnes with crews of 100 or more.

The Japanese built 126 more submarines after entering the war in late 1941, bringing their total to 189, of which 131 were lost in action by the end of the war.

At least 27 of these huge 'I Class' submarines patrolled in Australian waters. A total of 40 patrols were undertaken around our coastline from the Japanese naval base on the island of Truk, north of the Solomon Islands. Each patrol lasted several months.

'I Class' submarines were all-purpose vessels that could stay at sea for months at a time. They laid mines, reconnoitred enemy ports, collected weather and shipping data, attacked merchant shipping and bombarded shore installations. Some carried floatplanes in cylindrical metal hangars or midget submarines secured to the outer deck, which were used for reconnaissance of enemy ports and shipping.

The two-man submarines we refer to as 'midget' were actually 82 feet (25 metres) long and weighed almost 50 tonnes. Each carried two torpedoes and they could be used to attack enemy ships and installations, as happened in Sydney Harbour in May 1942.

When you realise that these 'midget' subs were carried strapped to the deck of the 'I Class' submarines, you get some idea of just how big the 'I Class' subs were.

The 27 Japanese submarines known to have operated along the east coast of Australia in 1942, 1943 and 1944 attacked at least 50 merchant vessels. The Japanese hoped to cut off supply lines to the war zones in New Guinea and the north and separate Australia from the rest of the Pacific.

Losses were often not reported due to military censorship and there was often uncertainty as to the definite cause of sinking. More than twenty sinkings were officially confirmed to be the result of Japanese submarine attacks on the east coast and another dozen or more were claimed by the Japanese submarine commanders but unconfirmed by the Allies. Certainly around 150,000 tonnes of merchant shipping was lost and 467 died in the attacks, including those killed when HMAS *Kuttabul* was sunk in the midget submarine attack in Sydney Harbour.

The three midget submarines that caused terror and chaos in Sydney Harbour were from a fleet of five 'I Class' submarines operating off the coast of Sydney in May 1942. Two of these carried floatplanes which made reconnaissance flights around Sydney Harbour on 23 and 30 May. The first flight was undetected and the second was seen by many and assumed to be a plane from the visiting warship USS *Chicago*, which was the target for the three midget subs which entered the harbour unde-tected on the night of 31 May 1942 and caused the havoc which spread terror throughout the city.

Two of the 'I Class' submarines returned a few nights later and shelled parts of Sydney from a few miles off shore, causing panic in the city and a fall in real estate prices in the eastern suburbs. Newcastle was also shelled and a number of merchant ships were torpedoed and sunk off the coast of New South Wales in the following weeks.

Few Australians at the time were aware how many vessels were lost in Australian waters to enemy submarines in WWII. A probable list, as accurate as can be compiled from Japanese accounts by individual submarine commanders, reads like this:

20/1/42 *Eidsvold*, 4184 tonnes—near Christmas Island
1/3/42 *Modjokerto*, 8806 tonnes—South of Christmas Island
1/3/42 *Parigi*, 1172 tonnes—off Fremantle
1/3/42 *Siantar*, 8867 tonnes—200 nm NW of Shark Bay
4/3/42 *Le Maire*, 3271 tonnes—NW of Cocos Islands

5/5/42 *John Adams*, 7180 tonnes—120 nm SW of Nouméa

7/5/42 *Chloe*, 4641 tonnes—35 nm from Nouméa

31/5/42 HMAS *Kuttabul*, 448 tonnes—Sydney Harbour

3/6/42 *Iron Chieftain*, 4812 tonnes—27 nm E of Sydney

4/6/42 *Iron Crown*, 3353 tonnes—40 nm SW of Gabo Island

12/6/42 *Guatemala*, 5527 tonnes—40 nm NE of Sydney

20/7/42 *George S. Livanos*, 4883 tonnes—15 nm E of Jervis Bay

21/7/42 *Coast Farmer*, 3290 tonnes—25 nm E of Jervis Bay

22/7/42 *William Dawes*, 7176 tonnes—off Tathra Head

25/7/42 *Cagou*, 2795 tonnes—NE of Sydney

25/7/42 *Tjinegara*, 9227 tonnes—92 nm SE of Nouméa

30/8/42 Trawler *Dureenbee*, 233 tonnes—off Moruya

18/1/43 *Kalingo*, 2047 tonnes—110 nm E of Sydney

18/1/43 Tanker *Mobilube*, 10,222 tonnes—60 nm E of Sydney

22/1/43 *Peter H. Burnett*, 7176 tonnes—420 nm E of Sydney

29/1/43 *Samuel Gompers*, 7176 tonnes—500 nm NE of Brisbane

30/1/43 *Giang Ann*, unknown tonnage—30 nm E of Newcastle

8/2/43 *Iron Knight*, 4812 tonnes—21 nm off Montague Island (one of the few ships sunk while in an escorted convoy)

10/2/43 *Starr King*, 7176 tonnes—150 nm E of Sydney

11/4/43 *Recina*, 4732 tonnes—20 nm off Cape Howe (sunk while sailing in an escorted convoy)

24/4/43 *Kowarra*, 2125 tonnes—160 nm N of Brisbane

26/4/43 *Limerick*, 8724 tonnes—20 nm SE of Cape Byron

27/4/43 *Lydia M. Childs*, 7176 tonnes—90 nm E of Newcastle

29/4/43 *Wollongbar*, 2239 tonnes—off Crescent Head NSW

5/5/43 *Fingal*, 2137 tonnes—off Nambucca Heads NSW

14/5/43 AHS *Centaur*, 3222 tonnes—30 nm E of Moreton Island

16/6/43 *I 174 Portmar*, 5551 tonnes—250 nm NE of Sydney (sunk while sailing in an escorted convoy)

22/6/43 *Stanvac Manilav* 10,245 tonnes—off Nouméa

22/6/43 two PT boats (each approximately 50 tonnes)—off Nouméa

*nm = nautical miles

Coastal shipping convoys were introduced early in the war and only six ships were lost while in a convoy or having fallen behind due to engine problems. All other ships lost to submarine activity were travelling independently, including the one ship Australians remember as being sunk by a submarine, the AHS *Centaur*.

The best known and most infamous submarine attack in Australia's WWII history occurred at 4 am on 14 May 1943, when the hospital ship AHS *Centaur*, a converted merchant vessel travelling just north of Brisbane with her markings fully lit as per the Geneva and Hague Conventions, was torpedoed by the Japanese KD7 class submarine *K177*, captained by Lieutenant Commander Hajime Nakagawa.

Prime Minister Curtin called sinking the *Centaur* 'an entirely inexcusable act' and General MacArthur said it demonstrated the 'limitless savagery' of the Japanese. The incident was used to boost the war effort and silence pacifists.

Not all the Axis submarines operating in Australian waters were Japanese. The 1800-tonne German U-boat *U862* gained the rare distinction of being the only German submarine to sink a vessel in the Pacific Ocean in WWII when it torpedoed the 7180-tonne SS *Robert J. Walker* off Moruya on Christmas Eve 1944.

Indeed the *U862* was the only German submarine known to operate in the Pacific at all in WWII!

U862 was part of a U-boat fleet that was based in Penang, in Japanese-controlled Malaya. She had made a successful sortie to the African coast in July and August 1944, sinking five Allied merchant ships and shooting down a Catalina aircraft before returning to base in Penang.

U862 has been described as a 'rogue German U-boat' whose captain, Heinrich Timm, apparently decided he would cruise around Australia on the way back to Europe on a whim because he had sailed in Australian waters before the war as an officer on a merchant ship.

It is far more likely that he was assigned to the task by the fleet command in Penang. The *U862* moved its base to Batavia (now Jakarta), left there in November 1944 and headed down the Western Australian coast. Timm then turned east across the Great Australian Bight and fired on the Greek tanker SS *Illios* 208 kilometres (129 miles) south-east of Adelaide. *Illios* returned fire with her 100-mm (4-inch) gun and *U862* submerged and headed south.

A search was mounted by three corvettes, HMAS *Lismore*, *Burnie* and *Maryborough*, and Beaufort aircraft flying from a base near Sale in Victoria, but the *U862* escaped, went around the bottom of Tasmania and then turned north. Proceeding up the New South Wales coast, she encountered the *Robert J. Walker* off Montague Island and used six torpedoes to sink her.

U862 then headed east, sailed around New Zealand and entered the harbour at Napier undetected at night before re-crossing the Tasman and retracing her course back to Batavia.

On 6 February 1945, 1120 kilometres (696 miles) south-west of Fremantle, *U862* sank the liberty ship SS *Peter Sylvester*, which was heading from Melbourne to Colombo, with US army supplies, 107 troops and 317 mules. The *U862* once again used six torpedoes to complete the sinking. Thirty-three lives were lost and some survivors of the *Peter Sylvester* drifted on rafts for 38 days before being picked up by Allied ships.

U862 was at sea testing radar equipment when Germany surrendered in May 1945. On arriving at Singapore, the crew were arrested by the Japanese as 'enemy personnel' and the submarine was seized and became the IJN *I–502*. It was surrendered to the Allies at the end of the war and scuttled by the British in the Strait of Malacca in February 1946.

The crew of the *U862* survived the war and were repatriated home in 1947. They were lucky. Being a submariner in WWII did not do a lot for your life expectancy. Not one of the five 'I Class' submarines off the coast of New South Wales in May and June 1942 survived the war. Indeed, only a small percentage of Axis submarines did survive. Japan lost 131 of her 189 submarines, while Germany had 1152 subs in operation and lost 785. In each case, that is almost 70 per cent.

On the other hand, the USA had 390 and lost 52, Britain had 220 and lost 75, and Russia lost 109 of its fleet of 282. So Allied losses amounted to around 32 per cent of available submarines.

There is an interesting sidelight to the Australasian cruise of the *U862*.

For decades after WWII there were stories of enemy troops on Australian soil, most of these stories were fanciful paranoid conspiracy theories at best, all part of the fear generated by the 'ring of menace'.

However, there were enemy troops on Australian soil; it did happen, and it happened several times.

After the war an ex-crew member of *U862* visited his brother who lived, like so many German-Australians, in South Australia. While fishing with his brother's mates on the Coorong, south-east of Adelaide, he commented that the area had not changed since he and other crew members of *U862* had gone ashore there looking for fresh water in 1944.

It has also been reported, and is quite probable, that German sailors went ashore from the *Passat/Storstad* near Wilsons Promontory looking for fresh water supplies in November 1941.

Japanese troops landed on the mainland on at least one occasion, and Murray Island in Torres Strait was used by one Japanese submarine crew as a source of fresh water and vegetables several times in 1942.

Murray Islanders gave accounts of landing parties from a Japanese submarine coming ashore to collect fresh water and fruit and vegetables from the islanders' gardens. The submarine apparently surfaced beside Dauar, one of the three volcanic islands that make up Murray Island, and crewmen came ashore to take on fresh water from the wells at the sardine factory and to obtain information about the area. The submarine also cruised slowly along the length of Murray Island on the surface.

Evidently a crew member of the submarine was a bêche-de-mer boat skipper in the Torres Strait before the war and knew quite a few of the islanders well. There are accounts of the submarine making quite a few visits to Murray Island.

In April 1942 the Japanese submarines *RO–33* and *RO–34* were sent to search for convoy routes and anchorages in advance of the planned assault on Port Moresby. They were later ordered to blockade Port Moresby and, on 7 August 1942, *RO–33* sank the Burns-Philp motor launch *Mamutu*, which was taking women and children to Daru to escape the Japanese bombing of Port Moresby.

The *RO–33* attacked on the surface and sank the *Mamutu* with her guns and then machine-gunned many of the survivors in the water just north of Murray Island. Only 28 of the 120 on board survived.

RO–33 was a small but well-armed submarine of 940 tonnes with a crew of 42 officers and men. It was almost certainly the *RO–33* that regularly visited Murray Island and put landing parties ashore during 1942.

On 29 August 1942, the destroyer HMAS *Arunta* used depth charges to sink *RO–33* 16 kilometres (10 miles) out of Port Moresby. There were no survivors.

Two years later, in January 1944, a Japanese army reconnaissance party of ten soldiers and fifteen Timorese, led by Lieutenant Susuhiko Mizuno, left in Timor in a fishing vessel, the *Hiyoshi Maru*. Their mission was to investigate reports received by Japanese navy sources that the United States navy was building a naval base at Admiralty Gulf.

They were given air cover for part of the voyage by a light bomber from the 7th Air Division, crewed by Staff Sergeant H. Aonuma and Hachiro Akai who spotted, fired at and attempted to bomb an Allied submarine they encountered en route.

The *Hiyoshi Maru* reached Browse Island at about 10 am on 18 January and stayed there for about three hours. They left the island at 1 pm and next morning entered an inlet on the Western Australian coast.

They anchored near shore at about 10 am and camouflaged the ship with tree branches. Three landing parties led by Lieutenant Mizuno and two sergeants explored different areas of the coast for about two hours.

They all returned to the ship and discussed what they had seen (mostly red rocks, small trees and old campfires). They went ashore again next day and explored until 2 pm and then returned to Timor with 8-mm movie footage of what they saw.

The area they explored was actually only 24 kilometres (15 miles) from the site of the proposed RAAF Truscott Airfield, construction of which was to start several weeks later.

Australia was totally unprepared to protect its enormous coastline in WWII. Axis submarines and German raiders operated all around our coasts, laying mines, sinking merchant ships and even coming ashore to find fresh water and explore the countryside.

Australia came out of WWII with a firm alliance established with the United States, a standing army, a policy of 'populate or perish', and a much less complacent attitude to protecting her borders.

The Australia which we know today is a result of the shock realisation, brought home to us by the events of WWII, that we are indeed 'girt by sea'—which can so easily lead to being 'ringed with menace'.

CHANGI, SANDAKAN AND THE BURMA RAILWAY

The British constructed Changi Prison as a civilian prison in 1936. Up until May 1944 the Japanese detained 3000 civilians in Changi Prison, which was built to accommodate 600. The nearby Selarang British Army Barracks housed the 50,000 British and Australian prisoners of war but the name 'Changi' also became used for the POW camp.

As far as Japanese POW camps during WWII were concerned, Changi was no better or worse than most. About 850 prisoners of war died there, a relatively low rate compared to the overall death rate of 27 per cent for prisoners of war in all Japanese POW camps.

Although the Japanese treatment of prisoners of war in WWII was generally inhumane and often so cruel that it is hard to comprehend, the prisoners in Changi were, at first, mostly responsible for their own day-to-day administration. A reasonably well equipped camp hospital operated, gardens were established and concert productions were staged. Much of the bad reputation of Changi itself comes from the period after May 1944, when all 12,000 Allied prisoners, including 5000 Australians, were crammed into the old Changi Prison, rations were cut and the authority of Allied officers over their troops was revoked.

The reason Changi is a name that is reviled in the history of WWII is mostly due to the fact that it was a staging post for places of extreme cruelty and horror, like Sandakan and the Burma Railway. In February 1942 there were 15,000 Australians in Changi but by June 1943 only 2500 remained. Most of the others were sent to work on the Thailand–Burma Railway, which ran 415 kilometres (258 miles) between Bangkok, Thailand, and Rangoon, Burma. It was built by 180,000 Asian labourers and 60,000 Allied prisoners of war working as slave labour. Some 16,000 Allied prisoners of war died during the construction. Almost half of these were British but around 2800 were Australian and similar numbers were Dutch. Some US and Canadian soldiers were also among the dead. It is estimated that 90,000 Asian labourers also died.

The railway had been surveyed by the British early in the 20th century and had been started and abandoned before the war. The project was revived in 1942 to speed up transport and communication for Japanese forces that relied on the sea route to Rangoon via Singapore and the Straits of Malacca. The Japanese aim was to complete the railway, through mountainous country and dense tropical jungle, by the end of 1943. To achieve this, groups of prisoners were transported to Thailand and Burma from Singapore, Java, Sumatra and Borneo, and worked from opposite ends of the line until the two parties met at Nieke in November 1943.

Prisoners of war were kept in camps along the line to provide maintenance and repair damage caused by Allied bombing. As POW camps were unmarked and were beside the track and near bridges and other vulnerable points, many men died as a result of these attacks. Food supplies, poor even by the normal low standards for Japanese POW camps, were irregular, totally inadequate and often contaminated. Men also had to work with malaria, dysentery and malnutrition, and hospitals were crude jungle huts where only those unable to walk were allowed to die. Although no drugs or hospital equipment were supplied by the Japanese, the devotion and skill of POW medical personnel like Sir Edward 'Weary' Dunlop saved thousands of lives.

Lieutenant Hiroshi Abe, who supervised a construction camp at Sonkrai, where more than 3000 prisoners of war died, was sentenced to death as a war criminal after the war, but his sentence was later commuted to fifteen years in prison.

The graves of the prisoners were moved from camp burial grounds to three war cemeteries after the war. Seven thousand are buried in the main cemetery in Kanchanaburi, 1750 at Chung Kai and 3600 at Thanbyuzayat. All three cemeteries are maintained by the Commonwealth War Graves Commission.

There are several museums along the track today. The largest of these is situated, along with an Australian memorial, at Hellfire Pass, where more lives were lost than anywhere else on the track. Only a portion of the railway, terminating just south of Hellfire Pass, is used today. Other parts of the track have been torn up and some made into walking trails.

The horrors of Changi and the Burma Railway remained vivid in the minds of Australians for generations after the war. As so many Australian troops ended up there after the fall of Singapore, almost everyone knew of someone who had been in Changi, where internment was often the prelude to the notorious Burma Railway where thousands died under appalling conditions. For this reason the name was reviled by many Australians whose sons, fathers, uncles and brothers suffered and died on the Burma Railway. For decades after the war, a large percentage of Australians boycotted Japanese products and there was strong resistance to trade with Japan.

The first repatriation to Australia, on cessation of hostilities, was an airlift by nine Catalina flying boats of the sick and wounded men from Changi. A crowd estimated at around 200,000 gathered around Sydney Harbour to watch them land at Rose Bay on 16 September 1945.

Sandakan

Some 2400 Allied prisoners captured in Singapore were sent, with 4000 Javanese civilians, to build an airfield at Sandakan on the eastern side of the island of Borneo.

As the airstrip neared completion in August 1943, some prisoners, including all officers, were sent to another camp at Kuching, also on Borneo. Those left behind were gradually starved to death until there were only 1900 left in early 1945 when the Allies successfully bombed the airfield.

With an Allied landing looming, camp commandant Captain Hoshijima decided to move the fittest 470 prisoners westward to Ranau, 250 kilometres (155 miles) away in the mountains. The men were given four days' rations for the ten-day march and those who fell were left to die or were shot. Conditions at Ranau were horrific and by June only six men were left alive. At the end of May, the new camp commander, Captain Takakuwa, sent another 536 prisoners to Ranau in groups of 50. This time the march took 26 days and the men were forced to forage for food. Only 183 prisoners reached Ranau on 24 June 1945.

There were 250 prisoners too weak to march still left at Sandakan. In June, 75 of them were forced to march until they dropped and were shot. None made it more than 50 kilometres (31 miles). Part of the camp at

Sandakan was destroyed to hide evidence of the conditions and cruelty. Most of the men who survived the marches died of dysentery and starvation in the weeks after, but around 30 prisoners were left alive at Ranau when WWII ended. The guards killed them during August, possibly up to twelve days after the surrender of Japan on 14 August.

Four thousand Indonesians, 1381 Australians and 641 British prisoners died at, or between, Sandakan and Ranau. Six Australians survived by escaping and being helped by locals: two during the march and four from Ranau. Of the six, only three lived long enough to give evidence at war crimes trials conducted at Rabaul and in Tokyo.

Hoshijima and Takakuwa were found guilty of causing the murders and massacres of prisoners of war and were hanged in April 1946. The Japanese conducted similar 'death marches' on a far larger scale with 75,000 prisoners, at Bataan, in the Philippines.

THE ENEMY WE SIMPLY DIDN'T UNDERSTAND

During World War II Australia's conflict with Japan was more than just a war between two armies, it was a war between two vastly different cultures and attitudes to life. Where the Australian soldiers were generally tough, laconic and easy-going, their Japanese opponents were obedient, fanatical and raised in the *bushido* tradition of 'death before dishonour'. When 1000 Japanese prisoners staged a mass riot and breakout at the prisoner of war camp at Cowra, in central New South Wales, Australians were terrified and paranoid. What we didn't understand was that they wanted to destroy themselves . . . not us. In fact, they had been ordered to do no harm to Australian civilians.

There were POW camps all around Australia during WWII. In New South Wales, there were camps at Liverpool and Long Bay Gaol and others at Bathurst, Orange, Hay and Yanco, as well as Cowra. The Japanese rarely surrendered. In the *bushido* code, which was part of the Japanese military ethos, surrender was a sign of shame and disgrace; death was more honourable than surrender. However, by August 1944, there were 2220 Japanese prisoners of war in Australia, including 550 merchant seamen. There were also 14,720 Italian POWs in Australia, most captured in North Africa, and 1600 Germans, mostly naval or merchant seamen.

Just outside Cowra, in the central west of New South Wales, about 300 kilometres (186 miles) by road from Sydney, was No. 12 Prisoner of War Compound (Camp 12), which housed 4000 military personnel and detained 'alien' civilians. At that time the town's population was just over 3000, so the prisoners outnumbered the locals.

Camp 12 was a large compound, covering 30 hectares, and was divided into four sections with well-lit, barbed-wire-fenced spaces in between for security. Two sections, A and C, held Italian prisoners. Camp D held the Korean and civilian detainees and the Japanese officers, and the 1100 Japanese non-commissioned officers (NCOs) and other ranks were held in Camp B.

Almost half of the Japanese prisoners of war in Australia were at Camp 12, along with 2000 Italians, some Koreans who had served in the Japanese military, and civilians from the Dutch East Indies (Indonesia) detained at the request of the Dutch.

Prisoners of war in Australia were treated in accordance with the Geneva Convention but cultural differences made relations between the Japanese prisoners of war and camp staff very unfriendly. A riot by Japanese at a New Zealand POW camp in February 1943 led to security being tightened at Cowra, and machine guns were installed to add to the rifles carried by the 22nd Garrison Battalion Militia who guarded the camp. They were mostly old or disabled veterans or young men considered physically unfit for front-line service. In early August, partly in response to the New Zealand riot, plans were made to separate the Japanese NCOs from the other ranks in Camp B and relocate all but the officers and NCOs to the POW camp at Hay.

The Japanese inmates had discussed escape plans for some time and, after the prisoners were informed of the relocation plans on 4 August, Sergeant Major Kanazawa, commander of Camp B, told hut leaders to explain the situation to their men and conduct a vote to see if there was support for a mass breakout. Evidently the final decision to break out was far from unanimous and some of the twenty hut leaders distorted the results, but the decision was made for a mass escape.

Strict ground rules were laid down. Any injured or disabled prisoners who could not join in were asked to restore their honour by committing suicide when the rest escaped. The huts were to be burned so there was nowhere for recaptured prisoners of war to return to, and it was agreed that civilians would not be harmed. Weapons were to be made from cutlery, baseball bats, timber, nails and wire; blankets would be carried to cover the barbed wire.

The men were divided into four groups. Two groups would climb the outer perimeter, which consisted of three fences and 10 metres (33 feet) of barbed wire entanglement. The other two groups would break into the space between the four camps, known as 'no-man's land' or 'Broadway' due to the powerful bright lights. One of these groups was designated to link up with the Japanese officers in Camp D and the other was to attack the outer gates and the 22nd Garrison Battalion Militia barracks. A bugle would sound at 2 am to start the operation.

The Japanese obviously saw the whole operation as a military exercise to restore their honour in death, rather than an escape to reach their homeland or annoy their enemies.

At 2 am a lone Japanese prisoner of war ran to the gates of Camp B and shouted a warning to the sentries. A bugle sounded and 1000 prisoners, in three separate mobs and all shouting '*Banzai*', began attacking the wire fences to the north, west and south. The sentries started firing as soon as the Japanese warning was shouted, firstly a warning shot was fired and then, as the mob appeared, the sentries started shooting to kill. The militia garrison was awake within minutes and two privates, Benjamin Hardy and Ralph Jones, soon manned the truck-mounted No. 2 Vickers machine gun and started firing into the mob.

By sheer weight of numbers, the two guards were soon overwhelmed and killed by a frenzied mob described later by Prime Minister John Curtin as having a 'suicidal disregard of life'. Hardy was clubbed to death and Jones stabbed. However, Private Jones had removed and hidden the machine gun's bolt while the Japanese were attacking and the gun could not be used by the prisoners against the guards. Both men were posthumously awarded the George Cross for bravery. Another guard, Charles Shepherd, was also stabbed to death near the top end of 'Broadway' during the riot.

The two groups who broke into 'Broadway' failed to breach the main gates or link up with the Japanese officers in Camp D. They attempted to storm the guard posts at either end, but were in direct firing line and remained pinned down for several hours.

Of the 378 Japanese who broke through the outer perimeter wire fences of Camp B, all those who remained alive, some 334, managed to escape. It took ten days to round up the survivors of the breakout. The RAAF, police, Australian Women's Battalion stationed at Cowra and army trainees conducted the round-up operations. Some escapees made it across country as far as Eugowra, more than 50 kilometres (31 miles) away. Many of the Japanese chose death rather than be recaptured. Two threw themselves under a train and some hanged themselves.

Two prisoners were shot by local civilians and several others by military personnel. Some pleaded to be shot when they were recaptured and some surrendered peacefully. Some died in suicide pacts, killed by their comrades.

Lieutenant Harry Doncaster of the 19th Australian Infantry Training Battalion was the only Australian killed in the pursuit, when he was attacked by a group of Japanese 11 kilometres (7 miles) north of Cowra.

In total, 231 Japanese soldiers were killed and 108 were wounded. Four Australians died, and another four were injured. No civilians were harmed. Cowra is the largest prisoner-of-war breakout ever recorded.

Inquiries were held into the breakout and the reactions of the media and the general public were twofold. There was an increase in the level of general distrust and paranoia about the enemy: the same sort of reaction that had been experienced over the Darwin bombings and the midget submarine attack. There was also puzzlement and a failure to understand the Japanese psyche. These men seemed so different with their focused and conditioned obedience to authority and narrow-minded cultural thinking, that most Australians simply thought they were weak-minded or insane. To many Australians, the Japanese appeared to be childlike, cruel and uneducated aliens.

When the camp was dismantled after the war, the puzzlement lingered on in the district and enough people were curious about the Japanese and their beliefs to begin to take steps to understand. Cowra was developed into a Centre of World Friendship. Those Japanese who died on Australian territory now lie in the Cowra War Cemetery, which was opened in 1963 and, in 1979, Cowra's famous Japanese Gardens were established. Tourists can also visit the ruins of POW Camp 12 and an avenue of cherry blossom trees links the Cowra War Cemetery and Japanese Gardens to the site.

A Strange Footnote: Mitsuo Fuchida, Sky Pilot

Truth is, inevitably, stranger than fiction. For me, this is the oddest story to come out of WWII.

Captain Fuchida, the architect and leader of the Darwin and Pearl Harbor raids, was about to be involved in the Battle of Midway when he had to undergo an emergency appendix operation on board the carrier *Akagi*.

Akagi was hit and exploded and sank during the battle and Fuchida broke both ankles when the explosions threw him from a rope ladder he was using to leave the ship onto a deck metres below. He survived and spent the rest of the war as a staff officer.

Fuchida was again apparently singled out by fate to survive against the odds when he was part of a group sent to Hiroshima the day after the atomic explosion to assess the damage. While all other members of Fuchida's party died of radiation poisoning, Fuchida suffered no symptoms.

In 1947, Fuchida met a group of returning Japanese prisoners of war and among them was his former flight engineer, Kazuo Kanegasaki, who was believed to have died at Midway.

Kanegasaki told Fuchida that, as prisoners of war, Japanese soldiers captured by the Allies were well treated and not tortured or abused. He related how a woman whose missionary parents had been murdered by Japanese troops in the Philippines had cared for the Japanese POWs. Hearing this, Fuchida, raised in the *bushido* belief of revenge for honour, was stunned and became obsessed trying to understand Christianity, although at first he couldn't find a Bible translated into Japanese.

His obsession eventually led to a meeting with the Christian evangelist Jacob DeShazer and conversion to Christianity. Fuchida became a member of the Worldwide Christian Missionary Army of Sky Pilots and spent the rest of his life evangelising in the United States, becoming a US citizen in 1960.

He died of a diabetes-related illness in 1976, aged 73.

PEACE

'P484'

We seem to be sure about winning this war
It's winning the peace that's the worry.
We know that the last was a failure that passed
To die in a chaos of flurry.

When asked by the mites what we did in the fights,
Our boasting and tales never cease;
It's just as well they never face us and say,
'And what did you do in the peace?'

Would we wave it aside as it only applied
To parliaments, mayors and kings?
Or be honest and say, 'My child, in my day
I failed in responsible things.

'I never could see that the world was just me
In thousands and thousands of men,
And that peace-terms were born in the things that I'd scorn
As being too trivial then.

'What things? Oh, a shake of the hand for the sake
Of straightening quarrels and strikes,
And saying "I'm wrong" to help things along,
For pride is the source of dislikes.'

When boosting this strife we've made ev'ry life
A servant to national claim,
And now ev'ry man must honestly plan
To make peace his personal aim,

By facing his wife, his office, his life,
From ill-feeling seeking release;
With an honest delight in setting things right,
Determined to hang on to peace.

PART V
FIGHTING THE COMMUNISTS

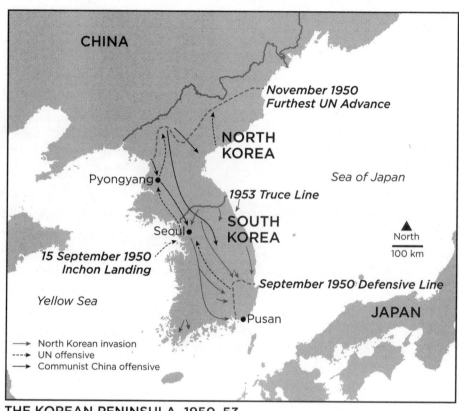

THE KOREAN PENINSULA, 1950–53

THE KOREAN WAR

After Japan defeated Russia in the Russian–Japanese war in 1905, Korea became a protectorate of Japan until annexed by the Japanese in 1910. The country was then governed as Japanese territory until Japan's unconditional surrender at the end of World War II in August 1945. During this time, Korean language was made illegal and teaching of Korean culture and history was banned in schools. The population were forced to use the Japanese language and worship at Japanese Shinto shrines was made compulsory. During WWII Koreans were forced to support the Japanese war effort and a large percentage of the 200,000 female sex slaves, known as 'comfort women', were Korean.

Soviet forces landed in the north of Korea at the very end of WWII and a dividing line along the 38th parallel of latitude separated the two areas of occupation after the war, with the Soviet army controlling the north and the United States controlling the south. The intention was always to reunite Korea as one nation, as had been agreed by the United States, United Kingdom and Chinese Republic at the Cairo conference during the war in 1943. In December 1945 a joint Soviet–American Commission was set up in order to oversee this process. As the Cold War developed, however, this became less and less achievable and the reunification of Korea became merely one element of the global political machinations and ideological propaganda war between the USSR, the Republic of China and what became known as 'The Free World', led by the United States of America.

Finally, in December 1948, the Americans submitted the question of reunification to the General Assembly of the United Nations, which voted to recognise the government of the Republic of Korea (the South) as the sole legal government of the country. On 25 June 1950, the Korean People's Army (KPA) crossed the 38th parallel and invaded the south.

The South Korean army and occupying US forces were completely unprepared for war and the KPA overran the south within a month, capturing the capital of Seoul and forcing the hastily assembled US forces and the army of the Republic of Korea (ROK) into an area known as the Pusan Perimeter, based around the port of Pusan (Busan) in the south-east of the peninsula.

The United Nations (UN) had reacted to the invasion by passing Resolution 83, which gave UN military assistance to South Korea. Sixteen UN nations supplied fighting units and five sent military hospitals and field ambulances. Australia was the first to send personnel from all three services: army, navy and air force, to support the US and Korean forces. The US had 140,000 combat troops in Korea at the height of the war, and Great Britain, Canada, France, Belgium, the Netherlands, Colombia, Ethiopia, South Africa, New Zealand, Turkey, Greece, Thailand, the Philippines and Luxembourg sent troops. Norway, Sweden, Denmark, India and Italy sent hospital and ambulance support.

US President Truman put General Douglas MacArthur in charge of the UN operation and MacArthur masterminded a daring plan to break out from Pusan in August 1950 and, at the same time, invade from the sea on the other (western) side of the peninsula at Incheon, just 27 kilometres (17 miles) from Seoul, which UN forces did on 15 September. This tactic broke the North Korean offensive and the UN troops pushed them back over the 38th parallel and drove north deep into North Korea.

Despite the fact that the American policy at this stage of the Cold War was one of 'containment' of communism, and the fact that China had been hinting at intervention, MacArthur pressed on towards the Chinese border at Yalu River and demanded the surrender of North Korea. The response from the north was the execution of prisoners of war and the murder of all foreigners in the territories still held by the KPA, along with many North Koreans who the government of Kim Il-sung decided were not sufficiently committed to communism.

In October 1950 Chinese forces crossed the Yalu River in a massive offensive that forced the UN army to retreat to the south of Seoul. MacArthur's forces counter-attacked in February 1951, took Seoul in March and again pushed north. In April, Truman replaced MacArthur with General Ridgway, who led the advance across the 38th parallel. The UN forces then halted just north of the border.

Armistice negotiations opened in July 1951 but were bogged down in detail and Cold War propaganda and were complicated by the fact that many North Korean and Chinese prisoners of war had no wish to be repatriated home. UN bombing raids continued and ground offensives included battles that became part of US military history, such as Heartbreak Ridge and Pork Chop Hill.

The armistice eventually went into effect on 27 July 1953 but, at the Geneva Conference, held to negotiate a peace treaty in 1954, no agreement was reached (although proposals were made which later affected the division on Vietnam). So, the war has never officially ended and the border remains almost as it was at the start—with a demilitarised zone along the 38th parallel, 400 kilometres (249 miles) long and 4 kilometres (2.5 miles) wide, it remains the most heavily militarised border in the world.

The Korean War was the most intense and bloodiest conflict of the 20th century. Fighting was continuous and relentless over the three years and one month of war. Troop losses, as percentages of combatants, were far greater than World War II.

Nearly four million Koreans and Chinese were killed—more than half the dead were Korean civilians. The US spent more than $30 billion fighting the Korean War and more than 300,000 American troops served in the conflict. US losses were 40,000 dead and 100,000 wounded.

Almost 17,000 Australians served, a number second only to the United States in the total of UN forces. Australian casualties numbered more than 1500, including 340 dead.

The Korean War is often thought of as the 'forgotten war' in the United States, and also in Australia. It seems to get lost in the aftermath of World War II and the hysteria of the Cold War. It has certainly been overshadowed by the Vietnam War in the minds of most Americans and Australians.

It is said that most Americans did not really know that the war was ever fought until the hugely popular television series *M.A.S.H.* used the war as the background setting for fictional characters operating in a fictional field hospital.

Sergeant Bill Collings, who later became an Australian Air Vice Marshal, once said, 'No one knew I was home from Korea. They used to ask, "What are those medals for?" They just didn't have a clue.'

In 2017 the sacrifices of the conflict were finally commemorated in a memorial on Anzac Parade in Canberra, the National Korean War Memorial.

THE DEAD DON'T CARE

Jack Sorensen

Oh sad, bewildered world: you have the reaping
Of that which you have sown throughout the years
And you have garnered all your hellish harvest
Of blood and tears.

There shall be spring clad days of dream contentment,
And halcyon nights that merge with hopeful dawn;
And there will come the solace of sad memories,
To those who mourn.

But you, and you, who gave yourselves to slaughter,
What matters it that other days be fair?
That ships of state, star-guided, find a haven?
The dead don't care.

THE STRANGE BATTLE OF SARIWON

Chris Coulthard-Clark

This battle was a bizarre one-sided action that occurred on 17 October 1950 during the United Nations (UN) counter-offensive launched against North Korean communist forces which had invaded the southern Republic of Korea. By 16 October the North Koreans were in rapid retreat and struggling to concentrate on their capital, Pyongyang, while American troops had occupied the village of Sohung little more than 70 kilometres directly to the south-east.

The 27th British Commonwealth Brigade (which included the 3rd Battalion of the Royal Australian Regiment, or 3RAR) was ordered to take over the advance the next day with the object of capturing Sariwon, an industrial town also reputed to be an important military training centre, located about 40 kilometres by road to the west of Sohung and only 54 kilometres south of Pyongyang. The brigade set off at 6.40 am, with two British companies of the Argyll and Sutherland Highland Regiment in the van sitting atop of Sherman tanks and riding in trucks.

Virtually no opposition was encountered until anti-tank and automatic fire was received from an enemy road-block 6 kilometres east of Sariwon. This resistance was quickly swept aside in a copybook attack by the Argylls, who then entered the heavily bombed and largely deserted town; while one company established a strongpoint, the other fanned out across the northern suburbs. Ordered to pass through and cut the road north-west of Sariwon, the Australian battalion advanced a further 8 kilometres across the rolling plain country through which the road passed before taking up a defensive position at last light.

Many North Korean units, falling back under pressure from the 24th US Infantry Division on the left flank, clearly had no idea that UN forces had taken Sariwon or even that they were in the area. Throughout the day large numbers of enemy continued to enter the town by the truckload and on foot from the south and south-west. The arrival at 6 pm of the main body of 27 Brigade was several times followed by scenes of absurd confusion, with trucks of both sides sometimes parking on opposite sides of the street without either being immediately aware of the other's identity. At least one party of Argylls was mistaken by North Koreans for Russian allies before the error was discovered and shooting began at very close quarters.

Groups of enemy who either escaped contact with the Argylls inside Sariwon or else bypassed the town began blundering into the blocking position established further along the road by 3RAR. The commander of the Australian battalion, Lieutenant Colonel Charles Green, was preparing to launch a coordinated attack on enemy positions in front of him early next morning, but instead found himself obliged to turn around his reserve company to face the way they had come to deal with enemy contacts at both ends of his perimeter. Meanwhile, a marching column of North Koreans stumbled upon 3RAR's second in command, Major Ian Ferguson, who was waiting with a party of six guides in an apple orchard between the battalion position and Sariwon for the arrival of the unit's ration vehicles. Again, the enemy at first took the strangers to be Russians, but shots were soon fired and the enemy column dispersed to adopt fire positions.

After Ferguson radioed for assistance, B Company under Major George Thirlwell was sent out to help clear the enemy presence away from the battalion's rear. Upon the arrival of these troops, Ferguson mounted a tank with Thirlwell and an interpreter and drove down the road calling on the North Koreans to surrender as they were surrounded. Deceived by this bold bluff, more than 1500 enemy soldiers were taken prisoner—Ferguson later claimed the total figure was 1982—along with their weapons, which included some anti-tank guns, many automatic weapons and mortars.

At 11 pm a convoy of the 7th US Cavalry Regiment, their vehicle lights turned on, drove into 3RAR's lines from the north. This unit had followed tracks to the east of the 27th Brigade's advance and reached the main road again at Hwangju, a few kilometres north of the Australian road-block.

The American movement had trapped further large numbers of enemy, and after a brisk fight another 1700 prisoners had been taken, with whom the 7th Cavalry returned.

The capture of Sariwon, and the accompanying North Korean losses of at least 215 personnel killed and a large number of prisoners, had been accomplished at a cost of just one man killed and three wounded (all among the Argylls). Although warmly praised for their part in the highly successful action by Major General Hobart Gay, commander of the 1st US Cavalry Division under whom the 27th Brigade had been placed, the Australians themselves understandably regarded the action as a pretty tame affair.

NO. 77 SQUADRON, RAAF

After the Japanese attack at Pearl Harbor in December 1941, Australia hastily formed three RAAF fighter squadrons, the 75th, 76th and 77th.

No. 77 Squadron was formed at Station Pierce, just north of Perth in Western Australia, in March 1942 and was the first squadron transferred to Darwin in August, with its 24 Curtis P40 Kittyhawks. It saw action defending Darwin from Japanese air raids and claimed the first Australian aerial 'kill' over the mainland—just after 5 am on 24 November 1942 when a Mitsubishi 'Betty' bomber was shot down during a bombing raid.

John Gorton, who would later become Australia's prime minister, was a pilot with No. 77 Squadron. In January 1942 Gorton had suffered horrific facial injuries when the RAF Hurricane he was flying crashlanded on an island south of Singapore after an aerial battle with Japanese fighter planes. He was rescued and taken to Singapore, which was being evacuated as the Japanese were advancing from the north. Gorton was put on a ship heading to Batavia (now Jakarta), but it was torpedoed by a Japanese submarine and he was again rescued, while afloat in an overcrowded life raft, taken to Batavia and finally transferred to Fremantle, where he recovered from his wounds and joined No. 77 Squadron.

While stationed in Darwin, Gorton was forced to land in the bush due to a faulty fuel gauge and both he and the aircraft were recovered after several days. The squadron relocated to Milne Bay in February and, on 18 March 1943, the engine of Gorton's Kittyhawk failed on take-off and the plane turned over. Gorton was sent back to Australia with the rank of flight lieutenant and became a flying instructor at the Mildura Training Unit. After the war, he had his face reconstructed but remained severely disfigured all his life.

When the Japanese attacked Milne Bay, No. 77 Squadron claimed four bombers and a fighter for the loss of one Kittyhawk in a battle that helped turn the tide of the war and inflict Japan's first defeat.

Relocated to Goodenough Island the Squadron flew ground-attack missions in New Britain and, in January 1944, was part of the two largest RAAF raids ever mounted, attacking targets in New Britain. The squadron then moved to the Admiralty Islands providing air cover for Allied shipping, moved again to western New Guinea to support the American coastal landings, and then moved to Morotai and conducted ground-attacks until hostilities ended in August 1945. The squadron's tally of aerial victories during the war was eleven enemy aircraft destroyed for the loss of eighteen pilots killed.

No. 77 Squadron did not go home when the war ended. It was deployed to Japan, with the Allied occupational forces, making surveillance patrols and training with new fighter aircraft, Mustangs. By the end of 1948, the squadron, stationed at Iwakuni, consisted of 40 Mustangs and 300 officers and men, and many of their families.

All RAAF personnel were about to return to Australia in June 1950, when plans changed suddenly. General MacArthur requested No. 77 Squadron be attached to the US Fifth Air Force when skirmishes along the border between North and South Korea precipitated the Korean War, which began on 25 June.

The Mustang was the best long-range ground-attack aircraft available at the time and so, on 2 July 1950, with the blessing of the Australian government, No. 77 Squadron became the first non-US unit to join the war as part of the UN force.

In the early phases of the war, the pilots of No. 77 Squadron regularly faced intense ground fire when flying in support of US Flying Fortresses during bombing raids. They also flew missions equipped with bombs, rockets and napalm to support UN troops retreating before the North Korean advance. The squadron's first fatality occurred on 7 July when Squadron Leader Graham Strout was killed during a bombing raid and became the first Australian, and the first non-American from the UN force, to die fighting in the Korean War.

By July the communists had taken Seoul and all of the Korean peninsula except the southern port of Pusan, and a last-ditch battle ensued
which was to turn the war in favour of the UN troops. During the month
of August 1950, as part of that action, No. 77 Squadron was credited with
destroying 35 enemy tanks, 212 other vehicles, eighteen railway engines
or cars, and thirteen fuel or ammunition dumps.

The squadron's part in the victory at Pusan earned recognition from
the highest political levels in the US and Australian Prime Minister
Menzies visited their base at Iwakuni in Japan and made a special
presentation to the squadron. In October, as the UN troops advanced
northward, No. 77 Squadron was transferred from Iwakuni to Pohang
Airport, on the east coast of South Korea, where they lived in freezing
conditions in tents. That same month China entered the war officially
and a counter-attack forced the UN base, and No. 77 Squadron, to
move back south to Pusan before the advance to the north by ground
forces pushed the communists back past Seoul and into North Korea
in 1951.

By this time, the squadron's Mustangs had become outdated and
were no match for the Russian-built MiG–15s now being flown by the
communist pilots. The Australian government attempted to replace
them with US-built Sabres, but there were none available at the time,
as those being built were all desperately needed by the US air force. The
government instead purchased British-built Gloster Meteors and the
squadron took delivery of 22 of these fighter planes at Iwakuni in April
1951 before transferring to an air base at Kimpo, north of Seoul in July.

Unfortunately, the Meteors were to prove no match for the MiG–15s
in air-to-air combat. On 29 August 1951 one Meteor was shot down by
a MiG–15 and the pilot captured, while another was badly damaged
in the same fight and limped home to Kimpo. On 1 December the
RAAF's biggest air-to-air battle of the war occurred in the skies over
North Korea when twelve Meteor F8s encountered a force of between
25 and 40 MiG–15s. The battle raged for less than fifteen minutes at
altitudes of between 20,000 and 30,000 feet (6000 and 9000 metres)
and, although two of the MiG–15s were shot down, No. 77 Squadron
lost three Meteors and three pilots, one presumed killed and two taken
prisoner.

After the war the Russian pilot, Lieutenant Colonel Sergey Vishnyakov,
wrote about the encounter in his memoirs:

I saw another Meteor leaving the battle. We overtook him and attacked . . . I managed to frame him in my sights and opened fire. My shells burst on the Meteor's wings and the pilot bailed out.

Although outnumbered, the Australian pilots performed well in what became known as the Battle of Sunchon. It was this action, however, that convinced the RAAF that the Meteor was no match for the MiG–15.

It was disappointing for the men of No. 77 Squadron to find themselves once more restricted to the role of air-to-ground attack, but the most successful operation was yet to come. It occurred at Wonsan on 16 March 1953. Military historian Chris Coulthard-Clark wrote this account of the event:

This was a resoundingly successful ground attack operation carried out along the east coast of North Korea by No. 77 Squadron of the Royal Australian Air Force (RAAF) on 16 March 1953. A pair of Meteor F.8 fighters on a dawn road patrol south of Wonsan sighted a Chinese convoy of about 140 trucks extending over a distance of roughly five kilometres. The column was moving slowly and virtually bumper to bumper on a narrow road running down from a saddleback, with steep cliffs and sheer drops on either side.

Vehicles at the head and rear of the line were attacked with rockets and destroyed, thereby trapping all the remaining trucks in between . . . more Meteors were requested from the squadron base at Kimpo . . . and by midday more than two-thirds of the convoy had been destroyed or damaged.

While strafing along the line of vehicles with cannonfire, the Meteor pilots had to zigzag to avoid the hazard posed by surrounding hills. Adding to the danger were the Chinese troops in the trucks, who dismounted and maintained a steady flow of small-arms fire; many of the soldiers climbed the adjoining heights to shoot across at the aircraft as they passed. Although several Meteors were hit, none were lost in what was described as 'one of the biggest lorry-busting forays in the Korean War'.

During the three years of the Korean War, No. 77 Squadron pilots flew into action 18,872 times and destroyed 3700 enemy buildings, 1408 enemy vehicles, 98 railway engines and carriages, and sixteen bridges—and shot down at least three and probably five MiG–15s. The squadron's losses were 37 pilots killed and seven captured by the enemy. Sixty aircraft, including more than 40 Meteors, were lost, five of which were shot down by MiG–15s.

On 22 September 1952, Flight Lieutenant, later Group Captain, Douglas Hurst, a veteran of WWII who had already flown 121 missions in Meteors, won the Distinguished Flying Cross when he:

> ... led a Squadron rocket attack against a dangerous build-up of enemy troops in North West Korea. Although met by intense and accurate anti-aircraft fire, this officer brilliantly led the Squadron in a low, daring attack, which successfully destroyed the target.

When No. 77 Squadron finally departed Iwakuni air base for Australia, on 19 November 1954, it had been based overseas continuously for eleven years. The squadron's excellent reputation was said to have played a part in America's willingness to ratify the ANZUS Pact in 1952.

THE BATTLE OF KAPYONG

The most famous and important battle fought by Australian ground troops in the Korean War took place in the Kapyong Valley, north of Seoul, in late April 1951.

With the coming of spring, the Chinese launched a massive offensive on the night of 22 April, with the aim of retaking Seoul and pushing south through the central part of the peninsula. A force of 330,000 enemy troops advanced along the valley towards Seoul, while a further 150,000 attacked UN defences further east in the central sector. Once again, their advance was rapid. The South Korean 6th Division, defending the Kapyong Valley, was vastly outnumbered and taken by surprise.

As South Korean forces held on grimly, a plan was put in place to defend the valley to their rear. On 23 April, the 3rd Battalion, Royal Australian Regiment (3RAR), of the 27th British Commonwealth Brigade, led by Lieutenant Colonel Bruce Ferguson, was given the task of defending the valley, if the South Korean forces failed to stop the Chinese onslaught.

The Australians were deployed on the high ground to the east and the 2nd Battalion, Princess Patricia's Canadian Light Infantry, occupied the hills on the western side of the valley. The 1st Battalion of the Middlesex Regiment, which had been further north supporting the South Korean 6th Brigade, fell back and took up a position directly beside the river to the west, at the rear of the Australian and Canadian troops.

Ahead of this defensive line, but also to the rear of the South Korean 6th Division, were the headquarters units' tanks and artillery. These units comprised the guns of the 16th New Zealand Field Regiment, fifteen Sherman tanks of the 72nd US Tank Battalion and a company of American heavy mortars.

As the Kapyong Valley was 7 kilometres (4.5 miles) wide at the point where the defences were established, a continuous defensive line was not possible and strong-points were set up, which it was hoped would block the enemy advance and contain the Chinese forces in the valley.

The Australians spent the day digging in and preparing defences and, by late afternoon, retreating South Korean troops appeared and passed through the defensive line. As the trickle of retreating troops became a flood around sunset, some Chinese troops following them managed to pass through the gaps in the defensive line and infiltrate between the positions held by A and B Companies of the 3rd Battalion (3RAR).

As night fell, the Chinese arrived in force and, when a full moon rose at 9.30 pm, they attacked en masse and the American tanks supporting 3RAR were overrun and forced to withdraw. Unfortunately, the tanks had been positioned ahead of the defensive line with no infantry support. The US heavy mortar unit also retreated, leaving its guns and vehicles behind.

While D Company held their position with little attention from the enemy and C Company were attacked only once during the night, A and B Companies, closer to the valley floor, faced wave after wave of assaults, each one precipitated by a barrage of mortar and artillery fire and showers of grenades. All these attacks were repelled until the Chinese were forced to attack over the bodies of their dead comrades. Some of the enemy troops who had breached the defensive line around sunset attacked A Company from the rear just before dawn, but were driven off.

At 3 am the New Zealand artillery regiment, which had been forced to retreat to a new position, came back into action. At 5 am, however, the 3rd Battalion headquarters was forced to retreat back inside the defensive line established to the rear of the Australian positions by the 1st Battalion of the Middlesex Regiment.

As the sun rose on 24 April, the Chinese, having failed to dislodge the Canadians on their right or the Australians on their left, were in an exposed position on the valley floor. UN reinforcements arrived in the shape of artillery, mortars and tanks, and the Chinese withdrew to safer positions and then moved higher up the side of the valley to attack D Company's position, which was on higher ground behind A and B Companies. This meant that A and B Companies were now in danger of being encircled and cut off. B Company was ordered to retreat to a higher position and did so, taking with them about 50 Chinese prisoners.

At this stage, a series of mishaps almost swung the battle in favour of the Chinese.

Firstly, it was decided to mount a counter-offensive that would be better served by the Australians of B company retaking their old position, and they were ordered back. The enemy were, however, now firmly entrenched and, despite a bayonet charge by the men of B Company that took them part way back, the Australians were forced to retreat.

Secondly, the men of D Company, who repelled relentless assaults on their position from 7.30 am until 2 pm, were napalmed by two US Corsair aircraft who had wrongly marked their location as an enemy position. Two men died in the 'friendly fire' and the attack was only called off when an officer ran into open view under enemy fire to display a marker panel to the pilots, which identified D Company as UN troops.

Meanwhile, C Company began to reinforce both A and B Companies and establish communication with headquarters. When the American 1st Marine Division radio operator told the A Company operator that he must be mistaken, as A Company had been wiped out the night before, Major Bernard O'Dowd had to take the phone and tell him, 'I've got news for you, we are still here and we are staying here.'

Shortly after the misdirected air strike, the Australians were ordered to leave their positions and withdraw through the Middlesex Regiment's defensive line. This was not easy as they were still busy engaging the enemy. A, B and C Companies made a tactical withdrawal along the higher ridges of the valley through the defensive position maintained by D Company. This was then followed by a fighting withdrawal, supported by New Zealand artillery from the 16th Field Regiment, down a ridge into the valley, where they finally disengaged the enemy and rejoined the rest of the brigade.

The price paid by the Australians in halting the Chinese advance and preventing the enemy from taking Seoul for the third time during the war was 32 men killed and 53 wounded. Lieutenant Colonel Bruce Ferguson, commander of 3RAR, was awarded the Distinguished Service Order, and the Australian and Canadian battalions received United States Presidential Distinguished Unit Citations for their part in the Battle of Kapyong. Chinese losses are unknown, but were at least 500 dead.

The Chinese, having failed to take the Canadian position, ended the assault and, by the afternoon of 25 April, the valley was secure and

US army units had linked up with the Canadian troops. By that time, however, the Australians were back at base, taking a well-deserved rest . . . after all, it was Anzac Day.

Captain Reg Saunders, who led the 3rd Battalion's C Company at Kapyong, later said:

> At last I felt like an Anzac, and I imagine there were 600 others like me.

By 29 April, the Chinese Spring Offensive had ground to a halt, at a defensive line north of Seoul.

THE MALAYAN EMERGENCY

The end of Japanese occupation in 1945 left Malaya's economy shattered. The country relied on exports of primary products like rubber, tin, palm oil, coffee and spices—and all of those industries required rebuilding. In the north of the country there was a long history of imported labour, largely from China but also from India. By the end of the 19th century, Singapore, Ipoh, Kuala Lumpur, Penang and the two northern tin-mining states of Perak and Selango all had Chinese majority populations.

During WWII the ethnic Chinese in Malaya suffered terribly under the Japanese, who regarded them as aliens in Malaya and had a policy of ethnic cleansing which involved burning Chinese businesses and schools and killing an estimated 90,000 Chinese Malays. The British-assisted resistance movement, the Malay People's Anti-Japanese Army (MPAJA) was made up of mostly Chinese and led by the Malay Communist Party (MCP), which had developed before WWII with the support of the Chinese Communist Party. In December 1945, the MPAJA, which had been 'unofficially' trained and armed by the British, was disbanded and offered incentives to hand in weapons. Not all its members, however, did so.

After WWII Britain desperately needed Malaya's tin and rubber for post-war recovery and re-established those industries with little consideration for the poverty-stricken workforce, many of whom had fought the Japanese with the MPAJA. This problem was exacerbated by the failure of a British plan to unite all provinces into a Malayan union—a federation in which all citizens, Malay, Chinese and Indian, would have equal rights. Ethnic Malays, however, did not favour the plan and the local rulers of the British-controlled states rejected it. Subsequently, when the British abandoned the proposal, the ethnic Chinese were left without civil rights as second-class citizens and felt betrayed by the British.

The Malayan Communist Party, led by Chin Peng, organised a number of strikes starting with a 24-hour general strike on 29 January 1946. Strike leaders and protesters were arrested, imprisoned and deported. Protests and strikes became more militant. In 1947 there were more than 300 strikes in Malaya organised by the MCP.

The situation escalated into the 'war' that became known as the 'Malayan Emergency' on the morning of 16 June 1948 at the Elphil rubber plantation near Sungai Siput in Perak province, when British plantation manager Arthur Walker was shot as he sat at his desk in his office. Another manager, John Allison, and his assistant, Ian Christian, were then tied up and executed by three young Chinese men.

In response to this incident, a state of emergency was declared in Perak two days later and, in July, this was extended to the entire country. The MCP and other leftist groups were outlawed and police were given power to detain anyone suspected of being a communist or assisting their activities.

The MCP reformed the MPAJA and transformed it into the Malayan National Liberation Army (MNLA), also known as the Malayan Races' Liberation Army (MRLA), which centred itself in the more remote rural areas of northern Malaya. Their first major move was to attack and occupy the town of Gua Musang in the province of Kelantan, east of Perak. From there the MNLA were able to organise attacks on British-owned rubber plantations and tin mines.

In the early months of the crisis, British planters and miners, who bore the brunt of the communist attacks, began to talk about government incompetence and being betrayed by Whitehall. Malayan security forces did not know how to fight an enemy based in the jungle and supported by the Chinese rural population, and did little except guard MCP targets, like mines and plantations.

In April 1950, British Army Director of Operations, General Sir Harold Briggs, was put in charge. His policy was to cut off the MNLA from their supporters and food supply. This entailed the forced relocation of some 500,000 people, including 400,000 ethnic Chinese, from villages on the fringes of the jungle to 'new villages', which were guarded camps surrounded by barbed wire, with police stations and floodlights.

At that time the British army was under-manned in Malaya. Its thirteen infantry battalions consisted of three British battalions, two battalions of the Malay regiment, seven Gurkha battalions, and an artillery regiment operating as infantry. Briggs brought in Royal Marines and a Special Air Service that specialised in reconnaissance, raiding and counter-insurgency.

The battle for the minds and hearts of the local population was the real struggle of the Malayan Emergency. The MCP demanded immediate independence and equal rights and full citizenship for all ethnic groups. Poverty and resentment to British rule and lack of civil rights fuelled the MNLA campaign and the British employed some interesting tactics, using fear and superstition to demonise the MNLA and scare the population into accepting 'protection'. There were also many acts of cruelty and several reported massacres of whole villages, British troops were accused of beheading enemy soldiers killed and captured, dehumanising local inhabitants and burning villages.

In Perak, there was an airdrop of leaflets into villages warning the locals that the guerrilla leader Perumal, who was of Indian descent, was 'a vicious man who had the power to make himself invisible'. The leaflet also contained a request from Queen Elizabeth asking locals to try to capture him alive. Perumal's advantage lay in the fact that he was related to many of the villagers and would often secretly visit workers' quarters at plantations, hand out gifts and sweets to the children, and tell the workers that he was trying to protect them from 'the British bullies'. Perumal was also known to kill workers who did not comply with his demands. His reign as local guerrilla leader, based on a mixture of persuasion, cajolery and terror, came to an end when he decided, near the end of the conflict, to save the lives of his guerrillas by surrendering. When he made the decision known to the group, he was shot and killed by his own men.

Although this was the type of local 'warfare' that, in many ways, typified the Malayan Emergency, it was also a very real national emergency. This became apparent when the British High Commissioner to Malaya, Sir Henry Gurney, was ambushed and killed on his way to a meeting at a resort 60 kilometres (37 miles) north of Kuala Lumpur on 7 October 1951.

The convoy included an armoured scout car, a police wireless van and an open Land Rover containing six policemen. After the police wireless van broke down, Gurney decided to go ahead without it and the vehicles were stopped by a hail of bullets from an ambush party of 40 MCP guerrillas 8 kilometres (5 miles) further on. The tyres on the cars were shot out, five of the six policemen were wounded and Gurney's chauffeur was killed. The High Commissioner then pushed his wife and private secretary onto the floor of the car, got out and sacrificed himself by attempting to draw the gunfire away from the car. The armoured scout car sped ahead to get help from a nearby police station and, although the guerrillas fired for another ten minutes before leaving the area, no one else was killed.

Two weeks after Gurney's assassination, Churchill's Conservative Party regained power in the United Kingdom and, in January 1952, General Sir Gerald Templer was appointed as Gurney's successor. He instituted a policy of close cooperation between the civil and military powers that finally began to undermine the terrorist threat.

Templer is generally credited with turning the conflict in favour of the British forces, who began the 'hearts and minds' policy, giving food and medical aid to rural communities and indigenous tribes, while constantly patrolling and pushing MNLA guerrillas deeper into the jungle and denying them food and other resources. This forced the MNLA to attack and take food from local tribes, which in turn destroyed the support they had previously enjoyed. Captured guerrillas were treated well and many changed sides as the tide turned against the MNLA who, in contrast, had a policy of never releasing any British troops alive.

It is estimated that, in General Templer's two-year term, the MNLA guerrilla numbers fell by 50 per cent, communist attacks fell from more than 500 a month to less than 100, and casualties, both military and civilian, declined from a peak of more than 200 a month to less than 40.

The first Australian involvement occurred in 1950 with the arrival of RAAF Dakotas from No. 38 Squadron, which were involved in troop movement and cargo transport, and in paratroop and leaflet drops. In July 1954, east of Ipoh, in Perak, five RAAF Lincolns of No. 1 Squadron joined six RAF Lincolns in a ten-day campaign known as 'Operation Termite', which involved bombing raids, air-to-ground attacks and paratroop drops.

That operation destroyed 181 communist camps and, while only thirteen guerrillas were confirmed killed and one captured, communist control of the district was ended.

When the 2nd Battalion, Royal Australian Regiment (2RAR), went into action in January 1956, the 'war' had entered a long, slow 'mopping up' phase that was mainly left to Australian troops operating as part of the

28th Commonwealth Brigade, who were tasked with guarding the 'new villages' and patrolling the surrounding areas.

In October 1957 the 3rd Battalion (3RAR) replaced the 2nd and continued driving the MNLA into the jungle areas of Perak and Kedah and, in April 1959, Perak was declared 'safe and secure'. By late 1959 most of the remaining communist fighters had crossed the border into Thailand. In October, the 1st Battalion (1RAR) replaced the 3rd and patrolled the border region. Although the Malayan government officially declared the emergency over in July 1960, 1RAR remained until October 1961 and 2RAR returned for a second tour and was involved in anti-communist operations, in Perlis and Kedah, until August 1963.

Through the latter stages of the Malayan Emergency, Australia also provided artillery, engineering infrastructure and built the main runway for the air force base at Butterworth, and RAN ships also served in Malayan waters.

Over its twelve-year timespan the Malayan Emergency involved 40,000 British and Commonwealth troops, and a maximum force of 8000 communist guerrillas. It was Australia's longest continuous military commitment of the twentieth century and more than 7000 Australians served during that time. Thirty-nine Australian servicemen died serving in Malaya, fifteen of them killed in action, and 27 were wounded.

SUNGEI BEMBAN

Chris Coulthard-Clark

This incident was the single most intense action fought by Australian ground troops during the Malayan Emergency, and took place on 22 June 1956 in the state of Perak about 1.5 kilometres south of the rubber-producing area of Sungei Siput. The clash began soon after 3 pm, when up to 25 communist terrorists, members of the 13/15th Independent Platoon of the Malayan Races Liberation Army, ambushed a five-man reconnaissance patrol from a platoon of A Company, 2nd Battalion of the Royal Australian Regiment (or 2RAR), about 400 metres north of the platoon's base at the Sungei Bemban reservoir.

The patrol was returning along a track which paralleled the pipeline leading from the reservoir to Sungei Siput when the guerrillas detonated a landmine and opened fire with submachine guns from well-prepared positions. The Australians suffered no casualties from the initial explosion, but in the following exchange of fire the patrol leader was killed outright and another man was critically wounded and soon died.

The position of the remaining four members of the patrol was perilous, since they could not see the enemy firing at them from concealed pits in the jungle undergrowth and shouting that they heard indicated that the guerrillas were receiving reinforcements from the north. The continuous volume of fire returned by the patrol's Bren gun ensured, however, that the ambushers did not immediately attempt to overrun them.

The sound of heavy firing quickly drew two other Australian parties to the scene. A second six-man patrol which had rested with the first barely fifteen minutes earlier was first to arrive. Hurrying south along the track, its members came to within 50 metres of where the ambush survivors were pinned down before they were also fired on from the ambush position. The patrol commander, Corporal L.H. Rodgers, sent four of his men to outflank the guerrillas from high ground to the north-east, while he and the remaining man (an Iban tracker)—both being wounded—attempted to hold the enemy's attention.

When the flanking group opened fire and began an assault, Rodgers and the tracker also charged forward. In the resulting fight, one of the four Australians in the flanking party was killed along with one guerrilla; another guerrilla was wounded as he fled into the jungle.

Meanwhile the platoon commander, Lieutenant A.W. Campbell, ran up along the track from the patrol base near the reservoir accompanied by two men. They arrived at the scene of the action just as the ambush party was dispersing, with a group of guerrillas observed moving into the undergrowth towards the south-east. Fire was still coming from the ambush position, however, but stopped after Campbell lobbed two hand grenades into it. As the remaining guerrillas split into two groups and fled, one lot heading south-east and the other crossing the track and making for the river to the west, Campbell and his men pursued the latter and succeeded in killing one guerrilla and recovering his weapon.

After a third six-man patrol which had originally been operating to the south-west of the reservoir also reached the area, Campbell conducted a sweep of the ambush site and also began the evacuation of the three members of his platoon who were now wounded, in addition to the three dead. A follow-up patrol launched the next morning found blood trails, which indicated that several guerrillas had sustained serious wounds, as well as the two terrorists whose bodies remained in the ambush position.

The enemy's presumed casualties could not, however, conceal the fact that the communists had nearly succeeded in wiping out an Australian patrol, and were only frustrated in this object by the vigorous reaction of a second patrol, which had fortuitously been present in the immediate vicinity.

THE INDONESIAN CONFRONTATION

This was an 'unofficial' war fought from 1963 to 1966 along the border of the Indonesian territory of Kalimantan and the Malaysian provinces of Sabah and Sarawak on the island of Borneo. It was fought between Indonesian troops and local Indonesian militia and Malaysian and British Commonwealth troops.

The cause of the confrontation was Indonesia's objection to the creation of the Malaysian Federation, which was a proposed union between Malaya, Singapore and the British protectorates on the island of Borneo. These were Sarawak, Brunei and North Borneo, which was later known as Sabah.

The conflict really began in December 1962, before the Malaysian Federation came into existence in September 1963, when armed insurgents, operating as the military wing of the Brunei People's Party (PRB) with Indonesian backing, attempted to seize power in the independent British protectorate of Brunei, only to be defeated by British troops rushed in from Singapore. As a result the Sultan of Brunei, who had been in favour of the Malaysian Federation, chose not to join and outlawed the PRB.

Throughout 1963 Indonesia, which was at that time led by President Sukarno, increased military activity along its borders in Borneo, as small parties of armed men began forming and incursions were frequently made into Malaysian territory to spread propaganda against the federation with Malaya. These more frequently became raids and sabotage missions—at first carried out by local militia known as 'volunteers' but later by Indonesian regular army units.

Sukarno had collaborated with the Japanese against the Dutch administration in WWII and declared Indonesian independence in August 1945. He became the first president and led resistance to Dutch recolonisation efforts by both diplomatic and military means until Indonesian independence was recognised by the Dutch in 1949. Indonesia had successfully annexed Dutch Papua with UN approval, even though a military attempt to take the territory had been defeated by the local population and the Dutch. Western powers supported the Indonesian claim in an attempt to appease Sukarno and move him away from his flirtation with communism. Sukarno strengthened ties with China and visited Beijing in 1956. He also accepted military aid from the USSR. By 1962, the Soviet bloc provided more aid to Indonesia than to any other non-communist nation.

On 15 September 1963, the day before Malaysia came into existence, Indonesia withdrew its embassy from Malaya and the British and Malayan embassies in Jakarta were stoned. Sukarno claimed the formation of Malaysia was 'neo-colonialism' and a threat to the region and Indonesia. Backed by the powerful Communist Party of Indonesia (PKI), he supported a communist insurgency in Sarawak, led by members of the local Chinese community, and Indonesian irregular forces were infiltrated into border areas of Sarawak.

Meanwhile, in Indonesia there was hyperinflation, political unrest and concern about the growing power of the PKI. In April 1965 Sukarno endorsed a PKI proposal for a new military force in Indonesia, consisting of armed peasants and workers. The idea was quickly rejected by Indonesia's generals and, when Major General Suharto was given operational command of the confrontation against Malaysia in 1965, he opened secret negotiations with the British, as he feared a communist takeover of the army should the confrontation continue and escalate.

Early on 1 October 1965, six army generals were kidnapped and executed in Jakarta by soldiers from the Presidential Guard, in an abortive coup that became known as the '30 September Movement'— supposedly aimed at protecting Sukarno. Suharto acted quickly to take control of the army and end the coup, announcing on radio that evening that the six generals had been kidnapped by 'counter-revolutionaries' and that the 30 September Movement planned to overthrow Sukarno. He vowed to crush the 30 September Movement and protect the president.

Suharto blamed the PKI and there followed an army and Islamist campaign to purge the Indonesian population, government and military of communists and leftists. PKI leaders were arrested and many executed and an estimated half a million Indonesians were killed in the unrest. The PKI was declared illegal and abolished. Indonesia lost interest in continuing the unofficial war with Malaysia and peace negotiations began in May 1966 before a final peace agreement was signed in Bangkok in August. In March 1967 Suharto took over as President of Indonesia.

Australians fought during the Indonesian confrontation as part of the British and Commonwealth force under overall British command. Two Australian battalions served in Sarawak, and operated in conflicts against communist militia and Indonesian regulars. Two squadrons of the Special Air Service, a troop of the Royal Australian Signals, several artillery batteries and parties of the Royal Australian Engineers were also involved, along with the Royal Australian Navy and several RAAF squadrons. During the confrontation, 3500 Australians served of which 23 were killed and eight were wounded.

OPERATION CLARET

Indonesian troops had been making incursions into Malaysian territory since the start of the confrontation and, towards the end of 1964, British forces in Borneo planned a series of secret patrols that ventured up to 10 kilometres (6 miles) into the Indonesian territory of Kalimantan. These were designed to catch the enemy off guard, disrupt troop movement and supply lines, and force the Indonesians into a state of constant worry and fear. When the 3rd Battalion, Royal Australian Regiment (3RAR), arrived in Sarawak in March 1965, they, too, carried out some of these clandestine patrols, which were given the collective codename 'Claret'.

24 May, Sungei Koemba

The 3rd Battalion was stationed on the Sarawak border 50 kilometres (31 miles) from Kuching, when B Company, commanded by Major William Broderick, made the first border crossing by Australian troops into Indonesian territory on 24 May 1965. From a patrol base overlooking the Koemba River, a reconnaissance party of four detected a noisy group of enemy soldiers camped beside the river. Next morning the main Australian force moved down a ridge towards the water, while a patrol with four Bren machine guns followed a track along the bank into an ambush position at a bend in the river.

Half an hour later, at 11.30 am, motors were heard and two boats, each about 10 feet (3 metres) long, appeared, each carrying five armed men. The patrol opened fire and all ten of the enemy were killed. At that very moment, the patrol sentry stationed on the right flank saw two similar boats appear around the bend only 10 metres from his hiding place. He opened fire and killed the five men in the first boat. The remaining boat ran ashore out of sight and the sentry then threw grenades into the place where the men from that boat appeared to be hiding, and sprayed the area with rapid fire.

As the Australians withdrew, the enemy commenced a barrage of small-arms fire from across the river and the main Australian force responded with well-directed artillery and mortar fire onto the enemy position. The Australian force recrossed the border without suffering any loss or injury—the time was 3 pm.

11–13 June, Second Sungei Koemba

A platoon of C Company 3RAR, under the command of Lieutenant Robert Guest, crossed the border on 11 June and set an ambush just downstream from the site of the previous action. They watched five boats pass carrying civilians and waited in hiding until 10.45 am on 12 June when a sentry signalled the approach of an enemy patrol of at least a dozen men on foot. Several minutes later, the enemy patrol saw the sentry, who opened fire and killed three of them. The others ran forward but the left flank of the Australian platoon turned away from the river and outflanked them.

One member of the Indonesian patrol escaped back along the track and one was seen crawling away badly wounded, the rest were killed. The Australian platoon collected weapons and identified the dead as members of the 440th Indonesian Battalion. They then withdrew under artillery cover and crossed the border next morning. The whole engagement had lasted less than ten minutes—there were no Australian casualties.

12–15 June, Kindau

On the same day that C Company was in action, a platoon from A Company 3RAR set an ambush along a track in thick jungle about 1.5 kilometres (one mile) over the border, with orders to intercept an Indonesian force that had entered Sarawak and would probably use the track when returning to Kalimantan. Three men were in hiding near a small creek on the eastern flank and four others, who had set two Claymore mines on the track, covered the western end. The main ambush party of fourteen men waited in between and a mortar party and reserves were situated a little way back in the jungle at a 'firm base'.

The ambush party remained quietly in position for three days until a group of between 60 and 100 Indonesians approached from the east with weapons slung over their shoulders. Lieutenant Douglas Byers counted until 25 of the enemy were in the trap and then sprung the ambush with a burst of submachine gun fire. Some of the enemy were only 5 metres from the Australian guns and half of those in the trap were killed in the first minute. The three at the head of the patrol ran west and were blown apart when the Claymore mines detonated.

Those in the rear of the enemy column regrouped and a firefight took place with grenades and rifles. The Indonesians managed to set up one machine gun and a mortar, but both were knocked out by return mortar fire and the encounter then became hand-to-hand combat until the Australians withdrew to their firm base while the enemy positions were being pounded by 100-mm (4-inch) and 137-mm (5.5-inch) artillery.

The platoon crossed the border two hours later, carrying one soldier who was shot in the knee and later discovered a second casualty, a private with a minor leg wound caused by shrapnel. The estimate of enemy dead was between 25 and 50. The engagement had lasted fifteen minutes.

This action was the first of the Operation Claret patrols to be made public, although the British and 3RAR were able to maintain the pretence that it took place in Malaysian territory.

10–13 July, Babang

A platoon from C Company 3RAR led by Lieutenant Robert Guest, who also led the second ambush on the Koemba River, left base on 10 July and next day set an ambush on a track leading from the Indonesian army base at Babang to the Malaysian border.

At midday on 12 July, 30 Indonesian soldiers approached from Babang. Although they were moving quietly and at the ready, their approach had been known for some time due to the sounds of disturbed wildlife in the jungle. When an Indonesian scout spotted one of C Company lying in wait and moved forward to investigate, there was no choice but to shoot him and spring the trap.

Six of the enemy were killed and five seriously wounded. The rest regrouped and attacked the Australians on the left flank of the ambush position, but were stopped by a Claymore mine as the Australians made a planned 200-metre withdrawal to their firm base, from where they called in defensive artillery fire before making good their escape without loss or injury. They then crossed the border and returned to base next day, having killed at least thirteen of the enemy, possibly more, and wounded at least five.

THE VIETNAM WAR

According to legend, the domestic history in Vietnam dates back to 2879 BC, when Kinh Dương Vương founded the state of Xích Qủy. Modern historians, however, seem to agree the first recognisable Vietnamese dynasty appeared as a Bronze Age culture around the Red River delta in the north sometime after 1000 BC.

Many dynasties ruled over the next 3000 years and there was a pattern of invasion and domination from China, especially in the north where the history of China and Vietnam is inextricably entangled. Large-scale wars were fought between the Vietnamese, Khmer, Laotian and Siamese people as empires and cultures rose and fell on the Indo-Chinese peninsula over the centuries.

After a period of more than 400 years of independence from China, Vietnam became a Chinese province again in 1407 AD, before establishing its independence once more, under the Lê Dynasty, from 1427 to 1527. This was followed by what is known as the 'Warlord Era', during which time four dynasties ruled over various parts of the country until the establishment of the Nguyễn Dynasty in 1802.

There is evidence of trade between Vietnam Indo-China and Europe as early as the time of the Roman Empire. Marco Polo visited Indo-China in the 13th century AD and trade with Europe began at around that time. While the Vietnamese remained free of European political domination until very late in the colonial era, Portuguese missionaries arrived as early as the 16th century and French Catholic missionaries arrived in force in the 17th and 18th centuries and converted around 10 per cent of the local population to Christianity.

In 1784 the French Roman Catholic prelate, Pigneau de Behaine, sailed to France to seek military backing for Nguyễn Ánh and signed the *Little Treaty of Versailles* with Louis XVI, which promised French military aid in exchange for trade concessions. De Behaine returned to Vietnam in 1788 with two ships, a regiment of Indian troops, and some mercenaries and volunteers to help Nguyễn Ánh overcome the Tây Sơn Dynasty and rule Vietnam. One of the volunteers, Jean-Marie Dayot, Europeanised and modernised Nguyễn Ánh's navy.

After he defeated the Tây Sơn Dynasty and took control of the country, Nguyễn Ánh tolerated Catholicism and employed some Europeans in his court as advisers, but his successors were less tolerant Confucians and resisted Westernisation and the church.

During the Catholic- and Siamese-supported Lê Văn Khôi revolt against the ruler Minh Mang in 1833, rebels held the French-built citadel in Saigon for two years until defeated. When the citadel was taken in 1835, 1800 people were massacred and the Roman Catholic Church declared 94 of those to be martyrs. Joseph Marchand, the French missionary who helped lead the revolt, was later tortured and killed. He was made a saint by Pope John Paul II in 1988.

Political instability, varying attitudes towards the French missionaries and frequent uprisings against the Nguyễns gave France many excuses to invade Vietnam. Napoleon III sent Admiral Pierre-Louis-Charles Rigault de Genouilly with gunships in 1858, to attack the northern port of Da Nang. Having failed to capture the port, de Genouilly went south and captured the city of Gia Dinh (Saigon, Ho Chi Minh City). From 1859 French troops expanded control over the Mekong Delta and, in 1867, the French created the colony of Cochinchina.

French troops invaded northern Vietnam in 1873 and again in 1882, established the French colony of Tonkin and took control over all of Vietnam in 1887. The central province of Annam was still ruled by the Nguyễn Dynasty as a French protectorate, while Tonkin had a French governor with local governments and Vietnamese officials, and Cochinchina was a colony ruled from France. Cambodia, with Laos, was added to Cochinchina in 1893.

Throughout the early 20th century the French suppressed nationalistic movements and exiled dissidents and others who hoped to gain independence and establish a republic, or return the country to dynastic rule. Many Vietnamese intellectuals looked to Japan as a model Asian nation that had modernised, but retained its own culture and some even set up Vietnamese independence societies in Japan.

The Japanese invaded in 1940 and used the Vichy French colonial administration as a puppet government. In 1941 Nguyễn Ái Quốc (Hồ Chí Minh), the son of a fiercely anti-French Confucian scholar and teacher and later imperial magistrate, arrived back in North Vietnam after living for three decades in Russia, China and France (where he had helped form the French Communist Party). He organised the Việt Minh front as a resistance movement against the Japanese and French. The Việt Minh collected intelligence on the Japanese in collaboration with the United States and support from China.

As the war neared an end, the Allied leaders had met in Potsdam in July 1945 and hatched a plan to divide Vietnam in half—this would restore French rule in the south, where the British would accept the Japanese surrender; and allow Chinese Nationalist leader, the anti-communist Chiang Kai-shek, to accept the surrender in the north. This plan went awry when General MacArthur forbade any reoccupation before he had received the Japanese surrender in Tokyo, which was actually set for 28 August, but a typhoon caused the ceremony to be postponed until 2 September.

In the meantime, Vietnamese nationalists of all parties had forced Bao Dai, the last emperor of the Nguyễn Dynasty, to abdicate and gained control of the whole country in September 1945. Hồ Chí Minh proclaimed the Democratic Republic of Vietnam (DRV) with himself as Chairman.

A bizarre situation occurred when Allied units arrived in Saigon on 11 September 1945 and were welcomed and guarded by fully armed Japanese and Việt Minh soldiers. Six months earlier in March the Japanese, expecting an American invasion of Indo-China following the fall of Manila, had disarmed the French and interned them. In Saigon the British occupation force, including Gurkha regiments, soon clashed with the Việt Minh, once it became known that they were there to reinstall French rule. An official war, the '1st Indochinese War', began in late 1946 between the Việt Minh and the French, who reinstated Bao Dai as Head of State and proclaimed Vietnam as a semi-independent state within the French Union in 1949.

France finally gave up her colonies in Indo-China in 1954 after Việt Minh forces won a victory in the Battle of Dien Bien Phu and the Geneva Conference divided Vietnam into two parts, with the communist DRV government ruling the north from Hanoi and the Republic of Vietnam, supported by the United States, ruling the south from Saigon.

The North Vietnamese government instituted 'land reform', which resulted in political oppression and executions, while President Diem, in South Vietnam, crushed political and religious opposition and thousands of his political opponents were killed and imprisoned.

The Geneva Accords had included an understanding that a nation-wide election be held in 1956 to finally reunite the country. President Diem, however, claimed that the people of the north could not vote freely, and encouraged by the United States, the south refused to participate. In 1960 the north declared its intention to remove Diem and reunite the country when it created the National Front for the Liberation of South Vietnam, which became known as the 'Viet Cong', and began a guerrilla war in the south.

The South Vietnamese army was unable to counter the Viet Cong and the later invasion by the North Vietnamese army. The United States—which had opposed the French being reinstalled in Vietnam, had worked with Hồ Chí Minh during WWII and had no objection to the creation of the Democratic Republic of Vietnam in 1945—found itself, in the post–Cold War environment, believing there was a desperate need to prevent the spread of communism in South-East Asia. By 1962 more than 11,000 United States military advisers had arrived in South Vietnam in what was the beginning of a commitment that would peak at more than 530,000 troops.

By the late 1960s there was increasing opposition in the United States to the war and, in 1969, President Richard Nixon announced the policy of 'Vietnamisation'—withdrawing US troops while giving massive financial support to the South Vietnamese army, which fought on for three years before Saigon fell to North Vietnamese forces in April 1975.

Millions lost their lives in the Vietnam War and millions more escaped as refugees as the region was destabilised to an extent that led to repercussions such as the war in Cambodia and the genocide of the Cambodian people by the Khmer Rouge.

AUSTRALIA IN VIETNAM

In 1962 Australia sent 30 military advisers to South Vietnam. By 1965 it became clear that the south was losing the struggle and the United States committed 200,000 troops and requested support from other nations. Australia dispatched the 1st Battalion, Royal Australian Regiment (1RAR), in June 1965.

In 1966 a task force, consisting of two battalions and a RAAF squadron of Iroquois helicopters, replaced 1RAR. Unlike 1RAR, the task force included conscripts called up under the National Service Scheme. A third RAAF squadron and destroyers of the Royal Australian Navy joined the conflict.

All nine battalions of the Royal Australian Regiment served in the war at one time or another—at the height of Australian involvement, we had 8500 troops in Vietnam.

In August 1966 a company of 6RAR was engaged in the Battle of Long Tan. During three hours of fierce fighting, it seemed the greatly outnumbered Australian force would be overrun, but the Viet Cong withdrew, leaving behind 245 dead. Eighteen Australians were killed and 24 wounded. The battle temporarily ended communist dominance in Phuoc Tuy province.

From 1970 Australia wound down its military effort in Vietnam. In December 1972 a detachment of advisers were the last Australian troops to come home. Their unit had seen continuous service in South Vietnam for ten and a half years. Australia's participation formally ended on 11 January 1973. The only force remaining was a platoon guarding the Australian embassy in Saigon.

In the weeks before the fall of Saigon on 30 April 1975, RAAF Hercules transports flew humanitarian missions to save civilian refugees and Vietnamese orphans before finally taking out embassy staff on 25 April. The war was the cause of great social and political dissent in Australia and many soldiers met a hostile reception and suffered long-term post-war problems on their return home.

The Vietnam War caused the greatest social division and political dissent the nation of Australia had experienced since the conscription issue and referenda that divided public opinion during World War I.

There was little opposition to Australia's participation in the war at first but, once conscription began and men were killed, opposition grew. In the early 1970s, more than 200,000 people participated in protest marches against conscription and the war in Australian cities. From 1966 to 1972 any Australian twenty-year-old male whose birth date was drawn from a barrel could be forced to do two years of full-time service in the army and be sent to combat duties in Vietnam. More than 15,000 of the 60,000 who served in Vietnam were national servicemen and more than 200 of them lost their lives.

Our last combat troops came home in March 1972, withdrawn by the McMahon Coalition Government, and one of the Whitlam ministry's first acts on being sworn in that year was to release the seven men who were in prison for resisting the draft. The RAAF did send personnel back to Vietnam in 1975 to assist with evacuations and humanitarian work during the war's final days.

Sixty thousand Australians, including ground troops, air force and navy personnel, served in Vietnam—520 Australians died and almost 2400 were wounded in the conflict.

GOODBYE TO VIETNAM

Stewart Law

I hand my rifle in,
Goodbye, Ho Chi Minh.
I climb aboard the plane,
Goodbye, dust and rain.
I leave The Nam behind,
But Nam won't leave my mind.

THE BATTLE OF LONG TAN

Chris Coulthard-Clark

The best-known battle of the Vietnam War in which Australians were involved, occurred in Phuoc Tuy Province on 18 August 1966. The action was fought a little over two months after the 1st Australian Task Force (1ATF)—comprising two infantry battalions of the Royal Australian Regiment (5RAR and 6RAR) and supporting arms—arrived in South Vietnam and established an operational base at Nui Dat, in the centre of Phuoc Tuy.

Shortly before 2.45 am on 17 August, Nui Dat was hit by a twenty-minute barrage from Viet Cong mortars and recoilless rifles firing from the east which left 24 personnel wounded, two seriously. As 5RAR was absent on operations to the north the base was not at full strength at this time, and was further weakened by having several elements of 6RAR also on patrol.

Nonetheless, the next morning B Company of 6RAR was sent out from the perimeter to locate the firing positions and establish in which direction the enemy responsible for the attack had withdrawn.

At midday on 18 August, D Company (commanded by Major Harry Smith) relieved B Company and took over the pursuit. That afternoon a sweep was begun of a rubber plantation north of the derelict village of Long Tan, situated 4 kilometres east of Nui Dat. At 3.40 pm 11 Platoon clashed briefly with a squad of six to eight Viet Cong, the enemy fleeing eastwards after one man was hit by Australian fire.

A weapon dropped by this party was found to be a Russian automatic AK47 rifle, a type not normally carried by VC Local Force units, and the fact that group had been dressed in khaki uniforms also drew comment within the company. It was not then realised, however, that such dress and equipment indicated the presence of enemy Main Force soldiers, not merely provincial troops.

Not long after resuming its advance, at 4.08 pm, 11 Platoon came under devastating small-arms fire and rocket-propelled grenades from its front and both flanks. The weight of this fire—believed to come from at least an enemy company-sized force—immediately pinned down the Australians, at the very moment when torrential monsoon rain broke across the area. Within less than twenty minutes this leading group of Australians had a third of its strength either killed or wounded, and was receiving mortar fire as well. Artillery counter-fire was called in, but shortly afterwards the aerial of the platoon's radio was shot away and communications were lost.

In response to 11 Platoon's plight, shortly after 5 pm 10 Platoon on the left flank was ordered to wheel south and move to its support. Within minutes 10 Platoon, too, came under heavy fire from three sides, its radio also hit and put out of action. Communications were restored shortly afterwards by a runner from company headquarters who carried a spare radio set through enemy fire—killing two enemy along the way—while calling out in the blinding rain until he found 10 Platoon's position. Still 100–150 metres short of 11 Platoon's location and unable to do anything to assist it to withdraw, 10 Platoon was ordered to fall back towards company headquarters. This movement was accomplished under cover of artillery fire, the wounded being carried back.

All this time 11 Platoon was still fighting hard, although cut off and with its effective strength of 28 men reduced to less than half. After its radio was repaired and contact restored, a steady hail of artillery was directed onto enemy positions. This initially had little effect on the leading VC assault troops, estimated to be from at least two companies, behind whom the weight of this fire fell. Despite the high risk involved, the sergeant now leading the Australian defence adjusted the barrage to within 50 metres of his position so that shells scythed through the enemy formations.

At 5.15 pm 12 Platoon set off from company headquarters towards the south-east in an attempt to link up with 11 Platoon and enable the survivors to be extricated. After pressing steadily forward for some 40 minutes, this group succeeded in reaching within about 75 metres of the embattled platoon before enemy pressure from three sides forced it to halt. With visibility down to about 70 metres in the rain, the commander of 12 Platoon ordered coloured smoke thrown to signal the presence and location of his men. Shortly afterwards, the dozen or so members of 11 Platoon able to do so raced to join them—though not before one was killed and two others wounded.

As this was happening, two RAAF UH–1B Iroquois helicopters had arrived overhead of company headquarters at 6 pm and managed to drop boxes of ammunition wrapped in blankets. This resupply was received at a critical moment, as the ammunition remaining within the company by this point was down to about 100 rounds.

By 6.10 pm 12 Platoon was back within the perimeter with what remained of 11 Platoon, and at last Smith had all the elements of his company that were still capable of fighting collected in one area. The action continued in heavy rain as darkness fell, the enemy engaging in repeated human wave assaults from the east, south-east and south. These attacks were broken up partly by D Company's fire, but mostly by the effective barrages called in by the attached forward observer, a New Zealander, from the regiment of three field batteries (two Australian, one New Zealand) operating in support of 1ATF from gun lines within the Nui Dat base.

Also available was the fire of a US battery of medium artillery.

As it happened, the conditions were technically near perfect for the type of support required of the guns on this occasion, and the slaughter caused among the enemy's ranks by the nearly 3500 artillery rounds fired during the battle was immense.

Meanwhile, at 5.45 pm, A Company of 6RAR had left Nui Dat mounted in M113 armoured personnel carriers under the personal orders of the unit's commanding officer, Lieutenant Colonel Colin Townsend. An element of the recently returned 5RAR was also placed on standby, while others took over the defence of 6RAR's sector of the base perimeter. At about 7 pm the carriers were able to reach D Company after fighting past groups of enemy encountered on the route through the plantation. A 30-strong party from B Company 6RAR, ordered to turn around while returning to Nui Dat once relieved by Smith at midday, also reached D Company's position on foot at this time. After the carriers made an easterly assault past the D Company position, continuing for 500 metres through the forming-up places being used by the enemy, they returned to join the defenders at 7.10 pm.

The Viet Cong were then still pressing an attack from the north-east but broke this off soon afterwards. All across the front, enemy figures were seen rising up from the ground and disappearing back among the rubber trees. The firing suddenly stopped, and although the augmented Australian force waited for a renewal of the enemy's major assaults, the battle was in fact over. Because of the dark, no attempt was made to secure the battlefield or locate the missing until next day, priority being given to evacuating D Company's many casualties.

The enemy force engaged in the action comprised the Viet Cong 275th Main Force Regiment reinforced by at least one North Vietnamese Army battalion, and a Local Force unit, D445 Battalion—a total of approximately 2500 men, as many as 1000 of whom actually came into direct contact with D Company. When the enemy forces eventually withdrew they left behind 245 bodies, although a further unknown number of killed had already been removed and others had been simply shredded into unidentifiable remains. In 1ATF, D Company lost seventeen of its 100 members killed and nineteen wounded—two of whom were not recovered until the following day, having spent a terrifying night watching the Viet Cong evacuate their casualties which were estimated to number in the hundreds. Three members of other Australian sub-units were wounded, one of whom later died, and three suffered such severe battle stress that they had to be evacuated.

The Australians' stunning victory did more than simply enhance their fighting reputation, since unquestionably the enemy force encountered by D Company had been preparing a decisive action against 1ATF— although opinion remains divided on whether this was to have been an attack on the Nui Dat base or a crushing ambush on part of the task force. This meeting/engagement destroyed the possibility of getting in an early politically wounding blow against the recent Australian deployment, and placed Viet Cong plans in the province on the back foot for some time.

This should not obscure the fact that 1ATF had been ill-prepared for a contest with an enemy force of the magnitude which materialised at Long Tan, or that the outcome of the action had come very close to being a catastrophe for the Australians.

THE ART OF WAR

Australia has a long tradition of sending artists to war as official war artists, to paint and draw both accurate and emotional representations of the people, places and conflicts with which the Australian military have been associated. While 22 official artists worked in World War I, 35 in World War II, and another fifteen in conflicts since then, there were only two official war artists to work during the Vietnam War as, for some reason, it was decided that the men chosen were required to undergo jungle training and take part in all the activities of an Australian soldier in Vietnam. This was a departure from normal practice for war artists and only applied in the Vietnam War.

Ken McFadyen from Preston, Victoria, had studied at the National Gallery School from 1954 to 1960 and was working as a set designer for the ABC when given an 'official artist' appointment. He trained in jungle warfare at Canungra, in Queensland, and arrived in Vietnam in August 1967 and served for seven months at Nui Dat, also visiting the base at Vung Tau several times and making tours of duty aboard the destroyer HMAS *Hobart* along the North Vietnamese coast.

As well as making large, accurate drawings of aircraft, he also drew detailed images of activities on the bases, and drew and painted while on patrol while carrying full combat equipment as well as his art materials. After his return to Australia, he received a further commission to produce a large painting of HMAS *Murchison* in action on the Han River during the Korean War.

Bruce Fletcher was the first official war artist to serve in Vietnam. Born in Melbourne in 1937, he also studied at the National Gallery School,

Prahran Technical College, Caulfield Technical College, Gordon Institute of Technology and RMIT, as well as privately under William Dargie, who had been an official war artist during WWII.

When he agreed to the appointment, Fletcher was already a very successful artist and highly regarded teacher of art. He was a finalist nine times between 1955 and 1961 in the Archibald Portrait Competition. Among his entries to become finalists were two self-portraits and others of Brigadier Langley, Victorian Premier Sir Henry Bolte and Sir Arthur Warner. His first solo exhibitions were held at the Athenaeum Gallery in 1961–62, from which paintings were bought by the National Gallery for their own collection and as gifts for Prince Charles.

Fletcher was commissioned as a lieutenant and served in the war from February to September 1967 but, just a few days after arriving, he made history by becoming the only Australian war artist to be wounded while serving in a war. This occurred when an automatic rifle taken from a captured Viet Cong soldier accidentally discharged while Fletcher was on an RAAF flight from Saigon to Vung Tau.

This meant Fletcher spent time at the hospital in Vung Tau, carefully recording all the base activities and the personnel stationed there. His sketches are a detailed gallery of daily life at Vung Tau and he later worked outdoors, complete with a plaster cast on his left leg and foot, and produced many pen drawings of army life, as well as a series of oil portraits accurately showing how soldiers looked when dressed and equipped for a variety of army duties.

After his time in Vietnam, he returned to teaching art and worked for the Australian War Memorial again in 1970, executing a very large painting of the Battle of Long Tan, which is displayed in the memorial collection in Canberra. He later held solo exhibitions at galleries throughout Australia, including the Hamilton Gallery, Benalla Art Gallery and Kew Gallery, and his works also hang in Buckingham Palace, the Australian National Collection, Monash University, Melbourne University, the offices of the *Herald and Weekly Times*, and in many private collections in Australia and overseas.

Bruce Fletcher once said that the treatment received by Vietnam veterans made him feel that they had been 'shat on' by anti-Vietnam sentiment after the war, and he often wished he'd never been a war artist. I, for one, am glad he was—his amazing painting of the Battle of Long Tan is a wonderful tribute to the men who served and those who died in the Vietnam War.

NEW YEAR AT BIEN HOA

Chris Coulthard-Clark

Bien Hoa was a series of contacts between units of the 1st Australian Task Force (1ATF) and communist forces in South Vietnam, which occurred between 24 January and 1 March 1968. Forewarned of the enemy's intention of launching a major offensive under cover of the Buddhist Tet festival (marking the Chinese Lunar New Year), 1ATF was moved from its normal operating base in Phuoc Tuy Province to assist in defending the vital Bien Hoa–Long Binh complex near Saigon.

The role of the Australians was to deny the Viet Cong and North Vietnamese Army forces access to the area and to suitable sites for launching rocket attacks on the military bases and installations. Initially only two battalions—2RAR and 7RAR—took part, but within a few days a company of 3RAR was also brought to assist with the defence of Fire Support Base 'Andersen', which was established about a kilometre north of the village of Trang Bom. Australian involvement—codenamed 'Operation Coburg'—began with a series of twelve minor patrol clashes up to 31 January which saw 22 enemy killed.

During early February the nature of these contacts changed, as the Australians found themselves increasingly encountering company-size groups from Viet Cong Main Force units in static base camps; in a further 29 clashes during this phase another 64 enemy were killed. The highlight of 1ATF's involvement in operations around Bien Hoa came later in the month, however, when the Andersen base was repeatedly subjected to major ground assaults. The first of these occurred on the night of 17–18 February, and was followed by further attacks on the night of 19–20 February and early on the morning of 28 February.

The base had been deliberately sited astride the Viet Cong lines of communication, so that it was fully expected that the enemy would make efforts to eliminate it. The first assault was preceded by a heavy rocket and mortar barrage, followed by two waves of infantry which hit the south-western portion of the perimeter manned by 3RAR's battalion echelon and mortar platoon, along with an American medium artillery battery. The perimeter wire was breached by the enemy, but the attack was driven back by the weight of machine-gun fire from armoured personnel carriers and the American gunners.

A second assault shortly afterwards, this time from the north, was stopped short of the wire by small-arms fire from the forward weapon pits. By the time of the second attack two nights later, the base had been reinforced by C Company of 3RAR. The enemy assault, launched from the south-east and preceded by heavy machine-gun fire, was stopped before reaching the wire. The attackers were able, however, to hit positions within the perimeter with rifle grenades and also struck the assault pioneer lines with two satchel charges. The final attack on 28 February also began with a mortar attack, but the assault wave was broken up by fire from the 3RAR mortars and the enemy was forced to withdraw to the east. Casualties on the last occasion were three Australians wounded.

VETERAN'S LAMENT

Stewart Law

I joined a peacetime army,
But some fool made a war.
My life was calm and balmy,
But that was all before.

I used to be real healthy,
I'd take on any chore,
Some say I was wealthy,
But that was all before.

My skin was clear, no rashes,
No funguses I bore,
No itchy spots or patches,
But that was all before,
Before the war in Vietnam;
Before I saw that place called Nam.

I used to sleep quite soundly,
But now my sleep is poor.
I didn't have these nightmares,
But that was all before.

I had a loving family,
Who loved me more and more,
We had a peaceful homelife,
But that was all before,

I used to be a young man,
With mates and friends galore,
I wasn't old and lonely,
But that was all before,
Before the war in Vietnam;
Before I saw that place called Nam.

AFTERWORD—OUR 100TH VC

Since the conclusion of the timespan covered by this collection of stories, Australia has sent troops to serve in conflicts in East Timor, the Gulf War, Iraq, Syria and, most notably, Afghanistan, where our involvement has lasted almost two decades. I felt this brief account deserved to be the final story in this collection.

On 22 June 2013, a platoon from the Australian 2nd Commando Regiment conducted a night-time raid on a Taliban-held village in Uruzgan province, Afghanistan. Shortly after landing by helicopter, a team led by Corporal Cameron Baird from Burnie in Tasmania, came under fire from several enemy positions. Corporal Baird quickly seized the initiative and led his team to attack the positions, killing six of the enemy and enabling the assault to continue.

Soon afterwards, another Special Operations task force team came under heavy enemy fire, resulting in its commander being seriously wounded. Without hesitation, Corporal Baird took his team to provide support. With complete disregard for his own safety, Corporal Baird charged the enemy positions and neutralised the new threat with grenades and rifle fire. With the main building now isolated, Corporal Baird drew the enemy fire and then moved to cover. This action enabled his team to regain the initiative.

On three separate occasions, Corporal Baird charged the enemy-held building. On the first occasion, he charged the door to the building, and engaged the enemy fire. He was forced to withdraw when his rifle ceased to function. He fixed the problem and again advanced under heavy fire, engaged the enemy through the door but had to take cover to reload. For a third time, he drew enemy fire away from his team and attacked the doorway. In this third attempt, the enemy was neutralised and the operation achieved its goal.

Corporal Baird was killed during the action.

In February 2014, Corporal Cameron Baird was posthumously awarded the Victoria Cross, becoming the 100th Australian serviceman, and at the time of writing, the most recent, to be awarded the honour.

ACKNOWLEDGEMENTS

I wish to sincerely thank Chris Coulthard-Clark (courtesy of Allen & Unwin) and my friends Martin Rossleigh and Peter Mace for their contributions to this collection.

Also:
- Jillian Dellit for her constant support, suggestions and proofreading.
- Chrissy Eustace for her help with graphics.
- Rebecca Kaiser for her continued support and encouragement.
- Tom Bailey-Smith for keeping it all on track.
- Susin Chow for her perceptive editing, attention to detail and ideas.
- Pamela Dunne for the proofread.
- Kim Wright at Mapgraphics for the maps.
- My wife, Robyn McMillan.
- George and Paul at 2GB.
- All at Allen & Unwin.

NOTE ON SOURCES

Some of the stories in this volume have appeared previously in collections published by Allen & Unwin, HarperCollins and ABC Books.

Sources used in researching these stories over the past twenty years are too many and varied to list, but I have constantly relied upon:

* The Australian War Memorial
* The National Library of Australia—especially Trove.

And the following two volumes:

* Coulthard-Clark, Chris, *The Encyclopaedia of Australia's Battles*, Allen & Unwin, 1998/2001/2010
* Salmaggi, Cesare, and Pallavisini, Alfredo, *2,194 Days of War*, Milan, 1977 (Translated from the Italian by Hugh Young, Windward, London, 1979)

Stories by other authors included here are from:

Baylebridge, W., *An Anzac Muster*, Angus & Robertson, Sydney, 1921.
Beeston, J.L., *Five Months at Anzac*, Angus & Robertson, Sydney, 1916.
Birdwood, W., *Khaki and Gown: An Autobiography*, Ward Lock, London, 1941.
Cavill, H.W., *Imperishable Anzacs*, William Brooks & Co., Sydney, 1916.
Hanman, E.F., *Twelve Months with The 'Anzacs'*, Watson, Ferguson Brisbane, 1916.
Hogue, O., *Trooper Bluegum at The Dardanelles*, Melrose, London, 1916.
Kingsford Smith, C., *My Flying Life*, David McKay Co., Philadelphia 1937.
Loch, F.S., *The Straits Impregnable*, John Murray, London, 1917.

Paterson, A.B., *Dispatches, Melbourne Argus/Sydney Morning Herald*, 1899.
Rossleigh, Martin, previously unpublished, 2019.

All poems are from *The Book of Australian Popular Rhymed Verse*, (Ed. J. Haynes) ABC Books, 2008, except *Lost With All Hands* and *What Price A VC?*, which appear courtesy of Peter Mace.

Jim Haynes is a first-generation Aussie whose mother migrated from the UK as a child during the Depression. His father arrived on a British warship at the end of World War II, met his mother and stayed. 'My parents always insisted we were Australian, not British,' says Jim.

Educated at Sydney Boys High School and Sydney Teachers' College, he taught for six years at Menindee, on the Darling River, and later at high schools in northern New South Wales and in London. Jim has also worked in radio and as a nurse, cleaner and sapphire salesman, and has two degrees in literature from the University of New England and a master's degree from the University of Wales in the UK.

Jim formed the Bandy Bill & Co Bush Band in Inverell in 1978. He also worked in commercial radio and on the popular ABC *Australia All Over* program. In 1988 he signed as a solo recording artist with Festival Records, began touring and had a minor hit with 'Mow Ya Lawn'. Other record deals followed, along with hits like 'Since Cheryl Went Feral' and 'Don't Call Wagga Wagga Wagga'.

Having written and compiled 27 books, released many albums of songs, verse and humour and broadcast his weekly Australiana segment on Macquarie Radio for fifteen years, Jim was awarded the Order of Australia Medal in 2016 'for service to the performing arts as an entertainer, author, broadcaster and historian'. He lives at Moore Park in Sydney with his wife, Robyn.